Lecture Notes in Computer Science 812

Edited by G. Goos and J. Hartmanis

Advisory Board: W. Brauer D. Gries J. Stoer

J. Karhumäki   H. Maurer
G. Rozenberg (Eds.)

Results and Trends
in Theoretical
Computer Science

Colloquium in Honor of Arto Salomaa
Graz, Austria, June 10-11, 1994
Proceedings

Springer-Verlag

Berlin Heidelberg New York
London Paris Tokyo
Hong Kong Barcelona
Budapest

Series Editors

Gerhard Goos
Universität Karlsruhe
Postfach 69 80
Vincenz-Priessnitz-Straße 1
D-76131 Karlsruhe, Germany

Juris Hartmanis
Cornell University
Department of Computer Science
4130 Upson Hall
Ithaca, NY 14853, USA

Volume Editors

Juliani Karhumäki
Department of Mathematics, University of Turku
SF-20500 Turku, Finland

Hermann Maurer
Institut für Grundlagen der Informationsverarbeitung
und Computergestützte neue Medien, TU Graz
Schießstattgasse 4a, A-8010 Graz, Austria

Grzegorz Rozenberg
Department of Computer Science, Leiden University
P. O. Box 9512, 2300 RA Leiden, The Netherlands

CR Subject Classification (1991): F, E.3, G.2-3

ISBN 3-540-58131-6 Springer-Verlag Berlin Heidelberg New York
ISBN 0-387-58131-6 Springer-Verlag New York Berlin Heidelberg

CIP data applied for

© Springer-Verlag Berlin Heidelberg 1994
Printed in Germany

Typesetting: Camera-ready by author
SPIN: 10131269   45/3140-543210 - Printed on acid-free paper

**To Arto Salomaa
from the TCS Community**

Professor Dr.Dr.h.c.mult. Arto Salomaa

PREFACE

This volume contains some 30 papers contributed in honor of Arto Salomaa on the occasion of his 60th birthday. It is based on the symposium "Important Results and Trends in Theoretical Computer Science" organized in Graz, Austria to celebrate this occasion.

Arto is a man of many worlds and we believe that it is the harmonious coexistence of all those worlds that is the key to Arto's success in life.

The world of science. Above all Arto is a scientist. He considers himself to be a writer - he draws as much pleasure from proving a new result as from writing it up. His scientific writings have had a big influence on the development of theoretical computer science - especially in Europe. He has written more than 300 papers and 9 books (translated into 6 languages). Many of those books are by now classics and they have had a big influence on the education of several generations of computer scientists. Arto also believes in the popularization of science and has been involved in many series of lectures on science for a general audience; he has also written many articles on science for newspapers. He has been a very popular teacher at his University of Turku, Finland, and also at the University of Western Ontario, Canada, the University of Aarhus, Denmark, and the University of Waterloo, Canada where he held visiting positions for longer periods of time. He travels a lot and had shorter visits to about 150 universities in Europe, North America and Asia. He has supervised 19 Ph.D. students - many of whom are today well-known scientists. He has also influenced the development of theoretical computer science by cooperating with many scientists - he has had 35 coauthors of papers and books. He has been an inspiring teacher and coauthor for many researchers in theoretical computer science.

Many of Arto's papers are major contributions to theoretical computer science in the sense that they either solve an important problem or they introduce a new and interesting research area. His published research covers quite a broad spectrum of mathematics and theoretical computer science. His first paper, on many-valued systems of logics, was published in 1959. Since then he has published in mathematical logic, automata theory, formal language theory, computability and cryptography (the interest in cryptography goes back to his childhood when he was already reading about classical cryptography and was the code breaker specialist of the famous Skeleton Gang in his native Turku in Finland).

His value for the scientific community extends far beyond the above. He has been on the program committee of most of the important conferences in theoretical computer science, he organized many conferences, he is an editor of many scientific journals and book series, he has been the president of the European Association for Theoretical Computer Science for the period 1979-1985, and he is currently the chairman of the Award Committee for the Gödel Prize. Arto has received a number of prestigious prizes in his native Finland. He has been honored for his contributions by receiving five honorary doctorates from universities in Finland and abroad. Although nobody keeps the record of such matters it must be among the highest number of honorary doctorates held by any computer scientist.

The world of family. His favorite place is his farm, Rauhala, in the remote country side in Finland, where he often stays with his wife Kaarina. The most happy days are the days when the whole family - his wife, son, daughter, son in law, and three grandchildren - are in Rauhala. When he is together with his grandchildren then every evening he has an hour for reading stories - the grandchildren anxiously await this event the whole day. He also reads stories to audiotapes for the times when his grandchildren are not with him.

The world of music. Arto loves classical music. He has an enormous collection of records, tapes and CD's with classical music. When he works on science either in his apartment in Turku or in his farm then the music (Beethoven, Bach,...) is very loudly on. In this way all "context" disappears and only the science and the music remains. He also talks of his own scientific writings in terms of symphonies and sonatas.

The world of sauna. The Finnish sauna is perhaps the most important regular event in Arto's life. He loves in particular the very old sauna on his farm - it is called Salosauna. While he stays on the farm an important part of the morning and the early afternoon is spent on the preparations for the sauna - then in the evening a sauna session follows. He believes that during the sauna "important" veins in the brain open and the mental ability increases significantly. There have been many instances when important open problems have been cracked either by Arto or by his friends during or after a Salosauna session. He regrets very much that he has not been born in sauna (it has not been unusual in former times that a child delivery in Finland took place in sauna). He is a real expert on sauna. Arto has written sauna-articles that have appeared in the EATCS Bulletin and has been trying to write a book on the subject several times. However he has postponed the project each time claiming that this is such an important topic and he is not ready for it yet.

The world of friends. Arto has a number of very close friends whom he calls brothers. They are a part of his family. To those friends and to his family he is Tarzan; members of his family and his brothers have then names such as Jane, Cheetah, Muviro, Korak, Bolgani. His writing talent extends far beyond scientific writings. It is always a pleasure for his friends to receive letters from Tarzan - they are full of stories and reflections about life.

In the above we have mentioned only the main aspects of Arto's life. We have not mentioned his hobbies such as the supikoira (the raccoon dog living in Finland), his expertise in the Turku language (the local dialect), and his admiration for the Toronto Blue Jays (he often wears a Toronto Blue Jays baseball shirt even to important official meetings).

We feel very privileged that we have been given the opportunity to organize this symposium and to edit this book in honor of our extraordinary friend.

We wish him a lot of success and a nice life in each of his worlds in the years to come.

June, 1994   Grzegorz, Hermann and Juhani

P.S.: We would like to thank all authors for complying with the desired format and schedule, Springer Verlag for the (as usual) excellent cooperation. And Ms. M. Lampl and Ms. Mags Woo for their excellent work in assembling the papers and for all necessary coordination between the authors and the editors.

TABLE OF CONTENTS

Generalizing Cook's Transformation to Imperative Stack Programs

Nils Andersen and Neil D. Jones

Department of Computer Science, University of Copenhagen, Universitetsparken 1,
DK-2100 Copenhagen, Denmark

Abstract. Cook's construction from 1971 [4] shows that any two-way
deterministic pushdown automaton (2DPDA) can be simulated in time
$\mathcal{O}(n)$, where n is the length of its input string, and the more general [5]
describes analogous results for other abstract machines. The goal of this
paper is to make Cook's result usable for a broader spectrum of practical
problems.

We introduce a family of one-stack programs that includes 2DPDAs,
and present a uniform way to *compile* any imperative stack program
into a new and often faster version by using memoization. The method
only explores the computational configurations that are *reachable on the
current input*, in contrast to Cook's method, and builds programs that
run in linear time if the original was a 2DPDA in program form. The
transformation applies to algorithms not previously dealt with by Cook's
method, *e.g.* fast computation of functions such as Fibonacci and $\binom{m}{n}$.

1 Introduction

Stephen A. Cook described a transformation in 1971 that can, for instance, improve program running times from exponential to linear (as functions of their input size). This is interesting in that it delineates a class of programs can be simulated *faster than they run*, by using a richer storage structure for memoization.

Cook's result inspired the now widely used Knuth-Morris-Pratt string matching algorithm; an example where a theoretical insight led to practically useful techniques.

The original formulations [4,5][1, Section 9.4] were in terms of a class of automata and dealt with deciding membership in formal languages, *i.e.* sets of strings, but work equally well on programs.

The method involves application of offline memoization, building a table to save the results of intermediate computational configurations, and so to avoid recomputation. The memoization table size is input-dependent, sometimes large but always linear in the number of the program's "surface configurations".

A surface configuration consists of a program point, the contents of the top of the stack, and the current values of all program variables (except the stack); the method is therefore particularly interesting for algorithms with a small number and range of program variables. Further, it is not necessary to count as part of the surface configuration variables of two kinds: those that do not vary after program initialization (*e.g.* regarding the input); and those that do not influence the control flow of the algorithm. We treat the former kind of variables as constants, and to avoid variables of the latter kind this paper uses a trick: instead of operations that only push or pop one item to or from the stack we allow a very general kind of stack operation. An operation of *arity* (a, b) will remove $a + 1$ elements from the stack and use them to determine $b + 1$ elements to be pushed.

Cook's table construction in effect *interprets* the program in an indirect way, and is general enough to handle deterministic and nondeterministic programs. This involves a nontrivial "bookkeeping" overhead. From an application viewpoint, another disadvantage is that table entries are made in a "speculative" or offline way, even if the program is deterministic — so that in practice most table entries turn out to be for computational configurations the program can never enter. Jones [7] (assuming the program to be deterministic) modifies Cook's approach to build the table online during simulation so that only the table entries actually needed are constructed, but is still in essence interpretive.

Bird [3] extends the transformation to computations with general values as input and output, as we also will do. However, Bird only treats programs of a very special form (built around a loop with a single pop instruction), and the memoizing transformation has to be done by hand.

Amtoft *et al.* [2] implement the method of [7], and use partial evaluation [8] to reduce the earlier methods' interpretive overhead [4,1,7]. During the development of this paper it was found that many of the proofs have strong similarities to ideas in [2]. Differences: our methods produce yet more efficient programs, and handle a significantly larger program class.

The present paper demonstrates a general method to *compile* a stack program directly into an equivalent online memoizing program that runs in linear time if the original was a 2DPDA in program form. It has no interpretive overhead at all, and significantly less other bookkeeping than any of the methods just mentioned, thus bringing Cook's general result closer to practical usability. As a by-product, the method also yields a proof of Cook's construction that is more perspicuous than the original (in [4,1,7]).

In Section 2 program notation and semantics is introduced, and Section 3 describes the transformation. In Section 4 the transformation is proven to be faithful, and the output program's running time is analyzed and proven to be proportional to a certain value computable from the program text. If the program uses only ordinary push and pop instructions, this value is at most the number of "surface configurations". If more complex stack operations are employed, the values pushed onto the stack and the amount by which the stack may increase also enter into the value.

A program to find the longest palindromic prefix of a string is used to illustrate the transformation, and in Sections 5 and 6 two further examples, the *subsequence problem* and computation of *binomial coëfficients* are presented. In the latter cases our method improves two exponential methods to ones whose execution times are bounded by products.

We conclude with some considerations of the applicability of the method.

2 Stack programs

The following is formulated in a way closer to daily programming practice than Cook's 2DPDA or auxiliary pushdown automata [4,5]. One difference is the use of an imperative programming style rather than transitions by sets of tuples as traditional in automata theory. Another difference is that the stack alphabet T is not necessarily finite, *e.g.* one may store integers there for future retrieval.

Notation: $[]$ denotes the empty stack, $A : S$ is the result of pushing A onto the stack S, and $\text{top}(S)$ is the topmost element of a non-empty stack S. List notation $[A_n, \ldots, A_2, A_1]$ denotes $A_n : \ldots : A_2 : A_1 : []$, stack $S \mathbin{+\!\!\!+} S'$ is stack S on top of (appended to) stack S', and in such a case S' is said to be a *bottom* of $S \mathbin{+\!\!\!+} S'$. For a natural number i, $i{\downarrow}S$ selects the i topmost elements of S, so $i{\downarrow}(A_n : \ldots : A_2 : A_1 : []) = A_n : \ldots : A_{n-i+1} : []$. The depth of S is written $|S|$, so $|[A_n, \ldots, A_1]| = n$.

For technical convenience we will generally assume that the "auxiliary store" or input tape scanning position is contained in the topmost stack element, but will on occasion break this convention by using an explicit *memory*.

2.1 Syntax

A *stack program* is a flow chart built with a collection of program statements labeled by a set L of *labels* $j, k, j', \ldots$ with a designated *initial label* j_0. Program statements refer to a *stack* S whose items are drawn from the *stack alphabet* T, which also contains the *bottom marker* Z.

A *stack function of arity* (a, b) is a function from T^{a+1} to T^{b+1}, for natural numbers a and b. Its use is to pop $a + 1$ stack items and then to push $b + 1$ values in their place. Thus a stack function of arity $(0,0)$ updates the stack top only, by convention containing the memory and/or input tape scanning position.

Programs have no read statements, so input must be coded into the memory, to be manipulated by predicates and stack functions during execution. The dependency on input does not appear explicitly in our program notation.

A stack program consists of an initializing program statement (init) and a mapping, associating with each program label j a unique statement which is either a test (**test**), a stack operation of arity (a, b) (**stackop**$_{a,b}$), or a terminal statement (**term**):

(init)	**begin** $S := [Z]$; **go_to** j_0
(test)	j: **if** $p(\text{top}(S))$ **then** **go_to** k^+ **else** **go_to** k^-
(stackop$_{a,b}$)	j: $S :=f= S$; **go_to** k
(term)	j: **end**

where j, k, k^+ and k^- are labels in L, p is a predicate over T, a and b are positive integers, and f is a stack function of arity (a, b).

A **stackop**$_{0,0}$ statement amounts to an ordinary assignment, a **stackop**$_{0,b}$ statement where $b > 0$ is a *push* statement of arity b, and a **stackop**$_{a,0}$ statement with

$a > 0$ is a *pop* statement of arity a. Many programs will only use stackop$_{a,b}$ statements where a or b (or both) are 0; but the use of other combinations can yield more efficient transformed programs, as will be seen in the Fibonacci and $\binom{m}{n}$ examples.

2.2 Semantics

A *program configuration* is its "total state", a pair (j, S) where j is the control point, and S is the current stack contents. A *surface configuration* is a pair (j, A_1) where $(j, [A_1, \ldots, A_n])$ is a program configuration.

Each stack program gives rise to a *next state relation* "$\triangleright$" on its set of program configurations. For technical reasons the relation is defined as ternary, also taking a stack argument. The significance of $(j, S) \triangleright_{S'} (j_1, S_1)$ is going to be "execution of the statement at label j with stack S leads in one step to label j_1 and new stack S_1 without using S' (which is a bottom part of both S and S_1)".

For a **test** statement

$$j: \text{ if } p(\text{top}(S)) \text{ then go\_to } k^+ \text{ else go\_to } k^-$$

define (for every bottom S' of S)

$$(j, A : S) \triangleright_{S'} (k^+, A : S)$$

if $p(A)$ holds, else

$$(j, A : S) \triangleright_{S'} (k^-, A : S)$$

In the case of a stackop$_{a,b}$ statement

$$j: \ S \ :=f= \ S; \ \text{go\_to } k$$

define

$$(j, A_a : \ldots : A_1 : A_0 : S) \triangleright_{S'} (k, B_b : \ldots : B_1 : B_0 : S)$$

where S' is any bottom of S, and $f(A_0, A_1, \ldots, A_a) = (B_0, B_1, \ldots, B_b)$. A small but necessary point: execution is assumed to terminate abnormally if a stackop$_{a,b}$ statement is reached with fewer than $a + 1$ elements on the stack or if a **test** statement is reached with an empty stack.

Notation "**push** A **onto** S" stands for "$S :=f= S$" where f is of arity $(0, 1)$, and $f(A_0) = (A_0, A)$. (Remark: A may be a function of A_0.) Similarly "**pop** S" stands for "$S :=f= S$" with f of arity $(1, 0)$, and $f(A_0, A_1) = (A_0)^1$.

The *multiple step state transition* relation is the reflexive transitive closure $\triangleright_S^*$ of $\triangleright_S$, and $\triangleright_S^+$ is its transitive closure. Symbols $\triangleright$, $\triangleright^+$ and $\triangleright^*$ denote $\triangleright_{[]}$, $\triangleright_{[]}^+$ and $\triangleright_{[]}^*$. For a given input, the *computation* with the stack program is the sequence

$$(j_0, [Z]) = (j_0, S_0) \triangleright (j_1, S_1) \triangleright \ldots \triangleright (j_n, S_n) \triangleright \ldots$$

---

[1] Note that these do not change A_0, in keeping with the convention that A_0 is the auxiliary memory, containing variables such as the input scanning position.

A computation may be infinite, or it may end if a **term** statement is met. In the latter case it is called a *terminating computation*, and the *length* of such a computation is the number of program configurations that it contains. The pairs (j, S_j) are called *reachable configurations*.

A stack program obviously has a unique computation, *i.e.* it is *deterministic* (the next state relation is a partial function).

Our main result is that any terminating stack program may be compiled into another *whose run time is linear in the number of reachable surface configurations*. This number may be much less than the number of *all* computational configurations (involving the stack) entered by the program in its computation, and it is in no case larger than $\#L \cdot \#T$ (the bound obtained by Cook).

2.3 Notational extensions

It is often convenient to work with ordinary program variables in addition to the stack, so a more detailed total configuration could be a triple (j, mem, S) with a state of the *memory* in addition to the previous components. The way our machinery deals with such an extension is to consider the memory to be part of the top of the stack. Changing the values of such ordinary program variables is done by an operation with a stack function of arity $(0, 0)$. Formally, therefore, the described situation is covered by a suitable extension of the stack alphabet T (although the extended alphabet is only used in the top of the stack and not relevant for items buried deeper in the stack).

In practical examples, we shall freely use ordinary variables, with an understanding of the underlying formal model as described. It will later become necessary to consider other variants, containing extra stacks, tables, *etc.* These can be fit into the framework just given by further extensions of the memory state set.

An example. Let us, as an example, consider the problem of finding the length of the longest palindromic prefix of a given string $t_1 t_2 \ldots t_n$, where each $t_i \in T_0 \backslash \{Z\}$ and T_0 is a fixed finite alphabet. (Since the result is a number, this problem is more general than a decision problem.) The problem may be solved by a stack algorithm in the following way: for decreasing values of i, $i = n, n - 1, n - 2, \ldots$, reversed prefixes $t_i \ldots t_2 t_1$, kept on the stack, are compared to the given string. During a comparison matching symbols are popped, but after a mismatch the stack can be restored by means of the given string, and the next shorter prefix can be tried.

This naïve approach has been programmed in Figure 1 where a PASCAL-like notation is used, rather than the strict formalism with labeled statements and explicit jumps. An ordinary variable i as explained above is also used.

The input consists of n and the current string t and has been coded into the program. The program may run in time $\mathcal{O}(n^2)$ due to the backing up needed for unsuccessful partial matches, exemplified by strings of the form $A^p B A^{3p}$.

```
S := [Z];
i := 0;
while i < n do begin
        i := i + 1;
        push t_i onto S
end;
{S = [t_n, ..., t_1, Z]}
i := 0;
while top(S) ≠ Z do begin  {invariant: S = [t_{h-i}, ..., t_1, Z], t_h ... t_{h-i+1} = t_1 ... t_i}
        if top(S) = t_{i+1} then i := i + 1
        else {restore} while i > 0 do begin
                push t_i onto S;
                i := i - 1
        end;
        pop S
end;
write("length of longest palindromic prefix is ", i)
```

Fig. 1. Naïve stack program to find for a given string $t_1 t_2 \ldots t_n$ the largest i such that $t_1 t_2 \ldots t_i$ is equal to its own reversal $t_i \ldots t_2 t_1$.

The variable i assumes values between 0 and n, so the size of the total alphabet T is $(\#T_0 + 1) \cdot (n + 1)$, and we shall see that the program can be simulated in a number of steps proportional to this value.

3 The improvement

The crucial observation (of both Cook's work and our own) is that in a computation, the entire series of configurations following any total configuration $(j, A : S)$ is determined by *the surface configuration (j, A) alone*, until (if ever) some symbol deeper in the stack than A is used or popped. Stated more formally:

For all stacks S the following equivalence holds:

$$(j, [A]) \triangleright^* (j', [A']) \text{ if and only if } (j, A : S) \triangleright_S^* (j', A' : S)$$

Thus any two steps that lead to the same configuration $(j, A : S)$ will repeat the same subcomputation, until (if ever) some symbol from S is used or popped, *i.e.* the subcomputation is functionally determined by surface configuration (j, A).

This may be exploited to optimize the program. Suppose $(j, A : S) \triangleright_S^*$ $(j', S' +\!\!+ S)$ where j' is a stackop$_{a,b}$ statement with $a \geq |S'|$. The first time $(j, A : S)$ is encountered, the program is run until $(j', S' +\!\!+ S)$ is entered. The surface part of this configuration is called the "terminator" in [1].

The pair (j', S') can then be stored for future reference, and if ever a configuration $(j, A : S_1)$ is entered again (for any S_1 at all), an immediate "short cut" can be taken to $(j', S' +\!\!+ S_1)$.

To do this we will add to the program a partial mapping from surface configurations, a table $dest : L \times T \to L \times T^*$, to remember the terminators (j', S'). Implementation note: $dest$ could be implemented by a hash table, so that the memory required need only be of the order of the number of surface configurations actually entered.

The following section works out the details and shows the new "compilation" technique.

3.1   Transformation

To keep track of surface configurations that have been met, but whose terminators have not yet been found, an auxiliary stack $dump$ is introduced; it will be driven in lockstep with S. Each entry in $dump$ is a list of surface configurations, so $dump$ is a list of lists.

We now modify **pgm** to give program **pgm'** that will, whenever a stackop$_{a,b}$ instruction with $a > 0$ is encountered, store the terminators of those surface configurations whose subcomputations have been completed. Further, **pgm'** may consult the $dest$ table to take a "shortcut" when a surface configuration is encountered whose terminator has already been computed. Let $dest_0$ denote the totally undefined mapping.

As a result, computations by **pgm'** are not in a one-to-one correspondence with those of **pgm**, but will avoid sometimes quite long recomputations.

At this stage only potential locations of the shortcuts are indicated, postponing the decisions as to which ones actually must be present.

The individual program statements of **pgm** are transformed as shown below, using the same labels and command forms in **pgm'** as in **pgm**.

(init)   **begin** $S := [Z]$; $dump := [[]]$; $dest := dest_0$; **go_to** j_0

(test) j: | potential shortcut; |
            if $p(\mathrm{top}(S))$ **then go_to** k^+ **else go_to** k^-

(stackop$_{0,b}$) j: | potential shortcut; | $S :=f= S$;
            for $i:=1$ **to** b **do push** $[]$ **onto** $dump$; **go_to** k

(stackop$_{a,b}$) j: **for** $i:=1$ **to** a **do begin**
where $a > 0$ **for** each (j', A') on the list $\mathrm{top}(dump)$ **do**
                  $dest(j', A') := (j, i{\downarrow}S)$;
           pop this list from $dump$
      end;
      $S :=f= S$;
      for $i:=1$ **to** b **do push** $[]$ **onto** $dump$; **go_to** k

(term) j: **end**

At the positions "potential shortcut;" in the table above one may or may not insert a call "$shortcut(j, top(S))$;" activating the following program segment

$shortcut(j, A) \equiv$
  if $dest(j, A) = (j', S')$ then begin
      pop S; push the symbols of S' onto S; go_to j'
  end else $\{dest(j, A)$ is undefined$\}$
      $top(dump) := (j, A) : top(dump)$

Strictly speaking, the construction "go_to j" where j is found by computation (as used in the program segment above) extends our program notation. It amounts to a Fortran "computed goto", or can be realized by insertion of a series of tests and jumps to statically known program points. (Note that this transformation is completely determined by the program text and thus only influences running time by a constant factor.)

The proof that the transformed program is as desired has two sides: it must be proven that it is a faithful simulation of the original one, and that it executes in linear time (in a sense later made precise).

4 Proofs

4.1 Faithfulness

Total configurations of **pgm′** are quadruples of the form $(j, S, dump, dest)$. Symbols ▶ and ▶* are used for the next state relation and the multiple step state transition, respectively, between these new total states. Recall that $dest_0$ is the totally undefined mapping.

Lemma 1 pgm′ only simulates pgm actions. *Assume that, in* **pgm′**:

$$(j_0, [Z], [[]], dest_0) \blacktriangleright^* (j, S, dump, dest)$$

Then

(a) **pgm** would do the same:
$$(j_0, [Z]) \rhd^* (j, S)$$

(b) entries in *dest* reflect subcomputations:
    if $dest(j', A') = (j'', S'')$, then $(j', [A']) \rhd^+ (j'', S'')$, and j'' labels a stackop$_{a,b}$ statement with $a > 0$

(c) information in *dump* is as intended:
    if some pair (j', A') is present in one of the lists on *dump*, say *dump* = $dump'' + [[\ldots, (j', A'), \ldots]] + dump'$, and S' is the bottom of the stack corresponding to $dump'$, $S = S'' + S'$ where $|S'| = |dump'|$, then

$$(j_0, [Z]) \rhd^* (j', A' : S') \rhd_{S'}^+ (j, S)$$

Proof. The three claims are proved simultaneously, by induction on the length of the computation in **pgm′**. First, all hold trivially for 0-step computations. Now consider

$$(j_0, [Z], [[]], dest_0) \blacktriangleright^* (j_1, S_1, dump_1, dest_1) \blacktriangleright (j, S, dump, dest)$$

and assume (a), (b) and (c) of the computation leading to $(j_1, S_1, dump_1, dest_1)$.

If the transition in **pgm′** from j_1 to j does not take a shortcut, (a) follows immediately; if a shortcut is taken, (a) follows inductively from (b).

Assume $dest(j', A') = (j'', S'')$. If $dest_1(j', A')$ was already defined, (b) holds. If not, $dest(j', A')$ must be defined by the statement at j_1. In that case $j_1 = j''$, j_1 must label a **stackop**$_{a,b}$ statement with $a > 0$, and (b) follows inductively from (c).

Finally, assume the premises of (c). If (j', A') was already present in $dump_1$, the conclusion follows as in the proof of (a) above. If (j', A') is added by the statement at j_1 we must have $j_1 = j'$, and the statement at j_1 must contain the call "*shortcut*$(j_1, \text{top}(S_1))$". In that case the conclusion of (c) follows inductively from (a). □

Lemma 2. *If a computation with* **pgm′** *inserts some pair* (j, A) *more than once into dump, then it does not terminate.*

Proof. Once a pair (j, A) is removed from $dump$, $dest(j, A)$ becomes defined, preventing (j, A) from ever being entered into $dump$ again. If, on the other hand, (j, A) is inserted into a $dump$ that contains this pair already, Lemma 1(c) implies that the computation will continue forever. □

We may now—the converse result is valid in the following form:

Lemma 3 pgm′ simulates all pgm actions. *If*

$$(j_0, [Z]) \triangleright^* (j, S)$$

then there will exist $S', dump', dest'$ *such that*

$$(j, S) \triangleright^*_{S'} (j', S') \text{ and}$$
$$(j_0, [Z], [[]], dest_0) \blacktriangleright^* (j', S', dump', dest')$$

Proof by induction on the length of the computation in **pgm**, using Lemma 1(b) above, if a shortcut is taken by **pgm′** at the final step. □

We may now draw the desired conclusion:

Theorem 4. *There is a terminating computation in* **pgm**

$$(j_0, [Z]) \triangleright^* (j, S)$$

if and only if there is a terminating computation in **pgm′**

$$(j_0, [Z], [[]], dest_0) \blacktriangleright^* (j, S, dump, dest)$$

for some dump and dest.

Proof by Lemma 1(a) and Lemma 3. □

4.2 Linearity

The running time of pgm' is dependent on the flow of control resulting from the inserted shortcuts. We shall use the sequencing structure of pgm as our reference. The terms "loop" and "execution path", in the criteria below, therefore refer to potential flows of control *before* the program is transformed.

Although the actual effect of a stackop$_{a,b}$ statement is not known until execution time, its influence on the height of the stack(s) may be determined statically: it will increase stack height by $b-a$, or decrease it by $a-b$, depending on whether $a \leq b$ or not. By adding the contributions from each statement it is therefore possible to determine how a particular path through the flow chart from a label j to a label j' will influence the stack height.

As detailed in the theorem below, the following is sufficient to ensure linearity. Any non-empty path from a label j to a label j' which does not decrease stack height must satisfy:

(1) If j labels a stackop$_{a,b}$ statement with $a > 0$ then the path must contain a shortcut.

(2) If $j = j'$ (*i.e.* if the path is a loop) then the path must contain a shortcut.

As a result of condition (2), there is a limit to how much a path through the flow chart may increase the stack, if the path does not contain a shortcut. Note also that condition (1) disallows stackop$_{a,b}$ statements with $0 < a \leq b$. On the other hand, if all stackop$_{a,b}$ statements satisfy $a = 0 \vee a > b$, then the conditions will hold if *all* potential shortcuts are added.

Theorem 5. *Assume that pgm' has been constructed in such a way that conditions (1) and (2) are satisfied. Let C denote the number of shortcuts, and let W be a bound on how much the stack height may increase along any path not containing any shortcut. Then if the computation with pgm' terminates, each statement is executed at most $2 \cdot (C \cdot \#T + 1) \cdot (W + 1)$ times.*

Proof. Assume $C \geq 1$. The case $C = 0$ is simpler.

By Lemma 1(b), if $dest(j, A) = (j', S')$ then j' labels a stackop$_{a,b}$ statement with $a > 0$. Each execution of $shortcut(j, A)$ will therefore either enter the pair (j, A) into *dump* or jump to a stackop$_{a,b}$ statement with $a > 0$. In the first case, let us use the terminology that execution of the shortcut "falls through". Since the computation is finite each pair (j, A), by Lemma 2, will be entered into *dump* at most once. Consequently, a shortcut will fall through at most $C \cdot \#T$ times during the computation.

By condition (1), if a shortcut does not fall through, the computation path leading to the next shortcut, if any, must decrease the height of the stack. Thus the increase in stack height, during the whole computation, cannot exceed the value $(C \cdot \#T + 1) \cdot W$. Taking the initialization with a single element into account one sees that the height of the stack is at most $C \cdot \#T \cdot W + W + 1$.

If a shortcut doesn't fall through, the execution path until the next shortcut (or to a terminal statement) must decrease stack height. This may therefore also happen at most $C \cdot \#T \cdot W + W + 1$ times.

Consequently at most $N = (C \cdot \#T + 1) \cdot (W + 1)$ shortcuts are executed during the computation.

Now consider any particular statement label j. If j is met several times during the computation without any intervening shortcut, then (by condition (2)) stack height is decreased. This may happen at most $C \cdot \#T \cdot W + W + 1 \le N - 1$ times.

There can be at most $N + 1$ remaining occurrences of j (separated by N shortcuts). The claim of the theorem follows. □

```
S := [Z]; dump := [[]];
initialize dest to the nowhere defined mapping;
i := 0;
while i < n do begin
      i := i + 1;
      push t_i onto S; push [] onto dump
end;
i := 0;
while top(S) ≠ Z do begin
      if top(S) = t_{i+1} then i := i + 1
      else
restore:
      if i > 0 then begin
            if dest(i, top(S)) is undefined then begin
                  add i to the list on top of dump;
                  push t_i onto S; push [] onto dump;
                  i := i - 1;
                  go_to restore
            end;
            i := dest(i, top(S))
      end;
      for each i' in the list on top of dump do dest(i', top(S)) := i;
      pop dump; pop S
end;
write("length of longest palindromic prefix is ",i)
```

Fig. 2. Linear stack program to find for a given string $t_1 t_2 \ldots t_n$ the largest i such that $t_1 t_2 \ldots t_i$ is equal to its own reversal $t_i \ldots t_2 t_1$.

Let us also formulate the result for the frequent simple case where the program deals with one element of the stack at a time. In other words: only **stackop** statements with arities $(0,0)$, $(0,1)$ and $(1,0)$ occur in **pgm**.

In this case it is convenient to attach shortcuts precisely to the **push** statements. The sufficient conditions are simplified into:

(2′) Each loop must contain a **push** or a **pop** statement.

Note that a path from a pop to a push statement now automatically leads to a shortcut, and that each loop that does not decrease the height of the stack must contain a shortcut.

Theorem 6. *Assume that* pgm *contains* C stackop$_{0,1}$ *statements and that the remaining* stackop$_{a,b}$ *statements have arities* $(0,0)$ *or* $(1,0)$. *Assume furthermore that* $(2')$ *is fulfilled and that in the transformation to* pgm$'$ *shortcuts are attached to all the* stackop$_{0,1}$ *statements. Then, if the computation with* pgm$'$ *terminates, in this computation*

- *there will be at most* $C \cdot \#T$ *executions of* push *statements*
- *there will be at most* $C \cdot \#T + 1$ *executions of* pop *statements*
- *each other statement will be executed at most* $2 \cdot (C \cdot \#T + 1)$ *times*

The proof is analogous to that of the general theorem: A push is only executed after a shortcut has fallen through, and that may happen at most $\#T$ times at each particular shortcut. Consequently, no more than $C \cdot \#T + 1$ elements are pushed onto the stack during the computation. This number therefore also bounds the number of executions of a pop statement.

The computation path between any two executions of any other statement must either decrease the stack, which may happen at most $C \cdot \#T + 1$ times, or not decrease the stack, in which case it must contain a shortcut. In the latter case, it must even contain a shortcut that falls through, which may happen at most $C \cdot \#T$ times.

This is the desired result. □

As an additional simplification, shortcuts may be omitted from parts of the program where the logic of the program puts a sufficiently low limit on the number of executions of the statements.

Only the surface configurations actually occurring at shortcuts need be taken into account in the computation of $C \cdot \#T$, and when considering how *dump* and *dest* could be organized. A similar simplification is sometimes also possible with regard to the *range* of *dest* (*e.g.* if there is only one stackop$_{a,b}$ statement with $a > 0$, the label component is unique and may be omitted).

Figure 2 shows a transformed version of the palindromic prefix algorithm where these improvements have been exploited. No shortcuts have been inserted in the initializing loop because it is obvious that the push is performed only once for each value of i.

Only one push and one pop remain, and they interrupt the remaining loops. The shortcut code is therefore only required at the push, and program labels need not be stored in *dump* or in *dest* (since if a shortcut is taken it will lead from the unique push to the unique pop).

A surface configuration is a value (of i) between 0 and n combined with a stack symbol. The running time (and the size of table *dest*) is thus $\mathcal{O}(n)$.

```
S := [Z];
i := 0;
j := 0;
tryNext:
if i = m then exit(success);
if m − i ≤ n − j then begin
      j := j + 1;
      push 0 onto S;
      go_to tryNext
end;
while j > 0 do begin
      if top(S) = 0 then begin
            pop S;
            i := i + 1;
            if xᵢ = yⱼ then begin
                  push 1 onto S;
                  go_to tryNext
            end
      end else pop S;
      i := i − 1;
      j := j − 1
end;
exit(failure)
```

Fig. 3. Naïve algorithm to determine if $x_1 x_2 \ldots x_m$ is a subsequence of $y_1 y_2 \ldots y_n$

5 Example: Subsequence problem

The m-n-subsequence problem is to determine, for given strings $x = x_1 x_2 \ldots x_m$ and $y = y_1 y_2 \ldots y_n$, whether x is a subsequence of y in the sense that $x = y_{j_1} y_{j_2} \ldots y_{j_m}$ for some indices $1 \le j_1 < j_2 < \ldots < j_m \le n$.

A straight-forward solution procedure would be to generate all the m-combinations $(j_1, j_2, \ldots, j_m)$ and check $\forall i = 1, 2, \ldots, m : x_i = y_{j_i}$ for each combination. Generation and checking can be done concurrently, proceeding in order of increasing values of i and backtracking as soon as a mismatch is found, by a program such as the one shown in Figure 3 where the combinations are generated in the natural reverse lexicographic order. (Another way in which this program might have been obtained is indicated in Section 7.) It is not difficult to see that the worst case running time of the program is $\Omega(\binom{n}{m})$. Our transformation will now convert this program to the program in Figure 4 which has the optimal running time[2] $\mathcal{O}(m(n − m + 1))$.

---

[2] Remark: After more careful thought, it becomes clear that one can also obtain this running time $\mathcal{O}(m(n − m + 1))$ by reprogramming Figure 3 to enumerate the combinations in true lexicographic order. Such insights, however, are nontrivial and not well suited to automation.

```
S := [Z];  dump := [[]];
initialize dest to the nowhere defined mapping;
i := 0;
j := 0;
tryNext:
if i = m then exit(success);
if m − i ≤ n − j then begin
        j := j + 1;
push0:  shortcut(push0);
        push 0 onto S; push [] onto dump;
        go_to tryNext
end;
while j > 0 do begin
        if top(S) = 0 then begin
pop0:       update(pop0);
            pop dump; pop S;
            i := i + 1;
            if x_i = y_j then begin
push1:          shortcut(push1);
                push 1 onto S; push [] onto dump;
                go_to tryNext
            end
        end else begin
pop1:       update(pop1);
            pop dump; pop S
        end;
        i := i − 1;
        j := j − 1
end;
exit(failure)
```

$shortcut(h)$ $\equiv$ if $dest(h, i, j, top(S)) = (h', i', j')$ then begin
$\qquad\qquad\qquad\qquad i := i'$; $j := j'$; go_to h'
$\qquad\qquad$ end else
$\qquad\qquad\qquad\qquad$ adjoin (h, i, j) to the list on top of $dump$

$update(h)$ $\quad\equiv$ for each (h', i', j') on the list on top of $dump$ do
$\qquad\qquad\qquad dest(h', i', j', top(S)) := (h, i, j)$

Fig. 4. Improved algorithm to determine if $x_1 x_2 \ldots x_m$ is a subsequence of $y_1 y_2 \ldots y_n$

The details of the transformation are as follows:

Each loop of the program contains a **push** or a **pop**, and in fact the program contains precisely two **push** statements and two **pop** statements, where one statement in each pair deals with the digit 0 and the other with 1. We introduce four labels, *push0*, *push1*, *pop0* and *pop1*, corresponding to these statements.

Only variables i and j change during computation, within ranges $0 \le i \le m$, $0 \le j \le n$, yielding time bound $m \cdot n$. In fact, the number of different pairs (i, j)

stacked on *dump* and used in *dest* is at most $m(n - m + 1)$, since the relation $1 \leq i \leq j \leq n - m + i \leq n$ will always hold when *shortcut* is called.

```
    S := [Z];
    push Z onto S;
    push the input pair ⟨ⁿ⁰ₖ₀⟩ onto S;
argument: shortcut;
    if (let ⟨ⁿₖ⟩ = top(S) in 0 < k < n) then begin
        pop ⟨ⁿₖ⟩ from S and push ⟨ⁿ⁻¹ₖ⟩ and ⟨ⁿ⁻¹ₖ₋₁⟩ instead;
        go_to argument
    end;
    {0 = k ∨ k = n}
    top(S) := 1;
result:
    swap(S);
    if top(S) is in IN then begin
        add;
        go_to result
    end;
    if top(S) is in IN × IN then go_to argument
    else {top(S) is Z} pop S;
top(S) contains the output
```

Fig. 5. Stack program to compute $\binom{n}{k}$

6 Example: Binomial coefficients

The following recursive definition of the binomial coefficients is valid for $0 \leq k \leq n$:

$$\binom{n}{k} = \begin{cases} 1 & \text{, if } 0 = k \vee k = n \\ \binom{n-1}{k} + \binom{n-1}{k-1} & \text{, if } 0 < k < n \end{cases}$$

It is easy to utilize this definition in a stack program. Let the stack alphabet

$$T = \mathbb{N} \times \mathbb{N} + \mathbb{N} + \{Z\}$$

consist of pairs of natural numbers (written in the form $\binom{n}{k}$, to be used as arguments) and individual natural numbers (used as results) in addition to the bottom marker (Z).

In the simple case ($k = 0$ or $k = n$) the argument pair $\binom{n}{k}$ is directly replaced by the result (1), but otherwise the top of the stack is replaced by the two subtasks $\binom{n-1}{k}$ and $\binom{n-1}{k-1}$.

Whenever the top of the stack exposes a value, the two top elements are swapped. An argument pair will initiate further computation, but if another value is revealed the two top elements may be added to form a new function result. When swapping uncovers the bottom marker, computation has finished.

The algorithm has been programmed in Figure 5. Initially an additional bottom marker is pushed onto the stack; when this marker reappears, just before termination, it is popped, and the result of the computation is left on the stack.

The program uses some *ad hoc* but hopefully self-explanatory notations for tests and operations. In addition to general pops and pushes there are four general stackoperations $S := f= S$ with stack functions f as detailed below:

- pop $\binom{n}{k}$ from S and push $\binom{n-1}{k}$ and $\binom{n-1}{k-1}$ instead corresponds to the f of arity $(0,1)$ where $f(\binom{n}{k}) = (\binom{n-1}{k-1}, \binom{n-1}{k})$
- top$(S) := 1$ corresponds to the f of arity $(0,0)$ where $f(\binom{n}{k}) = (1)$
- swap(S) corresponds to the f of arity $(1,1)$ where $f(v_0, v_1) = (v_1, v_0)$
- add corresponds to the f of arity $(1,0)$ where $f(v_0, v_1) = v_0 + v_1$

The running time of the program is $\mathcal{O}(\binom{n}{k})$, as is easily seen, and the main reason for this behaviour is the long-winded recomputation of many partial results.

The program may, however, be subjected to the transformation of Section 3.1 by inserting a shortcut at the label *argument*, as in Figure 5. Since the pair $\binom{n}{k}$ in the top of the stack at this point will always satisfy $0 \leq k \leq k_0$ and $0 \leq n - k \leq n_0 - k_0$, *dest* only needs $(n - k + 1)(k + 1)$ entries.

The transformed program in effect implements the method of "Pascal's triangle", using $(n - k)k$ additions to compute $\binom{n}{k}$. If more complex operations such as multiplications were allowed, faster methods could be devised.

Linearity (in the number of surface configurations) does not quite follow from Section 4.2, since condition (2) is satisfied but condition (1) is violated by the path from "*result*" via a negative outcome of the test "top(S) is in $\mathbb{N}$" and positive outcome of "top(S) is in $\mathbb{N} \times \mathbb{N}$" to *argument*, which does not decrease stack height and also does not contain a shortcut.

A more detailed analysis of the actual case reveals that our transformed program is still linear: Of the two argument pairs that are created by "pop $\binom{n}{k}$ from S and push ...instead" one is treated immediately by the next execution of the *argument*-loop; the other is eventually brought to the top of the stack when being swapped with the result value of the first pair. The offending path is therefore taken the same number of times as the number of executions of "pop $\binom{n}{k}$ from S and push ...instead" ($(n - k)k$ times).

6.1 Generalization

The structure used in Figure 5 may be adjusted to compute any function f with a recursive definition

$$f(x) = \begin{cases} c_1 & \text{, if } p_1(x) \\ \vdots & \vdots \\ c_q & \text{, if } p_q(x) \\ f(d_1(x), \ldots, d_r(x)) & \text{, otherwise} \end{cases} \qquad (*)$$

where $d_1, \ldots, d_r$ are decreasing functions in some well-founded ordering of the argument domain. Instead of **swap** a circular rotation of the topmost r elements of the stack could be used.

Our method may in this way be said to reinvent "course-of-values recursion" or "dynamic programming" for definitions of the form (*).

7 Conclusion

It has been shown how any stack program in a mechanical way may be transformed into a version that uses some extra tables (whose size is determined by the number of surface configurations), but such that the execution time of the transformed version is proportional to the number of surface configurations.

For this insight to be useful for a general computational problem one should first solve the problem by a stack program with a small number of surface configurations and then apply the transformation. In many cases, the first of these stages may require ingenuity; for example, to obtain the stack program for pattern matching from a naïve version using two pointers does not seem obvious.

An interesting source of stack programs arises as results of Floyd's transformation (in [6]) of non-deterministic programs to deterministic ones. These are obtained by "running the non-deterministic program in reverse", so to speak, using a stack to take care of the bookkeeping involved in backtracking.

```
i := 0;
j := 0;
while i < m do begin {x₁...xᵢ is a subsequence of y₁...yⱼ}
      if m − i > n − j then failure;
      j := j + 1;
      case choose(2) of
      0:    skip;
      1:    begin
                  i := i + 1;
                  if xᵢ ≠ yⱼ then failure
            end
      end case
end;
success
```

Fig. 6. Non-deterministic algorithm to determine whether $x_1 x_2 \ldots x_m$ is a subsequence of $y_1 y_2 \ldots y_n$

A particularly nice example of this procedure (suggested to us by Torben Mogensen[9]) is the non-deterministic program for the subsequence problem shown in Figure 6. This program is a straightforward product of the problem specification, but resolving non-determinism by systematically trying case 0 first and case 1 afterwards gives the deterministic program on Figure 3 which may be subjected to Cook's transformation, resulting in the program with optimal running time shown in Figure 4. (If the possibilities are examined in the order 1 first, then 0, the optimal program is produced directly.)

References

1. Alfred V. Aho, John E. Hopcroft, and Jeffrey D. Ullman, *The Design and Analysis of Computer Algorithms*, Addison-Wesley Publishing Company 1974.
2. Torben Amtoft Hansen, Thomas Nikolajsen, Jesper Larsson Träff, and Neil D. Jones, Experiments with Implementation of two Theoretical Constructions, p. 119–133 in Logic at Botik, *Lecture Notes in Computer Science* Vol. 363, Springer-Verlag 1989.
3. Richard S. Bird, Improving Programs by the Introduction of Recursion, *Communications of the ACM* Vol. 20 No. 11 (November 1977) 856–863.
4. Stephen A. Cook, Linear-Time Simulation of Deterministic Two-Way Pushdown Automata, p. 75–80 in C. V. Freiman (editor): *Information Processing 71*, North-Holland Publishing Company 1972.
5. Stephen A. Cook, Characterization of Pushdown Machines in Terms of Time-Bounded Computers, *Journal of the ACM* Vol. 18 No. 1 (January 1971) 4–18.
6. Robert W Floyd, Nondeterministic Algorithms, *Journal of the ACM* Vol. 14 No. 4 (October 1967) 636–644.
7. Neil D. Jones, A Note on Linear Time Simulation of Deterministic Two-Way Pushdown Automata, *Information Processing Letters* Vol. 6 No. 4 (1977) 110–112.
8. Neil D. Jones, Carsten Krogh Gomard, Peter Sestoft: *Partial Evaluation and Automatic Program Generation*, Prentice Hall International, 1993.
9. Torben Ægidius Mogensen: Personal communication, September 1993.

A Rewriting of Fife's Theorem about Overlap-free Words *

J. Berstel

LITP, Institut Blaise Pascal

Université Pierre et Marie Curie

4, place Jussieu

F-75252 Paris Cedex 05

Abstract

The purpose of this expository paper is to present a self-contained proof of a famous theorem of Fife that gives a full description of the set of infinite overlap-free words over a binary alphabet. Fife's characterization consists in a parameterization of these infinite words by a set of infinite words over a ternary alphabet. The result is that the latter is a regular set. The proof is by the explicit construction of the minimal automaton, obtained by the method of left quotients.

Introduction

One of the first results about avoidable regularities in words was Axel Thue's proof of the existence of an infinite overlap-free words over two letters. In two important papers [16, 17], Thue derived a great number of results in this and related topics. His papers were overseen for a long time (see [6] for a discussion) and his results have been rediscovered several times (e. g. by Morse [10]), when interest in combinatorics on words, both stimulated by symbolic dynamics and computer science, became more important.

Axel Thue also looked for a complete description of all overlap-free and square-free words. His main tools were morphisms and codes (in contemporary terminology). His aim was to express sets of infinite words as homomorphic images of what is now called a *minimal* set. He achieved this very quickly for overlap-free two-sided infinite words (since they form a minimal set), and in his second paper, obtained such a description for large families of square-free infinite words as a result of a more than thirty pages long investigation.

The description of one-sided infinite words, either square-free or overlap-free, is much more involved. It was E. D. Fife [4] who gave, among other deep results,

---

*Partially supported by PRC "Mathématiques et Informatique" and by ESPRIT BRA working group 6317 – ASMICS 2.

the first full "description" of the set of infinite overlap-free words. His clever method consists in decomposing each such word in longer and longer blocks, where each block is obtained from preceding ones by exactly one among three rules. Coding each rule by a new symbol, he obtains a "description" by an infinite word over a new, ternary alphabet. The truly remarkable result is that the set of all words obtained in this way is regular, that is recognized by a finite automaton (with five states, as we shall see).

The proof of this result is not quite easy. In the terminology of automata theory, it consists in computing the minimal automaton by the well-known method of derivatives (or left quotients). The purpose of this paper is to present this proof in this context. The paper is aimed to be self-contained, excepted for some basic facts on overlap-free words that can be found in Lothaire [9] and Salomaa [14].. After some preliminaries, we give two general, basic lemmas on overlap-free words. In the next section, we present the result of Fife. The last section is devoted to the proof.

Recently, two results have given new insights in this topic. J. Cassaigne [2] and A. Carpi [1] have presented encodings of finite overlap-free words that are similar to Fife's. Both act simultaneously on both ends of the words to be described. J. Cassaigne succeeded in giving explicit recurrence equations for the number of overlap-free words of a given length, a problem that was open for a while; A. Carpi also constructs automata but which are different from Cassaigne's for the description of overlap-free words.

1 Preliminaries

An *alphabet* is a finite set (of *symbols* or *letters*). A *word* over some alphabet A is a (finite) sequence of elements in A. The length of a word w is denoted by $|w|$. The *empty word* of length 0 is denoted by ε. An *infinite* word is a mapping from the set of nonnegative integers into A.

A *factor* of a word w is any word u that occurs in w, i. e. such that there exist word x, y with $w = xuy$. A *square* is a nonempty word of the form uu. A word is *square-free* if none of its factors is a square. Similarly, an *overlap* is a word of the form $xuxux$, where x is nonempty. The terminology is justified by the fact that xux has two occurrences in $xuxux$, one as a *prefix* (initial factor) one as a *suffix* (final factor) and that these occurrences have a common part (the central x). As before, a word is *overlap-free* if none of its factors is an overlap.

The set of words over A is denoted by A^*. A function $h : A^* \to B^*$ is a *morphism* if $h(uv) = h(u)h(v)$ for all words u, v. If there is a letter a such that $h(a)$ starts with the letter a, then $h^n(a)$ starts with the word $h^{n-1}(a)$ for all $n > 0$. If the set words $\{h^n(a)) \mid n \geq 0\}$ is infinite, the morphism is *prolongeable* in a and defines a unique infinite word say $\mathbf{x}$ by the requirement that all $h^n(a)$ are prefixes of $\mathbf{x}$. The word $\mathbf{x}$ is said to be obtained by iterating h on a, and $\mathbf{x}$ is also denoted by $h^\omega(a)$. Clearly, $\mathbf{x}$ is a fixed point of h. For a detailed discussion and results on iterating morphisms, see [3].

2 The Thue-Morse sequence

In this section, we recall some basic properties concerning the Thue-Morse sequence. Other properties and proofs can be found in Lothaire [9] and Salomaa [14].

Let $A = \{a, b\}$ be a two letter alphabet. Consider the morphism μ from the free monoid A^* into itself defined by

$$\mu(a) = ab, \qquad \mu(b) = ba$$

Setting, for $n \geq 0$,

$$u_n = \mu^n(a), \qquad v_n = \mu^n(b)$$

one gets

$$
\begin{aligned}
u_0 &= a & v_0 &= b \\
u_1 &= ab & v_1 &= ba \\
u_2 &= abba & v_2 &= baab \\
u_3 &= abbabaab & v_3 &= baababba
\end{aligned}
$$

$$\cdots$$

and more generally

$$u_{n+1} = u_n v_n, \qquad v_{n+1} = v_n u_n$$

and

$$u_n = \overline{v}_n, \qquad v_n = \overline{u}_n$$

where $\overline{w}$ (the *opposite* of w) is obtained from w by exchanging a and b. Words u_n and v_n are *Morse blocks*. It is easily seen that u_{2n} and v_{2n} are palindromes, and that $u_{2n+1} = v_{2n+1}^{\sim}$, where $w^{\sim}$ is the reversal of w. The morphism μ can be extended to infinite words; it has two fixed points

$$\mathbf{t} = abbabaabbaababbabaab \cdots = \mu(\mathbf{t})$$

$$\overline{\mathbf{t}} = baababbaabbabaababba \cdots = \mu(\overline{\mathbf{t}})$$

and u_n (resp. v_n) is the prefix of length 2^n of $\mathbf{t}$ (resp. of $\overline{\mathbf{t}}$). It is equivalent to say that $\mathbf{t}$ is the limit of the sequence $(u_n)_{n \geq 0}$ (for the usual topology on finite and infinite words), obtained by iterating the morphism μ.

The *Thue-Morse sequence* is the word $\mathbf{t}$. There are several other characterizations of this word. For instance, let t_n be the n-th symbol in $\mathbf{t}$, starting with $n = 0$. Then $t_n = a$ or $t_n = b$ according to the parity of the number of bits equal to 1 in the binary expansion of n. For instance, $bin(19) = 10011$, consequently $d_1(19) = 3$, and indeed $t_{19} = a$.

Theorem 2.1 [17](Satz 6) *The sequence $\mathbf{t}$ is overlap-free.*

What Thue actually shows is that a word w is overlap-free iff $\mu(w)$ is overlap-free.

3 Factorization of overlap-free words

The following lemmas have been given by many peoples independently (e. g. Shelton and Soni [15], Kobayashi [8], Restivo and Salemi [11], Kfoury [7].)

Lemme 3.1 *("Progression Lemma") Let $n \geq 0$ and let $x = uvwc$ be an overlap-free word of length $1 + 3 \cdot 2^n$, with $|u| = |v| = |w| = 2^n$ and $c \in A$. If u and v are Morse blocks, then w is a Morse block.*

Proof. By induction on n. The result is clear for $n = 0$. Assume $n \geq 1$. By assumption, x has the form

$$x = UVUVBCc, \quad \text{or} \quad x = UVVUBCc$$

where U and V are the Morse blocks of size 2^{n-1} and $|B| = |C| = 2^{n-1}$. By induction, both B and C are Morse blocks. It remains to show that $BC \neq UU$ and $BC \neq VV$.

If $x = UVUVBCa$, then $BC \neq UU, VV$ since otherwise x has an overlap. If $x = UVVUBCa$, then clearly $BC \neq UU$. Suppose $BC = VV$. Then $x = (UVV)^2 a$, but a can be neither the first letter of U nor the first letter of V without producing an overlap in x. The proof is complete. ■

Lemme 3.2 *("Factorization Lemma") Let x be an overlap-free word. There exist three words u, v, y, with $u, v \in \{\varepsilon, a, b, aa, bb\}$, such that*

$$x = u\mu(y)v.$$

Moreover, the triple (u, y, v) is unique if $|x| \geq 7$.

Proof. The result is straightforward by inspection if $|x| \leq 5$. Suppose $|x| \geq 6$. We show that x contains two consecutive Morse blocks ab or ba. The result then follows from the progression lemma.

By symmetry, we may suppose that x starts with a. The possible prefixes of x, developed up to an encounter of two consecutive Morse blocks ab or ba are:

$$aabaab, aabab, aabba, abaab, abab, abba$$

This shows that the prefixes are of the required form. To prove uniqueness, consider two triples (u, y, v) and (u', y', v') such that $x = u\mu(y)v = u'\mu(y')v'$. Since $|x| \geq 7$, one has $|y|, |y'| \geq 2$. But then the occurrences of $\mu(y)$ and $\mu(y')$ cannot overlap without being equal. This shows uniqueness. ■

As an illustration, we mention the following result, already known to A. Thue (for a related result, see T. Harju [5]):

Theorem 3.3 *The overlap-free squares over A are the words*

$$u_n^2, \quad (u_n v_n u_n)^2$$

for $n \geq 0$, their opposites, and their conjugates.

As a consequence, if xx is an overlap-free square, then $|x| = 3 \cdot 2^n$ or $|x| = 2^n$ for some n.

4 Fife's Theory

Let $X_n = \{u_n, v_n\}$ denote the set of Morse blocks of length 2^n and set $X = \bigcup_{n \geq 0} X_n$.

Let $w \in A^* X_1$. Thus w ends with ab or ba. The *canonical decomposition* of w is the triple

$$(z, y, \bar{y})$$

where y is the longest word in X such that

$$w = zy\bar{y}$$

In other terms, $(z, y, \bar{y})$ is the canonical decomposition of w iff $\bar{y}y$ is not a suffix of z. As an example, the canonical decomposition of $aabaabbabaab$ is

$$(aaba, abba, baab)$$

and that of $aabaabbabaababbaabbabaabbaababbaabbabaab$ is

$$(aabaabbabaababbaabbabaab, baababba, abbabaab)$$

Define now three mappings $\alpha, \beta, \gamma : A^* X_1 \rightarrow A^* X_1$, written on the right of their arguments like actions, as follows: let $w \in A^* X_1$ have the canonical decomposition $(z, y, \bar{y})$, then

$$\begin{aligned}
w \cdot \alpha &= zy\bar{y} \cdot \alpha = zy\bar{y}y\bar{y} = wyy\bar{y} \\
w \cdot \beta &= zy\bar{y} \cdot \beta = zy\bar{y}y\bar{y}y = wy\bar{y}y \\
w \cdot \gamma &= zy\bar{y} \cdot \gamma = zy\bar{y}y = w\bar{y}y
\end{aligned}$$

Setting

$$B = \{\alpha, \beta, \gamma\}$$

the word $w \cdot f$ is well defined for all $f \in B^*$. Since w is a prefix of $w \cdot \alpha$, $w \cdot \beta$ and $w \cdot \gamma$, the infinite word $w \cdot \mathbf{f}$ is well defined of any infinite word $\mathbf{f}$ over B. A finite or infinite word f over B is called a *description* of the finite or infinite word x if $x = ab \cdot f$ or $x = aab \cdot f$ (or symmetrically $x = ba \cdot f$ or $x = bba \cdot f$). Here are some examples:

$$\begin{aligned}
ab \cdot \alpha &= abaab \\
ab \cdot \beta &= ababba \\
ab \cdot \gamma &= abba \\
aba\ ab\ ba \cdot \alpha &= aba\ ab\ ba\ ab\ ab\ ba = abaabbaababba \\
aba\ ab\ ba \cdot \beta &= aba\ ab\ ba\ ab\ ba\ ba\ ab = abaabbaabbabaab \\
ab \cdot \gamma^\omega &= \mathbf{t} \\
aab \cdot \alpha &= aabaab = a(ab \cdot \alpha) \\
aab \cdot \alpha^3 \gamma &= aabaabbabaababbaabbabaabbaababbaabbabaab
\end{aligned}$$

The word

$$\begin{aligned}
u &= aaba\ abbabaab\ abbabaab\ baababba\ baababba\ abbabaab\ baababba\ baabbaa \\
&= (aab \cdot \alpha\alpha\beta\gamma)baababba\ baabbaa
\end{aligned}$$

of Restivo and Salemi [11] admits no description. As we shall see, this means that it is not the prefix of an infinite overlap-free word.

Proposition 4.1 *Every infinite overlap-free word admits a unique description.*

Proof. This is a simple application of the progression lemma.　　　■

Let

$$I = \{\alpha, \beta\}(\gamma^2)^* \{\beta\alpha, \gamma\beta, \alpha\gamma\}$$

and consider the set

$$F = B^\omega - B^* I B^\omega$$

of infinite words over B having no factor in I, and the set

$$G = \{\mathbf{f} \mid \beta\mathbf{f} \in F\}$$

Theorem 4.2 ("Fife's Theorem") *Let* $\mathbf{x}$ *be an infinite word over* A.
   (1)   *If* $\mathbf{x}$ *starts with* ab, *then* $\mathbf{x}$ *is overlap-free iff its description is in* F;
   (2)   *If* $\mathbf{x}$ *starts with* aab, *then* $\mathbf{x}$ *is overlap-free iff its description is in* G.

The set F of Fife's words is recognized by an automaton with 5 states, given in the following figure.

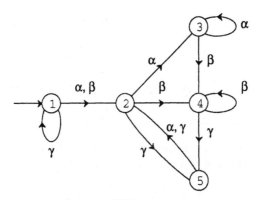

Fig. 1　Fife's automaton.

Fife's theorem has a number of consequences. Call a word w *infinitely extensible* if it is a prefix of an infinite overlap-free word. Then one has:

Corollaire 4.3 *A word* w *is infinitely extensible iff it is a prefix of a finite word that admits a description which is a prefix of a word in* F *or* G. *It is decidable whether a word is infinitely extensible.*

Indeed, it is easily seen that if w is a prefix of a word x that admits a (finite) description, then $|x| \leq 2|w|$. Another consequence is:

Corollaire 4.4 *The Thue-Morse* **t** *is the greatest infinite overlap-free word, for the lexicographic order, among those starting with the letter a.*

Proof. If one chooses $a < b$ and $\alpha < \beta < \gamma$ then indeed $\mathbf{f} \leq \mathbf{f}'$ implies $ab \cdot \mathbf{f} \leq ab \cdot \mathbf{f}'$. Now the greatest word in F is γ^ω and $\mathbf{t} = ab \cdot \gamma^\omega$ ∎

Observe that this result can also be proved directly, by arguing on the form of overlap-free words, and using the progression lemma.

5 Proof

We observe first that the second statement of the theorem is a consequence of the first statement. Indeed, let x be an infinite overlap-free word starting with aab, and let $\mathbf{f}$ be its description (which exists by the proposition). To prove that $\beta\mathbf{f}$ is in F, observe that

$$\mu(aab \cdot \mathbf{f}) = \mu(aab) \cdot \mathbf{f} = ababba \cdot \mathbf{f} = ab \cdot \beta\mathbf{f}$$

and since $aab \cdot \mathbf{f}$ is overlap-free iff $\mu(aab \cdot \mathbf{f})$ is overlap-free, the word $aab \cdot \mathbf{f}$ is overlap-free iff $ab \cdot \beta\mathbf{f}$ is overlap-free, thus iff $\beta\mathbf{f} \in F$.

It is convenient to use, for the proof, the notation n for $u_n = \mu^n(a)$, and symmetrically $\overline{n}$ for $v_n = \mu^n(b)$. (Consider n as a shorthand for μ^n.) For example

$$
\begin{aligned}
0 &= a, & \overline{0} &= b \\
1 &= ab, & \overline{1} &= ba \\
2 &= abba, & 3 &= abbabaab
\end{aligned}
$$

It follows that

$$
\begin{aligned}
1 \cdot \alpha &= 0\overline{2}, & n \cdot \alpha &= (n-1)\overline{(n+1)} \\
1 \cdot \beta &= 12, & n \cdot \beta &= n(n+1) \\
1 \cdot \gamma &= 2, & n \cdot \gamma &= n+1
\end{aligned}
$$

We denote by P the set of finite overlap-free words over A and by W those words over B that are description of words in P starting with $1 = ab$:

$$W = \{f \in B^* \mid 1 \cdot f \in P\}$$

Recall that

$$I = \{\alpha, \beta\}(\gamma^2)^*\{\beta\alpha, \gamma\beta, \alpha\gamma\}$$

Fife's theorem is a straightforward extension to infinite words of the following:

Theorem 5.1 *One has $W = B^* - B^*IB^*$.*

We start with a useful observation:

Proposition 5.2 *The set W is factorial : if $1 \cdot fgh$ is overlap-free, then $1 \cdot g$ is overlap-free.*

Proof. We show first that W is suffix-closed, by showing that if $\alpha f \in W$, then $f \in W$, and similarly for β and γ. Now

$$1 \cdot \alpha f = 0\overline{2} \cdot f = 0\overline{2 \cdot f} = 0\overline{\mu(1 \cdot f)}$$
$$1 \cdot \beta f = 12 \cdot f = 1\mu(1 \cdot f)$$
$$1 \cdot \gamma f = \mu(1 \cdot f)$$

This shows that in all three cases, the word $1 \cdot f$ is overlap-free.

We now prove that W is prefix-closed. Let $fg \in W$ and set $w = 1 \cdot fg$ and $u = 1 \cdot f$. Then $w = u \cdot g$ and u is a prefix of w. Consequently u is overlap-free and $f \in W$. This completes the proof. ∎

For the proof of 5.1, we compute the minimal automaton of the set W. This will be done by the method of quotients. For a word u and a set Y, we definie

$$u^{-1}Y = \{w \mid uw \in Y\}$$

We shall see that the minimal automaton of W is the automaton of the figure which recognizes $B^* - B^* I B^*$. This shows the theorem.

We start by the following easy properties:

Lemme 5.3 $(\alpha^2 \gamma)^{-1}W = (\alpha\beta\alpha)^{-1}W = (\alpha\gamma\beta)^{-1}W = \emptyset.$

Proof. It suffice to verify that the words $1 \cdot \alpha^2 \gamma$, $1 \cdot \alpha\beta\alpha$ and $1 \cdot \alpha\gamma\beta$ all have an overlap. Indeed:

$$1 \cdot \alpha^2 \gamma = abaabb\ abaabb\ a\ ababba$$
$$1 \cdot \alpha\beta\alpha = abaabbaababb\ abaabbaababb\ a$$
$$1 \cdot \alpha\gamma\beta = abaababb\ abaababb\ a\ abbabaab$$

∎

The following equations are more difficult:

Proposition 5.4 *The following equations hold for W* :
- (i) $W = \gamma^{-1}W$;
- (ii) $\alpha^{-1}W = \beta^{-1}W = (\alpha\gamma\alpha)^{-1}W = (\alpha\gamma\gamma)^{-1}W$;
- (iii) $(\alpha^2)^{-1}W = (\alpha^3)^{-1}W$;
- (iv) $(\alpha\beta)^{-1}W = (\alpha^2\beta)^{-1}W$;
- (v) $(\alpha\gamma)^{-1}W = (\alpha\beta\gamma)^{-1}W$.

Let P_a be the set of overlap-free words that have no prefix that is a square ending with the letter a. Thus $w \in P_a$ iff for each prefix $xcxc$ of w with c a letter, on has $c = b$. We show that $aw \in P \iff w \in P_a$, that is

$$P_a = a^{-1}P.$$

Indeed, let $w \in P_a$. If aw has an overlap, this overlap is a prefix of aw, and has the form $axaxa$. But then $xaxa$ is a prefix of w, a contradiction. Thus $w \in P_a$. The converse is straightforward. The set P_b is defined similarly. Set

$$W_a = \{f \in W \mid 1 \cdot f \in P_a\}, \quad W_b = \{f \in W \mid 1 \cdot f \in P_b\}$$

Then:

Proposition 5.5 *The following relations hold:*

(1) $f \in W \iff \gamma f \in W;$
   $f \in W_a \iff \gamma f \in W_b;$
   $f \in W_b \iff \gamma f \in W_a;$

(2) $\alpha f \in W \iff \alpha f \in W_b \iff f \in W_a;$

(3) $\beta f \in W \iff f \in W_a;$

(4) $\alpha^2 f \in W \Rightarrow \alpha^2 f \in W_a;$

(5) $\alpha\beta f \in W \Rightarrow \alpha\beta f \in W_a;$

(6) $\beta\gamma f \in W \Rightarrow \beta\gamma f \in W_a.$

Proof of proposition 5.4.

(i). From (1).

(ii). From (2) and (3), it follows that $\alpha f \in W \iff \beta f \in W$. Next

$$\alpha f \in W \iff \alpha f \in W_b \iff \gamma\alpha f \in W_a \iff \alpha\gamma\alpha f \in W$$
$$\alpha f \in W \iff f \in W_a \iff \gamma\gamma f \in W_a \iff \alpha\gamma\gamma f \in W$$

(iii). From (4) and (1), one obtains

$$\alpha^2 f \in W \Rightarrow \alpha^2 f \in W_a \Rightarrow \alpha^3 f \in W$$

the converse implication holds because W is prefix-closed.

(iv). From (5),

$$\alpha\beta f \in W \Rightarrow \alpha\beta f \in W_a \Rightarrow \alpha^2\beta f \in W$$

the converse implication holds because W is suffix-closed.

(v). From (ii),(6) and (2), one gets

$$\alpha\gamma f \in W \iff \beta\gamma f \in W \Rightarrow \beta\gamma f \in W_a \Rightarrow \alpha\beta\gamma f \in W \qquad \blacksquare$$

It remains to prove proposition 5.5. For this, we use the following lemma:

Lemme 5.6 *Let w be a word in P. Then*

(a) *if $w \in abaabbaX_1^*$, then $w \in P_a$;*

(b) *if $w \in aabbaX_1^*$, then $w \in P_b$;*

(c) *if $w \in abaabX_1^*$, then $w \in P_b$.*

Proof of proposition 5.5.

(1). First $1 \cdot f \in P \iff \mu(1 \cdot f) = 1 \cdot \gamma f \in P$. Next, let $f \in W_a$ and suppose $\mu(1 \cdot f) = ububv$. Then $|ub| \neq 3$, since otherwise $u = ab$ and $ubub = abbabb \notin X_1^*$, or $u = ba$ and $ubub = babbab \notin X_1^*$. Thus $|ub|$ is even, and $1 \cdot f \notin P_a$. The converse is immediate.

(2). One has $w = 1 \cdot \alpha f = 0\bar{2} \cdot f = abaabv$ for some $v \in X_1^*$, and by (c) of the lemma, one has $w \in P_b$. Thus $\alpha f \in W_b$. Next

$$\alpha f \in W_b \iff 0\bar{2} \cdot f \in P_b$$
$$f \in W_a \iff 1 \cdot F \in P_a \iff \bar{1} \cdot f \in P_b \iff \bar{2} \cdot f \in P_a$$

Thus it remains to show that $0\overline{2} \cdot f \in P_b \iff \overline{2} \cdot f \in P_a$. If $0\overline{2} \cdot f \in P_b$ then $\overline{2} \cdot f \in P_a$ since otherwise $\overline{2} \cdot f$ has an overlap. Conversely, if $\overline{2} \cdot f \in P_a$, then $0\overline{2} \cdot f = a\overline{2} \cdot f$ is overlap-free and, again by (c) of the lemma, it is in P_b.

(3). One has $w = 1 \cdot \beta f = 12 \cdot f = ababba \cdot f = \mu(aab \cdot f) = \mu(a(1 \cdot f))$. If $\beta f \in W$, then $w \in P$, whence $a(1 \cdot f) \in P$, and $f \in W$, and even $f \in W_a$. Conversely, if $f \in W_a$, then $a(1 \cdot f) \in P$, whence $w \in P$ and $\beta f \in W$.

(4). One has $w = 1 \cdot \alpha^2 f = 0\overline{1}3 \cdot f \in abaabbaX_1^* \cap P$, and by (a) of the lemma, $\alpha^2 f \in W_a$.

(5). One has $w = 1 \cdot \alpha\beta f = 0\overline{2}3 \cdot f \in abaabbaX_1^* \cap P$, and by (a) of the lemma, $\alpha\beta f \in W_a$.

(6). One has $w = 1 \cdot \beta\gamma f = 1\mu(2 \cdot f) = \mu(aabbav)$ for some $v \in X_1^*$. By statement (b) of the lemma, $aabbav \in P_b$, whence $w \in P_a$. ∎

Proof of the lemma.

(a). Suppose the conclusion is false. Then

$$w = abaabbaw' = uuv$$

where u end with an a. The word u has not length 3, hence it has even length, and is of the form $u = au'a$, with u' of even length. But then $u'aa$ is in X_1^*, a contradiction.

(b). Suppose the conclusion is false. Then

$$w = aabbaw' = uuv = (au'b)(au'b)v$$

Again, u is not of length 3, hence it has even length. Since $u'bau'b$ has odd length, the word bv is in X_1^*, and v starts by a letter a and w has an overlap, contradiction.

(c). Suppose the conclusion is false. Then

$$w = abaabw' = uuv = (au'b)(au'b)v$$

Again, u has even length because its length is not 3, and $bv \in X_1^*$, thus v starts with an a and w has an overlap, contradiction. ∎

This ends the proof of Fife's theorem. Let us mention again two finitary versions of this result, which are more complicated, due to J. Cassaigne and A. Carpi.

References

[1] A. CARPI, Overlap-free words and finite automata, *Theoret. Comput. Sci.* **115** (1993), 243–260.

[2] J. CASSAIGNE, Counting overlap-free binary words, in: *STACS'93*, Enjalbert, Finkel, Wagner (eds), Lect. Notes Comp. Sci.,**665**, Springer-Verlag, 1993, 216–225.

[3] K. Culik II and A. Salomaa, On infinite words obtained by iterating morphisms, *Theoret. Comput. Sci.* **19** (1982), 29–38.

[4] E. D. Fife, Binary sequences which contain no BBb, *Trans. Amer. Math. Soc.* **261** (1980), 115–136.

[5] T. Harju, On cyclically overlap-free words in binary alphabets, *The Book of L*, Springer-Verlag, 1986, 123–130.

[6] G.A. Hedlund, Remarks on the work of Axel Thue, *Nordisk Mat. Tidskr.* **15** (1967), 148–150.

[7] R. Kfoury, A linear time algorithm to decide whether a binary word contains an overlap, *Theoret. Inform. Appl.* **22** (1988), 135–145.

[8] Y. Kobayashi, Enumeration of irreducible binary words, *Discrete Appl. Math.***20** (1988), 221–232.

[9] M. Lothaire, *Combinatorics on Words*, Addison-Wesley, 1983.

[10] M. Morse, Recurrent geodesics on a surface of negative curvature, *Transactions Amer. Math. Soc.* **22** (1921), 84–100.

[11] A. Restivo, S. Salemi, Overlap-free words on two symbols, in: *Automata on infinite words*, Nivat, Perrin (eds), Lect. Notes Comp. Sci. .,**192**, Springer-Verlag, 1985, 198–206.

[12] G. Rozenberg, A. Salomaa, *The Mathematical Theory of L-Systems*, Academic Press, 1980.

[13] A. Salomaa, Morphisms on free monoids and language theory, in *Formal Language Theory : Perspectives and Open Problems*, pp. 141–166, Academic Press, 1980.

[14] A. Salomaa, *Jewels of Formal Language Theory*, Computer Science Press, 1981.

[15] R. Shelton, R. Soni, Chains and fixing blocks in irreducible sequences, *Discrete Math.***54** (1985), 93–99.

[16] A. Thue, Über unendliche Zeichenreihen, *Kra. Vidensk. Selsk. Skrifter. I. Mat.-Nat. Kl.*, Christiana 1906, Nr. 7.

[17] A. Thue, Über die gegenseitige Lage gleicher Teile gewisser Zeichenreihen, *Kra. Vidensk. Selsk. Skrifter. I. Mat.-Nat. Kl.*, Christiana 1912, Nr. 10.

[18] A. Thue, *Selected Mathematical Papers*, edited by T. Nagell, A. Selberg, S. Selberg, K. Thalberg, Universitetsforlaget, Oslo 1977.

Reconsidering the Jeep Problem
- Or How to Transport a Birthday Present to Salosauna -

Wilfried Brauer, Ute Brauer
Institut für Informatik
Technische Universität
D-80290 München

Abstract

The simple problem of how far a jeep can travel with a given amount of gasoline if intermediate gasoline dumps may be used is a nice example for problems which seem to have obvious recursive solution algorithms but which may become quite difficult if the problem specification is slightly changed. The classical version allows that arbitrarily small parts of the given amount of gasoline may be filled in the jeep's tank. Wood has restricted the problem to a discrete problem by requiring that the tank can be refilled only when it is empty and that it must be refilled completely, and that the gasoline is available only in cans of the size of the tank. In an earlier note we had shown, by using a new strategy, that the seemingly adequate algorithm given by Wood in analogy to the optimal solution to the classical version is not optimal. The new strategy however is also not optimal. In this note we discuss variants of the new strategy and try to get a better understanding of the influences of (small) changes in the problem specification to the solution algorithms.

The Problem and Earlier Results

The classical jeep problem (see [Fin], [Phi], [Gal]) is to compute how far a jeep may go when starting at a dump with n cans of gasoline, provided that it needs 1 canful to drive 1 unit distance and it is allowed to carry 2 canfuls of gasoline (including the contents of its tank). The optimal solution algorithm (see [Gal]) assumes that arbitrary fractions of a canful may be put into the tank.

Since this seems to be a bit unrealistic, a discrete variant was considered by D. Wood in [Woo]: It is only allowed to refill the tank, when it is empty and then 1 canful has to be filled in (thus 1 can can be transported). The following solution was proposed in [Woo]: With one canful transport $n - 1$ cans to the next dump and go on recursively. This gives the distance function $f_w(n) = 1 + 1 + \frac{1}{3} + \frac{1}{5} + \ldots + 1/(2n - 3)$. This seemed to be the natural adaptation of the classical optimal solution.

However in [Bra] we showed that $f_w(n)$ is not optimal for $n \geq 4$ by using a new strategy: With one canful transport only 1 can as far as possible. This means that, for even n, each second can is transported to a dump $\frac{1}{2}$ unit distance away - apart from the last one, which is moved to an auxiliary dump $\frac{3}{4}$ units away, and which is fetched in the next round with the last $\frac{1}{2}$ canful. This strategy should only be applied to even can numbers since if $n = 2k + 1$ then only k cans are used for the transportation of k cans and the last one is wasted.

Let $[x; n]$ denote the situation, that at position x there is a dump containing n cans. We then can describe the procedure by

$$[0; 2 \cdot (2k - 1)] \rightarrow [\frac{1}{2}; 2k - 2] \& [\frac{3}{4}; 1] \rightarrow [1; k] \qquad (1)$$

which means that the jeep starts at the dump at position 0 which contains $2 \cdot (2k - 1)$ cans. It then (in a first round) transports in each of $2k - 2$ round trips (each using up one tankful) one can to a dump at position $\frac{1}{2}$, and in the final trip one can is moved to position $\frac{3}{4}$, and the jeep stops at position $\frac{1}{2}$ with an empty tank. In a second round $k - 1$ cans are moved to a dump at position 1 in $k - 1$ round trips and one trip from position $\frac{1}{2}$ to position 1 which leaves $\frac{1}{2}$ canful in the tank such that the jeep may bring the can from position $\frac{3}{4}$ to position 1. This strategy gives better results than Wood's strategy for $n = 6$ and all $n \geq 12$. The distance function for this procedure is

$$f_{\kappa}(n) = f_{\kappa}(p(t)) = (t+3)/2 \quad \text{for} \quad p(t) \le n < p(t+1) \quad \text{and} \quad t \ge 1.$$

$$\text{where} \quad p(t) = \begin{cases} (2^{t+1}+4)/3 = 2 + 2 + 2^3 + \ldots + 2^{t-1} & \text{for } t \text{ even} \\ (2^{t+1}+2)/3 = 2 + 2^2 + 2^4 + \ldots + 2^{t-1} & \text{for } t \text{ odd} \end{cases}$$

Its asymptotic behaviour is $\frac{1}{2}\lfloor log_2(3n) \rfloor + 1$ while that of $f_w(n)$ is $\frac{1}{2}ln\,n + 1.98$. When we compare the two strategies we are lead immediately to the assumption that the new strategy performs better because it needs less backward trips.

Further Procedures

The algorithms given in [Bra] are not always optimal. We still conjecture optimality for $n = p(t)$ where t is odd. For other values of n we have found several other (and better) solutions by slightly weakening the basic strategic idea of moving only 1 can as far as possible with 1 canful - such that it now seems that there is perhaps no universally optimal solution, but different procedures for different series of can numbers.

Procedure (1) suggests to consider the following sequences of can numbers $h_s(n)$ where s is a (small) integer and $h_s(1) = s; h_s(n+1) = 4h_s(n) - 2, n \ge 1$. For example $s = 2$ gives the $p(t)$ where t is odd. Obviously $f_{\kappa}(h_s(n)) = f_{\kappa}(s) + n - 1$ for $n \ge 2$.

To be able to work efficiently also with can numbers like 3, 4, 5, 6, 7, 8, 9, and also with the $p(t)$ for even t, we allow several auxiliary dumps at varying distances, and we move sometimes two cans forward by using the same tank filling; the resulting modified distance function is denoted by $f_{\kappa m}$.

$$[0;3] \to [\frac{1}{3};2] \quad \text{gives} \quad f_{\kappa m}(3) = 2\frac{1}{3}$$

$$[0;4] \to [\frac{1}{2}+\frac{1}{6};2] \quad \text{gives} \quad f_{\kappa m}(4) = 2\frac{2}{3}$$

Both these values are optimal, since they are the same as in the classical case.

$$[0;5] \to [\frac{1}{4};2]\&[\frac{5}{8};1] \to [\frac{5}{8}+\frac{5}{24};2], \quad \text{i.e.} \quad f_{\kappa m}(5) = 2\frac{5}{6}.$$

This seems to be optimal also, since the distance for 5 cans in the classical case is $2\frac{13}{15}$.

More generally we obtain the following procedures:

$$[0; 2\cdot 2n] \to [\frac{1}{2}; 2n-2]\&[\frac{1}{2}+\frac{1}{8};2], n \ge 2 \tag{2}$$

$$[x; 2j+2]\&[x+a;2] \to [x+\frac{1}{2};j]\&[x+\frac{1}{2}+\frac{1}{2}a;1],\&[x+a;2] \to$$
$$\to [x+\frac{1}{2};j]\&[x+\frac{1}{2}+\frac{1}{8}+\frac{1}{2}a;2], j \ge 2 \tag{3}$$

$$[x; 4j+4]\&[x+a;2] \to [x+\frac{1}{2};2j+2]\&[x+\frac{4}{3}a;2] \to$$
$$\to [x+\frac{1}{2};2j+2]\&[x+\frac{3}{4}+\frac{2}{3}a;1] \to \tag{4}$$
$$\to [x+1;j]\&[x+1+\frac{4}{9}a;2], j \ge 2.$$

$$[x; 4]\&[x+a;2] \to [x+a;2]\&[x+\frac{1}{2}+\frac{1}{4}a;2] \tag{5}$$

Near the end of a jeep's tour we need the following procedure:

$$[x; 2] \& [x + a; 2] \to [x + \frac{1}{2} + \frac{1}{2}a; 1] \& [x + a; 2] \to$$
$$\to [x + \frac{1}{2} + \frac{1}{2}a + \frac{1}{3}(\frac{1}{2} + \frac{1}{2}a); 2] = [x + \frac{2}{3}(1 + a); 2] \tag{6}$$

For some odd n we also found a (possibly optimal) starting procedure:

$$[0; 7] \to [\frac{1}{4}; 2] \& [\frac{1}{2} + \frac{1}{16}; 2]$$
$$[0; 11] \to [\frac{1}{4}; 6] \& [\frac{5}{8}; 1] \to [\frac{3}{4}; 2] \& [\frac{3}{4} + \frac{1}{16}; 2]$$
$$[0; 4j + 5] \to [\frac{1}{4}; 2] \& [\frac{1}{2}; 2j] \& [\frac{1}{2} + \frac{1}{8}; 1] \to \tag{7}$$
$$\to [\frac{1}{4} + \frac{1}{2}; 1] \& [\frac{1}{2} + \frac{1}{8} + \frac{1}{8}; 1] \& [\frac{1}{2}; 2j] =$$
$$[\frac{1}{2}; 2j] \& [\frac{1}{2} + \frac{1}{4}; 2], j \ge 1.$$

Applying these procedures in the appropriate order gives the following values of f_{um}:

$$f_{um}(7) = \frac{3}{18}, f_{um}(11) = 3\frac{1}{3} + \frac{1}{8}$$
$$f_{um}(p(2j)) = f_u(p(2j)) + \frac{1}{16} \cdot (\frac{4}{9})^{j-2} \quad \text{for} \quad j \ge 2$$
$$f_{um}(2^k) = \frac{1}{2}k + \frac{3}{2} + \frac{1}{3}(1 - 2^{1-k}) \quad \text{for} \quad k \ge 1$$
$$f_{um}(2^k + 1) = \frac{1}{2}k + \frac{3}{2} + \frac{1}{3} \quad \text{for} \quad k \ge 1$$

Discussion

A problem arises when we consider the case $n = 10$. Obviously procedure (1) gives $[0; 10] \to [1; 3]$, and the optimal distance for $n = 3$ is $2\frac{1}{3}$. Thus it seems that the optimal distance for $n = 10$ should be $3\frac{1}{3} = f_u(h_3(2))$, since the jeep bringing 3 cans to position 1 by using procedure (1) always moves forward with a load of one can and never moves back behind a point where its tank was filled. Nevertheless already $f_{um}(9) = f_{um}(2^3 + 1) = 3\frac{1}{3}$. And indeed there is a better procedure for $n = 10$ by using procedures (5) and (6)

$$[0; 10] \to [\frac{1}{4}; 4] \& [\frac{1}{2} + \frac{1}{16}; 2] \to [1\frac{1}{4} + \frac{5}{32}; 2]$$

That is, the distance reachable with $n = 10$ is $\frac{7}{96}$ units larger than that reached with procedure (1), although the jeep goes back (and forth) more often.

Therefore the main reason why Wood's strategy is not optimal, probably is not the high number of backward tours.

From this we also have to conclude that we cannot assume that the composition of good procedures gives again a good procedure.

Also the values $f_u(h_a(n))$ need not be optimal (although for example $f_u(14) = f_u(h_4(2)) = 3\frac{2}{3}$ looks quite well).

To get a better understanding of the solution possibilities, we may look at some natural constraints on possible solutions. We then see for example, that the constraint to have only one intermediate dump gives Wood's solution, while the constraint to have fixed distances between dumps implies to allow for at least 2 dumps; therefore if fixed distances and at most 2 dumps are to be used then procedure (1) is the only solution.

It remains open to find other reasonable sets of restrictions which determine useful strategies and to find a generally optimal algorithm.

[Bra] Brauer, U., Brauer, W.: *A new approach to the jeep problem*, EATCS Bulletin **38** (1989) 145-153

[Fin] Fine, N.J.: *The jeep problem*, Amer. Math. Monthly, **54** (1947) 24-31

[Gal] Gale, D.: *The jeep once more or jeeper by the dozen*, Amer. Math. Monthly, **77** (1970) 493-501

[Phi] Phipps, C.G.: *The jeep problem, A more general solution*, Amer Math. Monthly, **54** (1947) 458-462

[Woo] Wood, D.: *Paradigms and Programming with PASCAL*, Computer Science Press, Rockville, 1984.

Learning Picture Sets from Examples

Anne Brüggemann-Klein, Petra Fischer, Thomas Ottmann

Institut für Informatik, Universität Freiburg
Rheinstr. 10–12, 79104 Freiburg, Germany
E-Mail: {brueggem | ottmann}@informatik.uni-freiburg.de

1 Introduction

The main purpose of this note is to establish a connection between three—at first glance—unrelated areas of computer science: Theory of automata and formal languages, computer graphics, and computational learning theory. Moreover, we demonstrate that this connection has been enabled by research carried out at the site of this colloquium and by people involved in it.

Already more than ten years ago, Maurer, Rozenberg, and Welzl [11] showed that formal languages can be used to describe pictures drawn in the Cartesian plane. A picture is described by a walk through the picture from a designated start point to a designated end point; that is; a sequence of the walking primitives l, r, u, and d that each denote a one-unit-length move in the Cartesian plane in the directions left, right, up, and down, respectively.

The description of a picture by a word over the alphabet $\Pi = \{l, r, u, d\}$ of the four single-step movements is not unique. The full language of all words that describe a given picture q forms a regular language of words over Π [11], called the *complete description language* of q and denoted by $des(q)$. Therefore, the class $\mathcal{B}_c$ of all the complete description languages of pictures in the plane is a subclass of the class of all regular languages over Π.

Instead of collecting *all* words that describe a given picture q into one language, $des(q)$, one can, for each picture q, also study the class $\mathcal{B}_q$ of the (uncomplete) *description languages*; that is, the *regular* languages of words over Π that describe q. In other words, $\mathcal{B}_q$ is the class of regular sublanguages of $des(q)$, for each picture q.

Finally, one can define directly operations on pictures (and picture sets) that correspond to concatenation and Kleene closure of words (and word languages). This leads to the notion of a regular picture set in a natural way.

Now we may ask whether restricting the whole class of the regular languages to $\mathcal{B}_c$ or to $\mathcal{B}_q$ or to regular picture sets reduces the complexity of regular sets essentially. Of course, in this form the question is too general for a rigorous study. In this note we discuss the question from a computational learning point of view.

The problem of identifying an unknown regular language from examples by a learning algorithm has been studied quite extensively; see [8, 13, 6] for surveys of the literature. To identify a regular language is understood as the task to construct a finite automaton or a regular expression that accepts or denotes the language, respectively. This is a very strong requirement for a learning algorithm. Valiant [16] has introduced a more liberal notion of PAC (probably approximately correct) learning that does not require the exact but only the approximate identification of an initially unknown language. In what follows we study the learnability of the above mentioned classes of picture description languages in the different learning models. We show that restricting regular languages to the description languages $\mathcal{B}_q$ of q does not ease the learning task. However, the class $\mathcal{B}_c$ has properties that can make learning a regular language in $\mathcal{B}_c$ quite easy. Learnability of regular picture sets is left open, except for a fairly specific case.

In the next two sections, we briefly recall the required notions on formal languages, computational learning, and regular picture sets. Section 4 states the results on learning a class $\mathcal{B}_q$, for a fixed picture q, and gives a brief sketch of the proofs. In Section 5 we discuss learning of $\mathcal{B}_c$ and, finally, in Section 6, learning of regular picture sets.

2 The Learning Paradigm of Exact Identification

Angluin [4] introduces the learning paradigm of exact identification that has since been applied to a growing number of domains, such as regular languages [1, 3, 15], reversible languages [2], context-free languages [14], and Boolean concepts [7].

Let U be a universe of objects. A *concept* is a subset of U, and a *class of concepts* is a set of concepts. Concepts are represented by words over some fixed finite alphabet Δ. A *representation system* for a class of concepts is a language of words over Δ, the representations, together with a mapping that maps a representation to the concept it represents.

As an example, we consider the universe $U = \Sigma^*$ of all words over a finite alphabet Σ. Then a concept is a language over Σ, and the regular languages over Σ form a class of concepts that may be represented by regular expressions.

The learner's task is to identify an unknown concept, the *target concept*, chosen from some specified class $\mathcal{C}$ of concepts. The goal of the learner is exact identification; that is, to compute a representation for the unknown concept. To gain knowledge on the target concept, the learner may put certain types of queries to a teacher, who returns the correct answers.

Following Angluin [3], we consider two types of queries, namely *membership queries* and *equivalence queries*. With membership queries, the learner proposes an object x; the reply is *yes* if x belongs to the target concept and *no* otherwise. With equivalence queries, the learner proposes a representation ρ (in the specified system) of a concept in $\mathcal{C}$. The reply is either *yes* or *no* and a counterexample. The reply *yes* is given if ρ represents the unknown concept; the reply *no* is given if ρ is wrong. In the latter case, the teacher also returns an arbitrary object x that ρ and the target concept classify differently.

Given a recursively enumerable set of representations, any class of concepts is trivially learnable with equivalence queries: Just pose an equivalence query for one representation after another, until the answer *yes* is received. So we are really interested in the efficiency of learning algorithms.

Angluin [3] describes a polynomial-time learning algorithm that uses both membership and equivalence queries to identify regular languages. The regular languages are represented by state-minimal deterministic finite automata (DFAs). Her learning algorithm is polynomial in the number of states of the minimal DFA for the target language and the length of the longest counterexample that is given in response to an equivalence query. In contrast, no polynomial-time learning algorithm can identify the regular languages either from equivalence queries or from membership queries alone [5, 12].

Previous work on computational learning tacitly assumes a canonical and unambiguous representation of objects from the universe. In this paper, we study the universe of pictures [11] that can be represented by words over the alphabet of single-step movements. A single picture is represented by many words, and there is no notion of a canonical representation.

Therefore we have to augment the framework of learning by representations of objects. Objects are represented by words over some fixed alphabet Γ. A *representation system* for a universe U is a language of words over Γ, the representations, together with a mapping that maps a representation to the object it represents. Learner and teacher communicate then via representations of objects.

We shall see in the next section how words serve as representations for pictures.

3   Picture Sets

We now introduce the required notions on pictures and picture sets in a quite intuitive manner; see [11] for a more formal presentation.

Let Π be the four-letter alphabet of single-step movements, $\Pi = \{l, r, u, d\}$. Every word w over Π represents a picture $pic(w)$ that consists of a connected set of one-unit-length lines in the square grid of the Cartesian plane. The picture $pic(w)$ is obtained from w as follows: Choose a point of the grid as the start of the picture and take a one-unit-length step to the left (right, up, down, respectively) for each occurrence of a letter l (r, u, d, respectively) in w such that the sequence of movements is the same as the sequence of letters in w. Thus, the word w describes a walk through the picture and the last point of the square grid reached along this walk is the end point of the picture.

We identify all pictures (considered as sets of one-unit-length lines) that can be translated into one another in the geometric sense. Therefore, strictly speaking, $pic(w)$ is an equivalence class of one-unit-length lines in the Cartesian square grid; see [11] for a rigorous formal definition.

There is an obvious way of drawing a picture as a planar graph with isooriented edges in the plane. Start and end points are marked by a circle and a square, respectively, as in Fig. 1.

Note that a word may traverse the same line of a picture several times. This fact immediately implies that there are infinitely many words that represent a given nonempty picture.

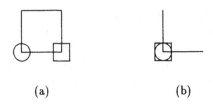

Fig. 1. The pictures that are represented by the words (a) *ruldr* and (b) *rludud*.

Example 1. The regular expressions $rl(rl)^*ud(ud)^*$ and $rlud(rlud)^*$ denote two regular languages over Π such that all words in both languages represent the same picture, namely the one in Fig. 1 (b).

Example 2. Any two distinct words w_1 and w_2 that are denoted by the regular expression r^* represent two distinct pictures $pic(w_1)$ and $pic(w_2)$.

We are interested in the class of regular languages over Π that represent a given picture q. A nonempty regular language L over Π is a *description language* of q if $pic(w) = q$ for each word w in L. Let $\mathcal{B}_q$ consist of all the description languages q.

The class $\mathcal{B}_q$ is a proper subclass of the class of all regular languages. The languages of $\mathcal{B}_q$ can be represented by finite automata or regular expressions. We study the problem of identifying a regular language from $\mathcal{B}_q$ in Section 4.

Second, for each picture q, we are interested in the language of *all* the words over Π that represent q, the *complete description language* of q. This language is denoted by $des(q)$. It is known that $des(q)$ is always a regular language [11].

Example 3. Let $q = pic(r)$. Then $des(q)$ is denoted by the regular expression $r(lr)^*$).

Note that the class $\mathcal{B}_c$ of the complete representation languages

$$\mathcal{B}_c = \{\, des(q) \mid q \text{ is a picture} \,\}$$

is also a proper subclass of the class of regular languages. The problem of identifying regular languages in $\mathcal{B}_c$ is studied in Section 5.

So far we have used regular languages to describe sets of pictures: For a language L over Π, let $pic(L)$ denote the set of all pictures that are represented by some word in L. Operations on word languages such as concatenation and Kleene star carry over to operations on picture sets via representations. There is, however, another, more direct way to define analogs of concatenation and Kleene star for sets of pictures.

Let p and q be two pictures with start and end points s_p, e_p and s_q, e_q, respectively. Then the concatenation pq of p and q is obtained by gluing the

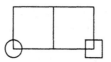

Fig. 2. The concatenation of two copies of the picture of Fig. 1 (a).

start point s_q and the end point e_p together. The picture pq has start point s_p and end point e_q; see Fig. 2.

We can now define the class of *regular picture sets* $\mathcal{P}$ inductively as follows: $\mathcal{P}$ is the minimal class of picture sets that satisfies the following properties:

1. The empty set $\emptyset$ is in $\mathcal{P}$.
2. For each picture q, the singleton set $\{q\}$ is in $\mathcal{P}$.
3. If B, B_1, and B_2 are in $\mathcal{P}$, then also
   (a) the union $B_1 \cup B_2$ is in $\mathcal{P}$,
   (b) the concatenation $B_1 B_2 = \{q_1 q_2 \mid q_1 \in B_1, q_2 \in B_2\}$ is in $\mathcal{P}$, and
   (c) the Kleene star $B^* = \bigcup_{i \geq 0} B^i$ is in $\mathcal{P}$, where B^i is defined inductively as follows: B^0 is the set that consists of the empty picture (the one that is denoted by the empty word) and $B^{i+1} = B^i B$.

There are different ways of denoting regular picture sets. One possible notation are the regular expressions over Π, since a set B of pictures is regular if and only if there is a regular word language L over Π such that $B = pic(L)$ [11].

4 Learning Description Languages

In this section, we consider the description languages of a fixed picture q. We demonstrate that identification of description languages of q is just as hard as identification of arbitrary regular languages.

If q is the empty picture, then $\mathcal{B}_q$ consists just of the language $\{\epsilon\}$. For any other picture q, however, $\mathcal{B}_q$ is an infinite yet still proper subclass of the class of regular languages. Nevertheless, from a learning point of view, each infinite class $\mathcal{B}_q$ is as complex as the full class of all regular languages.

Theorem 1. *For any nonempty picture q, learning of the class of regular languages can be reduced to learning of $\mathcal{B}_q$ within the same time bounds.*

Although this result holds true for any nonempty picture, for simplicity's sake we deal in this section only with the single picture that is represented by the word $udrl$.

Let $\mathcal{B}$ denote the class of description languages of the picture $des(udrl)$. The main idea is to encode regular languages over an arbitrary finite alphabet Σ as languages in $\mathcal{B}$ such that the learning of a language L over Σ can be reduced to the learning of the coded version of L.

The encoding is really quite simple. Let $\Sigma = \{a_1, \ldots, a_k\}$. Let h be the morphism from Σ^* to Π^* that maps a_i to $(ud)^i rl$. Finally, for each word w over Σ let $c(w) = udrl\, h(w)$.

Then for each word w over Σ, the word $c(w)$ represents the picture $des(udrl)$. The prefix $udrl$ of $c(w)$ asserts this property also for the empty word. The image $c(L)$ of a regular language L over Σ is $udrl\, h(L)$. Since homomorphic images of regular languages are also regular [10], $c(L) \in \mathcal{B}$.

A word w over Π is a *code word*, if there is an inverted image w' over Σ such that $c(w') = w$. If w is a code word, the inverted image w' is obviously unique. A regular language L over Π is a *code language* if each of its words is a code word. For a code language L, its inverted image L' consists of all inverted images of words in L.

Via the encoding c, we can now reduce learning of the class of regular languages over Σ to learning of $\mathcal{B}$. For any learning algorithm g for $\mathcal{B}$, we construct a learning algorithm g' for the class of regular languages over Σ, such that g', when working on the target language L over Σ, mimics exactly what g does when working on the target language $c(L)$.

In particular, if g poses a membership query for a word w over Π, then g' checks first whether w is a code word. If it is so, then g' replaces g's membership query for w with a membership query for the inverted image w' of w. On the other hand, if w is not a code word, then g' knows already that $w \notin c(L)$; therefore, it omits g's membership query and continues as g would with the answer *no*.

If g poses an equivalence query for a representation ρ of a regular language L over Π, then g' checks first whether L is a code language. If it is so, then g' computes from ρ a representation ρ' of the inverted image L' of L and replaces then g's equivalence query for ρ with an equivalence query for ρ'. If in response g' receives a counterexample w, then g' continues as g would when receiving $c(w)$ as its counterexample. Of course, if w is classified differently by the language represented by ρ' and the target language that g' is working on, then $c(w)$ is classified differently by the language represented by ρ and the coded target language that g is working on. On the other hand, if ρ does not represent a code language, then g' computes from ρ a word w over Π that belongs to the language of ρ but is not a code word. Then w serves as a counterexample to g for the hypothesis ρ, since w does not belong to the coded target language that g is working on. Therefore, g' omits g's equivalence query and continues as g would with w as its counterexample.

We only have to consider the case that g identifies a code language. Hence, if g outputs as its hypothesis the representation ρ of a code language L, then g' outputs a representation ρ' of the inverted image L' of L.

It is not hard to see that g' identifies a target language L over Σ if and only if g identifies the target language $c(L)$ over Π. Furthermore, g' poses at most as many queries as g does. Finally, the computing time of g' is polynomial in the computing time of g.

To prove the last claim, we just have to verify that all the coding and decoding g' does when simulating g can be carried out efficiently [9].

Lemma 2. *1. There is a linear-time algorithm that checks for a given word w over Π whether w is a code word. If it is so, the algorithm also computes the inverted image of w.*

2. There is a algorithm that checks for a given nondeterministic finite automaton M whether the language of M is a code language. If it is so, then the algorithm also computes an automaton for the inverted image of the code language. If it is not so, then the algorithm also computes a word w over Π that is accepted by M but is not a code word. The algorithm is linear in the number of transitions of M

5 Learning Complete Description Languages

Complete description languages have a property that make them easy or hard to learn, depending on the learning paradigm: Any two different complete description languages are disjoint; or, to put it differently, a single element of a complete description language determines the whole language.

The state-minimal DFA for the complete description language of the *comb* $pic(ud(rud)^n)$ (see Fig. 3) has on the order of 2^n many states.[1] It is therefore quite wasteful to represent complete description languages by DFAs. We'd rather represent the complete picture language $pic(q)$ by q itself or by a word that represents q. Each picture of size n (that is, that consists of n one-unit-length segments) can be represented by a word of length at most $2n$ [11]. Therefore, the representation of the language $des(q)$ is of a size that is linear in the size of q.

Fig. 3. A comb with 5 teeth.

Theorem 3. *There is a constant-time algorithm that learns complete description languages using just one query, an equivalence query.*

Proof. To learn complete description languages, we pose just one equivalence query, namely for the empty set. Since the empty set is not a complete description language, the answer is *no*; in addition, we receive a counterexample q. Since the

---

[1] Since each word in the complete description language has to describe the comb completely, a DFA has to keep track of the subset of the *teeth* that have already been visited.

target language and the empty set classify q differently, the counterexample q belongs to the target language. But now we have learned the target language: It is $des(q)$.

The constant-time algorithm we have just presented is, however, unreasonable, since it poses queries for sets it is not prepared to learn. We call a learning algorithm for a class C of concepts *reasonable* if it poses only equivalence queries for concepts in C.

In a reasonable learning algorithm for complete description languages, equivalence queries can be substituted for membership queries and vice versa. In fact, with a complete description language as the target language, a membership query for a picture q is answered with *yes* if and only if the equivalence query for $des(q)$ is answered with *yes*. Furthermore, if $des(q)$ is different from the target language, then q is a counterexample.

Theorem 4. *Let $\mathcal{B}_n = \{des(q) \mid q$ is a picture of size $n\}$. Each reasonable learning algorithm for $\mathcal{B}_n$ needs on the order of 2^n many queries in the worst case.*

Proof. Let g be a reasonable learning algorithm for $\mathcal{B}_n$. As we have noticed already, we may assume that g uses only membership queries. We apply Angluin's adversary technique [4] to find a target set that puts off the termination of g as long as possible. We run g answering all membership queries with *no* while at each point in time keeping track of the set S of the languages in $\mathcal{B}_n$ that are compatible with the answers we have given so far. We initialize S with $\mathcal{B}_n$. If g poses a membership query for picture q, we answer it with *no* and remove $des(q)$ from S. Since different complete description languages are disjoint, all remaining languages in S are compatible with the *no* answer to the membership query for q. As long as S contains more than one set, the algorithm g cannot stop; rather it has to pose another query to distinguish between the possible target languages that are still in S. Therefore, g has to pose $|\mathcal{B}_n| - 1$ many queries in the worst case. But there are at least 2^n many different pictures of size n.

6 Learning Picture Sets Directly

In this section we briefly discuss the problem of learning regular picture sets instead of learning regular languages of words describing a given picture. Of course, we need a representation system of the class of regular picture languages. Because regular picture sets have an inductively defined structure similar to regular languages of words, regular expressions can be used to represent them: Let E be a regular expression over the alphabet $\Pi = \{l, r, u, d\}$. Then E denotes both a regular language of words $L(E) \subseteq \Pi^*$ and a regular picture set $P(E)$ in $\mathcal{P}$, $P(E) = \{pic(w) \mid w \in L(E)\}$. Moreover, all regular picture sets can be obtained in this way [11].

There are, however, regular expressions over Π that denote different regular languages of words but represent the same picture set. Learning the class of regular picture languages asks for an algorithm that, for a given regular picture set as the target concept, poses membership or equivalence queries and outputs a regular expression that denotes the target set after finitely many steps. As for regular languages of words, we can show:

Theorem 5. *Membership queries are not sufficient for exact identification of regular picture sets.*

Proof. We apply Moore's technique [12] and assume, by contradiction, that the learning algorithm g identifies any given regular picture set from membership queries alone. First, we observe the behavior of g when the empty picture set $\emptyset$ is the target concept. During its computation, g poses membership queries for a finite number of pictures $q_1, \ldots, q_n$; all of them are answered with *no*. Let q be a picture that is different from any of the $q_1, \ldots, q_n$. Then we observe the behavior of g for the regular picture set $\{q\}$ as the target concept. Again, g poses membership queries for the pictures $q_1, \ldots, q_n$ and receives always the same answer *no* as before, since g is deterministic and the answers to membership queries are uniquely determined by the target set. Hence, g carries out exactly the same computation and, therefore, outputs the same result—a contradiction.

Because the representation of regular picture sets by regular expressions over Π is not unique and the same picture set can be described by regular expressions for different word languages, the coding technique of Section 4 cannot be applied to relate learning of regular word languages to learning of regular picture sets via reduction. Therefore, the question which subclasses of the class of regular picture languages are learnable in the various learning models is left open except for a very special case.

If we restrict ourselves to pictures with a canonical unique representation, the coding technique of Section 6 remains applicable. We briefly illustrate this for the class $\mathcal{P}_s$ of regular sets of staircase pictures that can be denoted by regular expressions over the two-letter alphabet $\{r, u\}$.

Theorem 6. *Learning of the class of regular languages can be reduced to learning of $\mathcal{P}_s$ with an at most polynomial time loss in efficiency.*

Proof. Let $\Sigma = \{a_1, \ldots, a_k\}$. We can encode any regular language L over Σ as a set of staircase pictures denoted by a regular expression over $\{r, u\}$ as follows. First, we define an encoding c of words over Σ by encoding the empty word by the empty picture and encoding a nonempty word $a_i w$ with first letter a_i, $1 \leq i \leq k$, as $c(a_i w) = pic(r^i u)c(w)$. Then we extend c to sets of words in the obvious way.

For each regular language L over Σ, the set $c(L)$ of codings is a regular set of staircase pictures that can be denoted by a regular expression over $\{r, u\}$.

It is decidable in polynomial time whether a regular expression E over $\{r, u\}$ denotes a set of staircase pictures that are encodings of words over Σ; if this is not the case, a staircase picture that is no code word can be computed within the same time bound. Furthermore, in linear time, we can decide whether a picture is an encoding of a word over Σ and compute their inverted image.

Since staircase pictures are uniquely represented by words over $\{r, u\}$, learning of regular sets of staircase pictures is just a special case of learning regular languages of words. It is an open question whether learning arbitrary regular picture sets can be reduced to learning regular word languages.

References

1. D. Angluin. A note on the number of queries needed to identify regular languages. *Information and Control*, 51(1):76–87, October 1981.
2. D. Angluin. Inference of reversible languages. *Journal of the Association of Computing Machinery*, 29(3):741–765, July 1982.
3. D. Angluin. Learning regular sets from queries and counterexamples. *Information and Computation*, 75(2):87–106, November 1987.
4. D. Angluin. Queries and concept learning. *Machine Learning*, 2:319–342, 1988.
5. D. Angluin. Negative results for equivalence queries. *Machine Learning*, 5:121–150, 1990.
6. D. Angluin. Computational learning theory: Survey and selected bibliography. In *Proceedings of the 24th Annual ACM Symposium on the Theory of Computing*, pages 351–369, New York, New York, 1992. ACM Press.
7. D. Angluin, M. Frazier, and L. Pitt. Learning conjunctions of horn clauses. In *Proceedings of the 31st Annual Symposium on Foundations of Computer Science*, pages 186–192. IEEE Computer Society Press, Los Alamitos, California, 1990.
8. D. Angluin and C. H. Smith. Inductive inference: Theory and methods. *Computing Surveys*, 15(3):237–269, September 1983.
9. P. Fischer. Lernalgorithmen für Bildbeschreibungssprachen. Master's thesis, Institut für Informatik, Universität Freiburg, March 1993.
10. J. E. Hopcroft and J. D. Ullman. *Introduction to Automata Theory, Languages and Computation*. Addison-Wesley Series in Computer Science. Addison-Wesley Publishing Company, Reading, MA, 1979.
11. H. A. Maurer, G. Rozenberg, and E. Welzl. Using string languages to describe picture languages. *Information and Control*, 54:155–185, 1992.
12. E. F. Moore. Gedanken-experiments on sequential machines. In C. E. Shannon and J. McCarthy, editors, *Automata Studies*, pages 129–153. Princeton University Press, Princeton, New Jersey, 1956.
13. L. Pitt. Inductive inference, DFAs, and computational complexity. Technical report UIUCDSCS-R-89-1530, Department of Computer Science, University of Illinois at Urbana-Champaign, Urbana, Illinois, July 1989.
14. Y. Sakakibara. Learning context-free grammars from structural data in polynomial time. *Theoretical Computer Science*, 76:223–242, 1990.
15. T. Shinohara. Polynomial time inference of extended regular pattern languages. In E. Goto, K. Furukawa, R. Nakajima, I. Nakata, and A. Yonezawa, editors, *RIMS Symposia on Software Science and Engineering*, pages 115–127, Berlin, 1983. Springer-Verlag. Lecture Notes in Computer Science 147.
16. L. G. Valiant. A theory of the learnable. *Communications of the ACM*, 27(11):1134–1142, November 1984.

Randomness as an Invariant for Number Representations

C. Calude[1] and H. Jürgensen[2]

[1] Computer Science Department, The University of Auckland,
Private Bag 92019, Auckland, New Zealand
[2] Department of Computer Science, The University of Western Ontario,
London, Ontario, N6A 5B7, Canada

Abstract. We show that the usual positional representations of a real number are either random, in the sense of Martin-Löf, for all bases or not so for any base. Thus, randomness is an invariant of number representations. All our proofs are constructive.

1. Introduction

A given real number **x** may be represented in many different ways. In addition to the usual representations with respect to a fixed base – like binary, octal, decimal, hexadecimal – representations have been proposed that deviate from this simple scheme (see for instance [3], [20], [30]). In this paper we focus on the usual representations of numbers. We refer to these as *natural positional representations* for lack of a better term.

Even for the natural positional representations, only very little is known about the connection between combinatorial properties of the representations of a number and properties of the number itself. We know of only one major exception: A number is rational if and only if its natural positional representation is ultimately periodic. This statement is true regardless of the base. For representations of numbers by continued fractions, on the other hand, the following is known: A number is rational if and only if its representation by continued fractions terminates; it is quadratic irrational, that is, a solution of a quadratic equation with integer coefficients, but not rational if and only if its representation by continued fractions is ultimately periodic.

It seems natural to ask the following question: *For a given class R of number representations, which combinatorial properties of number representations in this class are invariant under transformations between representations?* If P is such an invariant property, $r \in R$ is a number representation, and **x** is a real number, then a representation $r(\mathbf{x})$ of **x** according to r has property P if and only if, for every $r' \in R$, the representation $r'(\mathbf{x})$ of **x** according to r' has property P. Thus, relative to the class R, the property P can be considered as a property of the numbers themselves rather than of their representations. Of course, in formulating the above question one has to be slightly more careful as numbers may have more than one representation for a fixed representation system r.

Without loss of generality, we consider only numbers in the open interval $(0,1)$ in the sequel and for these only the property of randomness in the sense of Martin-Löf, that is, we ask the following question: *If the natural positional representation of a number $\mathbf{x} \in (0,1)$ at one base is an infinite random sequence, does this imply that the natural positional representation of this number at any other base is also an infinite random sequence?* Intuitively, the answer is "obviously yes!" Here is an "obvious proof:"

Consider bases Q and q and let $\mathbf{x} \in (0,1)$ be a real number with $r_Q(\mathbf{x})$ as natural positional representation, and assume that $r_Q(\mathbf{x})$ is a random sequence over the alphabet consisting of the digits $0, 1, \ldots, Q-1$. There is an injective recursive function f that computes, from the prefixes of $r_Q(\mathbf{x})$, successive prefixes – approximations – of a natural positional representation $r_q(\mathbf{x})$ of $\mathbf{x}$ with respect to base q. Suppose that $r_q(\mathbf{x})$ is not a random sequence over the alphabet consisting of the digits $0, 1, \ldots, q-1$. This means that we have lost "information" using the recursive function f. As f is injective and recursive, its inverse f^{-1} is a partial recursive function. Being a partial recursive function, f^{-1} cannot regain this lost information. However, $f^{-1}(r_q(\mathbf{x})) = r_Q(\mathbf{x})$ is a random sequence. Therefore, also $r_q(\mathbf{x})$ must be a random sequence.

This "proof" is *wrong!* The intuition seems to be based on two kinds of arguments: First, the base transformation is a recursive function which gives equal "preference" to all digits and cannot do much harm to a random sequence – the flaw with this argument is, that even very simple injective recursive functions can easily destroy much of randomness as shown by the following example due to von Mises [46], which is discussed in [8]: For an arbitrary binary sequence $x = x_1 x_2 \cdots$ consider the ternary sequence $y = y_1 y_2 \cdots$ given by $y_1 = x_1$ and $y_n = x_n + x_{n-1}$ for $n \geq 2$. The sequence y is never random even if x is, as, for instance, the sequences 02 and 20 do not occur in y.

The second intuitive argument is that for a base transformation there always is an inverse base transformation, and if the first one destroys randomness the second one cannot recover it. The core of the second idea may be correct; it is not clear, however, how it can be cast into rigorous terms as the base transformations involve computations on infinite sequences and approximations. The main difficulty arises from the fact that there is no *total* recursive and prefix-increasing mapping which, extended to infinite strings, transforms the *names* of irrational numbers with respect to one base into the corresponding *names* with respect to another base. This can be seen by analysing the rôle of carries in the sequence $0.x_1 q x_2 q x_3 q \cdots$ with $q > 1$ and $x_i \in \{0, \ldots, q-1\}$ for $i = 1, 2, \ldots$ when this sequence, considered as the natural positional representation of a real number at base $q+1$, is transformed into a natural positional representation of this number at base q. The transformation $x_1 x_2 \cdots x_n \mapsto y_1 y_2 \cdots y_n$ used in von Mises' construction, with $x_i \in \{0,1\}$ and $y_i \in \{0,1,2\}$ for $i = 1, 2, \ldots, n$, and the transformation

$$
x_1 x_2 \cdots x_n \mapsto
\begin{cases}
x_1 q x_2 q \cdots x_{\frac{n}{2}} q & \text{if } n \text{ is even}, \\
x_1 q x_2 q \cdots x_{\frac{n+1}{2}} & \text{if } n \text{ is odd},
\end{cases}
$$

used in this example, with $x_i \in \{0, 1, \ldots, q-1\}$ for $i = 1, 2, \ldots, n$, are both recursive, injective, length preserving; in the limit, they both destroy randomness.

The invariance studied in this paper is a quite subtle problem. On the one hand, a slight modification of von Mises' example, following a suggestion due to A. Szilard [50], results in a transformation of binary sequences into binary sequences that preserves randomness: Instead of the addition of integers, one uses modulo-2 addition. On the other hand, one has Gács' Reducibility Theorem (see [26], [11]) which asserts the existence of a recursive prefix-increasing function that maps – in the limit – the set of random sequences *onto* the set of all sequences over a given alphabet.

The intuitive answer is, nevertheless, correct. We prove that, *for the class of natural positional representations, randomness in the sense of Martin-Löf is a property of numbers rather than their representations.* Our proof relies on several equivalent characterizations of infinite random sequences. For background information, we refer to [43], [48], [13], [14], [15], [16], [19], [21], [40], [42], [5], [11], [6].

A related question – the one that was the starting point of this paper – is raised in [32]. Using the notion of principal congruence for sets of infinite sequences over a finite set as introduced in [31], one proves that the principal congruence for a single infinite sequence is the equality or, equivalently, the sequence is *disjunctive* if and only if every finite sequence occurs in the infinite sequence as a segment. Disjunctivity has a certain flavour of randomness, akin to that of normal numbers considered in the early discussions of randomness. By a result in [8] (see also [13], [10]) every random sequence is disjunctive, but the converse fails to be true. There exist disjunctive sequences like, for example, the Champernowne sequence

$$0123456789101112131415\ldots$$

over the alphabet $\{0, 1, 2, \ldots, 9\}$ [18], which are recursive and, therefore, not random [8].

In [32], many examples of numbers with disjunctive natural positional representations are given. A question raised there and left open both there and in the present paper is whether disjunctivity is an invariant property.

A property, weaker than randomness, but stronger than disjunctivity is that of (Borel) normality [1], [2], [10], [29]. By [47], a sequence $x = x_1 x_2 \cdots$ over a set $X = \{0, 1, \ldots, q-1\}$ is *Borel normal* if and only if, for any string y over X, the relative frequency of occurrences of y in $x_1 x_2 \cdots x_n$ tends to q^{-l} as $n \to \infty$ where l is the length of y, that is, in the limit the relative frequency of occurrences of y is equal to the *a priori* probability of y [22]. Borel normality is not, in general, an invariant property in the above sense [35]; see also [33], [44]. Note that it is not known whether the disjunctivity or the Borel normality of the Champernowne sequence is invariant under base transformations (see [17]).

Our paper is structured as follows: In Section 2, we introduce some notation. In Section 3, we review some definitions and results on random sequences. Sections 4 and 5 contain the result as announced above, that is, that randomness is indeed an invariant of numbers with respect to natural positional representations. The proof is achieved in two steps. First, in Section 4, we consider the transformation from base q to base q^m for any natural number m. In this case, sequential Martin-Löf tests turn out to be the appropriate proof tool and number representations do not play a rôle at all. In Section 5, we then consider the transformation from base $q + 1$ to base q, $q \geq 2$. For this transition, a characterization of randomness due to Solovay [49] seems to be the best tool. When combined, these transformations allow for the transition between any two bases while preserving randomness. All our proofs are constructive. For the transformation from base q to base q^m we also provide alternative proofs based on measure theoretic considerations. In Section 6 we state our main result. In Section 7, we discuss some of the consequences of our result and, in particular two different suggested proof methods, one based on a result due to Gács ([26]; see [42], p. 147, Exercise 2.15) and another one based on a result attributed to L. A. Levin ([28], [41]; see also [42], p. 266, Exercise 4.25).

2. Notation

The symbol $\mathbb{N}$ denotes the positive integers and $\mathbb{N}_0 = \mathbb{N} \cup \{0\}$. An alphabet is a non-empty, finite set. In the sequel, without special mention, every alphabet is assumed to have at least 2 elements.

Let X be an alphabet. Then X^* and X^ω are the sets of words and ω-words over X, respectively, that is, of finite and infinite sequences over X. Let X^+ denote the set of non-empty words. For $w \in X^\infty = X^* \cup X^\omega$, $|w|$ is the length of w (finite or infinite) and, for $n \in \mathbb{N}$, if $n \leq |w|$ then w_n is the nth symbol of w and $w(n)$ is the prefix of length n of w, that is, $w(n) = w_1 w_2 \ldots w_n$.

On X^* we consider two partial orders. The *prefix order* $\leq_p$ is defined by

$$u \leq_p v \iff v \in uX^*$$

for $u, v \in X^*$. The *standard order* $\leq_{\text{stand}}$ assumes an arbitrary, but fixed, total order $<_X$ on X. Then $u \leq_{\text{stand}} v$ if and only if $|u| < |v|$ or, when $|u| = |v|$, if $u = u'au''$, $v = u'bv''$ for $u', u'', v'' \in X^*$, $a, b \in X$, and $a \leq_X b$.

For $w \in X^*$ and $m \in \mathbb{N}_0$, X^m is the set of all words of length m, w^m is the the word $ww \cdots w$ composed of m copies of w, and wX^* is the set of words with w as a prefix. For $A, B \subseteq X^*$ let $AB = \{xy \mid x \in A, y \in B\}$.

There are some situations when $w \in X^\infty$ can also be considered as a word or ω-word over another alphabet, Y say. This happens, for example, when $Y = X^m$ for some $m \in \mathbb{N}$ and the length of w considered over the alphabet X is a multiple of m or infinite. To avoid confusion, we sometimes write w_X, w_Y, $|w|_X$, $|w|_Y$, $w_X(n)$, and $w_Y(n)$ in such cases.

For $q \in \mathbb{N}$, $q \geq 2$, let X_q be the alphabet $X_q = \{0, 1, \ldots, q-1\}$. The order $\leq_{X_q}$ is given by $0 <_{X_q} 1 <_{X_q} \cdots <_{X_q} q-1$. The elements of X_q are to be considered as the digits used in natural positional representations of numbers in the open interval $(0, 1)$ at base q, $q > 1$. Thus, an element $a \in X_q$ denotes both the symbol used in number representations and the numerical value in the range from 0 to $q-1$ which it represents. With a sequence $w \in X_q^\infty$ one associates its value $v_q(w) = \sum_{i=1}^{|w|} w_i q^{-i}$. Clearly, $v_q(w(n)) \to v_q(w)$ as $n \to |w|$.

If $v_q(w)$ is irrational then $v_q(w') = v_q(w)$ implies $w' = w$. On the other hand, for rational numbers there sometimes are two different natural positional representations. Since we are considering randomness properties of natural positional representations of numbers and since the natural positional representations of rational numbers are far from being random, this will not cause a problem in the sequel. Let $\mathbb{I}$ denote the set of irrational numbers in $(0, 1)$. Let r_q be defined on $\mathbb{I}$ as the inverse of v_q, that is, for an irrational number $\mathbf{x} \in (0, 1)$, $r_q(\mathbf{x})$ is the unique infinite sequence over X_q such that $\mathbf{x} = v_q(r_q(\mathbf{x}))$.

If X is an alphabet and $V \subseteq X^* \times \mathbb{N}$ then, for $i \in \mathbb{N}$, let $V_i = \{w \mid (w, i) \in V\}$. On $\mathbb{N}$ the symbol $|$ denotes divisibility, that is, $x \mid y$ if and only if x divides y. With $x\mathbb{N}$ defined as the set $\{xk \mid k \in \mathbb{N}\}$, we also write $y \in x\mathbb{N}$ instead of $x \mid y$.

The symbols $\to$ and $\overset{o}{\to}$ indicate total and partial mappings, respectively. For a mapping or a partial mapping β, $\text{dom}\,\beta$ denotes its domain.

Let X and Y be alphabets. A partial mapping $\beta : X^* \overset{o}{\to} Y^*$ is said to be *length preserving* if, for every $x \in \text{dom}\,\beta$, $|\beta(x)|_Y = |x|_X$. It is *prefix increasing* if, for $x, x' \in \text{dom}\,\beta$, $x \leq_p x'$ implies $\beta(x) \leq_p \beta(x')$. It is *suffix complete* if $x \in \text{dom}\,\beta$ implies $xX^* \subseteq \text{dom}\,\beta$.

For any alphabet X, let μ_X be the probability measure on X^ω obtained as the product measure induced by the uniform distribution on X. This measure has the property that $\mu_X(wX^\omega) = |X|^{-|w|}$ for $w \in X^*$. Under the usual identification of X^ω with $(0, 1)$ the measure μ_X coincides with the the Lebesgue measure on the interval $(0, 1)$ (see [11], Section 1.4, for details). Therefore, by slight abuse of terminology, we sometimes refer to μ_X as the Lebesgue measure on X^ω.

3. Background on Randomness

In this section we briefly review characterizations of randomness that we use in the sequel. Among the many equivalent definitions of random sequences, we base our definition on sequential Martin-Löf tests.

Definition 3.1. [43], [7] Let X be an alphabet with $|X| \geq 2$. A *Martin-Löf test* over X is a recursively enumerable set $V \subseteq X^* \times \mathbb{N}$ with the following properties for all $i \in \mathbb{N}$:

(1) $V_{i+1} \subseteq V_i$.
(2) $|X^n \cap V_i| < |X|^{n-i}/(|X| - 1)$ for all $n \in \mathbb{N}$.

A Martin-Löf test V is a *sequential Martin-Löf test* if, in addition, it has the following *sequentiality* property:

(3) For $x, y \in X^*$, if $x \leq_p y$ and $x \in V_i$ then $y \in V_i$.

The empty set is a sequential Martin-Löf test by definition.

Martin-Löf tests are useful tools for measuring randomness of (finite) strings ([43], [5], [42]) while sequential Martin-Löf tests are important measures of randomness of infinite sequences. Clearly, not every Martin-Löf test is a sequential Martin-Löf test.

For a Martin-Löf test V over the alphabet X, consider the function $m_V :$ $X^* \to \mathbb{N}_0$ given by

$$m_V(w) = \begin{cases} \max\{i \mid i \in \mathbb{N}, w \in V_i\}, & \text{if } w \in V_1, \\ 0, & \text{otherwise,} \end{cases}$$

for $w \in X^*$; m_V is called the *critical level* induced by V. One can consider $m_V(w)$ as the level at which w passes the test V for randomness. This leads to the following definition.

Definition 3.2. Let X be an alphabet and V a sequential Martin-Löf test over X. A sequence $w \in X^\omega$ is said to be V-*random* over X if and only if $\lim_{n \to \infty} m_V(w(n)) < \infty$. Let $\mathfrak{R}_X(V)$ denote the set of V-random sequences over X.

Remark 3.3. *Note that, for a sequential Martin-Löf test V and a sequence $w \in X^\omega$, the sequence $m_V(w(n))$ is monotonically increasing with $n \to \infty$ as $x \leq_p y$ implies $m_V(x) \leq m_V(y)$ for $x, y \in X^*$. This implies, in particular, that $\lim_{n \to \infty} m_V(w(n)) = \infty$ if and only if $m_V(w(n))$ is unbounded or, equivalently, if $w \notin \mathfrak{R}_X(V)$.*

Definition 3.4. Let X be an alphabet with $|X| \geq 2$. A sequential Martin-Löf test U over X is said to be *universal* if, for every sequential Martin-Löf test V over X, there is a constant c, depending on U and V, such that $V_{m+c} \subseteq U_m$ for all $m \in \mathbb{N}$.

Universal sequential Martin-Löf tests exist [43], [7]. If U is a universal sequential Martin-Löf test over X then $\mathfrak{R}_X(U) = \bigcap_V \mathfrak{R}_X(V)$ where the intersection is taken over all sequential Martin-Löf tests V over X [11]. Clearly, $\mathfrak{R}_X(U)$ does not depend on the specific choice of U. Therefore, let $\mathfrak{R}_X = \mathfrak{R}_X(U)$. The sequences $w \in \mathfrak{R}_X$ are the *(Martin-Löf) random* sequences over X.

For an arbitrary alphabet X, $|X| \geq 2$, the next two lemmata establish a natural connection between sequential Martin-Löf tests on the alphabets X and $Y = X^m$ with $m \in \mathbb{N}$.

Lemma 3.5. *Let X be an alphabet, $m \in \mathbb{N}$, $Y = X^m$, and let W be a sequential Martin-Löf test over Y. Then the set $V \subseteq X^* \times \mathbb{N}$ defined by $V_i = W_i X^*$ for $i \in \mathbb{N}$ is a sequential Martin-Löf test over X such that, for $k \in \mathbb{N}$ and $w \in X^{km}$, one has $m_V(w_X) = m_W(w_Y)$.*

Proof: Clearly, V is a recursively enumerable subset of $X^* \times \mathbb{N}$. If $y \in V_{i+1}$ then there is an $x \in W_{i+1}$ such that $x \leq_p y$. But $W_{i+1} \subseteq W_i$ implies $x \in W_i$ and, therefore, $y \in V_i$. This proves condition (1) of Definition 3.1.

Let $n \in \mathbb{N}$ and consider $X^n \cap V_i$. There are integers k and r such that $n = km + r$ and $0 \leq r < m$. It follows that $X^n \cap V_i = (Y^k \cap W_i)X^r$ and, therefore,

$$|X^n \cap V_i| = |Y^k \cap W_i| \cdot |X|^r < \frac{|Y|^{k-i} \cdot |X|^r}{|Y| - 1} = \frac{|X|^{n-mi}}{|X|^m - 1} \leq \frac{|X|^{n-i}}{|X| - 1}.$$

This proves condition (2).

Now consider $x \in V_i$ and $y \in X^*$ such that $x \leq_p y$. Then there is a $z \in W_i$ such that $z \leq_p x \leq_p y$ and, thus, $y \in V_i$. This proves condition (3).

Finally, let $k \in \mathbb{N}$ and $w \in X^{km}$. Then $m_V(w_X) = m_W(w_Y)$ follows from the fact that $X^{km} \cap V_i = (X^m)^k \cap W_i$ for all i. $\qquad\square$

In the situation of Lemma 3.5, the set W itself is only a Martin-Löf test over X, but never a sequential Martin-Löf test over X – except when $m = 1$, that is, $X = Y$ – as it fails the sequentiality condition, that is, condition (3) of Definition 3.1.

Lemma 3.6. *Let X be an alphabet, $m \in \mathbb{N}$, $Y = X^m$, and let V be a sequential Martin-Löf test over X. Then set $W \subseteq Y \times \mathbb{N}$ defined by $W_i = V_{(i+1)m} \cap Y^*$ for $i \in \mathbb{N}$ is a sequential Martin-Löf test over Y such that, for $k \in \mathbb{N}$ and $w \in X^{km}$, one has $(m_W(w_Y) + 1)m \leq m_V(w_X) < (m_W(w_Y) + 2)m$.*

Proof: Clearly, W is a recursively enumerable subset of $Y \times \mathbb{N}$. Moreover, one has $W_{i+1} = V_{(i+2)m} \cap Y^* \subseteq V_{(i+1)m} \cap Y^* = W_i$ for all $i \in \mathbb{N}$. Consider $n, i \in \mathbb{N}$. Then

$$|Y^n \cap W_i| = |X^{nm} \cap V_{(i+1)m}| < \frac{|X|^{nm-(i+1)m}}{|X| - 1} = \frac{|Y|^{n-i}}{|Y|(|X| - 1)} \leq \frac{|Y|^{n-i}}{|Y| - 1}.$$

Finally, suppose that $x, y \in Y^*$, $x \leq_p y$, and $x \in W_i$. Then $m \mid |y|$ and $x \in W_i = V_{(i+1)m} \cap Y^*$ implies $y \in V_{(i+1)m} \cap Y^* = W_i$. This shows that W is a sequential Martin-Löf test over Y.

Let $w \in X^{km} = Y^k$. The relation $X^{km} \cap V_{(i+1)m} = X^{km} \cap W_i$ implies that $(m_W(w_Y) + 1)m \leq m_V(w_X) < (m_W(w_Y) + 2)m$. $\qquad\square$

Combining Lemma 3.5 and Lemma 3.6, one finds that randomness over an alphabet X and over X^m are equivalent for infinite sequences.

Proposition 3.7. *Let X be an alphabet, $m \in \mathbb{N}$, and $Y = X^m$. Then $\mathfrak{R}_X = \mathfrak{R}_Y$.*

Proof: Let $w \in \mathfrak{R}_Y$ and assume that $w \notin \mathfrak{R}_X$. Then there is a sequential Martin-Löf test V over X such that $m_V(w_X(n))$ is unbounded. Consider the sequential Martin-Löf test W defined in Lemma 3.6 and $n \in \mathbb{N}$. It follows that

$$(m_W(w_Y(n)) + 1)m \leq m_V(w_X(nm)) < (m_W(w_Y(n)) + 2)m$$

and, therefore, $m_W(w_Y(n))$ is also unbounded, that is, $w \notin \mathfrak{R}_Y$, a contradiction.

Conversely, assume that $w \in \mathfrak{R}_X$, but $w \notin \mathfrak{R}_Y$. Then there is a sequential Martin-Löf test $W \subseteq Y^* \times \mathbb{N}$ such that $m_W(w_Y(n))$ is unbounded. By Lemma 3.5, a sequential Martin-Löf test V over X can be derived from W such that $m_V(w_X(nm)) = m_W(w_Y(n))$ for all $n \in \mathbb{N}$. Hence also $m_V(w_X(n))$ is unbounded and, therefore, $w \notin \mathfrak{R}_X$, again a contradiction. $\square$

An alternative proof of Proposition 3.7 can be obtained using Solovay's characterization of random sequences ([49]; see [14], [11]). This theorem is also used below in Section 5.2.

Theorem 3.8. ([49]) *A sequence $w \in X^\omega$ is random if only if, for every recursively enumerable set $A \subseteq X^* \times \mathbb{N}$ such that A_i is prefix-free for all $i \in \mathbb{N}$ and satisfies $\sum_{j \geq 1} \mu_X(A_j X^\omega) < \infty$, there is an $n \in \mathbb{N}$ such that for all $i \in \mathbb{N}$ with $i > n$ one has $w \notin A_i X^\omega$.*

To obtain a proof of Proposition 3.7 using Theorem 3.8, let $Y = X^m$. First, assume that $w \in X^\omega$ is random over Y. Let $A \subseteq X^* \times \mathbb{N}$ be recursively enumerable set satisfying the conditions of Theorem 3.8. We define a set $B \subseteq Y^* \times \mathbb{N}$ as follows. For every $i \in \mathbb{N}$, let

$$B_i = \{z \mid z \in A_i, |z| \in m\mathbb{N}\}$$
$$\cup \{zy \mid z \in A_i, y \in X^*, |z| \notin m\mathbb{N}, |y| < m, |zy| \in m\mathbb{N}\}.$$

Then B_i may be regarded as a subset of Y^*. Moreover, B_i is prefix-free as A_i is prefix-free. For $z \in X^*$ let

$$R_z = \{y \mid y \in X^*, |y| < m, |zy| \in m\mathbb{N}\}.$$

One computes

$$\mu_Y(B_i Y^\omega) = \sum_{w \in B_i} |Y|^{-|w|_Y}$$

$$= \sum_{w \in A_i \cap B_i} |Y|^{-|w|_Y} + \sum_{w \in B_i \setminus A_i} |Y|^{-|w|_Y}$$

$$= \sum_{w \in A_i \cap B_i} |Y|^{-\frac{|w|_X}{m}} + \sum_{\substack{z \in A_i \\ |z| \notin m\mathbb{N}}} \sum_{y \in R_z} |Y|^{-\frac{|zy|_X}{m}}$$

$$= \sum_{w \in A_i \cap B_i} |X|^{-|w|_X} + \sum_{\substack{z \in A_i \\ |z| \notin m\mathbb{N}}} \left(|X|^{-m\left(1 + \lfloor \frac{|z|}{m} \rfloor\right)} |R_z| \right)$$

$$= \sum_{w \in A_i \cap B_i} |X|^{-|w|_X} + \sum_{w \in B_i \setminus A_i} |X|^{-|w|_X}$$

$$= \mu_X(A_i X^\omega).$$

This shows that B satisfies the assumptions of Theorem 3.8 with respect to Y. Since w is random over Y there exists a natural number n such that, for all $i \geq n$, $w \notin B_i Y^\omega$. We prove that $w \notin A_i X^\omega$ for every $i \geq n$. Suppose, $w \in A_i X^\omega$ for some $i \geq n$. Then there is a $t \in \mathbb{N}$ such that $w(t) \in A_i$. If $m \mid t$ then $w(t) \in B_i$, hence $w \in B_i Y^\omega$, a contradiction. On the other hand, if m does not divide t then there is a word y with $|y|_X < m$ such that $wy \in B_i$ and $w(t + |y|) = wy$, hence $w \in B_i Y^\omega$, again a contradiction. This proves that w is random over X.

Conversely, assume that w is random over X. Let $B \subset Y^* \times \mathbb{N}$ be an recursively enumerable set satisfying the assumptions of Theorem 3.8 for Y. Let $A = B$, but considered as a subset of $X^* \times \mathbb{N}$. Clearly, A satisfies the assumptions of Theorem 3.8 for X. As w is random over X one has that $w \notin A_i X^\omega$ for almost all $i \in \mathbb{N}$ and, therefore, $w \notin B_i Y^\omega$ for almost all $i \in \mathbb{N}$, that is, w is random over Y.

Still another proof of Proposition 3.7, based on properties of measure preserving transformations, can be obtained from the following generalization of [48], Satz 6.5, derived in [9].

Theorem 3.9. ([9]) *Let X and Y be two alphabets, and let $\beta : X^* \overset{o}{\to} Y^*$ be a partial recursive, prefix increasing mapping such that, for the extension of β to X^ω, also denoted by β, one has that $w \in \operatorname{dom} \beta \cap X^\omega$ implies $\beta(w) \in Y^\omega$. If there is a constant K, $K \geq 1$, such that for all recursively enumerable prefix-free sets $S \subseteq Y^*$ the inequality*

$$\mu_X \left(\beta^{-1}(SY^\omega) \right) \leq K \cdot \mu_Y (SY^\omega)$$

holds true, then $\beta(w) \in \mathfrak{R}_Y$ for all $w \in \mathfrak{R}_X \cap \operatorname{dom} \beta$.

For an alternative proof of Proposition 3.7, based on Theorem 3.9, let $Y = X^m$ and $\beta : X^* \overset{o}{\to} Y^*$ given by $\operatorname{dom} \beta = (X^m)^*$ and $\beta(w_X) = w_Y$ for $w_X \in \operatorname{dom} \beta$. Let S be a prefix-free subset of Y^*. Then

$$\beta^{-1}(SY^\omega) = \bigcup_{w \in S} w_X X^\omega$$

and this union is disjoint. Hence

$$\mu_X \left(\beta^{-1}(SY^\omega) \right) = \mu_X \left(\bigcup_{w \in S} w_X X^\omega \right)$$
$$= \sum_{w \in S} |X|^{-|w|_X}$$
$$= \sum_{w \in S} |Y|^{-|w|_Y}$$
$$= \mu_Y (SY^\omega).$$

Thus, β satisfies the assumptions of Theorem 3.9 with $K = 1$.

4. Transformation from Base q to Base q^m

The goal of this paper is to prove that, if the natural positional representation with respect to a base q is random, then its natural positional representation is also random with respect to any other base p. The proof is achieved in two steps. First, in this section, we consider the case of $p = q^m$ for any $m \in \mathbb{N}$. In the next section, we then consider the case of $p = q - 1$. When combined, this allows for the transition between any two bases.

The transition from q to q^m is intuitively very simple. In $w \in X_q^\omega$ successive words of length m are considered as symbols in X_{q^m}. In this case, number representations do not play a rôle at all (see also [10]).

Theorem 4.1. Let $\mathbf{x} \in \mathbb{I}$ and $q \in \mathbb{N}$ with $q \geq 2$. Then $r_q(\mathbf{x}) \in \mathfrak{R}_{X_q}$ if and only if $r_{q^m}(\mathbf{x}) \in \mathfrak{R}_{X_{q^m}}$ for all $m \in \mathbb{N}$.

Proof: Let $m \in \mathbb{N}$, $m > 1$, and let $\alpha_m : X_q^m \to X_{q^m}$ be the bijection defined by

$$\alpha_m(0^m) = 0, \alpha_m(0^{m-1}1) = 1, \ldots, \alpha_m((q-1)^m) = q^m - 1,$$

that is, for $w \in X_q^m$, $\alpha_m(w) = q^m v_q(w)$. One extends α_m to a bijection of $(X_q^m)^\omega$ onto $X_{q^m}^\omega$ by

$$\alpha_m(w_1 w_2 \cdots) = \alpha_m(w_1 \cdots w_m)\alpha_m(w_{m+1} \cdots w_{2m}) \cdots$$

for $w_1 w_2 \cdots \in X_q^\omega$.

Let $\mathbf{x} \in \mathbb{I}$ and $w = r_q(\mathbf{x}) \in X_q^\omega$. The sequence w is in $\mathfrak{R}_{X_q}$ if and only if it is in $\mathfrak{R}_{X_q^m}$ by Proposition 3.7. Moreover, w is in $\mathfrak{R}_{X_q^m}$ if and only if $\alpha(w)$ is in $\mathfrak{R}_{X_{q^m}}$ as α_m is a bijection of X_q^m onto X_{q^m}. Clearly, $v_{q^m}(\alpha(w)) = \mathbf{x}$. $\square$

5. Transformation from Base $q+1$ to Base q

We now turn to the transition from base $q+1$ to base q. We need a function that achieves this transition. The obvious idea is to find an injective recursive mapping of X_{q+1}^* into X_q^* that preserves the number represented and is continuous in the topology generated by $\leq_p$. One can prove that such a function does not exist. As a consequence, one has to use a function with weaker properties and this leads to more complicated proofs than one would intuitively anticipate.

In the sequel, let $q \in \mathbb{N}$, $q \geq 2$. Let

$$D_q = \{w \mid w \in X_{q+1}^+, v_{q+1}(w) \leq 1 - q^{-|w|}\}.$$

Let β_q be the partial mapping of X_{q+1}^* into X_q^* with domain D_q and defined by

$$\beta_q(w) = \min\{z \mid z \in X_q^{|w|}, v_{q+1}(w) \leq v_q(z)\}$$

for $w \in D_q$ where the minimum is taken with respect to the standard order on X_q^*. Clearly, β_q is well-defined, D_q is recursive, and β_q is a partial recursive function.

5.1. Basic Properties of β_q

In this section we derive basic properties of natural positional representations and of the mapping β_q which are needed to establish our main result. The definition of β_q is based on the following idea: From the first n digits of the natural positional representation of a number in $\mathbb{I}$ at base $q+1$ one determines the first n digits of its representation at base q. In this sense β_q is a "continuous," partial recursive function the extension of which to the natural positional representations of irrational numbers in $\mathbb{I}$ is injective, and which also happens to preserve randomness. This function is not total because of "overflow carries" that would disturb continuity; fortunately, these discontinuities are very rare. Moreover, as a mapping of finite strings, β_q is surjective, but not injective; however, for every $u \in X_q^+$ the set $\beta_q^{-1}(u)$ is "small."

Lemma 5.1.1. *Let* $w \in X_{q+1}^\omega$ *and* $n \in \mathbb{N}$. *If* $w(n) \in D_q$ *then* $w(n+1) \in D_q$.

Proof: Assume the contrary, that is, for some $n \in \mathbb{N}$, $w(n) \in D_q$ and $w(n+1) \notin D_q$. Thus $v_{q+1}(w(n)) \le 1 - q^{-n}$ and $v_{q+1}(w(n+1)) > 1 - q^{-n-1}$. Using $v_{q+1}(w(n+1)) \le v_{q+1}(w(n)q)$ one obtains

$$1 - q^{-n-1} < v_{q+1}(w(n+1)) \le v_{q+1}(w(n)q) = v_{q+1}(w(n)) + \frac{q}{(q+1)^{n+1}}$$

$$\le 1 - q^{-n} + \frac{q}{(q+1)^{n+1}}$$

and, therefore,

$$\left(\frac{q+1}{q}\right)^{n+1} < \frac{q}{q-1},$$

a contradiction. $\qquad\qquad\square$

Remark 5.1.2. *By Lemma 5.1.1, the set* D_q *is a recursive open set with respect to the topology generated by* $\le_p$, *that is, if* $u \in D_q$ *and* $u \le_p v$, *then* $v \in D_q$.

Example 5.1.3. One has $0X_{q+1}^* \subseteq D_q$ as $v_{q+1}(0) = 0 \le 1 - q^{-1}$.

Lemma 5.1.4. *Let* $u, w \in X_q^*$. *Then* $u \le_p w$ *if and only if* $|u| \le |w|$ *and* $v_q(u) \le v_q(w) \le v_q(u) + q^{-|u|} - q^{-|w|}$.

Proof: If $u \le_p w$ then, obviously, $|u| \le |w|$ and

$$v_q(u) \le v_q(w) \le v_q(u) + \frac{q-1}{q^{|u|}} \left(\sum_{i=1}^{|w|-|u|} \frac{1}{q^i}\right) = v_q(u) + \frac{1}{q^{|u|}} - \frac{1}{q^{|w|}}.$$

Conversely, let $u = u_1 \cdots u_n$ and $w = w_1 \cdots w_m$ with $u_1, \ldots, u_n, w_1, \ldots, w_m \in X_q$ and $n \le m$. Assume that u is not a prefix of w, that is, there is i such that $i \le n$ and $u_i \ne w_i$. Moreover, we may assume that $u_j = w_j$ for all j with $j < i$. The inequality

$$v_q(u) \le v_q(w) \le v_q(u) + q^{-|u|} - q^{-|w|}$$

implies

$$0 \leq \sum_{j=i}^{n}(w_j - u_j)q^{m-j} + \sum_{j=n+1}^{m} w_j q^{m-j} \leq q^{m-n} - 1$$

where

$$(w_i - u_i), \ldots, (w_n - u_n) \in \{-(q-1), \ldots, -1, 0, 1, \ldots, (q-1)\}$$

and $w_{n+1}, \ldots, w_m \in X_q$.

Suppose that $w_i - u_i \geq 1$. Then the above inequality implies

$$q^{m-n} - 1 \geq q^{m-i} - (q-1) \sum_{j=i+1}^{n} q^{m-j} = q^{m-n},$$

a contradiction. Similarly, if $w_i - u_i \leq -1$ then, by the same inequality,

$$0 \leq -q^{m-i} + (q-1) \sum_{j=i+1}^{m} q^{m-j} = -1,$$

again a contradiction. □

Lemma 5.1.5. *Let $u, w \in X_{q+1}^{*}$ and $a \in X_q$ such that $u \in D_q$. Then $uw, uwa \in D_q$ and, if*

$$v_q(\beta_q(uwa)) \leq v_q(\beta_q(uw)) + \frac{q-1}{q^{|uw|+1}}$$

and

$$v_q(\beta_q(uw)) \leq v_q(\beta_q(u)) + \frac{1}{q^{|u|}} - \frac{1}{q^{|uw|}},$$

then

$$v_q(\beta_q(uwa)) \leq v_q(\beta_q(u)) + \frac{1}{q^{|u|}} - \frac{1}{q^{|uw|+1}}.$$

Proof: By Lemma 5.1.1, $uw, uwa \in D_q$. One computes

$$v_q(\beta_q(uwa)) \leq v_q(\beta_q(uw)) + \frac{q-1}{q^{|uw|+1}} \leq v_q(\beta_q(u)) + \frac{1}{q^{|u|}} - \frac{1}{q^{|u|w}} + \frac{q-1}{q^{|uw|+1}}$$

$$\leq v_q(\beta_q(u)) + \frac{1}{q^{|u|}} - \frac{1}{q^{|uw|+1}}$$

as

$$\frac{q-1}{q^{|uw|+1}} - \frac{1}{q^{|uw|}} = \frac{-1}{q^{|uw|+1}}.$$

□

Lemma 5.1.6. *If $u \in D_q$, $a \in X_q$, then $ua \in D_q$ and $v_q(\beta_q(ua)) \leq v_q(\beta_q(u)a)$.*

Proof: By Lemma 5.1.1, $ua \in D_q$. One computes

$$v_q(\beta_q(u)a) = v_q(\beta_q(u)) + \frac{a}{q^{|u|+1}}$$

$$\geq v_{q+1}(u) + \frac{a}{q^{|u|+1}} \geq v_{q+1}(u) + \frac{a}{(q+1)^{|u|+1}}$$

$$= v_{q+1}(ua)$$

and, therefore, $v_q(\beta_q(ua)) \leq v_q(\beta_q(u)a)$ by the definition of β_q. $\square$

Lemma 5.1.7. *Let $u, w \in X_{q+1}^*$ be such that $u \in D_q$. Then $uw, uwq \in D_q$ and*

$$v_{q+1}(uwq) \leq v_q(\beta_q(uw)) + \frac{q-1}{q^{|uw|+1}}.$$

Proof: By Lemma 5.1.1, $uw \in D_q$ and $uwa \in D_q$ for all $a \in X_{q+1}$. By the definition of β_q one has

$$v_q(\beta_q(uw)) \geq v_{q+1}(uw) = v_{q+1}(uwq) - \frac{q}{(q+1)^{|uw|+1}}.$$

Moreover, from $q \geq 2$ and $|uw| + 1 \geq |u| + 1 \geq 2$ it follows that

$$\frac{q-1}{q} \geq \left(\frac{q}{q+1}\right)^{|uw|+1}$$

and, therefore,

$$\frac{q-1}{q^{|uw|+1}} \geq \frac{q}{(q+1)^{|uw|+1}}.$$

$\square$

Lemma 5.1.8. *Let $u \in D_q$ and $v \in X_{q+1}^*$ with $u \leq_p v$. Then $v \in D_q$ and $\beta_q(u) \leq_p \beta_q(v)$.*

Proof: Let $u \in D_q$ and $u \leq_p v$. Then $v \in D_q$ by Lemma 5.1.1. By Lemma 5.1.4 it suffices to prove that $|\beta_q(u)| \leq |\beta_q(v)|$ and

$$v_q(\beta_q(u)) \leq v_q(\beta_q(v)) \leq v_q(\beta_q(u)) + q^{-|\beta_q(u)|} - q^{-|\beta_q(v)|}.$$

The first inequality follows from $|\beta_q(u)| = |u| \leq |v| = |\beta_q(v)|$. The second inequality is equivalent to

$$v_q(\beta_q(u)) \leq v_q(\beta_q(v)) \leq v_q(\beta_q(u)) + q^{-|u|} - q^{-|v|}.$$

From the definition of β_q and $u \leq_p v$ one has $v_q(\beta_q(v)) \geq v_{q+1}(v) \geq v_{q+1}(u)$ and, therefore, $v_q(\beta_q(v)) \geq v_q(\beta_q(u))$.

Let $v = uw$. We prove the remaining claim, that is, that

$$v_q(\beta_q(v)) \leq v_q(\beta_q(u)) + q^{-|u|} - q^{-|v|}$$

by induction on the length of w. For $|w| = 0$ nothing needs to be proved. Consider $w = w'a$ with $a \in X_{q+1}$ and assume that

$$v_q(\beta_q(uw')) \leq v_q(\beta_q(u)) + q^{-|u|} - q^{-|u|-|w'|}.$$

As $u \in D_q$, also $uw', uw'a \in D_q$ by Lemma 5.1.1. We distinguish two cases.

First, assume that $a \neq q$. Lemma 5.1.6 implies that

$$v_q(\beta_q(uw'a)) \leq v_q(\beta_q(uw')a) \leq v_q(\beta_q(uw')) + \frac{q-1}{q^{|uw'|+1}}.$$

Using the induction hypothesis and Lemma 5.1.5, one obtains

$$v_q(\beta_q(uw'a)) \leq v_q(\beta_q(u)) + \frac{1}{q^{|u|}} - \frac{1}{q^{|uw'a|}}$$

as required.

Now assume that $a = q$. By Lemma 5.1.7 one has

$$v_{q+1}(uw'q) \leq v_q(\beta_q(uw')) + \frac{q-1}{q^{|uw'q|}}$$

and, therefore, by the definition of β_q,

$$v_q(\beta_q(uw'q)) \leq v_q(\beta_q(uw')) + \frac{q-1}{q^{|uw'q|}} = v_q(\beta_q(uw')(q-1)).$$

Using the induction hypthesis and Lemma 5.1.5, one again obtains the required inequality. $\qquad \square$

Lemma 5.1.9. *Let $w \in X_{q+1}^\omega$ be such that $w(n_0) \in D_q$ for some $n_0 \in \mathbb{N}$. Then*

$$\lim_{n \to \infty} \beta_q(w(n))$$

exists and

$$v_{q+1}(w) = v_q\left(\lim_{n \to \infty} \beta_q(w(n))\right).$$

Proof: For $n, m \geq n_0$ with $n \leq m$ one has $w(n), w(m) \in D_q$ by Lemma 5.1.1 and, therefore, $\beta_q(w(n)) \leq_p \beta_q(w(m))$ by Lemma 5.1.8. Moreover, $|\beta_q(w(n))| = n \leq m = |\beta_q(w(m))|$ implies that $|\beta_q(w(n))|$ is strictly increasing as n increases. This proves the existence of the limit

$$\lim_{n \to \infty} \beta_q(w(n)) \in X_q^\omega.$$

For $n \geq n_0$ one has

$$v_{q+1}(w(n)) \leq v_q(\beta_q(w(n))) \leq v_{q+1}(w(n)) + q^{-n}$$

and, therefore,

$$v_{q+1}(w) = \lim_{n \to \infty} v_{q+1}(w(n)) \leq \lim_{n \to \infty} v_q(\beta_q(w(n)))$$

$$\leq \lim_{n \to \infty} \left(v_{q+1}(w(n)) + q^{-n}\right) = v_{q+1}(w)$$

as required. $\qquad \square$

Lemma 5.1.10. *Let* $w \in X_{q+1}^{\omega}$ *and* $w \neq qqq \cdots$. *Then* $w(n) \in D_q$ *for some* $n \in \mathbb{N}$.

Proof: Assume that $w(n) \notin D_q$ for all $n \in \mathbb{N}$, that is,

$$v_{q+1}(w(n)) > 1 - q^{-n}.$$

Then $\lim_{n \to \infty} v_{q+1}(w(n)) = 1$ and, therefore, $w = qqq \cdots$, a contradiction. $\square$

Lemma 5.1.11. β_q *is surjective and, for* $n \in \mathbb{N}$ *and* $u \in X_q^n$, *one has*

$$|\beta_q^{-1}(u)| \leq \left(\frac{q+1}{q}\right)^n + 1.$$

Proof: For $n \in \mathbb{N}$, a word $u \in X_q^n$ is the image of every $w \in X_{q+1}^n$ such that

$$v_{q+1}(w) \leq v_q(u) < v_{q+1}(w) + \frac{1}{q^n}.$$

As u ranges over X_q^n its values range over the numbers

$$\frac{0}{q^n}, \frac{1}{q^n}, \ldots, \frac{q^n - 1}{q^n}$$

and similarly, as w ranges over X_{q+1}^n its values range over the numbers

$$\frac{0}{(q+1)^n}, \frac{1}{(q+1)^n}, \ldots, \frac{(q+1)^n - 1}{(q+1)^n}.$$

Thus, to prove the surjectivity of β_q it suffices to prove that, for every $r \in \mathbb{N}_0$ with $r < q^n$, there is a $t \in \mathbb{N}_0$ with $t < (q+1)^n$ such that

$$\frac{t}{(q+1)^n} \leq \frac{r}{q^n} < \frac{t}{(q+1)^n} + \frac{1}{q^n}.$$

Given r, let

$$t = \left\lfloor \left(\frac{q+1}{q}\right)^n \cdot r \right\rfloor.$$

This choice of t satisfies the above inequality. Moreover, $0 \leq t < (q+1)^n$ as required.

This proves that β_q is surjective. For any given $u \in X_q^n$ with $v_q(u) = \frac{r}{q^n}$, the size of $\beta_q^{-1}(u)$ is bounded by $i + 1$ where $i \in \mathbb{N}_0$ is maximal with the property that, for some $t \in \mathbb{N}_0$ satisfying $0 \leq t < (q+1)^n$ and

$$\frac{t}{(q+1)^n} \leq \frac{r}{q^n} < \frac{t}{(q+1)^n} + \frac{1}{q^n},$$

one has

$$\frac{t+i}{(q+1)^n} \leq \frac{r}{q^n} < \frac{t+i}{(q+1)^n} + \frac{1}{q^n}.$$

Any such i has to satisfy

$$\frac{i}{(q+1)^n} \leq \frac{r}{q_n} - \frac{t}{(q+1)^n} < \frac{1}{q_n}.$$

This implies

$$i < \left(\frac{q+1}{q}\right)^n.$$

$\square$

Lemma 5.1.12. *Let $A \subseteq X_q^*$. Then*

$$\beta_q^{-1}(A)X_{q+1}^\omega = \bigcup_{x \in A} \bigcup_{u \in \beta_q^{-1}(x)} uX_{q+1}^\omega.$$

If A is prefix-free then $\beta_q^{-1}(A)$ is also prefix-free.

Proof: The first statement is obviously true. Suppose A is prefix-free and consider $u, v \in \beta_q^{-1}(A)$ such that $u \leq_p v$. Then $u, v \in D_q$ and, by Lemma 5.1.8, $\beta_q(u) \leq_p \beta_q(v)$. This implies that $\beta_q(u) = \beta_q(v)$ and, by the fact that β_q is length preserving, that $|u| = |\beta_q(u)| = |v|$, hence $u = v$. $\square$

In summary, we have proved that β_q is a partial recursive, length preserving, prefix increasing, suffix complete, and value-preserving function. Moreover, by Lemma 5.1.10, if $w \in \Re_{X_{q+1}}$ then β_q is defined on almost all prefixes of w. Note that β_q is not injective and that, in fact, there is no injective and length preserving function with domain D_q.

5.2. β_q Preserves Randomness

In this section we show that β_q preserves randomness. We prove this using Solovay's characterization of random sequences as stated in Theorem 3.8.

Lemma 5.2.1. *Let $w \in \Re_{X_{q+1}}$. Then $w(n) \in D_q$ for almost all $n \in \mathbb{N}$ and $\beta_q(w) = \lim_{n\to\infty} \beta_q(w(n))$ exists. Moreover, $\beta_q(w) \in \Re_{X_q}$.*

Proof: As $w \in \Re_{X_{q+1}}$, by Lemma 5.1.10, $w(n) \in D_q$ for almost all $n \in \mathbb{N}$. As β_q is length preserving and prefix increasing it follows that the limit $\beta_q(w) = \lim_{n\to\infty} \beta_q(w(n))$ exists. Using Theorem 3.8, we now show that $\beta_q(w) \in \Re_{X_q}$.

Let $A \subseteq X_q^* \times \mathbb{N}$ be a recursively enumerable set such that A_i is prefix-free for all $i \in \mathbb{N}$ and $\sum_{j\geq 1} \mu_{X_q}(A_j X_q^\omega) < \infty$. Consider the set $B \subseteq X_{q+1}^* \times \mathbb{N}$ defined by

$$B = \{(x, i) \mid x \in D_q, i \in \mathbb{N}, \beta_q(x) \in A_i\}.$$

The set B is recursively enumerable as D_q is recursive, A is recursively enumerable, and β_q is a partial recursive function. By definition,

$$B_i X_{q+1}^\omega = \beta_q^{-1}(A_i) X_{q+1}^\omega$$

and by Lemma 5.1.12,

$$\beta_q^{-1}(A_i) X_{q+1}^\omega = \bigcup_{x \in A_i} \bigcup_{u \in \beta_q^{-1}(x)} u X_{q+1}^\omega$$

for all $i \in \mathbb{N}$. For $x \in A_i$, as β_q is length preserving, one computes

$$\mu_{X_{q+1}} \left(\beta_q^{-1}(x) X_{q+1}^\omega \right) = \left| \beta_q^{-1}(x) \right| \cdot (q+1)^{-|x|}$$

$$\leq \left(\left(\frac{q+1}{q} \right)^{|x|} + 1 \right) \cdot (q+1)^{-|x|}$$

$$\leq 2 \left(\frac{q+1}{q} \right)^n \cdot (q+1)^{-|x|} = 2q^{-|x|}$$

using Lemma 5.1.11. Thus

$$\sum_{j \geq 1} \mu_{X_{q+1}}(B_j X_{q+1}^\omega) = \sum_{j \geq 1} \mu_{X_{q+1}} \left(\beta_q^{-1}(A_j) X_{q+1}^\omega \right)$$

$$= \sum_{j \geq 1} \mu_{X_{q+1}} \left(\bigcup_{x \in A_j} \beta_q^{-1}(x) X_{q+1}^\omega \right)$$

$$= \sum_{j \geq 1} \sum_{x \in A_j} \mu_{X_{q+1}} \left(\beta_q^{-1}(x) X_{q+1}^\omega \right)$$

(using the fact that $\beta_q^{-1}(A_j)$ is prefix-free by Lemma 5.1.12)

$$\leq \sum_{j \geq 1} \sum_{x \in A_j} 2q^{-|x|} = 2 \sum_{j \geq 1} \mu_{X_q}(A_j X_q^\omega) < \infty.$$

As w is a random sequence over X_{q+1}, there is an $n \in \mathbb{N}$ such that, for all $i > n$, one has $w \notin B_i X_{q+1}^\omega$. We show that there is $n_0 \geq n$ such that also $\beta_q(w) \notin A_i X_q^\omega$ for all $i > n_0$.

Assume the contrary, that is, $\beta_q(w) \in A_i X_q^\omega$ for infinitely many $i > n$. By Lemma 5.1.10 there is a $k_0 \in \mathbb{N}$ such that $w(k) \in D_q$ for all $k \in \mathbb{N}$ with $k \geq k_0$. As $\sum_{j \geq 1} \mu_{X_q}(A_j X_q^\omega) < \infty$ it follows that

$$\lim_{j \to \infty} \mu_{X_q}(A_j X_q^\omega) = 0$$

and, hence,

$$\lim_{j \to \infty} \min\{|x| \mid x \in A_j\} = \infty.$$

Thus, there is an $m_0 \in \mathbb{N}$ such that $m_0 > n$ and, for $j \in \mathbb{N}$ with $j \geq m_0$, one has $|u| \geq k_0$ for all $u \in A_j$. By assumption, there is an $i \geq m_0$ such that $\beta_q(w) \in A_i X_q^\omega$. As A_i is prefix-free there is a unique $k \in \mathbb{N}$ such that $\beta_q(w)(k) \in A_i$. Moreover, $k \geq k_0$ and, therefore, $w(k) \in D_q$ and $\beta_q(w(k)) = \beta_q(w)(k) \in A_i$. This implies $w(k) \in B_i$, hence $w \in B_i X_{q+1}^\omega$, a contradiction. $\qquad \square$

Using the property that β_q is value preserving, from Lemma 5.2.1 one obtains the following result.

Theorem 5.2.2. *Let $w \in \mathfrak{R}_{X_{q+1}}$ and $u \in X_q^\omega$ such that $v_{q+1}(w) = v_q(u)$. Then $u \in \mathfrak{R}_{X_q}$.*

Proof: From $w \in \mathfrak{R}_{X_{q+1}}$ it follows that $v_{q+1}(w)$ is irrational. Therefore, there is a unique $u \in X_q^\omega$ such that $v_{q+1}(w) = v_q(u)$. As $w(n) \in D_q$ for almost all n by Lemma 5.2.1, one has $u = \lim_{n \to \infty} \beta_q(w(n))$ by Lemma 5.1.9. By Lemma 5.2.1, $u \in \mathfrak{R}_{X_q}$. $\qquad\square$

6. Random Numbers

By combining Proposition 3.7 and Theorem 5.2.2 we derive the main result of this paper, that randomness is invariant with respect to transformations between natural positional representations of numbers in $(0, 1)$.

Theorem 6.1. *Let $p, q \in \mathbb{N}$ with $p, q \geq 2$ and let $w \in X_p^\omega$ and $v \in X_q^\omega$ be such that $v_p(w) = v_q(v)$. Then $w \in \mathfrak{R}_{X_p}$ if and only if $v \in \mathfrak{R}_{X_q}$.*

Proof: Without loss of generality, assume that $p < q$. Let m be the smallest integer such that $p^m \geq q$. By Proposition 3.7, $w \in \mathfrak{R}_{X_p}$ if and only if $w \in \mathfrak{R}_{X_{p^m}}$. Now let $q = p^m - i$. Applying Theorem 5.2.2 i times yields that $v \in \mathfrak{R}_{X_q}$ if and only if $w \in \mathfrak{R}_{X_{p^m}}$. $\qquad\square$

Corollary 6.2. *Let $\mathbf{x} \in \mathbb{I}$ and $q \in \mathbb{N}$ with $q \geq 2$. Then $r_q(\mathbf{x}) \in \mathfrak{R}_{X_q}$ if and only if $r_p(\mathbf{x}) \in \mathfrak{R}_{X_p}$ for all $p \in \mathbb{N}$ with $p \geq 2$.*

Proof: The statement is a direct consequence of Theorem 4.1 and Theorem 6.1. $\square$

Thus, randomness in the sense of Martin-Löf is invariant with respect to the natural positional representations of numbers in $\mathbb{I}$. Now consider an arbitrary real number $\mathbf{x}$. For $q \in \mathbb{N}$, $q \geq 2$, its natural positional representation over X_q consists of its sign $\mathrm{sgn}(\mathbf{x})$, a word $i_q(\mathbf{x}) \in X_q^*$ representing the integer part of $\mathbf{x}$, a dot, and a sequence $f_q(\mathbf{x}) \in X_q^\omega$ representing the fraction part of $\mathbf{x}$. We say that $\mathbf{x}$ is *random* (with respect to natural positional representations) if, for some q, the sequence $i_q(\mathbf{x})f_q(\mathbf{x})$ is in $\mathfrak{R}_{X_q}$. Note that $\mathbf{x}$ is random if and only if $f_q(\mathbf{x}) \in \mathfrak{R}_{X_q}$. Thus, if $\mathbf{x}$ is random, then also $q \cdot \mathbf{x}$ and $\mathbf{x}/q$ are random.

Theorem 6.1 implies that this concept of a random number is well-defined. Obviously, every random number is transcendental since algebraic numbers can be approximated recursively at every base using Newton's method, for instance, and this precludes randomness (see [8]).

7. Concluding Remarks

In the proof of the invariance of randomness with respect natural positional representations, the transition from base $q+1$ to base q turned out to be the most critical step. The possibility of sparse "overflow carries" implies that no total, recursive, injective, and prefix-increasing base transformation function exists. It is well-known that even simple recursive functions may destroy randomness (see von Mises' example described in the introduction). Our strategy was to exhibit a recursive set D_q which is open with respect to the topology generated by the prefix-order D_q, which has a strong "density" property (see Lemma 5.1.1), and on which a function β_q having all the desired properties can be constructed. It is important to realize in this context – and it is sometimes obscured by intuition – that the required function transforms *names* of numbers into *names* of numbers and it does not deal with the numbers themselves.

An earlier version of this paper was distributed as a technical report of The University of Western Ontario in early 1993 to some colleagues and also presented at a Dagstuhl seminar in May of 1993. Of the comments received, we discuss here two proposed modifications of our proof suggested by P. Gács, M. Li, and P. Vitányi.

In [28], [41], and also [42], p. 266, Exercise 4.25, it is suggested to use a result attributed to L. A. Levin in order to simplify the proof. Roughly, this result is as follows: *A recursive transformation of infinite sequences will map random sequences onto sequences which are random with respect to the induced measure on the image space*[3]. This statement captures part of the intuition described in the introduction of this paper. Applying this result to our situation does not seem to be straightforward, however. First, note that randomness in the sense of Martin-Löf has some very counter-intuitive properties when measures different from the Lebesgue measure are involved [4]. More importantly, in order to achieve our result, one would still have to find a recursive transformation of number representations and prove that it induces the Lebesgue measure. As pointed out earlier, this is the crucial part of our proof as well, being complicated because there is no such total recursive function with the required properties that converts *names* of numbers at base $q+1$ into *names* of the same numbers[4] at base q. In our proofs we do not need to establish that β_q induces the measure μ_{X_q} – we do not even know whether it does; the properties of β_q derived above are already sufficient to apply a direct measure theoretic argument (Theorem 3.8).

In [42], p. 202, Exercise 3.22, it is suggested that an invariance theorem for r-ary decoders ([26]; see [41] and [42], p. 147, Exercise 2.15) due to Gács can be used. Dealing with computers transforming strings written with respect to some fixed base into strings of natural numbers, it is shown that the base

---

[3] In this form, this statement does not seem to have been published. The references provided by Gács in [28] and Li in [41] and [42], that is, [37], [39], [38], [24], and [25] do not contain this result explicitly.

[4] The emphasis is on *names*. Very simple, intuitively convincing, but incorrect arguments are possible when this point is not carefully observed.

is asymptotically irrelevant for specifying all strings of natural numbers. As pointed out in greater detail in [12] (see also [11]), descriptional complexity in the binary and non-binary cases has crucial differences, some of which seem to be missed in [42]. In [12] we prove that there is no universal self-delimiting r-ary decoder that is a universal Chaitin computer. As a consequence, Gács' result does not seem to be applicable to the problem of this paper.

As randomness is an invariant of natural positional representations it is natural to view it as a property of numbers rather than of their representations. Having defined the random real numbers, the first question which naturally comes to mind is: How many real numbers are random? In measure-theoretical terms the answer is "almost all," using a classical theorem due to Martin-Löf which asserts that the set of random sequences has measure 1 (see [43], [6]). In topological terms the answer is "very few" as the set of random sequences is meagre [6]. Both results are constructively true. It is worth mentioning that under the usual identification of X^ω with $(0,1)$ the measure used in Martin-Löf's result coincides with the usual Lebesgue measure, which is not the case for the corresponding topologies.

Our study can be seen as a complementary approach to that in [36], since randomness in the sense of Martin-Löf corresponds to "maximal complexity."

Finally, other problems related to the algebraic and topological structure of random numbers will be treated elsewhere.

8. Acknowledgements

This work was supported by the Natural Sciences and Engineering Council of Canada under Grant OGP0000243.

9. References

1. É. Borel: Les Probabilités Dénombrables et leurs Applications Arithmétiques. *Rend. Circ. Mat. Palermo* **27** (1909), 247–271.

2. É. Borel: *Leçons sur la Théorie des Fonctions.* Gauthier-Villars, Paris, 2nd edition, 1914.

3. U. Brandt: Number Representations and Registers. *J. Inform. Process. Cybernetic, EIK* **28** (1992), 197–212.

4. C. Calude, I. Chiţescu: On Per Martin-Löf Random Sequences. *Bull. Math. Soc. Sci. Math. R. S. Roumanie* (N. S.) **26** (1982), 217–221.

5. C. Calude: *Theories of Computational Complexities.* North-Holland, Amsterdam, 1988.

6. C. Calude, I. Chiţescu: Random Sequences: Some Topological and Measure-Theoretical Properties. *An. Univ. Bucureşti, Mat.-Inf.* **2** (1988), 27–32.

7. C. Calude, I. Chiţescu: A Combinatorial Characterization of P. Martin-Löf Tests. *Internat. J. Comput. Math.* **17** (1988), 53–64.

8. C. Calude, I. Chiţescu: Qualitative Properties of P. Martin-Löf Random Sequences. *Boll. Unione Mat. Ital.* **(7) 3-B** (1989), 229–240.

9. C. Calude, H. Jürgensen: Randomness Preserving Transformations. Manuscript, November, 1993, in Preparation.

10. C. Calude: Borel Normality and Algorithmic Randomness. In G. Rozenberg, A. Salomaa (eds.), *Dëvelopments in Language Theory*, World Scientific, Singapore, 1994, in Press.

11. C. Calude: *Information and Randomness: An Algorithmic Perspective*. Springer-Verlag, Berlin, 1994, in Press.

12. C. Calude, H. Jürgensen: Coding without Tears. Manuscript, January, 1994, in Preparation.

13. G. J. Chaitin: On the Length of Programs for Computing Finite Binary Sequences: Statistical Considerations. *J. Assoc. Comput. Mach.* 16 (1969), 145–159. Reprinted in [15], 245–260.

14. G. J. Chaitin: *Algorithmic Information Theory*, Cambridge University Press, Cambridge, 1987; 3rd Printing 1990.

15. G. J. Chaitin: *Information, Randomness and Incompleteness. Papers on Algorithmic Information Theory.* World Scientific, Singapore, 1987; 2nd Edition, 1990.

16. G. J. Chaitin: *Information-Theoretic Incompleteness.* World Scientific, Singapore, 1992.

17. G. J. Chaitin: *Randomness in Arithmetic and the Decline and Fall of Reductionism in Pure Mathematics. EATCS Bull.* 50 (1993), 314–328.

18. D. G. Champernowne: The Construction of Decimals Normal in the Scale of Ten. *J. London Math. Soc.* 8 (1933), 254–260.

19. T. M. Cover, P. Gács, R. M. Gray: Kolomogorov's Contributions to Information Theory and Algorithmic Complexity. *The Annals of Probability* 17 (1989), 840–855.

20. K. Culik, A. Salomaa: Ambiguity and Decision Problems Concerning Number Systems. *Inform. and Control* 56 (1984), 139–153.

21. C. Dellacherie: Nombres au hazard. De Borel à Martin-Loef. *Gazette des Math.,* Soc. Math. France 11 (1978), 23–58.

22. W. Feller: *An Introduction to Probability Theory and Its Aplications.* Vol. 1, Chapman & Hall, London, John Wiley & Sons, New York, 2nd edition, 1958.

23. P. Gács (P. Gač): On the Symmetry of Algorithmic Information. *Dokl. Akad. Nauk SSSR* 218,6 (1974) 1265–1267, in Russian. English Translation: *Soviet Math. Dokl.* 15 (1974), 1477–1480.

24. P. Gács: *Komplexität und Zufälligkeit.* Dissertation, Frankfurt, 1978.

25. P. Gács: Exact Expressions for Some Randomness Tests. *Zeitschr. f. math. Logik und Grundlagen d. Math.* 26 (1980), 385–394.

26. P. Gács: Every Sequence is Reducible to a Random One. *Inform. and Control* 70 (1986), 186–192.

27. P. Gács: *Lecture Notes on Descriptional Complexity and Randomness.* Boston University, 1988, 62 pp., Unpublished Manuscript.

28. P. Gács: Personal Communication; Especially also Electronic Mail, November 2 and 3, 1993.

29. G. H. Hardy, E. M. Wright: *An Introduction to the Theory of Numbers.* Clarendon Press, Oxford, 5th Edition, 1979.

30. J. Honkala: On Unambiguous Number Systems with a Prime Power Base. *Acta Cybernetica* **10** (1992), 155–163.

31. H. Jürgensen, H. J. Shyr, G. Thierrin: Disjunctive ω-Languages. *EIK* **19** (1983), 267–278.

32. H. Jürgensen, G. Thierrin: Some structural properties of ω-languages. Сборник, XIII Национална Младежка Школа С Международно Участие "Приложение На Математиката В Техниката. *(13th National School with International Participation "Applications of Mathematics in Technology").* Sofia, 1988, 56–63.

33. D. E. Knuth: *The Art of Computer Programming,* Vol. 2, *Seminumerical Algorithms.* Addison-Wesley, Reading, Ma., 2nd Edition, 1971.

34. A. N. Kolmogorov: Three Approaches for Defining the Concept of 'Information Quantity.' *Problemy Peredachi Informatsii* **1** (1965), 3–11 (in Russian).

35. L. Kuipers, H. Niederreiter: *Uniform Distribution of Sequences.* John-Wiley & Sons, New York, 1974.

36. S. Labhalla, H. Lombardi: Répresentations des Nombres Réels par Développements en Base Entière et Complexité. *Theoret. Comput. Sci.* **88** (1991), 1771–182.

37. L. A. Levin: Laws of Information Conservation (Nongrowth) and Aspects of the Foundation of Probability Theory. *Problemy Peredachi Informatsii* **10,3** (1974), 30–35, in Russian. English Translation: *Problems of Information Transmission* **10** (1976), 206–210.

38. L. A. Levin: Uniform Tests of Randomness. *Dokl. Akad. Nauk SSSR* **227** (1976), 33-35, in Russian. English Translation: *Soviet Math. Dokl.* **17** (1976), 337–340.

39. L. A. Levin: Randomness Conservation Inequalities; Information and Independence in Mathematical Theories. *Inform. and Control* **61** (1984), 15–37.

40. M. Li, P. M. Vitányi: Kolmogorov Complexity and Its Applications. In J. van Leeuwen (ed.), *Handbook of Theoretical Computer Science,* Vol. A, North-Holland, Amsterdam, MIT Press, Boston, 1990, 187–254.

41. M. Li: Personal Communication; Especially also Electronic Mail, January 21, 1993.

42. M. Li, P. M. Vitányi: *An Introduction to Kolmogorov Complexity and Its Applications.* Springer-Verlag, Berlin, 1993.

43. P. Martin-Löf: The Defintion of Random Sequences. *Inform. and Control* **6** (1966), 602–619.

44. M. Mendes France: Suite de Nombres au Hasard (d'après Knuth). *Séminaire de Théorie des Nombres,* Université de Bordeaux I, 1974–1975, Exposé 6, 1–11.

45. R. von Mises: *Probability, Statistics and Truth.* G.Allen and Unwin Ltd., London, Macmillan, New York, 2nd Revised English Edition Prepared by Hilda Geiringer, 1961.

46. R. von Mises: *Mathematical Theory of Probability and Statistics.* Edited and complemented by Hilda Geiringer, Academic Press, New York, 1964.

47. I. Niven, H. S. Zuckerman: On the Definition of Normal Numbers. *Pacific J. Math.* **1** (1951), 103–110.

48. C. P. Schnorr: *Zufälligkeit und Wahrscheinlichkeit.* Lecture Notes Math. Vol. 218, Springer-Verlag, Berlin, 1981.

49. R. M. Solovay: *Draft of a Paper (or Series of Papers) on Chaitin's Work ... Done for the Most Part during the Period of Sept.–Dec. 1974*, Unpublished Manuscript, Thomas J. Watson Research Center, Yorktown Heights, New York, May, 1975, 215 pp.

50. A. Szilard: Personal Communication, November, 1993.

Cooperating Grammars' Systems: Power and Parameters*

Erzsébet Csuhaj-Varjú

Computer and Automation Research Institute
Hungarian Academy of Sciences
Kende u. 13 - 17.
H - 1111 Budapest
Hungary

Abstract. We give an overview on the results obtained about the connection between the power and some parameters of cooperating grammars' systems, and propose a method for comparing those CD grammar classes.

1 Introduction

Cooperative and distributed systems are in the focus of interest in the present day computer science. The development of concurrent (parallel) computers, the proliferation of computer networks, and the recognition that much human problem solving and activity involves groups of people, have provoked interest in cooperation and distribution in various scientific areas.

Highly elaborated formalisms in modelling cooperative/distributed systems can help in the better understanding of the nature of cooperation and distribution. The theory of formal grammars (formal language theory) is a promising tool for this purpose. We illustrate the idea by the following example. Consider some context-free grammars which cooperate in the interest of deriving words of a language. They share the sentential form that is rewritten by some grammar until a certain condition is met. Then, the grammar passes the string to the next grammar, and so on, until a terminal word is obtained. This model of cooperating grammars captures the main syntactic characteristics of the well-known blackboard model of problem solving. The blackboard architecture consists of a group of agents that jointly solve a problem by modifying the contents of a global database (the blackboard) from time to time until the solution is obtained. The agents can communicate with each other only through the blackboard that contains all information concerning the current state of the problem solving. Following similar ideas, cooperating/distributed grammar systems are candidates of appropriate models of various kinds of multiagent systems and they can help in enlightening such notions as cooperation, concurrency, cohabitation, etc. In addition to that formal language theory can be involved in these circumstances,

* Research supported by the Hungarian Scientific Research Foundation "OTKA", Grant No. 2571 and 4295 and by EC Cooperative Action IC 1000 ; Project ALTEC.

there is another argument for studying cooperation in grammatical terminology. In spite of that the main concern of "classic" formal language theory is the generation of a language by a single grammar (a generative device), the notion of a grammar and that of its functioning implicitly involves cooperation and distribution. What is a grammar? It is a multiagent system of productions (simple agents with bounded knowledge and influence) which have a common goal (the generation of a language) and also have separate individual goals (executing a derivation step). The derivation mode is the counterpart of the family of the strategies and the coordination mechanism used in the system. Thus, understanding cooperation and distribution (multiagent systems) means understanding the concept of the generative grammar and of its intricate intrinsic behaviour.

2 Development of the Area

The notion of the cooperating grammar system was introduced in 1978 in [30], motivated by two-level substitution mechanism. In 1986, some remarks were presented about the area of cooperating grammars as a possible generalized framework of regulated rewriting ([3]). A rather intensive study of the topic has been launched in [4] and [9] (1988-89), by discovering that the notion is a syntactic model of the blackboard architecture. ([4] appeared in 1990 but it was presented in 1988 at a conference.) A similar construction with a background from regulated rewriting, called the modular grammar, was published in 1989 ([1]). This is also the time when another grammatical model, the parallel communicating grammar system, was introduced ([36]) which is a theoretical framework for study parallel processing systems.

The first stream of investigations was strongly motivated by cooperative and distributed problem solving systems and focused on sequential cooperation. The research followed the coming main directions: finding boundaries of cooperating grammars' systems according to generative capacity and syntactic simplicity, comparison of structured/unstructured, controlled/uncontrolled systems and examining well-motivated extensions of the original model where the cooperating grammars are furnished with additional tools to help cooperation/communication. The spontaneous development of the research was strongly influenced by the formal language theoretic background. Important questions like concurrency, conflict, coherence, cohabitation were studied only in traces. However, the worth of cooperation was demonstrated by confirming that cooperation adds generative power and cooperating systems of grammars are useful in concise descriptions of language classes. A second phase of the investigations started in 1992 by introducing the colony ([26],[27]), a variant of simple grammar systems, which is a grammatical representation of multiagent systems with emergent behaviour. A third phase was launched in 1993 by defining teams in grammar systems, that is, groups of simultaneously working grammmars [24]. This step can be considered as the startpoint of the systematic investigation of the role of parallelism and synchronization in the cooperating grammars' area, although we should mention that such efforts can be traced earlier ([15]).

For detailed information and motivations the interested reader is referred to monographs [7] and [2] and to surveys [25],[14],[39]. The present research is branching into various directions: modelling life-like situations, ecosystems ([10]), and investigating synchronization, parallelism, complexity in CD grammar systems.

In this paper we give an overview on the results obtained about the connection between the power and some parameters of cooperating grammars' systems, and propose a method for comparing those CD grammar classes.

Throughout we assume the reader to be familiar with the basic notions of formal language theory.

We use the following notation for language and grammar classes: CF (context-free), REG (regular), RL (right-linear), MAT (matrix), MAT_{ac} (matrix with appearance checking), PR (programmed), PR_{ac} (programmed with appearance checking), UPR (unconditional programmed), OR (ordered), CS (context-sensitive). If λ-rules are allowed to use, then we add superscript λ to the above notations. The identical notation for the classes of languages and the classes of grammars does not lead to ambiguity because the presented theorems are concerned with equalities of language classes. We denote the class of finite languages by FIN and the class of recursively enumerable languages by RE. We also use classes of languages generated by L sytems: $0L$, $D0L$, $E0L$, $ED0L$, $ET0L$, $EDT0L$.

The reader can find their definitions and properties in [38], [17], [37].

3   CD Grammar Systems

The CD grammar system (the cooperating/distributed grammar system or, shortly, the grammar system) is a finite set of (usually Chomsky type) grammars which cooperate in deriving a common language.

Definition 1. A *CD grammar system* (of degree n) is a construct

$$\Gamma = (T, G_1, \ldots, G_n, S),$$

where T is an alphabet (the terminal alphabet of Γ), $G_i = (N_i, T_i, P_i)$, $1 \leq i \leq n$, are Chomsky grammars without axioms (the components of Γ) such that $T \subseteq \cup_{i=1}^n T_i$, and $S \in \cup_{i=1}^n N_i$ (the start symbol of Γ).

If S is replaced by a language L_S over $V_\Gamma^* = (\cup_{i=1}^n (N_i \cup T_i))^*$, then we speak of an *extended CD grammar system*.

T determines the *acceptance style* of the components according to termination. T is said to be of style

(i) *arb*, if $T \subseteq \cup_{i=1}^n T_i$,

(ii) *ex*, if $T = \cup_{i=1}^{n} T_i$,

(iii) *all*, if $T \subseteq \cap_{i=1}^{n} T_i$, and

(iii) *one*, if $T = T_i$, for some i, $1 \le i \le n$.

If $N_i = N$ and $T_i = T$, $1 \le i \le n$, for a given N and T, then Γ is *definitive* (or it has definitive nonterminals and terminals) and we write it in the form $\Gamma = (N, T, P_1, \ldots, P_n, S)$.

A CD grammar system $\Gamma = (T, G_1, \ldots, G_n, S)$ is *deterministic* if for each component $G_i = (N_i, T_i, P_i)$, $1 \le i \le n$, $A \to x_1 \in P_i$, $A \to x_2 \in P_i$, $A \in N_i$, implies $x_1 = x_2$.

Cooperation of grammars is realized by derivations.

Let $\Gamma = (T, G_1, \ldots, G_n, S)$ be a CD grammar system as above. The derivation relation $\Longrightarrow_{G_i}$ (in the case of definitive CD grammar systems written as $\Longrightarrow_{P_i}$) in components of Γ is defined as usual. We say a component is *competent* in (the derivation of) a sentential form, if it is able to apply at least one of its productions for that.

Definition 2. Let $\Gamma = (T, G_1, \ldots, G_n, S)$ be a CD grammar system as above.

We write $\Longrightarrow_{G_i}^{b}$, $\Longrightarrow_{G_i}^{\le k}$, $\Longrightarrow_{G_i}^{=k}$, $\Longrightarrow_{G_i}^{\ge k}$, for $k \ge 1$, for a derivation consisting of an arbitrary number of steps, of at least k steps, of exactly k steps, of at most k steps, respectively.

For $x, y \in (N_i \cup T_i)^*$ we write $x \Longrightarrow_{G_i}^{t} y$ if $x \Longrightarrow_{G_i}^{*} y$ and there is no z in $(N_i \cup T_i)^*$ such that $y \Longrightarrow_{G_i}^{*} z$.

For $f \in \{b, t\} \cup \{\le k, = k, \ge k | k \ge 1\}$, the language generated by Γ in the f-mode derivation (in f-derivation or in f-cooperation) is

$$L_f(\Gamma) = \{x \in T^* | S \Longrightarrow_{G_{i_1}}^{f} x_1 \Longrightarrow_{G_{i_2}}^{f} x_2 \ldots \Longrightarrow_{G_{i_m}}^{f} x_m = x, 1 \le i_j \le n, 1 \le j \le m\}.$$

t-cooperation is based on competence. In this case, the component grammar can start with the derivation if it is competent in the current sentential form and stops with the generation if it is no longer competent in the obtained string. f-derivations for $f \in \{\le k, = k, \ge k | k \ge 1\}$ are step-limited cooperation strategies.

In order to shorten the formulation of the statements and the definitions, throughout we use notations $M = \{b, t\} \cup \{\le k, = k, \ge k | k \ge 1\}$ and $A = \{arb, ex, all, one\}$.

A CD grammar system is heterogeneous (hybrid) if its each component has an individual cooperation strategy, otherwise the system is homogeneous.

A *heterogeneous CD grammar system* (of degree n) is a construct $\Gamma = (T, (G_1, f_1), \ldots, (G_n, f_n), S)$, where $T, G_1, \ldots, G_n, S$ are defined as in Definition 1 and $f_1, \ldots, f_n \in M$.

The language generated by Γ is

$$L(\Gamma) = \{x \in T^* | S \Longrightarrow_{G_{i_1}}^{f_{i_1}} x_1 \Longrightarrow_{G_{i_2}}^{f_{i_2}} x_2 \ldots \Longrightarrow_{G_{i_m}}^{f_{i_m}} x_m = x, 1 \le i_j \le n, 1 \le j \le m\}.$$

We denote by $CD_n X(f)$ the class of languages generated by CD grammar systems of degree at most n ($n \geq 1$) with components of type X, where $X \in \{CF, CF^\lambda, RL, REG\}$ and with derivation mode $f \in M$. If we would like to indicate the acceptance style, then we write $CDX(a, f)$ instead of $CDX(f)$, where $a \in A$. If we consider language classes generated by extended CD grammar systems with a single start word, then we replace CD by ECD. If a start language of type Z, for $Z \in \{FIN, REG, CF\}$, is taken into consideration, then we use $E_Z CD$ instead of CD in the above notations. Heterogeneous CD grammar systems are denoted by appending prefix H to the above notations and by omitting the reference to the derivation mode f. If we take only definitive CD grammar systems into account, then we change CD for CD' in the notations above.

Example:
We illustrate the notions by the following simple example:

Let $\Gamma = (\{a, b, c\}, G_1, G_2, G_3, S)$, where
$G_1 = (\{A, B\}, \{A', B', a, b, c\}, \{A \to aA'b, B \to cB'\})$,
$G_2 = (\{S, A', B'\}, \{A, B, a, b, c\}, \{S \to S, S \to AB, A' \to A, B' \to B\})$ and
$G_3 = (\{S, A, B, A', B'\}, \{a, b, c\}, \{A \to ab, B \to c\})$.
Then $L_{=1}(\Gamma) = L_b(\Gamma) = L_{\geq 1}(\Gamma) = \{a^n b^n c^m \mid n, m \geq 1\}$ and
$L_{=2}(\Gamma) = L_{\geq 2}(\Gamma) = L_t(\Gamma) = \{a^n b^n c^n \mid n \geq 1\}$.

We can observe that f-cooperation for $f \in \{t, = 2, \geq 2\}$ essentially increases the generative power: the obtained language is a non-context-free context-sensitive language.

An important subfield of the CD grammar systems' area is the theory of colonies.

Definition 3. A CD grammar system $\Gamma = (T, G_1, \ldots, G_n, S)$ is said to be a *colony* if $G_i = (\{S_i\}, T_i, P_i)$, $P_i \subseteq \{S_i\} \times T_i^+$, for $1 \leq i \leq n$, and $S = S_j$ for some j, $1 \leq j \leq n$.

Thus, a colony is a CD grammar system, where each component has exactly one nonterminal and all productions are nonrecursive. Derivation modes and languages associated with colonies are introduced in the obvious way with mentioning that step-limited derivation modes are defined for *extended* colonies (with a start word). To distinguish the class of languages generated by colonies from the class of languages generated by CD grammar systems in general, we use COL instead of CD in the notations.

4   Power: Strategy and Size

Cooperation strategy and size of CD grammar systems are candidates of parameters which have impact on the generative power. This conjecture is confirmed in the case of both sequential and parallel derivation modes.

4.1 Sequential Strategies

Sequential (non-simultaneous) cooperation strategies determine the order of the work of the components functioning in succession.

Competence-based strategies and step-limited strategies have a different character; the first type frequently leads to a (finite) hierarchy of language classes, the second type results in incomparability of classes of languages.

We first mention that in the case of context-free components b-cooperation is as powerful as $= 1$-cooperation and as $\leq k$-cooperation, for $k \geq 1$, and produces exactly the class of context-free languages. Acceptance styles and the number of components are with no effect on the generative power.

Theorem 4. ([4],[5]) *For $a \in A$, $k \geq 1$, $r \geq 1$,*

(i) $CD_r CF(a,1) = CD_r CDF(a, \leq k) = CD_r CF(a,b) = CF$ and
(ii) $CDCF(a,1) = CDCDF(a, \leq k) = CDCF(a,b) = CF$.

t-derivations add generative power; t-cooperating context-free grammars are as powerful as ET0L systems. This fact implies an expected property, namely, that the number of components, as a size parameter, induces only a finite hierarchy of language classes. Moreover, if three or more than three grammars cooperate, then the acceptance field has no impact on the generative power.

Theorem 5. ([4],[5])

(i) $CD_n CF(a,t) = ET0L$ for $n \geq 3$ and $a \in A$,
(ii) $CF = CD_1 CF(all,t) = CD_2 CF(all,t)$,
(iii) $CF = CD_1 CF(a,t) \subset E0L \subset CD_2 CF(a,t) \subseteq ET0L$ for $a \in \{arb, one\}$,
(iv) $CF = CD_1 CF(ex,t) \subset CD_2 CF(ex,t) \subseteq ET0L$.

According to hierarchies, the maximum of the number of productions in the components, as a size parameter, is with the same effect as the number of components in the CD grammar system. We should mention, however, that this property was shown only in that case if λ-rules are allowed to use.

For $n \geq 1, m \geq 1$ (including $n = \infty$, $m = \infty$ which denote that n, m are not bounded), we denote by $CD_{n,m} CF^\lambda$ the class of languages generated by context-free CD grammar systems with λ-rules and with at most n components, where each component has at most m productions. $DCD_{n,m} CF^\lambda$ denotes the class of languages generated by deterministic CD grammar systems corresponding to $CD_{n,m} CF^\lambda$.

Theorem 6. ([20]) *For $m \geq 5$*
$$CD_{\infty,5} CF^\lambda(t) = CD_{\infty,m} CF^\lambda(t) = CD_{\infty,\infty} CF^\lambda(t) = CDCF^\lambda(t) = ET0L.$$

Moreover, $DCD_{\infty,\infty}CF^{\lambda}(t) = DCD_{\infty,4}CF^{\lambda}(t)$ ([20]).

The number of components and the number of productions, as size parameters, together induce a doubly infinite hierarchy of languages in the case of both b-mode of derivation and t-mode of derivation.

Theorem 7. ([20]) *For all finite $n, m \geq 1$ and for $f \in \{b, t\}$ we have*
$$CD_{n,m}CF(f) \subset CD_{n+1,m}CF(f) \text{ and } CD_{n,m}CF(f) \subset CD_{n,m+1}CF(f).$$

Some properties are preserved by colonies. Although, t-cooperation is less effective in this case: colonies are able to generate only a proper subclass of the class of ET0L languages, namely the class of 1-restricted ET0L languages, denoted by $ET0L_{[1]}$.

Theorem 8. ([28]) *For $a \in \{arb, one, all\}$*

(i) $COLCF(a, t) = ET0L_{[1]} \subset ET0L$,
(ii) $COLCF(ex, t) \subset COLCF(a, t)$,
(iii) $COLCF(ex, b) \subset COLCF(a, b) = CF$,
(iv) $COLCF(a, b)$ *and* $COLCF(ex, t)$ *are incomparable,*
(v) $COLCF(ex, b)$ *and* $COLCF(ex, t)$ *are incomparable.*

[27] proves that in b-mode of derivation the hierarchy of languages generated by colonies with an increasing number of components is infinite.

The choice of the starting mechanism (a symbol, a word, a language) as a parameter can play an important role in changing the generative power. But, this holds only in the case of definitive CD grammar systems, CD grammar systems presented in the form of Definition 1 are out of interest from this point of view.

In [18] it was shown that $E_m CD'RL(f) = RLSM_m$, $m \geq 1$, where m refers to the number of nonterminal occurrences in the start word w and $RLSM_m$ denotes the class of right-linear simple matrix languages with matrices of size m. Thus, the special choice of starting mechanism and the restriction of the form of the grammar system, together, induce an infinite hierarchy of languages. Moreover, if we consider more general languages to start with, then we obtain the following interesting properties:

Theorem 9. ([21]) *For $f \in \{t\} \cup \{= k, \geq k | k \geq 1\}$*

(i) $E_{REG}CD'REG(f) \subset E_{CF}CD'REG(f) \subset E_{CF}CD'CF(f) = CD'CF(f)$,
(ii) $E_{REG}CD'REG(f)$ *is incomparable with* CF.

Step-limited derivation modes ($= k$, $\geq k$) have a character different from that of t-mode and b-mode derivations. It is of interest to note that in this case k behaves like a size parameter.

According to inclusions, so far, we have $CF \subset CDCF(f) \subseteq MAT$ for $f \in \{= k, \geq k | k \geq 1\}$ ([19].)

A more precise picture about the geography of languages of CD grammar systems with step-limited strategies is presented in [22].

Theorem 10. ([22]) *For $f \in \{= k, \geq k | k \geq 2\}$ and for $n \geq 2$*

(i) $CD_n CF(f)$ is incomparable with X, where
    $X \in \{0L, D0L, E0L, ED0L, T0L, EDT0L\}$;
(ii) $CD_n CF(f)$ is incomparable with $DCD_n CF(t)$;
(iii) $MAT_{ac}, ET0L$ contain languages not in $CDCF(f)$;
(iv) $CDCF(f)$ contains non-semi-linear languages.

Incomparability properties are preserved in the case of colonies, too.

Theorem 11. ([34])

(i) $COLCF_n(f)$ is incomparable with FIN, REG, LIN, CF
    for $f \in \{= k, \geq k | k \geq 2\}$ and for $n \geq 2$,
(ii) $COLCF(f)$ is incomparable with $COL(t)$;
(iii) $COLCF(= k_1)$, $COLCF(= k_2)$, $COLCF(\geq k_3)$ and $COLCF(\geq k_4)$ are
    pairwise incomparable for pairwise different k_1, k_2, k_3, k_4.

The above results demonstrate the impact of the size parameters on the generative power in the case of homogeneous systems. We close this section with an interesting size property of heterogeneous CD grammar systems. The statement implicitly refers to that, according to some properties, competence-based strategies dominate step-limited ones.

Theorem 12. ([32])
    $CF = HCD_1CF \subset HCD_2CF \subseteq HCD_4CF = HCD_nCF = HCDCF,$
    for $n \geq 5$.

4.2 Simultaneous Strategies

Cooperation implicitly presupposes simultaneous functioning of components, that is, such cases if more than one grammar becomes active at the same time.

Definition 13. A *team CD grammar system* (with (1) *prescribed teams*, and (2) of *variable size*) is a construct

$$\Gamma = (N, T, P_1, P_2, \ldots, P_n, w, Q_1, Q_2, \ldots, Q_m),$$

where $(N, T, P_1, \ldots, P_n, w)$ is a definitive extended CD grammar system with $w \in (N \cup T)^+$ and $Q_i \subseteq \{P_1, \ldots, P_n\}$, for $1 \leq i \leq m$. $Q_1, \ldots, Q_m$ are called *teams* of Γ.

Definition 14. Let $\Gamma = (N, T, P_1, P_2, \ldots, P_n, w, Q_1, Q_2, \ldots, Q_m)$ be a team CD grammar system as above.

A derivation step executed by a team $Q_i = \{P_{j_1}, P_{j_2}, \ldots, P_{j_s}\}$, $1 \leq i \leq m$, is defined as follows:

For $x, y \in (N \cup T)^*$ we write $x \Longrightarrow_{Q_i} y$ iff

$x = x_1 A_1 x_2 A_2 \ldots x_s A_s x_{s+1}$ and $y = x_1 y_1 x_2 y_2 \ldots x_s y_s x_{s+1}$,

where $x_l \in (N \cup T)^*$, $1 \leq l \leq s+1$, $A_k \to y_k \in P_{j_r}$, $1 \leq r \leq s$.

Derivation modes $\Longrightarrow_{Q_i}^b, \Longrightarrow_{Q_i}^{=k}, \Longrightarrow_{Q_i}^{\geq k}, \Longrightarrow_{Q_i}^{\leq k}$, $k \geq 1$, are defined according to Definition 2, respectively. (The team, as a whole, executes an arbitrary number of derivation steps, k, at least k, at most k steps.)

t-derivations are defined for a team Q_i by the following two variants:

(i) $x \Longrightarrow_{Q_i}^t y$ iff $x \Longrightarrow_{Q_i}^b y$ and for no component $P_{j_r} \in Q_i$, $1 \leq r \leq s$, and no z there is a derivation $y \Longrightarrow_{P_{j_r}} z$,

(ii) $x \Longrightarrow_{Q_i}^{t'} y$ iff $x \Longrightarrow_{Q_i}^b y$ and there is a component $P_{j_r} \in Q_i$, $j_r \in \{1, 2, \ldots, s\}$, for which no derivation $y \Longrightarrow_{P_{j_r}} z$ is possible.

(In the former case no component of Q_i can continue the derivation, in the latter case the team as a whole cannot go further.)

The language $L_f(\Gamma)$ generated by a team CD grammar system above in f-mode of derivation, where $f \in \{t'\} \cup M$, is

$$L_f(\Gamma) = \{x \in T^* \mid S \Longrightarrow_{Q_{i_1}}^f x_1 \Longrightarrow_{Q_{i_2}}^f x_2 \ldots \Longrightarrow_{Q_{i_m}}^f x_m = x, m \geq 1, 1 \leq i_j \leq n, 1 \leq j \leq m\}.$$

Components of CD grammar systems can be organized into teams in various ways: *teams of constant (bounded) size* (every team consists of the same (bounded) number of components), *free teams of constant (bounded) size* (there exists a positive integer s such that the teams are all sets consisting of s ($\leq s$) components) and teams emerging dynamically from the set of components having the same degree (a fixed degree) of competence. We should note that in the case of (free) teams of constant size (with more than one members) the definition is modified: we change the start symbol for a start word (to start we need sufficiently many nonterminals in the start word).

We denote by $PT_s CDCF(f)$ ($PT_{\leq s} CDCF(f)$) the class of languages generated by context-free CD grammar systems with prescribed teams of constant (bounded) size s, in the f-mode of derivation, where $f \in M \cup \{t'\}$. For free teams initial P is cancelled. If the team size is not bounded, but it is at least 2, then we change subscript s for $+$. If the team size is not bounded and single components as teams are taken into account, then we use $*$ instead of subscript s. For colonies we keep conventions and replace CD by COL.

There are two plausible expectations: first, team-work enhances the generative power, second, the size of teams and the choice of the team components have impact on the generative power. The first conjecture is confirmed. Surprisingly, for maximal derivations (t-modes and t'-modes) the second statement does not hold.

Nondeterministically chosen pairs of context-free grammars as teams in t-cooperation (in t'-cooperation) are as powerful as teams with prescribed components of variable size.

Theorem 15. ([33],[11])
$$T_s CDCF(f) = PT_s CDCF(f) = PT_s CD(f) = T_+ CD(f) = PR_{ac}$$
for $s \geq 2$ and $f \in \{t, t'\}$.

Thus, $T_s CDCF^\lambda(f) = PT_s CDCF^\lambda(f) = PT_s CDCF^\lambda(f) = T_+ CDCF^\lambda(f) = RE$.

In team organization, step-limited cooperation strategies are essentially less powerful than t-cooperations.

Theorem 16. ([33]) For $f \in \{b\} \cup \{\leq k, = k, \geq k| \geq 1\}$ and $s \geq 2$

(i) $PT_s CDCF(f) = PTCDCF(f) = PR$
(ii) $PT_s CDCF^\lambda(f) = PTCDCF^\lambda(f) = PR^\lambda$

We also can reach considerable generative power and economic organization of team-work if we choose colonies instead of general CD grammar systems. In [12] it is shown that $PT_{\leq 2} COLCF(b) = PR$.

But, the power of team-work can decrease if the teams are organized on the base of competence ([15]).

A colony works in *strongly competitive parallel way* if it works in team organization, uses b-mode of derivation and in each derivation step the actual team consists of all components that are competent on the current sentential form. If the team consist of a maximal number of competent components, then the colony works in *weakly competitive parallel way*. Let us denote the corresponding two classes of languages by $STCOLCF(b)$ and $WTCOL(b)$. Then, by [15],
$$CF \subset WTCOLCF(b) \subset UPR \subset PR \text{ and } STCOLCF(b) \subseteq MAT_{ac}.$$
Further results concerning teams organized on the base of competence and exitation levels can be found in [29].

5 Power and Structure

One expected way to improve cooperation is imposing an appropriate organizational structure or utilizing the intrinsic structure of the grammar system. External structures are composed of vertical and hierarchical relations among components; internal structures arise from the functioning of the system.

The following structural relation prescribes subsequency of the components.

Definition 17. A CD grammar system with a binary relation R is a construct $\Gamma = (N, T, P_1, \ldots, P_n, S, R)$, where $(N, T, P_1, \ldots, P_n, S)$ is a definitive CD grammar system and R is a binary relation over the set of components $\{P_1, \ldots, P_n\}$.

The language $L_f(\Gamma)$ generated by Γ in f-mode of derivation, for $f \in M$, is the set of all words $x \in T^*$ for which there is a derivation

$$S \Longrightarrow^f_{P_{i_1}} x_1 \Longrightarrow^f_{P_{i_2}} x_2 \ldots \Longrightarrow^f_{P_{i_m}} x_m = x, m \geq 1, 1 \leq i_j \leq n, 1 \leq j \leq m - 1,$$

such that $(P_{i_j}, P_{i_{j+1}}) \in R$.

We say that R is a priority relation if R is a partial order and the above notion of derivation is modified in the following way: for $x, y \in (N \cup T)^*$ we write $x \Longrightarrow^f_{P_i} y$ if, P_i is the maximal element according to R among all components P_k, $1 \leq k \leq n$, which are able to derive y from x in f-mode derivation.

In the case of t-cooperation binary relations and priority relations do not increase the generative power, but, by step-limited derivations a significant improvement can be reached.

We denote by $RCDCF(f)$ and $PCDCF(f)$ ($RCD_nCF(f)$ and $PCD_nCF(f)$, if the degree of the system is taken into account), the class of languages generated by context-free CD grammar systems with binary relations and with priority relations, respectively.

Theorem 18. ([4],[13],[33])

(i) $RCDCD(t) = PCDCF(t) = CDCF(t)$

(ii) $RCDCF(\leq k) = RCDCF(= k) = PR$ for $k \geq 1$, and,

(iii) $OR \subseteq PCDCF(= k) \subseteq MAT_{ac}$ for $k \geq 2$.

Moreover, [31] proves that for $f \in \{= k, \geq k | k \geq 1\}$ $PCD_nCF(f)$ contains a language not included in $CDCF(f)$.

A variant of organizing teams of CD grammar systems into local hierarchies is the *stratified grammar system*, motivated by Minsky's society model of mind ([30]). (A team is called a stratum in this variant).

An extended definitive team CD grammar system $\Gamma = (N, T, P_1, \ldots, P_n, Q_1, \ldots, Q_m, w)$, $w \in (N \cup T)^+$, is a stratified grammar system if the language generated by Γ in f-mode derivation, for $f \in M$, is defined as the set of all words $z \in T^*$ for which there is a derivation

$$S = x_0 \Longrightarrow^f_{Q_1} x_1 \Longrightarrow^f_{Q_2} x_2 \Longrightarrow^f_{Q_3} \ldots \Longrightarrow^f_{Q_i} x_i \Longrightarrow^f_{Q_{i+1}} x_{i+1} \Longrightarrow^f_{Q_{i+2}}$$
$$\ldots \Longrightarrow^f_{Q_r} x_r = z, \text{ where } 1 \leq i \leq r - 1, r \leq m.$$

In [6] it is shown that the class of languages generated by context-free stratified grammar systems in b-mode of derivation is included in MAT. It is an open question whether this inclusion is proper or not. For regular and for context-sensitive CD grammar systems stratified organization in the b-mode derivation does not imply increment of the generative power, the obtained languages classes are REG and CS.

Continuing the idea of imposing structures, [33] introduced a variant, where the the elements are not grammars but systems, which are also composed from systems, and so on, a finite number of times. Surprisingly, this kind of hierarchization does not add generative power in the case of t-mode and b-mode derivations.

Definition 19. A *hierarchized grammar system* of height h, $h \geq 0$, is a context-free grammar $\Gamma = (N, T, P, S)$, if $h = 0$, and a construct $\Gamma = (N, T, \gamma_1, \ldots \gamma_m, S)$ $m \geq 1$, if $h > 1$, where $\Gamma_i = (N, T, \gamma_1, S)$ $1 \leq i \leq m$, are hierarchized grammar systems of height $h - 1$.

Derivation step in a system of height 0 is a usual derivation step in a context-free grammar. For $h = 1$ derivation modes f, $f \in M$, correspond to that are used in a set of productions P. For a system $\Gamma = (N, T, \gamma_1, \ldots \gamma_m, S)$ of height h, $h \geq 2$, for $x, y \in (N \cup T)^*$, for some component γ_j we define

$$x \Longrightarrow_{\gamma_j}^{=k} y \text{ iff } x \Longrightarrow_{\gamma_{j,i_1}}^{=k} x_1 \Longrightarrow_{\gamma_{j,i_2}}^{=k} \ldots \Longrightarrow_{\gamma_{j,i_k}}^{=k} x_k = y, \text{ where } \gamma_{j,i_r}, 1 \leq r \leq$$

k, are components of γ_i. Derivation modes $\leq k$, $\geq k$, b come from the above definition in the obvious way, with mentioning that b-derivation corresponds to $= 1$-derivation.

We define $x \Longrightarrow_{\gamma_j}^{t} y$ iff $x \Longrightarrow_{\gamma_j}^{b} y$ and there is no $z \in (N \cup T)^*$, such that $y \Longrightarrow_{\gamma_j}^{=1} z$.

The language generated by a hierarchized grammar system Γ, as above, in derivation mode f is the set of all words over T^*, that can be obtained by f-derivation from S.

The family of languages generated by context-free hierarchized grammar systems of height at most h, $h \geq 1$, in the derivation mode f, $f \in M$, is denoted by $HY_h CDCF(f)$. By convention we put $HY_0 CDCF(f) = CF$ for all $f \in M$.

The induced language hierarchy is finite in the following derivation modes:

Theorem 20. ([33]) *For* $h \geq 1$

(i) $HY_h CDCF(t) = HY_1 CDCF(t)$,
(ii) $HY_h CDCF(f) = HY_1 CDCF(f)$ *for* $f \in \{b, =1, \geq 1\} \cup \{\leq k | k \geq 1\}$.

Summarizing the above results, we can observe that horizontal structures (teams) add generative power, but there are cooperation strategies and vertical organizations which do not imply increment of the generative capacity.

Not only external structures, but internal structures of the CD grammar systems are of interest. Such structures originate from the internal determinism of the system.

For a (definitive) context-free CD grammar system $\Gamma = (N, T, P_1, \ldots, P_n, S)$ let us denote by $SF_f(\Gamma)$ the set of sentential forms generated by Γ in f-mode of derivation. Let $dom(P_i) = \{A \mid A \rightarrow w \in P_i, A \in N\}$, $1 \leq i \leq n$.

Definition 21. For a definitive context-free CD grammar system Γ, as above, for $f \in M$, and for a sentential form $x \in SF_f(\Gamma) - T^*$ we denote by

$$wb(x, \Gamma) = card\{i \mid alph(x) \cap N \subseteq dom(P_i), 1 \leq i \leq n\}.$$

The *degree of weak branching* of Γ, in the derivation mode f, is

$$wb(\Gamma, f) = \max\{wb(x, \Gamma) \mid x \in SF_f(\Gamma) - T^*\}.$$

For $x \in SF_f(\Gamma)$ we denote by

$$sb(x, \Gamma, f) = card\{i \mid \text{ there is } y \in V_\Gamma^* \text{ such that } x \Longrightarrow_{P_i}^f y, 1 \leq i \leq n\}.$$

The *degree of strong branching* of Γ, in the derivation mode f, is

$$sb(\Gamma, f) = \max\{sb(x, \Gamma, f) \mid x \in SF_f(\Gamma)\}.$$

$sb(x, \Gamma, f)$ denotes the number of components that are able to to execute an f-derivation step; $wb(x, \Gamma, f)$ denotes the number of components which are completely competent in the current sentential form.

For $\alpha \in \{wb, sb\}$ and $L \in CD_nCF(f)$, $f \in M, n \geq 1$, we define $\alpha_f(L) = \min\{\alpha(\Gamma, f) \mid L = L_f(\Gamma)\}$.

We denote by $CD_nCF(f, \alpha(m)) = \{L \in CD_nCF(f) \mid L = L_f(\Gamma), \alpha(\Gamma, f) \leq m\}$ for $m \geq 1$.

The next series of equalities demonstrate that t-cooperation can be performed without much conflict : for every language L that can be generated by a context-free CD grammar system in t-cooperation there is an equivalent one in the case of which in each derivation step at most two components are able to continue t-cooperation.

Theorem 22. ([16])

(i) $CF = CDCF(t, sb(1)) \subset CDCF(t, sb(2)) = ET0L.$
(ii) $CDCF(t, wb(1)) = ET0L.$

Step-limited cooperation strategies need more than one completely competent components: for $f \in \{= k, \geq k \mid k \geq 1\}$ $CDCF(f) = CDCF(f, wb(2))$ ([16]). It is not known whether a similar result holds also for the parameter sb, and whether $CDCF(f) = CDCF(f, wb(1))$ holds or not.

To illustrate the power of the internal structure we mention that $CDCF(f, \alpha(1)) - CF \neq \emptyset$, for all $f \in \{= k, \geq k \mid k \geq 2\}, \alpha \in \{wb, sb\}$.

6 Power and the System Inside

Generative capacity is expected to depend on the relation of the cooperating grammars to each other. Differences and similarities can cover a wide range from the form of the presentation of the cooperating grammars to the role that the grammar plays in cooperation.

A natural demand is to examine situations in which similar grammars cooperate.

The following notion of similarity was introduced in [23].

Definition 23. Let N and T be two disjoint sets (of nonterminals and terminals), and let P_1 and P_2 be two sets of context-free rules contained in $N \times (N \cup T)^*$. We say that P_1 is similar to P_2 if there is a finite substitution $\mu : (N \cup T) \to (N \cup T)$ such that $\mu(A) \subseteq N$ for any $A \in N$, $\mu(A) \cap \mu(B) = \emptyset$ for $A, B \in N$, $A \neq B$, $\mu(a) \subseteq T$ for any $a \in T$, $\mu(a) \cap \mu(b) = \emptyset$ for $a, b \in T$, $a \neq b$, $P_2 \subseteq \mu(P_1) = \{v' \to w' | v' \in \mu(v), w' \in \mu(w), v \to w \in P_1\}$.

We denote by $SIMCDCF(f)$ the family of languages generated by context-free definitive CD grammar systems with pairwise similar components in f-mode of derivation, where $f \in M$. For the corresponding classes of languages generated by heterogeneous CD grammar systems we add prefix H to the notation and omit f.

The following statement expresses a very strong formal stability of the coooperating system. To reach the same generative power, components, independently from the strategy they use, can be chosen to be similar.

Theorem 24. ([8]) $SIMCDCF(f) = CDCF(f)$ for $f \in M$ and $HSIMCDCF = HCDCF$.

Moreover, in t-cooperation, components can be chosen to be both similar and reduced.

Theorem 25. ([8]) For any language $L \in CDCF(t)$, there is a reduced CD grammar system $\Gamma = (T, P_1, P_2, P_3, S)$ with pairwise similar components such that $L_t(\Gamma) = L$.

Differences in behaviour can be illustrated by such grammar systems which contain some extremely powerful components. Such a case is, for example, in which some components of the CD grammar systems can be fixed without any restriction of the generative power.

Definition 26. A p-tuple $(P_1, P_2, \ldots, P_p)$, where $P_1, P_2, \ldots, P_p$ are sets of context-free productions is called a (p, q, X, f)-universal CD grammar system for a language family $\mathcal{L}$ iff, for each $L \in \mathcal{L}$, there are sets $H_1, H_2, \ldots, H_q$ of context-free productions, disjoint sets N and T, and $S \in N$ such that the definitive CD grammar system $\Gamma = (N, T, P_1, P_2, \ldots, P_p, H_1, H_2, \ldots, H_q, S)$ generates in f-mode derivation L, where $f \in M$.

For $n, m \geq 1$, let us denote by $CD'_n CF_m(f)$ the class of languages generated by context-free definitive CD grammar systems with no more than n components and no more than m nonterminals. Then

Theorem 27. ([8]) *There is a $(2, 1, CF, t)$-universal CD grammar system for $CD'_n CF_m(t)$.*

But, for $m \geq 2$ there is no $(1, 1, CF, t)$-universal CD grammar system for $CD'_n CF_m(t)$.

7 Final Remarks

In the former sections we summarized important properties concerning language classes generated by classes of CD grammar systems with different parameters. The results demonstrate that some characteristics are with essential influence on the generative power. The questions that immediately arise are how to determine (to choose) appropriate parameters and how to compare classes of CD grammar systems (or single CD grammar systems) to each other according to the above parameters.

Despite the clear necessity, the systematic study of methods and of well-motivated concepts of comparison of CD grammar systems (classes of CD grammar systems) has not been started yet. One possible reason of this fact is that the research concentrates on such questions that come from language theory and computation. The crucial point in this circumstance is to find the base of comparison. Possible candidates are quantitative and qualitative properties of CD grammar systems. For example, size parameters (the number of components, the number of productions, the number of nonterminals) are quantitative properties. Qualitative properties are of a different character: existence/absence of external/internal structures, the way of component specification, the chosen strategy (strategies) and the generative power. Parameters and their relations to each other form a description of the CD grammar system (of the CD grammar system class). Descriptions can be optimal, stable, etc. (according to some parameters), and can be appropriate (feasible) for some CD grammar classes. Comparisons of descriptions provide comparisons of CD grammar systems. (Notice that the generative power is considered as a property, a component of the description. This is because we are interested in describing and representing the system and its functioning together.)

We illustrate descriptions by the following simple example:

(context-free components, t-cooperation, $ET0L$ language class, 3 components, unbounded number of productions, unbounded number of nonterminals, no external structure, internal structure with parameters $sb(2)$ and $wb(1)$, no restriction on the form of the components)

is a description. But,

(context-free components, t-cooperation, $ET0L$ language class, 3 components, unbounded number of productions, unbounded number of nonterminals, no explicit external structure, no explicit internal structure, similar components, reduced components)

is a description, too.

The two descriptions correspond to the same class of CD grammars with the same strategy. Moreover, by the above results, we know that some parameters are optimal (the number of components, for example) and the two descriptions are stable according to the change of some parameters (for example, general components are changed for similar components).

We can also derive some consequences according to the relation of size parameters (quantitative properties) and the chosen qualitative properties (similarity, structure, etc.). The descriptions are "balanced": quantitative properties are with not more influence than qualitative properties.

For future research, the theory of the above type of descriptions (comparisons and analysis) can play role in the development of CD grammar systems' area. Investigations in the corresponding languages, language classes, syntactic and computational complexity questions are of interest, but they do not exceed boundaries of language theory and computational theory. CD grammar systems are not only generative devices but systems, therefore their study according to different variants of systems' descriptions is of importance. This approach can also contribute to the theory of single grammars and languages, because, by means of the remark made in the Introduction, grammars can be considered as multiagent systems (cooperative systems of agents).

References

1. A. Atanasiu and V. Mitrana, The modular grammars. *Internat. J. Comp. Math.* 30 (1989), 101-122.
2. A. H. Bond, L. Gasser (Eds.), *Readings in Distributed Artificial Intelligence.* Morgan Kaufmann, San Mateo, 1988.
3. E. Csuhaj-Varjú, Some remarks on cooperating grammar systems. In: *Proc. Conf. Aut. Lang. Progr. Syst.* (I. Peák, F. Gécseg, Eds.), Budapest, 1986, 75 - 86.
4. E. Csuhaj-Varjú and J. Dassow, On cooperating/distributed grammar systems. *J. Inf. Process. Cybern. EIK* 26 (1990), 49-63.
5. E. Csuhaj-Varjú, J. Dassow and J. Kelemen, Cooperating/distributed grammar systems with different styles of acceptance. *Intern. J. Computer Math.* 42 (1992), 173 - 183.
6. E. Csuhaj-Varjú, J. Dassow, J, Kelemen and Gh. Păun, Stratified Grammar Systems. *Computers and Artif. Intell.*, accepted.
7. E. Csuhaj-Varjú, J. Dassow, J, Kelemen and Gh. Păun, *Grammar Systems.* Gordon and Breach Publ. House, to appear.
8. E. Csuhaj-Varjú, J. Dassow, V. Mitrana and Gh. Păun, Cooperation in Grammar Systems: Universality, Similarity, Timing. *Kybernetes*, accepted.

9. E. Csuhaj-Varjú and J. Kelemen, Cooperating grammar systems: a syntactical framework for the blackboard model of problem solving. In *Proc. AIICSR '89*, (I. Plander, Ed.), Elsevier, Amsterdam, 1989, 121 - 127.

10. E. Csuhaj-Varjú, J. Kelemen, A. Kelemenová and Gh. Păun, Eco(grammar) systems. A Preview. *12th Eur. Meeting on Cyb.and Systems Res.*, 1994, accepted.

11. E. Csuhaj-Varjú and Gh. Păun, Limiting the size of teams in cooperating grammar systems. *EATCS Bulletin* 51 (1993), 198-202.

12. E. Csuhaj-Varjú and Gh. Păun, Structured colonies: models of symbiosis/parasitism. *Annales Univ. Bucuresti, Ser. Comp. Sci.*, accepted.

13. J. Dassow, A remark on cooperating/distributed grammar systems controlled by graphs. *Wiss. Zeit. T.U. Magdeburg.* 35 (1991), 4-6.

14. J. Dassow and J. Kelemen, Cooperating/distributed grammar systems: a link between formal languages and artificial intelligence. *EATCS Bulletin* 45 (1991), 131-145.

15. J. Dassow, J. Kelemen and Gh. Păun, On parallelism in colonies. *Cybernetics and Systems* 24 (1993), 37-49.

16. J. Dassow, V. Mitrana, Gh. Păun and S. Vicolov, On determinism in cooperating distributed grammar systems. *Publicationes Math.*, to appear.

17. J. Dassow and Gh. Păun, *Regulated Rewriting in Formal Language Theory*. Springer-Verlag, Berlin, 1989.

18. J. Dassow and Gh. Păun, Cooperating/distributed grammar systems with regular components. *Computers and Artif. Intell.* 12 (1993), 71-82.

19. J. Dassow and Gh. Păun, On some variants of cooperating/distributed grammar systems. *Stud. Cerc. Mat.* 42 (1990),153-165.

20. J. Dassow, Gh. Păun and S. Skalla, On the Number and the Size of Components of Cooperating/Distributed Grammar Systems. Manuscript, 1993.

21. J. Dassow, Gh. Păun and S. Vicolov, On the Power of Cooperating/Distributed Grammar Systems with Regular Components. *Found. of Computing and Decision. Sci.* 18 (1993), 83-108.

22. J. Dassow, Gh. Păun and S. Vicolov, On the generative capacity of certain classes of cooperating grammar systems. *Fund. Informaticae*, accepted.

23. S. Ginsburg and O. Mayer, On strict interpretations of grammar forms. *LNCS 45*, Springer Verlag, Berlin, 1976, 294-298.

24. L. Kari, A. Mateescu, Gh. Păun and A. Salomaa, Teams in cooperating Grammar systems. Submitted.

25. J. Kelemen, Syntactic models of cooperative/distributed problem solving. *J. Exp. Th. Artif. Intell.* 3 (1991), 1-10.

26. J. Kelemen and A. Kelemenová, A subsumption architecture for generative symbol systems. In *10th Eur. Meeting on Cybern. and Syst. Res. '92* (R. Trappl, Ed.), World Scientific, Singapore, 1992, 1529 - 1536.

27. J. Kelemen and A. Kelemenová, A grammar-theoretic treatment of multiagent systems. *Cybernetics and Systems* 23 (1992) , 621-633.

28. A. Kelemenová and E. Csuhaj-Varjú, Languages of Colonies. *Theoretical Comp. Sci*, to appear.

29. A. Mateescu, V. Mitrana and A. Salomaa, Dynamic teams of cooperating grammar systems. *Annales Univ. Bucuresti, Ser. Comp. Sci.*, accepted.
30. R. Meersman and G. Rozenberg, Cooperating grammar systems. *Proc. MFCS'78 Symp. LNCS 64*, Springer-Verlag, Berlin, 1978, 364 - 374.
31. M. Minsky, *The Society of Mind.* Simon & Schuster, New York, 1988.
32. V. Mitrana, Hybrid cooperating distributed grammar systems. *Computers and Artif. Intell.* 12 (1993), 83-88.
33. V. Mitrana, Gh. Păun and G. Rozenberg, Structuring grammar systems by priorities and hierarchies. *Acta Cybernetica*, accepted.
34. Gh. Păun, On the generative capacity of colonies. *Kybernetika*, accepted.
35. Gh. Păun and G. Rozenberg, Prescribed teams of grammars. *Acta Informatica*, accepted.
36. Gh. Păun and L. Santean, Parallel communicating grammar systems: the regular case. *Annales. Univ. Bucuresti., Ser. Matem.-Inform.* 38 (1989), 55 - 63.
37. G. Rozenberg and A. Salomaa, *The Mathematical Theory of L Systems.* Academic Press, New York, 1980.
38. A. Salomaa, *Formal Languages.* Academic Press, New York, 1973.
39. L. Santean, Parallel communicating systems. *EATCS Bulletin* 42 (1990), 160-171.

Parallel pattern generation with one-way communications *

Karel Culik II[1] and Jarkko Kari[2]

[1] Dept. of Computer Science, University of South Carolina, Columbia, S.C. 29208
[2] Mathematics Department, University of Turku, 20500 Turku, Finland

Abstract. We study (static) patterns generated by Cellular Automata (CA). In particular, we consider CA with one-dimensional information flow (for each axis of coordinates) called one-way CA and CA with information flow only away from the center of coordinates, called one-way rooted CA. For example, we show that any pattern that can be generated by a one-way CA can be generated in linear time. The converse holds in the one-dimensional case. We show an interesting connection between patterns generated by CA, fixed points of CA and tilings of Euclidean spaces. We show that it is undecidable whether a CA converges to a pattern from a given finite configuration or from any configuration.

1 Introduction

An infinite pattern is a mapping that assigns colors to unit squares of the tesselation of the infinite plane. We are mainly interested in patterns generated by cellular automata (CA). Each cell of a CA represents one unit square of the tesselation. A partitioning of the CA state set represents a coloring, usually this partitioning is trivial, each state represents a different color. A CA generates a pattern if it converges to a limit configuration in the product topology, e.g. if each cell color (state) eventually becomes stable. The basic definitions of d-dimensional CA and patterns are in Section 2. We are mainly interested in one-way (rooted) CA, which are considered in Section 3. In two-dimensional one-way automaton the communication is restricted only to the west-to-east and south-to-north directions. In a one or two-dimensional rooted one-way CA the communication is restricted as shown in Fig. 3.

In Section 3 we show that a pattern is generated by a rooted d-dimensional one-way CA if and only if it can be composed from patterns generated by d-dimensional one-way CA in the d-dimensional quadrants. Thus we can concentrate on patterns generated by one-way CA.

In Section 4 we show that every pattern which is computed by a one-way CA is computed in linear time. In the one-dimensional case the converse holds, too: a pattern computed by an unrestricted CA in linear time can be computed by a one-way CA. We conjecture that this converse does not hold for higher dimensions. In the above we consider the trivial partition of states, i.e. each state

* Supported by the National Science Foundation under Grant No. CCR-9202396

represents a different color. The last result of Section 5 states that nontrivial colorings do not increase the generative power of one-dimensional CA running in linear time.

In Section 5 we established an interesting connection between patterns generated by CA, fixed points, and tilings of Euclidean spaces. A tiling of a plane, using a certain tile set, is valid if a certain local relation (matching) between the neighboring tiles is satisfied. It is clear that the patterns generated by a CA have to be fixed points of the CA mapping and consequently valid tilings of the corresponding tile set. We show that the converse holds, too. In the last section we show that it is undecidable whether a CA converges to a pattern from a given finite configuration or from any configuration.

2 Pattern generation by Cellular Automata

Definition 1. Let C be a finite set of colors, and let $d > 0$ be an integer. An *infinite d-dimensional pattern* is a mapping

$$P : \mathbf{Z}^d \longrightarrow C$$

that assigns colors to unit squares of an infinite d-dimensional Euclidean tessellation. Pattern P is called *recursive* if there exists an algorithm that, when given index $\bar{x} \in \mathbf{Z}^d$ of a square as input, computes its color $P(\bar{x})$. Color $c \in C$ is called *recursively enumerable* in pattern P if the set $\{\bar{x} \mid P(\bar{x}) = c\}$ is recursively enumerable, i.e. if there exists an algorithm that halts on input $\bar{x} \in \mathbf{Z}^d$ if $P(\bar{x}) = c$, and does not halt if $P(\bar{x}) \neq c$. Clearly a pattern P is recursive iff all colors in P are recursively enumerable. □

Frequently $C = \{$ "black", "white"$\}$, but patterns with more colors are studied as well. In this work patterns generated by Cellular Automata are considered.

Cellular Automata (CA) are discrete dynamical systems used for computer simulations of various natural phenomena. d-dimensional CA operate on the infinite d-dimensional Euclidean space divided into (d-dimensional) unit squares. The squares (referred to as cells) are indexed using integer coordinates. A finite *state set* S is fixed. At all times each cell is in one state of S. The cells alter their states synchronously at discrete time steps as specified by the *local transition rule* of the CA. The transition rule describes the new state of the cell as a function of the old states of some of the cell's neighbors. All cells use the same local rule. The *neighborhood* of the CA specifies the neighbors of a cell. Frequently used neighborhoods in the two-dimensional case are the *Moore* neighborhood and the *von Neumann* neighborhood. In the Moore neighborhood each cell has 9 neighbors: the cell itself and the eight surrounding cells. In the von Neumann neighborhood the neighbors of a cell are the four closest cells — the cells above, below, immediately to the right and to the left — as well as the cell itself.

A *configuration* of the CA is a mapping $\mathbf{Z}^d \longrightarrow S$ that specifies the states of all the cells. At each discrete time instance the present configuration of the CA is altered by applying the local rule simultaneously at all cells.

Definition 2. Let $d \in \mathbf{Z}_+$ be a positive integer, S a finite state set, $N = (\bar{x}_1, \bar{x}_2, \ldots, \bar{x}_n) \subset \mathbf{Z}^d$ a finite neighborhood vector of distinct elements of $\mathbf{Z}^d$, and $f : S^n \longrightarrow S$ a local transition function. Let $S^{\mathbf{Z}^d}$ denote the set of configurations $\mathbf{Z}^d \longrightarrow S$ over state set S. The 4-tuple $\mathcal{A} = (d, S, N, f)$ is a d-dimensional Cellular Automaton. It defines the global transition function $G_{\mathcal{A}} : S^{\mathbf{Z}^d} \longrightarrow S^{\mathbf{Z}^d}$ by

$$G_{\mathcal{A}}(c)(\bar{x}) = f\left(c(\bar{x} + \bar{x}_1), c(\bar{x} + \bar{x}_2), \ldots, c(\bar{x} + \bar{x}_n)\right) \; \forall c \in S^{\mathbf{Z}^d}, \bar{x} \in \mathbf{Z}^d.$$

□

One special state $q \in S$ is usually identified as the *quiescent state* of the Cellular Automaton. The quiescent state is assumed to satisfy $f(q, q, \ldots, q) = q$. This guarantees that if initially only finitely many cells are non-quiescent this is true on subsequent configurations as well. A configuration with a finite number of non-quiescent cells is called *finite*.

When the global function $G_{\mathcal{A}}$ is applied repeatedly to an initial configuration c_0, an infinite sequence $c_1, c_2, \ldots$ of configurations is obtained. This sequence describes the evolution of the CA. An evolution of infinite patterns is obtained if the states are interpreted as colors. Normally states represent distinct colors, which means that the set C of colors is the same as the state set S. Sometimes, however, a non-injective *coloring function* $S \longrightarrow C$ is applied. Then several states may represent the same color. The coloring function is extended in the obvious way to configurations, translating each configuration into an infinite pattern over the color set C. In the present article it is normally assumed that no coloring function is used — if a coloring is applied, it is specifically mentioned.

Now we are ready to define the infinite pattern generated by CA $\mathcal{A}$ from a finite initial configuration c_0.

Definition 3. Let $c_0, c_1, c_2, \ldots$ be the sequence of configurations obtained from c_0 by applying the CA rule $G_{\mathcal{A}}$ repeatedly. ($c_0, c_1, c_2, \ldots$ are assumed to be the colored configurations if coloring function is used.) The infinite pattern $c : \mathbf{Z}^d \longrightarrow C$ is generated by CA $\mathcal{A}$ from initial configuration c_0 if c is the limit of the sequence $c_0, c_1, \ldots$ in the product topology, i.e. if for every position $\bar{x} \in \mathbf{Z}^d$ there exists an integer $N_{\bar{x}}$ such that $c_i(\bar{x}) = c(\bar{x})$ for all $i \geq N_{\bar{x}}$.

The pattern c is generated *in time* $T : \mathbb{N} \longrightarrow \mathbb{N}$ if $N_{\bar{x}} \leq T(d(\bar{x}))$ for every $\bar{x} \in \mathbf{Z}^d$, where $d(x_1, x_2, \ldots, x_d) = |x_1| + |x_2| + \ldots |x_d|$ is the distance of cell $\bar{x}$ from the origin under the Manhattan-metric. The pattern is generated in *linear time* if it is generated in time $T(n) = an + b$ for some constants a and b. □

Example 1. Consider the following very simple two-dimensional CA $\mathcal{A}$ introduced by S. Ulam: The CA has two states, black and white. The white state is the quiescent state. The CA $\mathcal{A}$ uses the von Neumann neighborhood. A black cell never changes its state. A white cell turns black if and only if exactly one of its four closest neighbors is black. The fact that black states never become white guarantees that a limit exists for every initial configuration.

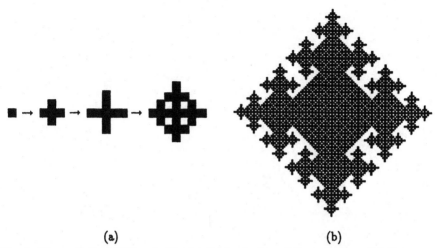

Fig. 1. The evolution of Ulam's CA: (a) the beginning of the evolution, (b) the pattern produced after 60 iterations

Fig. 1 shows the first iteration steps of A starting from an initial configuration containing just one black cell, as well as the pattern obtained after 60 iteration steps. Note the complex structure of the pattern even though the local rule of the CA is extremely simple. This "contradiction" between the simplicity of the local rule and the complexity of the pattern produced is typical for CA.

The infinite pattern generated by A in the limit no longer has the crystal-like structure visible in Fig. 1(b), which is due to the order in which the black states expand. The infinite pattern is a mixture of black and white cells with the following simple arithmetic characterization: A cell in position (x, y) is white if and only if $x, y \neq 0$ and the binary representations of both x and y have the same number of 0's in the end. Note also how the black cells form a connected loop-free graph (a tree). The pattern is generated in linear time $T(n) = 2n$. $\square$

Complex infinite patterns can be generated by CA. A portion of a periodic infinite pattern generated by a CA A is shown in Fig. 2. CA A is constructed first by digitalizing a photograph, then converting the digital image into a Weighted Finite Automaton (WFA) by the compression program from [4], then applying a Weighted Finite Transducer [2] to obtain the WFA generating one "tile", then constructing a CA generating this tile as shown in [1], and finally modifying the CA to periodically replicate the tile. We use a coloring mapping that maps the states of A to 64 levels of gray.

3 One-way (rooted) CA

In one-way Cellular Automata information may not move back and forth. Traditionally, one-way CA are defined in the one-dimensional case by requiring

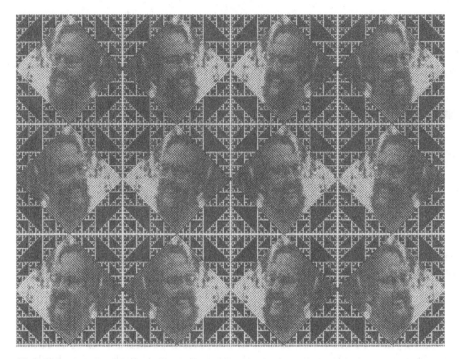

Fig. 2. A periodic pattern generated by CA A

the neighborhood to contain only non-positive elements. We want also to study higher dimensional one-way CA; on the other hand, to simplify notations we use only nearest neighbor neighborhoods. This is no severe restriction: an arbitrary (one-way) neighborhood can be simulated if a coloring function is used.

Definition 4. A d-dimensional CA with neighborhood vector N, where $N = (\bar{0}, -\bar{e}_1, -\bar{e}_2, \ldots, -\bar{e}_d)$, with $\bar{e}_i(j) = 1$ if $j = i$ and $\bar{e}_i(j) = 0$ if $j \neq i$, is called one-way. □

One draw-back of using one-way CA in pattern generation is the fact that interesting patterns can be generated from finite initial configurations only to one (d-dimensional) quadrant of the space — all other parts remain quiescent. Therefore, instead of full patterns $\mathbf{Z}^d \longrightarrow C$ it makes sense to talk about *one-sided* patterns generated by one-way CA, i.e about mappings $\mathbf{Z}_+^d \longrightarrow C$ that are restrictions of full patterns to $\mathbf{Z}_+^d$. The non-quiescent states of the initial configuration are placed in positions belonging to $\mathbf{Z}_+^d$ — other cells are initially quiescent and they also remain quiescent.

To generate full patterns with one-way communications, one can use *rooted one-way CA*. Strictly speaking, a rooted one-way CA is not a cellular automaton since different quadrants of the space apply different neighborhoods: The cell in position $\bar{x} = (x_1, x_2, \ldots, x_d)$ uses the neighborhood vector $(\bar{0}, \pm\bar{e}_1, \pm\bar{e}_2, \ldots, \pm\bar{e}_d)$, where the sign in front of $\bar{e}_i$ is '+' iff $x_i < 0$. The same local rule is used by all cells. Fig. 3 shows the communication structures of rooted one- and two-dimensional Cellular Automata.

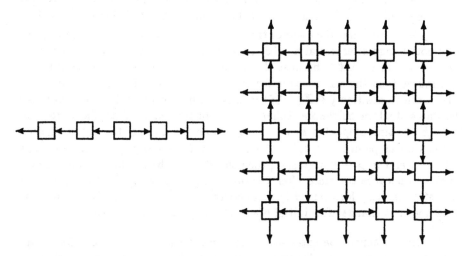

Fig. 3. Rooted one-way one-dimensional CA, and two-dimensional CA.

The following observation states that it is sufficient to concentrate on one-sided patterns generated by one-way CA.

Lemma 5. *A d-dimensional pattern P is generated by a rooted one-way CA iff its 2^d 'quadrants' are generated by one-way CA. More precisely, for every choice for $(p_1, p_2, \ldots, p_d) \in \{pos, neg\}^d$, the one-sided pattern P' defined by $P'(x_1, x_2, \ldots, x_d) = P(y_1, y_2, \ldots, y_d)$, $x_i \in \mathbf{Z}_+$, $y_i = x_i - 1$ if $p_i = pos$ and $y_i = -x_i$ if $p_i = neg$, is generated by a one-way CA. Coloring functions may need to be applied.*

Proof. ($\Longrightarrow$) : The one-way CA use the same local rule as the rooted CA do. The only difference concerns the cells that are on the sides of the quadrant: They also have to remember the states of the cells just outside the quadrant, and simulate them as well. This can be implemented in a straightforward manner. The coloring function ignores the additional states of the border cells.

($\Longleftarrow$) : The rooted CA uses 2^d distinct state sets for simulating the 2^d quadrants. A coloring function takes care of coloring the states in different quadrants appropriately. □

4 One-way vs. linear time pattern generation

First we show that one-way CA always define patterns in linear time.

Theorem 6. *If a d-dimensional one-way CA $\mathcal{A}$ converges to a (one-sided) pattern, it converges in linear time.*

Proof. Let n be the number of states in a d-dimensional CA $\mathcal{A}$ that converges to a one-sided pattern $P : \mathbf{Z}_+^d \longrightarrow C$. Let us prove using induction on $d(\bar{x}) = x_1 + x_2 + \ldots + x_d$ that the state of the cell in position $\bar{x} = (x_1, x_2, \ldots, x_d) \in \mathbb{N}^d$ does not change after initial $n \cdot d(\bar{x})$ time steps. This is certainly true for every cell situated in $\mathbb{N}^d \setminus \mathbf{Z}_+^d$, because those cells remain quiescent at all times.

Assume then the claim is true for all cells in positions $\bar{x}$, $d(\bar{x}) < k$, and consider a cell in position $\bar{y} \in \mathbf{Z}_+^d$, $d(\bar{y}) = k$. According to the inductive hypothesis the states of all the neighbors of that cell, except the cell itself, are fixed after initial $n(k-1)$ time steps. Let $s_0, s_1, \ldots, s_n$ denote the states of the cell in position $\bar{y}$ after time steps $n(k-1), n(k-1)+1, \ldots, nk$. Necessarily $s_i = s_{i+m}$, for some $0 \leq i < n$ and $m > 0$. If $s_i \neq s_{i+1}$, then the state of the cell in position $\bar{y}$ never stabilizes, because the state after $i + jm$ time steps is s_i, and after $i + jm + 1$ time steps is s_{i+1}, for every $j \geq 0$. Therefore $s_i = s_{i+1} = s_{i+2} = \ldots$, and the state does not change after initial $n(k-1) + i \leq nk$ time instances. □

Theorem 6 cannot be extended to the case when a coloring function is applied, not even in the one-dimensional case as shown by the following example.

Example 2. Consider the one-dimensional CA with four states 0, 1, 2 and 3, neighborhood $(-1, 0)$ and local transition function f defined as follows: $f(x, 3) = 1$ for all $x = 0, 1, 2, 3$, $f(3, x) = x+1$ for $x \leq 2$, and $f(0, x) = x+1$ for $1 \leq x \leq 2$. In all other cases the state does not change. State 0 is colored white, all other states black. Initially, all cells are in state 0 except the cell in position 1 which is in state 1. Position 1 changes states periodically $1 \rightarrow 2 \rightarrow 3 \rightarrow 1 \rightarrow 2 \rightarrow 3 \rightarrow \ldots$. Whenever the cell in position 1 enters stage 3, the state of the cell in position 2 is changed. In general, states 1, 2 and 3 are repeated periodically in every position $i > 0$. The length of the period is $3 \cdot 2^{i-1}$. Position $i > 1$ turns into state 1 for the first time after $3 \cdot 2^{i-1} + i - 5$ time steps, i.e. the black pattern is not generated in polynomial, but in exponential time. □

In one-dimensional case Theorem 6 can be reversed.

Theorem 7. *The restriction to $\mathbf{Z}_+$ of a one-dimensional pattern $P : \mathbf{Z} \longrightarrow C$ defined by an unrestricted CA $\mathcal{A}$ in linear time can be defined by a one-way CA.*

Proof. Let $P : \mathbf{Z} \longrightarrow S$ be a pattern defined in linear time by a one-dimensional CA $\mathcal{A}$. Assume that the neighborhood of $\mathcal{A}$ is included in $\{-m, -m+1, \ldots, m-1, m\}$. Assume also that $\mathcal{A}$ generates P in linear time $T(n) = an$, $a \in \mathbf{Z}_+$, $a \geq 2$. (Generation time $an + b$ can be changed to an by replacing the initial configuration c_0 by $G_{\mathcal{A}}^b(c_0)$.)

First, construct a CA that, after applying $\mathcal{A}$, shifts the configuration $2m$ cells to the right. Obviously, its neighborhood is included in $\{-3m, -3m+1, \ldots, -m\}$. Add a signal that starts in the origin and moves to the right with speed $2m + \frac{1}{a}$. On every a'th time step the signal makes a cell remember its present state on a separate layer. In this way, after ia time steps the state in position $2iam + i$ remembers its state, which is the same as $P(i)$. (In ia time steps the states have been shifted $2iam$ units to the right.) Once a state is copied to the separate layer it does not change or move to the right.

Finally, we group segments of $2am+1$ consecutive cells starting at the origin in blocks that will be the states of the one-way CA. As the simulation proceeds, each block will get exactly one state on the separate layer, and the basic layer gets filled with quiescent states (since the simulated configuration is shifted to the right faster than it expands to the left). A block that contains state s on the separate layer and quiescent states on the basic layer is identified with state s of the original CA. In this way the one-sided pattern $P_{|\mathbf{Z}_+}$ is generated. The neighborhood of the simulating CA is included in $\{-1, 0\}$ because the block size $2am + 1$ is greater than $3m$.

If the original CA uses a coloring function, the simulation remains unchanged. In fact, the simulating CA does not need any coloring function — the color can be stored on the separate layer instead of the state (see Theorem 8 below). □

It remains open whether Theorem 7 holds for higher dimensional CA. We conjecture that this is not the case. Namely, in two-dimensional case the cells on the border of the quadrant have very restricted behavior if one-way CA is used: in fact, they form a one-dimensional one-way CA. In two-way CA that work in linear time the border cells may depend on cells whose number is quadratic with respect to the distance of the cell from the origin. Therefore, general CA should be more powerful.

The next theorem states that coloring functions do not increase the power of linear time pattern generation in the case of one-dimensional CA.

Theorem 8. *A pattern P that is generated by a one-dimensional CA A in linear time using a coloring function is generated by another one-dimensional CA B in linear time without a coloring function. If A is one-way, so is B.*

Proof. We use the same construction as in the proof of Theorem 7. In the case of two-way CA, the simulation is done on two different layers that are shifted to the left and right, respectively, and there are signals in both directions. In the case of one-way CA, one simulating layer and one signal is sufficient as in the proof of Theorem 7.

The signal(s) make cells at regular intervals remember the *color* of their present state on a separate layer. The cells of CA B are blocks of A's cells as in the proof of Theorem 7. □

5   Fixed points and tilings

In this section we establish an important connection between patterns generated by CA, fixed points of CA, and tilings of Euclidean spaces.

Definition 9. A configuration $c \in S^{\mathbf{Z}^d}$ is a *fixed point* of CA $\mathcal{A}$ if $G_{\mathcal{A}}(c) = c$. □

Definition 10. A d-dimensional *tile set* is a 4-tuple $\mathcal{T} = (d, T, N, \psi)$, where $d \in \mathbf{Z}_+$ is the dimension, T is a finite set of tiles, $N = (\bar{x}_1, \bar{x}_2, \ldots, \bar{x}_n) \subset \mathbf{Z}^d$ a finite neighborhood vector of distinct elements of Z^d (as in Definition 2), and $\psi \subset T^n$ an n-ary relation. A mapping $t : \mathbf{Z}^d \longrightarrow T$ is a *tiling*. Tiling t is *valid* if

$$(t(\bar{x} + \bar{x}_1), t(\bar{x} + \bar{x}_2), \ldots, t(\bar{x} + \bar{x}_n)) \in \psi, \ \forall \bar{x} \in \mathbf{Z}^d.$$

In other words, the relation ψ is satisfied everywhere on valid tilings. □

Fixed points of CA and valid tilings coincide:

Lemma 11. *For each d-dimensional CA $\mathcal{A}$ there exists a d-dimensional tile set $\mathcal{T}$ such that the fixed points of $\mathcal{A}$ are precisely the valid tilings with tiles of $\mathcal{T}$. Conversely, for any tile set $\mathcal{T}$ there exists a CA $\mathcal{A}$ whose fixed points are precisely the valid tilings.*

Proof. Let a d-dimensional CA $\mathcal{A} = (d, S, N, f)$ be given. Assume the first element of the neighborhood vector N is $(0, 0, \ldots, 0)$. If it is not included in the neighborhood, add it there. Define the relation ψ on tile set $\mathcal{T} = (d, S, N, \psi)$ as follows:

$$(s_1, s_2, \ldots, s_n) \in \psi \iff f(s_1, s_2, \ldots, s_n) = s_1.$$

Conversely, given tile set $\mathcal{T} = (d, S, N, \psi)$ construct CA $\mathcal{A} = (d, S, N, f)$ in such a way that $f(s_1, s_2, \ldots, s_n) = s_1$ iff $(s_1, s_2, \ldots, s_n) \in \psi$. □

It is obvious that patterns generated by CA $\mathcal{A}$ have to be fixed points of $\mathcal{A}$, and consequently valid tilings of the corresponding tile set. The converse statement is proved by the following Theorem (for two-dimensional CA).

Theorem 12. *Let $\mathcal{T}$ be a two-dimensional tile set that admits at least one valid tiling. There exists a CA $\mathcal{A}$ and a finite initial configuration c_0 such that $\mathcal{A}$ started on c_0 converges to a valid tiling with tiles of $\mathcal{T}$.*

Proof. The tiling is constructed by adding new tiles as long as the tiling property is not violated. If a new tile cannot be placed, the process backtracks and changes earlier tiles.

The tiles are added in spiral-like order (see Fig. 4). At the head of the spiral tiles are tried one after the other. Once a tile is found that does not violate the tiling properties, the spiral is expanded by one position, and at the new position tiles are tried in the same fashion.

If, on the other hand, all tiles violate some tiling condition, the head backtracks one position in the spiral: the present cell is made quiescent, and the trial continues in the previous position of the spiral. Sometimes the process may need to backtrack to the very beginning of the spiral! Note that the cell in the head of the spiral can deduce both the next cell and the previous cell on the spiral just by checking which of its neighbors are quiescent. □

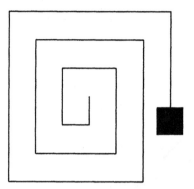

Fig. 4. The spiral

Corollary 13. *Because there exist two-dimensional tile sets that admit only non-recursive tilings [7], two-dimensional non-recursive patterns can be generated by Cellular Automata. In this case the speed of the pattern generation is very low: There is no recursive upper bound to the time complexity $T(n)$ — existence of such an upper bound would automatically mean that the pattern is recursive.*   □

Extending the proof of Theorem 12 to higher dimensional CA requires defining a path through all cells in such a way that at all times the cell at the head knows the next and previous cells on the path just by looking at the position of quiescent states in its neighborhood.

6   Decision problems

Not all CA converge and define a pattern. It is natural to question when this actually happens. How do we characterize CA that converge? There are different variants of this problem: The finite initial configuration may be given, or one may ask whether the CA converges for *any* (non-trivial) initial configuration. In this section we show that both variants are in general undecidable, even for one-dimensional one-way CA.

Every CA trivially converges when started on the quiescent configuration where all cells are in the quiescent state. Whether any other finite configuration leads to a convergent computation of a given CA is undecidable, even for one-dimensional one-way CA.

Theorem 14. *Given a one-dimensional one-way CA A it is undecidable whether there exists a finite non-quiescent initial configuration c_0 such that A converges when started on c_0.*

Proof. We use a reduction from the halting problem of Turing machines started on a blank tape. The reduction resembles the proof of Theorem 6.1 in [5] — the

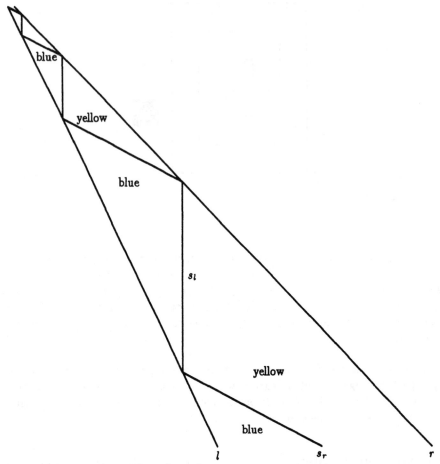

Fig. 5. Evolution of a valid configuration.

simulation is just done in "reversed time". Construct a one-dimensional one-way CA as follows. Its state set contains special "blinking" states K, K' that alternate regardless of their neighbors. State q is quiescent. There exist also two border states l and r, two signal states s_l and s_r, a yellow state y and a set B of blue states used in simulating the Turing machine.

A (one-sided) finite configuration is called valid, if it belongs to the ω-language

$$q^\omega \ \cup \ q^*lB^*\{s_l, s_r\}y^*rq^\omega.$$

Validity can be checked locally at all times. If the configuration is non-valid, the cell where the error occurs is changed to state K that will continue changing between K and K' for ever.

Border l moves to the right at speed $\frac{1}{4}$, leaving quiescent states q on its left side. (In fact, four states are needed to implement l — for simplicity we speak only of one state l, as well as state r etc.). Border r moves to the right with speed $\frac{3}{4}$. Signal s_r moves to the right with speed 1 cell/time step. When it meets border r, it is changed to s_l. Signal s_l does not move. When it hits l it becomes s_r and starts moving to the right. Valid configurations evolve as depicted in Fig. 5.

Inside the blue triangles, the computation of the Turing machine is simulated: The simulation is restarted from the blank tape whenever the signal s_l is turned into s_r. The Turing machine tape is shifted to the right with speed $\frac{5}{8}$, i.e. the speed of the center of the blue segment. If the Turing machine enters the halting state, state K is created on the simulating CA.

Clearly, if the Turing machine halts, the simulating CA sooner or later creates the blinking state K, and thus does not converge. The state K is created either if the configuration is not valid, or if inside a sufficiently large blue triangle the Turing machine under simulation halts. If the Turing machine does not halt, the initial configuration $ls_r rq^\omega$ converges to the quiescent configuration q^ω. $\square$

Theorem 15. *Given a CA A and a finite initial configuration c_0, it is undecidable whether A converges when started on c_0, even if only one-dimensional one-way CA are considered.*

Proof. Consider the CA constructed in the proof of Theorem 14. It halts on the initial configuration $ls_r rq^\omega$ iff the corresponding Turing machine does not halt when started on the blank tape. $\square$

Note, however, that the construction using the blue and yellow triangles is unnecessarily complicated for proving Theorem 15. A straightforward simulation of the Turing machine would be sufficient. In the proof of Theorem 14 the triangles are needed in order to guarantee that the Turing machine is simulated regardless of the initial configuration.

References

1. K. Culik II, How to Fire Almost any Pattern on Cellular Automaton. In *"Cellular Automata and Cooperative Systems"*. Boccara, Goles, Martinez, Picco (Eds.), Kluwer Academic Publishers, the Netherlands, 101–109, 1993.
2. K. Culik II and I. Fris, Weighted Finite Transducers in Image Processing. *Discrete Applied Mathematics*, to appear.
3. K. Culik II, J. Kari, Mechanisms for Pattern Generation. *Complex Systems*, submitted.
4. K. Culik II and J. Kari, Image-data Compression Using Edge-Optimizing Algorithm for WFA Inference, *Journal of Information Processing and Management*, to appear.
5. K. Culik II, J. Pachl and S. Yu, On the Limit Sets of Cellular Automata. *SIAM Journal on Computing* 18, 831-842 (1989).
6. John E. Hopcroft and Jeffrey D. Ullman, *Introduction to Automata Theory, Languages and Computation*. Addison-Wesley, Reading, Massachusetts (1979).
7. Dale Myers, Nonrecursive tilings of the plane II. *The Journal of Symbolic Logic* 39, 286-294 (1974).

Dynamic labeled 2-structures with variable domains

A. Ehrenfeucht
Department of Computer Science
University of Colorado at Boulder
Boulder, CO 80309, U.S.A.

G. Rozenberg
Department of Computer Science
Leiden University, P.O. Box 9512
2300 RA Leiden
The Netherlands
and
Department of Computer Science
University of Colorado at Boulder
Boulder, CO 80309, U.S.A.

all correspondence to the second author at his address in Leiden

Abstract

We consider the problem of making the notion of *dynamic labeled 2-structure* even more dynamic by allowing the domain of a dynamic labeled 2-structure to vary by either adding new elements or deleting some elements. To this aim we study in the framework of dynamic labeled 2-structures the operation of *disjoint union* (in combination with group-theoretic operations induced by *selectors*) and a more general operation of *amalgamated union*.

Introduction

A *labeled 2-structure* g, abbreviated $l2s$, consists of a finite domain $dom(g)$ and a labeling function lab_g which to every 2-edge over $dom(g)$ assigns a label from some alphabet Δ (a *2-edge over* $dom(g)$ is an ordered pair of different elements of $dom(g)$). The theory of 2-structures is quite well developed by now, and an essential part of it is dealing with the problems of hierarchical representations of $l2s's$ (see, e.g., [EhR1]).

A *l2s* may be seen as modeling relationships (expressed as labels from Δ) between the elements of its domain. In some situations it may be desirable that the relationships between the elements from a given domain are not static but rather that they change as the result of various transformations taking place *locally* in the domain. This consideration has led to the notion of a *dynamic labeled 2-structure* (see [EhR2]), abbreviated *dl2s*, where the local transformations take place in the elements of a given domain.

A possible intuition behind the notion of a dynamic labeled 2-structure is a network of processors. It consists of a set D of nodes - each node is a processor. The actions of a processor x consist of *output actions* O_x and *input actions* I_x. The relationships between the processors in a given global state of a network are represented by a *l2s* g with $dom(g) = D$ where for the 2-edge (x, y), $lab_g(x, y) = b$ says that b is the relationship between x and y in this global state. When an output action $\varphi \in O_x$ takes place in x it will affect the relationships between x and the other nodes by changing the label $lab_g(x, y)$ of each outgoing 2-edge (x, y) to $\varphi(lab_g(x, y))$. Analogously, an input action $\gamma \in I_x$ will change the label $lab_g(y, x)$ of each incoming 2-edge (y, x) to $\gamma(lab_g(y, x))$.

In order to make such a model "workable" one assumes that certain "natural" axioms are satisfied by the families $\{O_x : x \in D\}$ and $\{I_x : x \in D\}$ (see [EhR2]). It turns out that under these assumptions this model can be formalized as a group over the alphabet of labels Δ. Then applying an *output action* φ in a node x amounts to the *left multiplication* of the label $lab_g(x, y)$ of each outgoing 2-edge (x, y) by a symbol of Δ dependent on φ only, and applying an *input action* γ in a node x amounts to the *right multiplication* of the label $lab_g(y, x)$ of each incoming 2-edge (y, x) by a symbol of Δ dependent on γ only. Moreover the set of input and output actions available in each node are the same throughout the network, viz. *all* left- and right multiplications.

A dynamic labeled 2-structure is then a group Γ over an alphabet Δ and a set of *l2s's* which is closed under the operations of relabeling specified as above by the group Γ.

Clearly, in some situations it may be also desirable that the domain of a *l2s* (as well as the relationships between the elements of the domain) may change; thus one may *delete* some elements of the domain or one may *add* some elements to the domain. Such change of a domain is "standard" in the theory of graph grammars (see, e.g., [EKR]), and also in networks some processors may be deleted or some processors may be added to a network. In this paper we consider the problem of varying the domain of a *dl2s*.

A solution to the problem of enlarging domains that we discuss in this paper consists of using the operation of *disjoint union* for combining the domains of two *l2s's*, followed by the group operations as discussed above (called *selections*) over the new combined domain. We consider the basic properties of the so obtained *dl2s's*, and we define *decompositions* of *l2s's* and *dl2s's* (based on disjoint unions and selections). Then we compare these decompositions with grammatical substitutions as considered in graph grammars. Finally, in the last section we consider the use of the operation of *amalgamated union* for combining the domains of *dl2s's* - the operation of amalgamated union generalizes the operation of disjoint union.

The problem of decreasing domains is solved by the operation of *difference* which is derived from the operation of disjoint union.

0   Preliminaries

In this section we establish some basic terminology and notation concerning sets and functions. We also recall some basic notions concerning labeled 2-structures (see, e.g., [EhR1]).

For a set X, $|X|$ denotes the cardinality of X, and $E_2(X)$ denotes the set of all 2-*edges over* X, i.e., $E_2(X) = \{(u,v) : u,v \in X \text{ and } u \neq v\}$. The empty set is denoted by $\emptyset$. For a family $\mathcal{P}$ of sets, $\bigcup \mathcal{P}$ denotes the union of sets from $\mathcal{P}$. A *partition* of X is a family $\mathcal{P}$ of nonempty pairwise disjoint subsets of X such that $\bigcup \mathcal{P} = X$.

The identity mapping on X is denoted by id_X.

For groups $\Gamma_1 = (X, \circ)$ and $\Gamma_2 = (Y, \square)$ a bijection $\varphi : X \longrightarrow Y$ is an *antiisomorphism of* Γ_1 *onto* Γ_2 iff for all $u,v \in X, \varphi(u \circ v) = \varphi(v) \square \varphi(u)$. If $\Gamma_1 = \Gamma_2$, then φ is an *antiautomorphism* of Γ_1. A bijection $\varphi : X \longrightarrow X$ is an *involution* of Γ_1 iff $\varphi^2 = id_X$ and φ is an antiautomorphism of Γ_1.

Definition 0.1 A *labeled 2-structure* (abbreviated *l2s*) is a 3-tuple $g = (D, \Delta, \lambda)$, where D is a finite nonempty set, Δ is a finite alphabet, and λ is a function from $E_2(D)$ into Δ such that, for all $(x,y), (u,v) \in E_2(D)$, $\lambda(x,y) = \lambda(u,v)$ implies $\lambda(y,x) = \lambda(v,u)$.$\square$

The set of nodes D is called the *domain* of g, denoted $dom(g)$, λ is called the *labeling function* of g, denoted lab_g, and Δ is called the *alphabet* of g, denoted $alph(g)$. It is usually assumed that Δ is the *useful* alphabet, i.e., $\Delta = \{\lambda(x,y) : (x,y) \in E_2(D)\}$; then g may be given in the form (D, λ).

In the case that $|D| = 1, g$ is called a *singleton l2s*. As is the case with singleton sets, if $D = \{x\}$, then we may use x to denote g. If $g = (D, \Delta, \lambda)$ is a singleton *l2s*, then both Δ and λ are empty.

Remark 0.1 The condition imposed on the labeling function λ of g in the above definition is called the *reversibility condition*. Sometimes (see, e.g., [EhR1]) it is not required that *l2s's* satisfy the reversibility condition; then a *l2s* satisfying this condition is called *reversible*. Since it is technically convenient to consider reversible *l2s's* only, and since considering reversible *l2s's* only is not really a restriction (see, e.g., [EhR2]), we will consider reversible *l2s's* only. For this reason we have incorporated the reversibility condition in the definition of a *l2s*. $\square$

For a set Δ we will use $\mathbf{L2S}(\Delta)$ to denote the class of all *l2s's* g such that $alph(g) \subseteq \Delta$, and for a finite set D we will use $\mathbf{L2S}_D$ to denote the class of all *l2s's* g such that $dom(g) = D$; then $\mathbf{L2S}_D(\Delta)$ denotes the class of all *l2s's* g such that $dom(g) = D$ and $alph(g) \subseteq \Delta$.

A *l2s* g may be seen as a complete directed edge-labeled graph satisfying certain conditions, and so we may use the usual pictorial representations of directed graphs to specify *l2s's*. Hence, e.g., the following figure

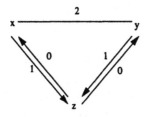

Figure 0.1

represents the *l2s* $g = (D, \Delta, \lambda)$ where
$D = \{x, y, z\}, \Delta = \{0, 1, 2\}, \lambda(x, z) = \lambda(y, z) = 1, \lambda(z, x) = \lambda(z, y) = 0$, and $\lambda(x, y) = \lambda(y, x) = 2$.
As usual the line without arrowheads between x and y represents the *symmetric* 2-edge (x, y), i.e., $\lambda(x, y) = \lambda(y, x)$.

For a *l2s* $g = (D, \lambda)$ and nonempty $X \subseteq D$, the *substructure of g restricted to X*, denoted $sub_g(X)$, is the *l2s* $h = (X, \lambda')$ where λ' equals λ restricted to $E_2(X)$. Hence, e.g., for the *l2s* g from Figure 0.1 and $X = \{z, y\}$, $sub_g(X)$ is the following *l2s*:

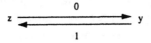

Figure 0.2

Labeled 2-structures $g_1 = (D_1, \lambda_1)$ and $g_2 = (D_2, \lambda_2)$ are *isomorphic*, denoted g_1 *isom* g_2, iff there exists a bijection $\varphi : D_1 \longrightarrow D_2$ such that, for all $(x, y) \in E_2(D_1)$, $\lambda_1(x, y) = \lambda_2(\varphi(x), \varphi(y))$. Hence this notion of isomorphism is *label preserving*, meaning that if φ maps $(x_1, y_1) \in E_2(D_1)$ into $(x_2, y_2) \in E_2(D_2)$ then the labels of (x_1, y_1) and (x_2, y_2) are equal.

The basic technical notion concerning *l2s's* is the notion of a clan. A set $X \subseteq D$ is a *clan of g* iff for all $x, y \in X$ and all $z \in D - X, \lambda(z, x) = \lambda(z, y)$.

Hence a clan of g is a subset of D such that each element z of D outside X "sees" all elements of X in the same way.

The set of all clans of g is denoted by $\mathcal{C}(g)$.

It follows directly from the definition of a clan that $\emptyset \in \mathcal{C}(g), D \in \mathcal{C}(g)$, and for each $x \in D, \{x\} \in \mathcal{C}(g)$; these clans are called the *trivial clans* - the set of trivial clans of g is denoted by $\mathcal{TC}(g)$. We call g *primitive* iff g has only trivial clans.

Example 0.1
For the *l2s* g from Figure 0.1, $\mathcal{C}(g) = \mathcal{TC}(g) \cup \{\{x, y\}\}$. Hence g is not primitive.
□

Let $g = (D, \lambda)$ be a *l2s* and let $\mathcal{P}$ be a partition of D into clans of g, i.e., $\mathcal{P} \subseteq \mathcal{C}(g)$ and $\bigcup \mathcal{P} = D$. The *quotient of g by $\mathcal{P}$*, denoted $g/\mathcal{P}$, is the *l2s* $(\mathcal{P}, \lambda')$ where for $X, Y \in \mathcal{P}, \lambda'(X, Y) = \lambda(x, y)$ where x is an arbitrary element of X and y is an arbitrary element of Y. The quotient $g/\mathcal{P}$ is well defined because it has been proved in [EhR1] that if U, Z are disjoint clans of g, then for all $u_1, u_2 \in U$ and all $z_1, z_2 \in Z, \lambda(u_1, z_1) = \lambda(u_2, z_2)$.

1 Dynamic labeled 2-structures

In this section we recall from [EhR2] some basic notions concerning dynamic labeled 2-structures; we also recall a number of results that will be used in this paper.

As explained in the introduction, the notion of a dynamic labeled 2-structure formalizes an intuitive notion of a network of processors and it is phrased in terms of groups. Before we recall the notion of a dynamic labeled 2-structure, we need a number of technical notions.

Let $\Gamma = (\Delta, \circ)$ be a (not necessarily finite) group, and let δ be an involution on Γ. Then one gets a class of transformations of $\mathbf{L2S}(\Delta)$ defined as follows.

An ordered pair $(a, b) \in \Delta \times \Delta$ is δ-*conjugated* iff $b = \delta(a)$. We wil use $cp_\delta(\Delta)$ to denote the set of all δ-conjugated pairs (on Δ). For a set D, a δ-*selector on* D is a function $\gamma : D \longrightarrow cp_\delta(\Delta)$. A δ-selector γ on D uniquely determines the function $tr_\gamma : \mathbf{L2S}_D(\Delta) \longrightarrow \mathbf{L2S}_D(\Delta)$, called the γ-*transformation* or γ-*selection* on $\mathbf{L2S}_D(\Delta)$, defined as follows. For a *l2s* $g = (D, \lambda), tr_\gamma(g)$ is the *l2s* $g' = (D, \lambda')$, where for each $(x, y) \in E_2(D), \lambda'(x, y) = a_x \circ \lambda(x, y) \circ b_y$ where $\gamma(x) = (a_x, b_x)$ and $\gamma(y) = (a_y, b_y)$. Thus $\gamma(x) = (a_x, b_x)$ means that a_x will affect the labels of the edges *outgoing* from x (through left multiplication) and b_x will affect the labels of the edges *incoming* to x (through right multiplication). A function from $\mathbf{L2S}_D(\Delta)$ into $\mathbf{L2S}_D(\Delta)$ is called a *selection* if it is a γ-selection for some δ-selector γ.

A *l2s* $g = (D, \lambda)$ such that, for each $(x, y) \in E_2(D), \delta(\lambda(x, y)) = \lambda(y, x)$ is called δ-*reversible*.

A set G of $l2s's$ is *compatible* with Γ iff all $l2s's$ in G have the same domain, and for each $g \in G$, $alph(g) \subseteq \Delta$. We say that G δ-*implements* Γ iff G is compatible with Γ, each $g \in G$ is δ-reversible, and for each $g \in G$ and each δ-selector γ, $tr_\gamma(g) \in G$. Also, we say that G *satisfies the single axiom property* (w.r.t. Γ and δ) iff G δ-implements Γ and there exists a $g \in G$ (called *an axiom* of G) such that for each $h \in G$ there exists a δ-selector γ such that $tr_\gamma(g) = h$.

We are ready now for the definition of a dynamic labeled 2-structure.

Definition 1.1 A *dynamic labeled 2-structure*, a *dl2s* for short, is a 3-tuple $\mathcal{A} = (\Gamma, \delta, G)$ where $\Gamma = (\Delta, \circ)$ is a (not necessarily finite) group, δ is an involution on Γ, and G is a set of $l2s's$ which satisfies the single axiom property (w.r.t. Γ and δ). $\quad\square$

Since in the above G δ-implements Γ, all $l2s's$ in G have the same domain. This common domain is called the *domain of* $\mathcal{A}$ (and the *domain of* G) and denoted by $dom(\mathcal{A})$ (and $dom(G)$).

Remark 1.1 The notion of a *dl2s* as defined in [EhR2] is more general than the one defined above.
(1) First of all, one considers in [EhR2] selectors more general than the δ-selectors defined above. Since it is proved in [EhR2] that (in a well defined sense) it suffices to consider only $dl2s's$ in which all $l2s's$ are δ-reversible, and the δ-selectors are exactly the selectors that preserve δ-reversibility, we consider δ-selectors only, and consequently we require in our definition that G δ-implements Γ.
(2) Secondly, the single axiom property is not required in the definition of a *dl2s* given in [EhR2]. A *single axiom dl2s* is defined in [EhR2] as a *dl2s* satisfying the single axiom property. Since in this paper we consider only single axiom $dl2s's$, in order to simplify the terminology we have required the single axiom property in Definition 1.1. $\quad\square$

In order to simplify the notation and the statements of the results, unless explicitly made clear otherwise, *in the rest of this paper we will consider an arbitrary but fixed group* $\Gamma = (\Delta, \circ)$ *and an arbitrary but fixed involution* δ *on* Γ. Consequently we may skip "δ" in terms like δ-selector, δ-conjugated, δ-reversibility and in notations like $cp_\delta(\Delta)$. We will also use e to denote the identity of Γ. All $l2s's$ g considered in the sequel of this paper are assumed to be δ-reversible and such that $alph(g) \subseteq \Delta$. Hence, notations like $\mathbf{L2S}(\Delta)$ or $\mathbf{L2S}_D(\Delta)$ will denote the appropriate classes of δ-reversible $l2s's$.

With Γ and δ fixed, a $dl2s$ $\mathcal{A} = (\Gamma, \delta, G)$ may be identified with G; consequently we will also refer to G as a $dl2s$. Since G satisfies the single axiom property, G may be *specified* by giving an axiom g of G (and so $\mathcal{A}$ may be specified by the 3-tuple (Γ, δ, g)). Then $G = \{tr_\gamma(g) : \gamma$ is a selector $\}$. For a $l2s$ h we will use $[h]$ to denote the set $\{tr_\gamma(h) : \gamma$ is a selector $\}$, and so $(\Gamma, \delta, [h])$ is a *dl2s*; thus according to the above convention, $[h]$ is a *dl2s*. We say that $[h]$ is *generated by* h; hence a *dl2s* G is generated by each of its axioms.

The *composition of selectors* γ_1, γ_2 (in this order) on a set D is the selector γ_2 *com* γ_1 on D defined by : for each $x \in D, (\gamma_2 \ com \ \gamma_1)(x) = (a_x^{(2)} \circ a_x^{(1)}, b_x^{(1)} \circ b_x^{(2)})$ where $\gamma_1(x) = (a_x^{(1)}, b_x^{(1)})$ and $\gamma_2(x) = (a_x^{(2)}, b_x^{(2)})$. Note that for a *l2s* $g = (D, \lambda), tr_{\gamma_2 com \gamma_1}(g)$ is the *l2s* $g' = (D, \lambda')$, where for each $(x, y) \in E_2(D)$, $\lambda'(x, y) = (a_x^{(2)} \circ a_x^{(1)}) \circ \lambda(x, y) \circ (b_y^{(1)} \circ b_y^{(2)}) = a_x^{(2)} \circ (a_x^{(1)} \circ \lambda(x, y) \circ b_y^{(1)}) \circ b_y^{(2)}$. Hence $tr_{\gamma_2 com \gamma_1}(g) = tr_{\gamma_2}(tr_{\gamma_1}(g))$ and so the class of selections on $\mathbf{L2S}_D(\Delta)$ is closed under composition.

As a matter of fact, for a given set (domain) D the set $SEL(D)$ of all selectors on D together with the operation *com* of composition of selectors as defined above is a group (see [EhR2]). In this group $(SEL(D), com)$ for a selector γ its inverse γ^{-1} is defined by : for each $x \in D, \gamma^{-1}(x) = (a_x^{-1}, b_x^{-1})$ where $\gamma(x) = (a_x, b_x)$; the selector γ with $\gamma(x) = (e, e)$ for each $x \in D$ is the identity of this group. Since $(SEL(D), com)$ is a group, the set $TR(D)$ of all selections tr_γ on $\mathbf{L2S}_D(\Delta)$ determined by selectors γ from $SEL(D)$ together with the operation of composition of functions also forms a group (see [EhR2]). In this group the inverse tr_γ^{-1} of a selection tr_γ is the selection $tr_{\gamma^{-1}}$, and the identity of this group is the selection tr_γ where $\gamma(x) = (e, e)$ for each $x \in D$.

Consequently for a *l2s* g the *dl2s* $[g]$ may be also defined as the smallest set G of *l2s's* such that $g \in G$, and if $h \in G$ and γ is a selector on $dom(h)$, then $tr_\gamma(h) \in G$.

It is convenient to be able to "apply" a selector on a set D to a set Y not necessarily equal to D. This is done as follows. Let γ be a selector on D and let Y be a set. The *extension of* γ *to* Y is the function $\gamma_Y : Y \longrightarrow cp(\Delta)$ defined by : for $x \in D \cap Y, \gamma_Y(x) = \gamma(x)$, and for $x \in Y - D, \gamma_Y(x) = (e, e)$. The γ-*selection on* $\mathbf{L2S}_Y(\Delta)$ is the function tr_{γ_Y}. Clearly if $Y = D$ then $\gamma = \gamma_Y$, and so $tr_\gamma = tr_{\gamma_Y}$. In the sequel of the paper, in order not to burden our notation too much, *we will write* γ *rather than* γ_Y *also to denote the extension of* γ *to a given domain* Y; since Y will always be clear from the context of considerations, this simplification should not cause any confusion.

The following (type of) selector turns out to be technically very useful in developing the theory of *dl2s's* (see [EhR2]).

Let $g = (D, \lambda)$ and let $x \in D$. The x-*selector for* g, denoted $sel_{g,x}$, is the selector γ on D such that $\gamma(x) = (e, e)$ and $\gamma(y) = ((\lambda(y, x))^{-1}, \delta((\lambda(y, x))^{-1}))$. The $sel_{g,x}$-selection is called the x-*translation of* g and denoted by $\tau_{g,x}$.

To simplify the notation we will write sel_x and τ_x whenever g is understood from the context of considerations.

Example 1.1

Let Γ be the group $(\{0, 1\}, +_2)$ where $+_2$ is the addition modulo 2, and let the involution δ be the identity on $\{0, 1\}$ (clearly δ is the only involution on Γ). Let g be the following *l2s* :

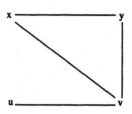

Figure 1.1

where the 2-edges shown are those labeled by 1 and those not shown are labeled by 0.

Then sel_x is the following selector:

$sel_x(x) = (0,0), sel_x(y) = (1,1), sel_x(u) = (0,0),$ and $sel_x(v) = (1,1).$

Consequently, $\tau_x(g)$ is the following $l2s$ h :

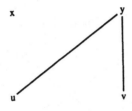

Figure 1.2

As a matter of fact for the given Γ and δ, $[g]$ consists of g, h, and the following seven $l2s's$:

Figure 1.3

Figure 1.4

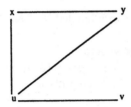

Figure 1.5

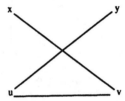

Figure 1.6

Figure 1.7

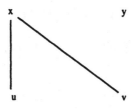

Figure 1.8

Figure 1.9

□

The notion of substructure carries over to $dl2s's$ as follows. Let $G = [g]$ be a $dl2s$ and let $X \subseteq dom(g)$ be nonempty. The *substructure of G determined by X*, denoted $SUB_G(X)$, is the $dl2s$ $[sub_g(X)]$.

It is easily seen that for each selector $\gamma, sub_{tr_\gamma(g)}(X) = tr_\gamma(sub_g(X))$. Since $G = [g] = \{tr_\gamma(g) : \gamma \in SEL(dom(g))\}, SUB_G(X) = [sub_g(X)] = \{tr_\gamma(sub_g(X)) : \gamma \in SEL(dom(g))\} = \{sub_{tr_\gamma(g)}(X) : \gamma \in SEL(dom(g))\} = \{sub_h(X) : h \in [g]\} = \{sub_h(X) : h \in G\}$. Thus the definition of $SUB_G(X)$ does not depend on the choice of an axiom of G.

The notion of a clan for $dl2s's$ is defined as follows.

Definition 1.2 Let G be a $dl2s$, and let $X \subseteq D$. X is a *clan of G* iff there exists $g \in G$ such that $X \in C(g)$. □

We will use $C(G)$ to denote the set of clans of G.

In the rest of this section we will recall from [EhR2] a number of results that will be used in the sequel of this paper.

Proposition 1.1 *Let G be a $dl2s$. For every $h \in G$, $G = [h]$.* □

Hence in a $dl2s$ G one can get any $g \in G$ from any other $h \in G$ by using a suitable selection. This implies that for each $dl2s$ G and each $l2s$ $h, G = [h]$ iff $h \in G$, and for all $l2s's$ g and $h, [g] = [h]$ iff $h \in [g]$. Thus for all $dl2s's$ G and H, either $G = H$ or $G \cap H = \emptyset$. Proposition 1.1 depends very essentially on assuming that we deal with single axiom $dl2s's$ (as done in Definition 1.1), see Remark 1.1(2)).

For a $l2s$ g we say that $X \subseteq dom(g)$ is *isolated in g* iff for each $z \in dom(g) - X$ and each $x \in X$, $lab_g(z, x) = e$.

Proposition 1.2 *Let G be a $dl2s$. If $X \in C(G)$, then there exists $g \in G$ such that X is isolated in g.* $\square$

The above result which says that each clan of a $dl2s$ G may be isolated in a $l2s$ belonging to G will be crucial in the technical considerations of this paper.

Let for a $dl2s$ G, $HOR(G)$ be the subset of G consisting of all $g \in G$ such that $\{x \in dom(g) : x$ is isolated in $g \} \neq \emptyset$. Note that by Proposition 1.2, $HOR(G) \neq \emptyset$.

Proposition 1.3 *Let G be a $dl2s$. If $h \in HOR(G)$, then $C(G) = C(h) \cup \{dom(G) - X : X \in C(h)\}$.* $\square$

Hence, by the above theorem, each $l2s$ h belonging to a $dl2s$ G, such that h contains at least one isolated element represents all clans of G either directly through its own clans or through the complements of its own clans.

The following example illustrates the usefulness of this result.

Example 1.2

Let Γ be the group of reals $\mathbf{R}$ with addition $+$, let the involution δ be the identity on $\mathbf{R}$, and let g be the following $l2s$:

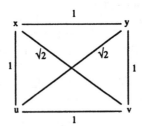

Figure 1.10

In order to compute the clans of [g] we consider the selector γ such that $\gamma(x) = (0,0)$, $\gamma(y) = (1 - \sqrt{2}, 1 - \sqrt{2})$, $\gamma(u) = (-1, -1)$, and $\gamma(v) = (0,0)$. Then $tr_\gamma(g)$ is the following $l2s$:

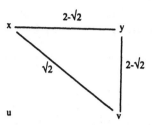

Figure 1.11

where we omit 2-edges labeled by 0. Hence u is isolated in $tr_\gamma(g)$ and consequently, by Proposition 1.3, the clans of $[g]$ are: $\emptyset, dom(g)$, the singletons over $dom(g)$, the complements of the singletons over $dom(g)$, and the sets $\{x, v\}$ and $\{y, u\}$. □

Proposition 1.4 *Let G be a dl2s. If $X \in \mathcal{C}(G)$, then $dom(G) - X \in \mathcal{C}(G)$.* □

The above result is intrinsic to $dl2s's$ - it does not hold for $l2s's$. It says in particular that complements of singletons are also clans in $dl2s's$; hence the notion of a *trivial clan for dl2s's* (i.e., a set which is a clan for *every* dl2s over a suitable domain) includes also the complements of singletons (in addition to the empty set, the whole domain and the singletons over a given domain). This is certainly not the case for $l2s's$; a *trivial clan for l2s's* is either the empty set or the whole domain or a singleton over a given domain.

Proposition 1.5 *Let G be a dl2s, let $g \in G$, let $X \in \mathcal{C}(g) - \{dom(g)\}$, and let γ be a selector. Then $\gamma(x_1) = \gamma(x_2)$ for all $x_1, x_2 \in X$ iff $X \in \mathcal{C}(tr_\gamma(g))$.* □

2 Disjoint Unions of *l2s*'s

The basic operation that we will use to combine two $l2s's$ into one $l2s$ with a larger domain is the operation of disjoint union. This is a well-known operation on graphs and we formulate it here for $l2s's$. We call $l2s's$ g and h *disjoint* iff $dom(g) \cap dom(h) = \emptyset$.

Definition 2.1 Let g, h be disjoint $l2s's$. The *disjoint union of g and h*, denoted $g + h$, is the $l2s$ (D, λ) where $D = dom(g) \cup dom(h)$, and for each $(x, y) \in E_2(D)$,
$$\lambda(x, y) = \begin{cases} lab_g(x, y) & \text{if } (x, y) \in E_2(dom(g)), \\ lab_h(x, y) & \text{if } (x, y) \in E_2(dom(h)), \\ e & \text{otherwise.} \end{cases} \qquad \square$$

We prove first that if a $l2s$ k is a disjoint union of g and h, then the domains of g and h are clans of the $dl2s$ generated by k.

Theorem 2.1 *Let* g, h *be disjoint* $l2s$*'s. Then* $dom(g) \in C([g + h])$ *and* $dom(h) \in C([g + h])$.

Proof: From the definition of disjoint union it follows directly that $dom(g) \in C(g + h)$ and $dom(h) \in C(g + h)$. Hence, by the definition of $C([g + h])$, it follows directly that $dom(g) \in C([g + h])$ and $dom(h) \in C([g + h])$. $\square$

Also the "inverse" of the above theorem holds. If X is a clan of a $dl2s$ G such that $X \neq \emptyset$ and $X \neq dom(G)$, then G is generated by the disjoint union of $l2s's$ g and h where $dom(g) = X$ and $dom(h) = dom(G) - X$.

Theorem 2.2 *Let* G *be a* $dl2s$. *For each* $X \in C(G)$ *such that* $X \neq \emptyset$ *and* $X \neq dom(G)$ *there exist* $g \in SUB_G(X)$ *and* $h \in SUB_G(dom(G) - X)$ *such that* $G = [g + h]$.

Proof: Let $X \in C(G)$. By Proposition 1.2, there exists $k \in G$ such that X is isolated in k. Let $g = sub_k(X)$ and $h = sub_k(dom(G) - X)$. Then, clearly, $k = g + h$. By Proposition 1.1, $G = [k]$ and so $G = [g + h]$. $\square$

3 Decompositions of $l2s$'s and of $dl2s$'s

We will give now a characterization of all $l2s's$ over Δ based on disjoint union and selections.

Definition 3.1 Let $\mathbf{SDU}(\Delta)$ be the class of $l2s's$ over Δ defined as follows.

1. All singleton $l2s's$ are in $\mathbf{SDU}(\Delta)$.

2. If $g \in \mathbf{SDU}(\Delta)$ and γ is a selector on $dom(g)$, then $tr_\gamma(g) \in \mathbf{SDU}(\Delta)$.

3. If g, h are disjoint $l2s's$ in $\mathbf{SDU}(\Delta)$, then $g + h \in \mathbf{SDU}(\Delta)$. $\square$

Theorem 3.1 $\mathbf{L2S}(\Delta) = \mathbf{SDU}(\Delta)$.

Proof: Clearly, it suffices to prove that $\mathbf{L2S}(\Delta) \subseteq \mathbf{SDU}(\Delta)$.
Let $g \in \mathbf{L2S}(\Delta)$.
We prove by induction on $|dom(g)|$ that $g \in \mathbf{SDU}(\Delta)$.
Base. $|dom(g)| = 1$.
Then $g \in \mathbf{SDU}(\Delta)$ by Clause 1 of the definition of $\mathbf{SDU}(\Delta)$.
Inductive assumption. Assume that $g \in \mathbf{SDU}(\Delta)$ whenever $|dom(g)| \leq n$ for a $n \geq 1$.
Inductive step. Let $|dom(g)| = n + 1$.

Let $G = [g]$ and let $x \in dom(g)$. Then $\{x\} \in \mathcal{C}(G)$. Thus by Theorem 2.2, $G = [k + h]$ for some $l2s's$ k and h such that $dom(k) = \{x\}$ and $dom(h) = dom(g) - \{x\}$. By the inductive assumption, $k, h \in \mathbf{SDU}(\Delta)$ and, by Clause 3 of the definition of $\mathbf{SDU}(\Delta)$, $k + h \in \mathbf{SDU}(\Delta)$. Since $g \in G$ and $G = [k + h]$, there exists a selector γ such that $tr_\gamma(k + h) = g$. Thus by Clause 2 of the definition of $\mathbf{SDU}(\Delta)$, $g \in \mathbf{SDU}(\Delta)$. □

Thus, by the above theorem, each $l2s$ g can be built up from singletons using disjoint unions and selections. This illustrates an advantage of having selectors (in $dl2s's$); the operation of disjoint union itself does not play a significant role in the theory of $l2s's$.

The above theorem leads then naturally to the following notion of a direct decomposition for $l2s$'s and for $dl2s$'s.

Definition 3.2   1. Let g, h be disjoint $l2s's$. A $l2s$ k *directly decomposes into* g, h, denoted $k \Longrightarrow g, h$, iff $k \in [g + h]$.

2. Let K, G, H be $dl2s's$. K *directly decomposes through* G, H, denoted $K \Longrightarrow G, H$, iff there exist $k \in K, g \in G$ and $h \in H$ such that $k \Longrightarrow g, h$. □

Hence $k \Longrightarrow g, h$ iff $k = tr_\gamma(g + h)$ for some selector γ, and $K \Longrightarrow G, H$ iff there exist $g \in G$ and $h \in H$ such that $K = [g + h]$.

Note that in the notations $k \Longrightarrow g, h$ and $K \Longrightarrow G, H$ the order of the arguments to the right of the arrow $\Longrightarrow$ is irrelevant, one may equivalently write $k \Longrightarrow h, g$ and $K \Longrightarrow H, G$. The reason that we use these notations is that we want to avoid the more cumbersome notations $k \Longrightarrow \{g, h\}$ and $K \Longrightarrow \{G, H\}$.

Example 3.1 Let Γ be the group $(\{0, 1\}, +_2)$, and let the involution δ be the identity on Γ (see Example 1.1).

Let g be the following $l2s$:

Figure 3.1

let h be the following $l2s$:

Figure 3.2

and let k be the following $l2s$:

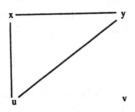

Figure 3.3

then $k \implies g, h$ because $k = tr_\gamma(g + h)$ where γ is the selector on $\{x, y, u, v\}$ such that $\gamma(x) = \gamma(y) = \gamma(v) = (1, 1)$, and $\gamma(u) = (0, 0)$. □

The iterative application of the direct decomposition relation can be represented by a decomposition tree. Hence, a decomposition tree representing a construction of a $l2s$ according to Theorem 3.1 will typically look as follows :

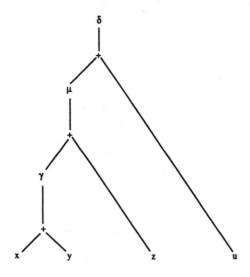

Figure 3.4

where γ, μ, δ are selectors, and x, y, z, u are singleton $l2s's$. Here we have combined already consecutive applications of selectors into one selector; moreover if several applications of disjoint union follow each other, then we separate them by the "identity" selectors.

If we now make one operation by first applying disjoint union and then the application of a selector, then such a derivation tree will look as follows :

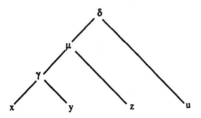

Figure 3.5

Here the labeling of an inner node by a selector β means that in this node the two arguments are combined by disjoint union and then the resulting $l2s$ is transformed by the selection tr_β. If β is the identity selector, then the result is the disjoint union of the two arguments - in this case we may as well label the node by $+$.

We will prove now that a direct decomposition of K amounts to decomposing K into clans.

Theorem 3.2 Let K, G, H be $dl2s's$. $K \Longrightarrow G, H$ iff there exists $X \in \mathcal{C}(K)$, $X \neq \emptyset$ and $X \neq dom(K)$, such that $G = SUB_K(X)$ and $H = SUB_K(dom(K) - X)$.

Proof:
1. Assume that $K \Longrightarrow G, H$.
Let $k \in K, g \in G$ and $h \in H$ be such that $k \Longrightarrow g, h$. Hence $K = [g + h]$. By Theorem 2.1, $dom(g) \in \mathcal{C}([g + h]) = \mathcal{C}(K)$. Let $X = dom(g)$. Clearly, $G = [g] = [sub_{g+h}(X)]$ and $H = [h] = [sub_{g+h}(dom(K) - X)]$, and so $G = SUB_K(X)$ and $H = SUB_K(dom(K) - X)$.
2. Assume that there exists $X \in \mathcal{C}(K)$ such that $G = SUB_K(X)$ and $H = SUB_K(dom(K) - X)$. Then by Theorem 2.2, $K = [g + h]$ for some $g \in G$ and $h \in H$. Hence $K \Longrightarrow G, H$. $\square$

Thus by Theorem 3.2 a direct decomposition of K is nothing else but decomposing K into two clans (a clan and its complement). As a matter of fact we can always decompose K into two trivial clans: a singleton $\{x\}$ and its complement $dom(K) - \{x\}$. The existence of such binary trivial decomposition is a major difference with the theory of $l2s's$: there one can always decompose a $l2s$ into singletons, but the complement of a singleton does not have to be a clan and so, in general, *binary* decompositions of $l2s's$ into trivial clans do not exist.

Example 3.2 (continues Example 1.2 from Section 1)
Let Γ, δ, and g be as in Example 1.2. Let g_1 be the following $l2s$:

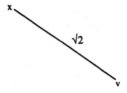

Figure 3.6

and let g_2 be the following $l2s$:

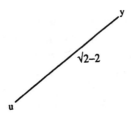

Figure 3.7

Let γ be the following selector:
$\gamma(x) = (0,0)$, and $\gamma(v) = (\sqrt{2}, \sqrt{2})$.
Then $tr_\gamma(x + v) = g_1$.
Let ω be the following selector:
$\omega(y) = (0,0)$, and $\omega(u) = (\sqrt{2} - 2, \sqrt{2} - 2)$.
Then $tr_\omega(y + u) = g_2$.

Let μ be the following selector :
$\mu(x) = (0,0), \mu(y) = (1,1), \mu(u) = (1,1)$, and $\mu(v) = (0,0)$.
Then $tr_\mu(g_1 + g_2) = g$.
Let g_3 be the following $l2s$:

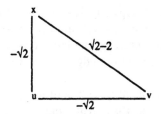

Figure 3.8

Let ζ be the following selector :
$$\zeta(x) = (1,1),\ \zeta(y) = (0,0),\ \zeta(u) = (\sqrt{2},\sqrt{2}),\ \text{and}\ \zeta(v)\ =\ (1,1).$$
Then $tr_\zeta(g_3 + y) = g$.
Let χ be the following selector:
$$\chi(x) = (-1,-1),\chi(u) = (1 - \sqrt{2}, 1 - \sqrt{2}),\ \text{and}\ \chi(v)\ =\ (-1,-1).$$
Then $tr_\chi(g_1 + u) = g_3$.
Hence we get the following two decompositions of g :

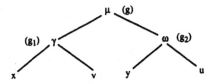

Figure 3.9

and

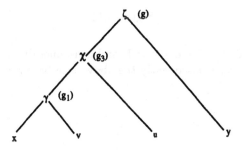

Figure 3.10

Example 3.3 Let Γ be the group $(\{0,1\}, +_2)$, and let δ be the identity involution on Γ, as considered in Examples 1.1 and 3.1. If we consider $l2s's$ with the label alphabet $\{0,1\}$, and we interpret the label 1 as "the presence of the edge" and the label 0 as "the absence of the edge", then we deal with (irreflexive and undirected) graphs.

Let g be such a $l2s$ with $|dom(g)| \geq 2$, and let $x_0, x_1, ..., x_n$ be an arbitrary ordering of the elements of $dom(g)$. Applying the x_n-selector τ_{x_n} to $g_n = g$ isolates x_n in g_n, applying the x_{n-1}-selector $\tau_{x_{n-1}}$ to $g_{n-1} = sub_g(dom(g) - \{x_n\})$ isolates x_{n-1} in g_{n-1}, ..., and finally applying the x_1-selector τ_{x_1} to $g_1 = sub_g(x_0, x_1)$ isolates x_1 in g_1. Consequently the following tree is a sequential decomposition tree for g (a decomposition tree is *sequential* if each inner node is such that at least one of its direct descendants is a leaf).

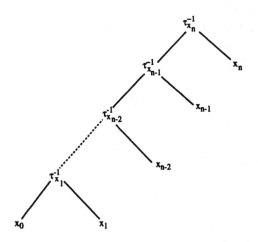

Figure 3.11

But in Γ we have $0^{-1} = 0$ and $1^{-1} = 1$, and consequently for each $x \in dom(g)$, $\tau_x^{-1} = \tau_x$. Consequently the above tree becomes :

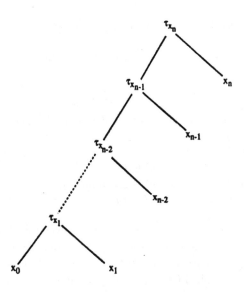

Figure 3.12

Hence, for each ordering $x_0, x_1, ..., x_n$ of the elements of $dom(g)$, the sequence $\tau_{x_1}, \tau_{x_2}, ..., \tau_{x_n}$ is a unique representation of g. Clearly,
τ_{x_1} can be represented by one bit which indicates whether $\tau_{x_1}(x_0) = (0, 0)$ or $\tau_{x_1}(x_0) = (1, 1)$,
τ_{x_2} can be represented by two bits which indicate which of the conjugated pairs $(0, 0), (1, 1)$ is the value of τ_{x_2} in x_0 and in x_1,
...
τ_{x_n} can be represented by n bits which indicate which of the conjugated pairs $(0, 0), (1, 1)$ is the value of τ_{x_n} in $x_0, x_1, ...,$ and x_{n-1}.

Altogether the sequence $\tau_{x_1}, \tau_{x_2}, ..., \tau_{x_n}$ can be represented by $\frac{n(n+1)}{2}$ bits. But the number of all graphs on the domain $0, 1, ..., n$ is $2^{\frac{n(n+1)}{2}}$ and hence any code for graphs on this domain must have at least $log_2(2^{\frac{n(n+1)}{2}}) = \frac{n(n+1)}{2}$ bits. Consequently the above way of coding graphs is optimal! $\square$

4 Comparison with Grammatical Substitution

The decompositions of $dl2s's$ as discussed in the previous section are based on the operations of disjoint union and selectors. Such decompositions give rise to decomposition trees. In the theory of graph grammars (see, e.g. [EKR]) the derivations of graphs are based on the operation of grammatical substitution.

Such derivations give rise to derivation trees. In this section we compare these operations.

We begin by defining the operation of grammatical substitution in the framework of $l2s's$.

Definition 4.1 Let g, h be $l2s's$ and let $x \in dom(g)$ be such that $(dom(g) - \{x\}) \cap dom(h) = \emptyset$. The *(grammatical) substitution of h for x in g*, denoted $g(x \longleftarrow h)$, is the $l2s$ f such that $dom(f) = (dom(g) - x) \cup dom(h)$, and for each $(z, y) \in E_2(dom(f))$,

$$lab_f(z, y) = \begin{cases} lab_g(z, y) & \text{if } (z, y) \in E_2(dom(g) - \{x\}), \\ lab_h(z, y) & \text{if } (z, y) \in E_2(dom(h)), \\ lab_g(z, x) & \text{if } z \in dom(g) - \{x\} \text{ and } y \in dom(h). \end{cases} \qquad \square$$

Note that, because the $l2s's$ we consider are δ-reversible, the definition of lab_f given above is complete and hence $g(x \longleftarrow h)$ is well defined.

The operation of grammatical substitution as defined above corresponds to the case of node label controlled (NLC) graph grammars (see, e.g., [EnR]) where the connection relation is hereditary, i.e., the labels of the edges adjacent to the mother node carry over without change to the edges adjacent to the daughter graph.

We will also need the following operation on $l2s's$ which is based on the disjoint union operation.

Definition 4.2 Let g, h, k be $l2s's$ such that $k = g + h$. Then h is the *difference of k and g*, written as $h = k - g$. $\qquad \square$

We will demonstrate now that the operation of substitution can be expressed by the operations of disjoint union and difference, and by selections as follows.

Theorem 4.1 Let g, h be $l2s's$ and let $x \in dom(g)$ be such that $(dom(g) - \{x\}) \cap dom(h) = \emptyset$. Then $g(x \longleftarrow h) = \tau_x^{-1}((\tau_x(g) - x) + h)$.

Proof: Let f_R be the $l2s$ $\tau_x^{-1}((\tau_x(g) - x) + h)$ with λ_R as its labeling function and let f_L be the $l2s$ $g(x \longleftarrow h)$ with λ_L as its labeling function.

We are going to prove that $f_L = f_R$.

First of all we notice that $dom(f_R) = (dom(g) - \{x\}) \cup dom(h) = dom(f_L)$. We let D denote this common domain.

In order to prove that $\lambda_L = \lambda_R$ consider an arbitrary $(z, y) \in E_2(D)$. We have three cases to consider

Case 1. $z, y \in dom(g) - \{x\}$.

Clearly, $\lambda_R(z, y)$ is the label of (z, y) in $\tau_x^{-1}\tau_x(g) = g$. Hence $\lambda_R(z, y) = lab_g(z, y)$.

By the definition of $g(x \longleftarrow h)$, $\lambda_L(z, y) = lab_g(z, y)$.

Hence $\lambda_L(z, y) = \lambda_R(z, y)$.

Case 2. $z \in dom(g) - \{x\}$ and $y \in dom(h)$.

By the definition of disjoint union, the label of (z, y) in $(\tau_x(g) - x) + h$ equals e. Hence, by the definition of τ_x^{-1}, $\lambda_R(z, y) = lab_g(z, x)$.

By the definition of $g(x \longleftarrow h)$, $\lambda_L(z, y) = lab_g(z, x)$.

Hence $\lambda_L(z, y) = \lambda_R(z, y)$.

Case 3. $z, y \in dom(h)$.

Since for each $t \in dom(h)$, $sel_x^{-1}(t) = (e, e)$, we get $\lambda_R(z, y) = lab_h(z, y)$. By the definition of $g(x \longleftarrow h)$, $\lambda_L(z, y) = lab_h(z, y)$.

Hence $\lambda_L(z, y) = \lambda_R(z, y)$.

From cases 1 through 3 it follows that $\lambda_L = \lambda_R$ and so $f_L = f_R$. Hence the theorem holds. $\quad\square$

There is also a result "dual" to the above theorem: the direct decomposition relation between *l2s's* can be expressed by substitution as follows. A *discrete doubleton* is a *l2sf* with $|dom(f)| = 2$ and such that $lab_f(x, y) = e$ where $dom(f) = \{x, y\}$.

Theorem 4.2 *Let k, g, h be l2s's such that $k \Longrightarrow g, h$. Then for every discrete doubleton f with $dom(f) = \{x, y\}$, $k = \beta((f(x \longleftarrow g))(y \longleftarrow h))$ for some selection β.*

Proof: Assume that $k \Longrightarrow g, h$. By the definition of the direct decomposition relation $k \in [g + h]$. If f is a discrete doubleton with $dom(f) = \{x, y\}$, then obviously $g + h = (f(x \longleftarrow g)) (y \longleftarrow h)$. Thus there exists a selection β such that $k = \beta((f(x \longleftarrow g))(y \longleftarrow h))$. $\quad\square$

5 Amalgamated Unions

In the previous sections we have considered constructions of *l2s's* using the operation of *disjoint* union (and selectors). In this section we will relax somewhat the disjointness condition and consider constructing a *l2s* from *l2s's* that do not have to be disjoint but have to "agree" on the intersection and be "independent" (disconnected) on the parts which lie outside the intersection. The operation we consider is the amalgamated union.

Definition 5.1 Let g, h be *l2s's* with $Z = dom(g) \cap dom(h)$ such that $sub_g(Z) = sub_h(Z)$, $dom(g) - Z \in C(g)$, and $dom(h) - Z \in C(h)$. The *amalgamated union of g and h*, denoted $g \oplus h$, is the *l2s* k such that $dom(k) = dom(g) \cup dom(h)$, and for each $(x, y) \in E_2(dom(k))$,

$$lab_k(x, y) = \begin{cases} lab_g(x, y) & \text{for } x, y \in dom(g), \\ lab_h(x, y) & \text{for } x, y \in dom(h), \text{ and} \\ e & \text{otherwise.} \end{cases} \qquad \square$$

Clearly, if in the above $Z = \emptyset$, then we get the disjoint union of g and h. Hence the operation of the amalgamated union generalizes the operation of disjoint union.

Example 5.1 Let Γ and δ be as in Examples 1.1 and 3.1. Let g be the following $l2s$:

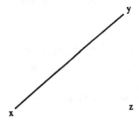

Figure 5.1

and let h be the following $l2s$:

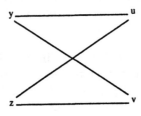

Figure 5.2

where the 2-edges shown are labeled by 1, and the missing 2-edges are labeled by 0.

Then $g \oplus h$ is the following $l2s$:

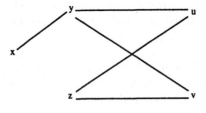

Figure 5.3

If we change h to either the following $l2s$ h_1 :

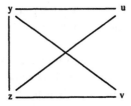

Figure 5.4

or to the following $l2s$ h_2 :

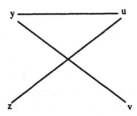

Figure 5.5

then neither $g \oplus h_1$ nor $g \oplus h_2$ are defined. The reason that $g \oplus h_1$ is not defined is that $sub_g(\{y,z\}) \neq sub_{h_1}(\{y,z\})$, and the reason that $g \oplus h_2$ is not defined is that $\{u,v\} \notin C(h_2)$. ☐

It follows directly from the definition of the amalgamated union, that if $k = g \oplus h$, then $sub_k(dom(g)) = g$ and $sub_k(dom(h)) = h$.

The following result gives a property of amalgamated union that is analogous to the property of disjoint union expressed by Theorem 2.1.

Theorem 5.1 Let g,h,k be $l2s's$ such that $k = g \oplus h$. Then $\mathrm{dom}(g) \in C([k])$ and $\mathrm{dom}(h) \in C([k])$.

Proof: By the definition of the amalgamated union, $dom(g) - (dom(g) \cap dom(h)) \in C(g)$. Hence from the definition of the amalgamated union it follows that $dom(k) - dom(h) \in C(k)$. Thus $dom([k]) - dom(h) \in C([k])$, and consequently, by Proposition 1.4, $dom(h) \in C([k])$.

Analogously one shows that $dom(g) \in C([k])$. ☐

We consider now the problem of decomposing a $dl2s$ using the amalgamated union and the covering of the domain by two (possibly overlapping) clans.

Theorem 5.2 Let K be a $dl2s$. Let $X_1, X_2 \in C(K)$ be such that $X_1 \cup X_2 = dom(K)$, and let $k \in K$ be such that for all $x \in X_1 - X_2$ and all $y \in X_2 - X_1$, $lab_k(x,y) = e$. Then $k = sub_k(X_1) \oplus sub_k(X_2)$.

Proof: By Proposition 1.4, $X_2 - X_1 \in C(K)$ and so there exists $h \in K$ such that $X_2 - X_1 \in C(h)$. By Proposition 1.1 there exists a selector γ such that $tr_\gamma(k) = h$.

We will show now thät γ has the same value on all elements of $X_2 - X_1$. To this aim assume to the contrary that there exist $y_1, y_2 \in X_2 - X_1$ such that $\gamma(y_1) \neq \gamma(y_2)$. Consider an arbitrary element $x \in X_1 - X_2$. Since from the assumptions about k we have $lab_k(x, y_1) = lab_k(x, y_2)$, we get $lab_h(x, y_1) = \gamma(x) \circ e \circ \delta(\gamma(y_1))$ and $lab_h(x, y_2) = \gamma(x) \circ e \circ \delta(\gamma(y_2))$. Thus $lab_h(x, y_1) \neq lab_h(x, y_2)$ which contradicts the fact that $X_2 - X_1 \in C(h)$. Consequently γ has the same value on all elements of $X_2 - X_1$.

Since $tr_{\gamma^{-1}}(h) = k$, by Proposition 1.5 it follows that $X_2 - X_1 \in C(k)$, and so $X_2 - X_1 \in C(sub_k(X_2))$.

By analogous reasoning we prove that $X_1 - X_2 \in C(sub_k(X_1))$.

Consequently, $k = sub_k(X_1) \oplus sub_k(X_2)$. □

Remark 5.1 It is important to notice here that if K, X_1, X_2 are as in the statement of Theorem 5.2, then a $k \in K$ satisfying the assumptions of Theorem 5.2 always exists. It simply suffices to consider a $k \in K$ such that X_2 is isolated in k; such a k exists by Proposition 1.2. □

The following result is analogous to Theorem 2.2 for disjoint unions.

Theorem 5.3 *Let k be a dl2s. If $X_1, X_2 \in C(K)$ are nonempty and such that $X_1 \cup X_2 = dom(K)$, then there exist l2s's g, h such that $g \in SUB_K(X_1)$, $h \in SUB_K(X_2)$, and $K = [g \oplus h]$.*

Proof: The theorem follows directly from Theorem 5.2 and Remark 5.1. □

Now one can define the direct decomposition relation $\Longrightarrow^{am}$ based on the amalgamated union analogously to the definition of the direct decomposition relation $\Longrightarrow$ based on disjoint union.

Definition 5.2 1. Let g, h be l2s's with $Z = dom(g) \cap dom(h)$ such that $sub_g(Z) = sub_h(Z)$, $dom(g) - Z \in C(g)$, and $dom(h) - Z \in C(h)$. A l2s k *directly am-decomposes* into g, h, denoted $k \Longrightarrow^{am} g, h$, iff $k \in [g \oplus h]$.

2. Let K, G, H be dl2s's. K *directly am-decomposes* through G, H denoted $K \Longrightarrow^{am} G, H$, iff there exist $k \in K, g \in G$, and $h \in H$, such that $k \Longrightarrow^{am} g, h$. □

Hence $k \Longrightarrow^{am} g, h$ iff $k = tr_\gamma(g \oplus h)$ for some selector γ, and $K \Longrightarrow G, H$ iff there exist $g \in G$ and $h \in H$ such that $K = [g \oplus h]$.

Then the proof of the following theorem is completely analogous to the proof of Theorem 3.2.

Theorem 5.4 *Let K, G, H be dl2s's. Then $K \Longrightarrow^{am} G, H$ iff there exist nonempty $X_1, X_2 \in C(K)$ such that $X_1 \cup X_2 = dom(K), G = SUB_K(X_1)$, and $H = SUB_K(X_2)$.* □

We move now to consider the quotient structure of the amalgamated union of two $l2s's$.

Let G be a $dl2s$, and let $\mathcal{P}$ be a partition of $dom(G)$ into clans ($\mathcal{P} \subseteq \mathcal{C}(G)$). The *quotient of G by $\mathcal{P}$*, denoted $G/\mathcal{P}$, is the $dl2s$ $[h/\mathcal{P}]$ where $h \in G$ is such that $\mathcal{P} \subseteq \mathcal{C}(h)$. The quotient $G/\mathcal{P}$ is well defined because (1) it is proved in [EhHR] that if $\mathcal{P}$ is a partition of $dom(G)$ into clans, then $\mathcal{P} \subseteq \mathcal{C}(h)$ for some $h \in G$, and (2) it follows from Propositions 1.1 and 1.5 that $[h_1/\mathcal{P}] = [h_2/\mathcal{P}]$ for all $h_1, h_2 \in G$ such that $\mathcal{P} \subseteq \mathcal{C}(h_1)$ and $\mathcal{P} \subseteq \mathcal{C}(h_2)$.

In the following, for a nonempty set X and a nonempty subset Y of X, $\mathcal{P}_{X,Y}$ denotes the partition of X consisting of Y and all singletons over $X - Y$. Also, we say that $dl2s's$ G and H are *isomorphic*, denoted G *isom* H, iff there exist $g \in G$ and $h \in H$ such that g *isom* h.

Theorem 5.5 *Let g, h, k be $l2s's$ such that $k = g \oplus h$ where $Z = dom(g) \cap dom(h) \neq \emptyset$. Then $[g]/\mathcal{P}_{dom(g),Z}$ isom $[k]/\mathcal{P}_{dom(k),dom(h)}$ and $[h]/\mathcal{P}_{dom(h),Z}$ isom $[k]/\mathcal{P}_{dom(k),dom(g)}$.*

Proof: Let γ be the selector on $dom(g)$ defined as follows: for each $x \in Z, \gamma(x) = ((lab_g(x,y))^{-1}, \delta(((lab_g(x,y))^{-1}))$, where y is an arbitrary element of $dom(g) - Z$, and for each $x \in dom(g) - Z, \gamma(x) = (e,e)$. Since $dom(g) - Z \in \mathcal{C}(g)$, γ is well defined.

Clearly, Z is isolated in $tr_\gamma(g)$. Thus by the definition of γ, $tr_\gamma(g) = sub_g(dom(g) - Z) + tr_\gamma(sub_g(Z))$. Hence $tr_\gamma(g)/\mathcal{P}_{dom(g),Z}$ is isomorphic with $sub_g(dom(g) - Z) + g'$, where g' is a singleton $l2s$.

Since for each $x \in dom(g) - Z$ and each $y \in dom(h) - Z, lab_k(x,y) = e$, we obtain that $tr_\gamma(k) = sub_g(dom(g) - Z) + tr_\gamma(h)$, and so $tr_\gamma(k)/\mathcal{P}_{dom(k),dom(h)}$ is isomorphic with $sub_g(dom(g) - Z) + k'$, where k' is a singleton $l2s$.

Since $tr_\gamma(g) \in [g]$ and $tr_\gamma(k) \in [k]$, $[g]/\mathcal{P}_{dom(g),Z}$ is isomorphic with $[k]/\mathcal{P}_{dom(k),dom(h)}$.

Analogously we prove that $[h]/\mathcal{P}_{dom(h),Z}$ is isomorphic with $[k]/\mathcal{P}_{dom(k),dom(g)}$. $\square$

6 Acknowledgements

The authors are indebted to J. Engelfriet and T. Harju for useful comments on the earlier versions of this paper, and to Mrs. M. Boon-van der Nat for the expert typing of this paper. The research presented here has been carried out within the framework of the ESPRIT BRA Actions "CALIBAN" and "COMPUGRAPH II".

References

[EhHR]   A. Ehrenfeucht, T. Harju and G. Rozenberg, Quotients and plane trees of group labeled 2-structures, Leiden University, Department of Computer Science, Technical Report No. 03, 1994.

[EhR1]   A. Ehrenfeucht and G. Rozenberg, Theory of 2-structures, parts I and II, *Theoretical Computer Science*, v. 70, 277-342, 1990.

[EhR2]   A. Ehrenfeucht and G. Rozenberg, Dynamic labeled 2-structures, *Mathematical Structures in Computer Science*, to appear.

[EnR]   J. Engelfriet and G. Rozenberg, Graph grammars based on node rewriting: an introduction to NLC graph grammars, in [EKR].

[EKR]   H. Ehrig, H.-J. Kreowski and G. Rozenberg (Eds.), Graph grammars and their application to computer science, *Lecture Notes in Computer Science* 532, Springer Verlag, Heidelberg, 1991.

Deciding the NTS Property of Context-Free Grammars

Joost Engelfriet *

Department of Computer Science, Leiden University
P.O.Box 9512, 2300 RA Leiden, The Netherlands

Abstract. An algorithm is presented that is a variation of the one of Senizergues in [4]. It decides the NonTerminal Separation property of context-free grammars in polynomial time. A straightforward generalization of the algorithm decides the NTS property of extended context-free grammars (but not in polynomial time).

It was shown in [4] that it is decidable whether an arbitrary context-free grammar is NTS. The algorithm in [4] takes exponential time in the worst case. It was recently shown in [3] that the NTS property can in fact be decided in polynomial time. This is not stated as such in [3], but immediately follows from the more general result, shown in Proposition 3.8 of [3], that it is decidable in polynomial time whether a monadic semi-Thue system is weakly confluent: the reversed productions of a (λ-free and chain-free) context-free grammar form a monadic semi-Thue system that is weakly confluent if and only if the context-free grammar is NTS.

Here we present an independent proof of the polynomial time decidability of the NTS property that is a variation of the decidability algorithm in [4]. We also show that the NTS property is decidable for extended context-free grammars, i.e., context-free grammars of which the productions have regular expressions as right-hand sides. We first recall some definitions and facts (see [1, 4]).

We consider context-free grammars $G = (X, V, P, Z)$ where X is the set of terminals, V the set of nonterminals, P the set of productions, and $Z \subseteq V$ the set of initial nonterminals. We assume that G is λ-free and chain-free (i.e., for every production $A \to \alpha$, $|\alpha| \geq 1$ and if $|\alpha| = 1$ then $\alpha \in X$). Such a grammar is NTS (*nonterminally separated*) if the following holds: for every $A, B \in V$ and $\alpha, \beta, \gamma \in (X \cup V)^*$, if $A \Rightarrow^* \alpha\beta\gamma$ and $B \to \beta$ is in P, then $A \Rightarrow^* \alpha B\gamma$. Note that this does not depend on Z.

Let $G = (X, V, P, Z)$ be a context-free grammar. A pair $\langle \alpha, \beta \rangle$ with $\alpha, \beta \in (X \cup V)^*$ is called a shift-reduce configuration. For two shift-reduce configurations we define the *shift-reduce step relation* $\vdash$ as follows (where $\alpha, \beta, \gamma \in (X \cup V)^*$, $b \in X$, and $A \in V$):

1. $\langle \alpha, b\beta \rangle \vdash \langle \alpha b, \beta \rangle$
   if no suffix of α is the right-hand side of a production in P, and

---

* Supported by ESPRIT BR Working Group No.6317 ASMICS

2. $\langle \alpha\gamma, \beta \rangle \vdash \langle \alpha A, \beta \rangle$

   if $A \to \gamma$ is in P, A is the "first" nonterminal that has a production with right-hand side γ (where we assume some fixed, but arbitrary order on V), and γ is the shortest suffix of $\alpha\gamma$ that is the right-hand side of a production in P.

A step of type 1 is a shift, and a step of type 2 is a reduction. We note that, in a step of type 2, it is irrelevant that γ is taken to be the shortest suffix of $\alpha\gamma$ that is the right-hand side of a production; we might as well take the longest suffix (or any other choice that makes $\vdash$ deterministic).

For $A \in V$, we define $\mathrm{LM}(G, A) = \{\alpha \in (X \cup V)^* \mid \langle \lambda, \alpha \rangle \vdash^* \langle A, \lambda \rangle\}$. Intuitively, $\mathrm{LM}(G, A)$ is the set of strings that are left-most reducible to A, where a reduction takes place as soon as the right-hand side of a production is detected. Obviously, if $\alpha \in \mathrm{LM}(G, A)$ then $A \Rightarrow^* \alpha$, but in general this is not true in the other direction. If G is an NTS grammar then $\alpha \in \mathrm{LM}(G, A)$ if and only if $A \Rightarrow^* \alpha$ (also because G is λ-free and chain-free). It should be clear from the definition of $\vdash$ that $\mathrm{LM}(G, A)$ is a deterministic context-free language over $X \cup V$.

Let $A \in V$ and $\alpha, \beta, \gamma \in (X \cup V)^*$. Let t be a derivation tree with root label A and yield$(t) = \alpha\beta\gamma$, and let M be the set of leaves of t that correspond to the indicated occurrence of β in yield(t) (the "marked" leaves). Then t is said to be *nearly essential* for the derivation $A \Rightarrow^* \alpha\beta\gamma$ if

1. the root is the only internal node of t that is an ancestor of all leaves in M, and
2. every internal node is ancestor of some leaf in M.

In [4] the test for the NTS property is based on the set of "essential" derivation trees, which is a finite subset of the (generally infinite) set of nearly essential derivation trees. For each such essential tree a right- (or left-) linear grammar is constructed. Since, for a given grammar G, there may exist exponentially many essential trees (in the size of the grammar), the algorithm in [4] takes exponential time. Here we will show that it suffices to construct only polynomially many right- (or left-) linear grammars. For the readers familiar with [4] we give the following exponential example.

Consider, for $n \in \mathbf{N}$, the context-free grammar G with productions $A \to aAc$, $A \to bAc$, $A \to d$ and $A \to c^n$. Then all the 2^n derivation trees for derivations $A \Rightarrow^* \alpha\beta\gamma$ with $\alpha \in \{a, b\}^n d$, $\beta = c^n$, and $\gamma = \lambda$, are essential. Note that this grammar is not NTS; adding the constant amount of productions $A \to aA \mid bA \mid cA \mid dA \mid AA \mid a \mid b \mid c$ makes it NTS.

We now turn to our polynomial time variation of the algorithm of [4]. It is based on the following two facts; the first fact is part of the proofs of Propositions 1 and 2 of [4].

Fact 1. A context-free grammar $G = (X, V, P, Z)$ is NTS iff the following holds, for all $A, B \in V$ and $\alpha, \beta, \gamma \in (X \cup V)^*$:
if $A \Rightarrow^* \alpha\beta\gamma$, $B \to \beta$ is in P, and there is a nearly essential derivation tree for $A \Rightarrow^* \alpha\beta\gamma$, then $\alpha B\gamma \in \mathrm{LM}(G, A)$.

Fact 2. Let $G = (X, V, P, Z)$ be a context-free grammar. For every $A \in V$ and every production $p = (B \to \beta)$, the language $E_{A,p} = \{\alpha B \gamma \mid A \Rightarrow^* \alpha \beta \gamma$ and there is a nearly essential derivation tree for $A \Rightarrow^* \alpha \beta \gamma\}$ is regular. Moreover, a right-linear grammar for $E_{A,p}$ can be constructed in polynomial time.

Before proving these facts we show that they imply the polynomial time decidability of the NTS property. It follows from Fact 1 that a grammar G is NTS iff $E_{A,p} \subseteq LM(G, A)$ for every $A \in V$ and $p \in P$. Consider a fixed A and p. It suffices to show that $E_{A,p} \cap LM(G, A)^c = \emptyset$ can be decided in polynomial time. Since $E_{A,p}$ is regular by Fact 2, and $LM(G, A)$ is a deterministic context-free language, the property can in fact be decided in polynomial time, provided grammars (or automata) for both $E_{A,p}$ and $LM(G, A)^c$ can be constructed in polynomial time. For $E_{A,p}$ this is shown in Fact 2. As observed in [1], a deterministic pushdown automaton D can be constructed that directly simulates the shift-reduce algorithm recognizing $LM(G, A)$. To decide between shifting or reducing, D should keep the top-most part of the pushdown α (the first element of the shift-reduce configuration) in its finite state. Clearly, it suffices that the state contains the longest suffix of α that is a prefix of a right-hand side of a production of G. Hence D needs polynomially many states only. From this it easily follows that D can be constructed in polynomial time. Since G is λ-free and chain-free, D always reads all of its input. Hence, an automaton recognizing $LM(G, A)^c$ is obtained by interchanging the final and nonfinal states of D. This shows the polynomial time decidability of the NTS property. We now prove Facts 1 and 2.

Proof of Fact 1. (Only if) Let G be NTS. If $A \Rightarrow^* \alpha \beta \gamma$ and $B \to \beta$ is in P, then (since G is NTS) $A \Rightarrow^* \alpha B \gamma$ and hence (since G is NTS) $\alpha B \gamma \in LM(G, A)$.
(If) Let the stated condition be true. To show that G is NTS, assume that $A \Rightarrow^* \alpha \beta \gamma$ and $B \to \beta \in P$. Let t be a derivation tree for $A \Rightarrow^* \alpha \beta \gamma$ and let M be the set of leaves of t that correspond to the occurrence of β in yield(t). Let x be the least internal node of t that is a common ancestor of all leaves in M. Considering the subtree t' of t rooted at x we obtain derivations $A \Rightarrow^* \alpha_1 A' \gamma_1$ and $A' \Rightarrow^* \alpha_2 \beta \gamma_2$ where x has label A', $\alpha = \alpha_1 \alpha_2$, and $\gamma = \gamma_2 \gamma_1$. Now consider the nearly essential derivation tree t'' obtained from t' by pruning all subtrees that are rooted at internal nodes of t' that are not ancestor of any leaf in M. Clearly, t'' is nearly essential for a derivation $A' \Rightarrow^* \alpha_2' \beta \gamma_2'$ with $\alpha_2' \Rightarrow^* \alpha_2$ and $\gamma_2' \Rightarrow^* \gamma_2$. The stated condition now implies that $\alpha_2' B \gamma_2' \in LM(G, A')$ and so $A' \Rightarrow^* \alpha_2' B \gamma_2'$. Hence $A \Rightarrow^* \alpha_1 A' \gamma_1 \Rightarrow^* \alpha_1 \alpha_2' B \gamma_2' \gamma_1 \Rightarrow^* \alpha_1 \alpha_2 B \gamma_2 \gamma_1 = \alpha B \gamma$. $\square$

Proof of Fact 2. Let $G = (X, V, P, Z)$, $A \in V$, and $p = (B \to \beta) \in P$. In what follows we will construct a (λ-free, but not necessarily chain-free) context-free grammar $G' = (X \cup V, V', P', Z')$ for the language $E_{A,p}$ which is itself not right- or left-linear but from which such a grammar can easily be constructed. In fact, $V' = \{S\} \cup V_L \cup V_R$ with $Z' = \{S\}$, $V_L \cap V_R = \emptyset$, $S \notin V_L \cup V_R$, and the productions of P' are also partitioned in three parts: productions with left-hand side S, right-linear productions that contain nonterminals from V_L only, and left-linear productions that contain nonterminals from V_R only. Clearly, any grammar of this form can be turned into an equivalent right-linear grammar (or finite automaton) in polynomial time.

Intuitively, a production of P' with left-hand side S simulates the production of P with left-hand side A that is applied at the root of a nearly essential derivation tree for some $A \Rightarrow^* \alpha\beta\gamma$. Such a production generates the B that replaces β, and it generates a prefix of α and a suffix of γ. The right-linear productions with nonterminals from V_L then generate the remainder of α (from left to right), and the left-linear productions with nonterminals in V_R generate the remainder of γ (from right to left). The generation of β is simulated in the nonterminals. To this aim every nonterminal from V_L contains a prefix of β, which is the part of β of which the generation still has to be simulated by this nonterminal. Similarly every nonterminal from V_R contains a suffix of β.

Thus, V_L consists of all $\langle Y, L, \phi \rangle$ where $Y \in V$, L stands for "Left", and ϕ is a non-empty prefix of β. Symmetrically, V_R consists of all $\langle \psi, R, Y \rangle$ where ψ is a non-empty suffix of β, R stands for "Right", and $Y \in V$. The productions of P' are defined as follows (where $\Rightarrow$ always refers to G).

(1) Productions with left-hand side S. For every production $A \to Y_1 \cdots Y_k$ in P, with $Y_i \in X \cup V$ for $1 \le i \le k$, P' contains the following productions.

(1.1) All productions $S \to Y_1 \cdots Y_{i-1} \langle Y_i, L, \phi \rangle B \langle \psi, R, Y_j \rangle Y_{j+1} \cdots Y_k$ where $1 \le i < j \le k$, $Y_i, Y_j \in V$, and there exists $\pi \in (X \cup V)^*$ such that $\beta = \phi \pi \psi$ and $Y_{i+1} \cdots Y_{j-1} \Rightarrow^* \pi$. Note that in the case that $i+1 = j$ the last condition means that $\beta = \phi\psi$.

(1.2) All productions $S \to Y_1 \cdots Y_{i-1} B \langle \psi, R, Y_j \rangle Y_{j+1} \cdots Y_k$ where $1 \le i < j \le k$, $Y_j \in V$, and there exists $\pi \in (X \cup V)^*$ such that $\beta = \pi\psi$ and $Y_i \cdots Y_{j-1} \Rightarrow^* \pi$.

(1.3) All productions $S \to Y_1 \cdots Y_{i-1} \langle Y_i, L, \phi \rangle B Y_{j+1} \cdots Y_k$ where $1 \le i < j \le k$, $Y_i \in V$, and there exists $\pi \in (X \cup V)^*$ such that $\beta = \phi\pi$ and $Y_{i+1} \cdots Y_j \Rightarrow^* \pi$.

(1.4) All productions $S \to Y_1 \cdots Y_{i-1} B Y_{j+1} \cdots Y_k$ where $1 \le i < j \le k$ and $Y_i \cdots Y_j \Rightarrow^* \beta$.

To explain the intuition behind the above productions, consider a nearly essential derivation tree for $A \Rightarrow^* \alpha\beta\gamma$ with production $A \to \delta$ applied at the root, and let $\delta = Y_1 \cdots Y_k$. Let M be the set of leaves corresponding to β. Then $Y_1, \ldots, Y_{i-1}$ are the symbols of δ that label leaves to the left of M, and $Y_{j+1}, \ldots, Y_k$ those that label leaves to the right of M. Furthermore, $\langle Y_i, L, \phi \rangle$ occurs in the production of P' if and only if Y_i is a nonterminal that generates both leaves in M and leaves not in M, and ϕ is the sequence of labels of the generated leaves in M. And a similar statement holds for $\langle \psi, R, Y_j \rangle$. This same intuition also explains the remaining productions.

(2) Productions with left-hand side in V_L. For every production $Y \to Y_1 \cdots Y_k$ in P, with $Y_i \in X \cup V$ for $1 \le i \le k$, P' contains the following productions.

(2.1) All productions $\langle Y, L, \phi \rangle \to Y_1 \cdots Y_{i-1} \langle Y_i, L, \phi_1 \rangle$ where $1 \le i \le k$, $Y_i \in V$, and there exists $\phi_2 \in (X \cup V)^*$ such that $\phi = \phi_1 \phi_2$ and $Y_{i+1} \cdots Y_k \Rightarrow^* \phi_2$. In the case that $i = k$ the last condition means that $\phi = \phi_1$.

(2.2) All productions $\langle Y, L, \phi \rangle \to Y_1 \cdots Y_{i-1}$ where $2 \le i \le k$ and $Y_i \cdots Y_k \Rightarrow^* \phi$.

(3) Productions with left-hand side in V_R. For every production $Y \to Y_1 \cdots Y_k$ in P, P' contains the following productions.

(3.1) All productions $\langle \psi, R, Y \rangle \rightarrow \langle \psi_1, R, Y_j \rangle Y_{j+1} \cdots Y_k$ where $1 \le j \le k$, $Y_j \in V$, and there exists $\psi_2 \in (X \cup V)^*$ such that $\psi = \psi_2 \psi_1$ and $Y_1 \cdots Y_{j-1} \Rightarrow^* \psi_2$. In the case that $j = 1$ the last condition means that $\psi = \psi_1$.

(3.2) All productions $\langle \psi, R, Y \rangle \rightarrow Y_{j+1} \cdots Y_k$ where $1 \le j \le k-1$ and $Y_1 \cdots Y_j \Rightarrow^* \psi$.

This concludes the construction of the grammar G' generating $E_{A,p}$. It remains to show that G' can be constructed in polynomial time from G. Let n be the size of G. Since the number of prefixes and suffixes of β is $O(n)$, G' has $O(n^2)$ nonterminals. Now consider the productions $S \rightarrow Y_1 \cdots Y_{i-1} \langle Y_i, L, \phi \rangle B \langle \psi, R, Y_j \rangle Y_{j+1} \cdots Y_k$ of P', corresponding to the production $A \rightarrow Y_1 \cdots Y_k$ of P, as defined in (1.1) above. There are $O(n^4)$ such productions in P', one for each choice of i, j, ϕ, and ψ. Note that the condition $Y_{i+1} \cdots Y_{j-1} \Rightarrow^* \pi$ can be verified in polynomial time. Similar statements hold for the productions of all other types. From these remarks it should be clear that G' can be constructed in polynomial time. □

We now turn to the decidability of the NTS property for extended context-free grammars. An extended context-free grammar (or extended BNF) has productions of which the right-hand sides are regular expressions over $X \cup V$. An alternative way of viewing this is as follows. An *extended context-free grammar* is a context-free grammar $G = (X, V, P, Z)$ such that P is infinite and for each nonterminal B the language $R_B = \{\beta \in (X \cup V)^* \mid B \rightarrow \beta \in P\}$ is regular. The regular languages R_B should be given effectively as regular expressions, finite automata, or right-linear grammars. In what follows we will assume that a deterministic finite automaton $\mathcal{A}$ is given, with state set Q, initial state q_0, and state transition function $\delta : Q \times (X \cup V) \rightarrow Q$, and that for each nonterminal B a set $F_B \subseteq Q$ of final states is given, such that, with this set of final states, $\mathcal{A}$ recognizes the language R_B. All the usual definitions for context-free grammars also apply to extended context-free grammars, including the definition of NTS.

The algorithm that decides the NTS property for extended context-free grammars is a variation of the one above. First of all, it should be clear that Fact 1 is still true in the extended case (with the same proof). Instead of Fact 2 we will show the following, closely related, fact.

Fact 3. Let $G = (X, V, P, Z)$ be an extended context-free grammar. For all $A, B \in V$, the language $E_{A,B} = \{\alpha B \gamma \mid A \Rightarrow^* \alpha \beta \gamma$ and there is a nearly essential derivation tree for $A \Rightarrow^* \alpha \beta \gamma$, for some $\beta \in R_B\}$ is regular. Moreover, a right-linear grammar for $E_{A,B}$ can be obtained effectively.

First we show, as before, that Facts 1 and 3 imply the decidability of the NTS property. By Fact 1, a grammar G is NTS iff $E_{A,B} \cap LM(G, A)^c = \emptyset$ for all $A, B \in V$. Since $E_{A,B}$ is regular by Fact 3, and since the deterministic context-free languages are (effectively) closed under complement and intersection with a regular language, it suffices to show that $LM(G, A)$ can be recognized by a deterministic pushdown automaton D. As before, D simulates the shift-reduce algorithm, with the first element α of the shift-reduce configuration on its pushdown. To decide between shifting or reducing, D keeps in its finite state the set

S of all states $q \in Q$ (of the finite automaton $\mathcal{A}$) such that $\delta(q_0, \gamma) = q$ for some suffix γ of α. When S contains a final state from some F_B, D makes a reduction, as follows. It pops symbols off its pushdown, simultaneously simulating automaton $\mathcal{A}$ backwards, starting with each of the final states in S (possibly for different B). To keep D deterministic, the backward simulation of $\mathcal{A}$ is with the usual subset construction. Thus, for each of the nonterminals B for which there is a final state in S, D keeps track of a set S_B of states of $\mathcal{A}$. As soon as q_0 turns up in one (or more) of the S_B, D stops popping because it knows that it just has popped the shortest suffix that is the right-hand side of a production. D then pushes the "first" B such that S_B contains q_0. Note that in order to keep track of the set S, D should in fact store S on its pushdown, each time it pushes a symbol. It should be clear that D can be obtained effectively from G.

This shows the decidability of the NTS property. It remains to prove Fact 3.

Proof of Fact 3. A grammar $G' = (X \cup V, V', P', Z')$ for the language $E_{A,B}$ can be defined in much the same way as in the proof of Fact 2. This time V_L consists of all $\langle Y, L, p \rangle$, and V_R of all $\langle q, R, Y \rangle$, with $p, q \in Q$. Intuitively, $\delta(q_0, \phi) = p$ for some prefix ϕ of some $\beta \in R_B$, and $\delta(q, \psi) \in F_B$ for some suffix ψ of β.

Moreover, G' is an extended context-free grammar. Since the regular languages are (effectively) closed under substitution, a right-linear grammar for $E_{A,B}$ can be constructed from G', due to the form of the productions (see the proof of Fact 2).

The productions of G' are very similar to those given in the proof of Fact 2. They are defined as follows.

(1) Productions with left-hand side S. For every production $A \to Y_1 \cdots Y_k$ in P, with $Y_i \in X \cup V$ for $1 \leq i \leq k$, P' contains the following productions.

(1.1) All productions $S \to Y_1 \cdots Y_{i-1} \langle Y_i, L, p \rangle B \langle q, R, Y_j \rangle Y_{j+1} \cdots Y_k$ where $1 \leq i < j \leq k$, $Y_i, Y_j \in V$, and there exists $\pi \in (X \cup V)^*$ such that $\delta(p, \pi) = q$ and $Y_{i+1} \cdots Y_{j-1} \Rightarrow^* \pi$. In the case that $i + 1 = j$ this condition means that $p = q$.

(1.2) All productions $S \to Y_1 \cdots Y_{i-1} B \langle q, R, Y_j \rangle Y_{j+1} \cdots Y_k$ where $1 \leq i < j \leq k$, $Y_j \in V$, and there exists $\pi \in (X \cup V)^*$ such that $\delta(q_0, \pi) = q$ and $Y_i \cdots Y_{j-1} \Rightarrow^* \pi$.

(1.3) All productions $S \to Y_1 \cdots Y_{i-1} \langle Y_i, L, p \rangle B Y_{j+1} \cdots Y_k$ where $1 \leq i < j \leq k$, $Y_i \in V$, and there exists $\pi \in (X \cup V)^*$ such that $\delta(p, \pi) \in F_B$ and $Y_{i+1} \cdots Y_j \Rightarrow^* \pi$.

(1.4) All productions $S \to Y_1 \cdots Y_{i-1} B Y_{j+1} \cdots Y_k$ where $1 \leq i < j \leq k$, and there exists $\beta \in R_B$ such that $Y_i \cdots Y_j \Rightarrow^* \beta$.

(2) Productions with left-hand side in V_L. For every production $Y \to Y_1 \cdots Y_k$ in P, with $Y_i \in X \cup V$ for $1 \leq i \leq k$, P' contains the following productions.

(2.1) All productions $\langle Y, L, p \rangle \to Y_1 \cdots Y_{i-1} \langle Y_i, L, p_1 \rangle$ where $1 \leq i \leq k$, $Y_i \in V$, and there exists $\phi \in (X \cup V)^*$ such that $\delta(p_1, \phi) = p$ and $Y_{i+1} \cdots Y_k \Rightarrow^* \phi$. In the case that $i = k$ the last condition means that $p = p_1$.

(2.2) All productions $\langle Y, L, p \rangle \to Y_1 \cdots Y_{i-1}$ where $2 \leq i \leq k$, and there exists $\phi \in (X \cup V)^*$ such that $\delta(q_0, \phi) = p$ and $Y_i \cdots Y_k \Rightarrow^* \phi$.

(3) Productions with left-hand side in V_R. For every production $Y \to Y_1 \cdots Y_k$ in P, P' contains the following productions.

(3.1) All productions $\langle q, R, Y \rangle \rightarrow \langle q_1, R, Y_j \rangle Y_{j+1} \cdots Y_k$ where $1 \leq j \leq k$, $Y_j \in V$, and there exists $\psi \in (X \cup V)^*$ such that $\delta(q, \psi) = q_1$ and $Y_1 \cdots Y_{j-1} \Rightarrow^* \psi$. In the case that $j = 1$ the last condition means that $q = q_1$.

(3.2) All productions $\langle q, R, Y \rangle \rightarrow Y_{j+1} \cdots Y_k$ where $1 \leq j \leq k - 1$, and there exists $\psi \in (X \cup V)^*$ such that $\delta(q, \psi) \in F_B$ and $Y_1 \cdots Y_j \Rightarrow^* \psi$.

This concludes the description of G'. It remains to show that G' is indeed an extended context-free grammar, and that it can be obtained effectively from G. For this we have to show that the languages $R'_C = \{\beta \in (X \cup V)^* \mid C \rightarrow \beta \in P'\}$ are regular (for each $C \in V'$), and can be obtained effectively from the regular languages R_C (for $C \in V$), i.e., from the automaton $\mathcal{A}$. This is based on the fact that for a given (extended) context-free grammar G and a regular language R, the language $\{\beta \in (X \cup V)^* \mid \beta \Rightarrow^*_G \pi \text{ for some } \pi \in R\}$ is regular, and can be obtained effectively from G and R (for an easy proof see Proposition 2.1 of [2]). From this fact, and the definition of P', it can easily be seen that a finite state transducer (even gsm mapping) τ can be constructed such that $R'_S = \tau(R_A)$. Similarly, $R'_{\langle Y, L, p \rangle}$ and $R'_{\langle q, R, Y \rangle}$ are (effectively) images of R_Y under appropriate finite state transductions. Since the class of regular languages is effectively closed under finite state transductions, this shows that G' is an extended context-free grammar that can be constructed from G. $\square$

References

1. L.Boasson, G.Senizergues; NTS languages are deterministic and congruential, J. of Comp. and Syst. Sci. 31 (1985), 332-342

2. R.V.Book; Decidable sentences of Church-Rosser congruences, Theor. Comput. Sci. 23 (1983), 301-312

3. K.Madlener, P.Narendran, F.Otto, L.Zhang; On weakly confluent monadic string-rewriting systems, Theor. Comput. Sci. 113 (1993), 119-165

4. G.Senizergues; The equivalence and inclusion problems for NTS languages, J. of Comp. and Syst. Sci. 31 (1985), 303-331

Homomorphic Representations by Products of Tree Automata*

Ferenc Gécseg

Department of Informatics
Attila József University
Szeged
Aradi vértanúk tere 1
HUNGARY

Abstract. In this paper we give necessary and sufficient conditions for sets of frontier-to-root tree automata to be homomorphically complete. Moreover, it is shown that–in contrast to the classical case–a homomorphically complete set not necessarily contains a one-element homomorphically complete subset. Similar results can be found in [6] for root-to-frontier (ascending) tree automata.

1 Notions and Notations

Sets of operational symbols will be denoted by Σ and Ω. Finite sets of operational symbols are called *ranked alphabets*. For the subset of Σ consisting of all l-ary operational symbols, we shall use the notation Σ_l ($l \geq 0$). By a Σ-*algebra* we mean a pair $\mathcal{A} = (A, \{\sigma^{\mathcal{A}} | \sigma \in \Sigma\})$, where $\sigma^{\mathcal{A}}$ is an l-ary operation on A if $\sigma \in \Sigma_l$ ($l \geq 0$). If there will be no danger of confusion, then we simply write $\mathcal{A} = (A, \Sigma)$. Moreover, every algebra $\mathcal{A} = (A, \Sigma)$ considered in this paper will be finite, i.e., A is finite and Σ is a ranked alphabet.

A finite subset R of nonnegative integers is a *rank type*. A set Σ of operational symbols is of rank type R, if for all nonnegative integers l, $\Sigma_l \neq \emptyset$ iff $l \in R$. A Σ-algebra is of rank type R if Σ is of rank type R. In the sequel R will be a fixed rank type. Moreover, to avoid trivial cases, we shall suppose that there is an $l \in R$ with $l > 0$. Furthermore, if Σ is a set of operational symbols and X is a set of variables, then the set of all Σ-trees over X will be denoted by $F_\Sigma(X)$. Subsets of $F_\Sigma(X)$ are ΣX-*forests*.

A *frontier-to-root* ΣX-*recognizer* is a system $\mathbf{A} = (\mathcal{A}, \alpha, A')$, where

1) $\mathcal{A} = (A, \Sigma)$ is an algebra,
2) $\alpha : X \to A$ is the *initial assignment*,
3) $A' \subseteq A$ is the set of *final states*.

* The results of this paper were obtained between September 1, 1992 and February 28, 1993 when the author, as a Research Professor of the Academy of Finland, worked with Arto Salomaa in Turku. The research was partially supported by the Hungarian National Foundation for Scientific Research Grant 2035.

In the sequel we shall speak simply of ΣX-recognizers or tree recognizers. The forest *recognized* by a tree recognizer $\mathbf{A}$ will be denoted by $T(\mathbf{A})$. Furthermore, a forest is *recognizable* if there is a tree recognizer which recognizes it.

Let $\Xi = \{\xi_1, \xi_2, \ldots\}$ be a countable set of auxiliary variables. For every $l \geq 0$, let Ξ_l denote the subset of the first l elements of Ξ.

By a *tree transducer* we mean a system $\mathfrak{A} = (\Sigma, X, A, \Omega, Y, P, A')$, where

1) Σ and Ω are ranked alphabets,
2) X and Y are the *frontier alphabets*,
3) A is the finite set of *states*,
4) P is a finite set of *productions* of the following two types:
   i) $x \to aq$ $(x \in X,\ a \in A,\ q \in T_\Omega(Y))$,
   ii) $\sigma(a_1, \ldots, a_l) \to aq(\xi_1, \ldots, \xi_l)$ $(\sigma \in \Sigma_l,\ l \geq 0,\ a_1, \ldots, a_l, a \in A,\ q \in T_\Omega(Y \cup \Xi_l))$,
5) $A' \subseteq A$ is the set of *final states*.

The transformation induced by the transducer $\mathfrak{A}$ will be denoted by $\tau_{\mathfrak{A}}$.

A tree transducer $\mathfrak{A}$ is *deterministic* if there are no two different productions in P with the same left side. Moreover, it is *completely defined* if for every $x \in X$ there is a production in P with left side x and for all $l \geq 0$, $\sigma \in \Sigma_l$ and $a_1, \ldots, a_l \in A$ there is a production in P with left side $\sigma(a_1, \ldots, a_l)$.

All tree transducers considered in this paper will be deterministic and completely defined. In this case $\mathfrak{A}$ can be built on the algebra $\mathcal{A} = (A, \Sigma)$, where for all $l \geq 0$, $\sigma \in \Sigma_l$ and $a_1, \ldots, a_l, a \in A$, $\sigma^{\mathcal{A}}(a_1, \ldots, a_l) = a$ iff there is a production $\sigma(a_1, \ldots, a_l) \to aq$ in P. Using this algebra $\mathcal{A}$, the tree transducer $\mathfrak{A}$ can be given in the form $\mathfrak{A} = (\mathcal{A}, X, \Omega, Y, P, A')$. In the sequel tree transducers will be given in such a form. It is also true that for an arbitrary algebra $\mathcal{A} = (A, \Sigma)$, one can give tree transducers $\mathfrak{A} = (\Sigma, X, A, \Omega, Y, P, A')$ such that $\mathfrak{A} = (\mathcal{A}, X, \Omega, Y, P, A')$.

A tree transformation $\tau : F_\Sigma(X) \to F_\Omega(Y)$ is *inducable* if there is a tree transducer $\mathfrak{A}$ with $\tau = \tau_{\mathfrak{A}}$.

A tree transducer $\mathfrak{A} = (\mathcal{A}, X, \Omega, Y, P, A')$ with $\mathcal{A} = (A, \Sigma)$ (tree recognizer $\mathbf{A} = (\mathcal{A}, \alpha, A')$) is *connected* if

$$\{a \mid \text{there is an } x \to aq \in P \text{ with } x \in X\}$$

generates $\mathcal{A}$. Moreover, $\mathfrak{A}$ is a *relabeling* if the productions have the following special forms: $x \to ay$ $(x \in X,\ a \in A,\ y \in Y)$ and $\sigma(a_1, \ldots, a_l) \to \sigma^{\mathcal{A}}(a_1, \ldots, a_l)\omega(\xi_1, \ldots, \xi_l)$ $(\sigma \in \Sigma_l,\ l \geq 0,\ a_1, \ldots, a_l \in A,\ \omega \in \Omega_l)$.

Let $\mathfrak{A}$ and $\mathfrak{B}$ be two tree transducers. It is said that $\mathfrak{A}$ and $\mathfrak{B}$ are *equivalent* if $\tau_{\mathfrak{A}} = \tau_{\mathfrak{B}}$. Moreover, let $\mathcal{K}$ be a class of tree transducers. Then a tree transducer $\mathfrak{A} \in \mathcal{K}$ is *minimal* in $\mathcal{K}$ if for every $\mathfrak{B} \in \mathcal{K}$ equivalent to $\mathfrak{A}$ we have $|A| \leq |B|$, where $\mathcal{A} = (A, \Sigma)$ is the algebra of $\mathfrak{A}$ and $\mathcal{B} = (B, \Sigma)$ is the algebra of $\mathfrak{B}$. (If $\mathfrak{A}$ and $\mathfrak{B}$ are equivalent tree transducers, then we shall suppose that their algebras are Σ-algebras for the same ranked alphabet Σ.)

Take the algebras $\mathcal{A}_i = (A_i, \Sigma^{(i)})$ $(i = 1, \ldots, k \succ 0)$ with rank type R and let

$$\varphi = \{\varphi_l : (A_1 \times \ldots \times A_k)^l \times \Sigma_l \to \Sigma_l^{(1)} \times \ldots \times \Sigma_l^{(k)} \mid l \in R\}$$

be a family of mappings, where Σ is an arbitrary ranked alphabet of rank type R. Then by the *product* of $\mathcal{A}_1, \ldots, \mathcal{A}_k$ with respect to Σ and φ we mean the algebra $\mathcal{A} = (A, \Sigma)$ with $A = A_1 \times \ldots \times A_k$ such that for arbitrary $l \in R$, $\sigma \in \Sigma_l$ and $(a_{11}, \ldots, a_{1k}), \ldots, (a_{l\bar{1}}, \ldots, a_{lk}) \in A$,

$$\sigma^{\mathcal{A}}((a_{11}, \ldots, a_{1k}), \ldots, (a_{l1}, \ldots, a_{lk})) =$$

$$(\sigma_1^{\mathcal{A}_1}(a_{11}, \ldots, a_{l1}), \ldots, \sigma_k^{\mathcal{A}_k}(a_{1k}, \ldots, a_{lk})),$$

where $(\sigma_1, \ldots, \sigma_k) = \varphi_l((a_{11}, \ldots, a_{1k}), \ldots, (a_{l1}, \ldots, a_{lk}), \sigma)$.

We shall introduce four operators on classes of algebras. Let $\mathcal{K}$ be a class of algebras of rank type R. Then

$\mathbf{P_g}(\mathcal{K})$ is the class of all products of algebras from $\mathcal{K}$,
$\mathbf{S}(\mathcal{K})$ is the class of all subalgebras of algebras from $\mathcal{K}$,
$\mathbf{H}(\mathcal{K})$ is the class of all homomorphic images of algebras from $\mathcal{K}$, and
$\mathbf{I}(\mathcal{K})$ is the class of all isomorphic copies of algebras from $\mathcal{K}$.

A set $\mathcal{K}$ of algebras of rank type R is *forest complete* if for all ranked alphabet Σ of rank type R and alphabet X, each recognizable ΣX-forest can be recognized by a tree recognizer built on an algebra from $\mathbf{P_g}(\mathcal{K})$.

A set $\mathcal{K}$ of algebras of rank type R is *transformation complete* if each inducable tree transformation $\tau : F_\Sigma(X) \rightarrow F_\Omega(Y)$ with Σ of rank type R can be induced by a tree transducer built on a Σ-algebra from $\mathbf{P_g}(\mathcal{K})$.

A set $\mathcal{K}$ of algebras of rank type R is *homomorphically* (*isomorphically*) *complete* if $\mathbf{HSP_g}(\mathcal{K})$ ($\mathbf{ISP_g}(\mathcal{K})$) is the class of all algebras of rank type R.

A set $\mathcal{K}$ of algebras of rank type R is *metrically complete* if for all inducable tree transformation $\tau : F_\Sigma(X) \rightarrow F_\Omega(Y)$ with Σ of rank type R and natural number m, there is a tree transducer $\mathfrak{A} = (A, X, \Omega, Y, P, A')$ built on an algebra $\mathcal{A} = (A, \Sigma)$ from $\mathbf{P_g}(\mathcal{K})$ such that $\tau(p) = \tau_{\mathfrak{A}}(p)$ for all $p \in F_\Sigma(X)$ with $h(p) \leq m$, where $h(p)$ denotes the height of p.

For notions and notations not defined in this paper, see [4].

2 Preliminary Results

The proof of the following result can be found in [4].

Theorem 1. *Let $T \subseteq F_\Sigma(X)$ be a recognizable forest. Then the minimal recognizer $\mathbf{A}$ with $T(\mathbf{A}) = T$ is a homomorphic image of every connected recognizer $\mathbf{B}$ with $T(\mathbf{B}) = T$.* □

Next we recall some notions and notations, and two results from [1].

Let $\tilde{F}_\Sigma(X \cup \Xi_n)$ denote the subset of all those trees from $F_\Sigma(X \cup \Xi_n)$ whose frontiers are $\xi_1 \ldots \xi_n$.

Let $p \in F_\Sigma(X \cup \Xi_n)$ ($n \geq 0$) be a tree. For an $i \in \{1, \ldots, n\}$ $\text{path}_i(p)$ is given in the following way:

(i) $\text{path}_i(p) = \lambda$ if $p = \xi_i$, where λ denotes the empty word,
(ii) $\text{path}_i(p) = \emptyset$ if $p \in (\Sigma_0 \cup X \cup \Xi_n) \setminus \{\xi_i\}$,

(iii) $\text{path}_i(p) = \{jw \mid w \in \text{path}_i(p_j),\ 1 \le j \le l\}$ if $p = \sigma(p_1, \ldots, p_l)$, $l > 0$, $\sigma \in \Sigma_l$, $p_1, \ldots, p_l \in F_\Sigma(X \cup \Xi_n)$.

Let ψ be a mapping of the set of all nonnegative integers into itself. A transducer $\mathfrak{A} = (\mathcal{A}, X, \Omega, Y, P, A')$ belongs to the class $\mathcal{K}(\psi)$ provided it satisfies the following conditions:

(i) if $\sigma(a_1, \ldots, a_l) \to aq \in P$ ($l > 0$, $\sigma \in \Sigma_l$, $a_1, \ldots, a_l, a \in A$), then $q \in \tilde{F}_\Omega(Y \cup \Xi_l)$, q does not contain any symbol from $\Omega_0 \cup Y$, and $|w| = \psi(i)$ holds for all $i \in \{1, \ldots, l\}$ and $w = \text{path}_i(q)$,

(ii) for any $a \in A$, there exist $l \ge 0$, $a_1, \ldots, a_l \in A$ and $p \in F_\Sigma(X \cup \Xi_{l+1})$ such that $p^{\mathcal{A}}(a, a_1, \ldots, a_l) \in A'$.

Take two tree transducers

$$\mathfrak{A} = (\mathcal{A}, X, \Omega, Y, P, A')$$

and

$$\mathfrak{B} = (\mathcal{B}, X, \Omega, Y, P', B'),$$

where $\mathcal{A} = (A, \Sigma)$ and $\mathcal{B} = (B, \Sigma)$. A mapping $\tau : A \to B$ is a *homomorphism* of $\mathfrak{A}$ into $\mathfrak{B}$ if

(i) τ is a homomorphism of $\mathcal{A}$ into $\mathcal{B}$,

(iia) $x \to \tau(a)q \in P'$ if $x \to aq \in P$ ($x \in X$, $a \in A$, $q \in F_\Omega(Y)$),

(iib) $\sigma(\tau(a_1), \ldots, \tau(a_l)) \to \tau(a)q \in P'$ if $\sigma(a_1, \ldots, a_l) \to aq \in P$ ($\sigma \in \Sigma_l$, $l \ge 0$, $a_1, \ldots, a_l, a \in A$, $q \in F_\Sigma(Y \cup \Xi_l)$),

(iii) $\tau(A') \subseteq B'$ and $\tau^{-1}(B') \subseteq A'$.

If τ is an onto homomorphism, then $\mathfrak{B}$ is a *homomorphic image* of $\mathfrak{A}$. If in addition, τ is one-to-one, then we speak about an *isomorphism*. If $A \subseteq B$ and τ is the natural embedding of A into B, then $\mathfrak{A}$ is a *subtransducer* of $\mathfrak{B}$. One can easily show that if the transducer $\mathfrak{B}$ is a homomorphic image of $\mathfrak{A}$, then $\tau_{\mathfrak{B}} = \tau_{\mathfrak{A}}$.

Let $\mathfrak{A} = (\mathcal{A}, X, \Omega, Y, P, A')$ be a transducer and ρ an equivalence relation on A. We say that ρ is a *congruence relation* of $\mathfrak{A}$ if the following conditions are satisfied:

(i) ρ is a congruence relation of $\mathcal{A}$,

(ii) if $\sigma(a_1, \ldots, a_l) \to aq_1$ and $\sigma(b_1, \ldots, b_l) \to bq_2$ are in P and $a_i \equiv b_i(\rho)$ ($i = 1, \ldots, l$), then $q_1 = q_2$ ($\sigma \in \Sigma_l$, $a_1, \ldots, a_l, a, b_1, \ldots, b_l, b \in A$, $q_1, q_2 \in F_\Omega(Y \cup \Xi_l)$),

(iii) A' is the union of certain blocks of the partition induced by ρ on A.

If ρ is a congruence relation of $\mathfrak{A}$, then we can define the *quotient transducer* $\mathfrak{A}/\rho = (\mathcal{A}/\rho, X, \Omega, Y, P', A'/\rho)$ by

$$P' = \{x \to a/\rho q \mid x \to aq \in P,\ x \in X\} \cup$$

$$\{\sigma(a_1/\rho, \ldots, a_l/\rho) \to a/\rho q \mid \sigma(a_1, \ldots, a_l) \to aq \in P, \sigma \in \Sigma_l\}.$$

One can easily show the usual connection between homomorphism and congruence relation: every transducer can be mapped homomorphically onto its quotient transducers, and conversely, every homomorphic image of a transducer is isomorphic to one of its quotient transducers.

For a transducer $\mathfrak{A} = (A, X, \Omega, Y, P, A')$, define the relation $\rho_{\mathfrak{A}}$ in the following way. Take two states a and b of $\mathfrak{A}$. Then $a \equiv b(\rho_{\mathfrak{A}})$ iff for all $n > 0$, $i \in \{1, \ldots, n\}$, $p \in F_{\Sigma}(X \cup \Xi_n)$ and $a_1, \ldots, a_{i-1}, a_{i+1}, \ldots, a_n \in A$, if

$$p(a_1\xi_1, \ldots, a_{i-1}\xi_{i-1}, a\xi_i, a_{i+1}\xi_{i+1}, \ldots, a_n\xi_n) \Rightarrow_{\mathfrak{A}}^* b_1 q_1$$

and

$$p(a_1\xi_1, \ldots, a_{i-1}\xi_{i-1}, b\xi_i, a_{i+1}\xi_{i+1}, \ldots, a_n\xi_n) \Rightarrow_{\mathfrak{A}}^* b_2 q_2$$

then $b_1 \in A' \Leftrightarrow b_2 \in A'$ and $q_1 = q_2$.

As it is noted in [1], the above $\rho_{\mathfrak{A}}$ is not a congruence relation of $\mathfrak{A}$ in general, but it will be a congruence relation if $\mathfrak{A}$ belongs to a class $\mathcal{K}(\psi)$. A transducer $\mathfrak{A} \in \mathcal{K}(\psi)$ is called *reduced* if $\rho_{\mathfrak{A}}$ is the equality relation on the state set of $\mathfrak{A}$.

Now we are ready to recall the next two results from [1].

Theorem 2. *Let $\mathfrak{A}, \mathfrak{B} \in \mathcal{K}(\psi)$ be connected transducers. Then they are equivalent iff $\mathfrak{A}/\rho_{\mathfrak{A}} \equiv \mathfrak{B}/\rho_{\mathfrak{B}}$.* $\square$

Theorem 3. *A transducer is minimal in $\mathcal{K}(\psi)$ if and only if it is both reduced and connected.* $\square$

In the rest of this paper ψ will be the mapping of all nonnegative integers into $\{1\}$. It is obvious that if $\mathfrak{A}$ is a relabeling, then $\mathfrak{A} \in \mathcal{K}(\psi)$.

We now prove

Theorem 4. *Let $\mathfrak{A} = (A, X, \Omega, Y, P, A') \in \mathcal{K}(\psi)$ be arbitrary with $A = (A, \Sigma)$ such that $A' = A$. Let $\mathfrak{B} = (B, X, \Omega, Y, P', B')$ be a connected transducer equivalent to $\mathfrak{A}$. There is a $\mathfrak{C} = (B, X, \Omega, Y, P'', B') \in \mathcal{K}(\psi)$ such that $\mathfrak{C}$ is equivalent to $\mathfrak{A}$.*

Proof. Let $B = (B, \Sigma)$. For an arbitrary $p \in F_{\Sigma}(X)$, if $p \Rightarrow_{\mathfrak{A}}^* aq$ ($a \in A$, $q \in F_{\Omega}(Y)$), then let us denote the state a by a_p. Similarly, if $p \Rightarrow_{\mathfrak{B}}^* bq$ ($b \in B$, $q \in F_{\Omega}(Y)$), then let us use the notation b_p for this b. Now for arbitrary $\sigma \in X \cup \Sigma_0$, $b \in B$, and $q \in F_{\Omega}(Y)$ if $\sigma \to bq \in P'$ then let $\sigma \to bq \in P''$. Moreover, for arbitrary, $m \in R$, $\sigma \in \Sigma_m$ and $a_{p_1}, \ldots a_{p_m} \in A$, if $\sigma(a_{p_1}, \ldots, a_{p_m}) \to \sigma^A(a_{p_1}, \ldots, a_{p_m})\omega \in P'$, then let $\sigma(b_{p_1}, \ldots, b_{p_m}) \to \sigma^B(b_{p_1}, \ldots, b_{p_m})\omega \in P''$. If the resulting transducer $\mathfrak{C}$ is deterministic, then it is obviously equivalent to $\mathfrak{A}$, $\mathfrak{C}$ can be built on the algebra B, and $\mathfrak{C} \in \mathcal{K}(\psi)$. We now show that $\mathfrak{C}$ is deterministic. Take arbitrary $m \in R$, $m > 0$, $\sigma \in \Sigma_m$ and $p_1, \ldots, p_m, p_1', \ldots, p_m' \in F_{\Sigma}(X)$ such that $b_{p_1} = b_{p_1'}, \ldots, b_{p_m} = b_{p_m'}$ and

$$\sigma(a_{p_1}, \ldots, a_{p_m}) \to \sigma^A(a_{p_1}, \ldots, a_{p_m})\omega \in P,$$

$$\sigma(a_{p_1'}, \ldots, a_{p_m'}) \to \sigma^A(a_{p_1'}, \ldots, a_{p_m'})\omega' \in P.$$

Let $\sigma(b_{p_1}, \ldots, b_{p_m}) \to bq \in P'$. Then $q \neq \xi_i$ for any $i = 1, \ldots, m$, since in the opposite case we would have

$$h(\tau_{\mathfrak{B}}(\sigma(p_1, \ldots, p_m)) \leq \max\{h(\tau_{\mathfrak{B}}(p_1)), \ldots, h(\tau_{\mathfrak{B}}(p_m))\},$$

which would contradict the assumption that $\mathfrak{B}$ is equivalent to $\mathfrak{A}$. Similarly, $q \in \Omega_0 \cup Y$ is impossible, too. Therefore, q has the form $q = \bar{\omega}(q_1, \ldots, q_l)$ for some $l > 0$, $\bar{\omega} \in \Omega_l$ and $q_1, \ldots, q_l \in F_{\Omega}(Y \cup \Xi_m)$. Thus, by the equivalence of $\mathfrak{A}$ and $\mathfrak{B}$, we get $\tau_{\mathfrak{A}}(\sigma(p_1, \ldots, p_m)) = \bar{\omega}(r_1, \ldots, r_l)$ and $\tau_{\mathfrak{A}}(\sigma(p'_1, \ldots, p'_m)) = \bar{\omega}(r'_1, \ldots, r'_l)$ for some $r_1, \ldots, r_l, r'_1, \ldots, r'_l \in F_{\Omega}(Y)$. Therefore, $\omega = \bar{\omega} = \omega'$, that is $\mathfrak{C}$ is deterministic. $\square$

From Theorem 4 we get the following corollaries.

Corollary 5. *Let $\mathfrak{A} = (A, X, \Omega, Y, P, A') \in \mathcal{K}(\psi)$ be minimal in $\mathcal{K}(\psi)$ with $A = (A, \Sigma)$ such that $A' = A$. Then $\mathfrak{A}$ is minimal in the class of all tree transducers.*

Proof. Let $\mathfrak{B} = (B, X, \Omega, Y, P', B')$ be an arbitrary connected transducer equivalent to $\mathfrak{A}$. Then, by Theorem 4, there is a $\mathfrak{C} = (C, X, \Omega, Y, P'', C') \in \mathcal{K}(\psi)$ such that $C = B$ and $\mathfrak{C}$ is equivalent to $\mathfrak{A}$. Therefore, $|A| \leq |B|$, where A is the base set of A and B is the base set of B. $\square$

Corollary 6. *Let $\mathfrak{A} = (A, X, \Omega, Y, P, A') \in \mathcal{K}(\psi)$ be minimal in $\mathcal{K}(\psi)$ with $A = (A, \Sigma)$ such that $A' = A$, and let $\mathfrak{B} = (B, X, \Omega, Y, P', B')$ be a connected transducer equivalent to $\mathfrak{A}$. Then A is a homomorphic image of B.*

Proof. Let $\mathfrak{C} \in \mathcal{K}(\psi)$ be the transducer given to $\mathfrak{B}$ in Theorem 4. By Theorems 2 and 3, $\mathfrak{A}$ is a homomorphic image of $\mathfrak{C}$. Therefore, A is a homomorphic image of B. $\square$

3 Results Concerning Homomorphic Completeness

The analogue of the next result is well-known for finita automata.

Theorem 7. *For a set $\mathcal{K}$ of algebras the following statements are equivalent:*

1) *$\mathcal{K}$ is homomorphically complete.*
2) *$\mathcal{K}$ is forest complete.*
3) *$\mathcal{K}$ is transformation complete.*

Proof. To show that 1) implies 2) and 3) it is enough to remark the following. If an algebra A is a homomorphic image of B, then for every recognizer $\mathbf{A} = (A, \alpha, A')$ there is a recognizer $\mathbf{B} = (B, \beta, B')$ such that $\mathbf{A}$ is a homomorphic image of $\mathbf{B}$, and similarly, for every transducer $\mathfrak{A} = (A, X, \Omega, Y, P, A')$ there is a transducer $\mathfrak{B} = (B, X, \Omega, Y, P', B')$ such that $\mathfrak{A}$ is a homomorphic image of $\mathfrak{B}$. Therefore, $T(\mathbf{A}) = T(\mathbf{B})$ and $\tau_{\mathfrak{A}} = \tau_{\mathfrak{B}}$.

Take an algebra $A = (A, \Sigma)$. For an arbitrarily fixed $l \in R$ with $l > 0$, let $\bar{\sigma}$ be a new l-ary operational symbol (i.e. $\bar{\sigma} \notin \Sigma$) which induces the following operation on A. Assume that $A = \{a_0, \ldots, a_{n-1}\}$. Then for any $a_{i_1}, \ldots, a_{i_l} \in A$ let

$$\bar{\sigma}(a_{i_1}, \ldots, a_{i_l}) = a_{i_1+1} \pmod{n}.$$

Set $\bar{\Sigma} = \Sigma \cup \{\bar{\sigma}\}$ and let $\bar{\mathcal{A}} = (A, \bar{\Sigma})$, where $\bar{\sigma}$ has the above realization in $\bar{\mathcal{A}}$ and $\sigma^{\bar{\mathcal{A}}}(b_1, \ldots, b_k) = \sigma^{\mathcal{A}}(b_1, \ldots, b_k)$ for arbitrary $\sigma \in \Sigma_k$, $k \in R$ and $b_1, \ldots, b_k \in A$. For the rest of the proof for any algebra $\mathcal{A} = (A, \Sigma)$ let $\bar{\mathcal{A}}$ be the algebra obtained from $\mathcal{A}$ by the above extension.

To prove that 2) implies 1) take an arbitrary algebra $\mathcal{A} = (A, \Sigma)$ with $A = \{a_0, \ldots, a_{n-1}\}$, and let $\bar{\mathbf{A}} = (\bar{\mathcal{A}}, \alpha, \{a_{n-1}\})$ be the tree recognizer, where $\alpha(x) = a_0$ for all $x \in X$. It can be immediately seen that $\bar{\mathbf{A}}$ is connected and reduced. Therefore, by Definition II.6.9 in [4], $\bar{\mathbf{A}}$ is minimal. By assumption 2), there is a product

$$\bar{\mathcal{B}} = (B, \bar{\Sigma}) = (\mathcal{B}_1 \times \ldots \times \mathcal{B}_k)[\bar{\Sigma}, \varphi]$$

with $\mathcal{B}_i = (B_i, \Sigma^{(i)}) \in \mathcal{K}$ $(i = 1, \ldots, k)$ such that $T(\bar{\mathbf{B}}) = T(\bar{\mathbf{A}})$ for a tree recognizer $\bar{\mathbf{B}} = (\bar{\mathcal{B}}, \beta, \bar{B}')$. Let $\bar{\mathbf{C}} = (\bar{\mathcal{C}}, \beta, \bar{C}')$ be the connected subrecognizer of $\bar{\mathbf{B}}$. Then, by Theorem 1, $\bar{\mathbf{A}}$ is a homomorphic image of $\bar{\mathbf{C}}$. Let $\mathcal{B} = (B, \Sigma)$ be the algebra obtained from $\bar{\mathcal{B}}$ by deleting $\bar{\sigma}$ in $\bar{\Sigma}$. Then $\mathcal{B} \in \mathbf{P}_\mathbf{g}(\mathcal{K})$ obviously holds. Moreover, if $\mathcal{C}$ is obtained from $\bar{\mathcal{C}}$ by deleting $\bar{\sigma}$ in $\bar{\Sigma}$, then $\mathcal{C}$ is a subalgebra of $\mathcal{B}$ and $\mathcal{A}$ is a homomorphic image of $\mathcal{C}$. Thus, $\mathcal{A} \in \mathbf{HSP}_\mathbf{g}(\mathcal{K})$.

To end the proof of Theorem 7, we shall show that 3) implies 1). Again take an arbitrary algebra $\mathcal{A} = (A, \Sigma)$ with $A = \{a_0, \ldots, a_{n-1}\}$. Let $\tilde{\mathfrak{A}} = (\bar{\mathcal{A}}, X, \Omega, X, P, A')$ be the relabeling with $A' = A$, $\Omega_i = \Sigma_i$ if $i \neq l$, and $\Omega_l = \Sigma_l \cup \{\bar{\sigma}_a \mid a \in A\}$. (Remember that l is the rank of the distinguished operational symbol $\bar{\sigma}$.) Moreover, P is defined as follows: $x \to a_0 x \in P$ $(x \in X)$ and

$$\sigma(a_{i_1}, \ldots, a_{i_m}) \to \sigma^{\mathcal{A}}(a_{i_1}, \ldots, a_{i_m})\sigma(\xi_1, \ldots, \xi_m) \in P$$

$(\sigma \in \Sigma_m, m \in R, a_{i_1}, \ldots, a_{i_m} \in A)$. Finally,

$$\bar{\sigma}(a_{i_1}, \ldots, a_{i_l}) \to a_{i_1+1} \pmod{n} \bar{\sigma}_{a_{i_1+1} \pmod{n}} (\xi_1, \ldots, \xi_l) \in P$$

for all $a_{i_1}, \ldots, a_{i_l} \in A$. It can be seen easily that $\tilde{\mathfrak{A}}$ is connected and reduced. Moreover, $\tilde{\mathfrak{A}}$ is in $\mathcal{K}(\psi)$. Thus, by Theorem 3, $\tilde{\mathfrak{A}}$ is minimal in $\mathcal{K}(\psi)$. By assumption 3) there is a product

$$\bar{\mathcal{B}} = (B, \Sigma) = (\mathcal{B}_1 \times \ldots \times \mathcal{B}_k)[\bar{\Sigma}, \varphi]$$

with $\mathcal{B}_i = (B_i, \Sigma^{(i)}) \in \mathcal{K}$ $(i = 1, \ldots, k)$ such that $\tilde{\mathfrak{B}}$ and $\tilde{\mathfrak{A}}$ are equivalent, where $\tilde{\mathfrak{B}} = (\bar{\mathcal{B}}, X, \Omega, X, P', B')$ is a suitable transducer. Let $\tilde{\mathfrak{C}} = (\bar{\mathcal{C}}, X, \Omega, X, P'', C')$ be the connected part of $\tilde{\mathfrak{B}}$, where $\bar{\mathcal{C}} = (C, \bar{\Sigma})$ is the subalgebra of $\bar{\mathcal{B}}$ generated by

$$\{b \mid x \to bq \in P' \text{ for some } x \in X, q \in F_\Sigma(X)\}.$$

By Corollary 6, $\bar{\mathcal{A}}$ is a homomorphic image of $\bar{\mathcal{C}}$. Again let $\mathcal{B} = (B, \Sigma)$ be the algebra obtained from $\bar{\mathcal{B}}$ by deleting $\bar{\sigma} \in \bar{\Sigma}$. Then $\mathcal{B} \in \mathbf{P}_\mathbf{g}(\mathcal{K})$. Moreover, if $\mathcal{C} = (C, \Sigma)$ is obtained from $\bar{\mathcal{C}}$ by deleting $\bar{\sigma}$ in $\bar{\Sigma}$, then $\mathcal{C}$ is a subalgebra of $\mathcal{B}$ and $\mathcal{A}$ is a homomorphic image of $\mathcal{C}$. Therefore, $\mathcal{A} \in \mathbf{HSP}_\mathbf{g}(\mathcal{K})$. $\square$

It is well-known (see [3]) that every homomorphically complete set of finite automata contains a single automaton which is homomorphically complete itself. The following result shows that this is not true for tree automata.

Theorem 8. *Let $t = |R|$. Then there is a t-element set of algebras which is homomorphically complete and minimal.*

Proof. Let $R = \{r_1, \ldots, r_t\}$. For every i $(1 \le i \le t)$, take the algebra $\mathcal{A}_i = (\{0,1\}, \Sigma^{(i)})$, where

$$\Sigma_l^{(i)} = \begin{cases} \{\sigma_0^{(i)}, \sigma_1^{(i)}\} & \text{if } l = r_i, \\ \{\sigma^{(i,l)}\} & \text{otherwise.} \end{cases}$$

Moreover,

$$\sigma_0^{(i)}(a_1, \ldots, a_{r_i}) = 0$$

and

$$\sigma_1^{(i)}(a_1, \ldots, a_{r_i}) = 1$$

for all $a_1, \ldots, a_{r_i} \in \{0,1\}$, and

$$\sigma^{(i,l)}(a_1, \ldots, a_l) = 0$$

for arbitrary $a_1, \ldots, a_l \in \{0,1\}$. Let $\mathcal{A} = (\{0,1\}, \Sigma)$ be an algebra which forms an isomorphically complete set. There exists such an algebra (see [5]). Take a mapping $\tau : \{0,1\}^t \to \{0,1\}$ given by

$$\tau((a_1, \ldots, a_t)) = \begin{cases} 0 \text{ if } a_1 + \ldots + a_t \text{ is even,} \\ 1 \text{ otherwise,} \end{cases}$$

where $(a_1, \ldots, a_t) \in \{0,1\}^t$.
Define the product

$$\mathcal{B} = (\{0,1\}^t, \Sigma) = (\mathcal{A}_1 \times \ldots \times \mathcal{A}_t)[\Sigma, \varphi]$$

in the following way. Take an $l = r_i \in R$, a $\sigma \in \Sigma_l$ and elements $(a_{11}, \ldots, a_{1t})$, $\ldots, (a_{l1}, \ldots, a_{lt}) \in \{0,1\}^t$. Let

$$\varphi^{(l)}((a_{11}, \ldots, a_{1t}), \ldots, (a_{l1}, \ldots, a_{lt}), \sigma) =$$

$$(\sigma^{(1,l)}, \ldots, \sigma^{(i-1,l)}, \sigma_0^{(i)}, \sigma^{(i+1,l)}, \ldots, \sigma^{(t,l)})$$

if $\sigma^{\mathcal{A}}(\tau(a_{11}, \ldots, a_{1t}), \ldots, \tau(a_{l1}, \ldots, a_{lt})) = 0$, and let

$$\varphi^{(l)}((a_{11}, \ldots, a_{1t}), \ldots, (a_{l1}, \ldots, a_{lt}), \sigma) =$$

$$(\sigma^{(1,l)}, \ldots, \sigma^{(i-1,l)}, \sigma_1^{(i)}, \sigma^{(i+1,l)}, \ldots, \sigma^{(t,l)})$$

if $\sigma^{\mathcal{A}}(\tau(a_{11}, \ldots, a_{1t}), \ldots, \tau(a_{l1}, \ldots, a_{lt})) = 1$. In the first case

$$\sigma^{\mathcal{B}}((a_{11}, \ldots, a_{1t}), \ldots, (a_{l1}, \ldots, a_{lt})) = (0, \ldots, 0, 0, 0, \ldots, 0),$$

and in the second case

$$\sigma^B((a_{11}, \ldots, a_{1t}), \ldots, (a_{l1}, \ldots, a_{lt})) = (0, \ldots, 0, 1, 0, \ldots, 0),$$

therefore, τ is a homomorphism of B onto A under the above choice of φ. Since A is isomorphically complete and the formation of the product is associative, $\{A_1, \ldots, A_t\}$ is homomorphically complete.

It remains to be shown that for any i ($1 \leq i \leq t$),

$$\mathcal{K}_i = \{A_1, \ldots, A_{i-1}, A_{i+1}, \ldots, A_t\}$$

is not homomorphically complete. To this it is enough to observe that in every product $A = (A, \Sigma)$ of algebras from $\mathcal{K}_i$ all the identities

$$\sigma_1(x_1, \ldots, x_{r_i}) = \sigma_2(x_1, \ldots, x_{r_i})$$

hold, where $\sigma_1, \sigma_2 \in \Sigma_{r_i}$. This, by Theorem 1 of [2], shows that for every i ($1 \leq i \leq t$) $\mathcal{K}_i$ is not metrically complete, which obviously implies that it is not homomorphically complete. □

By the proof of the above theorem we have the following results.

Corollary 9. *For every t with $1 \leq t \leq |R|$ there is a t-element set of algebras which is homomorphically complete and minimal.* □

Corollary 10. *For every t with $1 \leq t \leq |R|$ there is a t-element set of algebras which is metrically complete and minimal.* □

References

1. Ésik, Z.: Decidability results concerning tree transducers I. Acta Cybernet. **5** (1980) 1-20
2. Gécseg, F.: On a representation of deterministic frontier-to-root tree transformations. Acta. Sci. Math. **45** (1983) 177-187
3. Gécseg, F., Peák, I.: Algebraic theory of automata. Akadémiai Kiadó Budapest 1972
4. Gécseg, F., Steinby, M.: Tree Automata. Akadémiai Kiadó Budapest 1984.
5. Steinby, M.: On the structure and realizations of tree automata. in Second Coll. sur les Arbres en Algèbre et en Programmation Lille 1977 235-248
6. Virágh, J.: Deterministic ascending tree automata II. Acta Cybernet. **6** 1983 291-301

Identities and Transductions *

T. HARJU

Department of Mathematics, University of Turku, SF-20500 Turku, Finland

H.J. HOOGEBOOM   H.C.M. KLEIJN

Department of Computer Science, Leiden University, P.O.Box 9512
2300 RA Leiden, The Netherlands

Abstract. Let ι be the identity relation on the monoid A^*. It is shown that the problem $\iota \subseteq \tau$ is undecidable for rational transductions τ. On the other hand, the problems $\tau \subseteq \iota$ and $\tau = \iota$ are easily seen to be decidable.

1.   Introduction

We shall consider rational transductions $\tau : A^* \to B^*$ realized (defined or accepted) by finite (nondeterministic) transducers $T = (Q, A, B, \delta, q, F)$, where the transition relation δ is a mapping $\delta : Q \times A^* \to 2^{Q \times B^*}$. We refer to [1] for the theory of rational transductions.

A rational transduction τ is a multivalued mapping from the word monoid A^* into the word monoid B^*, where A^* and B^* are generated by the finite alphabets A and B, respectively. We shall also write τ as a relation in the usual way, i.e., $\tau \subseteq A^* \times B^*$. Define the *domain* of τ to be the regular set $\mathrm{dom}(\tau) = \{u \in A^* \mid u\tau \neq \emptyset\}$.

It is well-known, see [1] or [3], that the equivalence problem ($\tau_1 =? \tau_2$) and the inclusion problem ($\tau_1 \subseteq ? \tau_2$) of two rational transductions are undecidable, when the alphabets A and B are large enough. These undecidability results are usually proved by a reduction from the Post Correspondence Problem. Indeed, see [1], in this way it can be proved that it is undecidable whether or not a given rational transduction τ is *universal*, i.e., whether $\tau = \omega_{AB}$ holds, where $\omega_{AB} = A^* \times B^*$. That the corresponding inclusion problem $\omega_{AB} \subseteq \tau$ is undecidable as well, follows from this, because one can trivially decide if $\tau \subseteq \omega_{AB}$ holds.

In [7] Ibarra proved a strong undecidability result stating that one cannot decide the equivalence of two rational transducers with binary input alphabet and unary output alphabet. The proof in [7] reduces the emptiness problem of recursively enumerable languages to the equivalence problem of transducers.

---

*The authors are indebted to BRA Working Group 6317 ASMICS for its support.

Theorem 1.1. *It is undecidable whether or not $\tau = \tau_A$ for a given rational transduction $\tau : A^* \to a^*$, where $\tau_A : A^* \to a^*$ is defined by*

$$u\tau_A = \{a^i \mid |u| \le i \le 3 \cdot |u|\}$$

for a letter a, where A is a binary alphabet. ■

We use this theorem to prove that the identity inclusion problem for rational transductions is undecidable. For a subset $X \subseteq A^*$ we let $\iota_X = \{(u, u) \mid u \in X\}$ be the identity relation on X. In particular, ι_{A^*} is the identity for the whole free monoid A^*. We shall prove that it is undecidable whether or not $\iota_{A^*} \subseteq \tau$ for a given rational transduction $\tau : A^* \to A^*$.

2. Undecidable problem

The proof given for Theorem 1.1 in [7] reveals, in fact, a more detailed result. For this let A be an alphabet with at least two letters and let $a \in A$ be a fixed letter. Denote by $\mathcal{T}$ the family of all rational transductions, and let $\mathcal{T}_+$ be the family of rational transductions $\tau : A \to a^*$ such that τ is realized by a finite transducer $T = (Q, A, \{a\}, \delta, q, F)$ for which the transition relation $\delta : Q \times A \to 2^{Q \times a^*}$ satisfies the condition: $(p, a^k) \in \delta(q, x)$ implies $1 \le k \le 3$. In particular, such a T is nonerasing and does not read the empty word during its transitions.

Clearly, if $\tau \in \mathcal{T}_+$, then $\tau \subseteq \{(u, a^i) \mid |u| \le i \le 3 \cdot |u|\}$. Ibarra proved that it is undecidable whether or not $\tau = \{(u, a^i) \mid |u| \le i \le 3 \cdot |u|\}$ for transductions $\tau \in \mathcal{T}_+$ satisfying the sandwich condition

$$\{(u, a^i) \mid |u| \le i \le 3 \cdot |u|, i \ne 2 \cdot |u|\} \subseteq \tau \subseteq \{(u, a^i) \mid |u| \le i \le 3 \cdot |u|\}$$

for a binary alphabet A. In other words, this can be rewritten as follows.

Theorem 2.1. *It is undecidable whether or not for $\tau \in \mathcal{T}_+$, $a^{2 \cdot |u|} \in u\tau$ for all $u \in A^*$.* ■

This result appears as Lemma 3 of [4]. We shall now tranform this result into the following theorem.

Theorem 2.2. *Let A be a binary alphabet. It is undecidable whether or not $\iota_{A^*} \subseteq \tau$ for a rational transduction $\tau : A^* \to A^*$.*

Proof. Let $\tau : A^* \to a^*$ be a given rational transduction. Define a parity reducing transduction $\tau_P : a^* \to a^*$ as follows: $\mathrm{dom}(\tau) = \{a^{2n} \mid n \ge 0\}$ and $a^{2n}\tau_P = a^n$ for all n. Clearly, τ_P is a rational transduction (in fact, a rational function), and since the rational transductions are closed under compositions, see [1] or [3], also $\tau\tau_P : A^* \to a^*$ is a rational transduction. Further, $\tau\tau_P$ satisfies the following property: $a^{2 \cdot |u|} \in u\tau$ iff $a^{|u|} \in u\tau\tau_P$.

Next, consider the universalizing transduction $\tau_U : a^* \to A^*$, for which $a^n \tau_U = \{v \mid |v| = n\}$. Obviously, also τ_U is rational. We have now

$$a^{2 \cdot |u|} \in u\tau \iff (\forall v \in A^{|u|}): v \in u\tau\tau_P\tau_U \iff (\exists v \in A^{|u|}): v \in u\tau\tau_P\tau_U.$$

Therefore $a^{2 \cdot |u|} \in u\tau$ iff $(u, u) \in \tau\tau_P\tau_U$ from which we deduce that

$$\{(u, a^{2 \cdot |u|}) \mid u \in A^*\} \subseteq \tau \quad \Longleftrightarrow \quad \iota_{A^*} \subseteq \tau\tau_P\tau_U.$$

Hence, a decision procedure for the problem $\iota_{A^*} \subseteq \tau$ would yield such a procedure for the problem $\{(u, a^{2 \cdot |u|}) \mid u \in A^*\} \subseteq \tau$. However, the latter problem is undecidable by Theorem 2.1. ∎

We notice at this point that it is decidable whether or not a *simple* rational transduction is equal to Ibarra's transduction τ_A. This has been shown in [6].

Theorem 2.3. *It is decidable whether or not $\tau = \tau_A$ for a simple rational transduction τ, where τ_A is Ibarra's transduction.* ∎

We remind that a rational transduction τ is *simple*, if it can be realized by a (simple) finite transducer having a unique final state that is equal to its initial state. Clearly, Ibarra's transduction τ_A is simple.

The simple rational transductions were shown in [12] to coincide with the *morphic compositions*, i.e., with the monoid generated by all morphisms $\alpha \in \mathcal{H}$ and their inverse relations $\alpha^{-1} \in \mathcal{H}^{-1}$. In [9] the simple rational transductions are called *starry* transductions.

Now, for a simple rational transduction τ, $\tau^2 \subseteq \tau$, and hence the inclusion $\iota_{A^*} \subseteq \tau$ holds if and only if $(a, a) \in \tau$ for all input letters a. Thus in the simple case the identity inclusion problem is easily shown to be decidable.

Theorem 2.4. *It is decidable whether or not $\iota_{A^*} \subseteq \tau$ for a simple rational transduction τ.* ∎

The interesting point of the above observation comes from the fact that each rational transduction τ can be expressed as a composition $\tau = \mu\tau_s$ of an endmarking $\mu : A^* \to A^*m$, $u\mu = um$, and a simple rational transduction τ_s. We refer to [8], [9] and [12] for this result.

By Theorem 2.2 and the above observations, the endmarking plays a rather complicated role in the representations of rational transductions. This was observed before in [6] in the form of

Theorem 2.5. *It is undecidable whether or not a rational transduction is simple.* ∎

Finite substitutions are simple rational transductions. Indeed, a finite substitution τ is a transduction of the form $\alpha^{-1}\beta$ for two morphisms α and β, where α is a letter-to-letter morphism. By Theorem 2.4, one can decide whether or not $\iota_{A^*} \subseteq \tau$ for a finite substitution $\tau : A^* \to 2^{A^*}$. On the other hand, as shown in [10], it is undecidable whether or not $\iota_R \subseteq \tau$ for a regular set R and a finite substitution τ.

We end this section with an application to linear context-free languages.

For each rational transduction $\tau : A^* \to B^*$ we may design a linear context-free grammar G such that $L(G) = \{u\#v^{\text{rev}} \mid v \in u\tau\}$, where $\#$ is a special marker symbol and rev denotes reversal (mirror image). This construction uses a one-turn push-down automaton P, which simulates the (nondeterministic) finite transducer for τ by writing first the output of the transducer onto its stack, and then checking the stack against the remaining input word after the marker #. Since linear context-free languages coincide with the languages accepted by one-turn push-down automata, the claim for τ and $L(G)$ follows.

We have immediately from Theorem 2.2 the following corollary.

Theorem 2.6. *It is undecidable for linear context-free languages L whether or not* $\{u\#u^{\mathrm{rev}} \mid u \in A^*\} \subseteq L$. ∎

3. Decidable problems

In the other direction the inclusion problem $\tau \subseteq \iota_R$ is easily shown to be decidable for rational transductions τ and regular sets R. Indeed, the above inclusion holds just in case when $\tau = \iota_{\mathrm{dom}(\tau)}$ and $\mathrm{dom}(\tau) \subseteq R$, and in this case τ is a rational function. Since it is decidable whether or not a rational transduction is a partial function, see [11], and the equivalence problem is decidable for rational functions, the claim follows. Also, immediately from this we obtain that the equivalence problem $\tau = \iota_R$ is decidable.

Theorem 3.1. *The equivalence $\tau = \iota_R$ and the inclusion $\tau \subseteq \iota_R$ problems are decidable for rational transductions τ and regular sets R.* ∎

Another way to confirm the above result is to use Ehrenfeucht's Conjecture restricted to regular sets, see [2] or [5].

Theorem 3.2. *Let $S \subseteq C^*$ be a regular set over an alphabet C. There effectively exists a finite subset (test set) F of S such that any two morphisms $\alpha, \beta : C^* \to A^*$ satisfy*

$$(\forall u \in S): u\alpha = u\beta \iff (\forall u \in F): u\alpha = u\beta.$$

∎

By Nivat's Theorem, for each rational transduction $\tau : A^* \to B^*$ there is a regular set $S \subseteq C^*$ together with two morphisms $\alpha : C^* \to A^*$, $\beta : C^* \to B^*$ such that $\tau = \{(u\alpha, u\beta) \mid u \in S\}$. Now, consider the case $A = B$ and let F be the finite test set for S provided by Theorem 3.2. We obtain that $\tau \subseteq \iota_{A^*}$ if and only if $u\alpha = u\beta$ for all $u \in F$. Hence also the problem $\tau \subseteq \iota_{A^*}$ has a finite test set. From this Theorem 3.1 follows, since $\tau \subseteq \iota_R$ for a regular set R iff $\mathrm{dom}(\tau) \subseteq R$ and $\tau \subseteq \iota_{A^*}$.

References

[1] J. Berstel, *Transductions and context-free languages.* B.G. Teubner, Stuttgart (1979).

[2] K. Culik II and J. Karhumäki, Systems of equations over a free monoid and Ehrenfeucht's Conjecture, *Discrete Math.* *43* (1983) 139 – 153.

[3] S. Eilenberg, *Automata, Languages and Machines*. Vol A, Academic Press, New York (1974).

[4] A. Gibbons and W. Rytter, On the decidability of some problems about rational subsets of free partially commutative monoids, *Theoret. Comput. Sci.* *48* (1986) 329 – 337.

[5] T. Harju and J. Karhumäki, On the defect theorem and simplifiability, *Semigroup Forum* *33* (1986) 199 – 217.

[6] T. Harju and H.C.M. Kleijn, Decidability problems for unary output sequential transducers, *Discrete Appl. Math.* *32* (1991) 131 – 140.

[7] O.H. Ibarra, The unsolvability of the equivalence problem for ϵ-free NGSM's with unary input (output) alphabet and applications, *SIAM J. Comput.* *7* (1978) 524 – 532.

[8] J. Karhumäki and M. Linna, A note on morphic characterization of languages, *Discrete Appl. Math.* *5* (1983) 243 – 246.

[9] M. Latteux and J. Leguy, On the composition of morphisms and inverse morphisms, *Lecture Notes in Comput. Sci.* *154* (1983) 420 – 432.

[10] Y. Maon, On the equivalence of some transductions involving letter to letter morphisms on regular languages, *Acta Inf.* *23* (1986) 585 – 596.

[11] M.P. Schützenberger, Sur les relations rationnelles entre monoïdes libres, *Theoret. Comput. Sci.* *3* (1976) 243 – 259.

[12] P. Turakainen, A machine-oriented approach to composition of morphisms and inverse morphisms, *EATCS Bull.* *20* (1983) 162 – 166.

Decomposition of Infinite Labeled 2-structures

T. HARJU

Department of Mathematics, University of Turku, SF-20500 Turku, Finland

G. ROZENBERG

*Department of Computer Science, Leiden University, P.O.Box 9512
2300 RA Leiden, The Netherlands*

and

*Department of Computer Science, University of Colorado at Boulder
Boulder, Co 80309, U.S.A.*

Abstract. We generalize the decomposition theorem for finite 2-structures (from Ehrenfeucht and Rozenberg, *Theoret. Comput. Sci.* 70 (1990)) to infinite labeled 2-structures. It is shown that if an infinite labeled 2-structure g has at least one maximal prime clan, then its maximal prime clans form a partition of the domain of g, and the quotient w.r.t. this partition is linear, complete or primitive. Also, we show that the infinite primitive labeled 2-structures are upward hereditary, *i.e.*, if h is a primitive substructure of a primitive g, then h can be extended to a primitive substructure h' of g by adding one or two nodes to h.

1. Introduction

For a nonempty set D denote by

$$E_2(D) = \{(x, y) \mid x, y \in D, \ x \neq y\}$$

the complete set of (directed) *edges* between the elements of D. A *labeled 2-structure* (abbreviated as *ℓ2s*) $g = (D, \lambda, \Delta)$ is an edge-labeled directed graph with the *domain* D as its nodes, the set $E_2(D)$ as its edges and $\lambda : E_2(D) \to \Delta$ as its labeling function. In this paper the domain D and the set Δ of labels can be infinite.

In [2] labeled 2-structures were studied on finite domains. The main result of [2] states that for every (finite) *ℓ2s* $g = (D, \lambda, \Delta)$ the quotient w.r.t. the maximal prime clans is either linear (*i.e.*, a linear ordering of its nodes), or complete (*i.e.*, a complete graph), or primitive (*i.e.*, congruence free).

In this paper we shall prove that this basic result holds for those infinite labeled 2-structures that possess at least one maximal prime clan. Therefore the infinite $\ell 2s$'s can be divided into four categories: those whose quotient w.r.t. maximal prime clans are (1) linear, (2) complete, or (3) primitive, and those with (4) no maximal primes.

In [3] it was shown that every primitive $\ell 2s$ with n nodes has a primitive substructure of $n-1$ or $n-2$ nodes. We give an example demonstrating that this *downward hereditary property* of primitivity does not hold for infinite $\ell 2s$'s. Indeed, there is an infinite primitive $\ell 2s$, where removing any finite number of nodes results in a nonprimitive substructure. However, we show that the infinite primitive $\ell 2s$'s do have the following *upward hereditary property*: If h is a primitive substructure of a primitive g, then h can be extended to a primitive substructure h' of g by adding one or two nodes to h. The downward hereditary property of finite $\ell 2s$'s follows from this result, and, indeed, it improves the basic results of [3] by showing that any primitive substructure of a finite primitive g can be extended to g in small steps.

Decomposition of finite graphs has been studied in many papers. One should mention at least Gallai's article [5], which has inspired many other papers on the topic. One of these is Kelly's article [6], where decomposition and primitivity of infinite graphs is considered in the context of comparability graphs. In the present paper we have adopted the terminology of [2], which differs from that of [6]. We refer also to [1] for the history and applications of decomposition of graphs.

2. Preliminaries on labeled 2-structures

Let D be a nonempty set. For an edge $e = (x,y) \in E_2(D)$ we let $e^{-1} = (y,x)$ be the *inverse edge* of e.

Each labeled 2-structure g is determined uniquelly by its labeling function, and therefore we shall later identify an $\ell 2s$ with its labeling function. Hence we shall write $g : E_2(D) \to \Delta$ for an $\ell 2s$ $g = (D, \lambda, \Delta)$.

If the domain D of g is finite, then g is said to be a *finite* labeled 2-structure.

Let $X \subseteq D$ be a nonempty subset of $g : E_2(D) \to \Delta$. The *substructure induced by* X is the $\ell 2s$ $\mathrm{sub}_g(X) : E_2(X) \to \Delta$ such that $\mathrm{sub}_g(X)(e) = g(e)$ for all $e \in E_2(X)$.

The notion of a clan is central for the decomposition of labeled 2-structures. We say that a subset X is a *clan* of g, if for all $x, y \in X$ and $z \notin X$, $g(z,x) = g(z,y)$ and $g(x,z) = g(y,z)$. Clearly, the sets $\emptyset$, D and $\{x\}$ for all $x \in D$ are clans of g. We shall call these the *trivial clans* of g.

We shall denote by $\mathcal{C}(g)$ the family of clans of g, and by $\mathcal{C}^+(g)$ the family of all *nontrivial* clans of g. Further, if $X \in \mathcal{C}(g)$, then the substructure $\mathrm{sub}_g(X)$ is called a *factor* of g.

A $g : E_2(D) \to \Delta$ is said to be *reversible*, if for each label $b \in \Delta$ there is a unique *inverse label* $b^{-1} \in \Delta$ such that g satisfies the identity $g(e^{-1}) = g(e)^{-1}$ for all $e \in E_2(D)$. The family of reversible labeled 2-structures on the domain D and with the set of labels Δ will be denoted by $\mathcal{R}_\Delta^D$.

For a label $b \in \Delta$ of a reversible $g \in \mathcal{R}_\Delta^D$ we shall call the set $b^{\pm 1} = \{b, b^{-1}\}$

the *feature* of g determined by b. If the size $|b^{\pm 1}|$ of a feature determined by b is one, then $b = b^{-1}$ and in this case the label b is said to be *symmetric*.

Clearly, each (undirected) graph $G = (V, E)$ without loops can be interpreted as an $\ell 2s$ with two symmetric labels, say a and b, such that for each $e \in E_2(V)$, $g(e) = a = g(e^{-1})$, if $e \in E$, and $g(e) = b = g(e^{-1})$, if $e \notin E$. For this reason an $\ell 2s$ $g : E_2(D) \to \Delta$ is called a *graph*, if Δ consists of two symmetric labels.

As in [2] we may restrict ourselves to reversible $\ell 2s$'s, when the labeled 2-structures are studied with respect to their factors. To see this define for a $g : E_2(D) \to \Delta$ a new $\ell 2s$ $g' : E_2(D) \to \Delta \times \Delta$ by $g'(e) = (g(e), g(e^{-1}))$ for each $e \in E_2(D)$. Now, g' is clearly reversible, and as easily seen ([2]), $C(g) = C(g')$. Moreover, the preservation of clans is inherited by the substructures: for each substructure $\text{sub}_g(X)$ of g, $C(\text{sub}_g(X)) = C(\text{sub}_{g'}(X))$.

In the rest of the paper we shall consider reversible labeled 2-structures only.

3. Maximal clans and prime clans

For a family $\mathcal{A}$ of sets we shall denote

$$\cup \mathcal{A} = \bigcup_{A \in \mathcal{A}} A \quad \text{and} \quad \cap \mathcal{A} \bigcap_{A \in \mathcal{A}} A.$$

Further, we say that two sets A and B *overlap*, if $A \cap B$, $A \setminus B$ and $B \setminus A$ are nonempty.

The following lemma gives the basic properties of clans of an $\ell 2s$. The claims of this lemma are straightforward generalizations of [2].

Lemma 3.1. *Let* $g \in \mathcal{R}_\Delta^D$, *and let* $\mathcal{A} \subseteq C(g)$.

(1) $\cap \mathcal{A} \in C(g)$.

(2) *If* $\cap \mathcal{A} \neq \emptyset$, *then* $\cup \mathcal{A} \in C(g)$.

(3) *If* $A, B \in C(g)$ *and* $A \setminus B \neq \emptyset$, *then* $B \setminus A \in C(g)$. ∎

In particular, for each $g \in \mathcal{R}_\Delta^D$ and $A \subseteq D$ there exists the *smallest clan* $B \in C(g)$ such that $A \subseteq B$, since $D \in C(g)$ and $C(g)$ is closed under intersection. The clans of a $g \in \mathcal{R}_\Delta^D$ are inherited by a substructure h as follows.

Lemma 3.2. *Let* $h : E_2(F) \to \Delta$ *be a substructure of* $g \in \mathcal{R}_\Delta^D$. *If* $X \in C(g)$, *then* $X \cap F \in C(h)$. ∎

We say that a clan $A \in C(g)$ is *proper*, if $A \neq D$, and *maximal*, if it is maximal w.r.t. the inclusion relation among the proper clans. The family of maximal clans of g is denoted by $C_{\max}(g)$. Further, $P \subseteq D$ is called a *prime clan*, if it is a nonempty clan that does not overlap with any $B \in C(g)$. A prime clan P is *maximal*, if it is maximal w.r.t. the inclusion relation among the proper prime clans. We shall denote by $\mathcal{P}(g)$ and $\mathcal{P}_{\max}(g)$ the families of prime clans and maximal prime clans of g, respectively. Clearly, if $P_1, P_2 \in \mathcal{P}_{\max}(g)$, then

$P_1 \cap P_2 = \emptyset$. Note that a maximal prime clan is, by definition, always a proper clan.

An $\ell 2$s $g \in \mathcal{R}^D_\Delta$ is said to be *primitive*, if it has only trivial clans, and *special*, if it has only trivial prime clans. Further, g is *linear*, if there is a label $b \in \Delta$ that linearly orders the domain D: $x < y$ if and only if $g(x,y) = b$. Since g is assumed to be reversible, it follows that $x < y$ if and only if $g(y,x) = b^{-1}$ and thus the inverse label b^{-1} also linearly orders D. Moreover, g is said to be *complete*, if g has a symmetric label b such that $g(e) = b$ for all $e \in E_2(D)$.

The decomposition result of [2] is based on the partition of the domain into maximal prime clans. Notice that we may have that $\mathcal{C}_{\max}(g) = \emptyset$ and $\mathcal{P}_{\max}(g) = \emptyset$ as shown in the following example (from [6]). However, the nonempty trivial clans are always primes, and hence $\mathcal{P}(g) \neq \emptyset$.

Example 3.1. Let $D = \mathbb{Z} \times \{0,1\}$ and $\Delta = \{a,b\}$. Define an $\ell 2$s $g \in \mathcal{R}^D_\Delta$, where both of the labels a and b are symmetric, such that $g(e) = a$, if $e = ((n,0),(m,0))$ for $n, m \in \mathbb{Z}$ or $e = ((n,0),(m,1))$ for $n \in \mathbb{Z}$ and $m \leq n$; otherwise, $g(e) = b$.

Hence, in our terminology, g is a graph. In Figure 1 we have drawn a finite substructure of g, where we have omitted the label b, *i.e.*, each drawn edge has label a and if an edge is missing, then it has the label b in g.

We observe here that a node $(n,0)$ sees the nodes $(n,1)$ and $(n+1,1)$ differently, and the node $(n,1)$ sees the nodes $(n,0)$ and $(n-1,0)$ differently. Using these simple facts, we deduce that the clans of g are the trivial clans together with the infinite sets $A_n = \{((i,0),(j,1)) \mid i,j \leq n\}$ and $B_n = \{((i,0),(j,1)) \mid i \leq n, j \leq n+1\}$ for $n \in \mathbb{Z}$. We have also that $A_n \subseteq B_n \subseteq A_{n+1}$ for all n, and thus the family $\mathcal{C}^+(g)$ of nontrivial clans forms an infinite ascending chain. In particular, none of the clans overlap with another clan, and therefore all the nonempty clans of g are prime clans, $\mathcal{P}(g) = \mathcal{C}(g) \setminus \{\emptyset\}$. It follows that g has no maximal clans and no maximal prime clans. ∎

The next immediate result, see [2], is used to prove that quotients of labeled 2-structures are well-defined.

Lemma 3.3. *Let $A, B \in \mathcal{C}(g)$ be two disjoint clans of $g \in \mathcal{R}^D_\Delta$. There is a label $b \in \Delta$ such that $g(x,y) = b$ for all $x \in A$ and $y \in B$.* ∎

Let $\mathcal{A} \subseteq \mathcal{C}(g)$ be a partition of the domain D into disjoint clans of g. Such a partition is called a *clan partition* of g. For a clan partition $\mathcal{A}$ each substructure $\text{sub}_g(A)$ with $A \in \mathcal{A}$ is a factor of g. We define the *quotient* $g/\mathcal{A}$ of g by $\mathcal{A}$ as the reversible $\ell 2$s with domain $\mathcal{A}$ such that for all $A, B \in \mathcal{A}$, $(g/\mathcal{A})(A,B) = g(x,y)$, whenever $x \in A$ and $y \in B$. Clearly, by Lemma 3.3, the quotient is well-defined.

The proof of [2, Theorem 4.17(2)] does not use the finiteness of the domain, and hence we have in general the following statement.

Lemma 3.4. *Let $g \in \mathcal{R}^D_\Delta$, and let $\mathcal{A}$ be a clan partition such that $\mathcal{A} \subseteq \mathcal{P}(g)$. If $B \in \mathcal{P}(g/\mathcal{A})$, then $\cup B \in \mathcal{P}(g)$.* ∎

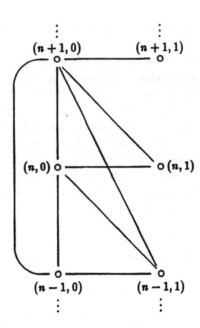

Figure 1: A 2-structure with no maximal primes

Although maximal clans may not exist in an infinite $\ell 2$s, there are clans that are maximal in certain subfamilies of clans. For a property p of subsets of an $\ell 2$s g, we shall say that A is a *locally maximal clan satisfying* p, if A is maximal (w.r.t. inclusion) among the clans possessing the property p. Note that, in general, a clan A that is locally maximal satisfying a property p does not need to be a proper clan.

Lemma 3.5. *Let* $g \in \mathcal{R}_\Delta^D$, $A \subset D$, *and let* $y \notin A$. *There exists a unique nonempty locally maximal clan* M *satisfying* $A \cap M = \emptyset$ *and* $y \in M$.

Proof. Consider the family

$$\mathcal{A} = \{X \mid X \in \mathcal{C}(g), A \cap X = \emptyset, y \in X\}.$$

This is nonempty, because $\{y\} \in \mathcal{A}$. Since $y \in \cap\mathcal{A}$, also $\cup\mathcal{A} \in \mathcal{C}(g)$ by Lemma 3.1(1). Clearly, $\cup\mathcal{A}$ satisfies the requirements of the claim. ∎

In particular, if $x, y \in D$ are distinct nodes of g, then there exists a locally maximal clan M satisfying $x \notin M$ and $y \in M$. It follows from this that for each node x, there is a locally maximal clan M satisfying $x \notin M$.

Notice that Lemma 3.5 does not state that the locally maximal clans should be nontrivial. Indeed, it can happen that such a clan is a singleton (take *e.g.* a primitive $\ell 2$s).

We say that a $g \in \mathcal{R}_\Delta^D$ satisfies the *maximal clan condition*, or *MCC* for short, (*maximal prime clan condition*, or *MPC* for short), if for each $x \in D$ there exists a maximal clan (maximal prime clan, resp.) containing x.

If g satisfies MPC, then $\mathcal{P}_{\max}(g)$ exists and it is a clan partition. Hence MPC implies that $g/\mathcal{P}_{\max}(g)$ is a well-defined quotient of g. Note that if g is finite, then it satisfies both MCC and MPC.

Theorem 3.1. *If $g \in \mathcal{R}_\Delta^D$ satisfies MCC, then it satisfies MPC. In fact, if $M \in \mathcal{C}_{\max}(g)$ then $M \in \mathcal{P}_{\max}(g)$ or $D \setminus M \in \mathcal{P}_{\max}(g)$.*

Proof. Assume that $M \in \mathcal{C}_{\max}(g)$. If $|M| = 1$, then clearly $M \in \mathcal{P}_{\max}(g)$. Suppose thus that M is nontrivial and assume that $M \notin \mathcal{P}(g)$.

There is a $Z \in \mathcal{C}(g)$, which overlaps with M, and, by Lemma 3.1(2), also $M \cup Z \in \mathcal{C}(g)$ and $Z \setminus M \in \mathcal{C}(g)$. By maximality of M, we have $M \cup Z = D$, and therefore $Z \setminus M = D \setminus M$. We shall prove that $D \setminus M$ is a maximal prime clan.

First of all, if $X \in \mathcal{C}(g)$ overlaps with $D \setminus M$, then X overlaps with M, and hence, by above, $X \setminus M = D \setminus M$, i.e., $D \setminus M \subseteq X$, which contradicts the assumption that X overlaps with $D \setminus M$. Therefore $D \setminus M \in \mathcal{P}(g)$.

In order to show that $D \setminus M$ is a maximal prime clan, assume that $D \setminus M \subset P$ for a $P \in \mathcal{P}(g)$. Now, since $P \in \mathcal{P}(g)$ and $M \in \mathcal{C}(g)$, we have that $M \subseteq P$. Thus $P = D$, and hence, indeed, $D \setminus M \in \mathcal{P}_{\max}(g)$. ∎

The converse of Theorem 3.1 does not hold. To see this consider $g \in \mathcal{R}_\Delta^D$, where $D = \mathbb{Z}$ is given its natural linear ordering, i.e., for the labels $b \neq b^{-1}$ define $g(n, m) = b$, if $n < m$, and $g(n, m) = b^{-1}$, if $n > m$. Now, g has only trivial prime clans. The proper clans of g are the intervals $[n, m] = \{i \mid n \le i \le m\}$, $[n, \infty) = \{i \mid n \le i\}$, and $(-\infty, m] = \{i \mid i \le m\}$ for all $n, m \in \mathbb{Z}$. In this example g has no maximal clans, but g satisfies MPC.

4. Special labeled 2-structures

In this section we generalize the basic decomposition results of [2] by showing that special ℓ2s's are primitive, linear or complete. We remind that an ℓ2s g is special, if its prime clans are trivial.

An ℓ2s $g : E_2(D) \to \Delta$ is called *angular*, [4], if each three node set $T = \{x, y, z\} \subseteq D$ induces a nonprimitive substructure $\mathrm{sub}_g(T)$. Angularity may be regarded as a weak version of transitivity. In an angular g a nonsymmetric label induces a partial ordering of the domain. However, a symmetric label may be nontransitive. Finite angular ℓ2s's were shown in [4] to have rather nice properties. Here we use this notion as a mid step towards the decomposition theorem.

Lemma 4.1. *Let $g \in \mathcal{R}_\Delta^D$ be special and nonprimitive, and let $x \in D$. Then there exists a nontrivial clan $A \in \mathcal{C}^+(g)$ with $x \in A$.*

Proof. By Lemma 3.5 there is a locally maximal clan B satisfying $x \notin B$. If B is nontrivial, then, since g is special, B overlaps with a $A \in \mathcal{C}^+(g)$. By Lemma 3.1(2), $A \cup B \in \mathcal{C}(g)$, and by maximality of B, $x \in A \cup B$. It follows that $x \in A$ as required by the claim.

On the other hand, if each locally maximal $B \in \mathcal{C}(g)$ satisfying $x \notin B$ is trivial, then $x \in A$ for each nontrivial $A \in \mathcal{C}(g)$. Moreover such a nontrivial A exists, since g is nonprimitive. This proves the claim. ∎

Lemma 4.2. *If $g \in \mathcal{R}_\Delta^D$ is special and nonprimitive, then g is angular.*

Proof. If g has at most three nodes, then the claim is obvious. Suppose then that $|D| > 3$, and let $T = \{x, y, z\}$ be a three node subset of D. We show that there is a clan $A \in \mathcal{C}(g)$ such that $|T \cap A| = 2$. This implies that g is angular, because now, by Lemma 3.2, $T \cap A$ is a nontrivial clan of $\mathrm{sub}_g(T)$.

Let $B \in \mathcal{C}(g)$ be the smallest clan such that $T \subseteq B$. If $B \neq D$, then there is an $X \in \mathcal{C}(g)$, which overlaps with B, since g is special. In this case, by Lemma 3.1, $B \setminus X \in \mathcal{C}(g)$ and $B \cap X \in \mathcal{C}(g)$, and either one of these has exactly two nodes of T. For, otherwise one of these clans would be a smaller clan than B containing T.

Assume then that $B = D$. By Lemma 4.1 there is a $Y \in \mathcal{C}^+(g)$ such that $y \in Y$. Since $Y \neq D = B$, we have that $x \notin Y$ or $z \notin Y$. Further, if $x \in Y$ or $z \in Y$, then $A = Y$ is a required clan. Suppose thus that $T \cap Y = \{y\}$. By Lemma 3.5 we may suppose that Y is locally maximal satisfying $y \in Y$ and $x, z \notin Y$. Since g is special, Y overlaps with some $Z \in \mathcal{C}^+(g)$. By Lemma 3.1, $Y \cup Z \in \mathcal{C}(g)$ and $Z \setminus Y \in \mathcal{C}(g)$. Further, by maximality of Y, x or z is in $Y \cup Z$. If $x \notin Z$ or $z \notin Z$, then $A = Y \cup Z$ is a required clan. On the other hand, if $x, z \in Z$, then $A = Z \setminus Y$ is a required clan, since $x, z \notin Y$ and $y \in Y$. This proves the claim. ∎

We say that a subset $X \subseteq D$ of $g \in \mathcal{R}_\Delta^D$ is a *connected component*, if there is a label $b \in \Delta$ such that

(1) for all distinct nodes $x, y \in X$ there is a finite path $e_1 e_2 \ldots e_n$, $e_i = (x_i, x_{i+1}) \in E_2(D)$ for $1 \leq i \leq n$, such that $x = x_1$, $y = x_{n+1}$ and $g(e_i) \in b^{\pm 1}$, and

(2) for all $z \notin X$, $g(z, x) \notin b^{\pm 1}$ for all $x \in X$.

Notice that in the definition of a connected component we do not distinguish between a label b and its inverse label b^{-1}. We say also that a connected component as above is a *b-connected component*.

We say that a $g \in \mathcal{R}_\Delta^D$ is *connected*, if D is the unique connected component for all labels $b \in \Delta$ that occur as a label of an edge. Notice that our definition of connectivity differs from that in [2].

The next lemma improves a result of [4].

Lemma 4.3. *Let $g \in \mathcal{R}_\Delta^D$ be angular. Each connected component of g is a prime clan. In particular, if g is special and angular, then g is connected.*

Proof. Let X be a b-connected component for a label $b \in \Delta$. We show that X is a clan. Assume to the contrary that there exists a $z \notin X$ and two nodes $x, y \in X$ such that $g(z, x) \neq g(z, y)$. By the definition of a b-connected component there is a path $e_1e_2 \ldots e_n$, $e_i = (x_i, x_{i+1}) \in E_2(D)$, such that $x = x_1$, $y = x_{n+1}$ and $g(e_i) \in b^{\pm 1}$. It follows that for some i, $g(z, x_i) \neq g(z, x_{i+1})$. On the other hand, since X is a connected component, $g(z, x_i) \notin b^{\pm 1}$ and $g(z, x_{i+1}) \notin b^{\pm 1}$. This contradicts the angularity of g: the substructure induced by $\{z, x_i, x_{i+1}\}$ is primitive. Therefore X is a clan of g.

To show that X is a prime clan suppose that a clan $A \in C(g)$ overlaps with X. Let $z \in A \setminus X$ and $y \in A \cap X$. Since X is a b-connected component and $X \setminus A \neq \emptyset$, there is a node $x \in X \setminus A$ such that $g(y, x) \in b^{\pm 1}$. However, this implies that $g(z, x) \in b^{\pm 1}$, because $A \in C(g)$ and $y, z \in A$. This contradicts the fact that X is a b-connected component, and proves that $X \in P(g)$. ∎

A $g \in \mathcal{R}_\Delta^D$ is monochromatic, if there is a label $b \in \Delta$ such that $g(e) \in b^{\pm 1}$ for all $e \in E_2(D)$.

The following lemma is obvious, because a monochromatic $g \in \mathcal{R}_\Delta^D$ is angular if and only if it is transitive w.r.t. its labels.

Lemma 4.4. *If $g \in \mathcal{R}_\Delta^D$ is angular and monochromatic, then it is either linear or complete.* ∎

Our first main result improves Lemma 4.2 by showing that angular and special g is either linear or complete.

Theorem 4.1. *A $g \in \mathcal{R}_\Delta^D$ is special if and only if g is primitive, linear or complete.*

Proof. In the one direction the claim is immediate, since if g is primitive, linear or complete, then clearly it is special.

Assume then that g is special and nonprimitive. By Lemma 4.2 we know that g is angular. By Lemma 4.4 it suffices to show that g is monochromatic.

By assumption there is a nontrivial $A \in C^+(g)$. Let $x \notin A$. By Lemma 3.1(2) there is a locally maximal clan Y ($= \cup\{C \mid A \subseteq C, x \notin C\}$) satisfying $A \subseteq Y$ and $x \notin Y$. Since g is special, there is a $B \in C^+(g)$ overlapping with Y. By maximality of Y, $x \in B \cup Y$, and hence $x \in B$. Choose then a node $z \in Y \setminus B$. Again, by Lemma 3.1(2), there is a locally maximal $X \in C(g)$ satisfying $B \subseteq X$ and $z \notin X$.

By above the clans X and Y overlap, and thus by Lemma 3.1, $X \cup Y \in C(g)$.

Assume first that $X \cup Y \neq D$. Now, since g is special, there is a clan Z that overlaps with $X \cup Y$. We have that $Z \cap X \neq \emptyset$, because otherwise $x \notin Z \cup Y$ and $Z \cup Y \in C(g)$ would contradict the maximality of Y. Therefore by Lemma 3.1, $Z \cup X \in C(g)$, and hence by maximality of X, $z \in Z$. Similarly we derive that $Z \cap Y \neq \emptyset$ and $y \in Z$.

We have also that $X \setminus Z \neq \emptyset$ or $Y \setminus Z \neq \emptyset$, because Z overlaps with $X \cup Y$. If $X \setminus Z \neq \emptyset$, then Lemma 3.1(3) implies that $Z \setminus X \in C(g)$ and, moreover, $z \in (Z \setminus X) \cap Y \neq \emptyset$. Therefore $(Z \setminus X) \cup Y \in C(g)$ contradicts maximality of Y. Similarly, $Y \setminus Z \neq \emptyset$ yields a contradiction.

Hence we must have that $X \cup Y = D$. Now, the clans $X \setminus Y$ and Y partition the domain D into two disjoint clans. By Lemma 3.3 there is a label b such that $g(u, v) = b$ for all $u \in X \setminus Y$ and $v \in Y$. Since g is angular, it follows from Lemma 4.3 that g is c-connected for all labels c. Hence, by above, g is monochromatic: $g(e) \in b^{\pm 1}$ for all $e \in E_2(D)$. ∎

The main decomposition theorem of [2] generalizes to infinite $\ell 2$s's as follows.

Theorem 4.2. Assume $g \in \mathcal{R}_\Delta^D$ has a maximal prime clan. Then g satisfies MPC, and $g/\mathcal{P}_{\max}(g)$ is linear, complete or primitive.

Proof. To prove the first claim let $x \in D$. Consider now the family of proper prime clans containing x:

$$\mathcal{P}_x = \{A \in \mathcal{P}(g) \mid x \in A \text{ and } A \neq D\}.$$

The family $\mathcal{P}_x$ is nonempty, since $\{x\}$ is in it. This family is linearly ordered by inclusion, i.e., for all $A_1, A_2 \in \mathcal{P}_x$, either $A_1 \subseteq A_2$ or $A_2 \subseteq A_1$, since $A_1 \cap A_2 \neq \emptyset$ and both are prime clans. Also, by Lemma 3.1(2), $M_x = \cup \mathcal{P}_x$ is a clan of g, and, it is a prime clan, because if a clan Z would overlap with M_x, then Z would overlap with some prime from $\mathcal{P}_x$. Therefore, either M_x is the unique maximal prime clan such that $x \in M_x$, or $M_x = D$. If the latter case holds, then for each $y \in D$, there is a prime $A \in \mathcal{P}_x$ such that $y \in A$, and consequently, there does not exist a maximal prime clan containing y. Hence, if $M_x = D$ for a node x, then $M_y = D$ for all $y \in D$. However, by assumption g has a maximal prime clan, say M, and therefore $M_y = M \neq D$ for all $y \in M$. Hence $M_x \neq D$, and so g satisfies MPC.

To prove the second claim, consider the clan partition $\mathcal{P}_{\max}(g)$ of D. By Lemma 3.4, if $Q \in \mathcal{P}(h)$ for $h = g/\mathcal{P}_{\max}(g)$, then $\cup Q \in \mathcal{P}(g)$. But in g the elements of Q are maximal prime clans, and hence either $\cup Q \in \mathcal{P}_{\max}(g)$ or $\cup Q = D$. We conclude that Q is a trivial clan of the quotient h. This shows that h is special, and hence the claim follows by Theorem 4.1. ∎

Theorem 4.2 does not imply that the factors of an $\ell 2$s g, for which $\mathcal{P}_{\max}(g)$ exists, would also have this maximal prime property. Indeed, for any $h \in \mathcal{R}_\Delta^D$ let x be a new node and b a new label, and define g on the domain $D \cup \{x\}$ such that h is a factor of g: $g(x, u) = b = g(u, x)$ for all $u \in D$. Clearly, $\mathcal{P}_{\max}(g) = \{D, \{x\}\}$ and $g/\mathcal{P}_{\max}(g)$ is a complete $\ell 2$s with two nodes. However, $\mathcal{P}_{\max}(h)$ may or may not exist.

Let us say that $g \in \mathcal{R}_\Delta^D$ is *fully decomposable*, if for each nonsingleton $P \in \mathcal{P}(g)$, the factor $\mathrm{sub}_g(P)$ has a maximal prime clan, and therefore by Theorem 4.2, $\mathcal{P}_{\max}(\mathrm{sub}_g(P))$ exists. Clearly, every finite g is fully decomposable.

In [2] a *shape* is defined for a (finite) $g \in \mathcal{R}_\Delta^D$ as $\mathcal{P}(g)$ together with the labeling

$$\sigma(P) = \mathrm{sub}_g(P)/\mathcal{P}_{max}(\mathrm{sub}_g(P))$$

for each prime $P \in \mathcal{P}$. Thus for infinite $\ell 2$s's, g has a shape if and only if it is fully decomposable.

We also say that a family $\mathcal{A}$ of sets satisfies the *ascending chain condition* (*ACC*, for short), if any increasing sequence $A_1 \subset A_2 \subset \ldots$ of sets of $\mathcal{A}$ is finite.

Theorem 4.3. *A $g \in \mathcal{R}_\Delta^D$ is fully decomposable if and only if $\mathcal{P}(g)$ satisfies ACC.*

Proof. Assume first that $g \in \mathcal{R}_\Delta^D$ is fully decomposable, and let $\mathcal{A}$ be an increasing sequence of proper prime clans of g. By Lemma 3.1, $\cup\mathcal{A} \in \mathcal{P}(g)$, and by assumption, $sub_g(\cup\mathcal{A})$ has a maximal prime clan, say M. By Lemma 3.2, each $A \in \mathcal{A}$ is also a prime of $sub_g(\cup\mathcal{A})$. Now M is a maximal prime clan in $sub_g(\cup\mathcal{A})$ and hence for each $A \in \mathcal{A}$ with $A \neq \cup\mathcal{A}$, we have $A \subseteq M$. Consider $\cup\mathcal{A}$. Since $\cup\mathcal{A} \setminus M \neq \emptyset$, the preceeding implies that $\cup\mathcal{A} \in \mathcal{A}$, and hence, indeed, $\mathcal{A}$ is finite.

On the other hand, if $\mathcal{P}(g)$ satisfies ACC, then obviously g is fully decomposable. ∎

Assume $g \in \mathcal{R}_\Delta^D$ is fully decomposable. Still the depth of $\mathcal{P}(g)$ may be infinite, *i.e.*, there may exist an infinite descending chain of prime clans.

Example 4.1. Let g be the labeled 2-structure on $\mathbf{Z} \times \{0,1\}$ of Example 3.1 (see, Figure 1), and let A_n and B_n for $n \in \mathbf{Z}$ be defined as in Example 3.1. Each $sub_g(A_n)$ has an infinite descending chain of prime clans $(A_i, i = n-1, n-2, \ldots)$, but every ascending chain of prime clans is finite. Indeed, B_{n-1} is a maximal prime of $sub_g(A_n)$, and A_n is a maximal prime clan of $sub_g(B_n)$. ∎

5. Primitive labeled 2-structures

It was shown in [3] that finite primitive ℓ2s's are downward hereditary in the following sense.

Theorem 5.1. *Let $g \in \mathcal{R}_\Delta^D$ be a finite primitive ℓ2s on n nodes. There is a primitive substructure h of g that has $n-1$ or $n-2$ nodes.* ∎

We show first that this result does not hold for infinite ℓ2s's. Indeed, in the next example we present a primitive ℓ2s g, where one has to remove infinitely many nodes before obtaining a primitive substructure.

Example 5.1. Define $g \in \mathcal{R}_\Delta^D$ on the domain $D = \mathbf{Z}$ as follows: $g(n,m) = b$, if $|n - m| = 1$, and otherwise, $g(n,m) = c$. Hence g is a graph, in fact, an infinite path without chords. It is easy to check that g is primitive. Now let $F \subseteq \mathbf{Z}$, $h = sub_g(D \setminus F)$ and $n \in F$. Consider the lower and upper sets $L = \{m \mid m < n\}$ and $U = \{m \mid m > n\}$. Now, for each $m \in L$ and $k \in U$, we have that $g(m,k) = c$ by the definition of g, and hence $L \cap (D \setminus F)$, $U \cap (D \setminus F) \in \mathcal{C}(h)$. Therefore, if h is a primitive substructure, we must have that either $L \cap (D \setminus F) = \emptyset$ and $U \cap (D \setminus F) = D \setminus F$ or $L \cap (D \setminus F) = D \setminus F$ and $U \cap (D \setminus F) = \emptyset$, which implies that $F = L$ or $F = U$. Both L and U are infinite, and so F must be infinite, if h is primitive. Consequently removing a finite number of nodes from g results in a nonprimitive substructure. ∎

Although the downward hereditary property does not hold for infinite $\ell 2s$'s, the upward hereditary property does. This is the content of the following result, the proof of which is based on the main idea (Claim 1 below) of the proof of Theorem 5.1 in [3].

Theorem 5.2. *Let $g \in \mathcal{R}_\Delta^D$ be primitive, and let $h = \mathrm{sub}_g(X)$ be a proper primitive substructure of g with $|X| > 2$. There exists a $Y \subseteq D$ such that $X \subseteq Y$, $1 \leq |Y \setminus X| \leq 2$ and the substructure $\mathrm{sub}_g(Y)$ is primitive.*

Proof. Assume to the contrary that for all $V \subseteq D \setminus X$ with $1 \leq |V| \leq 2$, $\mathrm{sub}_g(X \cup V)$ is nonprimitive. We shall write for each $y, z \in D \setminus X$, $h_y = \mathrm{sub}_g(X \cup \{y\})$ and $h_{zy} = \mathrm{sub}_g(X \cup \{z, y\})$, for short.

Claim 1. *For each $y \notin X$, h_y has a unique nontrivial clan Z_y, and either*
(1) $Z_y = X$ *(and y is called global), or*
(2) $|Z_y| = 2$ *and $y \in Z_y$ (and y is called local).*

For the proof of Claim 1 suppose $Z \in C^+(h_y)$. By Lemma 3.2, $Z \cap X \in C(h)$, and hence this is a trivial clan of h, since h is primitive. It follows that either $Z = X$ or $Z \cap X$ is a singleton and $Z = \{y, x\}$ for some $x \in X$.

For the uniqueness, assume $|Z| = 2$, and therefore that $y \in Z$. Now, $X \notin C(h_y)$, because otherwise $X \setminus Z \in C^+(h_y)$ by Lemma 3.1 and by the fact that $|X| \geq 3$. Here $y \notin X \setminus Z$ and $X \setminus Z \neq X$ contradicting the above requirements. Finally, if $|Y| = 2$ is also a clan of h_y, then $y \in Z \cap Y$, and hence $Z \cup Y \in C(h_y)$ must also be a clan of two nodes, i.e., $Y = Z$. This proves that h_y has a unique nontrivial clan as specified in (1) and (2). This proces Claim 1.

We shall denote the set of all local nodes by L, and the set of all global nodes by G. Moreover, let $\tau : L \to X$ be the function such that $Z_y = \{y, \tau(y)\}$ is the unique clan of h_y for a local $y \in L$. Since g is primitive, $X \notin C(g)$ and hence $L \neq \emptyset$.

Claim 2. $G = \emptyset$.

We shall show that $X \cup L$ is a clan of g. Since g is assumed to be primitive, the claim follows from this.

Let $z \in G$ and $y \in L$. There exists a $Y \in C^+(h_{yz})$. By Lemma 3.2, $Y \cap X \in C(h)$, and therefore either (i) $X \subseteq Y$, or (ii) $|Y \cap X| \leq 1$, since h is primitive.

In Case (i), since y is local, clearly $y \in Y$, and consequently $Y = X \cup \{y\}$. In this case $g(z, y) = g(z, x)$ for all $x \in X$.

Suppose then that $|Y \cap X| \leq 1$. If $z \in Y$, then by Lemma 3.2, $Y \cap (X \cup \{z\}) \in C(h_z)$. Now, by Claim 1, h_z has a unique nontrivial clan X, since $z \in G$, and hence $Y \cap (X \cup \{z\})$ is trivial in h_z. This means that $Y \cap (X \cup \{z\}) = \{z\}$. Since Y is a nontrivial clan of h_{yz}, we must have that $Y = \{z, y\}$. However, now $g(y, x) = g(z, x)$ for all $x \in X$, and thus $z \in G$ implies that $y \in G$. This contradicts the choice of $y \in L$. Thus we conclude that $z \notin Y$, and consequently $y \in Y$. Again, by Lemma 3.2, $Y = Y \cap (X \cup \{y\}) \in C(h_y)$, and thus by Claim 1, $Y = Z_y$. It follows that $Y \cup X \in C(h_{yz})$, since $\mathrm{dom}(h_{yz}) = (Y \cup X) \cup \{z\}$. But now $g(z, x) = g(z, y)$ holds for all $x \in X$. We conclude that $X \cup L \in C(g)$.

Claim 3. If $\tau(u) \neq \tau(v)$ for $u, v \in L$, then $Z_u \in \mathcal{C}(h_{uv})$ and $Z_v \in \mathcal{C}(h_{uv})$.

For this let $Y \in \mathcal{C}^+(h_{uv})$. As in above, Lemma 3.2 implies that $|Y \cap X| \leq 1$.

Since $|X| \geq 3$ and $h = \text{sub}_g(X)$ is primitive, there exists a node $x \in X \setminus \{\tau(u), \tau(v)\}$ such that $g(x, \tau(u)) \neq g(x, \tau(v))$. This implies that also $g(x, u) \neq g(x, v)$, because $Z_u = \{u, \tau(u)\} \in \mathcal{C}(h_u)$ and $Z_v = \{v, \tau(v)\} \in \mathcal{C}(h_v)$. It follows that if $u \in Y$ and $v \in Y$, then also $x \in Y$, that is, in this case $Y = \{x, u, v\}$. However, by Lemma 3.2, $\{x, u\} = Y \cap (X \cup \{u\}) \in \mathcal{C}(h_u)$, and hence $x = \tau(u)$. This contradicts the choice of x. We conclude that either $u \in Y$ or $v \in Y$ but not both. Since $|Y| \geq 2$, $|Y \cap X| = 1$.

Assume (without restriction) that $u \in Y$. Now, by Claim 1, $Y \cap (X \cup \{u\}) \in \mathcal{C}(h_u)$ implies that $Y = Z_u$, and hence, indeed, $Z_u \in \mathcal{C}(h_{uv})$. Consequently $g(v, u) = g(v, \tau(u))$. We have also that $g(v, \tau(u)) = g(\tau(v), \tau(u))$, since $Z_v \in \mathcal{C}(h_v)$. We conclude that $Z_v \in \mathcal{C}(h_{uv}$. Thus the claim follows.

Let now $x \in X$ be a node such that $x = \tau(y)$ for some $y \in D \setminus X$, and set $A = \tau^{-1}(x)$. Hence $A \subseteq D \setminus X$ consists of those (local) nodes y for which $Z_y = \{y, x\}$. If $A = \{y\}$, then Claim 3 implies that $Z_y \in \mathcal{C}(h_{yz})$ for all $z \in D \setminus X$, from which it would follow that $Z_y \in \mathcal{C}(g)$ contradicting the primitivity of g. Hence we may suppose that $|A| \geq 2$.

By assumption, g is primitive and hence there is a node $z \notin A$ such that $g(z, y_1) \neq g(z, y_2)$ for some $y_1, y_2 \in A$. It follows that $g(z, u) \neq g(z, x)$ for some $u \in A$, and hence $Z_u \notin \mathcal{C}(h_{zu})$. By Claim 3, $z \in X$, since by assumption, $z \notin A$. However, by the definition of $A = \tau^{-1}(x)$, for all $v \in X$ with $v \neq x$, $g(v, y_1) = g(v, y_2)$, for all $y_1, y_2 \in A$. This shows that $z \notin X$, which is a contradiction, and proves the theorem. ∎

Theorem 5.2 is also closely connected to a result of [7], where it was proved that every primitive tournament (*simple tournament*, in the terminology of [7]) with n nodes can be embedded in a primitive tournament with $n + 1$ or $n + 2$ nodes.

It follows from Theorem 5.1 that each finite $\ell 2s$ has a small primitive substructure of 3 or 4 nodes. Although, as demonstrated by Example 5.1, Theorem 5.1 does not hold for infinite $\ell 2s$'s, this particular corollary holds for infinite $\ell 2s$'s. We shall reduce this claim to the following result of [6] (Theorem 3.6 and Corollary 3.7 in [6]), which is here stated in our terminology. Below we interpret a directed graph as a reversible $\ell 2s$ with one symmetric and one antisymmetric feature.

Theorem 5.3. Let g be an angular $\ell 2s$ with at least three nodes. If g is a primitive graph or a primitive directed graph, then g contains a primitive substructure of four nodes. ∎

Let $g \in \mathcal{R}_\Delta^D$ and let $b \in \Delta$. Let us define the b-digraph of g as the $\ell 2s$ g_b, for which

$$g_b(e) = \begin{cases} b & \text{if } g(e) = b \\ b^{-1} & \text{if } g(e) = b^{-1} \\ a & \text{if } g(e) \notin b^{\pm 1} \end{cases}$$

where a is a symmetric label different from b. Clearly, if the label b is symmetric, then g_b is a graph, and if b is not symmetric, then g_b is a directed graph.

Theorem 5.4. *Let $g \in \mathcal{R}_\Delta^D$ be an angular $\ell 2s$. The following conditions are equivalent:*

(1) g is primitive.
(2) g_b is primitive for all $b \in \Delta$.
(3) g_b is primitive for some $b \in \Delta$.

Proof. Assume first that g is primitive and angular. Let $b \in \Delta$, and suppose to the contrary that g_b has a nontrivial clan X. Define

$$Y = \{y \mid y \notin X, \; g(y, x_1) \neq g(y, x_2) \text{ for some } x_1, x_2 \in X\}.$$

We shall show that $X \cup Y$ is a nontrivial clan of g. First of all, since g is connected by Lemma 4.3, there exists a $z \notin X$ such that $g(z, x) \in b^{\pm 1}$ for some $x \in X$. Further, $X \in \mathcal{C}(g_b)$ implies that $z \notin Y$. We conclude that $X \cup Y$ is a proper subset of D. Consider then any $u \notin X \cup Y$. By definition of Y, we have that $g(u, x_1) = g(u, x_2)$ for all $x_1, x_2 \in X$. Let $y \in Y$. Hence there are $x_1, x_2 \in X$ such that $g(y, x_1) \neq g(y, x_2)$. Since g is angular, both the substructures induced by $\{u, y, x_1\}$ and $\{u, y, x_2\}$ must have a 2-element clan. This is possible only if $g(u, y) = g(u, x_1)$. Consequently, $g(u, y) = g(u, x)$ for all $y \in Y$ and $x \in X$, and $X \cup Y \in \mathcal{C}^+(g)$, which contradicts the primitivity of g. We have shown that condition (1) implies condition (2).

Clearly, (3) follows from (2), and (1) follows from (3). Hence the claim follows. ∎

By Theorem 5.3 and Theorem 5.4 we have the following result.

Theorem 5.5. *Let $g \in \mathcal{R}_\Delta^D$ be primitive. Then g has a primitive substructure of 3 or 4 nodes.* ∎

Acknowledgement. The authors are in debt to BRA Working Groups ASMICS and COMPUGRAPH for their support.

References

[1] Buer, H. and R.H. Möhring, A fast algorithm for the decomposition of graphs and posets, *Math. Oper. Res. 8* (1983) 170 – 184.

[2] Ehrenfeucht, A. and G. Rozenberg, Theory of 2-structures, Parts I and II, *Theoretical Computer Science 70* (1990) 277 – 303 and 305 – 342.

[3] Ehrenfeucht, A. and G. Rozenberg, Primitivity is hereditary for 2-structures *Theoretical Computer Science 70* (1990) 343 – 358.

[4] Ehrenfeucht, A. and G. Rozenberg, Angular 2-structures, *Theoretical Computer Science 92* (1992) 227 – 248.

[5] Gallai T., Transitiv orientierbare Graphen, *Acta Math. Acad. Sci. Hungar.* *18* (1967) 25 – 66.

[6] Kelly, D., Comparability graphs, in Rival.I (ed): *Graphs and Order*, Reidel, Dordrecht 1985, 3 – 40.

[7] Moon, J.W., Embedding tournaments in simple tournaments, *Discrete Math.* 2 (1972) 389 – 395.

An Iteration Property of Lindenmayerian Power Series

Juha Honkala
Department of Mathematics
University of Turku
20500 Turku, Finland

Abstract. We establish an iteration property of Lindenmayerian power series. As an application we derive results on the series generating power of L systems.

1 Introduction

Formal power series play an important role in many diverse areas of theoretical computer science and mathematics [1,9,10,14]. The classes of power series studied most often in connection with automata, grammars and languages are the rational and algebraic series. In language theory formal power series often provide a powerful tool for obtaining deep decidability results [9,14]. A brilliant example is the solution of the equivalence problem for finite deterministic multitape automata given by Harju and Karhumäki [3].

In [9] Kuich and Salomaa gave a power series approach to formal language theory by using an algebraic notion of convergence. In [6-8] Kuich generalized the Kleene theorem, the Parikh theorem and the equivalence between context-freeness and acceptance by pushdown automata to complete semirings.

The framework of [9] was used in [4] to define Lindenmayerian power series, i.e., series obtained by morphic iteration. These series are generated by suitably modified L systems. We give a simple example.

Suppose A is a semiring and Σ is a finite alphabet. Denote the semiring of formal polynomials over Σ with coefficients in A by $A<\Sigma^*>$ and assume that $h : A<\Sigma^*> \rightarrow A<\Sigma^*>$ is a semiring morphism. Such a morphism necessarily satisfies $h(\lambda) = \lambda$. We suppose also that $h(a \cdot \lambda) = a \cdot \lambda$ holds for every $a \in A$. Finally, assume $\omega \in A<\Sigma^*>$. Now define the sequence $r^{(i)} (i \geq 0)$ by $r^{(0)} = \omega, r^{(i+1)} = h(r^{(i)})$. Then $\lim r^{(i)}$, if it exists, is a morphically generated series. Of course, we have to specify the convergence used in the limit process. In our work we allow also more complicated iteration. Instead of $r^{(i+1)} = h(r^{(i)})$ we might have, e.g., $r^{(i+1)} = ah_1(r^{(i)}) + h_2(r^{(i)})h_3(r^{(i)})$, where a is a letter and h_1, h_2, h_3 are, not necessarily distinct, morphisms of $A<\Sigma^*>$.

In this paper we continue the study of Lindenmayerian series by establishing a basic iteration property of these series. By the well known iteration lemma for regular languages, if $L \subseteq \Sigma^*$ is an infinite regular language, there exist words $u, v, w \in \Sigma^*$ such that

$$uw^*v \subseteq L.$$

Hence, we can repeat the nonempty subword w an arbitrary number of times provided that we prefix the resulting word by u and suffix it by v. The analogous result for Lindenmayerian series can be stated as follows. Suppose r is a Lindenmayerian series with an infinite support. Then there exist morphisms h and g and a word w such that

$$\{h(g^n(w)) \mid n \geq 0\} \subseteq \mathrm{supp}(r)$$

and the left-hand side is infinite. Notice that the application of h corresponds to the words u and v used above. This iteration property can be utilized in the study of Lindenmayerian series in much the same way as the pumping lemma is used in the study of regularity, see [13]. In particular, earlier results about combinatorial properties of HD0L languages can be utilized to give examples of series which are not Lindenmayerian.

For the motivation and background of our work, we refer to [4,5].

2 Definitions

We assume that the reader is familiar with the basic notions concerning semirings and formal power series (see [9]). For completeness, we specify the following.

The semiring of nonnegative real numbers is denoted by $\mathbf{R}_+$.

If A is a semiring and Σ is an alphabet, not necessarily finite, the *semiring of formal power series with coefficients in A and (noncommuting) variables in Σ* is denoted by $A \ll \Sigma^* \gg$. If $r \in A \ll \Sigma^* \gg$ we denote

$$r = \sum_{w \in \Sigma^*} (r, w)w \quad \text{and} \quad \mathrm{supp}(r) = \{w \mid (r, w) \neq 0\}$$

The set $\mathrm{supp}(r)$ is called the *support* of r. The subsemiring of $A \ll \Sigma^* \gg$ consisting of the series having a finite support is denoted by $A < \Sigma^* >$. The elements of $A < \Sigma^* >$ are referred to as *polynomials*.

If $L \subseteq \Sigma^*$ is a language, the series $\mathrm{char}(L) \in A \ll \Sigma^* \gg$ is defined by

$$\mathrm{char}(L) = \sum_{w \in L} w$$

and called the *characteristic series* of L. If $r, s \in A \ll \Sigma^* \gg$, the *Hadamard product* $r \odot s \in A \ll \Sigma^* \gg$ of r and s is defined by

$$(r \odot s, w) = (r, w)(s, w), \quad w \in \Sigma^*.$$

In the sequel we need a notion of convergence. We follow [9].

A *sequence* in A is a mapping $\alpha : \mathbf{N} \to A$. The set of all sequences in A is denoted by $A^{\mathbf{N}}$. If $\alpha \in A^{\mathbf{N}}$, we denote $\alpha = (\alpha(n))$. For $\alpha \in A^{\mathbf{N}}$ and

$c \in A$, we define $c\alpha$ and αc in $A^{\mathbf{N}}$ by $(c\alpha)(n) = c\alpha(n)$ and $(\alpha c)(n) = \alpha(n)c$, for all $n \geq 0$, respectively. For $\alpha_1, \alpha_2 \in A^{\mathbf{N}}$, we define $\alpha_1 + \alpha_2$ in $A^{\mathbf{N}}$ by $(\alpha_1 + \alpha_2)(n) = \alpha_1(n) + \alpha_2(n)$, for all $n \geq 0$. Finally, for $\alpha \in A^{\mathbf{N}}$ and $a \in A$, the sequence $\alpha_a \in A^{\mathbf{N}}$ is defined by $\alpha_a(0) = a, \alpha_a(n+1) = \alpha(n)$, for all $n \geq 0$.

A set $D \subseteq A^{\mathbf{N}}$ is called a *set of convergent sequences* in A if the following conditions (D1) - (D3) hold.

(D1) $1 \in D$ where $1(n) = 1$ for all $n \geq 0$.
(D2) (i)   If $\alpha_1, \alpha_2 \in D$ then $\alpha_1 + \alpha_2 \in D$.
    (ii)   If $\alpha \in D$ and $c \in A$ then $c\alpha, \alpha c \in D$.
(D3)   If $\alpha \in D$ and $a \in A$ then $\alpha_a \in D$.

Let D be a set of convergent sequences in A. A mapping $\lim : D \to A$ satisfying the following conditions $(\lim 1) - (\lim 3)$ is called a *limit function* (on D).

$(\lim 1)$ $\lim 1 = 1$.
$(\lim 2)$ (i) If $\alpha_1, \alpha_2 \in D$ then $\lim(\alpha_1 + \alpha_2) = \lim \alpha_1 + \lim \alpha_2$.
      (ii) If $\alpha \in D$ and $c \in A$ then $\lim c\alpha = c \lim \alpha$ and $\lim \alpha c = (\lim \alpha)c$.
$(\lim 3)$ If $\alpha \in D$ and $a \in A$ then $\lim \alpha_a = \lim \alpha$.

If D is a set of convergent sequences in A and $\lim$ is a limit function on D, the pair $\mathcal{D} = (D, \lim)$ is called a *convergence* in A.

If $\mathcal{D} = (D, \lim)$ is a convergence in A, a convergence $\mathcal{D}' = (D', \lim')$ in $A \ll \Sigma^* \gg$ can be defined by

$$D' = \{\alpha \in (A \ll \Sigma^* \gg)^{\mathbf{N}} \mid \text{for every } w \in \Sigma^*, \text{ we have } ((\alpha(n), w)) \in D\}$$

and

$$\lim' \alpha = \sum \lim(\alpha(n), w)w, \alpha \in D'.$$

For the proof see [9].

If A is a semiring there exists a convergence $\mathcal{D} = (D, \lim)$ in A defined by

$$D = \{\alpha \in A^{\mathbf{N}} \mid \text{there exists an } n_\alpha \text{ such that } \alpha(n) = \alpha(n_\alpha) \text{ for all } n \geq n_\alpha\}$$

and

$$\lim \alpha = \alpha(n_\alpha) \text{ for } \alpha \in D.$$

We denote by $\mathcal{D}_d = (D_d, \lim_d)$ the convergence in $A \ll \Sigma^* \gg$ which is obtained when the convergence $\mathcal{D} = (D, \lim)$ defined above is transferred to $A \ll \Sigma^* \gg$ as explained above. $\mathcal{D}_d$ is called the *discrete convergence*.

Suppose A is a commutative semiring and $h : \Sigma^* \to A < \Sigma^* >$ is a monoid morphism. (Here $A < \Sigma^* >$ is regarded as a multiplicative monoid.) Then we extend h to a semiring morphism

$$h : A < \Sigma^* > \to A < \Sigma^* >$$

by

$$h(P) = \sum(P, w)h(w), \ P \in A<\Sigma^*> .$$

Notice that the assumption of commutativeness is needed in the verification that indeed $h(r_1 r_2) = h(r_1)h(r_2)$ for $r_1, r_2 \in A<\Sigma^*>$. In the sequel we always tacitly extend a morphism $h \in \text{Hom}(\Sigma^*, A<\Sigma^*>)$ to a semiring morphism $h : A<\Sigma^*> \rightarrow A<\Sigma^*>$ as explained above. Notice that $\text{Hom}(\Sigma^*, A<\Sigma^*>)$ can be identified with the set

$$\{h : A<\Sigma^*> \rightarrow A<\Sigma^*>| \ h \text{ is a semiring morphism and}$$

$$h(a \cdot \lambda) = a \cdot \lambda \text{ for any } a \in A\}.$$

In what follows X is a denumerably infinite alphabet of variables. Furthermore, Σ will always be a finite alphabet.

Definition 2.1. Suppose A is a commutative semiring and Σ is a finite alphabet. An *interpretation* φ over (A, Σ) is a mapping from X to $\text{Hom}(\Sigma^*, A<\Sigma^*>)$.

Definition 2.2. A *Lindenmayerian series generating system*, shortly, an *LS* system, is a 5-tuple $G = (A \ll \Sigma^* \gg, \mathcal{D}, P, \varphi, \omega)$ where A is a commutative semiring, Σ is a finite alphabet, $\mathcal{D}$ is a convergence in $A \ll \Sigma^* \gg, P$ is a polynomial in $A < (X \cup \Sigma)^* >, \varphi$ is an interpretation over (A, Σ) and ω is a polynomial in $A<\Sigma^*>$.

The series generated by an *LS* system is obtained by iteration. Before the precise definition we need a notation.

Suppose $P(x_1, \ldots, x_n) \in A < (X \cup \Sigma)^* >$ and $s^{(1)}, \ldots, s^{(n)} \in A \ll \Sigma^* \gg$, where A is a commutative semiring. Then the series $P(s^{(1)}, \ldots, s^{(n)})$ is defined recursively as follows:

$$a(s^{(1)}, \ldots, s^{(n)}) = a, \ a \in A,$$

$$w(s^{(1)}, \ldots, s^{(n)}) = w, w \in \Sigma^*,$$

$$x_i(s^{(1)}, \ldots, s^{(n)}) = s^{(i)}, 1 \leq i \leq n,$$

$$(P_1 + P_2)(s^{(1)}, \ldots, s^{(n)}) = P_1(s^{(1)}, \ldots, s^{(n)}) + P_2(s^{(1)}, \ldots, s^{(n)}),$$

$$(P_1 P_2)(s^{(1)}, \ldots, s^{(n)}) = P_1(s^{(1)}, \ldots, s^{(n)}) \cdot P_2(s^{(1)}, \ldots, s^{(n)}),$$

$$P_1, P_2 \in A < (X \cup \Sigma)^* > .$$

Definition 2.3. Suppose $G = (A \ll \Sigma^* \gg, \mathcal{D}, P(x_1, \ldots, x_n), \varphi, \omega)$ is an *LS* system. Denote $h_i = \varphi(x_i)$ for $1 \leq i \leq \text{n}$. Define the sequence $(r^{(j)})(j = 0, 1, \ldots)$ recursively by

$$r^{(0)} = \omega,$$

$$r^{(j+1)} = P(h_1(r^{(j)}), \ldots, h_n(r^{(j)})), j \geq 0.$$

If $\lim r^{(j)}$ exists we denote

$$S(G) = \lim r^{(j)}$$

and say that $S(G)$ is the *series generated* by G. The sequence $(r^{(j)})$ is the *approximation sequence associated* to G. A series r is called an *LS series* if there exists an *LS* system G such that $r = S(G)$. A series r is an *LS series with* $\omega = 0$ if there exists an *LS* system $G = (A \ll \varSigma^* \gg, \mathcal{D}, P, \varphi, 0)$ such that $r = S(G)$.

In this paper we study extended *LS* series in the sense of the following definition.

Definition 2.4. An ELS *system* is a construct $G = (A \ll \varSigma^* \gg, \mathcal{D}, P, \varphi, \omega, \Delta)$ where $U(G) = (A \ll \varSigma^* \gg, \mathcal{D}, P, \varphi, \omega)$ is an *LS* system called the *underlying system* of G and $\Delta \subseteq \varSigma$. If $S(U(G))$ exists, G generates the series

$$S(G) = S(U(G)) \odot \mathrm{char}(\Delta^*).$$

A series r is called an ELS *series* if there exists an ELS system G such that $r = S(G)$. A series r is called an ELS *series with* $\omega = 0$ if there exists an ELS system $G = (A \ll \varSigma^* \gg, \mathcal{D}, P, \varphi, 0, \Delta)$ such that $r = S(G)$.

For examples and basic properties of *LS* and ELS series see [4,5].

3 The Iteration Property

Before the main result we need a lemma which states in a precise way the following fact. Consider a word $w \in \varSigma^*$ and an *LS* system $G = (\mathbf{R}_+ \ll \varSigma^* \gg, \mathcal{D}_d, P, \varphi, 0)$ with the approximation sequence $(r^{(i)})$. It is well known that $r^{(i)} \le r^{(i+1)}$ for each i. Now, if $S(G)$ exists, there is a bound $i(w)$ such that $r^{(i)}$ for $i \ge i(w)$ contains no "new" terms with support w.

We call a polynomial $P(x_1, \ldots, x_m)$ *individualized* if each variable x of P occurs in exactly one word $w(x)$ of supp(P) and has a unique occurrence in $w(x)$. Hence, for example, $2x_1 + x_2 x_3$ is individualized but $x_1 + x_1 x_2$ and x_1^2 are not.

Suppose now that $G = (\mathbf{R}_+ \ll \varSigma^* \gg, \mathcal{D}_d, P(x_1, \ldots, x_m), \varphi, 0)$ is an *LS* system, where P is individualized. Denote the approximation sequence associated to G by $(r^{(i)})$. Consider the algebraic system

$$z = P(x_1 z, \ldots, x_m z) \tag{1}$$

with the one variable z and one equation. Denote the approximation sequence of (1) by $(z^{(i)})$. Define the sequence $(s^{(i)})$ where $s^{(i)} \in \mathbf{R}_+ < (\{x_1, \ldots, x_m\} \cup \varSigma)^* >$ by

$$s^{(0)} = 0, z^{(i+1)} = z^{(i)} + s^{(i+1)}.$$

Next define the mapping ψ from $\bigcup_{i \ge 0} \mathrm{supp}(z^{(i)})$ to $\mathbf{R}_+ < \varSigma^* >$ recursively by

$$\psi(w) = w, w \in \Sigma^*,$$
$$\psi(u_0 x_{i_1} v_1 u_1 x_{i_2} v_2 u_2 \ldots x_{i_k} v_k u_k) = u_0 \varphi(x_{i_1})(\psi(v_1)) u_1 \varphi(x_{i_2})(\psi(v_2)) u_2 \ldots$$
$$\varphi(x_{i_k})(\psi(v_k)) u_k,$$

whenever $u_0 x_{i_1} u_1 x_{i_2} u_2 \ldots x_{i_k} u_k (k \geq 1)$ belongs to supp(P) and $v_1, \ldots, v_k \in \bigcup_{i \geq 0}$ supp$(z^{(i)})$. It is not difficult to see that ψ is well defined. Finally, extend ψ to a partial mapping

$$\psi : \mathbf{R}_+ < (\{x_1, \ldots, x_m\} \cup \Sigma)^* > \to \mathbf{R}_+ < \Sigma^* >$$

by

$$\psi(\sum a_j w_j) = \sum a_j \psi(w_j),$$

where $a_j \in \mathbf{R}_+, w_j \in \bigcup_{i \geq 0}$ supp$(z^{(i)})$.

Lemma 1. Suppose $S(G)$ exists. Then
(i) $\psi(z^{(i)}) = r^{(i)}$ and
(ii) for any $w \in \Sigma^*, (\psi(s^{(i)}), w) = 0$ for almost all i.

Proof. Claim (i) follows inductively. Suppose $w \in \Sigma^*$. Because $S(G)$ exists, there is a positive integer $i(w)$ such that $(S(G), w) = (r^{(i)}, w)$ for $i \geq i(w)$. Now claim (ii) follows because $r^{(i)} = \sum_{0 \leq j \leq i} \psi(s^{(j)})$. $\qquad\square$

Now we are ready to establish the basic iteration property of Lindenmayerian power series.

Theorem 2. Suppose $G = (\mathbf{R}_+ \ll \Sigma^* \gg, \mathcal{D}_d, P(x_1, \ldots, x_m), \varphi, 0, \Delta)$ is an ELS system such that $S(G)$ exists. Then there exists an integer N such that for any $w \in \Sigma^*$, if

$$(S(G), w) \neq 0 \text{ and } |w| \geq N$$

then there exist an alphabet Σ_1, a word $\overline{w} \in \Sigma_1^*$ and morphisms $g : \mathbf{R}_+ < \Sigma_1^* > \to \mathbf{R}_+ < \Sigma_1^* >$ and $h : \mathbf{R}_+ < \Sigma_1^* > \to \mathbf{R}_+ < \Sigma^* >$ such that the series

$$s = \sum_{n=1}^{\infty} h(g^n(\overline{w})) \odot \text{char}(\Delta^*)$$

has an infinite support, $w \in$ supp(s) and

$$\text{supp}(s) \subseteq \text{supp}(S(G)).$$

Proof. Denote $r = S(U(G))$.

Suppose $w \in \Sigma^*$ is a word such that $(S(G), w) \neq 0$ and $|w| \geq N$. Here N is an integer to be chosen later on. Then there exist a word $u_{10} x_{11} u_{11} \ldots x_{1k} u_{1k}$ of supp(P) and words $w_{11}, \ldots, w_{1k} \in$ supp(r) such that

$$w \in \text{supp}(u_{10} h_{11}(w_{11}) u_{11} \ldots h_{1k}(w_{1k}) u_{1k})$$

where $h_{1\alpha} = \varphi(x_{1\alpha})$ for $1 \leq \alpha \leq k$. Choose one of the words $w_{1\alpha}$, as long as possible, and denote it by w_1. Hence there exist $u_1, v_1 \in \Sigma^*$ and $h_1 \in \{\varphi(x_1), \ldots, \varphi(x_m)\}$ such that

$$w \in \text{supp}(u_1 h_1(w_1)v_1) \quad \text{and} \quad \text{supp}(u_1 h_1(r)v_1) \subseteq \text{supp}(r).$$

In a similar way we find $u_2, v_2, w_2 \in \Sigma^*$ where $w_2 \in \text{supp}(r)$ and $h_2 \in \{\varphi(x_1), \ldots, \varphi(x_m)\}$ such that

$$w_1 \in \text{supp}(u_2 h_2(w_2)v_2) \quad \text{and} \quad \text{supp}(u_2 h_2(r)v_2) \subseteq \text{supp}(r).$$

Continue the process until two words w_i and $w_j (i < j)$ satisfy $\text{Alph}(w_i) = \text{Alph}(w_j)$. (Here $\text{Alph}(w)$ stands for the minimal alphabet of w.) It is clear that we can give an estimate for N which guarantees the existence of such i and j.

It follows that there exist $u, v, \overline{u}, \overline{v} \in \Sigma^*$ such that

$$w \in \text{supp}(uh(w_i)v),$$

$$\text{supp}(uh(r)v) \subseteq \text{supp}(r),$$

$$w_i \in \text{supp}(\overline{u}g(w_j)\overline{v}),$$

$$\text{supp}(\overline{u}g(r)\overline{v}) \subseteq \text{supp}(r),$$

where $h = h_1 \ldots h_i$ and $g = h_{i+1} \ldots h_j$. Denote

$$s_n = \overline{u}g(\overline{u}) \ldots g^n(\overline{u})g^{n+1}(w_j)g^n(\overline{v}) \ldots g(\overline{v})\overline{v},$$

$n \geq 0$. It is seen inductively that

$$\text{supp}(s_n) \subseteq \text{supp}(r)$$

and that $\text{supp}(s_n)$ contains words with minimal alphabet contained in $\text{Alph}(w_i)$. Hence, for any n, $\text{supp}(uh(s_n)v)$ contains words in Δ^*. By Lemma 1, the series

$$s = \sum_{n=0}^{\infty} uh(s_n)v \odot \text{char}(\Delta^*)$$

has an infinite support. Furthermore, $w \in \text{supp}(s)$ and

$$\text{supp}(s) \subseteq \text{supp}(S(G)).$$

Finally, choose two new letters $a, b \notin \Sigma$ and denote $\Sigma_1 = \Sigma \cup \{a, b\}$. Extend h and g by defining $h(a) = u, h(b) = v, g(a) = a\overline{u}, g(b) = \overline{v}b$. Then

$$s = \sum_{n=1}^{\infty} h(g^n(\overline{w})) \odot \text{char}(\Delta^*)$$

where $\overline{w} = aw_jb$. $\qquad\qquad\qquad\qquad\qquad\qquad\qquad\qquad\qquad\qquad\square$

For the definitions and results concerning L systems needed below, see [12].

Corollary 3. Suppose $G = (\mathbf{R}_+ \ll \Sigma^* \gg, \mathcal{D}_d, P, \varphi, 0, \Delta)$ is an ELS system such that $S(G)$ exists and has an infinite support. Then $\text{supp}(S(G))$ contains an infinite $HD0L$ language. More specifically, there exist an alphabet Σ_1, a word $w \in \Sigma_1^*$ and morphisms $g : \Sigma_1^* \to \Sigma_1^*, h : \Sigma_1^* \to \Sigma^*$ such that

$$\{h(g^n(w)) \mid n \geq 0\} \subseteq \text{supp}(S(G))$$

where

$$h(g^n(w)) \neq h(g^m(w)) \text{ if } n \neq m$$

and the sequence (α_n) defined by

$$\alpha_n = \mid h(g^n(w)) \mid$$

is a D0L length sequence.

Proof. Denote again $r = S(U(G))$. It follows by the proof of Theorem 2, that there are words $u, v, \overline{u}, \overline{v}, w, w_i, w_j \in \Sigma^*$ and morphisms $h, g : \Sigma^* \to \mathbf{R}_+ < \Sigma^* >$ satisfying $h(\sigma), g(\sigma) \in \Sigma^* \cup \{0\}$ for all $\sigma \in \Sigma$ such that

$$w = uh(w_i)v,$$

$$\text{supp}(uh(r)v) \subseteq \text{supp}(r),$$

$$w_i = \overline{u}g(w_j)\overline{v},$$

$$\text{supp}(\overline{u}g(r)\overline{v}) \subseteq \text{supp}(r)$$

and

$$w \in \Delta^*, \text{Alph}(w_i) \subseteq \text{Alph}(w_j).$$

Next, define Σ_1 and $\overline{w}$ and extend h and g as in the proof of Theorem 2. It follows that

$$\{h(g^n(\overline{w})) \mid n \geq 1\} \subseteq \text{supp}(S(G))$$

where the left-hand side is infinite. It is easy to see that we can assume without restriction that $h(\sigma) \neq 0$ and $g(\sigma) \neq 0$ for all $\sigma \in \Sigma_1$.

Now, denote

$$\beta_n = \mid h(g^n(\overline{w})) \mid.$$

Because (β_n) is an **N**-rational sequence, it can be decomposed into PD0L length sequences. This implies the claim. $\qquad \square$

4 Consequences

Corollary 3, in connection with various combinatorial properties of HD0L languages, makes it possible to give examples of simply defined series which are not ELS series. No such examples are previously known.

Theorem 4. Neither of the series given below is generated by an ELS system $G = (\mathbf{R}_+ \ll \Sigma^* \gg, \mathcal{D}_d, P, \varphi, 0, \Delta)$:
(i) $s_1 = \sum_{n \geq 1} a^{n!}$,
(ii) $s_2 = \sum_{n \geq 1} (a^n b)^n$.

Proof. (i) No subsequence of $(n!)$ is a D0L length sequence, see [11 or 12, Theorem I.3.8].

(ii) If $L_2 \subseteq \text{supp}(s_2)$ is an infinite HD0L language, $\{b\}$ is rare in L_2, but not nonfrequent in L_2. This contradicts [2, Theorem 1]. Alternatively, see [12, Theorem V.2.1]. □

Other examples of nonlindenmayerian series can be given along similar lines. We conclude this section with a different application of Theorem 2.

Theorem 5. Suppose $G = (\mathbf{R}_+ \ll \Sigma^* \gg, \mathcal{D}_d, P, \varphi, 0, \Delta)$ is an ELS system such that $S(G)$ exists. Then it is decidable whether or not $S(G)$ is a polynomial.

Proof. Let N be the (effectively computable) integer given in Theorem 2. It suffices to decide whether $\text{supp}(S(G))$ has a word of length at least N. This can be decided by the method of the proof of Theorem 5.2 of [4]. □

References

[1] J. Berstel and C. Reutenauer, *Rational Series and Their Languages* (Springer -Verlag, Berlin, 1988).

[2] A. Ehrenfeucht and G. Rozenberg, On proving that certain languages are not ET0L, *Acta Inform.* 6 (1976) 407-415.

[3] T. Harju and J. Karhumäki, The equivalence problem of multitape finite automata, *Theoret. Comput. Sci.* 78 (2) (1991) 347-355.

[4] J. Honkala, On morphically generated formal power series, *Theoret. Inform. and Appl.*, to appear.

[5] J. Honkala, On Lindenmayerian series in complete semirings. In A. Salomaa and G. Rozenberg, eds., *Developments in Language Theory* (World Scientific) to appear.

[6] W. Kuich, The Kleene and the Parikh theorem in complete semirings. In: T. Ottmann, ed., *Automata, Languages and Programming* (Springer-Verlag, Berlin, 1987) 212-225.

[7] W. Kuich, ω-continuous semirings, algebraic systems and pushdown automata. In: M.S. Paterson, ed., *Automata, Languages and Programming* (Springer-Verlag, Berlin, 1990) 103-110.

[8] W. Kuich, Automata and languages generalized to ω-continuous semirings, *Theoret. Comput. Sci.* 79 (1991) 137-150.

[9] W. Kuich and A. Salomaa, *Semirings, Automata, Languages* (Springer-Verlag, Berlin, 1986).

[10] J. van Leeuwen, ed., *Handbook of Theoretical Computer Science* (Elsevier, Amsterdam, 1990).

[11] A. Paz and A. Salomaa, Integral sequential word functions and growth equivalence of Lindenmayer systems, *Inform. and Control* 23 (1973) 313-343.

[12] G. Rozenberg and A. Salomaa, *The Mathematical Theory of L Systems* (Academic Press, New York, 1980).

[13] A. Salomaa, *Formal Languages* (Academic Press, New York, 1973).

[14] A. Salomaa and M. Soittola, *Automata-Theoretic Aspects of Formal Power Series* (Springer-Verlag, Berlin, 1978).

Comparing Descriptional and Computational Complexity of Infinite Words *

Juraj Hromkovič[1], Juhani Karhumäki[2] and Arto Lepistö[2]

[1] Department of Mathematics and Computer Science, University of Paderborn,
33098 Paderborn, Germany
[2] Department of Mathematics, University of Turku
SF-20500 Turku, Finland

Abstract. This paper searches for connections between descriptional and computational complexities of infinite words. In the former one the complexity is measured by the complexity of the mechanism used to generate infinite words, typical examples being iterated morphisms, iterated dgsm's and double D0L TAG systems. In the latter on the complexity is measured by resourses used by Turing machines to generate infinite words.

1 Introduction

During the last twenty years infinite words over a finite alphabet has been under a very active investigation. The two major aspects studied have been combinatorial properties of infinite words, for example their power-freeness, cf. [Lo], and possibilities of recognizing languages consisting of infinite words by certain devices, for example by different variations of finite automata, cf. [PP].

On the other hand complexity aspects of infinite words has attracted much less attention as they, in our opinion, would have deserved. In particular, there seems to be very little litterature on a low level complexity of infinite words, while there are several important results on a high level complexity due to Kolmogorov complexity theory, cf. [LV] or the original papers, [Ch], [Ko], [So]. Apparently this is connected to the fact that it seems to be extremely difficult to show that a given infinite word is not of a certain complexity, cf. [HK].

Of course, complexity results of languages of finite words apply directly to infinite words by interpreting an infinite word as the set of its prefixes. However, this identification overlooks some essential features of complexity of infinite words, cf. e.g. Theorem 3.3.

Our goal here is to find out some basic facts on complexity of infinite words, which hopefully motivate further research on this field. In particular, we want to compare two different types of complexities, descriptional and computational ones.

---

* This research was supported by the Academy of Finland under Project 11181, as well as by SAV Grant No 88.

By the descriptional complexity, which, in fact, has been implicitly one of the important trends in combinatorics of words, we mean the complexity, which is measured by the fact how complicated mechanism is needed to generate a considered infinite word. Typical mechanisms used in the litterature are iterated morphisms, deterministic gsm's and double D0L TAG systems, cf. [Th], [AG] and [CK] respectively. It is natural to say that words generated by iterating a morphism are of lower descriptional complexity than words obtained by iterating a dgsm.

On computational complexity theory the complexity is measured how much resources, such as time or space, is needed in the generation of an infinite word by a Turing machine. Here we require that the machine computes an infinite word, that is we consider infinite computations, and the complexity is determined by the amount of resources needed to output the ith letter of the considered infinite word.

The structure of this paper is as follows.

In Section 2 we fix our computational model - multitape Turing machine - used to define the time and space complexities of an infinite word, as well as the corresponding complexity classes $GSPACE(f) = \{$infinite words generated in space $f(n)\}$ and $GTIME(g) = \{$infinite words generated in time $g(n)\}$ for some functions $f, g : \mathbb{N} \to \mathbb{N}$. The basic mechanisms used to classify the descriptional complexity of infinite words are also recalled here.

Section 3 shows that there is no hierarchy of space complexity classes below $\log n$, i.e. $GSPACE(\mathcal{O}(1)) = GSPACE(f) = \{$ultimately periodic infinite words $\}$ for every $f(n) = o(\log n)$. This should be compared, in one hand, to the well known fact that for the ordinary complexity classes such hierarchies exist, and on the other hand, to the fact proved in [HK] that above $\log n$ such hierarchies exist, indeed $GSPACE(f) \subset GSPACE(g)$, if only $g(n) \geq f(n) \geq \log n$ for all n and $f(n) = o(g(n))$.

In Section 4 we show that infinite words obtained by iterating a morphism, i.e. defined by the simplest iterative devices, are in the second smallest space complexity class $GSPACE(\log n)$.

In Section 5 we deal with infinite words obtained by iterating a deterministic gsm. Such words can possess very complex combinatorial properties, as shown by the Kolakoski infinite word Kol, cf. [L], or by the infinite word Bin, cf. Section 4, which contains all binary encodings of natural numbers. Despite of that we show that all infinite words obtained by exponentially growing dgsm's, for example the above Kol, are in the class $GSPACE(\log n)$.

In Section 6 we consider words obtained by double D0L TAG systems. As shown in [CK] this class contains very complicated infinite words. However, from the computational point of view this is not so; we show that all words obtained by exponentially growing such devices are in the space class $GSPACE(\log^2 n)$.

Finally, in Section 7 we conclude with some open problems.

2 Definitions and notations

In this section we fix our computational model - multitape Turing machine - used to define the time and space complexities of infinite words, as well as recall basic mechanisms used to generate infinite words.

Our computational model is *multitape* (or *k-tape*) *Turing machine, MTM* (or *k-TM*) for short, which consist of

- a finite state control;

- k infinite one-way working tapes each of which contains one two-way read/write head;

- one infinite output tape containing one one-way write-only head.

Depending on the current state and the k symbols read by heads on the working tapes the machine makes the following actions (corresponding one step in a computation):

(i)   It changes the current state to a new one;

(ii)   It writes a symbol on the output tape and moves the head on the output tape one unit to the right, or it does not do anything on the output tape;

(iii)   Each head on a working tape writes a symbol from the finite working alphabet on the currently scanned square and possibly moves to the neighboring square in the right or left.

A *configuration* of a k-*TM* is $Q = (w, p, x_1, \ldots, x_k)$ where w is a content of the output tape, p is a state and each x_i is a content of ith working tape including the position of the head. For a configuration Q, $\bar{Q} = (p, x_1, \ldots, x_k)$ is referred to as its *internal configuration*. *Initial configuration* is the one where all tapes are empty, i.e. containing only blank symbols. As usual *a computation* is a sequence of (consecutive) configurations $Q_0, Q_1, \ldots, Q_n, \ldots$ where Q_0 is the initial one and the machine moves from Q_i to Q_{i+1} in one step. We call the sequence $\bar{Q}_0, \bar{Q}_1, \ldots, \bar{Q}_n, \ldots$ the corresponding *internal computation*.

Next we define our central notions how a *MTM* generates an infinite word.

An *infinite word* $w \in \Sigma^\omega$ *is generated by a MTM* M if the computation $D = Q_0, Q_1, \ldots$ of M has the following properties:

(i) D is infinite;

(ii) Q_0 is the initial configuration of M, i.e. all the tapes are empty;

(iii)   In each configuration Q_i the content of the output tape is a prefix of w;

(iv)   For each i there exists an index j such that $j > i$ and the content of the output tape in Q_i is a proper prefix of that in Q_j.

Let M be a MTM generating a word w. The *time* and *space complexities* of M are functions $T_M : \mathbb{N} \to \mathbb{N}$ and $S_M : \mathbb{N} \to \mathbb{N}$ defined as follows:

$T_M(n) = i_n$, where Q_{i_n} is the first configuration of the computation of M having the prefix of w of length n on the output tape.

$S_M(n) = \max\{S(Q_i) \mid i = 0, \ldots, T_M(n)\}$, where $S(Q_i)$ is the space complexity of the configuration Q_i measured as the maximum of the lengths of words on working tapes.

Finally, we define the complexity classes dealt with in this paper in a standard way: For any $s, t : \mathbb{N} \to \mathbb{N}$

$GTIME(t) = \{w \in \Sigma^\omega \mid \exists \text{ a } MTM \ M \text{ generating } w \text{ and } T_M(n) \le t(n) \text{ for all } n\}$;

$GSPACE(s) = \{w \in \Sigma^\omega \mid \exists \text{ a } MTM \ M \text{ generating } w \text{ and } S_M(n) \le s(n) \text{ for all } n\}$;

$GTIME - SPACE(t, s) = \{w \in \Sigma^\omega \mid \exists \text{ a } MTM \ M \text{ generating } w \text{ and } T_M(n) \le t(n), S_M(n) \le s(n) \text{ for all } n\}$.

It follows from the speed-up argument, as in ordinary complexity theory, that, for example, any $w \in \Sigma^\omega$ which can be generated by a MTM in space $\mathcal{O}(f)$ is in the class $GSPACE(f)$.

The most commonly used method, introduced already by Thue [Th], to generate infinite words is to iterate a morphism $h : \Sigma^* \to \Sigma^*$. In order to obtain a unique infinite word it is normally assumed that h satisfies a so-called *prefix-condition*, i.e. for some letter a, a is a proper prefix of $h(a)$. Then, if h is nonerasing, there exists the limit

$$w = \lim_{i \to \infty} h^i(a).$$

Natural generalizations of this method are to use more powerful mappings in the iteration, such as deterministic gsm's, or to further rewrite the result of the iteration by some rules, such as using another morphism, cf. for example [AG], [Lo] and [Sa].

A unified general approach to generate infinite words in the above framework was developed in [CK]. A central notion here is *double D0L TAG system* which consist of two infinite one-way tapes each of which containing a one-way read-only head and a one-way write-only head. In each step of the generation both read-only heads read a symbol and move to the next square while the write-only heads write the corresponding outputs to the first empty squares of these tapes. Consequently, the rewriting rules are of the form

$$\begin{pmatrix} a \\ b \end{pmatrix} \to \begin{pmatrix} \alpha \\ \beta \end{pmatrix}, \quad a, b \in \Sigma, \ \alpha, \beta \in \Sigma^+. \tag{1}$$

This model was introduced to capture simultaneously the two generalizations of iterating a morphism: iterating a deterministic gsm and iterating a morphism and then mapping by another morphism (cf. [CK]). Consequently, double D0L TAG systems were used to generate infinite words rather than pairs of infinite words, that is the result is read from the first tape.

For our purposes it is preferable to view a double D0L TAG system as an iterative device as follows: Let a double D0L TAG system G be given by (1), and assume that for some letters a and b, a is a proper prefix of α and b is a proper prefix of β. Now, (1) can be extended to a morphism $H : (\Sigma \times \Sigma)^* \to \Sigma^* \times \Sigma^*$, and consequently, can be viewed as a mapping $F : \Sigma^* \times \Sigma^* \to \Sigma^* \times \Sigma^*$ defined as

$$F(x,y) = H(\mathrm{pref}_l(x), \mathrm{pref}_l(y)) \quad \text{with} \quad l = \min\{|x|, |y|\}.$$

It follows that $F^i(a, b)$ is always well defined, and moreover, that the components of $F^{i-1}(a, b)$ are proper prefixes of the corresponding components of $F^i(a, b)$. Hence, there exist infinite words w and v such that

$$(w, v) = \lim_{i \to \infty} F^i(a, b). \tag{2}$$

We call $F^i(a, b)$ the ith *iterate* of G, in particular $F^0(a, b) = (a, b)$. A word generated by a double D0L TAG system is the limit of the first component of (2). Here G is called *exponential* if there exist constants K and σ such that $|\Pi_j \cdot (F^i(a, b))| \geq K\sigma^i$ for all $i \geq 0$ and $j = 1, 2$, where Π_j denotes the jth projection.

We conclude this section with a few remarks. The approach illustrated above to generate infinite words measures the descriptional complexity rather than computational one. More complicated devices are needed to generate more complicated words. However, the actual complexity to generate considered words, which is the main theme of this paper, is not directly obtainable from the models. On the other hand the following conclusions can be drawn easily.

Fact 2.1. *Each $w \in \Sigma^\omega$ generated by iterating a morphism belongs to $GTIME-SPACE(n^2, n)$.*

This follows immediately since the difference of the positions of the reading and writing heads can be stored in a linear space and each step of the rewriting can be simulated by traversing the working tape. Obviously, the result extends to the words obtained by iterating a deterministic gsm or even double D0L TAG system.

Fact 2.2. *Each $w \in \Sigma^\omega$ generated by iterating a morphism can be generated in linear space and real-time by a two head Turing machine.*

Indeed, if two heads are allowed the above traversing can be avoided and the result follows. Also Fact 2.2 can be extended similarly as Fact 2.1.

As a convention we assume throughout that all morphisms, dgsm's etc. are nonerasing.

3 Infinite words with the smallest complexity

In this section we look at the smallest space complexity classes. From the computational point of view this is clearly the class $GSPACE(\mathcal{O}(1))$, while from the descriptional point of view it seems to be the class of ultimately periodic infinite words. We show that these two classes coincide. Moreover we prove a gap theorem showing that there exists no space complexity class between $GSPACE(\mathcal{O}(1))$ and $GSPACE(\log n)$. Therefore $GSPACE(\log n)$ can be referred to as the second smallest space complexity class.

We recall that infinite words w of the form $w = xy^\omega$, with $x, y \in \Sigma^+$, are called *ultimately periodic*.

Lemma 3.1. *Each ultimately periodic word $w = xy^\omega$ belongs to $GTIME - SPACE(n, \mathcal{O}(1))$.*

Proof. Clearly, finite words x and y can be stored in the states of a finite automaton which can produce w in a real time.

□

Next we show not only the converse of Lemma 3.1 but also that there is no hierarchy between $GSPACE(\mathcal{O}(1))$ and $GSPACE(\log n)$.

Lemma 3.2. *Let $f : \mathbb{N} \to \mathbb{N}$ be a function satisfying $f(n) = o(\log n)$. Then each $w \in GSPACE(f)$ is ultimately periodic.*

Proof. Assume that $w \in GSPACE(f)$ with $f(n) = o(\log n)$, and let M be a $k - TM$ generating w. Hence $S_M(n) = o(\log n)$. Let the number of states of M be b and the cardinality of the working alphabet be d. Then the number of distinct internal configurations in the initial part $Q_0, Q_1, \ldots, Q_{T_M(n)}$ of the computation of M is bounded by

$$b \cdot (d+1)^{k \cdot S_M(n)} \cdot (S_M(n))^k \leq c^{S_M(n)}$$

for some suitably chosen constant c. By the assumption $S_M(n) = o(\log n)$ there exists an n_0, and hence also the smallest n_0, such that

$$n_0 \geq c^{S_M(n_0)} + 1.$$

Now, consider the initial part $Q_0, Q_1, \ldots, Q_{T_M(n_0)}$ of the computation of M generating the prefix of w of length n_0. Since $T_M(n_0) \geq n_0 \geq c^{S_M(n_0)} + 1$ there exist such $i, j \in \{0, 1, \ldots, T_M(n_0)\}$ that $Q_i = \{w_1, g_1, x_{11}, \ldots, x_{1k}\}$, $Q_j = \{w_2, g_2, x_{21}, \ldots, x_{2k}\}$, and moreover $g_1 = g_2$ and $x_{1j} = x_{2j}$ for $j = 1, \ldots, k$. Hence, since M is deterministic the internal computation of M must be

$$\bar{Q}_0, \bar{Q}_1, \ldots, \bar{Q}_i(\bar{Q}_{i+1}, \ldots, \bar{Q}_j)^\omega.$$

We assumed that w is infinite, so that $w_2 = w_1 y$ for some nonempty word y. Consequently, $w = w_1 y^\omega$ proving the lemma.

□

Now we can state the main results of this section which are immediate consequences of Lemmas 3.1 and 3.2.

Theorem 3.3. *For $w \in \Sigma^\omega$ the following conditions are equivalent:*

(i) $w \in GSPACE(\mathcal{O}(1))$;

(ii) w *is ultimately periodic.*

Theorem 3.4. *For any function $f : \mathbb{N} \to \mathbb{N}, f(n) = o(\log n)$ the following equalities hold true:*

$$GTIME - SPACE(n, \mathcal{O}(1)) = GSPACE(\mathcal{O}(1)) = GSPACE(f).$$

4   Infinite words generated by iterating a morphism

As we showed in Section 3 the second smallest space complexity class is $GSPACE(\log n)$. Here we prove that all infinite words obtained by iterating a morphism are in this class.

We start with a simple lemma.

Lemma 4.1. *Let y be a word in Σ^+ and $h : \Sigma^* \to \Sigma^*$ a nonerasing morphism. There exists a MTM M which for a given i computes the length of $h^i(y)$ and uses at most $\log_2(|h^i(y)|)$ squares of any working tape.*

Proof. We assume that i is given in binary form in the first working tape, and that Σ is ordered, say $\Sigma = \{1, \ldots, k\}$. M operates as follows:

(i)   It writes the number of the occurrences of letter l in y, for $l = 1, \ldots, k$ to the $(l + 1)$st working tape;

(ii)   Assuming that the contents of the tapes $2, \ldots, k + 1$ coincide with the number of letters $1, \ldots, k$ in $h^j(y)$ respectively, M computes and stores to these tapes the numbers of the corresponding letters in $h^{j+1}(y)$;

(iii)   This is repeated i times and then the contents of the tapes $2, \ldots, k + 1$ are summed up.

Clearly, the above, in particular (ii), can be realized by a $(k + 2) - TM$. Moreover, if the computations are carried out in binary numbers the machine works within the required space.

$\square$

For a word $w = a_1 \ldots a_n, a_i \in \Sigma$, we denote $a_j = j[w]$. Then we can prove.

Theorem 4.2. *Let $w \in \Sigma^\omega$ be an infinite word obtained by iterating a morphism h, i.e. $h^i(a)$ is a prefix of w for all i. Then $w \in GSPACE(\log n)$.*

Proof. Let $h(a) = ax$ where $x = b_1 \ldots b_m$ and $a, b_1, \ldots, b_m \in \Sigma$. Denote $w_i = h^i(a)$ and $w_{j,i} = h^i(b_j)$ for $i \geq 0$ and $j = 1, \ldots, m$. Then clearly

$$w_i = w_{i-1} w_{1,i-1} \cdots w_{m,i-1}.$$

A *MTM* M computing the jth letter of w in space $\mathcal{O}(\log j)$ is constructed as follows.

First M computes the smallest index i_0 such that

$$|w_{i_0}| > j,$$

as well as the value $|w_{i_0-1}|$. By Lemma 5.1, this is possible. Then M knows that

$$j[w] = (j - |w_{i_0-1}|)[w_{1,i_0-1} \cdots w_{m,i_0-1}].$$

Now, by several applications of Lemma 5.1 M computes the smallest m_0 such that

$$j - |w_{i_0-1}| < \Sigma_{j=1}^{m_0} |w_{j,i_0-1}|.$$

After this point M knows that

$$j[w] = j_0[w_{m_0,i_0-1}],$$

where

$$j_0 = j - |w_{i_0-1}| - \Sigma_{j=1}^{m_0-1} |w_{j,i_0-1}|.$$

Now M repeats the whole process: It computes the smallest i_1 such that

$$|h^{i_1}(b_{m_0})| = |w_{m_0,i_1}| > j_0.$$

After at most i_0 iterations M knows the value $j[w]$.

Besides applications of Lemma 5.1, M performs only simple arithmetic operations, and hence operates in the required logarithmic space.

$\square$

Of course, the converse of Theorem 5.2 is not true, as shown by the following example.

Example 4.3. Consider the infinite word

$$\text{Bin} = \text{bin}(1)2\text{bin}(2)2\ldots\text{bin}(j)2\ldots \in \{0,1,2\}^\omega,$$

where $\text{bin}(n)$ is the binary encoding of the number n. Clearly, $\text{bin}(j+1)$ can be computed from $\text{bin}(j)$ without any extra space, so that $\text{Bin} \in GSPACE(\log n)$. On the other hand, Bin is not obtainable by iterating a morphism, of [CK]. Its obvious modification where $\text{bin}(j)$ is replaced by its reverse $r(\text{bin}(j))$ is, however, obtainable by iterating a dgsm, since a dgsm can compute the function $r(\text{bin}(j)) \mapsto r(\text{bin}(j+1))$.

5 Infinite words generated by iterating a dgsm

In this section we consider infinite words generated by iterating a deterministic gsm, and show that if the considered dgsm mapping τ is exponentially growing, i.e. $\tau^i(a)$ is of exponential length in i, then the generated word belongs to the second smallest space complexity class $GSPACE(\log n)$.

Theorem 5.1. *Let $w \in \Sigma^\omega$ be an infinite word obtained by iterating an exponentially growing dgsm. Then $w \in GSPACE(\log n)$.*

Proof. Let α be an infinite word generated by an exponential dgsm G with σ and λ as the output and new state functions and q_0 as the initial state, i.e.

$$\alpha = \lim_{i \to \infty} \tau^i(a)$$

where τ is the dgsm mapping defined by G.

We show how the letter in the nth position of α can be computed in $\mathcal{O}(\log n)$ space. Let the nth letter be in the ith iterate of τ, i.e.

$$|\tau^{i-1}(a)| < n \leq |\tau^i(a)|.$$

We associate with n an $(i+1)$-tuple

$$A(n) = (\gamma_0, \gamma_1, \ldots, \gamma_i) \tag{3}$$

called the history of n as follows:

Let us denote the above nth letter in α (which we are supposed to compute) by a_i. Further let

$$seq(n) = a_0 \, (= a), a_1, a_2, \ldots, a_i$$

be the sequence of occurrences of letters in α such that a_{j-1} derives a_j in the generation of α by τ, and let

$$state(n) = q_0, q_1, \ldots, q_{i-1}$$

be the sequence of the states of the dgsm such that a_j is scanned in the state q_i. Now, clearly for $j = 1, \ldots, j$, a_j occurs in

$$\beta_j = \sigma(a_{j-1}, q_{j-1}),$$

let us say, as the p_j's letter, and we are ready to fix the components of (3) in the following way

$$\gamma_0 = (a_0, 1, q_0)$$

$$\gamma_j = (\beta_j, p_j, q_j), \text{ for } j = 1, \ldots, i-1,$$

and

$$\gamma_i = p_i.$$

It follows immediately that

(i) $A(n)$ can be stored in space $\mathcal{O}(i)$,

and

(ii) the letter a_i can be concluded from $A(n)$, in fact $a_i = p_i[\sigma(p_{i-1}(\beta_{i-1}), q_{i-1})]$.

Further since $|\tau^i(a)|$ is exponential in i we have $\mathcal{O}(i) = \mathcal{O}(\log n)$ so that it remains to be shown that $A(n)$ can be computed in space $\mathcal{O}(\log n)$. This, in turn, follows if we can show that $A(n+1)$ can be computed from $A(n)$ by using only a constant amount of additional space.

In order to prove this let $A(n)$ be given. There are three cases.

First, if

$$p_i < |\sigma(p_{i-1}[\beta_{i-1}], q_{i-1})|$$

then $A(n+1)$ is obtained from $A(n)$ by setting $\gamma_i = p_i + 1$.

Second, if

$$p_j < |\sigma(p_{j-1}[\beta_{j-1}], q_{j-1})|$$

and

$$p_k = |\sigma(p_{k-1}[\beta_{k-1}], q_{k-1})|, \quad \text{for } k > j, \tag{4}$$

we set

$$\gamma_j = (\beta_j, p_j + 1, \lambda(p_j[\beta_j], q_j)),$$

and recursively, assuming that $\gamma_{j+t-1} = (\beta_{j+t-1}, p_{j+t-1}, q_{j+t-1})$, and

$$\gamma_{j+t} = (\sigma(p_{j+t-1}[\beta_{j+t-1}], q_{j+t-1}), 1, \lambda(p_{j+t}[\beta_{j+t}], q_{j+t}), \text{ for } t = 1, \ldots, i - j - 1,$$

and

$$\gamma_i = 1.$$

Third, if (4) holds for all $k \leq i$, we define a new γ-value γ_{i+1}, but otherwise follow the lines of the second case:

$$\gamma_0 = (a, 1, q_0)$$

$$\gamma_t = (\sigma(1[\beta_{t-1}], q_{t-1}), 1, \lambda(p_t[\beta_t], q_t)), \quad \text{for } t = 1, \ldots, i,$$

where $\gamma_{t-1} = (\beta_{t-1}, 1, q_{t-1})$, and

$$\gamma_{i+1} = 1.$$

This completes the proof of Theorem 5.1.

□

Theorem 5.1 leads to a few natural comments. First, many combinatorially complicated infinite words are obtained by iterating a dgsm. A typical example is the Kolakoski word, cf. [L],

$$\text{Kol} = 2211212212211\ldots ,$$

which is obtained from word 2 by iterating a dgsm which is represented in the Fig. 1.

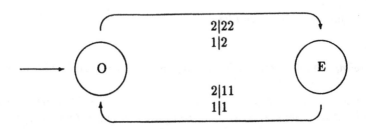

Fig. 1. A dgsm generating Kolakoski word

Second, as pointed out in Example 4.3, it is not necessary in Theorem 5.1 that a dgsm is exponential.

Third, although in many concrete examples, like in the above Kolakoski word, we know that the word is obtained by iterating an *exponential* dgsm, in general the problem whether a given dgsm is exponential is undecidable.

Theorem 5.2 *It is undecidable whether a given dgsm is exponential.*

Proof. Let M be an arbitrary 1-tape Turing machine, x its input and a a letter in the alphabet of M, but not in x. We define a dgsm τ which carries out the computations

$$x_i \mapsto x_{i+1} \ , \text{ for } i \geq 0,$$

where x_i corresponds to the ith configuration of M on input x. Of course, we can assume here that the computation of M is infinite simply by demanding that $x_{i+j} = x_i$, for all $j \geq 0$ and all halting configurations x_i of M. Clearly, such a dgsm exists.

Now, we modify τ such that it maps its starting letter \$ into $\$x_0\cent$ and $\cent$ into itself and it behaves as above unless x_i contains a letter a, in which case it is otherwise identity but duplicates each occurrence of a. Again, it is obvious that such a dgsm, say τ', exists.

It follows from the above construction that

τ' is exponential, if and only if M prints a letter a on input x.

Clearly, the latter problem is undecidable, so that our proof is complete.

□

6 Infinite words generated by a double D0L TAG system

As a third iterative mechanism to generate infinite words we consider double D0L TAG systems of [CK]. This is very powerful mechanism. Indeed contrary to the other two mechanisms we have considered, it is not known any concrete example of an infinite word which cannot be generated by this mechanism - although by a diagonalization argument such words clearly exist.

Despite of the above the computational complexity of infinite words generated by double D0L TAG systems is not very high. We are not able to show that these words, even under certain restrictions still would lay in the second smallest space complexity class, but we do can prove the following.

Theorem 6.1 *Let $w \in \Sigma^\omega$ be generated by an exponential double D0L TAG system. Then $w \in GSPACE(\log^2 n)$.*

Proof. Let α be an infinite word generated by an exponential double D0L TAG system G with Σ as the alphabet, say

$$\alpha = \Pi_1 \lim_{i \to \infty} F^i(a, b)$$

where F is the morphism $(\Sigma \times \Sigma)^* \mapsto \Sigma^* \times \Sigma^*$ defined by G and Π_1 (resp. Π_2) is the projection to the first (resp. second) component. Denote further

$$\alpha = a_0 a_1 a_2 \ldots a_n \ldots \quad , a_i \in \Sigma.$$

We give an algorithm to compute a_n in space $\mathcal{O}(\log^2 n)$. We describe our algorithm only on an intuitive level and leave its straightforward implementation by a MTM to the reader.

The input for our algorithm is a number n given in binary. Let i be such that

$$|\Pi_1(F^{i-1}(a, b))| < n \leq |\Pi_1(F^i(a, b))|.$$

Our algorithm computes for consecutive values of $j = 1, 2, \ldots$ the letters

$$t[\Pi_1(F^j(a, b))], \tag{5}$$

for $t = 1, \ldots, |\Pi_1(F^j(a, b))|$, and

$$v[\Pi_2(F^j(a, b))], \tag{6}$$

for $v = 1, \ldots, |\Pi_2(F^j(a, b))|$, and stops when t reaches value n. In more details the algorithm works recursively as follows. To compute a_n assume that all the letters in (5) and (6) for all values of $j = i - 1$ can be computed. Using this assumption the pairs

$$(t[\Pi_1(F^{i-1}(a, b))], t[\Pi_2(F^{i-1}(a, b))])$$

for $t = \min(|\Pi_1(F^{i-1}(a,b))|, |\Pi_2(F^{i-1}(a,b))|)$, are computed one after another (reusing the space). At the same the count of the sum

$$\Sigma_{u=1}^t |\Pi_1(F(u[\Pi_1(F^{i-1}(a,b))], u[\Pi_2(F^{i-1}(a,b))]))| \qquad (7)$$

is kept until for the first time it reaches the value $\geq n$. When this happens the value a_n is obtained.

The space needed to compute (7) (or its analog for the other component) is linear in i. Consequently, since the depth of the recursion is i, the total need for space is $\mathcal{O}(i^2)$. Now, finally from the facts that $|\Pi_k(F^i(a,b))|$ are exponential in i, it follows that the space requirement in terms of the size n of the input is $\mathcal{O}(\log^2 n)$ as required.

□

The above proof proposes two comments. First, it can immediately extended to any numbers of tapes. Second, the requirement that the system is exponential is rather strong, it means that the lengths of iterates in both components grow exponentially.

7   Concluding remarks

We have investigated the computational complexity of certain infinite words obtained by iterating certain types of mappings considered in the litterature, namely morphisms, deterministic gsm's and double D0L TAG systems. We showed, by three different constructions, that the space complexity of such words are $\mathcal{O}(\log n)$ for morphisms and exponential dgsm's and $\mathcal{O}(\log^2 n)$ for exponential double D0L TAG systems. In particular, we were not able to separate these mappings by the computational complexity of the words they generate. On the contrary out results hint that the computational complexity of infinite words obtained by an iterative mapping seems to be rather low.

Maybe the separation of some of these classes could be achieved by considering simultaneously time and space. A step to that direction can be a result in [HK] showing that the binary word encoding consecutive binary numbers can not be generated simultaneously in real time and in space $\mathcal{O}(n/\log n)$ by a MTM having only a binary alphabet.

It follows that an obvious topic for further research is to consider the time complexity of infinite words, as well as the combined time-space complexity.

We conclude with a few concrete open problems. The first two asks whether our Theorems 5.1 and 6.1 can be generalized.

Problem 1. Are all words generated by dgsm's in $GSPACE(\log n)$?

Problem 2. Are all words generated by double D0L TAG systems in the class $GSPACE(\log^2 n)$ or even in the class $GSPACE(\log n)$?

Finally, as a very interesting but probably difficult problem we state

Problem 3. Give a concrete infinite word w and prove that it cannot be generated in linear time and logarithmic space by a MTM, or even more strongly, that it cannot be generated in logarithmic space.

References

[AG] J.M. Autebert, J.Gabaró: Iterated GSM's and Co-CFL. Acta Informatica 26(1989), 749-769.

[CK] K. Culik II and J. Karhumäki: Iterative devices generating infinite words. IJFCS (to appear).

[Ch] G.J. Chaitin: On the length of programs for computing finite binary sequences:statistical considerations. J.Assoc.Comp.Mach. 16(1969), 145-159.

[HK] J. Hromkovic and J. Karhumäki: Two lower bounds on complexity of infinite word generation, manuscript (1993).

[Ko] A.N. Kolmogorov: Three approaches to the quantitative definition of information. Problems Inform. Transmission 1(1968), 662-664.

[LV] M. Li, P.M.B. Vitányi: Kolmogorov complexity and its applications. In: Handbook of Theoretical Computer Science A - Algorithms and Complexity (Jan van Leeuwen, ed.), Elsevier, Amsterdam, New York-Oxford-Tokyo & The MIT Press, Cambridge 1990, 187-254.

[L] A. Lepistö: Repetitions in Kolakoski Sequence. In: Developments in Language Theory (G. Rozenberg and A. Salomaa, eds.), World Scientific, Singapore 1994.

[Lo] M. Lothaire: Combinatorics on Words. Addison-Wesley, Reading, Massachusetts 1981.

[PP] D. Perrin and J.-E. Pin: Mots Infinis. Technical Report 93.40. LITP, Paris 1993.

[Sa] A. Salomaa: Jewels of formal language theory. Computer Science Press, Rockville, Maryland 1981.

[So] R.J. Solomonoff: A formal theory of inductive inference. Part 1 and Part 2. Inform. and Control 7(1964), 1-22 and 224-254.

[Th] A.Thue: Über unendliche Zeichenreihen. Norske Vid. Selsk. Skr., I Mat. Nat. KI., Kristiania 7(1906), 1-22.

On Some Open Problems Concerning the Complexity of Cellular Arrays

Oscar H. Ibarra [*] *and Tao Jiang* [†]

Abstract. We give a brief account of the progress that has been made in the last few years concerning the computational complexity of cellular arrays, and cite a few important open problems that remain unresolved.

Key words: Cellular array, computational complexity, one-way communication, mesh-connected, tree-connected.

1. Introduction

One of the earliest and simplest models of parallel computation is the cellular array (also called cellular automaton). They have been studied extensively in the literature. Early papers have studied these machines in the context of formal language recognition - their recognition power, closure and decision properties, and their relationships to other models of computation, such as Turing machines, linear bounded automata, pushdown automata, and finite automata. In later papers, the study of these arrays has focused on their abilities to perform numeric and nonnumeric computations in various areas such as computational linear algebra, signal and image processing, graph problems, string processing, sorting, computational geometry, database, dynamic programming, etc. Such arrays, whose processors need no longer be "finite-state", have also been called systolic arrays.

There remains a number of important and fundamental open problems concerning the computational complexity of cellular arrays. In this paper, we review some of these questions, and give a brief summary of the progress that has been made in the recent past in resolving some of them, including questions concerning one-way communication versus two-way communication, linear-time versus real-time, serial input versus parallel input, space-efficient simulation of one-way arrays, etc.

The paper has six sections, including this section. In the rest of Section 1, we recall the definition of a linear cellular array and a related model called linear iterative array. Generalizations of these models are also defined. Section 2 gives sequential machine characterizations of the arrays, which are useful in proving many of the results. Section 3 looks at the one-way versus two-way question, while Section 4 investigates the complexity of linear-time linear arrays. Section 5 discusses the complexity of one-way mesh-connected arrays. Finally, Section 6 studies briefly the complexity of tree-structured arrays.

---

[*] Research was supported in part by NSF Grant CCR-8918409. Address: Department of Computer Science, University of California, Santa Barbara, CA 93106, USA. Email: ibarra@cs.ucsb.edu.

[†] Research was supported in part by NSERC Operating Grant OGP0046613. Address: Department of Computer Science, McMaster University, Hamilton, Ontario L8S 4K1, Canada. Email: jiang@maccs.mcmaster.ca.

1.1. Linear cellular arrays

One of the simplest models of parallel computation is the *linear cellular array* (LCA) [BUCH84, KOSA74, SMIT70, SMIT71, SMIT72]. An LCA is a one-dimensional array of n identical finite-state machines (called nodes) that operate synchronously at discrete time steps by means of a common clock (see Figure 1). The input $a_1a_2 \cdots a_n$, where a_i is in the finite alphabet Σ, is applied to the array in parallel at time 0 by setting the states of the nodes to $a_1, a_2, \cdots, a_n$. The state of a node at time t is a function of its state and the states of its left and right neighbors at time t-1. We assume that the leftmost (rightmost) node has an "imaginary" left (right) neighbor whose state is $ at all times. We say that $a_1a_2 \cdots a_n$ is accepted by the LCA if, when given the input $a_1a_2 \cdots a_n$, the leftmost cell eventually enters an accepting state. The LCA has time complexity T(n) if it accepts inputs of length n within T(n) steps. Clearly, for a nontrivial computation, $T(n) \geq n$. If $T(n) = cn$ for some real constant $c \geq 1$, then the LCA is called a *linear-time* LCA. When $T(n) = n$, it is called a *real-time* LCA. Note that an LCA without time restriction is equivalent to a linear-space bounded deterministic TM.

Figure 1. An LCA.

A restricted version of an LCA is the *one-way* linear cellular array (OLCA) [DYER80]. In an OLCA, the communication between nodes is one-way, from left to right. The next state of a node depends on its present state and that of its left neighbor (see Figure 2). An input is accepted by the OLCA if the rightmost node of the array eventually enters an accepting state. The time complexity of an OLCA is defined as in the case of an LCA.

Figure 2. An OLCA.

Although OLCA's have been studied extensively in the past (see, *e.g.*, [BUCH84, CHOF84, DYER80, IBAR85b, IBAR86, UMEO82]) a precise characterization of their computational complexity with respect to space- and/or time-bounded TM's is not known. For example, it is not known whether linear space-bounded deterministic TM's are more powerful than OLCA's, although a positive answer seems likely.

1.2. A related model: linear iterative arrays

Another simple model that is closely related to linear cellular arrays is the *linear iterative array* [COLE69, HENN61, IBAR85b, IBAR86]. The structure of an LIA is similar to an LCA, as shown in Figure 3. (Note that here we assume that the size of the array is bounded by the length of the input. In some papers, the array is assumed to be infinite.) The only difference between an LIA and an LCA is that in an LIA the input $a_1a_2 \cdots a_n$ is fed serially to the leftmost node. Symbol a_i, $1 \leq i \leq n$, is received by the leftmost node at time i-1; after time n-1, it receives the endmarker $. That is, $ is not consumed and always available for reading. At time 0, each cell is in a distingushed quiescent state q_0. As in an LCA, the state of a node at time t is a function of its state and the states of its left and right neighbors at time t-1. For the leftmost node, the next state depends on its present state and the input symbol. An OLIA is defined in a straightforward way.

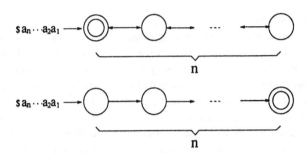

Figure 3. An LIA and an OLIA.

For a nontrivial computation, the time complexity of an LIA is at least n, and the time complexity of an OLIA is at least 2n. So, an LIA operating n steps is called a real-time LIA and an OLIA operating in 2n steps is called a *pseudo-real-time* OLIA.

It is relatively easy to show that an LIA and an LCA can efficiently simulate each other. We will focus on fast simulations between LCA, OLCA, and OLIA in this paper.

1.3. Mesh-connected arrays

Mesh-connected cellular arrays (MCA's) and *mesh-connected iterative arrays* (MIA's) are the two-dimensional analogs of LCA's and LIA's. Here we are mostly interested in the arrays with one-way communication. A one-way mesh-connected iterative array (OMIA) and a one-way mesh-connected cellular array (OMCA) are shown in Figure 4.

1.4. Tree-structured arrays

A *tree cellular array* (TCA) is a full binary tree of depth log n as shown in Figure 5 [DYER81]. The input $a_1 \cdots a_n$ is applied to the leaves in parallel at time 0 by setting the states of the bottom nodes to $a_1 \cdots a_n\$^k$ (from left to right), where k is the smallest nonnegative integer such that n+k is a power of 2. All internal nodes are initially set to the quiescent state. The next state of a node is determined by the current states of the node and its parent and children. A one-way TCA (OTCA) is a TCA with one-way (*i.e.*, bottom-up) communication between nodes. Thus, the next state of a node is determined only by the current states of the node and its children. Clearly, for a nontrivial computation, a TCA (OTCA)

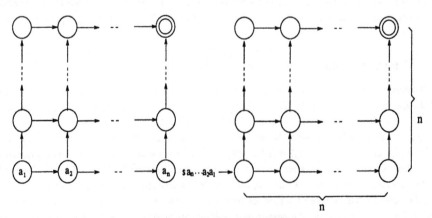

Figure 4. An OMCA and an OMIA.

has time complexity at least log n since it takes at least log n steps for the root to enter a non-quiescent state.

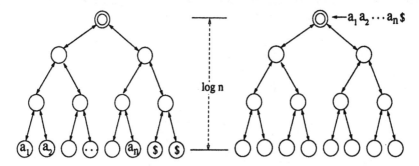

Figure 5. A TCA and a TIA.

The only difference between a *tree iterative array* (TIA) and a TCA is their input modes [CULI86]. See Figure 5. Again, here we assume that the tree has a log n bounded depth.

To simplify the presentation, we introduce the following notations.

1. For any class C of machines and function T(n), C(T(n)) denotes the machines in C operating in time T(n).

2. Let C_1 and C_2 be two classes of machines. $C_1 \subseteq C_2$ means that every machine M_1 in C_1 can be simulated by some machine M_2 in C_2. $C_1 \subset C_2$ means that $C_1 \subseteq C_2$ and there is a machine in C_2 that cannot be simulated by any machine in C_1.

2. Characterizing the computation of linear arrays

There is a nice way to represent the computation of a linear iterative or cellular array using its time-space diagram (or unrolling). The representation can be described in terms of a sequential machine. Sequential machine characterizations of various types of iterative and cellular arrays have been given in [IBAR85a, IBAR85b, IBAR86]. In particular, there is a sequential machine, called SMI, which is equivalent to an OLIA, and a sequential machine, called SMC, which accepts the *reverse* of the language accepted by an OLCA.

An SMI is a restricted on-line single tape TM. It consists of a semi-infinite worktape (bounded at the left by a special marker ¢) and a finite-state control with an input terminal from which it receives the serial input $a_1 a_2 \cdots a_n \$$. Each a_i, $1 \le i \le n$, comes from a finite input alphabet Σ, which does not contain $. The symbol $ is used as the endmarker for the input. The SMI operates as follows. Initially, all cells of the worktape (to the right of ¢) contain λ's (where λ is the blank symbol). The read-write head (RWH) makes left-to-right sweeps of the worktape as follows. A left-to-right sweep begins with the RWH scanning ¢ and the machine in a distinguished start state q_0. The machine then reads the input symbol a_i (starting with i=1) and moves right (of ¢) into some state different from q_0. It continues to move right, rewriting symbols scanned by non-λ symbols and changing states (except into q_0), until the RWH scans a λ. When the RWH reaches λ, it rewrites λ by a non-λ symbol different from $ and resets to the left boundary marker ¢ in state q_0. Then it begins the next left-to-right sweep. When the endmarker $ is read, the machine operates just like on any input a_i, except that at the end of the left-to-right sweep, the machine rewrites λ by a right boundary marker $. The machine then continues making left-to-right sweeps between ¢ and $ as before, but without expanding the work space. (The $ is never rewritten.) We assume that the input endmarker $ is not consumed when read by the machine, and is always available for reading. The worktape profile of 6 (left-to-right) sweeps of the SMI is shown in Figure 6. The string

$a_1a_2 \cdots a_n$ is accepted by an SMI M if, after reading the input $a_1a_2 \cdots a_n\$$, M eventually enters an accepting state at the end of some left-to-right sweep, *i.e.*, when the RWH reaches the right boundary marker $\$$. The sweep complexity $S(n)$ of an SMI on string $a_1a_2 \cdots a_n$ is the least number of sweeps needed to accept it. Clearly, if the computation is nontrivial, $S(n) \geq n+1$.

Sweep	Input	Worktape
0		¢
1	a_1	¢Z_1^1
2	a_2	¢$Z_1^2 Z_2^1$
3	a_3	¢$Z_1^3 Z_2^2 Z_3^1$
4	$\$$	¢$Z_1^4 Z_2^3 Z_3^2$$\$$
5	$\$$	¢$Z_1^5 Z_2^4 Z_3^3$$\$$
6	$\$$	¢$Z_1^6 Z_2^5 Z_3^4$$\$$

Figure 6. The worktape profile of an SMI on input $a_1a_2a_3\$$.

The structure of an SMC is similar to that of the SMI, except that the semi-infinite worktape of an SMC is bounded at the right. The SMC operates as follows. Initially, all cells of the worktape (to the left of ¢) contain λ's, and the RWH is on the rightmost λ. The RWH makes left-to-right sweeps of the worktape as follows. A left-to-right sweep begins with the RWH scanning λ and the machine in a distinguished start state q_0. The machine then reads the input symbol a_i (starting with $i = 1$), rewrites λ by a non-λ symbol, and moves right into some state different from q_0. When the RWH reaches ¢, it resets to the rightmost cell which contains λ in state q_0. Then it begins the next left-to-right sweep. When the input endmarker $\$$ is read, the machine rewrites λ by the left boundary marker $\$$. The machine then continues making left-to-right sweeps between $\$$ and ¢ without expanding the work space. The worktape profile of 6 sweeps of the SMC is shown in Figure 7. Like the SMI, the string $a_1a_2 \cdots a_n$ is accepted by the SMC if, when given the input $a_1a_2 \cdots a_n\$$, the machine eventually enters an accepting state at the end of some left-to-right sweep. The sweep complexity $S(n)$ of an SMC on string $a_1a_2 \cdots a_n$ is the least number of sweeps needed to accept it.

Sweep	Input	Worktape
0		¢
1	a_1	Z_1^1¢
2	a_2	$Z_2^1 Z_1^2$¢
3	a_3	$Z_3^1 Z_2^2 Z_1^3$¢
4	$\$$	$\$$$Z_3^2 Z_2^3 Z_1^4$¢
5	$\$$	$\$$$Z_3^3 Z_2^4 Z_1^5$¢
6	$\$$	$\$$$Z_3^4 Z_2^5 Z_1^6$¢

Figure 7. The worktape profile of an SMC on input $a_1a_2a_3\$$.

The relations between the arrays and the sequential machines are given by the following theorem.

Theorem 2.1. Let $S(n) \geq n+1$. Then

1. $SMI(S(n)) = OLIA(S(n)+n-1)$;

2. A language is accepted by an SMC in $S(n)$ sweeps if and only if its reverse is accepted by an OLCA in $S(n)-1$ steps.

3. One-way versus two-way for linear arrays

The question of whether one-way communication reduces the power of a linear array has remained open for over a decade. In particular, we do not know if OLCA = LCA and if OLIA = LIA. The following result shows that an LIA and an LCA can simulated each other with a delay of at most n steps [IBAR85b].

Theorem 3.1. For any $T(n) \geq n$,

1. $LCA(T(n)) \subseteq LIA(T(n)+n)$;

2. $LIA(T(n)+n) \subseteq LCA(T(n)+n)$.

Hence LIA = LCA. It seems difficult to precisely characterize the computational complexity of an OLCA or an OLIA. Nevertheless, it has been shown in [CHAN88b] that OLIA's are actually very powerful since they can simulate linear time-bounded alternating TM's.

Theorem 3.2.

1. Every linear time-bounded alternating TM can be simulated by an OLIA.

2. $NSPACE(n^{1/2}) \subseteq OLIA$.

3. Every language accepted by a multihead two-way PDA operating in $c^{n/\log n}$ time (for some constant c) can be accepted by an OLIA. Thus, every context-free language is accepted by an OLIA.

4. The class of languages accepted by OLIA's is an AFL closed under intersection, complementation, and reversal. (An AFL is a family of languages containing at least one nonempty language which is closed under the operations of union, concatenation, Kleene +, ε-free homomorphism, inverse homomorphism, and intersection with regular sets [HOPC79].)

Clearly, OLCA $\subseteq$ OLIA. On the other hand, it has also been shown (quite surprisingly) that every OLIA can be simulated by an OLCA [IBAR87]. The difficulty arises from the fact that in an OLIA, *every* node of the array has access to *each* symbol of the input string, whereas in an OLCA, the i-th cell can only access the first i symbols of the input.

Theorem 3.3. OLCA = OLIA.

We sketch the proof briefly. By Theorem 2.1, it suffices to show that every SMI M_1 can be simulated by an SMC M_2. Suppose that the size of the tape alphabet of M_1 is k. Imagine that each cell of M_2 is split into 3 subcells. M_2 could begin by using markers to partition its subcells into 3 contiguous regions A, B and C of equal size. If M_2 had knowledge of n no matter where its RWH is, it could work by moving the input string x into region C, and then using region A as a k^n counter to assist in systematically generating each possible input string y of size n, in region B. Region C is used to first simulate M_1 on y and then to check if y = x. However, M_2 can know n only when its RWH is on the right endmarker. This problem can be resolved by iterating the above procedure n times. In the i-th iteration, M_2 works on the prefix of x of length i, using regions A, B and C of size i each. That is, in the i-th iteration, all possible strings of length i are generated, simulated, and checked against the prefix of x of length i.

Remark. The above simulation of an OLIA by an OLCA involves an exponential slow-down. It would be interesting to know if the slow-down can be made polynomial.

It follows that the results in Theorem 3.2 also hold for OLCA's. These results answer in the affirmative some open questions in [DYER80], *e.g.*, whether OLCA languages are closed under operations such as concatenation and reversal, and whether OLCA's accept context-free languages.

Corollary 3.4.

1. Every linear time-bounded alternating TM can be simulated by an OLCA.

2. $NSPACE(n^{1/2}) \subseteq OLCA$.

3. Every language accepted by a multihead two-way PDA operating in $c^{n/\log n}$ time (for some constant c) can be accepted by an OLCA. Thus, every context-free language is accepted by an OLCA.

4. The class of languages accepted by OLCA's is an AFL closed under intersection, complementation, and reversal.

It seems unlikely that OLCA = LCA. On the other hand, by the above corollary and the fact that LCA = DSPACE(n), proving OLCA $\subset$ LCA would imply $NSPACE(n^{1/2}) \subset DSPACE(n)$, which would be an improvement of Savitch's well-known result [SAVI70]. This should explain why the one-way communication versus two-way communication problem for linear arrays is hard.

4. Complexity of linear-time linear arrays

The following important issues concerning LCA's operating in O(n) time still remain unresolved as of today.

1. Is LCA(n) = LCA(O(n))?

2. Is every context-free language accepted by a real-time LCA?

3. Is the class of real-time LCA languages closed under reversal? under concatenation?

4. Is LCA(O(n)) = LCA?

The first question was asked in [BUCH84]. The last 3 questions were raised in [SMIT72]. In fact, the following seemingly easier question is also open:

5. Is LCA(n) = LCA?

Below we review the partial results that have been obtained in this area. In particular, we will show that

a. LCA(n) = OLCA(O(n)) $\supset$ OLCA(n).

b. LCA(n) = LCA(O(n)) if and only if the class of real-time LCA languages is closed under reversal.

This result is rather interesting since it provides a method of proving/disproving the equivalence of two classes of LCA's in terms of a closure operation.

c. If the class of real-time LCA languages is closed under reversal, then it is also closed under concatenation.

d. OLCA $\subset$ LCA implies LCA(O(n)) $\subset$ LCA.

4.1. Linear-time versus real-time for the arrays

The following result [CHOF84] holds because, when the alphabet is unary, a real-time OLCA can only accept a regular language and a linear-time OLCA can accept the language $\{0^{2^n} \mid n>0\}$.

Theorem 4.1. OLCA(n) $\subset$ OLCA(O(n)).

We now consider relations between linear/real -time LCA, OLCA, and OLIA. The proofs make essential use of the following speed-up lemma, which is interesting in its own right [IBAR85] (see also [BUCH84], [IBAR86], [SMIT72]).

Lemma 4.2. Let T(n) $\geq$ 0 and M be an OLIA (LCA, OLCA) operating in time 2n+T(n) (n+T(n), n+T(n)). We can effectively construct an OLIA (LCA, OLCA) equivalent to M which operates in time 2n+T(n)/k (n+T(n)/k, n+T(n)/k) for any positive integer k.

It follows from the above lemma that any linear-time OLIA (LCA, OLCA) can be converted to one that operates in time $(2+\varepsilon)n$ $((1+\varepsilon)n, (1+\varepsilon)n)$ for any positive real constant ε.

The relations between linear time-bounded LCA, OLCA, and OLIA are summarized in the following theorem [IBAR88b].

Theorem 4.3.

1. $LCA(n) = OLCA(O(n)) = OLIA(2n)$.

2. $LCA(O(n)) = OLIA(O(n))$.

Hence, $LCA(O(n)) \supset OLCA(O(n))$ if and only if $OLIA(O(n)) \supset OLCA(O(n))$. This contrasts with the equivalence of OLIA and OLCA when there is no restriction on the time.

Next we establish the relations between the open questions listed above. We will first state the results in terms of the OLIA and then give the relations between the open questions as corollaries.

Theorem 4.4. $OLIA(O(n)) = OLIA(2n)$ if and only if the class of pseudo-real-time OLIA languages is closed under reversal.

Here is a sketch of the proof. The "if" part holds since the class of linear-time OLIA languages is closed under reversal. For the "only if" part, assume that the class of pseudo-real-time OLIA languages is closed under reversal. We show that every linear-time OLIA can be simulated by a pseudo-real-time OLIA. By Theorem 2.1 and Lemma 4.2, it suffices to prove that every 2n-sweep SMI can be simulated by an n-sweep SMI.

Let M_1 be a 2n-sweep SMI and $L_1 = L(M_1)$ be the language accepted by M_1. Define another language L_2 as follows:
$$L_2 = \{a_1 a_2 \cdots a_n \#^m \mid a_1 a_2 \cdots a_n \in L_1, n \leq m < 2n\},$$
where # is a padding symbol not in the input alphabet of M_1. It is easy to see that L_2 can be accepted by an n-sweep SMI, *i.e.*, L_2 is a pseudo-real-time OLIA language. By the assumption that the class of pseudo-real-time OLIA languages is closed under reversal,
$$L_2^R = \{\#^m a_1 a_2 \cdots a_n \mid a_n \cdots a_2 a_1 \in L_1, n \leq m < 2n\}$$
is also a pseudo-real-time language and accepted by an n-sweep SMI M_2. Now define another language
$$L_3 = \{a_1 \cdots \hat{a}_i \cdots a_n \mid a_n \cdots a_i \cdots a_1 \in L_1, n/4 \leq i < n/2\},$$
where $\hat{a}_i$ is a composite symbol consisting of symbol a_i and marker $\wedge$. It is possible to show that L_3 is accepted by an n-sweep SMI M_3. Using M_3, we can construct an n-sweep SMI M_4 to accept L_2^R, by iteratively guessing a correct location for $\wedge$.

From Theorems 4.3 and 4.4, we have the following corollary.

Corollary 4.5. $LCA(O(n)) = LCA(n)$ if and only if the class of real-time LCA languages is closed under reversal.

Interestingly, the class of real-time OLCA languages is closed under reversal [CHOF84]. Whether it is closed under concatenation is still open. The following partial result is shown in [IBAR87].

Theorem 4.6. The concatenation of two real-time OCA languages is a linear-time OLCA language.

We do not know if the same result holds for LCA languages, *i.e.*, whether the concatenation of two real-time CA languages is a linear-time LCA language. However, it has been shown that if the class of real-time CA languages is closed under reversal, then it is also closed under concatenation [IBAR88b].

Theorem 4.7. If the class of pseudo-real-time OLIA (or real-time LCA) languages is closed under reversal, then it is also closed under concatenation.

When the alphabet is unary, the closure is known [IBAR88b].

Theorem 4.8. The class of unary real-time LCA languages is closed under concatenation.

It would be interesting to know whether the class of unary real-time LCA languages is identical to the class of unary linear-time LCA languages. We conjecture the answer to be negative. Since real-time LCA's can accept fairly difficult unary languages (*e.g.*, the set of primes, the set of perfect squares, etc), it is even hard to find a promising candidate language.

4.2. A discussion of some candidate languages

In [BUCH84], Bucher and Culik conjectured that the language $L = \{0^n 1^m \mid m, n \geq 1$ and m divides $n\}$ is not a real-time LCA language. Since L^R is a real-time LCA language, this would imply that the class of real-time LCA languages is not closed under reversal. Unfortunately the conjecture is not true as it has been shown in [IBAR88b] that L is a real-time LCA language.

Informally, the reason that L is a real-time LCA language is that it is basically a "bounded language" (*i.e.*, $L \subseteq a_1{}^* a_2{}^* \cdots a_k{}^*$ for some distinct symbol $a_1, a_2, \cdots, a_k$). In fact, there is a large class of bounded languages accepted by real-time LCA's.

Let N be the set of natural numbers and k be a positive integer. A set $Q \subseteq N^k$ is a semilinear set [HARR78] if there exist positive integers $m, r_1, \ldots, r_m$ and vectors v_j^i in N^k for $1 \leq i \leq m$, $0 \leq j \leq r_i$ such that

$$Q = \bigcup_{i=1}^{m} \{v_0^i + \sum_{j=1}^{r_i} t_j v_j^i \mid t_j \text{ in } N\}.$$

The language, L_Q, defined by Q is the set $\{a_1^{x_1} \cdots a_k^{x_k} \mid (x_1, \ldots, x_k)$ in $Q\}$, where $a_1, \cdots, a_k$ are distinct symbols. L_Q is called a semilinear language. Note that the language L above is bounded but not semilinear. The next two results are from [IBAR87].

Theorem 4.9. Every semilinear language is accepted by a real-time LCA.

Corollary 4.10 Let L be a language accepted by a one-way multihead PDA, and $L \subseteq a_1{}^* \cdots a_k{}^*$ for distinct symbols $a_1, \ldots, a_k$. Then L is accepted by a real-time LCA.

Ibarra and Jiang [IBAR88b] also proposed a language $L_1 = \{ x^n \# x \mid n \geq 1, x \in \{0,1\}^+ \}$, and conjecture that L is not a real-time LCA language. Note that L_1^R is a real-time LCA language. But it was later shown that L_1 is actually accepted by a real-time LCA.

4.3. Linear-time LCA versus nonlinear-time LCA

Many conjecture that $LCA(O(n)) \subset LCA$. Note that Paterson's result (*i.e.*, $NTIME_1(n^2) \subseteq DSPACE(n)$, where $NTIME_1(n^2)$ is the class of languages accepted by one-tape nondeterministic Turing machines in time $O(n^2)$) [PATE72] does not help unless we can show that the class of linear-time LCA languages is properly contained in $NTIME_1(n^2)$, which is probably even harder. The next result relates this conjecture to the one-way versus two-way problem. The implication holds because $LCA(O(n)) = OLIA(O(n)) \subseteq OLCA$.

Corollary 4.11. If $OLCA \subset LCA$, then $LCA(O(n)) \subset LCA$.

The question of whether $LCA(n) \subset LCA$ seems to be easier to answer. Of course, a negative answer to questions concerning the closure properties under reversal or concatenation would imply a positive answer to this problem, because we know that the class of LCA languages is closed under both reversal and concatenation.

4.4. A summary of open questions and results

The following diagram summarizes what are currently known about the closure properties of various LCA, OLCA and OLIA language classes and their inclusion relations. Here, a single box means the closure under reversal (but the closure under concatenation is open), and a double box means the closure under both reversal and concatenation. A vertical bold line means inclusion and a line with marker / means that the inclusion is proper.

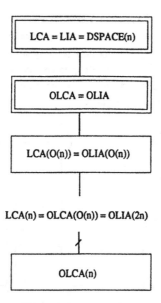

Figure 8. The status diagram.

5. The complexity of one-way mesh-connected arrays

We now consider mesh-connected arrays, especially the ones with one-way communication. Theorem 3.3 can be easily extended to OMCA and OMIA.

Theorem 5.1. OMCA = OMIA.

The one-way communication versus two-way communication question can be answered for mesh-connected arrays, because of the following space-efficient simulation result for OMCA's and OMIA's [CHAN88a].

Theorem 5.2. OMCA = OMIA $\subseteq$ DSPACE($n^{3/2}$).

Remark. It is unclear if the the above space bound is the best possible. In fact, we do not know if OMCA's are more powerful than OLCA's. We also do not know the relationship between OMCA's and LCA's.

Since MCA = MIA = DSPACE(n^2), we obtain that one-way mesh-connected arrays are weaker than their two-way counterparts. In general, for time-bounded one-way arrays, we have the following simulation.

Theorem 5.3. For every T(n), OMCA(T(n)) $\subseteq$ DSPACE(n log T(n)) and and OMIA(T(n)) $\subseteq$ DSPACE(n log T(n)).

The next theorem gives an upper bound on the time complexity of a one-way array.

Theorem 5.4. Each OMCA (or OMIA) operates in $O(c^n)$ time for some constant c>0.

Note that Theorems 5.3 and 5.4 together do not imply Theorem 5.2. Both Theorems 5.3 and 5.4 actually work for a larger class of arrays called *uniform conglomerates* [CHAN88a]. Theorem 5.2 was obtained by exploring the regularity of a mesh.

OMCA's and OMIA's are quite powerful. They can accept fairly complex languages efficiently. For example, the following result can be shown [IBAR86]:

Theorem 5.5. OMIA's (OMCA's) can accept context-free languages in 2n−1 time (3n−1 time), which is optimal with respect to the model of computation.

Theorem 5.5 is an improvement of a result in [KOSA74] which showed that context-free languages can be accepted by two-way mesh-connected iterative arrays in linear time.

In our definition of an MCA (or an MIA, or their one-way versions), the number of nodes is the square of the length of the input. It is also interesting to consider mesh-connected arrays where the number of nodes is equal to the length of the input. Denote these models as MCA_1 and MIA_1. The one-way version of these arrays are shown in Figure 9.

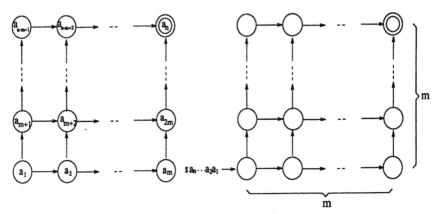

Figure 9. An $OMCA_1$ and an $OMIA_1$. (Here, $m = n^{1/2}$.)

We do not know if $OMCA_1 = OMIA_1$. Clearly each $OMCA_1$ can be simulated by an $OMIA_1$. It seems difficult to prove the converse. The technique in the proof of Theorem 3.3 does not work anymore since an $OMCA_1$ can only count up to $O(c^{n^{1/2}})$. We also do not know if $OMCA_1 = OLCA$, if $OMIA_1 = OLIA$, and if $OMCA_1$'s and $OMIA_1$'s can simulate linear time-bounded alternating TM's. The best we have is the following, which can be shown using the ideas in Theorem 3.2.

Theorem 5.6. Every $O(n^{1/2})$ time-bounded alternating TM can be simulated by an $OMIA_1$.

It is not obvious how to extend the above result to $OMCA_1$.

6. The complexity of tree-structured arrays

In this section, we study the computational complexity of TIA's and TCA's. Clearly, both TIA's and TCA's are equivalent to linear space-bounded TM's. We will give efficient simulations between a TIA, a TCA, and an LIA. We also show that both a sublinear-time TCA and a real-time TIA can accept languages which are complete for P with respect to log-space reductions, thus making it unlikely that sublinear-time TCA languages or real-time TIA languages can be accepted by TM's in polylog space. In contrast, every OTCA can be simulated by a $\frac{\log^2 n}{\log\log n}$ space-bounded TM. It follows from the space hierarchy theorem that the class of OTCA languages is properly contained in the class of languages accepted by $S(n)$ space-bounded TM's for any $S(n)$ which grows faster than $\frac{\log^2 n}{\log\log n}$. OTCA's are quite powerful in that they can accept interesting languages. *E.g.*, the set of palindromes is accepted by an OTCA in $O(n^3)$ time.

6.1. Fast simulations between TCA's, TIA's and LCA's

Since TCA's and TIA's have the same structure, one would expect fast simulation between the two models. The only difficult part in the simulation is how to set up the initial configuration properly. The next theorem is given in [IBAR89a].

Theorem 6.1.

1. $TCA(T(n)) \subseteq TIA(T(n)+O(n))$.

2. $TIA(T(n)) \subseteq TCA(T(n)+O(n))$.

A TCA can simulate an LCA without loss of time by wrapping the array of nodes of the LCA around the tree as in [CULI86], and let every node of the TCA simulate three nodes of the LCA. Thus we have

Theorem 6.2. $LCA(T(n)) \subseteq TCA(T(n))$.

It is easy to show that every TCA can be simulated by an LCA with a slow-down n, *i.e.*, $TCA(T(n)) \subseteq LCA(nT(n))$ for any $T(n)$. Interestingly, we can improve the slow-down to $O(n/\log n)$ [IBAR89b]. The simulation is realized by embedding an n-node full binary tree into an n-node linear array with a dilation $O(n/\log n)$. The construction uses the idea of horizontal trees introduced in [PATE81]. The slow-down factor $O(n/\log n)$ is optimal with respect to stepwise simulation, since one can show that for any embedding of a log n-depth full binary tree in a $(2^{1+\log n}-1)$-node linear array, the dilation $\geq (2n-2)/\log n$. An embedding f is any injective mapping from the nodes of an array A to the nodes of another array B. The dilation of the embedding f is the maximum distance between the images of nodes adjacent in array A. The simulation is not trivial because the nodes have only a finite number of states and thus the standard message routing scheme cannot be implemented on an LCA.

Theorem 6.3. For any function $T(n)$, $TCA(T(n)) \subseteq LCA(nT(n)/\log n)$.

6.2. Space-efficient simulation of OTCA's

Now we investigate the space complexity of TCA and OTCA languages. First we show that an OTCA can be simulated by a $\frac{\log^2 n}{\log\log n}$ space-bounded deterministic TM. The next lemma is needed for proving this result. Although it is an open problem whether every TCA (or linear space-bounded TM) can be made to operate in polynomial time, the answer is positive for OTCA's [IBAR89a].

Lemma 6.4. Every OTCA A operates in n^c time for some constant c depending only on A.

An interesting corollary of Lemma 6.4 is the following.

Corollary 6.5. The class of OTCA languages is closed under intersection, union, and complementation.

The next result is also proven in [IBAR89a].

Theorem 6.6. Let $T(n)$ be a function such that log $T(n)$ is space-constructible. Then every language accepted by a $T(n)$ time-bounded OTCA A can be accepted by a $\frac{\log n \log T(n)}{\log\log T(n)}$ space-bounded TM.

From Lemma 6.4 and Theorem 6.6, we have

Corollary 6.7. $OTCA \subseteq DSPACE(\frac{\log^2 n}{\log\log n})$.

Corollary 6.8. $OTCA \subset TCA$ and $OTCA \subset OLCA$.

On the other hand, an OTCA can be actually quite powerful. For example, it has been shown in [DYER81,IBAR89a] that the set of balanced parentheses and the set of palindromes are accepted by an OTCA. It remains open if the space bound in Corollary 6.7 is tight.

We now show that it is unlikely that Corollary 6.7 holds for a sublinear-time TCA. In [IBAR84], it was shown that a *trellis automaton* (TA) [CULI84] can accept a language L which is complete for P (= languages accepted by deterministic polynomial-time TM's) with respect to log-space reductions. It follows that if L can be accepted by a $\log^k n$ space-bounded TM for some k, then every language in P can be accepted by some $\log^k n$ space-bounded TM, which is very unlikely. Since a linear-time LIA can simulate a TA [BUCH84], L is accepted by a linear-time LIA. It is easy to show that a TCA can accept a padded version of L. Thus, we have

Theorem 6.9. For every real constant $\varepsilon > 0$, there is a language L_ε accepted by a TCA operating in n^ε time which is complete for P with respect to log-space reductions.

Now, we know that a TIA has to use at least n steps. The next result is an analog of Theorem 6.9 for the case of TIA's.

Theorem 6.10. A real-time TIA can accept a language which is complete for P with respect to log-space reductions.

It is unlikely that the n^ε-time in Theorem 6.9 can be reduced, because of the following fact [IBAR89a].

Theorem 6.11. $TCA(O(\log^k n)) \subseteq DSPACE(\log^{k+2} n)$.

References

[BUCH84] Bucher, W. and K. Culik II, On real time and linear time cellular automata, *R.A.I.R.O. Informatique theorique/Theoretical Infomatics* 18-4, 1984, pp. 307-325.

[CHAN81b] Chandra, A., D. Kozen and L. Stockmeyer, Alternation, *J. ACM* 28-1, 1981, pp. 114-133.

[CHAN88a] Chang, J., O. Ibarra, and M. Palis, Efficient simulations of simple models of parallel computation by space-bounded TMs and time-bounded alternating TMs, in the *Proceedings of the 14th ICALP*, 1988, Finland; expanded version in *Theoretical Computer Science* 68, 19-36, 1989.

[CHAN88b] Chang, J., O. Ibarra, and A. Vergis, On the power of one-way communication, *J. ACM* 35, 1988, pp. 697-726.

[CHOF84] Choffrut, C. and K. Culik II, On real-time cellular automata and trellis automata, *Acta Inform.* 21, 1984, pp. 393-409.

[COLE69] Cole, S., Real-time computation by n-dimensional iterative arrays of finite-state machines, *IEEE Trans. Comput.* 18-4, 1969, pp. 346-365.

[CULI84] Culik II, K., J. Gruska, and A. Salomaa, Systolic trellis automata: Part I, *Internat. J. Comput. Math.* 15, 1984, pp. 195-212.

[CULI86] Culik II, K., O. Ibarra, and S. Yu, Iterative Tree Arrays with Logarithmic Depth, *Intern. J. Computer Math.* 20, 1986, pp. 187-204.

[DYER80] Dyer, C., One-way bounded cellular automata, *Information and Control* 44, 1980, pp. 54-69.

[DYER81] Dyer, C. and Rosenfeld, A., Triangle Cellular Automata, *Information and Control* 48, 1981, pp. 54-69.

[HARR78] Harrison, M., Introduction to formal language theory, *Addison-Wesley*, 1978.

[HENN61] Hennie, F., Iterative arrays of logical circuits, *MIT Press, Cambridge, Mass.*, 1961.

[HOPC79] Hopcroft, J. and J. Ullman, Introduction to automata theory, languages, and computation, *Addison-Wesley*, 1979.

[IBAR84] Ibarra, O. and S. Kim, Characterizations and computational complexity of systolic trellis automata, *Theor. Comput. Sci.* 29, 1984, pp. 123-153.

[IBAR85a] Ibarra, O., S. Kim, and S. Moran, Sequential machine characterizations of trellis and cellular automata and applications, *SIAM J. Computing* 14, 1985, pp. 426-447.

[IBAR85b] Ibarra, O., M. Palis, and S. Kim, Some results concerning linear iterative (systolic) arrays, *J. of Parallel and Distributed Computing* 2, 1985, pp. 182-218.

[IBAR86] Ibarra, O., S. Kim, and M. Palis, Designing Systolic Algorithms using sequential machines, *IEEE Trans. on Computers* C35-6, 1986, pp. 31-42; extended abstract in *Proc. 25th IEEE Symposium on Foundations of Computer Science*, 1984, pp. 46-55.

[IBAR87] Ibarra, O. and Jiang, T., On one-way cellular arrays, *SIAM J. on Computing* 16, 1987, pp. 1135-1154; prelim. version in *Proc. 13th ICALP*, 1987, Karlsruhe, West Germany.

[IBAR88a] Ibarra O., and M. Palis, Two-dimensional systolic arrays: characterizations and applications, *Theoretical Computer Science* 57, 1988, pp. 47-86.

[IBAR88b] Ibarra, O. and T. Jiang, Relating the power of cellular arrays to their closure properties, *Theoretical Computer Science* 57, 1988, 225-238.

[IBAR89a] O. Ibarra, T. Jiang, and J. Chang, On iterative and cellular tree arrays, *Journal of Computer and System Sciences* 38, 1989, pp. 452-473.

[IBAR89b] Ibarra, O. and T. Jiang, Optimal simulation of tree arrays by linear arrays, *Inform. Process. Lett.* 30, 1989, pp. 295-302.

[KOSA74] Kosaraju, S., On some open problems in the theory of cellular automata, *IEEE Trans. on Computers C-23, 1974, pp. 561-565.*

[PATE72] Paterson, M., Tape bounds for time-bounded Turing machines, *J. Comp. System Sci.* 6, 1972, pp. 116-124.

[PATE81] Paterson, M., W. Ruzzo, and L. Snyder, Bounds on minmax edge length for complete binary trees, *Proc. 13th ACM Symposium on the Theory of Computing*, 1981, pp. 293-299.

[SAVI70] Savitch, W., Relationships between nondeterministic and deterministic complexities, *J. Comp. System Sci.* 4, 1970, pp. 177-192.

[SMIT70] Smith, A., III, Cellular automata and formal languages, *Proc. 11th IEEE Ann. Symp. on Switching and Automata Theory*, 1970, pp. 216-224.

[SMIT71] Smith, A., III, Cellular automata complexity trade-offs, *Information and Control* 18, 1971, pp. 466-482.

[SMIT72] Smith, A., III, Real-time language recognition by one-dimensional cellular automata, *J. Comp. System Sci.* 6, 1972, pp. 233-253.

[UMEO82] Umeo, H., K. Morita, and K. Sugata, Deterministic one-way simulation of two-way real-time cellular automata and its related problems, *Inform. Process. Lett.* 14, 1982, pp. 159-161.

Power of controlled insertion and deletion

Lila Kari

Academy of Finland and Department of Mathematics[1]

University of Turku

20500 Turku

Finland

Abstract

The paper investigates classes of languages obtained as the closure of certain atomic languages under some insertion and deletion operations. Each of the classes studied is closed under an insertion operation, a deletion operation and an iterative insertion one. The operations are controlled and have been chosen as stated in order to allow an increase as well as a decrease of the length of the words in the operands. The iterative operation has been included in each class to provide an infinite growth of the strings.

1 Introduction

Language operations have been studied intensively in formal language theory. One of the main goals of the theory is to represent a family of languages as the closure of some atomic languages with respect to some operations. The theory of abstract families of languages (AFL) deals with operations, many operations appear in formal language theory applications, and so on.

This paper analyzes the generative power of some insertion and deletion operations defined in [4]. The operations are generalizations of catenation and left/right quotient and among them we can list *insertion, parallel insertion, controlled insertion, scattered insertion, deletion, parallel deletion, controlled deletion, scattered deletion*. For a comprehensive study of these and other operations as well as of various related topics see [4], [5], [6], [7], [8], [10].

The operations needed in our study are defined in Section 2 and some closure properties necessary for our investigation are proved in Section 3.

In Section 4 we focus on classes of languages which contain the singleton letters, the empty word, the empty set and are closed under an insertion operation,

---

[1] The work reported here is part of the project 11281 of the Academy of Finland

a deletion operation and an iterative insertion one. Finally, the mirror image operator and the union with the empty word are added for technical reasons.

Our results have the following uniform structure. The classes obtained properly contain the family of regular languages. Moreover, the class whose operations are sequential is properly included in the family of context-free languages. The one whose operations are parallel is included in the family of context-sensitive languages and contains non-context-free languages.

Let Σ be a finite alphabet and Σ^* the set of all words over Σ, including the empty word λ. The length of a word $w \in \Sigma^*$ is denoted by $\lg(w)$. The left quotient of a word u by a word v is defined by "$v \backslash u = w$ iff $u = vw$", and the right quotient u/v is defined analogously. The mirror image of a word u is denoted by $\mathrm{Mi}(u)$. For two languages L_1, L_2 over Σ,

$$L_1 - L_2 = \{u|\, u \in L_1 \text{ and } u \notin L_2\}, \quad L_1^c = \Sigma^* - L_1.$$

In the sequel REG, CF, CS will denote the family of regular, context-free and context-sensitive languages respectively. For unexplained formal language notions the reader is referred to [9].

2 Controlled insertion and deletion

The simplest and most natural generalization of catenation is the *sequential insertion* (see [4]). Given two words u and v, instead of catenating v at the right extremity of u, the new operation inserts v in an arbitrary place in u. Notice that the sequential insertion of two words is a finite set of words and that their catenation is an element of this set. However, catenation cannot be obtained as a particular case of sequential insertion because we cannot force the insertion to take place at the right extremity of the word. This brings up the notion of *control*: each letter determines what can be inserted after it. The catenation operation will then be obtained by using a particular case of *controlled insertion*.

Let L be a language over the alphabet Σ. For each letter a of the alphabet, let $\Delta(a)$ be a language over an alphabet Σ_a. The Δ- controlled insertion into L (shortly, *insertion*), is defined as:

$$L \leftarrowtail \Delta = \bigcup_{u \in L} (u \leftarrowtail \Delta), \text{ where } u \leftarrowtail \Delta = \{u_1 a v_a u_2|\, u = u_1 a u_2, v_a \in \Delta(a)\}.$$

The function $\Delta : \Sigma \longrightarrow 2^{\Sigma'^*}$, where $\Sigma' = \bigcup_{a \in \Sigma} \Sigma_a$ is called a *control function*.

The insertion is an $(n + 1)$-ary operation, where n is the arity of Σ, the domain of the control function.

The catenation can be now expressed as $L_1 L_2 = h(L_1 \# \leftarrowtail \Delta)$, where $\Delta(\#) = L_2$, $\Delta(a) = \emptyset$, $\forall a \in \Sigma$ and h is the morphism defined by $h(\#) = \lambda$, $h(a) = a$, $\forall a \in \Sigma$.

Note that the empty word does not occur in the result of the insertion. Indeed, the notion of control implies the presence of at least one letter in the word in which the insertion is performed. Therefore we have

$$(L_1 \xleftarrow{} \Delta) = (L_1 - \{\lambda\}) \xleftarrow{} \Delta.$$

In the following we shall define a parallel variant of insertion.

Let L be a language over Σ and $\Delta : \Sigma \longrightarrow 2^{\Sigma'^*}$ a control function satisfying $\Delta(a) \neq \emptyset$, $\forall a \in \Sigma$. The Δ-controlled parallel insertion into L (shortly, *parallel insertion*) is defined as:

$$L \xLeftarrow{} \Delta = \bigcup_{u \in L} (u \xLeftarrow{} \Delta), \text{ where}$$

$$u \xLeftarrow{} \Delta = \{a_1 v_1 a_2 v_2 \ldots a_k v_k \mid u = a_1 \ldots a_k, k \geq 1, a_i \in \Sigma,$$

$$\text{and } v_i \in \Delta(a_i), 1 \leq i \leq k\}.$$

For example, if $L = \{cd, \lambda, bdc, f^2\}$ and Δ is the control function defined by $\Delta(c) = \{a\}$, $\Delta(d) = \{\lambda, e\}$, $\Delta(b) = \{\lambda\}$, $\Delta(f) = \{f\}$ then,

$$L \xLeftarrow{} \Delta = \{cad, cade, bdca, bdeca, f^4\}.$$

Note that in the previous definition the control function cannot have the empty set as its value. This condition has been introduced because of the following reasons. If there would exist a letter $a \in \Sigma$ such that $\Delta(a) = \emptyset$, then all the words $u \in L$ which contain a would give $u \xLeftarrow{} \Delta = \emptyset$. This means that these words would not contribute to the result of the parallel insertion. Consequently, we can introduce, without loss of generality, the condition $\Delta(a) \neq \emptyset$, $\forall a \in \Sigma$.

For each of the above mentioned variants of insertion, a "dual" deletion operation can be also considered. Let L be a language over the alphabet Σ. For each letter a of the alphabet, let $\Delta(a)$ be a language over Σ. The Δ-controlled deletion from L (shortly, *deletion*) is defined as:

$$L \xmapsto{} \Delta = \bigcup_{u \in L} (u \xmapsto{} \Delta), \text{ where}$$

$$u \xmapsto{} \Delta = \{u_1 a u_2 \in \Sigma^* \mid u = u_1 a v u_2 \text{ for some} \\ u_1, u_2 \in \Sigma^*, a \in \Sigma \text{ and } v \in \Delta(a)\}.$$

The function $\Delta : \Sigma \longrightarrow 2^{\Sigma^*}$ is called a control function.

For example, if $L = \{abba, aab, bba, aabb\}$ and Δ is the control function $\Delta(a) = b$, $\Delta(b) = a$, then $L \xmapsto{} \Delta = \{aba, abb, aa, bb, aab\}$. As a language operation, the Δ-controlled deletion has the arity $\text{card}(\Sigma) + 1$.

Notice that if λ belongs to L, λ does not contribute to the result of the deletion:

$$L \xmapsto{} \Delta = (L - \{\lambda\}) \xmapsto{} \Delta, \forall L \subseteq \Sigma^*, \Delta : \Sigma \longrightarrow 2^{\Sigma^*}.$$

A parallel variant of the deletion will be defined in the sequel. Let $u \in \Sigma^*$ be a word and $\Delta : \Sigma \longrightarrow 2^{\Sigma^*}$ be a control function which does not have $\emptyset$ as its value. The set $u \longmapsto \Delta$ is obtained by finding all the non-overlapping occurrences of av_a, $v_a \in \Delta(a)$, in u, and by deleting v_a from them. Here v_a may be different for different occurrences of a in the same word. Between any two occurrences of words of the type av_a, $v_a \in \Delta(a)$, in u, no other words of this type may remain.

Let L be a language over an alphabet Σ and $\Delta : \Sigma \longrightarrow 2^{\Sigma^*}$ be a control function such that $\Delta(a) \neq \emptyset$, $\forall a \in \Sigma$. The Δ- controlled parallel deletion from L (shortly, *parallel deletion*) is formally defined as:

$$L \longmapsto \Delta = \bigcup_{u \in L} (u \longmapsto \Delta), \text{ where}$$

$$
\begin{aligned}
u \longmapsto \Delta = \quad & \{u_1 a_1 u_2 a_2 \ldots u_k a_k u_{k+1} \mid k \geq 1, a_j \in \Sigma, 1 \leq j \leq k, \\
& u_i \in \Sigma^*, 1 \leq i \leq k+1, \text{ and there exist } v_i \in \Delta(a_i), 1 \leq i \leq k, \\
& \text{such that } u = u_1 a_1 v_1 \ldots u_k a_k v_k u_{k+1}, \text{where} \\
& \{u_i\} \cap \Sigma^* (\cup_{a \in \Sigma} a\Delta(a)) \Sigma^* = \emptyset, \ 1 \leq i \leq k+1.\}
\end{aligned}
$$

The last line is a formalization of the condition that no word av_a, $v_a \in \Delta(a)$, may occur in u between $a_i v_i$, $1 \leq i \leq k$, $v_i \in \Delta(a_i)$.

For example, if $L = \{abababa, a^3 b^3, abab\}$ and $\Delta(a) = b$, $\Delta(b) = a$, then

$$L \longmapsto \Delta = \{a^4, ab^3, a^2 b^2, ab^2 a^2, a^3 b, a^3 b^2, a^2, ab^2\}.$$

The arity of the Δ-controlled parallel deletion is $\text{card}(\Sigma) + 1$.

As in the case of deletion, if the empty word belongs to L, this does not influence the result of the parallel deletion:

$$L \longmapsto \Delta = (L - \{\lambda\}) \longmapsto \Delta, \ \forall L \subseteq \Sigma^*, \Delta : \Sigma \longrightarrow 2^{\Sigma^*}, \Delta(a) \neq \emptyset, \forall a \in \Sigma.$$

3   Closure properties

This section contains some closure properties of the families of the Chomsky hierarchy under iterated insertion and iterated parallel insertion. These closure properties will later be used in establishing the position of the investigated classes of languages relative to the Chomsky hierarchy.

Let L be a language over Σ and $\Delta : \Sigma \longrightarrow 2^{\Sigma'^*}$ be a control function. The Δ-controlled insertion of order k into L is defined as

$$
\begin{aligned}
L \longleftarrow^0 \Delta &= L, \\
L \longleftarrow^{k+1} \Delta &= (L \longleftarrow^k \Delta) \longleftarrow \Delta, \ k \geq 0.
\end{aligned}
$$

The Δ-controlled iterated insertion into L (shortly, *iterated insertion*) is then defined as

$$L \longleftarrow^* \Delta = \bigcup_{k=0}^{\infty} (L \longleftarrow^k \Delta).$$

If the control function is $\Delta : \Sigma \longrightarrow 2^{\Sigma'^{*}}$ and $\Sigma' - \Sigma \neq \emptyset$, we put $\Delta(a) = \emptyset$ for $a \in \Sigma' - \Sigma$.

Our first results show that the family of regular languages is not closed under iterated insertion, whereas the families of context-free and context-sensitive languages are closed under it.

Proposition 1 *The family of regular languages is not closed under iterated insertion.*

Proof. Take $L = \{ab\}$ and the control function Δ defined by:

$$\Delta : \{a, b\} \longrightarrow 2^{\{a,b\}^{*}}, \Delta(a) = \Delta(b) = \{ab\}.$$

Then $L = \{ab\} \leftarrowtail^{*} \Delta$ equals the Dyck language of order one, which is not a regular language. $\qquad \Box$

Proposition 2 *The family of context-free languages is closed under iterated insertion.*

Proof. Let L be a language generated by the context-free grammar $G = (N, \Sigma, S, P)$ and $\Delta : \Sigma \longrightarrow 2^{\Sigma'^{*}}$ be a control function. The fact whether or not $\lambda \in L$ is irrelevant to the result of the insertion into L. Therefore, if $\lambda \in L$ then $L \leftarrowtail^{*} \Delta = [(L - \{\lambda\}) \leftarrowtail^{*} \Delta] \cup \{\lambda\}$. Consequently we can assume, without loss of generality, that L is a λ-free language. Assume that for every $a \in \Sigma$, the language $\Delta(a)$ is generated by the context-free grammar $G_a = (N_a, \Sigma_a, S_a, P_a)$, that the nonterminal sets $N, N_a, a \in \Sigma$, are pairwise disjoint and $\Sigma' = \cup_{a \in \Sigma} \Sigma_a$. Assume further that the grammar G satisfies the following properties (see [9], pp.55-56): *(i)* S does not appear on the right side of any production of P, *(ii)* if $\lambda \in L(G)$ the only production of P with λ as the right side is $S \longrightarrow \lambda$, *(iii)* all the productions of P (except eventually $S \longrightarrow \lambda$) are of the form $A \longrightarrow BC$, $A \longrightarrow a$, $A, B, C \in N$, $a \in \Sigma$. Assume that also the grammars G_a, $a \in \Sigma$ satisfy similar properties.

Construct the context-free grammar:

$$\begin{aligned}
G' &= (N', \Sigma \cup \Sigma', S, P'), \\
N' &= N \cup (\cup_{a \in \Sigma} N_a), \\
P' &= P \cup (\cup_{a \in \Sigma} P_a) \cup \\
&\quad \{A \longrightarrow aS_a \mid A \in N', a \in \Sigma, A \longrightarrow a \in P \cup (\cup_{a \in \Sigma} P_a)\}.
\end{aligned}$$

It is not difficult to prove that $L(G') = L \leftarrowtail^{*} \Delta$. $\qquad \Box$

Proposition 3 *The family of context-sensitive languages is closed under iterated insertion.*

Proof. Let L be a language generated by the context-sensitive grammar $G = (N, \Sigma, S, P)$ and $\Delta : \Sigma \longrightarrow 2^{\Sigma'^{*}}$ be a control function. The fact whether or not $\lambda \in L$ is irrelevant to the result of the insertion into L. Therefore, if $\lambda \in L$ then $L \hookleftarrow^* \Delta = [(L - \{\lambda\}) \hookleftarrow^* \Delta] \cup \{\lambda\}$. Consequently we can assume, without loss of generality, that L is a λ-free language. Assume that, for every $a \in \Sigma$, the language $\Delta(a)$ is generated by the context-sensitive grammar $G_a = (N_a, \Sigma_a, S_a, P_a)$, that the nonterminal sets N, N_a, $a \in \Sigma$, are pairwise disjoint and $\Sigma' = \cup_{a \in \Sigma} \Sigma_a$. Assume further that the grammar G satisfies the properties (i) and (ii) from Proposition 2 together with (iii) every rule of P containing a terminal letter is of the form $A \longrightarrow a$ where $A \in N$ and $a \in \Sigma$ (see [9], pp.19-20). Assume that also all G_a, $a \in \Sigma$ satisfy similar properties.

Construct the context-sensitive grammar:

$$
\begin{aligned}
G' = {} & (N', \Sigma \cup \Sigma', S, P'), \\
N' = {} & N \cup (\cup_{a \in \Sigma} N_a) \cup \{\#\}, \\
P' = {} & P \cup (\cup_{a \in \Sigma}(P_a - \{S_a \longrightarrow \lambda\})) \cup \\
& \{A \longrightarrow a \# S_a \# \mid A \in N', a \in \Sigma, A \longrightarrow a \in P \cup (\cup_{a \in \Sigma} P_a)\}.
\end{aligned}
$$

Define now the morphism $h : \Sigma'^* \longrightarrow \Sigma'^*$ by $h(\#) = \lambda$, $h(a) = a$ for all $a \neq \#$. It is not difficult to show that

$$
h(L(G')) = L \hookleftarrow^* \Delta,
$$

and that h is a 3-linear erasing with respect to $L(G')$. We conclude that CS is closed under iterated insertion. $\qquad\square$

The *iterated parallel insertion* can be defined starting from the parallel insertion. The formal definition can be obtained by replacing in the definition of iterated insertion $\hookleftarrow$ with $\Leftarrow$. Observe, however, that the iterated parallel insertion can be defined only when the control function Δ, defined on Σ, has as values languages over the same alphabet Σ.

The following results show that the family of regular and of context-free languages are not closed under iterated parallel insertion but the family of context-sensitive languages is closed under it.

Proposition 4 *The family of regular and the family of context-free languages are not closed under iterated parallel insertion.*

Proof. Take $L = \{a\}$ and the control function Δ defined by $\Delta(a) = a$. Then, $L \Leftarrow^* \Delta = \{a^{2^n} \mid n \geq 0\}$, which is not a context-free language. $\qquad\square$

Proposition 5 *The family of context-sensitive languages is closed under iterated parallel insertion.*

Proof. Let L be a language generated by the context-sensitive grammar $G = (N, \Sigma, S, P)$, and let $\Delta : \Sigma \longrightarrow 2^{\Sigma^*}$ be a control function, $\Delta(a) \neq \emptyset$, $\forall a \in \Sigma$. Assume that, for every $a \in \Sigma$, the language $\Delta(a)$ is generated by the context-sensitive grammar $G_a = (N_a, \Sigma_a, S_a, P_a)$, that the nonterminal sets N, N_a, $a \in$

Σ are pairwise disjoint and that $\cup_{a \in \Sigma} \Sigma_a \subseteq \Sigma$. Assume further that all the above grammars satisfy the requirements of Proposition 3. The fact whether or not $\lambda \in L$ does not affect the result of parallel insertion into L. If λ belongs to L then $L \longleftarrow^* \Delta = [(L - \{\lambda\}) \longleftarrow^* \Delta] \cup \{\lambda\}$. Consequently we will assume, without loss of generality, that L is λ-free.

We can construct then the following grammar:

$$
\begin{aligned}
G' &= (N', \Sigma', S', P'), \\
\Sigma' &= \Sigma \cup \{\$, \#\}, \\
N' &= N \cup (\cup_{a \in \Sigma} N_a) \cup \{S', X\}, \\
P' &= P \cup (\cup_{a \in \Sigma} (P_a - \{S_a \longrightarrow \lambda\})) \cup \\
& \quad \{S' \longrightarrow X S', S' \longrightarrow \$S\#, X\$ \longrightarrow \$X\} \cup \\
& \quad \{Xa \longrightarrow aX \mid a \in \Sigma, \lambda \in \Delta(a)\} \cup \\
& \quad \{Xa \longrightarrow aS_a X \mid a \in \Sigma\} \cup \\
& \quad \{Xa\# \longrightarrow aS_a\# \mid a \in \Sigma\} \cup \\
& \quad \{Xa\# \longrightarrow a\# \mid a \in \Sigma, \lambda \in \Delta(a)\},
\end{aligned}
$$

where $S', X, \$, \#$ are new symbols which do not occur in any of the given alphabets.

Intuitively, the grammar G' works as follows. First, a sentential form of the type $X^n \$w\#$, $w \in L$ is generated, where n represents the number of parallel iterations that will be made into w. X starts to move to the right. When crossing a letter a, it generates at its left a start symbol of $\Delta(a)$. The rules $S_a \longrightarrow \lambda$ are never needed. When X reaches the right extremity of the sentential form, it disapears.

The language $L(G')$ is context-sensitive. Indeed, all rules of G' except the ones of the form $Xa\# \longrightarrow a\#$ are length-increasing. However, the application of such a rule during a minimal derivation of a word $\alpha \in L(G)$ is always preceded by the application of a rule $Xa \longrightarrow aS_a X$. If this wouldn't be the case, our X would represent a dummy iteration step, in which all the inserted words are empty. This would further imply that the derivation for α is not minimal, as α could be obtained with a shorter derivation where the dummy iteration step is omitted.

The rule $Xa \longrightarrow aS_a X$ increases the length of the sentential form by one and the rule $Xa\# \longrightarrow a\#$ decreases its length by one. Combining these observations we conclude that the longest sentential form in a terminal derivation of α has the length smaller than or equal to $\lg(\alpha) + 1$.

Consequently, for all words $\alpha \in L(G')$ the workspace of α is smaller than $2\lg(\alpha)$ and, according to the workspace theorem (see, for example [9], pp.93-97), $L(G')$ is a context-sensitive language.

If we consider now the morphism $h : (\Sigma \cup \{\$, \#\})^* \longrightarrow \Sigma^*$, defined by $h(\$) = h(\#) = \lambda$ and $h(a) = a$ for $a \in \Sigma$ it can be proved that $h(L(G')) = L \longleftarrow^* \Delta$. Clearly, h is 3-linear erasing with respect to the language $L(G')$. $\qquad \square$

4 Power of operations

Let S be the smallest class of languages which contains $\emptyset$, the language $\{\lambda\}$, the singleton letters and is closed under union with the empty word, mirror image, insertion, iterated insertion and deletion with singletons. The union with lambda has been added because λ cannot occur in the result of insertion and deletion. If this operation wouldn't have been used, the class S would not contain any language L with $\lambda \in L$, except $\{\lambda\}$.

The following result should be compared with the characterization of REG as the smallest class containing singleton letters, the empty set and closed under union, catenation and catenation closure.

Theorem 1 S *is contained in the family of context-free languages and properly contains the family of regular languages.*

Proof. In order to show that REG $\subseteq S$ we will prove the closure of S under catenation, union and catenation closure.

Catenation. Let L_1, L_2 be two languages in S, over the alphabet Σ. If $\#$ is a new symbol which does not belong to Σ, let Δ_1, Δ_2 be the control functions:

$$\Delta_1 : \{\#\} \longrightarrow 2^{\Sigma^*}, \quad \Delta_2 : \Sigma \cup \{\#\} \longrightarrow 2^{\Sigma^*},$$
$$\Delta_1(\#) = L_2, \qquad \Delta_2(\#) = L_1, \ \Delta_2(a) = \emptyset, \forall a \in \Sigma.$$

The following equality holds:

$$\#L_1L_2 = (\{\#\} \leftarrow\!\!\mid \Delta_1) \leftarrow\!\!\mid \Delta_2.$$

The Δ_1-controlled insertion performs the task of catenating the symbol $\#$ and the language L_2. The Δ_2-controlled insertion inserts the language L_1 in the language $\#L_2$, at the right of $\#$, realizing thus the catenation $\#L_1L_2$.

If we define now the control function:

$$\Delta_3 : \Sigma \cup \{\#\} \longrightarrow 2^{(\Sigma \cup \{\#\})^*}, \Delta_3(\#) = \emptyset, \Delta_3(a) = \#, \forall a \in \Sigma,$$

we have that:

$$
\begin{aligned}
L_1L_2 &= \text{Mi}(\text{Mi}(\#L_1L_2) \mapsto \Delta_3), & \text{if } \lambda \notin L_1 \cap L_2, \\
L_1L_2 &= \text{Mi}(\text{Mi}(\#L_1L_2) \mapsto \Delta_3) \cup \{\lambda\}, & \text{if } \lambda \in L_1 \cap L_2.
\end{aligned}
$$

The role of the Δ_3-controlled deletion is to delete the symbol $\#$ in every word of $\text{Mi}(\#L_1L_2)$. This operation could be performed only after Mi transferred the symbol $\#$ to the right extremity of the words. This transfer was needed because the first letter of a word cannot be erased by deletion. Finally, Mi was used again, in order to obtain the desired language from its mirror image.

The catenation L_1L_2 has been obtained from $L_1, L_2, \{\#\}, \emptyset \in S$ by using the operations union with lambda, mirror image, insertion and deletion with singletons. Therefore, the class S is closed under catenation.

Union. We will show first that the union of two letters is a language belonging to S. Indeed, let $\{a\}, \{b\}$ be two singleton letters. Let $\#$ be a letter different from a and b and define the control function Δ_4 by:

$$\Delta_4 : \{a, b, \#\} \longrightarrow 2^{\{a,b,\#\}^*}, \Delta_4(\#) = a, \Delta_4(a) = b, \Delta_4(b) = \emptyset.$$

The following relation holds:

$$\{\#a, \#b\} = \{\#ab\} \mapsto \Delta_4.$$

The Δ_4- controlled deletion was used to obtain a set of two elements from a singleton. The additional symbol $\#$ was needed in order to make possible the deletion at the left extremity of the word ab.

If we define now the control function:

$$\Delta_5 : \{a, b, \#\} \longrightarrow 2^{\{a,b,\#\}^*}, \Delta_5(a) = \Delta_5(b) = \#, \Delta_5(\#) = \emptyset,$$

we obtain the requested set:

$$\{a, b\} = \mathrm{Mi}(\{\#a, \#b\}) \mapsto \Delta_5.$$

The role of the Δ_5-controlled deletion was to delete the symbol $\#$ and the mirror image transferred it to the right extremity of every word, to allow its deletion. Observe that another application of Mi is not needed.

As we have obtained the set $\{a, b\}$ starting from the sets $\emptyset$, $\#$, a, b and $\{\#ab\}$ (which belongs to S as S is closed under catenation) and applying only insertion, deletion with singletons and mirror image, we conclude that it belongs to S.

Returning now to the general case, let L_1, L_2 be two languages in S, over the alphabet Σ. Let $\#_1, \#_2$ be two symbols which do not occur in Σ and Δ_6, Δ_7 be the control functions:

$$\Delta_6 : \{\#_1, \#_2\} \longrightarrow 2^{\Sigma^*}, \quad \Delta_7 : \Sigma \cup \{\#_1, \#_2\} \longrightarrow 2^{\{\#_1, \#_2\}^*},$$
$$\Delta_6(\#_1) = L_1, \qquad \Delta_7(\#_1) = \#_2,$$
$$\Delta_6(\#_2) = L_2, \qquad \Delta_7(\#_2) = \#_1, \Delta_7(a) = \emptyset, \forall a \in \Sigma.$$

The following equality is now obvious:

$$\#_1\#_2 L_1 \cup \#_2\#_1 L_2 = (\{\#_1, \#_2\} \leftarrowtail \Delta_6) \leftarrowtail \Delta_7.$$

Indeed, the Δ_6-controlled insertion inserts L_1 after $\#_1$ and L_2 after $\#_2$, yielding thus $\#_1 L_1 \cup \#_2 L_2$. The Δ_7-controlled insertion inserts then $\#_2$ after $\#_1$ and $\#_1$ after $\#_2$.

If we further define the control functions :

$$\Delta_8 : \Sigma \cup \{\#_1, \#_2\} \longrightarrow 2^{(\Sigma \cup \{\#_1, \#_2\})^*}, \Delta_9 : \Sigma \cup \{\#_2\} \longrightarrow 2^{(\Sigma \cup \{\#_2\})^*},$$

$$\Delta_8(a) = \#_1, \forall a \in \Sigma \cup \{\#_2\}, \quad \Delta_9(a) = \#_2, \forall a \in \Sigma,$$
$$\Delta_8(\#_1) = \emptyset, \qquad\qquad\qquad \Delta_9(\#_2) = \emptyset,$$

then

$$L_1 \cup L_2 = \mathrm{Mi}((\mathrm{Mi}(\#_1\#_2 L_1 \cup \#_2\#_1 L_2) \mapsto \Delta_8) \mapsto \Delta_9),$$
$$\text{if } \lambda \notin L_1 \cup L_2,$$
$$L_1 \cup L_2 = \mathrm{Mi}((\mathrm{Mi}(\#_1\#_2 L_1 \cup \#_2\#_1 L_2) \mapsto \Delta_8) \mapsto \Delta_9) \cup \{\lambda\},$$
$$\text{if } \lambda \in L_1 \cup L_2.$$

The role of the Δ_8-controlled deletion was to erase the symbol $\#_1$ and that of the Δ_9-controlled deletion to erase $\#_2$. We needed two deletions because only deletion with singletons had to be used. The role of the mirror image operator has been similar as in the previous cases.

We have obtained $L_1 \cup L_2$ starting with the languages $L_1, L_2, \#_1, \#_2, \emptyset$ in S and with the set $\{\#_1, \#_2\}$ (which consists of two letters and therefore belongs to S) by applying only insertion, mirror image, union with λ and deletion with singletons. Therefore $L_1 \cup L_2$ is in S, that is, S is closed under union.

Catenation closure. Let L be a language in S, over the alphabet Σ, and let $\#$ be a letter which does not belong to Σ. If Δ_{10} is the control function defined as:

$$\Delta_{10} : \Sigma \cup \{\#\} \longrightarrow 2^{\Sigma^*}, \Delta_{10}(\#) = L, \Delta_{10}(a) = \emptyset, \forall a \in \Sigma,$$

then

$$\#L^* = \{\#\} \leftharpoondown {}^* \Delta_{10}.$$

Indeed, the Δ_{10}-controlled insertion inserts words from L only to the right of $\#$, assuring that the insertion amounts to catenation. Defining finally the control function

$$\Delta_{11} : \Sigma \cup \{\#\} \longrightarrow 2^{(\Sigma \cup \{\#\})^*}, \Delta_{11}(a) = \#, \forall a \in \Sigma, \Delta_{11}(\#) = \emptyset,$$

the catenation closure of L will be

$$L^* = \mathrm{Mi}(\mathrm{Mi}(\#L^*) \mapsto \Delta_{11}) \cup \{\lambda\}.$$

With the help of the mirror image operator, which puts $\#$ to the end of words, the Δ_{11}-controlled deletion erases the letter $\#$ from all the words in $\#L^*$. Finally, Mi restores the form of the words from L.

We have obtained L^* starting from $L, \emptyset$ and $\{\#\}$ in S and using iterated insertion, mirror image, union with λ and deletion with singletons. Therefore, S is closed under catenation closure.

As S contains the singleton letters and is closed under catenation, union and catenation closure, it follows that it contains all the regular languages. According to Proposition 1 the inclusion is proper.

The inclusion $S \subseteq CF$ follows from the fact that CF is closed under mirror image, insertion, deletion with singletons (see [4]) and iterated insertion (see Proposition 2). $\square$

In the following we will be able to prove that the inclusion $S \subseteq$ CF is actually strict. For this, an auxiliary result is needed.

Lemma 1 (Pumping lemma) *For each language L in S there exists a natural n_0 such that every word $w \in L$ with $lg(w) > n_0$ possesses a decomposition $w = w_1 w_2 w_3$ satisfying:*

- $w_2 = w_2' w_2''$,

- *there exists a nonempty word u such that $w_1 w_2' u^k w_2'' w_3 \in L$ for all $k \geq 0$.*

Proof. The constant n_0 is defined by structural induction, based on the construction of L using the operations of S.

If L equals a singleton letter, the empty set or the empty word, we define $n_0 = 1$. The operations $\cup \{\lambda\}$, and Mi do not change n_0.

We now consider, in succession, $L \leftarrowtail \Delta$, $L \leftarrowtail^* \Delta$ and $L \mapsto \Delta$ and assume that L and $\Delta(a)$, $a \in \Sigma$, satisfy the lemma with the constants n, respectively n_a, $a \in \Sigma$.

Insertion. Take $n_0 = 2n + \max\{n_a | a \in \Sigma\} + 1$ and let w be a word in $L \leftarrowtail \Delta$, $w = w_1 w_2 w_3$ with $lg(w_2) > n_0$.

Being a result of the insertion, the word w is of the form $w = \alpha_1 a w_a \alpha_2$, where $w_a \in \Delta(a)$. One of the following cases holds:

(a) the word w_2 is a subword of α_1 or α_2 or of w_a. In this case the lemma holds as we can directly apply the induction hypothesis.

(b) the word w_2 is a subword of $\alpha_1 a$ and then we can apply the induction hypothesis for the part of w_2 which lies in α_1.

(c) we have that either

    – the length of the portion of w_2 in $\alpha_1 a$ is greater than $n + 1$

    – the length of the portion of w_2 in w_a is greater than n_a

    – the length of the portion of w_2 in α_2 is greater than n.

(If none of these cases happens, the length of w_2 becomes smaller than or equal to n – a contradiction.) In all cases, by applying the induction hypohesis we are able to pump inside the portion of w_2 which lies inside α_1, w_a, respectively α_2.

Iterated insertion. Take $n_0 = 2n + \max\{n_a | a \in \Sigma\} + 1$ and a word w in $L \leftarrowtail^* \Delta$ be of length greater than n_0. There exists a natural $k \geq 0$ such that $w \in L \leftarrowtail^k \Delta$. We shall show that w satisfies the requirements of the lemma by induction on k, the number of iterations.

If $k = 0$ then $w \in L$ and the lemma holds.

Assume now that the lemma holds for words in $L \leftarrowtail^k \Delta$ and let $w = w_1 w_2 w_3$ be a word in $L \leftarrowtail^{k+1} \Delta$, of length greater then n_0. Then, w is of the form $w = \alpha_1 a w_a \alpha_2$ where $\alpha_1 a \alpha_2$ belongs to $L \leftarrowtail^k \Delta$ and w_a to $\Delta(a)$.

If w_2 is a subword of α_1, w_a or α_2 then we can directly apply the induction hypothesis.

If w_2 is a subword of $\alpha_1 a$ we can apply the induction hypothesis for the portion of w_2 which lies in α_1.

If w_2 overlaps with w_a and $\alpha_1 a$ then we can choose $u = w_a$. The words obtained by pumping w_a near a will belong to the $L \leftarrowtail^* \Delta$ according to the definition of the iterated insertion.

If w_2 overlaps with w_a and α_2 then again we can choose $u = w_a$ (pump w_a between a and α_2).

Deletion. Take $n_0 = 2n+1$ and take $w = w_1 w_2 w_3$ a word in $L \longmapsto \Delta$ of length greater than n_0. Then there exists a word $w' \in L$, $w' = \alpha_1 a w_a \alpha_2$, $w_a \in \Delta(a)$ such that $w = \alpha_1 a \alpha_2$.

If w_2 is a subword of α_1 or of α_2, we are through.

If w_2 is a subword of $\alpha_1 a$ the we can apply the induction hypothesis to the portion of w_2 which lies in α_1.

Otherwise, either the overlapping portion of w_2 and α_1 is longer than n or the overlapping portion of w_2 and α_2 is longer than n. In both cases we can apply the induction hypothesis to the overlapping portion.

$\square$

Languages in S are constructed from certain atomic ones by applying some operations. Consequently, to every language L in S, a formula describing the "construction history" of L can be associated. Such a formula is analogous to a regular expression. Observe that the definition of the constant in Lemma 1 is based on this formula. Analogous constants for regular languages are customarily defined in terms of the automaton, rather than in terms of the regular expression.

Proposition 6 *The family S is strictly included in the family of context-free languages.*

Proof. Consider the language $L = \{a^n b^n \mid n \geq 0\}$. L is a context-free language but it does not belong to the family S.

Indeed, if L would belong to S, there would exist a constant n_0 such that every word $w \in L$ with $\lg(w) > n_0$ possesses a decomposition satisfying the requirements of Lemma 1.

The word $u \in \{a, b\}^+$ from Lemma 1 that can be pumped into w, producing words that still belong to L, can be of one of the following forms:

- $u = a^r$, $r > 0$. In this case, by pumping u into w we obtain words in which the number of occurrences of a is arbitrarily large whereas the number of occurrences of b is constant – a contradiction with the form of words in L.

- $u = b^r$, $r > 0$. A similar argument proves that this case also leads to a contradiction.

- u contains both letters a and b. By pumping u into w we are able to produce words where the occurrences of a's and b's alternate arbitrarily many times – a contradiction with the definition of L.

As all the possible ways of choosing u led to contradictions, we conclude that our initial assumption that the language L belongs to S was false. □

Theorem 2 *The family S is not closed under intersection.*

Proof. We will prove that there exist two languages $L_1, L_2 \in S$ whose intersection is not a context-free language. As, according to Theorem 1, $S \subseteq CF$, this will imply that S is not closed under intersection.

Let L_1 be the language defined by:

$$L_1 = \{\#\} \leftarrow^* \Delta_1,$$

where Δ_1 is the control function $\Delta_1 : \{\#, a, b, d\} \longrightarrow 2^{\{\#, a, b, d\}^*}$ defined by:

$$\Delta_1(\#) = \{a\#b\#, b\#a\#, d\#\}, \Delta_1(a) = \Delta_1(b) = \Delta_1(d) = \emptyset.$$

Claim. $L_1 = \{w \in \#(\Sigma\#)^* \mid N_a(w) = N_b(w)\}$, where $\Sigma = \{a, b, d\}$.

" $\subseteq$ " This inclusion is obvious, as we insert an equal number of a's and b's at every iteration step.

" $\supseteq$ " We will show by induction on n that if w is a word in the right member of the equality satisfying $N_a(w) = N_b(w) = n$, then $w \in L_1$.

$n = 0$. Let $w = \#(d\#)^p$, where $p \geq 0$. Then we have:

$$w \in \{\#\} \leftarrow^p \Delta_1 \subseteq \{\#\} \leftarrow^* \Delta_1,$$

as w is obtained by p insertions of $d\#$ next to the first symbol $\#$.

$n \mapsto n + 1$. Assume the statement true for numbers up to n and let w be a word in $\#(\Sigma\#)^*$, containing $n + 1$ letters a and $n + 1$ letters b. The word w is of one of the forms:

$$w = \#\alpha a\#(d\#)^m b\#\beta, m \geq 0, \alpha, \beta \in (\Sigma\#)^*,$$
$$w = \#\alpha b\#(d\#)^m a\#\beta, m \geq 0, \alpha, \beta \in (\Sigma\#)^*.$$

Assume that the first case holds, the other one being similar. Consider the word $w' = \#\alpha\beta$. According to the induction hypothesis, w' is a word in L_1. Therefore we have:

$$w \in \{w'\} \leftarrow^{m+1} \Delta_1 \subseteq \{\#\} \leftarrow^* \Delta_1.$$

Indeed, w is obtained from w' by inserting first $a\#b\#$ at the right extremity of α and then inserting m times $d\#$ at the right extremity of $a\#$. We conclude that $w \in L_1$ and the claim is proved.

If we define now the control function $\Delta_2 : \{\#, a, b, d\} \longrightarrow 2^{\{\#,a,b,d\}^*}$ by:

$$\Delta_2(\#) = \{d\#b\#, b\#d\#, a\#\}, \Delta_2(a) = \Delta_2(b) = \Delta_2(d) = \emptyset,$$

one can prove, as before, that:

$$L_2 = \{\#\} \longleftarrow^* \Delta_2 = \{w \in \#(\Sigma\#)^* | \ N_b(w) = N_d(w)\}.$$

It is easy to show that:

$$L_1 \cap L_2 = \{w \in \#(\Sigma\#)^* | \ N_a(w) = N_b(w) = N_d(w)\},$$

which is not a context-free language. As L_1 and L_2 belong to $S \subseteq CF$, it follows that S is not closed under intersection. $\square$

The remaining part of this section will deal with similar questions concerning the generative power, in case all insertions and deletions are replaced with their parallel counterparts. The families thus obtained properly contain REG and are contained in CS. Their relation with the class of context-free languages as well as their relation with S remains open.

Let $\mathcal{P}$ be the smallest class of languages which contains the empty set, the language $\{\lambda\}$, the singleton letters and is closed under mirror image, union with λ, parallel insertion, iterated parallel insertion and parallel deletion with singletons.

Theorem 3 $\mathcal{P}$ *is contained in the family of context-sensitive languages and properly contains the family of regular languages.*

Proof. The fact that $\mathcal{P}$ contains REG can be shown using the proof of Theorem 1. The control functions that appear in the proof have the value $\emptyset$ for some arguments. However, in the case of parallel insertion (parallel deletion), the control function cannot have the empty set as its value. We will modify the functions as follows. Let $ be a new symbol which does not occur in any of the alphabets used in Theorem 1. For every insertion and iterated insertion (resp. deletion) the control function gets the value λ (resp. the value $) for all those letters for which it had previously the value $\emptyset$. After this change, one notices that if we replace everywhere in the proof the insertion, iterated insertion, deletion with singletons with parallel insertion, iterated parallel insertion, parallel deletion with singletons respectively, the same relations hold. This happens because, in all the cases occurring in the proof of Theorem 1, the parallel insertion or deletion will amount in fact to insertion or deletion.

According to Proposition 4, the inclusion REG$\subseteq \mathcal{P}$ is proper.

The inclusion of $\mathcal{P}$ in CS follows from the fact that CS is closed under mirror image, parallel insertion, parallel deletion with singletons (see [4]) and iterated parallel insertion (see Proposition 5). $\square$

Let $\mathcal{P}'$ be the smallest class of languages containing the empty set, $\{\lambda\}$, the singleton letters and closed under mirror image, union with λ, parallel insertion, iterated parallel insertion and parallel deletion. The difference between $\mathcal{P}$ and $\mathcal{P}'$ is that, in the case of $\mathcal{P}$, the parallel deletion is restricted to the case where only singletons are erased.

Theorem 4 $\mathcal{P}'$ *is a Boolean algebra properly containing the family of regular languages.*

Proof. The family $\mathcal{P}$ is included in $\mathcal{P}'$, therefore $\mathcal{P}'$ properly contains the family of regular languages.

It will be showed in the following that $\mathcal{P}'$ is closed under complementation. Let L be a language in $\mathcal{P}'$, over the alphabet Σ, and let $\#, \$$ be letters which do not occur in Σ. Then,

$$\{\#\$\} \cup \#L^c\$\$ = \#\Sigma^*\$\$\# \longmapsto \Delta_1,$$

where Δ_1 is the control function:

$$\Delta_1 : \Sigma \cup \{\#, \$\} \longrightarrow 2^{(\Sigma \cup \{\#, \$\})^*}, \Delta_1(\#) = L\$, \Delta_1(a) = \Delta_1(\$) = \#, \forall a \in \Sigma.$$

Indeed, given a word $w = \#u\$\$\# \in \#\Sigma^*\$\$\#$, the Δ_1-controlled parallel deletion:

- if $u \in L$, erases both $u\$$ and the last $\#$, yielding $\#\$$;

- if $u \in \Sigma^* - L$, erases only the last $\#$, yielding $\#u\$\$$.

One can use the control function Δ_2 to erase the marker $\$$, where

$$\Delta_2 : \Sigma \cup \{\#, \$\} \longrightarrow 2^{(\Sigma \cup \{\$, \#\})^*},$$

$$\Delta_2(\#) = \Delta_2(\$) = \Delta_2(a) = \$\$, \forall a \in \Sigma.$$

Consequently we have:

$$\#L^c = (\{\#\$\} \cup \#L^c\$\$) \longmapsto \Delta_2.$$

Using now the control function Δ_3 to erase the marker $\#$:

$$\Delta_3 : \Sigma \cup \{\#\} \longrightarrow 2^{(\Sigma \cup \{\#\})^*}, \Delta_3(\#) = \Delta_3(a) = \#, \forall a \in \Sigma,$$

we obtain,

$$\begin{aligned} L^c &= \text{Mi}(\text{Mi}(\#L^c) \longmapsto \Delta_3), && \text{if } \lambda \in L, \\ L^c &= \text{Mi}(\text{Mi}(\#L^c) \longmapsto \Delta_3) \cup \{\lambda\}, && \text{if } \lambda \notin L. \end{aligned}$$

The language $\#\Sigma^*\$\$\#$, can be obtained from the singleton letters by using catenation and catenation closure. As, in order to obtain L^c, we have started from Σ, $\$$, $\#$ and L, and we have used only the operations of $\mathcal{P}'$, we deduce that $L^c \in \mathcal{P}'$. Being closed under complementation and union, $\mathcal{P}'$ is closed also under intersection. Consequently $\mathcal{P}'$ is a Boolean algebra. □

References

[1] R.V.Book, M.Jantzen, C.Wrathall. Monadic Thue systems. *Theoretical Computer Science*, 19(1982), pp.231-251.

[2] M.Jantzen. Semi-Thue systems and generalized Church-Rosser properties. *Proc.Fete des Mots*, Rouen, France, 1982, pp.60-75.

[3] T.Kimura. Formal description of communication behaviour. *Proc. Johns Hopkins Conf. on Information Sciences and Systems* (1979).

[4] L.Kari. On insertion and deletion in formal languages. *Ph.D. Thesis*, University of Turku, 1991.

[5] L.Kari. Insertion and deletion of words: determinism and reversibility. *Lecture Notes in Computer Science*, vol.629, 1992, pp.315-327.

[6] L.Kari. Generalized derivatives. *Fundamenta Informaticae*, vol.18, nr.1, 1993, pp.27-40.

[7] L.Kari, A.Mateescu, Gh.Paun, A.Salomaa. Deletion sets. To appear in *Fundamenta Informaticae*.

[8] L.Kari, A.Mateescu, Gh.Paun, A.Salomaa. On parallel deletions applied to a word. To appear in *RAIRO*.

[9] A.Salomaa. *Formal Languages*. Academic Press, New York, 1973.

[10] L.Sântean. Six arithmetic-like operations on languages. *Revue Roumaine de Linguistique*, Tome XXXIII, 1988, Cahiers de linguistique theorique et applique, Tome XXV, 1988, No.1, Janvier-Juin, pp.65-73.

From Colonies
to Eco(grammar)systems
An Overview

Alica Kelemenová
Institute for Informatics
Slovak Academy of Sciences
Dúbravská 7, 842 35 Bratislava, Slovakia
e-mail: kelemenova@savba.sk

Jozef Kelemen
Department of Applied Informatics
University of Economics
832 20 Bratislava, Slovakia
e-mail: kelemen@vseba.sk

1 Societies of Agents as Systems of Grammars

This contribution demonstrates a possibility to study societies of entities which act autonomously in their common environment – *societies of agents* – using tools and techniques of the *theory of formal grammars and languages*.

Informally, we will consider an *agent* as a sensor/effector system that operates within an environment and changes states of that environment by acts performed in it. In present days, this conception of agents becomes to be popular namely in robotic research (where agents are considered to be physically embodied robotic systems situated in real physical environments), and in software design where agents operate in (symbolic) software environments such as databases, operating systems, or computer networks.

In theoretical computer science, esp. in the theory of formal grammars, languages, and automata, however, only properties of single agents have been studied. The agents have been described as grammars, automata, or in some similar ways, and collections of agents have been considered only as families of grammars, and the study concentrated towards the understanding of features of such families.

Recently, however, collections of agents are more and more frequently embedded in physical or symbolic environments (containing other agents, too). Several important problems appear in connection with such *societies of agents*. From experimental point of view, some of them are studied e.g.

in [10] or [11]. For instance, the capabilities of societies of several agents to change the states of a shared environment, an influence of some properties of an environment into the behavior of collections of agents, the role of strategy followed by a society of (communicating) agents in behavior of the society, etc. can be investigated. However, *agents in social level* are only beginning to influence the relevant research in theoretical computer science. (The above mentioned experimentations [10] and [11] have been in certain extent connected with the theoretical approach presented in this contribution in [5].)

One of the first attempts to study (communicating) collections of agents in the framework of the theory of formal grammars and languages –*the theory of grammar systems* – has been developed during eighties (see [8] for more bibliographical details). The monographical presentation of recent results of the topic is just appearing [1].

An important and well motivated situation is when as elementary as possible – so called *purely reactive* – agents without any shared strategy of cooperation take part in a cohabitation in an environment. "Elementary" is here related both to the individual properties of agents as well as to the global properties of societies of agents. Individual properties take the form of allowed rules in agents, while the global properties are given by the type of the global behavior of the society of agents in which the autonomous behaviors of individual agents result.

The central aim of this contribution is to recapitulate two approaches towards societies of purely reactive agents situated in symbolic environments. Formally, a purely reactive agent will be modelled by a *grammar (with right-linear productions)* which determines a finite behavior as the corresponding *finite language* generated by this grammar. We will first consider societies of simple agents – *colonies*. A colony behaves in a symbolic environment and changes its states only through acts performed by the simple agents – the *components of the colony*. Each state of the environment of a colony will be modelled by a (finite) string of symbols. The states may change only as results of acts performed by agents. So, the set of all possible states of an environment will be considered as a language generated by agents forming the colony. The environment itself is in the case of colonies quite passive – it does not change its state in certain sense autonomously, but only through the activities of agents.

In the case of colonies we are facing with two restrictions: First, because of the lack of environments' own dynamics we may find colonies as a quite restrictive model of real situations when agents act in environments with their own dynamics of changes. From this reason we will consider a more realistic situation when in order to change its parts, which are not influenced in a given moment by any agent, environments use their own rules.

The second restriction is connected with the conception of agents of colonies. The agents are not able to change their "internal states", they do not to "develop".

In order to overcome above mentioned restrictions on colonies, we extend colonies onto a more complicated type of societies which we will call *ecosystems*.

The agents in an ecosystem will be characterized not only by their actions in the environment but also by the rules used for their own (parallel Lindenmayer-style) inner development.

Environments of ecosystems will be modelled by the language defined by the formal grammars which models laws of changes of their states. Environment develops on the base of rules (applied in Lindenmayer-style, again), everywhere, where no action of any agent can occur. The formal model – the *eco(grammar)system* – will consist of purely reactive agents (as in the case of colonies) situated in environments which change their states not exclusively through agents acts, but also according their own laws of changes.

Because of the use of the theory of formal grammars and languages in the following, we will suppose the reader to be familiar with that theory in certain details (e.g. in the extent presented in [13], [14]).

2 Colonies – the Basic Model

A colony is a collection of (very simple) grammars operating in common string either in sequential or parallel manner. By a "very simple" we mean a *regular grammar* producing a *finite language*.

In this section we present definition of basic model of a colony as well as definitions of many of its variation which result from different motivations.

Definition: *A colony C is a 3-tuple $C = (\mathcal{R}, V, T)$, where*

(i) $\mathcal{R} = \{R_i : 1 \leq i \leq n \}$ is a finite set of regular grammars $R_i = (N_i, T_i, P_i, S_i)$ producing finite languages $L(R_i) = F_i$ for each i. R_i will be referred to as *a component of C*.

(ii) $V = \bigcup_{i=1}^{n}(T_i \cup N_i)$ is *an alphabet of the colony*, and

(iii) $T \subseteq V$ is *a terminal alphabet of the colony*.

We note that terminal symbol of one grammar can occur as a nonterminal symbol of another grammar.

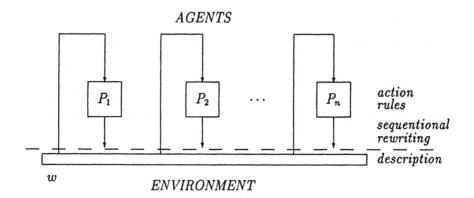

Fig.1: A colony

The activity of components in a colony is realized by string transformation on common tape. Elementary changes of strings are determined by a *basic derivation step*:

For $x, y \in V^*$ we define $x \overset{b}{\Longrightarrow} y$ iff

$$x = x_1 S_i x_2, \ y = x_1 z x_2, \text{ where } z \in F_i \text{ for some } i, 1 \leq i \leq n.$$

Language determined by a colony $\mathcal{C}$ starting with the word $w_0 \in V^*$ is given by

$$L(\mathcal{C}, w_0) = \{v | \ w_0 \overset{b}{\Longrightarrow}{}^* v, \ v \in T^*\}.$$

If it is sufficient for formulation and solution of problems, components are characterized simply by pairs (S_i, F_i), where strings in F_i do not contain the symbol S_i.

3 Variations of the Basic Model

Due to wide possibilities how to determine and interpret colonies there are many natural variants of them. They differ in

(1) the definition of single derivation step
(2) the choice of terminal alphabet or other termination mode.
(3) global characterization of derivation process (additional limitations and controls of derivation process can be considered)

3.1 Variants of the Derivation Step

Basic differences among the definitions of derivation steps are due to the number of components used in one step (sequential/parallel model) as well as to the amount of start symbols (of components), rewritten in one step by each component.

3.1.1 Sequential Models

In a colony with sequential derivation *exactly one component* takes place in a derivation step. The basic derivation step $\overset{b}{\Longrightarrow}$ is a sequential derivation step in which one component changes one letter of string.

In a sequential model discussed in [9], in the derivation step (denoted here by $\overset{t}{\Longrightarrow}$) one component is used to rewrite all occurrences of its start symbol in string (not necessary by the same word).

Formally, for $x, y \in V^*$ we define a *terminal* derivation step

$$x \overset{t}{\Longrightarrow} y \quad \text{iff} \quad x = x_1 S_i x_2 S_i x_3 \ldots x_m S_i x_{m+1},$$
$$y = x_1 w_1 x_2 w_2 x_3 \ldots x_m w_m x_{m+1},$$
$$x_1 x_2 \ldots x_{m+1} \in (V - \{S_i\})^*,$$
$$\text{where } w_j \in F_i, \text{ for each } j, 1 \le j \le m$$
$$\text{and for some } i, 1 \le i \le n$$

In [12], intermediate situations between $x \overset{b}{\Longrightarrow} y$ and $x \overset{t}{\Longrightarrow} y$ are studied for a given k, where exactly (less then, more than) k occurrences of S_i are rewritten.

Formally, for $x, y \in V^*$ and $k \ge 1$, we define the derivation steps "$= k$","$\le k$" and "$\ge k$" as follows:

$$x \overset{=k}{\Longrightarrow} y \quad \text{iff} \quad x = x_1 S_i x_2 S_i \ldots x_k S_i x_{k+1},$$
$$y = x_1 w_1 x_2 w_2 \ldots x_k w_k x_{k+1},$$
$$\text{where } w_j \in F_i, 1 \le j \le k,$$
$$\text{and for some } i, 1 \le i \le n;$$
$$x \overset{\le k}{\Longrightarrow} y \quad \text{iff} \quad x \overset{=k'}{\Longrightarrow} \text{ for some } k' \le k;$$
$$x \overset{\ge k'}{\Longrightarrow} y \quad \text{iff} \quad x \overset{=k'}{\Longrightarrow} \text{ for some } k' \ge k.$$

3.1.2 Parallel Models

Following [4], by a parallel model we mean that all components of a colony, which *can* work *must* work simultaneously on the tape and each of them rewrites at most one occurrence of its start symbol. The case when more components (S_i, F_i) have the same associated nonterminal S_i requires a special discussion:

 * If (S, F_i), and (S, F_j) are two components of a colony C and if (at least) two symbols S appear in a current string, then both these components must be used, each rewriting one occurrence of S.

* If only one S appears in a current string, then each component *can* be used, but not both in parallel, hence in such a case we discuss two possibilities

(i) derivation is blocked – *strongly competitive parallel* way of derivation, and

(ii) derivation continues and maximal number of components is used, nondeterministically chosen from all the components which can be used – *weakly competitive parallel* way of derivation.

This corresponds to the following derivation steps:

For $x, y \in V^*$ define a *strongly competitive parallel* derivation step by

$$x \overset{sp}{\Longrightarrow} y \text{ iff } x = x_1 S_{i_1} x_2 S_{i_2} ... x_k S_{i_k} x_{k+1},$$

$y = x_1 z_{i_1} x_2 z_{i_2} ... x_k z_{i_k} x_{k+1}, z_{i_j} \in F_{i_j}, 1 \le j \le k,$

$i_u \ne i_v$ for all $u \ne v, 1 \le u, v \le k,$

(one component is allowed to rewrite at most one

occurrence of its startsymbol)

$|x|_{S_t} > 0$ implies $i_j = t$ for some j, $1 \le j \le k$

(if component F_t *can* be used, then it *must* be used).

For $x, y \in V^*$ define a *weakly competitive parallel* derivation step by

$$x \overset{wp}{\Longrightarrow} y \text{ iff } x = x_1 S_{i_1} x_2 S_{i_2} ... x_k S_{i_k} x_{k+1},$$

$y = x_1 z_{i_1} x_2 z_{i_2} ... x_k z_{i_k} x_{k+1}, z_{i_j} \in F_{i_j}, 1 \le j \le k,$

$i_u \ne i_v$ for all $u \ne v, 1 \le u, v \le k,$

(one component is allowed to rewrite at most one

occurrence of its startsymbol)

$|x|_{S_t} > 0$ implies $S_t = S_{i_j}$ for some j, $1 \le j \le k,$

k is the maximal integer with the previous properties.

If start symbols of all components in a colony are different, then both $\overset{sp}{\Longrightarrow}$ and $\overset{wp}{\Longrightarrow}$ define the same relation denoted by $\overset{p}{\Longrightarrow}$.

3.2 On Terminal Sets of Colonies

According to different selections of the terminal set of a colony we can distinguish colonies with different styles of acceptance [9].

We say that colony $C = (\mathcal{R}, V, T)$ with components $R_i = (N_i, T_i, P_i, S_i)$, $(1 \le i \le n)$ and with $alph(L_i) = T_i$ has an acceptance style

(i) "arb" if $T \subseteq \bigcup_{i=1}^{n} T_i$;

(ii) "one" if $T = T_i$ for some i $(1 \leq i \leq n)$;

(iii) "ex" if $T = \bigcup_{i=1}^{n} T_i$;

(iv) "all" if $T = \bigcap_{i=1}^{n} T_i$;

(v) "dist" if $T = (\bigcup_{i=1}^{n} T_i) - (\bigcup_{i=1}^{n} N_i)$.

The *language* generated by $\mathcal{C}$ with the derivation step $\overset{x}{\Longrightarrow}$ for $x \in \{b, t, = k, \leq k, \geq k, sp, wp, p\}$ starting with word $w_0 \in V^*$ is defined as

$$L_x(\mathcal{C}, w_0) = \{v : w_0 \overset{x}{\Longrightarrow}^* u, \ v \in T^*\},$$

where $\overset{x}{\Longrightarrow}^*$ denotes the reflexive and transitive closure of $\overset{x}{\Longrightarrow}$.

The corresponding families of languages we denote by COL_x or by COL_x^f in order to stress the property $f \in \{one, arb, ex, all, dist\}$ of terminal sets. If we are looking for colonies with exactly n components, we use $COL_x(n)$ and $COL_x^f(n)$.

3.3 Variations of Control and Limitations of Derivation Process

Additional mechanisms used for derivation in colonies are time delays of components, hypothesis languages and transducer-colony pairs.

A time delay, associated to each component of a colony, was studied in [7]. It determines a minimal time period between two consecutive uses of a component.

Definition: A *colony with delay* is a quadruple

$$C_T = (\mathcal{R}, V, T, d),$$

where $(\mathcal{R}, V, T)$ is a colony, and $d = (d_1, \ldots, d_k)$ is a vector of nonnegative integers called a *delay vector* of the colony C_T.

A derivation step of a colony with delay is defined for pairs $\langle w, t \rangle$, where w is a string and t is a n-tuple of integers (determining possible active components of a colony).

Definition: Let $C_T = (\mathcal{R}, V, T, d)$ be a colony with delay.
$\langle w_1, t \rangle \Longrightarrow_{C_T} \langle w_2, t' \rangle$ iff
$w_1 = x_1 S_j x_2$,
$t = (t_1, \ldots, t_n)$ with $t_j = 0$ for some j, $1 \leq j \leq n$
$w_2 = x_1 z x_2$ for some $z \in L(G_j)$,
$t' = (t'_1, \ldots, t'_k)$, where $t'_j = d_j$ and $t'_i = max\{0, m_i - 1\}$ for all i, $i \neq j$.

Note: $d = (0, \ldots, 0)$ corresponds to the basic definition of colonies. The derivation step for a colony without delay corresponds to t being the zero vector.

Definition: Let $\mathcal{C}_T = (\mathcal{R}, V, T, d)$ be a colony with delay. A *language* defined for a colony $\mathcal{C}_T$ with axiom w_0 and with start delay vector t_0 is the set

$$L(\mathcal{C}_T, w_0, t_0) = \{w \in T^* : \langle w_0, t_0 \rangle \Longrightarrow^*_{\mathcal{C}_T} \langle w, t \rangle\}.$$

The corresponding family of languages is denoted by $\mathcal{DCOL}$.

A colony is a model of a system designed for solving certain problems, hence it is supposed that its actions tend to some expected results. This can be captured in colony terms e.g. by considering a target language for selecting the sentential forms generated by the colony, as it was introduced in [12].

Definition: A *colony with a (regular) hypothesis language* is a quadruple

$$\mathcal{C_H} = (\mathcal{R}, V, T, H),$$

where $(\mathcal{R}, V, T)$ is a colony and H is a regular language in $V^* - T^*$.

For $f \in \{*, t\} \cup \{\leq k, = k, \geq k : k \geq 1\}$ and i $(1 \leq i \leq n,)$ the colony accepts a derivation $x \overset{f}{\Longrightarrow} y$ only if $y \in H$ or $y \in T^*$.

The *language generated* by $\mathcal{C_H}$ in the mode f starting with w_0 is the set

$$
\begin{aligned}
L_f(\mathcal{C_H}, w_0) = \{x \in T^* \mid & w_0 \overset{f}{\Longrightarrow} w_1 \overset{f}{\Longrightarrow} \ldots \overset{f}{\Longrightarrow} w_s = x, \\
& s \geq 1, 1 \leq i_j \leq n, 1 \leq j \leq s, \text{ and} \\
& w_j \in H, 1 \leq j \leq s - 1\}.
\end{aligned}
$$

(No hypothesis is made about the last string, the terminal word.)

We denote by $HCOL_f(n)$, $HCOL_f$ $(n \geq 1, f$ as above) the families of languages obtained in this way, which correspond to families $COL_f(n)$ and COL_f.

Another way to increase the generative power of colonies is considered in [12]. It is supposed that the components "speak different languages," and a transducer is required to intermediate them.

Definition: A *colony-transducer pair* is a couple (C, g), where $C = (\mathcal{R}, V, T)$ is a colony, and $g = (V, V, Q, s_0, F, P)$ is a generalized sequential machine (gsm) (Q is the set of states, s_0 is the initial state, F is the set of final states, P is the set of translation rules of the form $sa \to xs'$, $s, s' \in Q$, $a \in V$, $x \in V^+$).

The *language* generated by (C, g) in the mode f starting with w_0 is

$$L_f(C, g, w_0) = \{x \in T^* \mid w \Longrightarrow^f_{i_1} w_1 \Longrightarrow g(w_1) \Longrightarrow^f_{i_2} w_2 \Longrightarrow g(w_2) \Longrightarrow \cdots$$
$$\cdots \Longrightarrow^f_{i_s} w_s = x, s \geq 1, 1 \leq i_j \leq n, 1 \leq j \leq s\}.$$

By $TCOL_f(n)$, $TCOL_f(\, n \geq 1, f$ as above) we denote corresponding families of languages.

Some further interesting and well motivated variants of colonies appear in [3].

4 Generative Power of Colonies

Generative power is the most intensively studied topic of colonies. We compare classes of languages defined by colonies, study their relation to the classes of Chomsky hierarchy and to the classes characterized by L systems. We shall discuss first COL classes and then their versions restricted to n components in the colonies $COL(n)$.

4.1 Relations between COL Classes

First, we discuss classes with sequentional derivations. Four of properties for T given in Section 3.2 lead to the same class of languages.

Theorem [9]: For $x \in \{b, t\}$

$$COL^{ex}_x \subset COL^{one}_x = COL^{all}_x = COL^{dist}_x = COL^{arb}_x.$$

For $f \in \{one, arb, all, dist\}$
a) $COL^{ex}_b \subset COL^f_b \subset COL^f_t$
b) Families COL^f_t and COL^{ex}_t are incomparable.
c) Families COL^{ex}_b and COL^{ex}_t are incomparable.

All following results are due to the acceptance style "arb".

Some cases for the number of consecutive derivation steps of components produce equivalent classes of languages.

Theorem [12]: $COL_{=1} = COL_{\leq k} = COL_{\geq 1}$ for all $n \geq 1, k \geq 1$.

The cases $= k$ and $\geq k$ are of interest, each.

Theorem [12]: Families $COL_{=k_1}, COL_{=k_2}, COL_{\geq k_3}, COL_{\geq k_4}$ with different k_1, k_2, k_3, k_4 are pairwise incomparable.

The family COL_t is incomparable with each of $COL_{=k}, COL_{\geq k}, k \geq 2$.

Now, we shall deal with classes of languages defined by colonies with restricted derivations.

Theorem[7,12]: $COL \subset DCOL_T$

$\qquad COL_f \subseteq HCOL_f$ for all f

$\qquad COL_f \subset HCOL_f \cap TCOL_f$ for $f \in \{= k, \geq k \mid k \geq 2\}$.

For classes with parallel derivations the following is known:

Theorem[4]: $COL_b = COL_p \subset COL_{sp}$.

4.2 Comparison with Traditional Classes of Languages

By traditional classes of languages we mean classes of languages defined by Chomsky-type grammars and classes of languages defined by L systems.

Theorem[9]: $COL_b^{ex} = nrpCF$,

where $nrpCF$ states for languages determined by the pure context-free grammars with no production of type $Z \to xZy$ for $xy \in V^*$.

$\qquad CF \subset COL_t^{arb} = EPT0L_{[1]}$,

where $EPT0L_{[1]}$ is the family of languages generated by propagating $ETOL$ systems having at most one rule $X \to x, x \neq X$, in each table.

$\qquad COL_t^{ex} = nrFPT0L_{[1]}$,

where $nrFPT0L_{[1]}$ is the family of languages generated by $FPT0L_{[1]}$ systems with no recursive rule.

Theorem[4]: $COL_{wp} \subset ETOL_{[1]}$

Theorem[12]: $COL_f = CF$, for $f \in \{= 1, \leq k, \geq 1\}$.

Theorem [12]: $TCOL_f = CS$ and $HCOL_f = CS$ for $f \in \{t, = 1, \geq 1\} \cup \{\leq k : k \geq 1\}$.

Theorem [4]: $COL_p = CF$

$\qquad COL_{sp} \subseteq MAT_{ac}$

$\qquad COL_{wp} \subset 1lETOL$ and $COL_w \subset MAT_{ac}$.

Theorem[12]: The families $FIN, REG, LIN, CF, MAT_{fin}$ are incomparable with $COL_{=k}, COL_{\geq k}$ for $k \geq 2$.

4.3 The Role of the Number of Components

In general, increasing of the number of components leads to the increase of the generative power of colonies. In more detail:

Theorem [12]: $COL_{=1}(n) \subset COL_{=1}(n+1), n \geq 1$,

$\qquad COL_t(n) \subset COL_t(n+1), n \geq 1$.

$\qquad COL_f(n) \subset COL_f(n+1), n \geq 1, f \in \{= k, \geq k \mid k \geq 2\}$.

$\qquad COL_f(n) \subseteq HCOL_f(n), n \geq 1$, for all f.

Comparing colonies with n components and traditional classes of languages we have:

Theorem[9,12]: $COL_f(1) \subseteq FIN$
for $n \geq 1$, and for all f, and it is equality for $f \in \{t, = 1, \geq 1\} \cup \{\leq k \mid k \geq 1\}$.

Theorem[12]: $COL_f(n) \subset CF$, for $f \in \{= 1, \leq k, \geq 1\}$ and $n \geq 1$.

Theorem[12]: The families $FIN, REG, LIN, CF, MAT_{fin}$ are incomparable with each of $COL_{=k}(n), COL_{\geq k}(n)$ for $n \geq 2$ and $k \geq 2$.

$COL_t(2)$ is incomparable with REG, LIN, MAT_{fin}, but $COL_t(2) \subset CF$.

5 Eco(grammar)systems

An eco(grammar)system consists of two mutually influencing parts, an environment characterized by an $0L$ scheme and a collection of agents characterized by inner developmental rules and action rules working sequentially in environment.

Definition [2]: An *eco(grammar)system* (*EG system* for short) is a pair

$$\mathcal{E} = (E, \mathcal{R}),$$

where

- $E = (V_E, P_E)$ is an $0L$ scheme,

- $\mathcal{R} = \{O_i : O_i = (V_O, P_i, \varphi_i, R_i, \psi_i), 1 \leq i \leq n \}$, where $O_i = (V_O, P_i, \varphi_i, R_i, \psi_i)$ for i $(1 \leq i \leq n)$ is an *agent schemes* of i-th type, and

  - V_O is an alphabet common for all O_i,
  - P_i is a finite set of $(0L)$ rules over V_O (possibly with the distinguished symbol $\sqcup$ – the separator – on the right hand sides of rules),
  - $\varphi_i : V_E^* \longrightarrow 2^{P_i}$,
  - R_i is a finite set of (pure) rewriting rules of the form $x \to y$ with $x, y \in V_E^*$
  - $\psi_i : V_O^* \longrightarrow 2^{R_i}$.

The above items are interpreted as follows:

- E describes the environment behaving according the rules P_E over the alphabet V_E, and ;

- $O_i = (V_O, P_i, \varphi_i, R_i, \psi_i)$ for i $(1 \leq i \leq n)$ represents the agents of the i-th type, where

- V_O is an alphabet of agents, (the same for all agents);
- P_i is the set of rules for the evolution of the agents of i-th type;
- φ_i is the mapping, which selects rules of P_i for actual evolution in dependence of current *environment* state;
- R_i is the set of rules for the actions of the agents of i-th type in the environment;
- ψ_i is the mapping, which selects the rules of R_i for the actual action of the agent, depending on its current state.

Derivation in an EG system is defined for its configuration, given by a string for its environment and by strings for the agents.

Definition: A *configuration* of the EG system $\mathcal{E} = (E, \mathcal{R})$ is an $(n+1)$-tuple

$$(w_E, W_1, W_2, \ldots, W_n),$$

where $n = card(\mathcal{R})$, $w_E \in V_E^*$ is the current evolution state of the environment, and $W_i = \{w_{i1}, \ldots, w_{ik_i}\}$ is a finite subset of V_O^+ (possibly with multiple occurrences of the same word), where $w_{i1}, \ldots, w_{ik_i}$ are evolution states of all agents of the i-th type currently occurring in $\mathcal{E}$.

Fig.2 presents an eco(grammar)system with its components and with the interplay of model components.

225

AGENTS

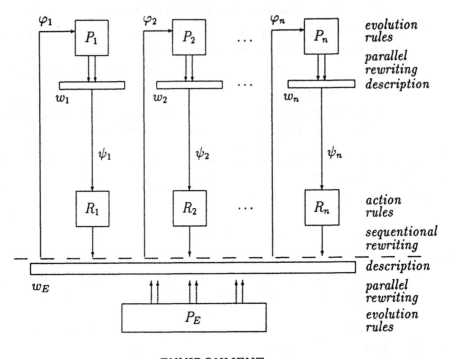

ENVIRONMENT

Fig.2: An eco(grammar)system

5.1. Functioning of the Model

To describe the behavior of an EG system $\mathcal{E}$ we explain the role of the $\sqcup$, first. The separator $\sqcup$ (appearing on the right hand side of productions) is used to change the number of agents. We assume that

$$w \sqcup \varepsilon = \varepsilon \sqcup w = w$$

holds for the separator and for the empty word ε.

Moreover, in order to deal with multiple occurrences of the same words in sets, we introduce an operator s with arguments in $(V_0 \cup \{\sqcup\})^*$ and values in the set of nonempty words, where a multiple occurrence of the same word is allowed. (To stress the multiplicity in sets we use $\{'$ and $\}'$ instead of $\{$ and $\}$, respectively.) Following rules for s are claimed:

$$s(\varepsilon) = \emptyset$$
$$s(w_1 \sqcup w_2 \sqcup \ldots \sqcup w_n) = \{'w_1, w_2, \ldots, w_n\}'$$

Derivation step of an EG system $\mathcal{E}$ is a relation $\Longrightarrow_{\mathcal{E}}$ between its configurations.

Definition: Let $(w_E, W_1, \ldots, W_n)$ and $(w'_E, W'_1, \ldots, W'_n)$ be configurations of an EG system $\mathcal{E} = (E, \mathcal{R})$ with $W_i = \{'w_{i1}, \ldots, w_{ik_i}\}'$ and $W'_i = \{'w'_{i1}, \ldots, w'_{ik_i}\}'$, $(1 \leq i \leq n)$, and $m = \sum_{i=1}^{n} k_i$.

We define

$$(w_E, W_1, \ldots, W_n) \Longrightarrow_{\mathcal{E}} (w'_E, W'_1, \ldots, W'_n)$$

iff:

1. $W'_i = \bigcup_{t=1}^{k_i} s(w'_{it})$ for $w_{it} \Longrightarrow_{\varphi_i(w_E)} w'_{it}$, and $1 \leq i \leq n$.

(The union here is treated in the sense of sets with multiple occurrences of elements, too.)

2. $w_E = z_1 x_1 z_2 x_2 \ldots z_m x_m z_{m+1}$,
   $w'_E = z'_1 y_1 z'_2 y_2 \ldots z'_m y_m z'_{m+1}$,

where for every w_{ij} $(1 \leq i \leq n, 1 \leq j \leq k_i)$ exactly one rule $x_r \to y_r$ of $\psi_i(w_{ij})$ is used, and $z_r \Longrightarrow_{P_E} z'_r$, $(1 \leq r \leq m+1)$.

($\Longrightarrow$ in points 1. and 2. denotes L system mode of derivation.)

Informally, the EG systems increase the number of agents – new agents appear – whenever the symbol $\sqcup$ occurs in the rules used in a derivation step. The number of agents of the system decreases – some agent disappears – in the case when its state becomes ε (see special rules for $\sqcup$ above.)

The state of the environment is modified in one derivation step in such a way that each agent modifies exactly one symbol of environment by its action rule of the sets $\psi_i(w_{it})$, and all the remained symbols are rewritten simultaneously by the evolution rules of the set P_E.

Given an EG system $\mathcal{E}$ and a starting configuration σ_0 a *language of configurations* of $\mathcal{E}$ is given by

$$L(\mathcal{E}, \sigma_0) = \{\sigma_i : \sigma_0 \Longrightarrow_{\mathcal{E}}^* \sigma_i\}.$$

The language of the environment is defined by

$$L_E(\mathcal{E}, \sigma_0) = \{w_E \in V_E^* : (w_E, W_1, \ldots, W_n) \in L(\mathcal{E}, \sigma_0)\}$$

We shall illustrate EG systems in next two sections. First, we characterize unary deterministic ecosystems, and then we give an example of EG system with nonstable size of agents.

We restrict ourselves to the case when $\varphi_i(w) = P_i$ for arbitrary w in V_E^* and $\psi_i(v) = R_i$ for arbitrary $w \in V_O^*$. In such a case we write an agent scheme in form $O_i = (V_O, P_i, R_i)$.

5.2 Unary Deterministic EG Systems

An EG system is *deterministic (with respect to the environment)* if P_E, R_1, $\ldots, R_n$ are deterministic sets of rules.

An EG system is unary if it is the system with environmental alphabet being a single letter $V_E = \{a\}$.

A unary deterministic EG system without separator is an EG system $\mathcal{E} = (E, \mathcal{R})$, where $E = (\{a\}, \{a \to a^k\})$ and $\mathcal{R} = (O_i : 1 \leq i \leq n\}$ for $O_i = (V_O, P_i, \{a \to a^{s_i}\})$. Assume for the starting configuration that $w_{0E} = a^m$ and that $W_{0,i}$ are singletons. Put $s = \sum_{i=1}^{n} s_i$.

Definition: Let $\mathcal{E} = (E, \mathcal{R})$ be a unary deterministic EG system with starting configuration $(a^m, W_1, \ldots, W_n)$, and $W_i = \{w_i\}$ for every i.

$\mathcal{E}$ is of the type 0 (or it is *blocked*) if $a^x \in L_E(\mathcal{E}, a^m)$ for $x < n$.

$\mathcal{E}$ is of the type 1 (it *stagnates*) if for all $t \geq t_0$ there is an x_0 such that $a^m \Longrightarrow^t a^x$ and $n \leq x \leq x_0$.

$\mathcal{E}$ is of the type 2 (it *grows (develops)*) otherwise.

Theorem: It is decidable for the behavior of a unary deterministic EG system $\mathcal{E}$ whether it is of the type 0, 1 or 2.

Proof: Let $\mathcal{E}$ be a unary deterministic system specified above. The derivation step in $\mathcal{E}$ has the form $a^x \Longrightarrow a^{(x-n)k+s}$.

In the case $m < n$, the development of an environment in $\mathcal{E}$ is blocked, and the language of the environment is a singleton containing the axiom.

Assume $m \geq n$. We shall discuss the cases $k = 0$, $k = 1$ and $k > 1$ separately.

(i) For $k = 0$ a derivation step is of the form $a^x \Longrightarrow a^s$. This gives a blocked derivation for $s < n$ and a stagnating derivation for $s \geq n$. In both cases the language of the environment is finite, with one or two words.

(ii) For $k = 1$ a derivation step is of the form $a^x \Longrightarrow a^{x+s-n}$.

This gives a blocked derivation if for some $t_0 > 0$, $m + t_0(s - n) \leq n$ holds. This implies $s < 2n - m$. The language of the environment has two words.

Stagnating derivation arises when $s = n = m$. Language of environment consists of the axiom.

The environment grows for $s \geq 2n + m$ and $s \neq n$, and corresponding language of environment is $L = \{a^{m+t(s-n)} : t \geq 0\}$.

(iii) Assume $k \geq 1$. Then $a^x \Longrightarrow a^{(x-n)k+s}$, and ε is of

the type 0 iff $k^i(m - n) < \sum_{j=0}^{i-1}(n - s)$ for some i,

the type 1 iff $k^i(m - n) = \sum_{j=0}^{i-1}(n - s)$ for all i,

the type 2 iff $k^i(m - n) \geq \sum_{j=0}^{i-1}(n - s)$ for all i.

Equalities $k^i(m-n) = \sum_{j=0}^{i-1}(n-s)$ hold for all i iff

$$\frac{k^i}{k^i-1}(m-n) = \frac{1}{k-1}(n-s), \quad \text{for all} \ \ i$$

iff $m = n = s$.

Inequalities $k^i(m-n) > \sum_{j=0}^{i-1}(n-s)$ hold for all i iff

$$(1 + \frac{1}{k^i-1})(m-n) > \frac{1}{k-1}(n-s) \ \text{i.e.} \ s > m - k(m-n).$$

In all other cases the derivation is blocked.

The following table summarizes the previous results.

type 0	$m < n$
	$m \geq n, k = 0, s < n$
	$m \geq n, k = 1, s < 2n - m$
	$m \geq n, k > 1, s \leq m - k(m-n)$
type 1	$m \geq n, k = 0, s \geq n$
	$m = n, k = 1, s = n$
	$m = n, k > 1, s = n$
type 2	$m \geq n, k = 1, s \geq 2n - m$
	$m \geq n, k > 1, s > m - k(m-n)$

5.3 Emergence of Life-Like Features

The birth is included to our model using the separator ⊔. We capture in this way an asexual reproduction. In order to treat sexual reproduction one can extend action rules of agents from the environment also on another agents.

The death of the agent is expressed in our model by $w_{ij} = \varepsilon$. The *life* of the agent is the period starting with its birth and ending with its death.

We say an EG system is with *unchanged population* if there is no birth and death in the system; an EG system is *constant* if all configurations have the same number of agents; it is *increasing (decreasing)* if the number of births is greater (is smaller) than the number of deaths in the EG system. We speak about EG systems with *finite (infinite) environment* if the language of its environment is finite (infinite). We speak about a *periodical (aperiodical) birth (death) sequence* if birth (death) happens periodically (aperiodically) in the sequence of configurations.

Following statments illustrate a wide variety of EG systems with different behavior.

The death results that the language of the environment leads out from the class of 0L languages even in the simplest case, when the system consists of one agent with finite life without any reproduction.

Theorem [2]: There exists an EG system with one agent of finite life and with finite but non-0L environment.

Theorem [2]: There exists an EG system with finite unchanged population and with finite environment such that there is an infinite ultimately aperiodical sequence in the behavior of the environment.

Theorem [2]: There exists an EG system with exponentially growing population with periodical birth and no death of agents, where every agent makes a real change in the environment and the language of the environment is an infinite D0L language with almost locally catenative behavior.

Other life like phenomena, particularly symbiosis and parasitism, are analyzed for colonies in [3]. The structured colonies with weak/strong dependence relations are defined and relation of corresponding classes of languages to context sensitive languages are discussed.

REFERENCES

1. Csuhaj-Varjú, E., Dassow, J., Kelemen, J., Păun, Gh: *Grammar Systems*. Brighton: Gordon & Breach (in press)

2. Csuhaj-Varjú, E., Kelemen, J., Kelemenová, A., Păun, Gh.: Eco(grammar)systems – a preview. In: *Proc. 13th European Meeting on Cybernetics and Systems Science*, Vienna, April 1994 (accepted)

3. Csuhaj-Varjú, E., Păun, Gh.: Structured colonies: models of symbiosis and parasitism. *Annals Univ. Bucuresti, Computer Science Series* (accepted)

4. Dassow, J., Kelemen, J., Păun, Gh.: On parallelism in colonies. *Cybernetics and Systems 24* (1993) 37–49

5. Kelemen, J.: Multiagent symbol systems and behavior-based robots. *Applied Artificial Intelligence 7* (1993) 419-432

6. Kelemen, J., Kelemenová, A.: A subsumption architecture for generative symbol systems. *Cybernetics and Systems Research'92*, R. Trappl. ed., World Scientific, Singapore, 1992, pp. 1529-1536

7. Kelemen, J., Kelemenová, A.: A grammar-theoretic treatment of multiagent systems. *Cybernetics and Systems 23* (1992) 210–218

8. Kelemen, J., Mlichová, R.: Bibliography of Grammar Systems. *Bulletin of the EATCS 48* (1992) 210-218

9. Kelemenová, A., Csuhaj-Varjú, E.: Languages of Colonies. *Theoretical Computer Science 132* (accepted)

10. Mataric, M. J.: Designing emergent behaviors: from local interactions to collective intelligence. In: *From Animals to Animates, Proc. 2nd International Conference on Simulation of Adaptive Behavior*, J. A. Meyer, H. Roitblat, and S. Wilson, eds., Cambridge, Mass.: The MIT Press, 1992, pp. 135-183

11. Parker, L. E.: Adaptive action selection for cooperative agent teams. In: *From Animals to Animates, Proc. 2nd International Conference on Simulation of Adaptive Behavior* J. A. Meyer, H. Roitblat, and S. Wilson, eds., Cambridge, Mass.: The MIT Press, 1992, pp. 442-450

12. Păun, Gh.: On generative capacity of colonies. *Kybernetika* (accepted)

13. Rozenberg, G., Salomaa, A.: *The Mathematical Theory of L Systems.* New York: Academic Press, 1980

14. Salomaa, A.: *Formal Languages.* New York: Academic Press, 1973

ON THE MULTIPLICITY EQUIVALENCE PROBLEM FOR CONTEXT-FREE GRAMMARS

WERNER KUICH

Institut für Algebra und Diskrete Mathematik
Technische Universität Wien
Wiedner Hauptstraße 8-10, A-1040 Wien

Meinem Freund Arto zum 60. Geburtstag gewidmet.

Abstract. Two context-free grammars are called multiplicity equivalent
iff all words over the common terminal alphabet are generated with the
same degree of ambiguity. Generalizing a technique introduced by D. Raz,
we show for some classes of context-free grammars that their multiplicity equivalence problem is decidable.

1. Introduction

The result of Harju, Karhumäki [3], which showed the decidability of
the equivalence problem for deterministic multitape finite automata by
algebraic methods has again raised interest to solve the same problem
for deterministic pushdown automata, i. e., for deterministic context-free
languages. Raz [8], [9] has, in two versions of a paper, introduced a
new technique which allows to decide the multiplicity equivalence of
certain context-free grammars. This technique is described in Section 2.
In Section 3 we will generalize this technique and in Section 4 we will
apply the results of Section 3 to certain classes of context-free
grammars.

The decidability of the multiplicity equivalence by the technique of Raz
[8], [9] depends on the following result of Kuich, Salomaa [4]:

Corollary 16.19. *It is decidable whether or not two given formal power series in* $\mathbb{Q}^{alg}\langle\!\langle c(\Sigma^*)\rangle\!\rangle$ *are equal.* $\qquad\square$

Here $c(\Sigma^*)$ denotes the free commutative monoid generated by the alphabet Σ.

We now assume the reader to be familiar with the basic notions and results concerning context-free grammars and languages (see Salomaa [10]) and algebraic formal power series (see Kuich, Salomaa [4]).

If Σ is an alphabet, then $|w|_a$ denotes the number of occurences of the symbol $a\in\Sigma$ in the word $w\in\Sigma^*$. If $\Sigma=\{a_1,\ldots,a_m\}$, the *Parikh mapping* $\psi:\Sigma^*\to\mathbb{N}^m$ is the morphism defined by $\psi(a_i)=(0,\ldots,1,\ldots,0)$, where the 1 stands at position i and the addition of vectors is componentwise. This yields $\psi(w)=(|w|_{a_1},\ldots,|w|_{a_i},\ldots,|w|_{a_m})$.

In the sequel we only consider ε-free context-free grammars G with terminal alphabet $\Sigma=\{a_1,\ldots,a_m\}$ such that for all words over Σ the number of different leftmost derivations with respect to G is finite. The number of different leftmost derivations for the word w is called *degree of ambiguity* of w and is denoted by $d(G,w)$. Since $d(G,w)$ is finite for all $w\in\Sigma^*$, the formal power series $\sum_{w\in\Sigma^*}d(G,w)w$ is in $\mathbb{N}^{alg}\langle\!\langle\Sigma^*\rangle\!\rangle$.

Let G_1 and G_2 be two context-free grammars with terminal alphabet Σ. Then G_1 and G_2 are called *multiplicity letter equivalent*, denoted by $G_1\sim_\# G_2$, iff for all $(n_1,\ldots,n_m)\in\mathbb{N}^m$

$$\sum_{\psi(w)=(n_1,\ldots,n_m)} d(G_1,w) = \sum_{\psi(w)=(n_1,\ldots,n_m)} d(G_2,w).$$

Since $\sum_{w\in\Sigma^*}d(G_l,w)c(w) = \sum_{\alpha\in c(\Sigma^*)}\left(\sum_{c(w)=\alpha}d(G_l,w)\right)\alpha$, $l=1,2$, where $c(w)$ is the commutative version of w, is in $\mathbb{N}^{alg}\langle\!\langle c(\Sigma^*)\rangle\!\rangle$, this definition allows us to express the above quoted Corollary 16.19 of Kuich, Salomaa [4] in terms of the theory of context-free grammars:

Theorem 1.1. *It is decidable whether or not two given context-free grammars are multiplicity letter equivalent.* $\qquad\square$

The next definition is the crucial one. Two context-free grammars G_1 and G_2 are *multiplicity equivalent*, denoted by $G_1 \sim G_2$, iff for all words $w \in \Sigma^*$

$$d(G_1, w) = d(G_2, w).$$

With the notation $\text{diff}(G_1, G_2, w) = d(G_1, w) - d(G_2, w)$ we have

$$G_1 \sim G_2 \quad \text{iff} \quad \text{diff}(G_1, G_2, w) = 0 \text{ for all } w \in \Sigma^*.$$

As usual, G_1 and G_2 are called *equivalent*, denoted by $G_1 \equiv G_2$, iff $L(G_1) = L(G_2)$. Observe that, for unambiguous context-free grammars G_1 and G_2,

$$G_1 \sim G_2 \quad \text{iff} \quad G_1 \equiv G_2.$$

Hence, the decidability of the multiplicity equivalence for the members of a class of context-free grammars would imply the decidability of the equivalence for the unambiguous context-free grammars of this class, i. e., the decidability of the equality of the generated context-free languages. This would also show the decidability of the equivalence for the deterministic context-free grammars of this class.

A language is called *acommutative* iff its Parikh mapping is injective. In this case, two context-free grammars are multiplicity letter equivalent iff they are multiplicity equivalent. Hence, Corollary 16.19 of Kuich, Salomaa [4] yields at once the next result.

Theorem 1.2. *It is decidable whether or not two given context-free grammars which generate acommutative languages are multiplicity equivalent.* □

Example. If $L(G_1), L(G_2) \subseteq a_1^* \ldots a_m^*$ then it is decidable whether or not $G_1 \sim G_2$. (See Ginsburg [2] for the theory of bounded context-free languages.) □

A language over a one-letter alphabet is always acommutative. This yields the next result.

Corollary 1.3. *It is dedidable whether or not two given context-free grammars that generate languages over $\Sigma = \{a_1\}$ are multiplicity equivalent.* □

The following remark is in order. A context-free grammar G that generates a language over $\Sigma = \{a_1\}$ always generates a regular language. But in general, there is no regular grammar G' such that $d(G', a_1^n) = d(G, a_1^n)$ for all $n \geq 0$. These facts are due to

$$\mathbb{B}^{rat} \langle\!\langle a_1^* \rangle\!\rangle = \mathbb{B}^{alg} \langle\!\langle a_1^* \rangle\!\rangle \qquad \text{and} \qquad \mathbb{N}^{rat} \langle\!\langle a_1^* \rangle\!\rangle \subsetneqq \mathbb{N}^{alg} \langle\!\langle a_1^* \rangle\!\rangle.$$

Example. Consider the context-free grammar $G = (\{S\}, \{a_1\}, \{S \rightarrow a_1 SS, S \rightarrow a_1\}, S)$. We obtain, for all $n \geq 0$,

$$d(G, a_1^{2n+1}) = \frac{(2n)!}{n!(n+1)!}, \qquad d(G, a_1^{2n}) = 0.$$

The language $L(G) = \{a_1^{2n+1} \mid n \geq 0\}$ is regular. But there exists no regular grammar G' such that $d(G', a_1^n) = d(G, a_1^n)$ for all $n \geq 0$. □

2. Previous results by D. Raz

In this section we cover some of the results of Raz [8], [9]. Most of the constructions and proofs are modified versions of those of Raz [8], [9].

The basic idea of Raz [8] is to construct, for a given context-free grammar G with terminal alphabet $\Sigma = \{a_1, \ldots, a_m\}$, a context-free grammar G' such that, for all $w \in \Sigma^*$,

$$d(G', w) = \sum_{w' \leq w} d(G, w').$$

Here the summation is over all words $w' \in \Sigma^*$ that are less or equal to w, where $\leq$ is the following partial order over Σ^* (total lexicographic order on Σ^n, $n \geq 0$):

$$w_1 \leq w_2 \qquad \text{iff} \qquad |w_1| = |w_2|, \; w_1 = va_i v_1, \; w_2 = va_j v_2, \; i < j,$$
$$\text{or } w_1 = w_2.$$

This means that a_1 is the least and a_m is the largest element of Σ.

Let G_1 and G_2 be context-free grammars. Let G_1' and G_2' be context-free grammars such that, for all $w \in \Sigma^*$,

$$d(G_l', w) = \sum_{w' \leq w} d(G_l, w'), \quad l = 1, 2.$$

Then, for all $w \in \Sigma^*$, we have

$$\text{diff}(G_1', G_2', w) = \sum_{w' \leq w} \text{diff}(G_1, G_2, w')$$

Construction 2.1. Let $G = (\Phi, \Sigma, P, S)$ be a context-free grammar in binary Greibach normal form, i. e., all the productions are of the form

$$A \to aA_1A_2, \quad A \to aA_1, \quad A \to a, \qquad A, A_1, A_2 \in \Phi, \ a \in \Sigma.$$

Let $\bar{G} = (\bar{\Phi}, \Sigma, \bar{P}, \bar{S})$ be the context-free grammar defined by
  (i) $\bar{\Phi} = \Phi \cup \Phi' \cup \Phi'' \cup \{\bar{S}\}$, where Φ' and Φ'' are primed and double-primed versions of Φ, respectively, and $\bar{S}$ is a new start variable;
 (ii) $\bar{P} = P \cup P_0 \cup P_1 \cup P_2 \cup \{\bar{S} \to S, \ \bar{S} \to S''\}$, where
    $P_0 = \{A' \to b, \ A'' \to c \mid A \to a \in P, \ b, c \in \Sigma, \ c > a\}$,
    $P_1 = \{A' \to bA_1', \ A'' \to aA_1'', \ A'' \to cA_1' \mid A \to aA_1 \in P, \ b, c \in \Sigma, \ c > a\}$,
    $P_2 = \{A' \to bA_1'A_2', \ A'' \to aA_1''A_2', \ A'' \to aA_1A_2'', \ A'' \to bA_1'A_2' \mid$
$$A \to aA_1A_2 \in P, \ b, c \in \Sigma, \ c > a\}.$$
Then we obtain

$$d(\bar{G}, w) = \sum_{w' \leq w} d(G, w') \qquad \text{for all } w \in \Sigma^*. \qquad \square$$

Theorem 2.2. *For a given context-free grammar G, where $d(G, w)$ is finite for all words w, a context-free grammar G' can be effectively constructed such that, for all w,*

$$d(G', w) = \sum_{w' \leq w} d(G, w').$$

Proof. By Theorems 14.9, 14.31 and 14.6 of Kuich, Salomaa [4] (the basic semiring is $\mathbb{N}$) we can transform the grammar G into a multiplicity equivalent context-free grammar G'' in binary Greibach normal form. Now we apply Construction 2.1 yielding $G'=\bar{G}''$. □

In the sequel, we denote the grammar G' of Theorem 2.2 by $I(G)$. Iteration of this construction yields the context-free grammars $I^s(G)$, $s \geq 0$: $I^0(G) = G$, $I^{i+1}(G) = I(I^i(G))$, $i \geq 0$.

Before studying some of the properties of the context-free grammars $I^s(G)$, $s \geq 0$, we need two combinatorial lemmas and one more grammatical construction.

Lemma 2.3. Let $a_{k,i} \in \mathbb{R}$, $k \geq 0$, $i \geq 1$, and assume $a_{k,i} = \sum_{1 \leq j \leq i} a_{k-1,j}$ for all $k,i \geq 1$. Then, for $k,i \geq 1$,

$$a_{k,i} = \sum_{1 \leq j \leq i} \binom{k+i-j-1}{k-1} a_{0,j}.$$

Proof. Let $B_k(z) = \sum_{i \geq 1} a_{k,i} z^i = \frac{1}{1-z} B_{k-1}(z)$, $k \geq 1$, be the generating function of the $a_{k,i}$. The equation $B_k(z) = \frac{1}{(1-z)^k} B_0(z)$, $k \geq 1$, implies $a_{k,i} = \sum_{1 \leq j \leq i} a_{0,j} \cdot c_{k,i,j}$, where $c_{k,i,j}$ is the coefficient of z^{i-j} in $(1-z)^{-k}$. The Binomial Expansion yields

$$c_{k,i,j} = \binom{k+i-j-1}{k-1}.$$ □

Lemma 2.4. Let $a_{k,i} \in \mathbb{R}$, $k \geq 0$, $i \geq 1$, and assume $a_{k,i} = \sum_{1 \leq j \leq i} a_{k-1,j}$ for all $k,i \geq 1$. Let now $k,t \geq 1$ be fixed. Assume $a_{s,t} = 0$ for all $1 \leq s \leq k$ and $|\{j \mid a_{0,j} \neq 0, 1 \leq j \leq t\}| \leq k$. Then $a_{0,j} = 0$ for all $1 \leq j \leq t$.

Proof. Assume that $a_{0,s_1}, a_{0,s_2}, \ldots, a_{0,s_l}$, $l \leq k$, are possibly unequal to 0. Since $a_{s,t} = 0$, we obtain by Lemma 2.3

$$\sum_{1 \leq j \leq l} \binom{s+t-s_j-1}{s-1} a_{0,s_j} = 0, \qquad 1 \leq s \leq k.$$

The determinant of the $l \times l$-matrix with i,j-entry

$$\binom{i+t-s_j-1}{i-1}$$

is unequal to 0. Hence $a_{0,s_j} = 0$ for $1 \leq j \leq l$. □

Theorem 2.5. *Let G_1 be a context-free grammar and G be a regular grammar. Then a context-free grammar G' can be effectively constructed such that*

$$d(G',w) = d(G_1,w) \cdot d(G,w).$$

Proof. By Theorems 14.9, 9.18 and Corollary 13.6 of Kuich, Salomaa [4] (the basic semiring is $\mathbb{N}$), the formal power series

$$\sum_{w \in \Sigma^*} d(G_1,w) \cdot d(G,w)w \quad = \quad \sum_{w \in \Sigma^*} d(G_1,w)w \odot \sum_{w \in \Sigma^*} d(G,w)w$$

is $\mathbb{N}$-algebraic in a constructive sense. (Here, $\odot$ denotes the Hadamard product.) □

In terms of grammars, the construction given in the proof of Theorem 6.7 of Salomaa [10] yields a grammar G' with the properties stated in Theorem 2.5. In the sequel, we denote the grammar G' of Theorem 2.5 by $G_1 \odot G$.

Lemma 2.6. *Let $k,n \geq 0$. Assume that G_1 and G_2 are context-free grammars such that, for all $1 \leq s \leq k$, $\mathrm{diff}(\mathsf{I}^s(G_1),\mathsf{I}^s(G_2),a_m^n) = 0$. Furthermore, assume that $k_n = |\{w \mid \mathrm{diff}(G_1,G_2,w) \neq 0, w \in \Sigma^n\}| \leq k$. Then $k_n = 0$.*

Proof. Denote, for $1 \leq i \leq |\Sigma|^n$, the i-th word in the lexicographic order over Σ^n by $w_i^{(n)}$. The equalities

$$d(\mathsf{I}^s(G_l),w_i^{(n)}) = \sum_{1 \leq j \leq i} d(\mathsf{I}^{s-1}(G_l),w_j^{(n)}), \qquad l=1,2,$$

imply the equality

$$\mathrm{diff}(\mathsf{I}^s(G_1),\mathsf{I}^s(G_2),w_i^{(n)}) = \sum_{1 \leq j \leq i} \mathrm{diff}(\mathsf{I}^{s-1}(G_1),\mathsf{I}^{s-1}(G_2),w_j^{(n)}).$$

We are now in the position to apply Lemma 2.4: Define

$$a_{s,i} = \mathrm{diff}(\mathsf{I}^s(G_1),\mathsf{I}^s(G_2),w_i^{(n)}) \text{ and } t = |\Sigma|^n,$$

i. e., $w_t^{(n)} = a_m^n$. By our assumptions, we have $|\{j \mid a_{0,j} \neq 0, 1 \leq j \leq t\}| \leq k$ and $a_{s,t} = \mathrm{diff}(\mathsf{I}^s(G_1),\mathsf{I}^s(G_2),a_m^n) = 0$ for all $1 \leq s \leq k$. Hence, for all $1 \leq j \leq |\Sigma|^n$, $a_{0,j} = \mathrm{diff}(G_1,G_2,w_j^{(n)}) = 0$, i. e., $k_n = 0$. □

Theorem 2.7. *Let G be a regular grammar with $d(G,w) = 1$, $w \in a_m^+$, and $d(G,w) = 0$, otherwise. Let G_1 and G_2 be context-free grammars. Then*

$$G_1 \sim G_2 \quad \textit{iff} \quad I^s(G_1) \odot G \sim I^s(G_2) \odot G \textit{ for all } s \geq 1.$$

Proof. Assume that $G_1 \sim G_2$ is not valid. Then there exists an $n \geq 1$ such that $k_n > 0$, contradicting Lemma 2.6. $\qquad \square$

Let $k \geq 0$. Two context-free grammars G_1 and G_2 are called *k-length close* iff, for all $n \geq 0$, $k_n \leq k$, where k_n is defined in Lemma 2.6. Obviously, $G_1 \sim G_2$ iff they are 0-length close.

Theorem 2.8. *Let G be a regular grammar with $d(G,w) = 1$, $w \in a_m^+$, and $d(G,w) = 0$, otherwise. Let G_1 and G_2 be context-free grammars that are k-length close for some $k \geq 0$. Then*

$$G_1 \sim G_2 \quad \textit{iff} \quad I^s(G_1) \odot G \sim I^s(G_2) \odot G \textit{ for all } 1 \leq s \leq k.$$

Proof. Our assumptions yield $k_n \leq k$ for all $n \geq 0$, where k_n is from Lemma 2.6. $I^s(G_1) \odot G \sim I^s(G_2) \odot G$ implies by Lemma 2.6 $k_n = 0$ for all $n \geq 0$, i.e., $\mathrm{diff}(G_1, G_2, w) = 0$ for all $w \in \Sigma^n$, $n \geq 0$. This means $G_1 \sim G_2$. $\square$

Corollary 2.9. *Let G_1 and G_2 be context-free grammars that are k-length close for some $k \geq 0$. Then it is decidable whether or not G_1 and G_2 are multiplicity equivalent.*

Proof. Apply Corollary 1.3. $\qquad \square$

Recently, in a series of papers, Andrasiu, Dassow, Paun, Salomaa [1] and Paun, Salomaa [5], [6], [7] introduced and considered thin and slender languages. For $k \geq 0$ a language $L \subseteq \Sigma^*$ is called *properly k-thin* iff L contains at most k words of length n for all $n \geq 0$, i.e., $|L \cap \Sigma^n| \leq k$. A language is *slender* iff it is properly k-thin for some $k \geq 0$.

Corollary 2.10. *It is decidable whether or not two context-free grammars generating slender languages are multiplicity equivalent.*

Proof. Let G_1 and G_2 generate properly k_1- and k_2-thin context-free languages. Then G_1 and G_2 are (k_1+k_2)-length close. Apply Corollary 2.9. ☐

Corollary 2.11. *Let G_1 and G_2 be unambiguous context-free grammars. Furthermore, let $L(G_1)$ be slender. Then it is decidable, whether or not $L(G_1) = L(G_2)$.*

Proof. By Andrasiu, Dassow, Paun, Salomaa [1], it is decidable for an unambiguous context-free grammar whether or not it is slender. If G_2 is not slender, $L(G_2)$ is different from $L(G_1)$. If G_2 is slender, apply Corollary 2.10. Since G_1 and G_2 are unambiguous, $L(G_1) = L(G_2)$ iff $G_1 \sim G_2$. ☐

As mentioned earlier, the results presented in the first part of this section are due to Raz [8]. Theorem 2.2 is Lemma 5 of [8]; Theorem 2.7 is Algorithm A of [8]; Theorem 2.8, Corollary 2.9 are Theorem 9 of [8] (but $I^S(G_1) \sim I^S(G_2)$ is replaced by our condition $I^S(G_1) \odot G \sim I^S(G_2) \odot G$); Corollary 2.10 is Corollary 10 of [8]; and Corollary 2.11 is Corollary 11 of [8].

We now turn to Raz [9]. The basic idea in this paper is to construct, for a given context-free grammar G with terminal alphabet $\Sigma = \{a_1, \ldots, a_m\}$, a context-free grammar G' such that, for all $w \in \Sigma^*$,

$$d(G',w) = o(w)\,d(G,w).$$

Here, $o(w) = i$ iff w is the i-th word of length n in the lexicographic order on Σ^n, where $|w| = n$.

Let G_1 and G_2 be context-free grammars. Let G_1' and G_2' be context-free grammars such that, for all $w \in \Sigma^*$,

$$d(G_l',w) = o(w)\,d(G_l,w), \qquad l=1,2.$$

Then, for all $w \in \Sigma^*$, we have

$$\mathrm{diff}(G_1',G_2',w) = o(w)\,\mathrm{diff}(G_1,G_2,w).$$

Construction 2.12. Let $G = (\Phi, \Sigma, P, S)$ be a context-free grammar in binary Greibach normal form. Let $\bar{G} = (\bar{\Phi}, \Sigma, \bar{P}, \bar{S})$ be the context-free grammar defined by

(i) $\bar{\Phi} = \Phi \cup \Phi' \cup \Phi'' \cup \{\bar{S}\} \cup \{T_b^a \mid a, b \in \Sigma\}$, where Φ' and Φ'' are primed and double-primed versions of Φ, respectively, and $\bar{S}$ and T_b^a are new variables;

(ii) $\bar{P} = P \cup P_0 \cup P_1 \cup P_2 \cup \{\bar{S} \to S, \bar{S} \to S'\} \cup \{T_b^a \to a \mid a, b \in \Sigma\}$, where

$P_0 = \{A' \to T_c^a, A'' \to T_b^a \mid A \to a \in P, b, c \in \Sigma, c < a\},$

$P_1 = \{A' \to aA_1', A' \to T_c^a A_1'', A'' \to T_b^a A_1'' \mid A \to aA_1 \in P, b, c \in \Sigma, c < a\},$

$P_2 = \{A' \to aA_1 A_2', A' \to aA_1' A_2'', A' \to T_c^a A_1'' A_2'', A'' \to T_b^a A_1'' A_2'' \mid$
$$A \to aA_1 A_2 \in P, b, c \in \Sigma, c < a\}.$$

Then we obtain

$$d(\bar{G}, w) = o(w)\, d(G, w) \qquad \text{for all } w \in \Sigma^*. \qquad \square$$

Theorem 2.13. *For a given context-free grammar G, where $d(G, w)$ is finite for all words w, a context-free grammar G' can effectively be constructed such that, for all w,*

$$d(G', w) = o(w)\, d(G, w).$$

Proof. Analogous to the proof of Theorem 2.2; use Construction 2.12 instead of Construction 2.1. $\qquad \square$

In the sequel, we denote the grammar G' of Theorem 2.13 by $K(G)$. Iteration of this construction yields the context-free grammars $K^s(G)$, $s \geq 0$: $K^0(G) = G$, $K^{i+1}(G) = K(K^i(G))$, $i \geq 0$. We have

$$d(K^s(G), w) = o(w)^s\, d(G, w)$$

and

$$\text{diff}(K^s(G_1), K^s(G_2), w) = o(w)^s\, \text{diff}(G_1, G_2, w)$$

for context-free grammars G, G_1, G_2 and all $s \geq 0$, $w \in \Sigma^*$.

Lemma 2.14. *Let $k \geq 0$. Assume that G_1 and G_2 are context-free grammars such that, for all $0 \leq s \leq k-1$,*

$$K^s(G_1) \sim_\# K^s(G_2).$$

Furthermore, let $(n_1, \ldots, n_m) \in \mathbb{N}^m$ and assume that

$$k_{n_1, \ldots, n_m} = |\{w \mid \text{diff}(G_1, G_2, w) \neq 0, \psi(w) = (n_1, \ldots, n_m)\}| \leq k.$$

Then $k_{n_1, \ldots, n_m} = 0$.

Proof. There are at most k different words $w \in \Sigma^*$, $\psi(w) = (n_1, \ldots, n_m)$, such that possibly $\text{diff}(G_1, G_2, w) \neq 0$. Denote these words by $w_1, \ldots, w_l$, $l \leq k$. We have, for all $s \geq 0$,

$$\sum_{1 \leq i \leq l} \text{diff}(K^s(G_1), K^s(G_2), w_i) = \sum_{1 \leq i \leq l} o(w_i)^s \text{diff}(G_1, G_2, w_i).$$

Hence, by our assumption $K^s(G_1) \sim_\# K^s(G_2)$, we obtain, for all $0 \leq s \leq l-1$,

$$\sum_{1 \leq i \leq l} o(w_i)^s \text{diff}(G_1, G_2, w_i) = 0.$$

Since the Vandermonde matrix is nonsingular, we obtain $\text{diff}(G_1, G_2, w_i) = 0$ for all $1 \leq i \leq l$, i. e., $k_{n_1, \ldots, n_m} = 0$. $\square$

Theorem 2.15. *Let G_1 and G_2 be context-free grammars. Then*

$$G_1 \sim G_2 \quad \text{iff} \quad K^s(G_1) \sim_\# K^s(G_2) \text{ for all } s \geq 1.$$

Proof. Assume that $G_1 \sim G_2$ is not valid. Then there exists $(n_1, \ldots, n_m) \in \mathbb{N}^m$ such that $k_{n_1, \ldots, n_m} > 0$ contradicting Lemma 2.14. $\square$

Let $k \geq 0$. Two context-free grammars G_1 and G_2 are called *k-letter count close* iff, for all $(n_1, \ldots, n_m) \in \mathbb{N}^m$, $k_{n_1, \ldots, n_m} \leq k$, where $k_{n_1, \ldots, n_m}$ is defined in Lemma 2.14. Obviously $G_1 \sim G_2$ iff they are 0-letter count close.

Theorem 2.16. *Let G_1 and G_2 be context-free grammars that are k-letter count close for some $k \geq 0$. Then*

$$G_1 \sim G_2 \quad \text{iff} \quad K^s(G_1) \sim_\# K^s(G_2) \text{ for all } 0 \leq s \leq k-1.$$

Proof. Our assumptions yield $k_{n_1, \ldots, n_m} \leq k$ for all $(n_1, \ldots, n_m) \in \mathbb{N}^m$, where

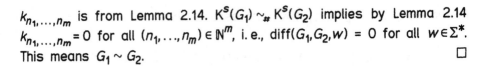

$k_{n_1,\ldots,n_m}$ is from Lemma 2.14. $K^s(G_1) \sim_\# K^s(G_2)$ implies by Lemma 2.14 $k_{n_1,\ldots,n_m} = 0$ for all $(n_1,\ldots,n_m) \in \mathbb{N}^m$, i.e., $\text{diff}(G_1,G_2,w) = 0$ for all $w \in \Sigma^*$. This means $G_1 \sim G_2$. □

Corollary 2.17. *Let G_1 and G_2 be context-free grammars that are k-letter count close for some $k \geq 0$. Then it is decidable whether or not G_1 and G_2 are multiplicity equivalent.*

Proof. Apply Theorem 1.1. □

Clearly, Corollaries 2.10 and 2.11 are at once proved again by Corollary 2.17.

As mentioned earlier, the results presented in the second part of this section are due to Raz [9]. Theorem 2.13 is Lemma 6 of [9]; Theorem 2.16 and Corollary 2.17 are Theorem 8 of [9].

3. Generalizations

In this section we will generalize the results of Raz [8], [9] as presented in Section 2. Before stating one of these generalizations, we have to generalize the combinatorial Lemma 2.4.

Lemma 3.1. *Let $a_{k,i} \in \mathbb{R}$, $k \geq 0$, $i \geq 1$, and assume $a_{k,i} = \sum_{1 \leq j \leq i} a_{k-1,j}$ for all $k, i \geq 1$. Let $k, l > 0$ and $t_0 = 1 \leq t_1 < \ldots < t_l$. Assume $a_{s,t_r} = 0$ for all $1 \leq s \leq k$, $1 \leq r \leq l$ and, for all $0 \leq r \leq l-1$, $|\{j \mid a_{0,j} \neq 0, t_r \leq j \leq t_{r+1}\}| \leq k$. Then $a_{0,j} = 0$ for all $1 \leq j \leq t_l$.*

Proof. The proof is by induction on l. For $l = 1$, Lemma 3.1 is identical to Lemma 2.4. Hence, assume $l > 1$. By definition, let $s_0 = 1, s_1 = t_2, \ldots, s_{l-1} = t_l$. Then we obtain by Lemma 2.4

$$\{j \mid a_{0,j} \neq 0, s_0 \leq j \leq s_1\} = \{j \mid a_{0,j} \neq 0, t_1 \leq j \leq t_2\}.$$

Hence, for all $0 \leq r \leq l-2$, $|\{j \mid a_{0,j} \neq 0, s_r \leq j \leq s_{r+1}\}| \leq k$. We obtain now by our induction hypothesis $a_{0,j} = 0$ for all $1 \leq j \leq s_{l-1} = t_l$. □

Theorem 3.2 is a generalization of Theorem 2.8.

Theorem 3.2. *Let $k,l > 0$. Let G be an unambiguous regular grammar. Assume that G_1 and G_2 are context-free grammars such that, for all $n \geq 1$, the following condition is satisfied: There exist words $v_0 = a_1^n < v_1 < \ldots$ $\ldots < v_{l-1} < v_l = a_m^n$ of length n in $L(G)$ such that*

$$|\{w \mid \mathrm{diff}(G_1, G_2, w) \neq 0, \, v_r \leq w \leq v_{r+1}\}| \leq k \qquad \text{for all } 0 \leq r \leq l-1.$$

Moreover, assume that

$$I^s(G_1) \odot G \sim I^s(G_2) \odot G \qquad \text{for all } 1 \leq s \leq k.$$

Then $G_1 \sim G_2$.

Proof. Let $n \geq 1$. Define $a_{s,i}$ as in the proof of Lemma 2.6:

$$a_{s,i} = \mathrm{diff}(I^s(G_1), I^s(G_2), w_i^{(n)}).$$

By $I^s(G_1) \odot G \sim I^s(G_2) \odot G$ we obtain

$$a_{s,o(v_r)} = 0 \text{ for } 1 \leq s \leq k, \, 0 \leq r \leq l.$$

Our condition and Lemma 3.1 yield $\mathrm{diff}(G_1, G_2, w) = 0$ for all w with $1 \leq o(w) \leq |\Sigma|^n$, i.e., for all words of length n. $\qquad \square$

We now use a construction slightly different from that in Theorem 3.2.

Lemma 3.3. *Let $k,l > 0$. Let G be an unambiguous regular grammar. Assume that G_1 and G_2 are context-free grammars such that, for some $n \geq 1$, the following conditions are satisfied:*

(i) There exist words $v_0 = a_1^n < v_1 < \ldots < v_{l-1} < v_l$ of length n in $L(G)$ such that

$$|\{w \mid \mathrm{diff}(G_1, G_2, w) \neq 0, \, v_r \leq w \leq v_{r+1}\}| \leq k \qquad \text{for all } 0 \leq r \leq l-1.$$

(ii) $\mathrm{diff}(I(K^s(G_1)) \odot G, I(K^s(G_2)) \odot G, w) = 0$ for all $0 \leq s \leq k-1$, $w \in \Sigma^n$.

Then $\mathrm{diff}(G_1, G_2, w) = 0$ for all $w \in \Sigma^n$, such that $w \leq v_l$.

Proof. The proof is by induction on *l*. Let *l* =1. There are at most *k* words *w*, $w \leq v_1$, of length *n* such that possibly diff(G_1, G_2, w) $\neq 0$. Denote these words by $w_1, \ldots, w_{k'}$, $k' \leq k$. Condition (ii) yields diff($l(K^s(G_1)) \odot G$, $l(K^s(G_2)) \odot G, v_1$) = 0 for $0 \leq s \leq k-1$, i. e.,

$$o(w_1)^s \text{diff}(G_1, G_2, w_1) + \ldots + o(w_{k'})^s \text{diff}(G_1, G_2, w_{k'}) = 0$$

for $0 \leq s \leq k'-1$. By the nonsingularity of the Vandermonde matrix we obtain

$$\text{diff}(G_1, G_2, w_1) = \ldots = \text{diff}(G_1, G_2, w_{k'}) = 0.$$

Hence diff(G_1, G_2, w) = 0 for all words $w \leq v_1$ of length *n*.

Let now *l* >1. By definition let $u_0 = a_1^n, u_1 = v_2, \ldots, u_{l-1} = v_l$. Then we obtain (by the case *l* =1)

$$\{w \mid \text{diff}(G_1, G_2, w) \neq 0, u_0 \leq w \leq u_1\} = \{w \mid \text{diff}(G_1, G_2, w) \neq 0, v_1 \leq w \leq v_2\}.$$

Hence, for all $0 \leq r \leq l-2$, $|\{w \mid \text{diff}(G_1, G_2, w) \neq 0, u_r \leq w \leq u_{r+1}\}| \leq k$. We obtain now by our induction hypothesis diff(G_1, G_2, w) = 0 for $w \leq u_{l-1} = v_l$. □

Our next theorem is similar to Theorem 3.2.

Theorem 3.4. *Let* $k, l > 0$. *Let* G *be an unambiguous regular grammar. Assume that* G_1 *and* G_2 *are context-free grammars such that, for all* $n \geq 1$, *the following condition is satisfied: There exist words* $v_0 = a_1^n < v_1 < \ldots \ldots < v_{l-1} < v_l = a_m^n$ *of length* *n* *in* $L(G)$ *such that*

$$|\{w \mid \text{diff}(G_1, G_2, w) \neq 0, v_r \leq w \leq v_{r+1}\}| \leq k \qquad \text{for all } 0 \leq r \leq l-1.$$

Moreover, assume that

$$l(K^s(G_1)) \odot G \sim l(K^s(G_2)) \odot G \qquad \text{for all } 1 \leq s \leq k-1.$$

Then $G_1 \sim G_2$.

Proof. Conditions (i) and (ii) of Lemma 3.3 are satisfied by our assumptions for all $n \geq 1$. □

Before our last generalization, we need three lemmas.

Lemma 3.5. *Let* $k \geq 1$, $p \geq 2k+1$. *Let* $l \geq 0$ *and, for all* $0 \leq j \leq l$, $k_j \in \mathbb{Z}$ *with* $0 \leq |k_j| \leq k$. *Then*

$$k_0 + k_1 p + \ldots + k_l p^l = 0 \quad \text{implies} \quad k_j = 0 \text{ for all } 0 \leq j \leq l.$$

Proof. The proof is by induction on l. Since for $l=0$ Lemma 3.5 is valid, we proceed with $l>0$. The equation $k_0 + k_1 p + \ldots + k_l p^l = 0$ implies $|k_l| p^l \leq k \cdot (p^l - 1)/(p-1)$. Hence, $|k_l| p^{l+1} \leq (k + |k_l|) p^l - k$. If $k_l \neq 0$, this inequality implies $p^{l+1} \leq 2k p^l$, i.e., $p \leq 2k$. This contradicts the assumption $p \geq 2k+1$. $\qquad\square$

Lemma 3.6. *For a given context-free grammar* G, *for* $a \in \Sigma$ *and* $p \geq 1$, *a context-free grammar* G' *can be effectively constructed such that, for all* w, $d(G',w) = p^{|w|_a} d(G,w)$.

Proof. In the productions of G, replace each occurrence of $a \in \Sigma$ by the new nonterminals T_j and add productions $T_j \to a$, $1 \leq j \leq p$. $\qquad\square$

In the sequel, we denote the grammar G' of Lemma 3.6 by $L_p^a(G)$.

A context-free grammar G is called *d-ambiguous* iff $d(G,w) \leq d$ for all $w \in \Sigma^*$.

Lemma 3.7. *Let* G *be an unambiguous regular grammar. Assume that* G_1 *and* G_2 *are d-ambiguous context-free grammars such that, for some* $n, l \geq 1$ *and* $a \in \Sigma$, *the following conditions are satisfied:*

(i) *There exist words* $v_0 = a_1^n < v_1 < \ldots < v_{l-1} < v_l$ *of length* n *in* $L(G)$ *such that for all* $0 \leq r \leq l-1$ *and words* w_1, w_2,

$$v_r \leq w_1 < w_2 \leq v_{r+1}, \ |w_1|_a = |w_2|_a \quad \text{imply}$$
$$\text{diff}(G_1, G_2, w_1) = 0 \ \text{or} \ \text{diff}(G_1, G_2, w_2) = 0.$$

(ii) $\text{diff}((l(L_{2d+1}^a(G_1)) \odot G, l(L_{2d+1}^a(G_2)) \odot G, w) = 0$ *for all* $w \in \Sigma^n$.

Then $\text{diff}(G_1, G_2, w) = 0$ *for all* $w \in \Sigma^n$, *such that* $w \leq v_l$.

Proof. The proof is by induction on l. Let $l=1$. By condition (ii), we obtain

$$\text{diff}(l(L^a_{2d+1}(G_1)), l(L^a_{2d+1}(G_2)), v_1) = \sum_{v_0 \le w \le v_1} (2d+1)^{|w|_a} \text{diff}(G_1, G_2, w) = 0.$$

By condition (i), there exists for each exponent j at most one word w, $v_0 \le w \le v_1$, such that $\text{diff}(G_1, G_2, w) \ne 0$ and $|w|_a = j$. Hence, Lemma 3.5 implies $\text{diff}(G_1, G_2, w) = 0$ for all words w, $v_0 \le w \le v_1$.

Let now $l > 1$. By definition, let $u_0 = a_1^n$, $u_1 = v_2, \ldots, u_{l-1} = v_l$. Then we obtain (by the case $l = 1$) that condition (i) is valid also for $u_0, u_1, \ldots, u_{l-1}$. Application of our induction hypothesis yields $\text{diff}(G_1, G_2, w) = 0$ for all words w, $u_0 = v_0 \le w \le u_{l-1} = v_l$. $\square$

Theorem 3.8. *Let G be an unambiguous regular grammar. Assume that G_1 and G_2 are d-ambiguous context-free grammars such that, for all $n \ge 1$, some $l \ge 1$ and some $a \in \Sigma$, the following conditions are satisfied:*

(i) There exist words $v_0 = a_1^n < v_1 < \ldots < v_{l-1} < v_l = a_m^n$ of length n in $L(G)$ such that, for all $0 \le r \le l-1$ and words w_1, w_2,

$$v_r \le w_1 < w_2 \le v_{r+1}, \ |w_1|_a = |w_2|_a \quad \text{imply}$$
$$\text{diff}(G_1, G_2, w_1) = 0 \ \text{or} \ \text{diff}(G_1, G_2, w_2) = 0.$$

(ii) $l(L^a_{2d+1}(G_1)) \odot G \sim l(L^a_{2d+1}(G_2)) \odot G.$

Then $G_1 \sim G_2$.

Proof. Conditions (i) and (ii) of Lemma 3.7 are satisfied by our assumptions for all $n \ge 1$. $\square$

4. Applications

We now apply the results of Section 3. A class $\mathfrak{G}$ of context-free grammars has a *decidable multiplicity equivalence problem* iff, whenever G_1 and G_2 are in $\mathfrak{G}$, then $G_1 \sim G_2$ is decidable.

The classes of context-free grammars generating acommutative, bounded and slender languages have a decidable multiplicity equivalence problem (by Theorem 1.2; by Corollary 12 of Raz [9]; by Corollary 2.10; respectively). By help of these classes we define new classes of context-free grammars that also have a decidable multiplicity equivalence problem.

We consider languages of the form

$$L_1 = \bigcup_{\alpha \in L} \alpha a_m L_\alpha,$$

where $L \subseteq \Sigma^*$ and $L_\alpha \subseteq (\Sigma - \{a_m\})^*$, $\alpha \in L$. Let $n > 0$ be fixed, consider all words of length n in the language $L a_m^+$ and order these words:

$$\alpha_1 a_m^{n - |\alpha_1|} < \alpha_2 a_m^{n - |\alpha_2|} < \ldots < \alpha_{l-1} a_m^{n - |\alpha_{l-1}|},$$

$\alpha_r \in L$, $1 \le r \le l-1$. Extend this notation by $\alpha_0 = a_1^n$ and $\alpha_l = \varepsilon$.

Each word $w \in L_1$ of length n has the form $w = \alpha_r a_m v$, $v \in L_{\alpha_r}$, $|v| = n - |\alpha_r| - 1$, where r is uniquely determined. Moreover, we have the inequalities

$$\alpha_{r-1} a_m^{n - |\alpha_{r-1}|} < w \le \alpha_r a_m^{n - |\alpha_r|}.$$

We now consider two conditions on all L_α, $\alpha \in L$:

(1) L_α is properly k-thin for some $k \ge 0$. (Hence, $L_\alpha = \emptyset$ is allowed; in this case $\alpha a_m L_\alpha = \emptyset$.)
(2) If $v_1, v_2 \in L_\alpha$, $|v_1| = |v_2|$, then $|v_1|_{a_1} \ne |v_2|_{a_1}$.

Assume now that condition (1) holds for all L_α. Then we obtain, for all $0 \le r \le l-1$,

$$|\{w \mid \alpha_r a_m^{n - |\alpha_r|} \le w \le \alpha_{r+1} a_m^{n - |\alpha_{r+1}|}, w \in L_1\}| \le k+1.$$

Consider now two context-free grammars G_1 and G_2 that generate languages of the considered form

$$L(G_1) = \bigcup_{\alpha \in L} \alpha a_m L_\alpha^1, \qquad L(G_2) = \bigcup_{\alpha \in L} \alpha a_m L_\alpha^2,$$

such that condition (1) holds for L_α^1 and L_α^2. Let G be an unambiguous regular grammar generating the language La_m^+. Then we obtain by Theorem 3.2 that $I^s(G_1) \odot G \sim I^s(G_2) \odot G$, $1 \le s \le k+1$, implies $G_1 \sim G_2$. By Theorem 3.4 we obtain that $I(K^s(G_1)) \odot G \sim I(K^s(G_2)) \odot G$, $0 \le s \le k$, implies $G_1 \sim G_2$. Either of these implications yields the next theorem.

Theorem 4.1. *Consider the class $\mathfrak{L}$ of context-free languages of the form*

$$\bigcup_{\alpha \in L} \alpha a_m L_\alpha,$$

where La_m^+ is a regular acommutative, bounded or slender language and, for all $\alpha \in L$, L_α is a properly k-thin language, $k \ge 0$, not containing a_m. Then the class of context-free grammars generating languages in $\mathfrak{L}$ has a decidable multiplicity equivalence problem. □

For the proof of our next theorem, we assume that condition (2) holds for all L_α. Consider two d-ambiguous context-free grammars G_1, G_2 that generate languages

$$L(G_1) = \bigcup_{\alpha \in L} \alpha a_m L_\alpha^1, \qquad L(G_2) = \bigcup_{\alpha \in L} \alpha a_m L_\alpha^2,$$

such that condition (2) holds for L_α^1 and L_α^2. Let G be an unambiguous regular grammar generating the language La_m^+. Then we obtain by Theorem 3.8 that $I(L_{2d+1}^{a_1}(G_1)) \odot G \sim I(L_{2d+1}^{a_1}(G_2)) \odot G$ implies $G_1 \sim G_2$.

A definition is needed before our last theorem. A context-free grammar G is of *bounded ambiguity* iff there exists a $d \ge 1$ such that G is d-ambiguous.

Theorem 4.2. *Consider the class $\mathfrak{L}$ of context-free languages of the form*

$$\bigcup_{\alpha \in L} \alpha a_m L_\alpha,$$

where La_m^+ is a regular acommutative, bounded or slender language and, for all $\alpha \in L$, L_α is a language not containing a_m and satisfying condition (2). Then the class of context-free grammars of bounded ambiguity generating languages in $\mathfrak{L}$ has a decidable multiplicity equivalence problem. □

References

[1] M. Andrasiu, J. Dassow, Gh. Paun, A. Salomaa: *Language-theoretic problems arising from Richelieu cryptosystems.* Theoretical Computer Science **116** (1993), 339–357.

[2] S. Ginsburg: *The Mathematical Theory of Context-Free Languages.* McGraw-Hill, 1966.

[3] T. Harju, J. Karhumäki: *The equivalence problem of multitape finite automata.* Theoretical Computer Science **78** (1991), 347–355.

[4] W. Kuich, A. Salomaa: *Semirings, Automata, Languages.* Springer, 1986.

[5] Gh. Paun, A. Salomaa: *Thin and slender languages.* To appear in: Discrete Applied Mathematics.

[6] Gh. Paun, A. Salomaa: *Closure properties of slender languages.* Theoretical Computer Science **120** (1993), 293–301.

[7] Gh. Paun, A. Salomaa: *Decision problems concerning the thinness of DOL languages.* Bulletin of the EATCS **46** (1992), 171–181.

[8] D. Raz: *Deciding multiplicity equivalence of certain context-free languages.* Manuscript (1993), first version.

[9] D. Raz: *Deciding multiplicity equivalence of certain context-free languages.* Manuscript (1993), second version, to appear in Proceedings of the Conference on Developments in Language Theory (G. Rozenberg, A. Salomaa eds.), World Scientific Publ. Co., 1994.

[10] A. Salomaa: *Formal Languages.* Academic Press, 1973.

On General Solution of Word Equations

G.S. Makanin[1]   H. Abdulrab[2]

Abstract:

We define in this article an approach to tackle the problem of the computation of the general solution of word equations. Parametric transformation, Nielsen's transformation and Rouen's transformation allowing to collect in one transformation some unbounded sequences of elementary transformations are given.

1 Introduction, Definitions and Notations

Let Π be a free monoid with a countable alphabet of generators

$$a_1, a_2, ..., a_k, ... \qquad (1)$$

A *coefficientless* equation in Π is given by an alphabet of word variables

$$x_1, x_2, ..., x_n \qquad (2)$$

and a *left noncancellable* equality

$$\varphi(x_1, x_2, ..., x_n) = \psi(x_1, x_2, ..., x_n) \qquad (3)$$

A list $X_1, X_2, ..., X_n$ of words on the alphabet (1) is called a *solution* of the equation (2), (3) whenever the words $\varphi(X_1, X_2, ..., X_n)$ and $\psi(X_1, X_2, ..., X_n)$ coincide.

If $\varphi(x_1, x_2, ..., x_n)$ and $\psi(x_1, x_2, ..., x_n)$ are empty words, the equation (2), (3) is called *trivial*.

Coincidence of two words P and Q will be denoted by P == Q.

The morphisms e_{pq} (p, q = 1,..., n) on a free monoid with generators x_1, x_2, ..., x_n are defined as follows:

— The morphisms e_{pq}, $p \neq q$, called *nondegenerated* morphisms, are determined by the mappings: $x_q \to x_p x_q$, and $x_j \to x_j$ if $j \neq q$.

— The morphisms e_{pp}, called *degenerated* morphisms, are determined by the mappings: $x_p \to 1$, and $x_j \to x_j$ if $j \neq q$.

Two types of *elementary transformations* of the equation (2), (3), called *nondegenerated* and *degenerated* elementary transformations, are defined:

---

[1] Steklov Mathematical Institute, Vavilova 42, 117966, Moscow GSP-1, Russia
[2] LIR/LITP, INSA de Rouen, BP 08, 76131 Mont Saint Aignan Cedex, France

— The nondegenerated transformation $x_p \rightarrow x_q x_p$, where $p \neq q$, can be applied to the equation (2), $x_p \varphi_1(x_1, x_2, ..., x_n) = x_q \psi_1(x_1, x_2, ..., x_n)$. The result of the application of this nondegenerated transformation is given by the alphabet (2) and the equality $x_p(\varphi_1)^{e_{qp}} = (\psi_1)^{e_{qp}}$.

— The degenerated transformation $x_p \rightarrow 1$, can be applied to the equation (2), $x_p \varphi_1(x_1, x_2, ..., x_n) = \psi(x_1, x_2, ..., x_n)$. The result of the application of this degenerated transformation is the equation given by the alphabet $x_1, ..., x_{p-1}, x_{p+1}, ..., x_n$ and the equality $(\varphi_1)^{e_{pp}} = (\psi)^{e_{pp}}$, after all possible left cancellations.

A sequence of equations

$$Y_0 \rightarrow Y_1 \rightarrow, ..., \rightarrow Y\tau \tag{4}$$

connected by elementary transformations is called a *finished sequence* associated with Y_0, if $Y\tau$ is trivial.

Any finished sequence associated with the equation (2), (3) contains at most n degenerated transformations.

The number $n - s$, where s is the minimal number of all degenerated transformations in finished sequences associated with the equation (2), (3), is called the *rank* of this equation.

The transformation

$$\begin{cases} x_1 \rightarrow W_1(x_1, ..., x_n) \\ .... \\ x_n \rightarrow W_n(x_1, ..., x_n) \end{cases} \tag{5}$$

resulting from all the successive applications of elementary transformations in any finished sequence of the equation (2), (3) is called a *principal solution* of the equation (2), (3).

For each solution $X_1, ..., X_n$ of the equation (2), (3) there exists a principal solution (5) and a list $L_1, ..., L_n$ of words on the alphabet (1) such that $X_i == W_i(L_1, ..., L_n)$, for all $i = 1, ..., n$.

For each principal solution (5) and each list $L_1, L_2 ..., L_n$ of words on the alphabet (1), the list of words $W_1(L_1, ..., L_n), ..., W_n(L_1, ..., L_n)$ is a solution of the equation (2), (3).

Thus the *general solution* of any equation in Π is described by the set of all finished sequences of elementary transformations of this equation.

We are interested in describing the general solution by functions associating with the variables of the equation the set of all their principal solutions. In other words, we are interested in "getting rid" of the equality predicate (3).

An expression of the form

$$\alpha(x_1, x_2 ..., x_n)... = \beta(x_1, x_2 ..., x_n)...$$

will be called the *prefix-equation* of the equation

$$\alpha(x_1, x_2 ..., x_n) \varphi(x_1, x_2 ..., x_n) = \beta(x_1, x_2 ..., x_n) \psi(x_1, x_2 ..., x_n)$$

if $\alpha(x_1, x_2 \ldots, x_n)$ and $\beta(x_1, x_2 \ldots, x_n)$ are minimal nonempty words, such that every variable x_i occurs in $\alpha(x_1, x_2 \ldots, x_n)$ if and only if it occurs in $\beta(x_1, x_2 \ldots, x_n)$.

If each variable of (2) occurs in the prefix-equation, it is called *nondegenerated*. Otherwise, it is called *degenerated*.

An *elementary* equation is defined by the alphabet (2) and the equality
$$x_1 x_2 \ldots x_n = x_{i_1} x_{i_2} \ldots x_{i_n}$$
where $i_1, \ldots, i_n$ is a permutation of $1, \ldots, n$, and $i_1 \neq 1, i_n \neq n$.

By $\partial(X_i)$, where X_i is a word on the alphabet (1), we denote the length of the word X_i.

By $[A_i]_{i=1}^q$ where A_i is any word, we denote the word $A_1 A_2 \ldots A_q$.

By a *directed equation* in Π, we mean an equation of the form $x_t \varphi(x_1, \ldots, x_n) = x_s \psi(x_1, \ldots, x_n)$ with the additional condition $\partial(x_t) > \partial(x_s)$.

This directed equation will be written as follows $x_t \varphi(x_1, \ldots, x_n) \to x_s \psi(x_1, \ldots, x_n)$.

We introduce the countable table of the natural parameters
$$\lambda_{11}, \ldots, \lambda_{1u}, \ldots$$

$$\ldots\ldots\ldots\ldots\ldots\ldots$$

$$\lambda_{p1}, \ldots, \lambda_{pu}, \ldots$$

$$\ldots\ldots\ldots\ldots\ldots\ldots$$

The set of all linear polynomials of the form $k_0 + \sum\limits_{i=1}^{r} k_i \lambda_{pi}$, where $r, k_0, k_1, \ldots, k_r$, are natural numbers will be denoted by **Lp**.

A word C on an arbitrary alphabet is called *simple*, if there exists no word D such that $C == D^m$, with $m > 1$. In particular, a simple word is not empty.

Define inductively a *parametric word* as follows:

— Any word on the alphabet (2) is a parametric word.

— If A is a parametric word, λ is a natural parameter, then A^λ is a parametric word.

— If A and B are parametric words, then AB is a parametric word.

A parametric word w represents a set of words obtained by substituting each parameter of w by all its integer values. A parametric word w is *identical* to a list of parametric words $p_1, \ldots, p_n$ if the set of words that represents w coincide with those of $p_1, \ldots, p_n$.

The following problems are posed:

1. How to indicate the first word variable in a parametric word?

2. How to indicate the first occurrence of a certain word variable in a parametric word?

3. How to left-cancellate a couple of parametric words?

4. How to divide a parametric word into a set of parametric words in all the possible ways?

These problems can be easily solved by means of the *division of natural parameters*. Consequently, it is possible to transform and to use parametric words in the same way as usual words.

Consider the table of parametric words

$$x_1, x_2 , \ldots\ldots, x_n$$
$$C_1^{\lambda 11}, \ldots, C_1^{\lambda 1w}, \ldots$$
$$\ldots\ldots\ldots\ldots\ldots$$ (6)
$$C_p^{\lambda p1}, \ldots, C_p^{\lambda pw}, \ldots \qquad (p \geq 0)$$

where C_1 is a word on the alphabet $x_1, x_2, \ldots, x_n$, and where for each $q = 1, \ldots, p-1$, C_{q+1} is a word on the alphabet

$$x_1, x_2 , \ldots\ldots, x_n$$
$$C_1^{\lambda 11}, \ldots, C_1^{\lambda 1w}, \ldots$$
$$\ldots\ldots\ldots\ldots\ldots$$ (7)
$$C_q^{\lambda q1}, \ldots, C_q^{\lambda qw}, \ldots$$

Every word of the table (6) is called a *parametric letter*.

The alphabet (6) is called the *p-layer* alphabet of *parametric letters*.

The word C_i ($i = 1, \ldots, p$) is called the *base* of the letters of the *ith* layer of the alphabet (6).

The alphabet (6) will be called the alphabet of *normal* parametric letters if for any value of parameters, every base C_r on the alphabet (6) remains nonempty and simple word.

A transformation of natural parameters $\lambda_{qi} \to L_{qi}$, $L_{qi} \in \mathbf{L_q}$, can be applied to the p-layer alphabet of the parametric letters (6) by substituting every occurrence of the letter $C_q^{\lambda qi}$ in the words $C_{q+1}, \ldots, C_p$ on this alphabet by the word $C_q^{L qi}$, respectively.

The result of the application of the transformation of natural parameters to the alphabet of (normal) parametric letters is an alphabet of (normal) parametric letters.

An *exponential* equation in free monoid is given by the p-layer alphabet of normal parametric letters (6) and the equality of words

$$\Phi(x_1, x_2, \ldots, x_n, \ldots, \lambda_{st}, \ldots) = \Psi(x_1, x_2, \ldots, x_n, \ldots, \lambda_{st}, \ldots) \qquad (8)$$

on this alphabet.

A finite table of natural numbers $\{\ldots \Lambda_{st} \ldots\}$ corresponding to the parameters $\{\ldots \lambda_{st} \ldots\}$ of (8) is called *solution* of the exponential equation (6), (8) whenever the words $\Phi(x_1, x_2, \ldots, x_n, \ldots, \Lambda_{st}, \ldots)$ and $\Psi(x_1, x_2, \ldots, x_n, \ldots, \Lambda_{st}, \ldots)$ coincide.

A *parametric* equation in free monoid is given by the p-layer alphabet of the parametric letters (6) and the equality of words

$$\Phi(x_1, x_2, \ldots, x_n, \ldots, \lambda_{st}, \ldots) = \Psi(x_1, x_2, \ldots, x_n, \ldots, \lambda_{st}, \ldots) \qquad (9)$$

on this alphabet.

A list of words $X_1, X_2 ..., X_n$ on the alphabet (1) and a finite table of natural numbers $\{ ... \Lambda_{st} ...\}$ corresponding to parameters $\{ ... \lambda_{st}...\}$ of (9) is called a *solution* of the parametric equation (6), (9) whenever the words $\Phi(X_1, ..., X_n, ..., \Lambda_{st},...)$ and $\Psi(X_1, ..., X_n, ..., \Lambda_{st}, ...)$ coincide

A parametric equation (6), (9), is called a *normal* parametric equation, if (6) is an alphabet of normal parametric letters. A parametric equation (6), (9) is called a *trivial* parametric equation, if $\Phi(x_1, ..., x_n, ..., \lambda_{st}, ...)$ and $\Psi(x_1, ..., x_n, ..., \lambda_{st} , ...)$ are empty words.

2 General Scheme of our Approach

In this section we discuss the main ideas that we propose for describing the general solution of word equations.

First, we suppose that each variable occurs in each hand-member of the equation (otherwise, it is sufficient to concatenate the word $x_1x_2...x_n$ at the right of each hand-member, and to use the new equation obtained after the concatenation).

The prefix-equation p associated with an equation e can be seen as the "fundamental" part of e. Remark that if p is an elementary equation, then the set of the solutions of e is a subset of the set of the solutions of p.

The general solution of elementary equations can be described using elementary transformations. Theses transformations ensure (only in the case of elementary equations) a finite process for describing the general solution.

In our approach we suppose that the general solution can be computed by induction on the number of variables.

Equations with one variable are isomorphic to systems of linear diophantine equations. The general solution of such a system can be effectively computed.

To compute the general solution of an equation e with n variables, $n > 1$, we propose to start by finding a finite graph connected by all the nondegenerated transformations of e. (New types of transformations deduced from the case of n-1 variables can be used. This point will be developed later in this section). All the transformations can be applied only on the "active" part of the equation: its prefix-equation.

Thus prefix-equations (more precisely, nondegenerated prefix-equations at this step) can be seen as the nodes of a graph. They are connected by nondegenerated transformations.

If in any branch of this graph we obtain an elementary prefix-equation, then this branch is finished be applying elementary transformations to this elementary equation. These elementary transformations give rise in this case, as mentioned above, to a finite graph associated with the elementary equation.

Then, for each node of such a graph one can apply degenerated transformations. Applying such transformations produces equations with less than n variables. In which case (as well as for degenerated prefix-equations) the computation of the general solution is supposed known by induction.

Elementary transformations gives in general an infinite graph describing the general solution. One of the main questions to solve, in order to obtain a finite graph of nondegenerated transformations, is to find powerful transformations that can allow to "fuse" unbounded sequences of transformations, and to "factorize" the initial infinite graph into a finite graph.

Parametric transformations introduced in Section 3 can replace sequences where one variable is transformed unboundedly.

Nielsen's transformations described in Section 4 can replace sequences where two variables are transformed unboundedly.

Rouen's transformations given in Section 5 can replace sequences where three variables are transformed unboundedly.

In this framework, the general solution of equations with coefficients (or with constants) $\varphi(x_1, x_2 ..., x_n, a_1, a_2, ..., a_m) = \psi(x_1, x_2 ..., x_n, a_1, a_2, ..., a_m)$ is reduced to the case of coefficientless equations. In fact, it is sufficient to replace each coefficient a_i by a new variable y_i, and to respect the following three rules:

1) An equation of the form $y_i\varphi(x_1, ..., x_n, y_1, y_2, ..., y_m) = y_j\psi(x_1, ..., x_n, y_1, y_2, ... a_m)$, with $i \neq j$, has no solution.

2) No degenerated transformation of the form $y_i \to 1$ is allowed.

3) Nondegenerated transformations to each equation of the form $x_i\varphi(x_1,..., x_n, y_1, y_2 ..., y_m) = y_j\psi(x_1, ..., x_n, y_1, y_2 ..., a_m)$, are only applied to the directed equation $x_i\varphi(x_1, ..., x_n, y_1, y_2 ..., y_m) \to y_j\psi(x_1, ..., x_n, y_1, y_2 ..., a_m)$.

3 Parametric Transformation

Let the equation (2), (3) in free monoid Π be of the form

$$x_1 \varphi(x_1, x_2, ..., x_n) = \alpha(x_2, ..., x_n) \ x_1 \ \psi(x_1, x_2, ..., x_n) \qquad (10)$$

where $\alpha(x_2, ..., x_n)$ is a nonempty word. It is easy to see that sequences of nondegenerated transformations $x_1 \to \alpha(x_2, ..., x_n)x_1$ can be applied to the equation (2), (10) unboundedly. This cause forces us to introduce an additional transformation which will be called *parametric transformation*.

Define, by a joint induction, *parametric equations* and *parametric transformations*: (Detailed study of parametric transformations and parametric equations is given in [1]).

— Equation (2), (3) is a parametric equation.

— If a parametric equation has the form (10), then the parametric transformation is given by

$$x_1 \to (\alpha(x_2, ..., x_n))^\lambda x_1 \qquad (11)$$

where λ is a natural parameter which does not occur in the parametric equation.

— The result of the application of the transformation (11) to the equation (10) is the parametric equation:

$$x_1 \varphi((\alpha(x_2, ..., x_n))^\lambda x_1, x_2, ..., x_n) = \alpha(x_2, ..., x_n) \; x_1 \; \psi((\alpha(x_2, ..., x_n))^\lambda x_1, x_2, ..., x_n)$$

with the additional condition: $\partial(x_1) < \partial(\alpha(x_2, ..., x_n))$.

— The result of the application of an elementary transformation to a parametric equation is a parametric equation.

Using parametric transformations leads to deal with parametric equations. But we have to remember that any diophantine equation is equivalent to some exponential equation in a free monoid. For example the equation $y^2 = z^3 + 1$ is equivalent to $(a_1{}^y)^y = ((a_1{}^z)^z)^z a_1$, and there exists no algorithm to determine the solvability of diophantine equations.

However, we show in [1] that starting with a word equation (2), (3), and applying the transformation $x_1 \to (\alpha(x_2, ..., x_n))^\lambda x_1$, where λ is a new natural parameter gives rise to some particular parametric equations: in the obtained parametric equation can arise the product $\lambda*L$, where λ is a natural parameter, L is a linear polynomial from natural parameters different from λ, and the parameter λ occurs in the equation only in the product $\lambda*L$.

We particularly show in [1] that in this case we must replace each occurrence of the product $\lambda*L$ in the equation by the parameter λ. Informally, this result is obtained by introducing some *normalisations* of parametric equations (6), (9), which are applied to the bases C_s of the alphabet (6) in order to use only simple and nonempty bases. Then, the essential step consists of the following: rather than using the transformation $x_1 \to (\alpha(x_2, ..., x_n))^\lambda x_1$, when $\alpha(x_2, ..., x_n) = (\beta(x_2, ..., x_n))^k$, where $\beta(x_2, ..., x_n)$ is a simple word, we use the transformation $x_1 \to (\beta(x_2, ..., x_n))^\lambda x_1$.

Let Y_0 be an equation (2), (3) in a free monoid Π and

$$Y_0 \to Y_1 \to ,..., \to Y\tau \tag{12}$$

be a finished sequence of parametric equations, connected by elementary and parametric transformations.

The transformation

$$\begin{cases} x_1 \to W_1(x_1, x_2 ..., x_n, \lambda_1, ..., \lambda_t) \\ .... \\ x_n \to W_n(x_1, x_2 ..., x_n, \lambda_1, ..., \lambda_t) \end{cases} \tag{13}$$

which results from successive applications of elementary and parametric transformations in some finished sequences associated with the equation (2), (3) is called the *principal parametric solution* of the equation (2), (3).

For every solution $X_1, ..., X_n$ of the equation (2), (3) there exists a principal parametric solution (13), a list $K_1, ..., K_n$ of words on the alphabet (1) and a list of natural numbers $\Lambda_1, ..., \Lambda_s$ such that $X_i == W_i (K_1, ..., K_n, \Lambda_1, ..., \Lambda_s)$ for all $i = 1, ..., n$.

For every principal parametric solution (13), every list $K_1, ..., K_n$ of words on the alphabet (1) ; and every list of natural numbers $\Lambda_1, ..., \Lambda_s$, the list of words

$$W_1 (K_1, ..., K_n, \Lambda_1, ..., \Lambda_s), ..., W_n (K_1, ..., K_n, \Lambda_1, ..., \Lambda_s)$$

is a solution of the equation (2), (3).

4 Nielsen's Transformation

Let a parametric equation in Π be of the form

$$x_1\alpha(x_3, ..., x_n)\, x_2\, \varphi(x_1, x_2, ..., x_n) = x_2\beta(x_3,..., x_n)\, x_1\, \psi(x_1, x_2 ..., x_n) \quad (14)$$

where $\alpha(x_3, ..., x_n)\, \beta(x_3, ..., x_n)$ is a nonempty word. We can apply to this equation the parametric transformations

$$x_1 \rightarrow (x_2\, \beta(x_3, ..., x_n))^{\lambda_1}\, x_1$$
$$x_2 \rightarrow (x_1\, \alpha(x_3, ..., x_n))^{\mu_1}\, x_2$$

$$..\quad (15)$$

$$x_1 \rightarrow (x_2\, \beta(x_3, ..., x_n))^{\lambda_\omega}\, x_1$$
$$x_2 \rightarrow (x_1\, \alpha(x_3, ..., x_n))^{\mu_\omega}\, x_2$$

for any natural number ω. This cause forces us to introduce an additional transformation, which will be called *Nielsen's transformation*.

A vector of natural numbers

$$[q, k_1, m_1, ..., k_q, m_q] \quad (16)$$

will be called Nielsen's vector if $k_2, ..., k_q, m_1, ..., m_{q-1} > 0$. Trivial Nielsen's vector has the form [0]. A variable will be called *Nielsen's parameter* if its values are Nielsen's vectors.

By *Nielsen's function* $N[w, A, B]$ we mean any function (whose Nielsen's vector is $w = [q, k_1, m_1, ..., k_q, m_q]$; A, B are two morphisms) that maps into the morphism $[A^{k_i}\, B^{m_i}]_{i=1}^q$.

We denote by the expression $N[v, A, B]$, where v is Nielsen's parameter ; A and B are two morphisms, the set of values of the function $N[v, A, B]$, for all the values of Nielsen's parameter v.

Nielsen's transformation applied to the parametric equation (14) has the form

$$\begin{cases} x_1\rightarrow x_1 N[v, e_{21}\, \beta(e_{31}, ..., e_{n1}),\, e_{12}\, \alpha(e_{32}, ..., e_{n2})] \\ x_2\rightarrow x_2 N[v, e_{21}\, \beta(e_{31}, ..., e_{n1}),\, e_{12}\, \alpha(e_{32}, ..., e_{n2})] \end{cases} \quad (17)$$

The result of the application of Nielsen's transformation (17) to the equation (14) is the two-parametric equation

$$x_1\, \alpha(x_3, ..., x_n)\, x_2\, \varphi(x_1 N[v, e_{21}\, \beta, e_{12}\, \alpha],\, x_2 N[v, e_{21}\, \beta, e_{12}\, \alpha]\, x_3, ..., x_n) = x_2\, \beta(x_3, ..., x_n)\, x_1\, \psi(x_1 N[v, e_{21}\, \beta, e_{12}\, \alpha]\, x_2 N[v, e_{21}\, \beta, e_{12}\, \alpha]\, x_3, ..., x_n) \quad (18)$$

with the additional condition

$$\begin{cases} \partial(x_1) < \partial(x_2 \, \beta(x_3, \, ..., \, x_n)) \\ \partial(x_2) < \partial(x_1 \alpha(x_3, \, ..., \, x_n)) \end{cases}$$

A two-parametric equation has three kinds of variables: word variables, natural parameters and Nielsen's parameters. It can be written under the form:

$$\varphi(x_1, \, ..., \, x_n, \, \lambda_1, \, ..., \, \lambda_s, \, \nu_1, \, ..., \, \nu_z) = \psi(x_1, \, ..., \, x_n, \, \lambda_1, \, ..., \, \lambda_s, \, \nu_1, \, ..., \, \nu_z)$$

Example:

Here, the graph of prefix-equations of equations with two variables is shown.

Now we show how to deduce from this graph the graph of prefix-equations of the equation $x_1{}^2x_2{}^3x_1 = x_2{}^2x_1{}^3x_2$

Applying to (*) the degenerated transformation e_{11} gives $x_1x_1{}^{\lambda\nu}x_1{}^{\nu}x_1{}^{\lambda\nu+4\nu}x_1{}^{\nu} = x_1x_1{}^{\nu}(x_1{}^{\lambda\nu+\nu}x_1{}^{\nu})^2x_1{}^{\nu}$. After replacing the product $\lambda\nu$ by λ we obtain: $x_1x_1{}^{\lambda}x_1{}^{\nu}x_1{}^{\lambda+4\nu}x_1{}^{\nu} = x_1x_1{}^{\nu}x_1{}^{2\lambda+4\nu}x_1{}^{\nu}$. This equation is isomorphic to the linear diophantine equation: $2\lambda + 6\nu + 1 = 2\lambda + 6\nu + 1$, whose solutions are any naturals λ, ν.

Principal solutions obtained in this finished sequences are:

$$\begin{cases} x_1 \to x_2x_1 & \to x_2{}^{\lambda+1}x_1 & \to (x_1x_2)^{\lambda+1}x_1 \to (x_1^N x_2^N)^{\lambda+1}x_1^N & \to x_1{}^{\nu(\lambda+1)+\nu} \\ x_2 \to x_2 & \to x_2 & \to x_1x_2 & \to x_1^N x_2^N & \to x_2{}^{\nu} \end{cases}$$

◆

5 Rouen's Transformation

It is easy to find some equations in free monoid, for which only three indicated variables will be transformed unboundedly. In order to collect all these transformations into one transformation, we introduce an additional transformation, which we call *Rouen's transformation*.

Rouen's transformation has the form

$$\begin{cases} x_1 \rightarrow x_1{}^{R[...]} \\ x_2 \rightarrow x_2{}^{R[...]} \\ x_3 \rightarrow x_3{}^{R[...]} \end{cases}$$

where R[...] is Rouen's function.

A finite graph of prefix-equations (connected by all the nondegenerated transformations) of equations with three variables is constructed in [2], where the set of *Rouen's prefix-equations* is defined by all the prefix-equations appearing in the diagrams N, I, II,... XX presented in [2]. This graph allows us to define Rouen's function. Diagrams I, II, IV, and V, called in annexe R_1, R_2, R_3 and R_4 respectively, determine Rouen's function allowing to collect in one transformation any sequence of nondegenerated transformations of three variables. The Other diagrams correspond to Nielsen's and parametric functions.

It is proved in [2] that using finite applications of nondegenerated parametric and Nielsen's transformations, we can reduce any equation with three variables to Rouen's function.

Rouen's transformation can be defined from Rouen's function in the same way as in section 4. We show here, as an example, how to define first Rouen's transformations according to the first component R_1.

Let a parametric equation in Π be of the form

$$x_1 \alpha(x_4, ..., x_n)\, x_2\, \beta(x_4, ..., x_n)x_3 = x_3\gamma(x_4, ..., x_n)\, x_2\, \delta(x_4, ..., x_n)x_3 \qquad (19)$$

A vector of vectors of natural numbers is called first *Rouen's vector* if it has the form:

$$[\omega\, ;\, \lambda_{11}, \lambda_{21}, ..., \lambda_{v_11}\, ;\, \alpha_{11}, \alpha_{21}, ..., \alpha_{\beta_11}\, ;\, ...\, ;\, \lambda_{1\omega}, \lambda_{2\omega}, ..., \lambda_{v_\omega\omega}\, ;\, \alpha_{1\omega}, \alpha_{2\omega}, ..., \alpha_{\beta_\omega\omega}] \qquad (20)$$

A variable will be called *Rouen's first parameter* if its values are Rouen's first vector.

By *First Rouen's function* R[ω, A_{12}, A_{13}, A_{21}, A_{23}, A_{31}, A_{32}] we mean any function (whose Rouen's first vector is (20), A_{ij} are morphisms), that maps into the morphisms

$$\left[\left[A_{31}A_{12}^{\lambda_{ij}}A_{21}\right]_{i=1}^{v_j}\,\left[A_{13}A_{32}^{\alpha_{ij}}A_{23}\right]_{i=1}^{\beta_j}\right]_{j=1}^{\omega}.$$

We can collect any sequence of transformations where three variables are transformed unboundedly in the equation (19) by applying Rouen's first function, with:

$$A_{12} = e_{12}\alpha(e_{42}, ..., e_{n2}), A_{13} = e_{13}\alpha(e_{43}, ..., e_{n3}), A_{21} = e_{21}\delta(e_{41}, ..., e_{n1}), A_{23} =$$
$$e_{23}\beta(e_{43}, ..., e_{n3}) A_{31} = e_{31}\gamma(e_{41}, ..., e_{n1}), A_{32} = e_{32}\gamma(e_{42}, ..., e_{n2}).$$

6 Perspectives and Open Works

Now we are interested in constructing the graph of all the nondegenerated transformations of equations with four variables, in order to obtain the new transformation corresponding to the case where four variables are transformed unboundedly.

An algorithm simplifying and optimising the application of parametric transformations for equations with four variables is given in [3]. Next open step consists in the application of this algorithm to get the new transformation. The following steps consist in generalising this construction for n variables and in studying the use of degenerated transformations.

Using the technique of prefix-equations is sufficient for constructing the graph of all the nondegenerated transformations and obtaining new transformations. A complementary study of the whole structure of transformed equations (and not only their prefix-equations) is initiated in [4]. Its application in the case of three variables, as well as its relationship with the graph of [2] is given in [5].

References:

[1] *Parametric Word Equations*, G.S. Makanin, and H. Abdulrab, *Rapport LITP 93.43, July 93.*

[2] *Transformations of Word Equations with Three Variables: Rouen's Function*, G.S. Makanin, and H. Abdulrab, *Rapport LITP 93.44, July 93.*

[3] *Transformations Algorithm of Word Equations with Four Variables*, G.S. Makanin, and H. Abdulrab, *Rapport LITP 93.49, September 93.*

[4] *Bunches of Formal Parametric Equations*, G.S. Makanin, H. Abdulrab and M.N. Maksimenko, *Rapport LITP 93.62, December 93.*

[5] *Bunches of Formal Parametric Equations with Three Variables*. G.S. Makanin, H. Abdulrab and M.N. Maksimenko, LIR, Research rapport, 1994.

Raven's function R1

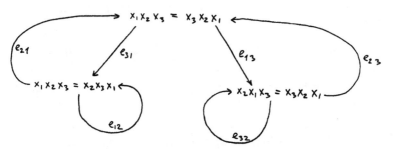

$$\left[\left[e_{31}e_{12}^{\lambda_{ij}}e_{21}\right]_{i=1}^{\gamma_j}\left[e_{13}e_{32}^{\alpha_{ij}}e_{23}\right]_{i=1}^{\beta_j}\right]_{j=1}^{\omega}$$

Raven's function R2

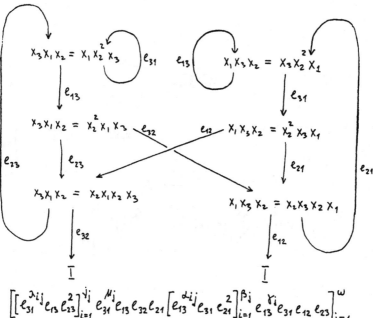

$$\left[\left[e_{31}^{\lambda_{ij}}e_{13}e_{23}^{2}\right]_{i=1}^{\gamma_j}e_{31}^{\mu_j}e_{13}e_{32}e_{21}\left[e_{13}^{\alpha_{ij}}e_{31}e_{21}^{2}\right]_{i=1}^{\beta_j}e_{13}^{\gamma_i}e_{31}e_{12}e_{23}\right]_{j=1}^{\omega}$$

Raven's function R3

$$\left[\left[e_{31}^{\lambda_{ij}}\,e_{13}\,e_{23}^{2}\right]_{i=1}^{\gamma_{j}}\,e_{31}^{\mu_{i}}\,e_{13}\,e_{32}\,e_{21}\,e_{13}\left[e_{32}^{\lambda_{ij}}\,e_{23}\,e_{13}^{2}\right]_{i=1}^{\beta_{j}}\,e_{32}^{\gamma_{i}}\,e_{23}\,e_{31}\,e_{12}\,e_{23}\right]_{j=1}^{\omega}$$

Raven's function R4

$$\left[\left[e_{23}\,e_{31}^{\rho_{ij}}\,e_{13}\right]_{i=1}^{\beta_{j}}\left(e_{32}\,e_{12}^{2}\,(e_{32}\,e_{12})^{\rho\beta_{ij}}\right)^{\lambda_{ij}}\right]_{j=1}^{\sigma}$$

On (Left) Partial Shuffle

Alexandru Mateescu

Academy of Finland and Department of Mathematics,
University of Turku, SF-20700 Turku, Finland

Abstract. We introduce a new operation between languages, called *left partial shuffle* or shortly *partial shuffle*. The need for the partial shuffle operation is strongly motivated by the theory of concurrent processes and by the practice of concurrent programming. Whereas the (classical) shuffle is useful to define free or pure parallel composition of concurrent processes, the partial shuffle provides an operation able to define the parallel composition of concurrent processes that possibly have *critical sections*. Indeed critical sections frequently exist inside concurrent processes.

1. Introduction

The aim of this paper is to introduce a new operation between languages able to define the parallel composition of concurrent processes such that the processes may contain critical sections or mutual exclusion of tight subprocesses. In certain circumstances, it may be necessary to ensure that parts of two concurrent processes do not run concurrently. These parts are so called *critical sections*. According to [1] a critical section is a part of a process which must not be executed concurrently with a critical section of another process. More precisely, once one process has entered its critical section, another process may not enter (its critical section or any other action) until the first process exits its critical section. Mutual exclusion is said to apply between critical sections and any other sections. On the other hand, it is assumed that any noncritical section of a process can be executed concurrently with any noncritical section of another process.

A first algebraic development of processes starts in [11], namely *CCS*. An important contribution on this line is the paper [2] that is the starting point for a more algebraic theory of concurrent processes. Here we have to emphasize that the free or pure parallel compositions of concurrent processes lead in a natural way to the shuffle operation, a well-known operation in the theory of formal languages.

Throughout this paper the reader may consult the monograph [14] for all unexplained notions of formal languages.

An important operations with languages that has an important role in this paper is the *shuffle* operation. We like to mention here that this operation was studied in many papers, for instance : [6], [9], [13], [15], etc. as well as in many monographs, for example the recent monograph [12].

---

* Research supported by the Academy of Finland, Project 11281.

Definition 1. The *shuffle* operation between words, denoted $⊔⊔$, is defined recursively by :

$$(au⊔⊔bv) = a(u⊔⊔bv) \cup b(au⊔⊔v),$$

and

$$(u⊔⊔\lambda) = (\lambda⊔⊔u) = \{u\},$$

where $u, v \in \Sigma^*$ and $a, b \in \Sigma$. □

The shuffle operation is extended in a natural way to languages :

Definition 2. The *shuffle* of two languages L_1 and L_2 is :

$$L_1⊔⊔L_2 = \bigcup_{u \in L_1, v \in L_2}(u⊔⊔v).$$

□

Remark 3. The shuffle operation is a commutative and associative operation on $\mathcal{P}(\Sigma^*)$ and, moreover $\{\lambda\}$ is the unit element. Therefore, $\mathcal{M}_{⊔⊔} = (\mathcal{P}(\Sigma^*), ⊔⊔, \{\lambda\})$ is a commutative monoid. Another important property is that:

$$\mathcal{S} = (\mathcal{P}(\Sigma^*), \cup, \emptyset, ⊔⊔, \{\lambda\})$$

is a commutative semiring. □

For general results concerning the theory of semirings, the reader may consult the monographs [4] or [8].

Let Σ be an alphabet and assume that $\Sigma = \Gamma \cup \Delta$, where $\Gamma \cap \Delta = \emptyset$. Note that Γ or Δ can be empty. Intuitively the symbols from Γ are elementary actions from critical sections, i.e., a critical section is a nonempty word over Γ, whereas a noncritical section is a word over Δ. Throghout this paper we assume that processes have a very simple structure, i.e. a process is a word over Σ.

Notations.

$$M_0 = \Gamma^*,$$
$$M_{k+1} = \Gamma^*(\Delta^+\Gamma^+)^k\Delta^+\Gamma^* \cup \{\lambda\}, k \geq 0.$$

Remark 4. Note that :

   (i) $\bigcup_{k \geq 0} M_k = \Sigma^*$.
   (ii) if $i \neq j$, then $M_i \cap M_j = \{\lambda\}$.
   (iii) for any $w \in \Sigma^+$, there exists a unique $k, k \geq 0$, such that $w \in M_k$.

□

Definition 5. Let w be in Σ^+. The *Δ-degree* of w is :

$$deg_\Delta(w) = k, \text{ where } w \in M_k.$$

By definition, $deg_\Delta(\lambda) = 0$. □

Comment. Note that for any nonempty word w, deg_Δ has a unique value (see Remark 4).

Let $\mathcal{P}(M_k)$ be the set of all subsets of M_k. We'll define a binary operation on $\mathcal{P}(M_k)$ as follows :

Definition 6. Let A, B be subsets of M_k. The *left partial $k-\Delta$-shuffle* or shortly, $k-\Delta$-*shuffle* of A with B, is by definition :

$$A \lfloor\!\rfloor_\Delta B = \bigcup_{x \in A, y \in B} x \lfloor\!\rfloor_\Delta y,$$

where, if :

$$x = u_0 v_1 u_1 \ldots v_k u_k,$$

$$y = u_0' v_1' u_1' \ldots v_k' u_k',$$

with $u_0, u_0', u_k, u_k' \in \Gamma^*, u_i, u_i' \in \Gamma^+, i = 1, \ldots, k-1, v_i, v_i' \in \Delta^+, i = 1, \ldots, k$, then :

$$x \lfloor\!\rfloor_\Delta y = u_0 u_0'(v_1 \lfloor\!\rfloor v_1') u_1 u_1' \ldots (v_k \lfloor\!\rfloor v_k') u_k u_k'.$$

By definition,

$$x \lfloor\!\rfloor_\Delta \lambda = \lambda \lfloor\!\rfloor_\Delta x = \{x\}.$$

$\square$

Comment. A decomposition of x (y) like in the above definition will be called a *canonical decomposition with respect to Δ* or, shortly, a *canonical decomposition*, when Δ is understood from the context.

Remark 7. Note that $x \lfloor\!\rfloor_\Delta y = xy$ if $\Delta = \emptyset$ ($\Sigma = \Gamma$), and $x \lfloor\!\rfloor_\Delta y = x \lfloor\!\rfloor y$ if $\Gamma = \emptyset$ ($\Sigma = \Delta$).
Moreover, for any $x, y \in \Delta$, it follows that :

$$x \lfloor\!\rfloor_\Delta y \subseteq x \lfloor\!\rfloor y.$$

$\square$

Comment. The above remark explains the terminology way this operation, i.e. $\lfloor\!\rfloor_\Delta$, is called *partial shuffle*.

Lemma 8. For any alphabet Σ and for any $\Delta, \Delta \subseteq \Sigma$ the ordered system:

$$S_{\Delta,k} = (\mathcal{P}(M_k), \cup, \emptyset, \lfloor\!\rfloor_\Delta, \{\lambda\})$$

is a (noncommutative) semiring. $\square$

Definition 9. If $A \subseteq M_k, k \geq 0$, then the *$\Delta$-shuffle closure* of A is:

$$A^{\lfloor\!\rfloor_\Delta} = \bigcup_{i \geq 0} A^{(i)_\Delta}, \text{ where}$$

$$A^{(0)_\Delta} = \{\lambda\} \text{ and } A^{(i+1)_\Delta} = A \lfloor \lfloor \rfloor_\Delta A^{(i)_\Delta}.$$

□

Comment. Note that $A^{\lfloor \lfloor \rfloor_\Delta}$ is the submonoid generated by A, with respect to $\lfloor \lfloor \rfloor_\Delta$, in the semiring $S_{\Delta,k}$.

We will now extend the Δ-shuffle operation to arbitrary words from Σ^*. The new operation will be denoted by $\lfloor \lfloor \rfloor_\Delta$, too.

Definition 10. Let x, y be in Σ^+ such that $deg_\Delta(x) = n$ and $deg_\Delta(y) = m$. Assume that

$$x = u_0 v_1 u_1 \ldots v_n u_n,$$

$$y = u_0' v_1' u_1' \ldots v_m' u_m',$$

with $u_0, u_0', u_n, u_m' \in \Gamma^*, u_i \in \Gamma^+, i = 1, \ldots, n-1, v_i \in \Delta^+, i = 1, \ldots, n,$
$u_i' \in \Gamma^+, i = 1, \ldots, m-1, v_i' \in \Delta^+, i = 1, \ldots, m.$ Then the *left Δ partial shuffle* (or shortly Δ *partial shuffle* or *partial shuffle*) of x with y is :

$$x \lfloor \lfloor \rfloor_\Delta y = \begin{cases} u_0 u_0' (v_1 \lfloor \lfloor \rfloor v_1') u_1 u_1' \ldots (v_n \lfloor \lfloor \rfloor v_n') u_n u_n' v_{n+1}' u_{n+1}' \ldots v_m' u_m', & \text{if } n \le m, \\ u_0 u_0' (v_1 \lfloor \lfloor \rfloor v_1') u_1 u_1' \ldots (v_m \lfloor \lfloor \rfloor v_m') u_m u_m' v_{m+1} u_{m+1} \ldots v_n u_n, & \text{otherwise.} \end{cases}$$

By definition :

$$x \lfloor \lfloor \rfloor_\Delta \lambda = \lambda \lfloor \lfloor \rfloor_\Delta x = \{x\}.$$

□

Example 11. Assume that $\Sigma = \{a, b, c, d\}$ and let x and y be words over Σ :
$x = acdbccac$ and $y = badad$.
(i) Consider that $\Delta = \{c, d\}$ and note that $deg_\Delta(x) = 3$ and $deg_\Delta(y) = 2$. Using Definition 10, we obtain that :

$$x \lfloor \lfloor \rfloor_\Delta y = aba(cd \lfloor \lfloor \rfloor d)ba(cc \lfloor \lfloor \rfloor d)ac.$$

(ii) Assume now that x, y are the same, but $\Delta = \{b, c, d\}$. It follows that $deg_\Delta(x) = 2$ and $deg_\Delta(y) = 3$ and :

$$x \lfloor \lfloor \rfloor_\Delta y = a(cdbcc \lfloor \lfloor \rfloor b)aa(c \lfloor \lfloor \rfloor d)ad.$$

(iii) As above, except that $\Delta = \{d\}$. Note that $deg_\Delta(x) = 1$ and $deg_\Delta(y) = 2$ and, in this case :

$$x \lfloor \lfloor \rfloor_\Delta y = acba(d \lfloor \lfloor \rfloor d)bccacad.$$

□

Lemma 12. $(\mathcal{P}(\Sigma^*), \lfloor \lfloor \rfloor_\Delta, \{\lambda\})$ is a (noncommutative) monoid.

Proof. First, observe that $\{\lambda\}$ is the unit element. It remains to show that $\lfloor\lfloor\rfloor_\Delta$ is an associative operation on $\mathcal{P}(\Sigma^*)$. Let x, y, z be in $\mathcal{P}(\Sigma^+)$ with $deg_\Delta(x) = i, deg_\Delta(y) = j, deg_\Delta(z) = k$. Assume that x, y, z have the canonical decompositions:

$$x = u_0 v_1 u_1 \ldots v_i u_i,$$

$$y = u_0' v_1' u_1' \ldots v_j' u_j',$$

$$z = u_0'' v_1'' u_1'' \ldots v_k'' u_k''.$$

Observe that :

$$(x\lfloor\lfloor\rfloor_\Delta y)\lfloor\lfloor\rfloor_\Delta z = u_0 u_0' u_0''(v_1\lfloor\lfloor\rfloor v_1'\lfloor\lfloor\rfloor v_1'')u_1 u_1' u_1'' \ldots (v_s\lfloor\lfloor\rfloor v_s'\lfloor\lfloor\rfloor v_s'')u_s u_s' u_s''.$$

$$\cdot(v_{s+1}^{(1)}\lfloor\lfloor\rfloor v_{s+1}^{(2)})u_{s+1}^{(1)}u_{s+1}^{(2)} \ldots (v_r^{(1)}\lfloor\lfloor\rfloor v_r^{(2)})u_r^{(1)}u_r^{(2)}v_{r+1}^{(2)}u_{r+1}^{(2)} \ldots v_t^{(2)}u_t^{(2)},$$

where $s = min(i, j, k), r = min(\{i, j, k\} - \{s\}), t = max(i, j, k)$
and, moreover :
if $i \leq j \leq k$, then $v_p^{(1)} = v_p', u_p^{(1)} = u_p', v_q^{(2)} = v_q'', u_q^{(2)} = u_q''$, else
if $i \leq k \leq j$, then $v_p^{(1)} = v_p'', u_p^{(1)} = u_p'', v_q^{(2)} = v_q', u_q^{(2)} = u_q'$, else
if $j \leq i \leq k$, then $v_p^{(1)} = v_p, u_p^{(1)} = u_p, v_q^{(2)} = v_q'', u_q^{(2)} = u_q''$, else
if $j \leq k \leq i$, then $v_p^{(1)} = v_p'', u_p^{(1)} = u_p'', v_q^{(2)} = v_q, u_q^{(2)} = u_q$, else
if $k \leq i \leq j$, then $v_p^{(1)} = v_p, u_p^{(1)} = u_p, v_q^{(2)} = v_q', u_q^{(2)} = u_q'$, else
if $k \leq j \leq i$, then $v_p^{(1)} = v_p', u_p^{(1)} = u_p', v_q^{(2)} = v_q, u_q^{(2)} = u_q$,
where $p = s + 1, \ldots, r$ and $q = s + 1, \ldots, t$.
It follows that $\lfloor\lfloor\rfloor_\Delta$ is an associative operation. $\square$

Corollary 13. For any alphabet Σ and for any $\Delta, \Delta \subseteq \Sigma$,
$S_\Delta = (\mathcal{P}(\Sigma^*), \cup, \emptyset, \lfloor\lfloor\rfloor_\Delta, \{\lambda\})$ is a (noncommutative) semiring. $\square$

Remark 14. Note that, if $x, y \in \Sigma^*$, then for any $t \in x\lfloor\lfloor\rfloor_\Delta y$,

$$deg_\Delta(t) = max(deg_\Delta(x), deg_\Delta(y)).$$

$\square$

Notation. For any $k, k \geq 0$,

$$H_k = \bigcup_{i \leq k} M_i.$$

Lemma 15. For any alphabet Σ, for any subset $\Delta, \Delta \subseteq \Sigma$ and for any $k, k \geq 0$,

$$\mathcal{H}_{\Delta,k} = (\mathcal{P}(H_k), \cup, \emptyset, \lfloor\lfloor\rfloor_\Delta, \{\lambda\})$$

is a (noncommutative) semiring.

Proof. It follows from Lemma 12 and Remark 14. $\square$

2. Partial shuffle operation and Chomsky's hierarchy

Let REG, CF, CS, RE be the classes of regular, context-free, context-sensitive and recursively enumerable languages .

Theorem 16.

(i) if $R_1, R_2 \in REG$, then $(R_1 \lfloor\lfloor\rfloor_\Delta R_2) \in REG$.

(ii) if $R \in REG$ and $L \in CF$, then $(R \lfloor\lfloor\rfloor_\Delta L) \in CF$ and $(L \lfloor\lfloor\rfloor_\Delta R) \in CF$.

(iii) if $L_1, L_2 \in CF$, then not necessarily $(L_1 \lfloor\lfloor\rfloor_\Delta L_2) \in CF$.

(iv) if $L_1, L_2 \in CS$, then $(L_1 \lfloor\lfloor\rfloor_\Delta L_2) \in CS$.

(v) if $L_1, L_2 \in RE$, then $(L_1 \lfloor\lfloor\rfloor_\Delta L_2) \in RE$.

Proof. (i) Assume that L_i is accepted by the finite deterministic automaton $A_i = (Q_i, \Sigma, \delta_i, q_0^i, F_i)$, $i = 1.2$. We will define a nondeterministic finite automaton $A = (Q, \Sigma, \delta, Q_0, F)$ such that $L(A) = L_1 \lfloor\lfloor\rfloor_\Delta L_2$. By definition : $Q = Q_1 \times Q_2 \times \{1, 2, 3\}$, $Q_0 = \{(q_0^1, q_0^2, i) \mid 1 \le i \le 3\}$, $F = F_1 \times F_2 \times \{1, 2, 3\}$. An element of Q will be denoted by $[p, q, k]$ instead of (p, q, k). The transition function δ is defined as follows.

$$\delta([p, q, 1], a) = \delta([p, q, 3], a) = \{[\delta_1(p, a), q, 1], [p, \delta_2(q, a), 2]\}, \forall a \in \Gamma.$$

$$\delta([p, q, 2], a) = \{[p, \delta_2(q, a), 1]\}, \forall a \in \Gamma.$$

$$\delta([p, q, k], b) = \{[\delta_1(p, b), q, 3], [p, \delta_2(q, b), 3]\}, \forall b \in \Delta \text{ and } \forall k \in \{1, 2, 3\}.$$

It is easy to observe that $L(A) = L_1 \lfloor\lfloor\rfloor_\Delta L_2$. Intuitively, A tries to guess in words over Γ^+ if it is possible to switch from the automaton A_1 to A_2. At most one switch is possible for words in Γ^+. The remaining construction of A is like in the case of the ordinary shuffle, $\lfloor\lfloor\rfloor$.

(ii) The proof is similar with the above, except that one automaton is a pushdown automaton. Hence, one component must simulate the behaviour of a pushdown automaton. Thus, the resulting pushdown automaton uses its finite control to simulate the finite deterministic automaton that accepts the language R.

(iii) It is well-known that the class CF is not closed under shuffle, hence CF is not closed under $\lfloor\lfloor\rfloor_\Delta$ either.

(iv) Note that L_i is accepted by a nondeterminisic Turing machine M_i of space complexity $\mathcal{O}(n)$, $i = 1, 2$. One can define a nondeterministic Turing machine of space complexity $\mathcal{O}(n)$ that try to guess for an input w if there are scattered subwords u, v of w such that $w \in u \lfloor\lfloor\rfloor_\Delta v$. The resulting Turing machine is of space complexity $\mathcal{O}(n)$.

(v) Similar to the case (iv). $\qquad\qquad\square$

3. Equations and systems of equations

Note that the semirings $S_{\Delta,k}$, $\mathcal{H}_{\Delta,k}$ and S_Δ are ω-complete semirings, i.e. any increasing sequence $(A_n)_{n \ge 0}$ of elements has the supremum in the corresponding semiring. The supremum of an increasing sequence $(A_n)_{n\geq 0}$ will be denoted by $\bigvee A_n$. Moreover, any of the above semirings has a first element, the empty set, $\emptyset$.

Lemma 17. Let a, B be in S_Δ. The equation $X = A \sqcup\!\sqcup_\Delta X \cup B$ has the (minimal) solution $X_0 = A^{\sqcup\!\sqcup_\Delta} \sqcup\!\sqcup_\Delta B$.

Proof. Consider the function :

$$\varphi : \mathcal{P}(\Sigma^*) \to \mathcal{P}(\Sigma^*), \varphi(C) = A \sqcup\!\sqcup_\Delta C \cup B.$$

It is easy to verify that φ is a ω-continuous function, i.e. φ commutes with the supremum of increasing sequences of elements from S_Δ. Therefore, by Kleene's fixed point theorem φ has a least fix point, $X_0 = \bigvee_n \varphi^{(n)}(\emptyset)$, where $\varphi^{(n)}$ means $\overbrace{\varphi \circ \varphi \ldots \circ \varphi}$ if $n > 0$, and the identity function if $n = 0$. In our case, we obtain that $X_0 = A^{\sqcup\!\sqcup_\Delta} \sqcup\!\sqcup_\Delta B$. $\square$

Corollary 18. The result of the above lemma remains true, if the semiring S_Δ is replaced with any of the semirings $S_{\Delta,k}$, $\mathcal{H}_{\Delta,k}, k \geq 0$. $\square$

Definition 19. Let A be in S_Δ , $A \neq \emptyset$. The Δ-*degree* of A is :

$$deg_\Delta(A) = max\{deg_\Delta(x) \mid x \in A\},$$

if maximum does exist and ∞ otherwise.
By definition, $deg_\Delta(\emptyset) = 0$. $\square$

Remark 20. Let A, B be nonempty subsets of Σ^* such that $deg_\Delta(A)$ and $deg_\Delta(B)$ are finite.
The Δ-degree of the solution X_0 of the equation $X = A \sqcup\!\sqcup_\Delta X \cup B$ is :

$$deg_\Delta(X_0) = max(deg_\Delta(A), deg_\Delta(B)).$$

(Observe that $deg_\Delta(A^{\sqcup\!\sqcup_\Delta}) = deg_\Delta(A)$ and use then Lemma 17 and Remark 14.) $\square$

Let $X = \{X_1, \ldots, X_n\}$ be a set of variables such that $X \cap \Sigma = \emptyset$.

Definition 21. A *monomial* over S_Δ with variables in X is a finite string of the form :

$$A_1 \sqcup\!\sqcup_\Delta A_2 \sqcup\!\sqcup_\Delta \cdots \sqcup\!\sqcup_\Delta A_n, \text{ where } A_i \in X \text{ or } A_i \in \Sigma^*, i = 1, \ldots, n.$$

A *polynomial* $p(X)$ over S_Δ is a finite union of monomials.
A *system of equations* over S_Δ is a finite set of equations :

$$E = \{X_i = p_i(X) \mid i = 1, \ldots, n\},$$

where $p_i(X)$ are polynomials.
The *solution* of E is a n-tuple $(L_1, \ldots, L_n)$ of languages over Σ, with the property that $L_i = p_i(L_1, \ldots, L_n)$ and the n-tuple is minimal with this property, i.e.

if $(L'_1, \ldots, L'_n)$ is another n-tuple that satisfies E then $(L_1, \ldots, L_n) \leq (L'_1, \ldots, L'_n)$ (where the order is defined componentwise with respect to the inclusion). $\square$

As in the case of Lemma 13, see also [8], one can show that :

Theorem 22. Any system of equations over S_Δ ($S_{\Delta,k}$, $\mathcal{H}_{\Delta,k}, k \geq 0$) has a unique solution. $\square$

4. Rational and algebraic languages with respect to partial shuffle

Definition 23. A language L is (partial shufle) *algebraic* over Σ if and only if L is the component of the solution of a system of equations over S_Δ. $\square$

Notation.

$$Alg - ps_{\Sigma,\Delta} = \{L \mid L \text{ is } \Delta\text{-algebraic over } \Sigma\}.$$

$$Alg - ps_\Sigma = \bigcup_{\Delta \subseteq \Sigma} Alg - ps_{\Sigma,\Delta}$$

$$Alg - ps = \{L \mid \exists \Sigma, L \in Alg - ps_\Sigma\}.$$

$\square$

Definition 24. The family of (partial shuffle) *rational* languges over the semiring $S_{\Sigma,\Delta}$ is the smallest family of languages denoted $Rat - ps_{\Sigma,\Delta}$ such that :

(i) if $F \subseteq \Sigma^*$, F finite, then $F \in Rat - ps_{\Sigma,\Delta}$.
(ii) if $A, B \in Rat - ps_{\Sigma,\Delta}$, then $A \cup B$, $A \lfloor\rfloor_\Delta B$ and $A^{\lfloor\rfloor\Delta}$ are in $Rat - ps_{\Sigma,\Delta}$. $\square$

Notation.

$$Rat - ps_\Sigma = \bigcup_{\Delta \subseteq \Sigma} Rat - ps_{\Sigma,\Delta}.$$

$$Rat - ps = \{L \mid \exists \Sigma, L \in Rat - ps_\Sigma\}.$$

$\square$

Definition 25. A monomial is *rational* iff it is of the form $\alpha \lfloor\rfloor_\Delta Y$ or of the form α, where Y is a variable and $\alpha \in \Sigma^*$. A polynomial is *rational* iff it is a finite union of rational monomials. A system $E = \{X_i = p_i(X) \mid i = 1, \ldots, n\}$ is *rational* if each polynomial p_i is a rational polynomial, $i = 1, \ldots, n$. $\square$

The following theorem recovers one fundamental result :

Theorem 26. The following assertions are equivalent :

(i) $L \in Rat - ps_{\Sigma,\Delta}$.
(ii) L is a component of the solution of a rational system of equations over the semiring $S_{\Sigma,\Delta}$.

Proof. It follows straight from the general theory of semirings, see [8] or [4]. $\square$

Comment. From the above theorem, it follows that $Rat - ps \subseteq Alg - ps$.

The next pumping lemma can be derived as in the classical case :

Lemma 27. Let $L, L \subseteq \Sigma^*$ be in $Rat - ps$. There exist $\Delta \subseteq \Sigma$ and $n > 0$ such that, for any $w \in L$ with $\mid w \mid \geq n$, there exist $x, y, z \in \Sigma^*$ such that :
(i) $w = x \lfloor\lfloor\rfloor_\Delta y \lfloor\lfloor\rfloor_\Delta z$.
(ii) $0 < \mid y \mid < n$.
(iii) $x \lfloor\lfloor\rfloor_\Delta y^{\lfloor\lfloor\rfloor_\Delta} \lfloor\lfloor\rfloor_\Delta z \subseteq L$. $\square$

5. Properties of $Rat - ps$ and $Alg - ps$

Remark 28. Assume that

$$E = \{X_i = p_i(X) \mid i = 1,\ldots,n\},$$

is a rational system of equations over $S_{\Sigma,\Delta}$. We can extend Remark 20 for the components of the solution of E, i.e. :
(i) for any $X_i, i = 1,\ldots,n$, component of the solution of E:

$$deg_\Delta(X_i) < \infty.$$

(ii) moreover, for any $X_i, i = 1,\ldots,n$, component of the solution of E,

$$deg_\Delta(X_i) < max\{deg_\Delta(\alpha) \mid \alpha \text{ coefficient in } E\}.$$

$\square$

As consequence for the case $\Delta = \emptyset$, $x \lfloor\lfloor\rfloor_\Delta y = xy$, we obtain:

Lemma 29.
(i) $REG \subset Rat - ps$.
(ii) $CF \subset Alg - ps$.
(iii) $Alg - ps \subset CS$.
and all above inclusions are strict.
Proof. (i) - (ii) Obviously the inclusions are true. It is enough to consider $\Delta = \emptyset$.
Assume that $\Sigma = \{a, b, c\}$ and $\Delta = \{b\}$. Note that $L = \{abc\}^{\lfloor\lfloor\rfloor_\Delta} = \{a^n b^n c^n \mid n \geq 0\} \in Rat - ps$ and hence it is also in $Alg - ps$. On the other hand L is neither in REG nor in CF.

(iii) One can easily define a nondeterministic Turing machine of space complexity $\mathcal{O}(n)$ such that, for an partial shuffle algebraic system of equations, for a fixed component and for an arbitrary input w, the machine verifies whether or not w is in the considered component of the solution. Here we must point out that the system can be considered without coefficients λ and thus, in the Kleene's iterations the length of words is strictly increasing. Therefore, $Alg - ps \subseteq CS$.

Consider the language :

$$L = \{a^n b^{n^2} \mid n > 0\}.$$

Obviously, $L \in CS$ but note that the length of words in L is a set that is not semilinear. One can show that for any $K \in Alg - ps$, the set $\{\mid w \mid \mid w \in K\}$ is a semilinear set. Thus, L cannot be in $Alg - ps$ and hence the inclusion is strict.

□

Lemma 30. The class $Rat - ps$ is incomparable with the class CF.

Proof. Assume that $\Sigma = \{a,b\}$ and $\Delta = \{b\}$. Observe that $\{ab\}^{\sqcup\!\sqcup_\Delta} = \{a^n b^n \mid n \geq 0\} \in Rat - ps \cap CF$. Now, consider $\Sigma = \{a,b,c\}$ and $\Delta = \{b\}$. Note that $\{abc\}^{\sqcup\!\sqcup_\Delta} = \{a^n b^n c^n \mid n \geq 0\} \in Rat - ps$ but is not in CF.

Let L be the language, $L = \{a^n b^n \mid n \geq 0\}^*$. Obviously, $L \in CF$. Note that $L \notin REG$, thus Δ cannot by empty. If $\Delta = \{a\}$ or $\Delta = \{b\}$, then $deg_\Delta(L) = \infty$ and thus, by Remark 28, L cannot be in $Rat - ps$.

Finally, if $\Delta = \{a,b\}$, then using pumping lemma (Lemma 27) it is easy to conclude that $L \notin Rat - ps$.

□

Lemma 31. $Rat - ps \subset Alg - ps$ and the inclusion is strict.

Proof. Obviously, $Rat - ps \subseteq Alg - ps$. Consider the equation :

$$X = (ab) \sqcup\!\sqcup_\Delta X \sqcup\!\sqcup_\Delta (cd) \cup \{\lambda\},$$

where $\Gamma = \{a,c\}$ and $\Delta = \{b,d\}$. It is easy to observe that the solution of this equation is the language :

$$L = \bigcup_{n \geq 0} ((ab)^{(n)\sqcup\!\sqcup_\Delta} \sqcup\!\sqcup_\Delta (cd)^{(n)\sqcup\!\sqcup_\Delta}).$$

Thus, we obtain that :

$$L = \{a^n c^n u \mid u \in \Delta^*, N_b(u) = N_d(u) = n, n \geq 0\}.$$

Using Lemma 27 we deduce that $L \notin Rat - ps$ and therefore $Rat - ps$ is a strict subclass of $Alg - ps$.

□

Comment. From Lemma 29, Lemma 30 and Lemma 31, we obtain the following diagram, where the arrows mean strict inclusion:

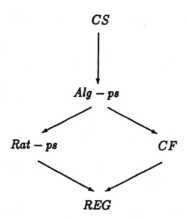

$$CS$$

$$Alg - ps$$

$$Rat - ps \qquad CF$$

$$REG$$

Theorem 32. The class $Rat - ps$ is an anti-AFL, i.e. it is not closed under any of the following six operations : union, catenation, Kleene star, intersection with regular languages, morphic direct and inverse images.

Proof. Rat − ps is not closed under union.
The language $L_1 = \{a^n b^n \mid n \geq 0\}$ is in $Rat - ps$ (see the proof of Lemma 26) The language $L_2 = (ab)^*$ is regular and hence is in $Rat - ps$ (see Remark 29 (i)). The language $L_1 \cup L_2$ is not in $Rat - ps$. Observe that if $\Delta = \emptyset$, then $L_1 \cup L_2$ is not regular and hence is not $Rat - ps$. If $\Delta = \{a\}$ or $\Delta = \{b\}$ then $deg_\Delta(L) = \infty$ and hence, by Remark 28, $L_1 \cup L_2$ cannot be in $Rat - ps$. The remaining case, $\Delta = \{a, b\}$ leads to the same conclusion, by Lemma 27.

Rat-ps is not closed under catenation.
Consider again the above languages. By a similar argument we obtain that $L_1 L_2$ is not in $Rat - ps$.

Rat-ps is not closed under Kleene star.
It is easy to observe that L_1^* is not in $Rat - ps$, despite that L_1 is in $Rat - ps$.

Rat-ps is not closed under intersection with regular languages.
Assume that $L_3 = (ab)^*(cd)^*$ and $L_4 = \bigcup_{n \geq 0}(ab)^n(cd)^{(n)\Delta}$. Note that, for $\Delta = \{c, d\}$ we obtain that $L_4 = (abcd)^{\text{Ш}\Delta}$ and, thus L_4 is in $Rat-ps$. But, $L_5 = L_3 \cap L_4 = \{(ab)^n(cd)^n \mid n \geq 0\}$ is not in $Rat - ps$ (use Lemma 27).

Rat-ps is not closed under morphic direct images.
Let h be the homomorphism : $h(a) = ab$ and $h(b) = cd$. Observe that $h(L_1) = L_5 \notin Rat - ps$.

Rat-ps is not closed under morphic inverse images.
Assume that $L_6 = (ab)^{\text{Ш}\Delta}$. Note that L_6 is the Dyck languge over $\{a, b\}$. Define the morphism : $h(x) = a^2, h(y) = b$. Observe that for any $n \geq 0$ there are words $w = x^n y^{2n} \in h^{-1}(L_6)$. $(h(x^n y^n) = a^{2n}b^{2n} \in L_6)$. Now, using Lemma 27 for such words we obtain that $h^{-1}(L_6) \notin Rat-ps$. For instance, for $\Delta = \{x, y\}, x^n y^{2n} \text{Ш}_\Delta xy^2$ contains the word $xyx^n y^{2n+1} \notin h^{-1}(L_6)$. The possibilities : $\Delta = \emptyset, \Delta = \{x\}$ and $\Delta = \{y\}$ lead to the same conclusion. $\qquad \square$

Corollary 33. The class $Rat - ps$ is not closed neither under intersection nor under complementation.

Proof. Nonclosure under intersection follows directly by Theorem 32.

Consider the language, $L = \{a^n b^n \mid n \geq 0\}$. Note that $L \in Rat - ps$ if and only if $\Delta = \{a\}$ or $\Delta = \{b\}$, but, in any of these cases the complement of L has the $\Delta-$ degree ∞ and hence cannot be in $Rat - ps$. $\qquad\square$

Now, we consider some properties of the class $Alg - ps$.

Theorem 34. For any Σ and for any Δ, $\Delta \subseteq \Sigma$, the class $Alg - ps_{\Sigma,\Delta}$ is closed under : union, $\bigsqcup_\Delta$ and $\bigsqcup_\Delta$-closure.

Proof. Let L_1, L_2 be in $Alg - ps_{\Sigma,\Delta}$. There exist E_1 and E_2 algebraic systems of equations such that L_i corresponds to the X_i component of the solution. Without loss of generality, we can assume that E_1 and E_2 have disjoint sets of variables.

Let X_3 be a new variable and define the system of algebraic equations :

$$E_3 = E_1 \cup E_2 \cup \{X_3 = X_1 \cup X_2\}.$$

Obviously, the component of the solution of E_3, corresponding of X_3 is $L_3 = L_1 \cup L_2$. For proving closure under $\bigsqcup_\Delta$ define E_3 as being :

$$E_3 = E_1 \cup E_2 \cup \{X_3 = X_1 \bigsqcup_\Delta X_2\}.$$

Finally, for the $\bigsqcup_\Delta$-closure define :

$$E_3 = E_1 \cup \{X_3 = X_1 \bigsqcup_\Delta X_3 \cup \{\lambda\}\}.$$

$\qquad\square$

Comment. Concerning decidable properties of $Rat - ps$ we can easily show that the membership problem, the emptiness problem, the infinity problem are decidable problems.

Theorem 35 For $L_1, L_2 \in Rat - ps$ it is undecidable :
(i) whether or not $L_1 \cap L_2 = \emptyset$.
(ii) whether or not $card(L_1 \cap L_2) = \infty$.

Proof. (i) Let $PCP(\alpha, \beta)$ be an instance of the Post Correspondence Problem. Assume that $\alpha = (\alpha_1, \ldots, \alpha_n)$, $\beta = (\beta_1, \ldots, \beta_n)$ are Post's lists, where $\alpha_i, \beta_i, \ldots, i = 1, \ldots, n$ are nonempty words over $\{a, b\}$. Define $\Sigma = \{a, b, c\}$, $\Delta = \{c\}$ and consider the finite set K_α,

$$K_\alpha = \{ba^i c\alpha_i \mid \alpha_i \text{ in } \alpha, i = 1, \ldots, n\}.$$

and let L_1 be , $L_1 = K_\alpha \bigsqcup_\Delta K_\alpha^{\bigsqcup_\Delta}$. Note that $L_1 \in Rat - ps$ and moreover,

$$L_1 = \{ba^{i_1} ba^{i_2} b \ldots ba^{i_r} c^r \alpha_{i_1} \alpha_{i_2} \ldots \alpha_{i_r} \mid r \geq 1\}.$$

Analogously,

$$L_2 = \{ba^{j_1} ba^{j_2} b \ldots ba^{j_s} c^s \beta_{j_1} \beta_{j_2} \ldots \beta_{j_s} \mid s \geq 1\}.$$

is a language in $Rat - ps$. Note that, $L_1 \cap L_2 \neq \emptyset$ if and only if $PCP(\alpha, \beta)$ has a solution.

(ii) It follows like in case (i) that $card(L_1 \cap L_2) = \infty$ if and only if $PCP(\alpha, \beta)$ has a solution.

$\square$

Comment Note that the above problems are decidable for the classical family of rational (regular) languages.

6. Conclusions

There are several problems concerning the partial shuffle operation that have not been studied in this paper, as for instance : grammars and automata for langues in $Rat - ps$ ($Alg - ps$), pumping lemma for languages in $Alg - ps$. The syntactic monoids (see [7] for such monoids associated to codes or [10] for syntactic monoids associated to shuffle operation). The study of such monoids can be related to the theory of models, see [7] and thus one can obtain a uniform theory for concurrency that involves syntax and semantics in the same approach.

Here we have to mention that the existence of critical sections in processes was considered (in an axiomatic way) in [2]. For instance, in [2], page 128, the first example shows that :

$$\mathcal{M}(a : b \parallel c : d) = \{abcd, cdab\}.$$

Note that there is no Δ such that $(ab \lfloor \lfloor \rfloor_\Delta cd) = \{abcd, cdab\}$. Thus, our approach is different from the approach from [2].

One can also criticize our partial shuffle. First, in practice, very often some atomic (elementary) action, say the symbol a, can be in $\Delta \cap \Gamma$, i.e. in some context a appears in a critical section and the same a can be used in some noncritical section in another context. This difficulty can be solved by considering a copy of a, say a' and a is in Δ, whereas a' is in Γ.

Another major aspect is that, in some sense, when we defined $p \lfloor \lfloor \rfloor_\Delta q$ the leftmost operator, i.e. p has some priority compared with the process q, i.e., whenever two critical sections, say s_1 from p and s_2 from q are concurrent, the section s_1 is performed first. (see Definition 10). Perhaps a more suitable name for our partial shuffle is *left partial shuffle*. In order to overcome this situation, one has to do important changes. Define $\Gamma' = \{[v] \mid v \in \Gamma^+\}$,where [and] are new symbols that are not in Σ . Note that Γ' is an infinite set. Consider the monoid $M = (\Delta \cup \Gamma')^*$ (observe that this monoid is not finited generately). If $x \in \Sigma^*$ has the canonical decomposition $x = u_0 v_1 u_1 \ldots v_n u_n$ then the corresponding word in M is : $\bar{x} = [u_0]v_1[u_1] \ldots v_n[u_n]$. We will use the same convention for y. Consider again the Definition 10, as follows :

Definition 10'. Let x, y be in Σ^+ such that $deg_\Delta(x) = n$ and $deg_\Delta(y) = m$. Assume that

$$x = u_0 v_1 u_1 \ldots v_n u_n,$$
$$y = u'_0 v'_1 u'_1 \ldots v'_m u'_m,$$

with $u_0, u'_0, u_n, u'_m \in \Gamma^*, u_i \in \Gamma^+, i = 1, \ldots, n-1, v_i \in \Delta^+, i = 1, \ldots, n$, $u'_i \in \Gamma^+, i = 1, \ldots, m-1, v'_i \in \Delta^+, i = 1, \ldots, m$.

Then the *(commutative) partial shuffle* of $\bar{x}$ with $\bar{y}$, denoted $\bar{x} \sqcup \!\sqcup'_\Delta \bar{y} =$, is :

$$com([u_0],[u'_0])(v_1 \sqcup\!\sqcup v'_1)com([u_1],[u'_1]) \ldots (v_n \sqcup\!\sqcup v'_n)com([u_n],[u'_n])v'_{n+1} \cdots u'_m,$$

if $n \leq m$, or if $n > m$, then

$$com([u_0],[u'_0])(v_1 \sqcup\!\sqcup v'_1)com([u_1],[u'_1]) \ldots (v_m \sqcup\!\sqcup v'_m)com([u_m],[u'_m])v_{m+1} \cdots u_n,$$

where $com(A)$ means the commutative closure of the set A.

Note that com is applied to symbols from Γ', i.e., the symbols between the brackets "[" and "]" are not commuted anymore. Also, it is important to emphasize that $\sqcup\!\sqcup'_\Delta$ continues to be an associative operation and even commutative. Assuming that we don't use the brackets "[" and "]", the resulting operation $\sqcup\!\sqcup'_\Delta$ is not associative. Note that this approach leads to partial commutation, see [3] for new results in this area.

On the other hand, there are several new and specific problems concerning partial shuffle. We mention one that it seems to be nontrivial. Concurrent processes are rather complex objects. From practical reasons a process can be considered as parallel with respect to some actions and nonparallel (sequential) with respect to other actions. For example, assume that $\Sigma = \{a,b,c\}$ and the process is defined by the equation :

$$X = a \sqcup\!\sqcup X \cup bX \cup c$$

or in a more algebraic theory of processes :

$$X = a \parallel X + b.X + c,$$

where $\parallel$ means the parallel composition of processes, "." is the sequential composition of processes and $+$ is the nondeterministic choice. Note that the above equation has a unique minimal solution in $\mathcal{P}(\Sigma^*)$. This can be proved using Kleene's fixed point theorem. But, the above equation involves both, $\sqcup\!\sqcup$ and "." operations. Hence this equation cannot be considered neither in the semiring $(\mathcal{P}(\Sigma^*), \cup, \emptyset, \sqcup\!\sqcup, \{\lambda\})$ nor in the semiring $(\mathcal{P}(\Sigma^*), \cup, \emptyset, ., \{\lambda\})$. Hence, for complex systems that involve several operations $\sqcup\!\sqcup'_\Delta$ for different Δ, the theory of semirings is difficult to use. A more general framework is necesary to be defined in order to cover such situations.

7. References

1. T. Axford; Concurrent Programming Fundamental Techniques for Real Time and Parallel Software Design, John Wiley & Sons, New York, 1989.
2. J.A. Bergstra, J.W. Klop; Process Algebra for Synchronous Communication, *Information and Control*, 60 (1984), 109-137.
3. V. Diekert; Rewriting, Möbius Functions and Semi-Comutations, Proceedings of FCT'93, LNCS 710, Springer-Verlag, (1993) 1-15.
4. J.S. Golan; The Theory of Semirings with Application in Mathematics and Theoretical Computer Science, Longman Scientific and Technical, 1992.

5. M. Ito, G. Thierrin, S.S. Yu; Shuffle-closed Languages (to appear).

6. M. Jantzen; Extending Regular Expressions with Iterated Shuffle, *Th. Comp. Sci.*, **38** (1985) 223-247.

7. H. Jürgensen; Syntactic Monoids of Codes, Report 327, Dept.Comp.Sci., The University of Western Ontario, 1992.

8. W. Kuich, A. Salomaa; Semirings, Automata, Languages, EATCS Monographs on Theoretical Computer Science, Springer-Verlag, Berlin, 1986.

9. M. Latteux, G. Rozenberg; Commutative One-Counter Languages Are Regular, *Journal of Computer and System Sciences* **29** (1984), 54-57.

10. A. Mateescu; On Scattered Syntactic Monoids, Proceedings of FCT'93, LNCS 710, Springer-Verlag, (1993) 386-395.

11. R. Milner; A Calculus of Communicating Systems, LNCS 92, Springer-Verlag, Berlin, 1980.

12. C. Reutenauer; Free Lie Algebras, Clarendon Press, Oxford, 1993.

13. J. Sakarovitch, I. Simon; Subwords, in Combinatorics on Words, M. Lothaire (ed.), Addison-Wesley, Read. Mass., 1983.

14. A. Salomaa; Formal Languages, Academic Press, New York, 1973.

15. G. Thierrin, S.S. Yu; Shuffle Relations and Codes, *Journal of Information and Optimization Sciences*, **12** , 3 (1991) 441-449.

Learning Theoretical Aspects is Important but (Sometimes) Dangerous

H. Maurer

Graz University of Technology, Austria
and University of Auckland, New Zealand
hmaurer@iicm.tu-graz.ac.at

I am dedicating this paper to my friend Arto Salomaa on the occasion of his 60th birthday.

Hermann Maurer

Abstract

In science-education the discussion on the role of theory teaching has been going on for decades. Some persons claim that without a deep and thorough foundation in theory no serious work or understanding is possible, others tend to belittle theory as something on the fringes, for university professors only, as much and as little important as some kinds of esoteric forms of art.

In this paper we take a more balanced view, leaning towards supporting theory, yet not without reservations. We discuss in this paper first what we believe should be obvious anyway: that theory is important, even if some aspects may not seem to lend themselves to any applications; that certain aspects of theory are, however, likely to be and remain esoteric and their pursuit is indeed as much or as little justified as the support of alpine ski racing or formula-one motorsport, or experiments in modern art, or all those other things that make life interesting for a comparatively small group of people, yet probably do not really contribute to the overall benefit of humanity ... if there is any way to define such a benefit! However, we then show that in teaching and using theory there are some very real dangers involved that one should be aware of: theoretic results may stifle (!) attempts to solve problems because they are theoretically so hard that nobody wants to get involved in them; learning theory by means of formalisms may hide important intuitive notions; and learning in certain situations may indeed be detrimental, rather than helpful!

Above observations, just based on a few examples, show the complexity of teaching, and seem to indicate that interest in and research into how to teach properly is indeed an important matter. It is typical for Arto Salomaa that he has not only been a leader in theoretical research, but has much watched out for the borderline where theory becomes too esoteric and has been involved in a number of teaching experiments such as COSTOC and JUCS mentioned in the final section of this paper.

1 Introduction: Teaching Theoretical Aspects Is Important

There can be no doubt that research in and teaching theoretical aspects is as important in computer science as in any other area.

Without understanding the theoretical underpinning many investigations will remain superficial; without careful theoretical studies many problems could never be solved. Yet sometimes theoreticians are accused of working in an "ivory tower", of producing "esoteric results one after another with no apparent merit whatsoever."

The latter accusations may indeed be sometimes true. There may well be cases when complete theories will never be of any "practical" use. But who can tell?

Who could have predicted that investigations into prime numbers and factoring of large integers would at some stage be of crucial importance for public-key cryptography [Salomaa 1990], an area of dramatic importance for all kinds of computer applications when high security, digital signatures or unorthodox protocols are required. Who could have guessed that the theory of uniform distribution of multiples of irrational numbers modulo 1 would allow the development of superb hashing algorithms [Ottmann 1993]? And it is certainly no coincidence that theoretical results led to the breakthrough in areas as diverse as the dictionary problem in data structures starting with the AVL trees of Adelson, Velskii and Landis, the matrix-multiplication algorithms faster than $O(n^3)$ as started by Strassen, the post office problem solution based on Voronoi diagrams, entirely new ways of looking at formal language and automata theory using power series [Kuich 1986], at developmental processes using L-systems [Salomaa 1980], new text compression techniques that can revolutionize the storage of information [Bell 1990] or new ways of compressing pictures as pioneered in e.g. [Barnsley 1988] and [Culik II 1993] ...just to mention some very theoretical results that have had or will have tremendous "practical" impact.

Thus, although areas of theory sometimes may look esoteric it is hard to tell whether they might not become applicable at some stage. But even if this may not be the case: developing a theory can be as beautiful and rewarding as painting a picture or composing a symphony – and who has ever doubted the value of such undertakings? Working with theory and discovering new truths is as natural as discovering new territories: if explorers are allowed to answer the question "why do you go there?" by saying "because it is there!", then so can theoreticians. Learning to understand deep theoretical results sharpens the brain more than many other activities. And like when trying to climb a mountain it is often not best to take the most direct route but to explore the surroundings and possible alternatives first, for solving a specific concrete and pragmatic problem it will often pay off to first examine the whole area carefully for having a solid basis to then hopefully solve it!

After all this defence of theory, the rest of this paper voices a word of caution concerning what and how we teach theoretical aspects. First, we have to continously fight the temptation to teach what we know rather than what is important: maybe numerical solutions of differential equations are more important than learning all cases of types of equations that can be solved analytically (they never occur in practice); maybe teaching hashing with average $O(1)$ performance for dictionary problems should receive much more attention than tree-like data structures (although the latter are more fun to teach: the author knows this from many years of teaching such things!), etc. Second, and this is the main statement of this paper: theoretical results should be always seen with a grain of salt or else they will sometimes distract from possible solutions; and formalisms – as important as they are – tend to sometimes hide important intuitive notions.

We discuss these matters in the next three sections; thereby establishing that teaching theoretical aspects is not without dangers. But knowing of them will hopefully help to avoid them!

2 Theory May Stifle Progress

In the last section we have argued that theory is and must remain an important part of science in education, particularly also of computer science teaching.

It is worth noting however that it is also very important to teach students that theoretical results have to be taken with a grain of salt:

It is important to understand that algorithms requiring $O(n)$ time are asymptotically worse than algorithms requiring $O(\log n)^m$, even for large m, since such results may eventually lead to a much better understanding of a problem and eventually to "useful" results. But is has to be made clear that $(\log n)^m$ for even moderately large m is clearly larger than n for all reasonably interesting values of n. It is important to understand that the median of n numbers can be found without sorting (which would require $O(n \log n)$ steps) in "linear time" even if the $O(n)$ algorithms known will only be better than the brute force sorting methods for ridiculously large n, etc.

Such examples abound, and all good teachers make sure that students are not deceived by things like the O-notation to always consider asymptotically better algorithms automatically superior to other ones. However, there are more critical cases which are less well known and less widely discussed that merit particular attention: there are problems that are known to be NP-complete, some even known to be undecidable, suggesting that they cannot be tackled efficiently. However, in a number of cases simple and for practical purposes absolutely satisfactory techniques do exist.

Let me demonstrate this using one example that I have encountered in practise.

Since we were fed up with correcting thousands of exercises on differentiating functions of one variable in elementary calculus classes at some stage we decided to write a computer program that would generate arbitrarily many examples, would allow students to differentiate the functions, type in the result and tell the students if they had correctly solved the problem or not. First, it turned out to be more difficult than expected to generate arbitrarily many examples of increasing difficulty automatically [Gillard 1990], but this is an aside. The real problem is this: once the computer has generated a function, it can easily differentiate it, giving an expression U. The student differentiating the same function arrives at an expression V. The program now has to decide if U and V represent identical functions. According to well-known results by Richardson (see [Richardson 1968], [Caviness 1970] and [Wang 1974]) this problem is undecidable even for rather limited classes of functions.

Hence it appears that our goal, to write a program providing a rich repertoire of differentiation problems and checking the correctness of the student's work was doomed from the beginning. However, surprise, surprise: although it is undecidable on principle to decide whether two expressions U and V in one variable x denote the same function, in practice the problem is easy to solve. We just select 100 random values for the variable x and evalute both U and V at those 100 points: if they agree, we can assume with sort-of 100 % probability that U and V represent the same function. If there is a disagreement for some of the 100 x values, clearly U and V denote different functions. Although we have not yet been able to properly establish the probability that above method works it has worked so well in practice that we can indeed completely rely on it. We believe we will be able to show (with C. Calude and D. Stefanescu) that the probability can be made arbitrary small with only little effort.

Above example demonstrates an important issue: theoretical results may indicate that problems are very hard, and thus may stifle (by scaring) research on pragmatically acceptable solutions: this is true for a number of undecidable problems, but also for NP complete problems. For instance, the problem to determine an optimal route ("travelling salesman problem") is known to be NP-complete; yet very good approximations can be computed easily ....

3 Formalisms May Hide Intuition

The comparative linguist Lee Whorf has claimed most convincingly that "our language influences how we think". Although there is much truth in this observation it is worthwhile to point out that not all our thoughts are based on language: we indeed think also in terms of "mental imgry", hence the importance of new visual languages as alluded to in [Carlson 1992] and [Lennon 1994]. That conceptualisation is possible without words is actually best seen by considering animals: surely cats don't have a language, yet they are clearly able to "learn" and to "conceptualize"!

Nevertheless, without proper language ...including the language of mathematical formalisms ...many phenomena would still be ellusive. Following Lee Whorf's speculations, both the Chinese and the Italians knew about electricity in the sense of "jerking frog-legs" or "static electricity": yet, it was Luigi Galvani who had the right mathematical formalism to go from a qualitative observation of the phenomenon "electricity" to the quantitative study resulting (eventually) in electric generators, motors, transformers, etc.

Physics without the formalism of differential equations seems as unconceivable as chemistry without its formulae. Yet, for all the advantage of formulae they also have inherent dangers. To drive the point home, let me just explain one example.

We all know of Pythagoras theorem "$a^2 + b^2 = c^2$", reading "the sum of the areas of the squares of the shorter sides of a right-angled triangle is equal to the area of the square of the longest side of such triangle." We all understand this result ...or do we?

It was in the science museum in San Diego where I first realised to my dismay that, in a sense, I never had understood the theorem properly. There was a display with four sides. The first side contained a right angled triangle with three squares erected over its sides, the largest one filled with a red fluid. By turning the triangle, the fluid would flow into the two other squares, eventually filling them exactly, hence establishing "$a^2 + b^2 = c^2$". Great!

The second side of the display showed the same triangle, this time with equilatral triangles erected on top of the sides instead of the squares. Again, the largest was filled with red liquid and turning it, it filled exactly the two other triangles. The next two displays were similar, with the triangles replaced by semicircles and then by some weired X-mas tree-like shape...

Although as mathematician it is clear to me that "$a^2 + b^2 = c^2$" certainly implies also "$ta^2 + tb^2 = tc^2$" for any t (thus explainig the experiments with the equilateral triangles, the semicircles, or arbitrary shapes whose area would be proportional to the square of the length of the sides involved) the formulation of Pythagoras theorem had for ever and ever been associated in my brain with "squares" that the display came as genuine "revelation" ...and as proof how formalisms can hide the "true" intuitive meaning!!

Hence, whenever we teach formalisms, as necessary as this may be, we better make sure that the intuitive ideas hidden behind the formalisms do not get burried!

4 Learning may sometimes be detrimental!

Edgar Dijkstra, one of the "purist" in his approach to programming is well-known for essentially claiming that "any person learning programming by starting with BASIC or FORTRAN will never be a good programmer: such person will be spoilt for life."

Allan Kay has proven with his famous "tennis experiment" that learning a sport activity the wrong way will make it extremely hard to ever be good in that activity.

Both of above statements can be reduced to an experience we are all fairly familiar with: unlearning bad habits is very difficult!

In this sense most of us accept that learning the "right thing the right way" (whatever that may mean!) is indeed very important. However, it appears that the situation is still more complex than that. It seems that even the order in which the "right things" are learnt is essential, since knowledge acquired later may tend to hide knowledge that we have had before. The classical example comes from a test carried out by Allan Kay.

Kay used "Turtle Graphics" to ask persons of various age groups to solve the "circle problem". Surprisingly, performance decreased with increasing knowledge. Before explaining the "circle experiment" let us briefly review (a version of) Turtle Graphics, sufficient for our purposes.

Turtle Graphics is a simple programming language; it has the usual notion of variables, assignment-statements, conditionals, loops, and procedures and a few special commands for drawing "with a pen" on the screen. (The terminology "Turtle Graphics" comes from the fact that in one variant a small turtle-like robot actually moves around on a sheet of paper and leaves a trace if its pen is "down".)

The only special commands we will need for our explanations are:

go-startposition : this command places the pen at a designated point on the screen (e.g. center of screen) facing in a designated direction (e.g. to the right)

draw-point : draws a point in the current position of the pen

move-pen (n): moves the pen n points in the current direction; this draws n points if the pen is "down", else just repositions the pen

turn-pen (n): turns the direction of the pen *n* degrees counter-clockwise

lift-pen : lifts the pen up

put-down-pen : puts the pen down

Now we can turn our attention to the "circle experiment". In this experiment, groups of school-age children were asked to write a Turtle Graphic program that would draw an approximation of a circle.

All members of the youngest group solved the program easily, essentially writing something like the PROGRAM 1 below:

PROGRAM 1:

```
go-startposition;
put-down-pen;
for  i:  = 1  to 360  do
   begin
       move-pen(5);
       turn (1)
   end;
```

Thus, all members of this groups realised that a "circle has constant curvature" hence can be approximated by a polygon with 360 equally long sides, adjacent sides differing in direction by 1 degree.

The members of the second group were older and better trained in mathematics. All managed to solve the problem, some developing something similar to PROGRAM 1 above, others with more difficulty, eventually ending up with something like PROGRAM 2:

PROGRAM 2:

```
go-startposition;
lift-pen;
for  i:  = 1  to 360  do
   begin
       move-pen (100);
       put-down-pen;
       draw-point;
       lift-pen;
       turn (180);
       move-pen;
       turn (181)
   end;
```

PROGRAM 2 clearly draws an approximation of a circle with radius 100 using the concept that a "circle is the locus of all points with same distance from a center". PROGRAM 2 draws 360 points 100 units away from the startposition of the pen. Students using this approach seem to have "forgotten" the easier and more intuitive approach using constant curvature!

However, the worst is yet to come. The third test group with the oldest children (close to leaving high-school) who had had some training in algebra and analytic geometry did still much worse: only a few ended up with PROGRAM 1, some with PROGRAM 2 and some got so bogged down in the details of extracting square-roots that they never finished something akin to PROGRAM 3 (that would draw a semi-circle). Most members of the age-group wrote immediately:

$$x^2 + y^2 = r^2$$
$$x^2 + y^2 = 10000$$
$$y = \sqrt{10000 - x^2}$$

and now (for $x = 1, 2, \ldots, 100$) would go x steps to the right, then y steps up (drawing a point) and then $2y$ steps down (drawing a point) in compliance with above formulae.

PROGRAM 3:

```
for  x :  = 0  to  100  do
   begin
       y:= sqrt (10000 - x**2);
       go-startposition;
       lift-pen;
       move-pen (x);
       turn(90);
       move-pen (y);
       put-down-pen;
       draw-point;
       lift-pen;
       turn (180);
       move-pen (2*y);
       put-down-pen;
       draw-point
   end;
```

Thus, members of the oldest group used all the formalism they had learned rather than simpler notions available to them: intuitive rather than formal understanding may "buy" more natural approaches, a fact that we should continuously be aware of!

References

[Bell 1990]   Bell, T.C., Cleary, J.G., Witten, I.H.: Text Compression; Prentice Hall, Engelwood Cliffs (1990).

[Barnsley 1988] Barnsley, M.F.: Fractals Everywhere; Academic Press, New York (1988).

[Calude 1994]   Calude, C., Maurer, H., Salomaa, A.: JUCS - the Journal of Universal Computer Science; Report, Department of Computer Science, University of Auckland (1994); submitted for publication elsewhere.

[Carlson 1992]   Carlson, P., Maurer, H.: Computer Visualization, a Missing Organ and a Cyber-Equivalency; Collegiate Microcomputers 10, 2 (1992), 110-116.

[Caviness 1970] Caviness, B.F.: On Canonical Forms and Simplification; J.ACM 17, (1970), 385-396.

[Culik II 1993] Culik II, K., Kari, J.: Image Compression Using Weighted Finite Automata; Computer and Graphics 17,3 (1993), 305-313.

[Gillard 1990]   Gillard, P., Maurer, H., Stone, M.G., Stubenrauch, R.: Automatic Problem Generation Does Not Work; Proc. 6th Symposium Did. Mathematik, Klagenfurt/Austria (1990), 191-197.

[Huber 1989]   Huber, F., Makedon, F., Maurer, H.: HyperCOSTOC - a Comprehensive Computer-Based Teaching Support System J.MCA 12 (1989), 293-317.

[Kuich 1986]   Kuich, W., Salomaa, A.: Semirings, Automata, Languages; EATCS Monographs 5, Springer Pub.Co, Heidelberg/New York (1986).

[Lennon 1994]   Lennon, J., Maurer, H.: MUSLI - A MUlti-Sensory Language Interface; Proc. ED-MEDIA' 94, Vancouver, Canada (1994).

[Ottmann 1993]   Ottmann, Th., Widmayer, P.: Algorithmen und Datenstrukturen; Reihe Informatik 70, BI Mannheim (1993).

[Richardson 1968] Richardson, D.: Some Unsolvable Problems Involving Elementary Functions of a Real Variable; J. Symbolic Logic 33 (1968), 514-520.

[Salomaa 1980]   Salomaa, A., Rozenberg, G.: The Mathematical Theory of L Systems; Academic Press, London (1980).

[Salomaa 1988]   Salomaa, A.: Computation and Automata; COSTOC Computer Collection, vol. 5 (1988).

[Salomaa 1989]   Salomaa, A.: Cryptography and Data Security; COSTOC Computer Collection, vol. 32 (1989).

[Salomaa 1990]   Salomaa, A.: Public-Key Cryptography; EATCS Monography 23, Springer Pub.Co, Heidelberg/New York (1990).

[Wang 1974]   Wang, P.S.: The Undecidability of the Existence of Zeros of Real Elementary Functions, J.ACM 21, 4 (1974), 586-589.

Bisimulation, Games, and Logic

Mogens Nielsen and Christian Clausen

BRICS**
Computer Science Department
Aarhus University
Ny Munkegade
DK–8000 Aarhus C, Denmark

Abstract. In a recent paper by Joyal, Nielsen, and Winskel, bisimulation is defined in an abstract and uniform way across a wide range of different models for concurrency. In this paper, following a recent trend in theoretical computer science, we characterize their abstract definition game-theoretically and logically in a non-interleaving model. Our characterizations appear as surprisingly simple extensions of corresponding characterizations of interleaving bisimulation.

1 Introduction

An important ingredient of the theory of concurrency is the notion of *behavioral equivalence* between processes; what does it mean for two systems to be equal with respect to their communication structures? There is no unique answer to this question, but, undoubtedly, one of the most popular and successful answers was given by Park [Par81]: Two processes (or states s and s' of two transition systems) are equivalent, or *bisimilar*, if for all actions a, every a-derivative of s is bisimilar to some a-derivative of s', and vice versa.

One of the measures of success for a behaviour equivalence is its accompanying *theory*. And here bisimulation is particularly rich in results. Let us mention just three examples of elegant and powerful characterizations.

The first classical characterization is in terms of the existence of a bisimulation relation over states of the associated transition systems: Two transition systems are *bisimilar* iff there is a relation S over states such that the initial states are related, and

- whenever $s \, S \, s'$ and $s \xrightarrow{a} s_1$, there is a transition $s' \xrightarrow{a} s'_1$ such that $s_1 \, S \, s'_1$, and
- whenever $s \, S \, s'$ and $s' \xrightarrow{a} s'_1$, there is a transition $s \xrightarrow{a} s_1$ such that $s_1 \, S \, s'_1$.

The process of exploring whether two transition systems are bisimilar or not can be viewed as a *game* between two persons, Player and Opponent, taking turns [Sti93]. This provides an operational setting in which bisimulation may be

---

** Basic Research In Computer Science,
Centre of the Danish National Research Foundation.

understood experimentally. Player tries to prove the systems bisimilar, whereas Opponent intends otherwise. The game is opened by Opponent who chooses a transition from the initial state of one of the systems. This transition must be matched by Player with an equally labelled transition from the initial state of the other system. The new states form the starting point for the next pair of moves, and so forth. The play continues like this *forever*, in which case Player wins, or until either Player or Opponent is unable to move, in which case the opposition wins. This game is *characteristic* for bisimulation in the sense that two transition systems are bisimilar iff Player has a *winning strategy*, i.e. iff Player is able to win every game starting from the initial states.

Another important ingredient of the theory is the associated language of logical assertions. The logic, known as *Hennessy-Milner logic* [HM85] , is a modal logic in which the modalities are indexed by actions. As such, it captures precisely the discrimination power of bisimulation: Two systems are bisimilar iff they satisfy the same logical assertions. For verification and analysis, the Hennessy-Milner logic is most interesting in conjunction with *recursion*. In such logic, it is possible to express properties like deadlocks, invariants, inevitability, etc. [Sti93]. Also this very expressive logic is characteristic for bisimulation.

In the transition system model of CCS and CSP, parallelism is treated as *non-deterministic interleaving* of atomic actions. As a result, the CCS-processes $a \parallel b$, which can do the atomic actions a and b in parallel, is bisimilar to the process $a.b + b.a$, which non-deterministically chooses to do either "a *followed by* b" or "b *followed by* a". In fact, the associated transition systems are isomorphic. Abstracting away from the names of the states, both transition systems are represented by the system of Fig. 1. Due to this identification, the transition system

Fig. 1. A transition system representing both $a \parallel b$ and $a.b + b.a$.

model is usually called an *interleaving model*, and bisimulation is traditionally called *interleaving bisimulation* when confusion is possible.

Interpreted at the machine level, non-deterministic interleaving corresponds to parallel processes sharing a single CPU. Opposed to this, Petri nets [WN94] model the *physical disjointness* of parallel processes. The processes $a \parallel b$ and $a.b + b.a$ are represented by the labelled nets of Fig. 1 [Old91].

The leftmost net consists of two independent events labelled a and b, whereas the rightmost net is a purely (nondeterministic) sequential net.

Many other closely related *non-interleaving* models have been suggested, e.g. the *asynchronous transition systems* of [Bed88, Shi85] and the *transitions systems with independence* of [WN94].

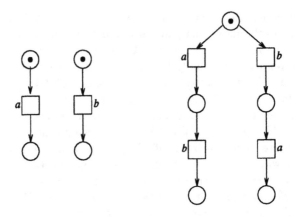

Fig. 2. Labelled Petri nets representing $a \parallel b$ and $a.b + b.a$.

What is now the appropriate generalization of bisimulation to these "independence models"? Many attempts have been made to answer this question. Unfortunately, with almost just as many different answers. Moreover, many of the proposed equivalences are incomparable. (See [GG89] and [GKP92] for definitions and comparisons of some of them.)

Apparently, the problem is that the step from interleaving models to independence models opens up for variations when trying to define an equivalence at the concrete level. [JNW93] reports on a promising attempt to define bisimulation in a *uniform* way across a wide range of different models for concurrent computation, including those described previously. However, the abstract definition is intangible. In order to obtain a better understanding of the equivalence, it is necessary to find concrete characterizations, which are indispensable for practical purposes. As a first measure of success, it is observed in [JNW93] that the abstract definition specializes to interleaving bisimulation in the case of ordinary transition systems.

In the context of an independence model, we shall denote the abstract equivalence by **Pom**$_L$-*bisimilarity*. The thoughts behind this choice of name will become clear later. In [JNW93], a concrete characterization of **Pom**$_L$-bisimilarity is given in the model of *event structures*, which may be thought of as *unfoldings* of nets or transition systems with independence. Interestingly, their characterization is not equal to any previously published equivalence; in fact, it is a strengthening of the history-preserving bisimulation [GG89, RT88].

In this paper, we give concrete characterizations of **Pom**$_L$-bisimilarity in the model of transition systems with independence. As a matter of fact, our choice of model is not essential, in the sense that our results could equally have been formulated and proved for nets or asynchronous transition systems.

It turns out that surprisingly small twists of the game [Sti93] and relation [Mil89] characterizations of interleaving bisimulation lead to characterizations of **Pom**$_L$-bisimilarity. On the logical side, the Hennessy-Milner logic is extended with a backwards modality. The logic is characteristic for **Pom**$_L$-bisimilarity, when restricted to systems without *auto-concurrency*, i.e. to systems where no two consecutive and independent transitions are equally labelled. This restriction is necessary and has to do with the fact that our logic is based on *labels*. By strengthening the language of logical assertions, we can eliminate this restriction.

We present here our results without detailed proofs, for which we refer to [NC94].

2 An Abstract Equivalence

In [JNW93], a uniform definition of bisimulation across a range of different models for parallel computation is presented. The aim of this section is to rephrase briefly parts of this work.

A model of computation is represented as a category. For a specific model, **M**, a choice of observation is any subcategory **P** of **M**. Typically, a choice of observation is a selection of "observation objects" of **M**, and **P** is then the corresponding full subcategory.

Given a model **M** and a choice of observation **P**, where **P** is a subcategory of **M**, a morphism $f : X \to Y$ is said to be **P**-*open* in **M** iff whenever a square

$$
\begin{array}{ccc}
P & \xrightarrow{\ p\ } & X \\
\scriptstyle m \downarrow & & \downarrow \scriptstyle f \\
Q & \xrightarrow[\ q\ ]{} & Y
\end{array}
$$

commutes, i.e. $f \circ p = q \circ m$, there is a morphism $p' : Q \to X$ such that the "triangles" in

$$
\begin{array}{ccc}
P & \xrightarrow{\ p\ } & X \\
\scriptstyle m \downarrow & \nearrow \scriptstyle p' & \downarrow \scriptstyle f \\
Q & \xrightarrow[\ q\ ]{} & Y
\end{array}
$$

commute, i.e. $p' \circ m = p$ and $f \circ p' = q$.

In the familiar example of **M** being a category of transition systems and **P** being sequences of labels (see [JNW93] for details), it turns out that open maps correspond to the well-known zig-zag morphisms of [Ben84].

Definition 1. Assume **P** is a subcategory of **M** and define two objects X and X' of **M** to be **P**-*bisimilar* iff there is a span of **P**-open morphisms f and f' with common domain Y:

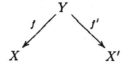

□

Using that pullbacks of **P**-open maps are themselves **P**-open, it can be shown that **P**-bisimilarity is an equivalence relation provided that **M** *has* pullbacks.

The category of transition systems turns out to have pullbacks, and the notion of **P**-bisimilarity (**P** again being sequences of labels) turns out to coincide precisely with (strong) bisimilarity in the sense of [Mil89].

The interesting question is what you get when you lift this abstract characterization to non-interleaving models. One choice of model made in [JNW93] is transition systems with independence. Transition systems with independence are precisely what their name suggests, namely ordinary transition systems with an additional relation expressing when one transition is independent of another. The independence relation expresses which actions can happen in parallel.

Definition 2. A *transition system with independence* is a structure

$$X = (S, i, L, Tran, I)$$

where

- S is a set of *states* with a distinguished *initial state* i,
- L is a set of *labels*,
- $Tran \subseteq S \times L \times S$ is a set of *transitions*[3], and
- $I \subseteq Tran^2$ is an *independence relation* which is irreflexive and symmetric.

Moreover, we require the following axioms to hold:

1. $s \xrightarrow{a} s_1 \sim s \xrightarrow{a} s_2 \Rightarrow s_1 = s_2$
2. $s \xrightarrow{a} s_1 \ I \ s_1 \xrightarrow{b} u \Rightarrow \exists s_2. \ s \xrightarrow{a} s_1 \ I \ s \xrightarrow{b} s_2 \ I \ s_2 \xrightarrow{a} u$
3. (a) $s \xrightarrow{a} s_1 \prec s_2 \xrightarrow{a} u \ I \ w \xrightarrow{b} w' \Rightarrow s \xrightarrow{a} s_1 \ I \ w \xrightarrow{b} w'$
   (b) $w \xrightarrow{b} w' \ I \ s \xrightarrow{a} s_1 \prec s_2 \xrightarrow{a} u \Rightarrow w \xrightarrow{b} w' \ I \ s_2 \xrightarrow{a} u$

where the relation $\prec$ between transitions is defined by

$$s \xrightarrow{a} s_1 \prec s_2 \xrightarrow{a} u \Leftrightarrow \exists b. \ s_1 \xrightarrow{b} u \ I \ s \xrightarrow{a} s_1 \ I \ s \xrightarrow{b} s_2 \ I \ s_2 \xrightarrow{a} u,$$

and $\sim$ is the least equivalence relation including $\prec$. $\qquad \square$

The $\sim$-equivalence classes should be thought of as *events*. Thus, Axiom 1 asserts that the occurrence of an event at a state yields a unique state. Similarly, Axiom 3 asserts that independence respects events. Axiom 2 describes the intuitive property of independence that whenever two independent transitions occur consecutively, they can also occur in the opposite order. Hence, if $s \xrightarrow{a} s_1 \xrightarrow{b} u$ are independent transitions there is an "independence square"

---

[3] As usual, a transition $(s, a, s_1) \in Tran$ is written as $s \xrightarrow{a} s_1$.

Moreover, Axiom 1 implies the uniqueness of s_2. So we are justified in saying that s_2 (or $s \xrightarrow{b} s_2 \xrightarrow{a} u$) is *the* completion of $s \xrightarrow{a} s_1 \xrightarrow{b} u$.

Notice that an ordinary labelled transition system can be viewed as a transition system with independence having empty independence relation. Furthermore, the standard labelled case graph of a labelled (safe) net, with two transitions being independent iff they represent firings of independent (in net terminology) events, is a transition system with independence [WN94]. As an example the transition system with independence above is the representation of the CCS-expression $a \parallel b$ or its corresponding net from 1 (following [WN94]).

For later use, we introduce some terminology. For a transition $t = (s \xrightarrow{a} s_1)$ we shall write $src(t)$, $tgt(t)$, and $\ell(t)$ for s, s_1, and a, respectively. The set $Seqs(X)$ consists of those transition sequences $\bar{t} = t_0 t_1 \cdots t_{n-1}$ in X beginning at the initial state ($src(t_0) = i$) which are consecutive ($src(t_{i+1}) = tgt(t_i)$). Transition sequences are always indexed from zero. We write $(\bar{t})_i$ or simply t_i for the i'th transition in $\bar{t}$. The length of $\bar{t}$ is referred to as $|\bar{t}|$. When nothing else is stated, a transition system with independence X is assumed to have components S, i, L, $Tran$, and I.

The category **TI** has transition systems with independence as objects. For the remaining part of this paper we fix a set L and restrict ourselves to those transition systems with independence that have labelling set L. As morphisms in the category $\mathbf{TI}_L$ we choose the fiber-morphisms of [WN94]:

Definition 3. Let $X = (S, i, L, Tran, I)$ and $X' = (S', i', L', Tran', I')$ be transition systems with independence. A *morphism* f from X to X' is a function $f : S \to S'$ such that

- $f(i) = i'$
- for all transitions $s \xrightarrow{a} s_1$ in X, $f(s) \xrightarrow{a} f(s')$ in X'
- $s \xrightarrow{a} s_1 \; I \; u \xrightarrow{b} u_1$ in X implies $f(s) \xrightarrow{a} f(s_1) \; I' \; f(u) \xrightarrow{b} f(u_1)$ in X' □

As observations is is naturally to take Pratt's pomsets [Pra86]. We identify the category $\mathbf{Pom}_L$ of pomsets with its full and faithful embedding in $\mathbf{TI}_L$ (for details see [JNW93]). The category $\mathbf{TI}_L$ has pullbacks, so $\mathbf{Pom}_L$-bisimilarity is an equivalence relation in $\mathbf{TI}_L$. The following proposition characterizes $\mathbf{Pom}_L$-open morphisms in $\mathbf{TI}_L$ [JNW93].

Proposition 4. *A morphism $f : Y \to X$ in $\mathbf{TI}_L$ is $\mathbf{Pom}_L$-open iff it is zig-zag and reflects consecutive independence, i.e. iff it has the following properties:*

- *whenever r is reachable and $f(r) \xrightarrow{a} s_1$ there is a state r_1 in Y such that $r \xrightarrow{a} r_1$ & $f(r_1) = s_1$, and*
- *whenever r is reachable, $r \xrightarrow{a} r_1$ and $r_1 \xrightarrow{b} r_2$ are transitions in Y, and*

$$f(r) \xrightarrow{a} f(r_1) \; I \; f(r_1) \xrightarrow{b} f(r_2),$$

we also have $r \xrightarrow{a} r_1 \; I \; r_1 \xrightarrow{b} r_2$.

On event structures [JNW93] **Pom**$_L$-bisimilarity turns out to be a slight strengthening of the history-preserving bisimilarity originally defined in [GG89, RT88]. In fact, the same strengthening has been studied in [Bed91] in which the equivalence is denoted *hereditary* history-preserving bisimilarity. The strengthening is illustrated by the following event structures, here identified with their embeddings in **TI**$_L$.

Example 1. Consider the following "event structures":

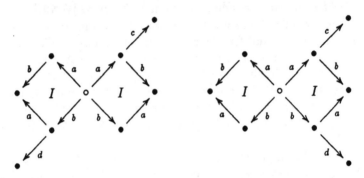

The circles indicate the initial states. These "event structures" are history-preserving bisimilar but *not* hereditary history-preserving bisimilar.   ☐

One result on **Pom**$_L$-bisimilarity for **TI**$_L$ mentioned in [JNW93] is the fact that two **TI**$_L$-objects are **Pom**$_L$-bisimilar iff their unfolded event structures are **Pom**$_L$-bisimilar. The natural question is now: Does **Pom**$_L$-bisimilarity for **TI**$_L$ have characterizations in the spirit of e.g. the relational, game-theoretical, and logical characterizations of bisimulation for standard transition systems? This question is answered positively in the next sections.

3 Game Characterizations

Following a new trend in the area of program semantics, we first present a game-theoretical characterization of **Pom**$_L$-bisimilarity. The game defined can be viewed as a "backtracking" extension of Stirling's game [Sti93]. We then show that the equivalence induced by the backtracking game can be characterized by the existence of a bisimulation relation over paths, satisfying a certain "backtracking property".

3.1 Basic Definitions

The following definitions are inspired by [AJ92].
    A *game* is a structure $\Gamma = (C, c_0, \triangleright, \lambda, W)$ where

   − C is a set of *configurations* with a distinguished *initial configuration* c_0,

- $\triangleright \subseteq C^2$ is a set of *moves*. Formally, a *play* of Γ is a (possibly infinite) sequence of moves

$$c_0 \cdot c_1 \cdot c_2 \cdot \ldots,$$

such that $c_0 \triangleright c_1 \triangleright c_2 \triangleright \cdots$. The set $Pos(\Gamma)$ of *positions* consists of all finite plays. The meta-variable p ranges over positions.
- $\lambda : Pos(\Gamma) \to \{O, P\}$ is a function indicating whose *turn* it is to move in a given *position* (an element of $Pos(\Gamma)$, defined below) of a play, and
- $W \subseteq Pos(\Gamma)$ is a set of *winning positions*.

We require all plays to be *alternating*, i.e. we require $\triangleright$ and λ together to satisfy that if $\lambda(p \cdot c) = Q$ and $c \triangleright c'$ then $\lambda(p \cdot c \cdot c') = \overline{Q}$, where $\overline{P} = O$ and $\overline{O} = P$. Furthermore, Opponent should start every play. This is expressed by demanding $\lambda(c_0) = O$.

In defining when a game is won we take Player's point of view: A *play p is won (by P)* if one of the following conditions hold:

- p is infinite,
- p is finite and $\lambda(p) = O$, or
- $p \in W$.

If p is not won, it is *lost*.

A *strategy* is a partial function $\sigma : Pos(\Gamma) \to C$ such that

$$\sigma(p \cdot c) = c' \text{ implies } c \triangleright c'.$$

We reserve the words strategy for Player and *counter-strategy* for Opponent and use σ and τ to range over strategies and counter-strategies, respectively. Player is said to *follow her strategy* σ in a play $c_0 \cdot c_1 \cdot \ldots \cdot c_n \cdot c_{n+1} \cdots$ iff $\lambda(c_0 \cdot c_1 \cdot \ldots \cdot c_n) = P$ implies $c_{n+1} = \sigma(c_0 \cdot c_1 \cdot \ldots \cdot c_n)$. Similarly, we can define when Opponent follows his strategy.

The intuition behind W is the following. As soon as Player can force Opponent to a position $p \in W$, she has won p and all extensions of p. We reflect this intuition by demanding that W is closed under $\triangleright$, i.e. that $p \cdot c \in W$ whenever $p \in W$. To avoid a play $p \in W$ to continue forever, we require all strategies to be undefined on winning positions, i.e. $\sigma(p)$ is undefined whenever $p \in W$.

The set $Plays(\sigma, \tau)$ of plays in which both Player and Opponent follow their strategies is easily seen to be prefix-closed. This leads to the following definition of *the play of a strategy σ against a counter-strategy τ*:

$$\langle \sigma | \tau \rangle = \bigsqcup \{p \mid p \in Plays(\sigma, \tau)\},$$

where the least upper bound refers to the prefix-ordering. Finally, σ is said to be a *winning strategy* iff $\langle \sigma | \tau \rangle$ is won for any counter-strategy τ. Similarly, we define τ to be a *winning counter-strategy* iff $\langle \sigma | \tau \rangle$ is lost for any σ.

Any game of the above kind possesses the nice property that there can be no ties, and hence there is either a winning strategy or a winning counter-strategy.

Proposition 5. *For any game, there is a winning strategy iff there is no winning counter-strategy.*

Proof. See [NC94]. □

3.2 A Characteristic Game for Interleaving Bisimulation

The first game considered is a "sequence variant" of the game defined by Stirling [Sti93]. Given two ordinary transition systems X and X' we take as configurations (ordered) pairs of *transition sequences* with the pair consisting of empty sequences as initial configuration. Informally, a play progresses as follows. Opponent starts out by first choosing either X or X' and then a transition from the initial state of the system chosen. If Player can't match the move with an equally labelled transition from the initial state of the other system, she loses. Otherwise, she chooses such a matching transition, and it's again Opponent's turn to move. He chooses a system, not necessarily the same as before, and a transition of that system leading out of the state arrived at in the previous pairs of moves. Again, Player is required to match with an equally labelled transition in the other system. The play continues like this *forever*, in which case Player wins, or until either Player or Opponent is *stuck* (unable to move), in which case the other participant wins.

The above description is now formalized to fit the basic definitions of games. We define the *interleaving game* between transition systems X and X' to be $\Gamma(X, X') = (C, c_0, \rhd, \lambda, W)$ where

- $C = Seqs(X) \times Seqs(X')$. As a convention, writing configurations $(\bar{t}, \bar{t}')$, $(\bar{t}t, \bar{t}')$, and $(\bar{t}, \bar{t}'t')$ implicitly means that $|\bar{t}| = |\bar{t}'|$.
- $c_0 = (\varepsilon, \varepsilon)$.
- $\lambda : Pos(\Gamma(X, X')) \to \{O, P\}$ is defined by taking

$$\lambda(\bar{t}, \bar{t}') = O \quad \text{and} \quad \lambda(\bar{t}t, \bar{t}') = \lambda(\bar{t}, \bar{t}'t') = P.$$

- $W = \emptyset$.
- $\rhd \subseteq C^2$ is defined by the rules

$$
\begin{array}{lll}
(\bar{t}, \bar{t}') \rhd (\bar{t}t, \bar{t}') & \text{if } \bar{t}t \in Seqs(X) \\
(\bar{t}, \bar{t}') \rhd (\bar{t}, \bar{t}'t') & \text{if } \bar{t}'t' \in Seqs(X') \\
(\bar{t}t, \bar{t}') \rhd (\bar{t}t, \bar{t}'t') & \text{if } \bar{t}'t' \in Seqs(X') \ \& \ \ell(t') = \ell(t) \\
(\bar{t}, \bar{t}'t') \rhd (\bar{t}t, \bar{t}'t') & \text{if } \bar{t}t \in Seqs(X) \ \& \ \ell(t) = \ell(t')
\end{array}
$$

Just like Stirling's game, the game $\Gamma(X, X')$ is *characteristic* for interleaving bisimulation in the following sense.

Theorem 6. *Two transition systems X and X' are bisimilar iff Player has a winning strategy in $\Gamma(X, X')$.*

Proof. Small modifications of the reasoning of Stirling [Sti93]. $\square$

The game presented above has the property that if X and X' exhibit infinite behaviour, then there exist infinite plays, even if both systems are finite state. For some purposes this property is undesirable, and can indeed can be eliminated by choosing the set W of winning positions appropriately. To be concrete, we might in $\Gamma(X, X')$ have chosen W to consist of those positions p which are duplicate-free in the sense that no two configurations $(\bar{t}, \bar{t}'), (\bar{r}, \bar{r}')$ in p have $tgt(\bar{t}) = tgt(\bar{r})$

and $tgt(\bar{t}') = tgt(\bar{r}')$. By the pigeonhole principle this modification of $\Gamma(X, X')$ would bound the length of any play by $2 \cdot |S| \cdot |S'| + 1$ where $|S|$ and $|S'|$ are the number of states in X and X', respectively. Furthermore, it is quite easy to see that the characterization result also holds for the modified game.

3.3   Allowing Opponent to Backtrack

Throughout this paper we shall take "backtrack" to mean *trace backwards* within *the present observation*.

With this interpretation, backtracking in an ordinary transition system means to trace backwards *along* the transition sequence observed. In terms of games, we can express this by allowing Opponent to do backwards moves like

$$(\bar{t}t, \bar{t}'t') \rhd (B, \bar{t}, \bar{t}'t'),$$

where the B is a directive to Player to play backwards on the longer of the sequences. Player must match with the move

$$(B, \bar{t}, \bar{t}'t') \rhd (\bar{t}, \bar{t}').$$

It is easy to see that these additional rules do *not* give Opponent more opportunities to beat Player, nor the other way around.

Proposition 7. *Two transition systems are bisimilar iff Player has a winning strategy in their associated game with backtracking.*

Backtracking in an independence model is much more interesting. Consider a simple transition system with independence X

consisting of a single independence square. Since $i\xrightarrow{a}s_1$ and $s_1\xrightarrow{b}u$ are independent, the sequence $\bar{t} = i\xrightarrow{a}s_1\xrightarrow{b}u$ in X represents the observation "a and b in parallel". Another representative of this observation is the sequence $i\xrightarrow{b}s_2\xrightarrow{a}u$, so this gives us two ways to backtrack within $\bar{t}$: Either along $s_1\xrightarrow{b}u$, leaving behind the sequence $i\xrightarrow{a}s_1$, or along $s_2\xrightarrow{a}u$ leaving behind the sequence $i\xrightarrow{b}s_2$.

In terms of the net representation of $a \parallel b$ from Section 1 this amounts to the following: After firing the a-transition followed by the b-transition you may naturally backtrack on the a-transition, since the firing of the b-transition has in no way affected the post-conditions of the a-transition.

In the above example the event represented by $i\xrightarrow{a}s_1$ has an occurrence – namely $s_2\xrightarrow{a}u$ – ending in u. We say that $i\xrightarrow{a}s_1$ is *backwards enabled* in the sequence $i\xrightarrow{a}s_1\xrightarrow{b}u$. In general, a transition t_i of a sequence $\bar{t}$ is said to be backwards enabled iff it by repeated use of Axiom 2 of Definition 2 can be "pushed to last position in $\bar{t}$." By Axiom 3, this is equivalent to requiring t_i to be independent of all transitions t_j in $\bar{t}$ with $j > i$. This leads to the following formal definition.

Definition 8. For $\bar{t} = t_0 \cdots t_{n-1}$, a sequence in a transition system with independence X, and $i \in \{0, \ldots, n-1\}$, we define

$$t_i \in BEn(\bar{t}) \text{ iff } \forall j \in \{i+1, \ldots, n-1\}. t_j \ I \ t_i,$$

where I is the independence relation in X. If $t_i \in BEn(\bar{t})$ we define $\delta(i, \bar{t})$ to be the result of deleting the event corresponding to t_i, i.e.

$$\delta(i, \bar{t}) = t_0 \cdots t_{i-1} s_{i+1} \cdots s_{n-1},$$

where $s_{i+1} \prec t_{i+1}, \ldots, s_{n-1} \prec t_{n-1}$ as in the following figure in which the squares are the unique completions defined in Section 2.

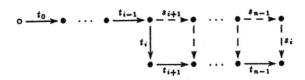

□

The backtracking game on transition systems with independence is a simple extension of the previously defined (forward) game. By introducing rules like

$$(\bar{t}, \bar{t}') \triangleright (i, \delta(i, \bar{t}), \bar{t}') \text{ if } t_i \in BEn(\bar{t})$$

we allow Opponent to backtrack on transitions which are backwards enabled. The index i is a request to Player to play backwards on the i'th transition of the longer of the sequences. So the only way Player can respond to such moves is to use the rule

$$(i, \delta(i, \bar{t}), \bar{t}') \triangleright (\delta(i, \bar{t}), \delta(i, \bar{t}')) \text{ if } t'_i \in BEn(\bar{t}'),$$

provided, of course, that t'_i is backwards enabled in $\bar{t}'$. Formally, we define the backtracking game $\Gamma(X, X')$ on transition systems with independence X and X' to be the structure $(C, c_0, \triangleright, \lambda, W)$:

- $C = \omega \times Seqs(X) \times Seqs(X') \cup Seqs(X) \times Seqs(X')$. Conventionally, writing configurations $(i, \delta(i, \bar{t}), \bar{t}')$ and $(i, \bar{t}, \delta(i, \bar{t}'))$ implicitly means that $|\bar{t}| = |\bar{t}'|$.
- $c_0 = (\varepsilon, \varepsilon)$.
- $\lambda : Pos(\Gamma(X, X')) \to \{O, P\}$ is defined by taking $\lambda(\bar{t}, \bar{t}') = O$ and $\lambda(\bar{t}t, \bar{t}') = \lambda(\bar{t}, \bar{t}'t') = \lambda(i, \delta(i, \bar{t}), \bar{t}') = \lambda(i, \bar{t}, \delta(i, \bar{t}')) = P$.
- $W = \emptyset$.

- $\triangleright \subseteq C^2$ is defined by the following rules:

$$
\begin{array}{ll}
(\bar{t}, \bar{t}') \triangleright (\bar{t}t, \bar{t}') & \text{if } \bar{t}t \in Seqs(X) \\
(\bar{t}, \bar{t}') \triangleright (\bar{t}, \bar{t}'t') & \text{if } \bar{t}'t' \in Seqs(X') \\
(\bar{t}t, \bar{t}') \triangleright (\bar{t}t, \bar{t}'t') & \text{if } \bar{t}'t' \in Seqs(X') \ \& \ \ell(t') = \ell(t) \\
(\bar{t}, \bar{t}'t') \triangleright (\bar{t}t, \bar{t}'t') & \text{if } \bar{t}t \in Seqs(X) \ \& \ \ell(t) = \ell(t')
\end{array}
$$

$$
\begin{array}{ll}
(\bar{t}, \bar{t}') \triangleright (i, \delta(i, \bar{t}), \bar{t}') & \text{if } t_i \in BEn(\bar{t}) \\
(\bar{t}, \bar{t}') \triangleright (i, \bar{t}, \delta(i, \bar{t}')) & \text{if } t_i' \in BEn(\bar{t}') \\
(i, \delta(i, \bar{t}), \bar{t}') \triangleright (\delta(i, \bar{t}), \delta(i, \bar{t}')) & \text{if } t_i' \in BEn(\bar{t}') \\
(i, \bar{t}, \delta(i, \bar{t}')) \triangleright (\delta(i, \bar{t}), \delta(i, \bar{t}')) & \text{if } t_i \in BEn(\bar{t})
\end{array}
$$

Definition 9. Two transition systems with independence X and X' are Γ-*equivalent* iff Player has a winning strategy in $\Gamma(X, X')$. $\square$

With a simple example we will now illustrate how backtracking distinguishes parallelism from non-deterministic interleaving.

Example 2. Consider the transition systems with independence representing the CCS-processes $a \parallel b$ and $a.b + b.a$:

These systems are interleaving bisimilar but *not* Γ-equivalent, as we are able to define a winning counter-strategy τ as follows (here, p ranges over all appropriate positions):

$$
\tau(\varepsilon, \varepsilon) = (i \xrightarrow{a} s_1, \varepsilon)
$$
$$
\tau(p \cdot (i \xrightarrow{a} s_1, i' \xrightarrow{a} s_1')) = (i \xrightarrow{a} s_1 \xrightarrow{b} u, i' \xrightarrow{a} s_1')
$$
$$
\tau(p \cdot (i \xrightarrow{a} s_1 \xrightarrow{b} u, i' \xrightarrow{a} s_1' \xrightarrow{b} u')) = (0, i \xrightarrow{b} s_2, i' \xrightarrow{a} s_1' \xrightarrow{b} u')
$$

The point is, of course, that Player is unable to backtrack on index 0 in the sequence $i' \xrightarrow{a} s_1' \xrightarrow{b} u'$, as these transitions are dependent. $\square$

Distinguishing the transition systems with independence of Example 2 is, in fact, a minimum demand on any reasonable generalization of bisimulation to independence models. And following the reasoning of Example 2, the reader should not be surprised that backtracking may be used by Opponent to detect the partial order structures of configurations. However, it is more surprising that Γ-equivalence coincides exactly with the abstractly derived **Pom$_L$**-bisimilarity of Section 2. As a more interesting example, the reader may check that Opponent has a winning counter-strategy in the game associated with the systems of Example 1.

Before formulating and proving this it is convenient to introduce our relational characterization of **Pom$_L$**-bisimilarity.

Definition 10. A relation $T \in Seqs(X) \times Seqs(X')$ is a δ-*bisimulation* between X and X' iff it satisfies the following axioms:

$\mathbf{A_{init}}$: $\varepsilon \, T \, \varepsilon$

$\mathbf{A_{bisim}}$:

    1. $\bar{\iota} \, T \, \bar{\iota'}$ & $\bar{\iota}t \in Seqs(X) \Rightarrow \exists t'. (\ell'(t') = \ell(t)$ & $\bar{\iota}t \, T \, \bar{\iota'}t')$

    2. $\bar{\iota} \, T \, \bar{\iota'}$ & $\bar{\iota'}t' \in Seqs(X') \Rightarrow \exists t. (\ell(t) = \ell'(t')$ & $\bar{\iota}t \, T \, \bar{\iota'}t')$

$\mathbf{A_\delta}$: $\bar{\iota} \, T \, \bar{\iota'} \Rightarrow ((t_i \in BEn(\bar{\iota}) \Leftrightarrow t'_i \in BEn(\bar{\iota'}))$ & $(t_i \in BEn(\bar{\iota}) \Rightarrow \delta(i, \bar{\iota}) \, T \, \delta(i, \bar{\iota'})))$

We define X and X' to be δ-*bisimilar* iff there exists a δ-bisimulation between them. $\square$

The axiom $\mathbf{A_{bisim}}$ is the usual "bisimulation axiom", here formulated on sequences rather than states. So this formulation is also a simple extension of a well-known concept.

Theorem 11. δ-*equivalence coincides with* $\mathbf{Pom}_L$-*bisimilarity.*

Proof. Suppose X and X' are $\mathbf{Pom}_L$-bisimilar. Then there is a transition system with independence Y and a span of $\mathbf{Pom}_L$-open maps:

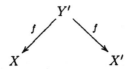

Using the obvious extensions of f and f' to sequences, we now define a relation $T \subseteq Seqs(X) \times Seqs(X')$ by

$$T = \{(f(\bar{r}), f'(\bar{r})) \mid \bar{r} \in Seqs(Y)\}.$$

It is straightforward to show that T is a δ-bisimulation.

The other direction is more involved. The proof hinges on the fact that backtracking, here represented by the axiom $\mathbf{A_\delta}$, is strong enough to enforce *isomorphism*: Whenever sequences $\bar{\iota}$ and $\bar{\iota'}$ are related by a δ-bisimulation, they represent isomorphic pomsets. Suppose now that X and X' are δ-bisimilar and let T be a witnessing δ-bisimulation. We can then define a transition system with independence Y with states those pomsets corresponding to pairs $(\bar{\iota}, \bar{\iota'})$ of T. To any state of Y, i.e. a pomset corresponding to a pair $(\bar{\iota}, \bar{\iota'})$, we associate $f(\bar{\iota}, \bar{\iota'}) = tgt(\bar{\iota})$ and $f'(\bar{\iota}, \bar{\iota'}) = tgt(\bar{\iota'})$. It can be shown that this defines $\mathbf{Pom}_L$-open morphisms $f : Y \to X$ and $f' : Y \to X'$. See [NC94] for details. $\square$

Theorem 12. Γ-*equivalence coincides with* $\mathbf{Pom}_L$-*bisimilarity.*

Proof. We prove that Γ-equivalence coincides with δ-bisimilarity. The result then follows from Theorem 11.

For one direction, assume X and X' are Γ-equivalent, and let σ be a winning strategy in $\Gamma(X, X')$. Define a relation $T \subseteq Seqs(X) \times Seqs(X')$ by

$$\bar{\iota} \, T \, \bar{\iota'} \text{ iff } p \cdot (\bar{\iota}, \bar{\iota'}) \in Plays(\sigma, \tau) \text{ for some play } p \text{ and counter-strategy } \tau.$$

It is straightforward to verify that T is a δ-bisimulation.

For the other direction, suppose X and X' are δ-bisimilar and let $T \subseteq Seqs(X) \times Seqs(X')$ be a witnessing δ-bisimulation. We define a partial function $\sigma : Pos(\Gamma(X, X')) \to C$ in the following way:

- Whenever $\bar{t}\ T\ \bar{t}'$ and $\bar{t}t \in Seqs(X)$, choose t' such that $\bar{t}'t' \in Seqs(X')$ and $\bar{t}t\ T\ \bar{t}'t'$. Then, for all $p \cdot (\bar{t}t, \bar{t}') \in Pos(\Gamma(X, X'))$, define
$$\sigma(p \cdot (\bar{t}t, \bar{t}')) = (\bar{t}t, \bar{t}'t').$$

In a similar way, σ is defined to respond to moves on the right-hand side.
- Whenever $\bar{t}\ T\ \bar{t}'$ and $t_i \in BEn(\bar{t})$, we know, since T satisfies $\mathbf{A}_\delta$, that $t'_i \in BEn(\bar{t}')$ and $\delta(i, \bar{t})\ T\ \delta(i, \bar{t}')$. For all $p \cdot (i, \delta(i, \bar{t}), \bar{t}') \in Pos(\Gamma(X, X'))$ we define
$$\sigma(p \cdot (i, \delta(i, \bar{t}), \bar{t}')) = (\delta(i, \bar{t}), \delta(i, \bar{t}')).$$

Here, too, there is a symmetric definition.

By construction, σ is a strategy. To argue that σ is winning, suppose towards contradiction that there is a counter-strategy τ such that $\langle \sigma | \tau \rangle$ is lost. In a case-analysis of the last move, a contradiction with the maximality of $\langle \sigma | \tau \rangle$ can easily be obtained. $\qquad\square$

4 A Path Logic

Just as interleaving bisimulations can be characterized as a relation over paths, we can interpret the Hennessy-Milner logic over paths rather than states. Following [HS85], we may add a past tense modality $@$, where a is a label, and obtain a logic which still characterizes bisimulation for ordinary transition systems. However, interpreted over transition systems with independence, we obtain a logic which is easily shown to be sound for $\mathbf{Pom}_L$-bisimilarity. Furthermore, the logic is *complete* if we restrict to systems which do not exhibit *auto-concurrency*, i.e. systems in which no two consecutive and equally labelled transitions are independent.

Let **Assn** be the following language of assertions:

$$A ::= \neg A \mid \bigwedge_{j \in J} A_j \mid \langle a \rangle A \mid @A.$$

By convention, *true* is the conjunction over the empty set.

Definition 13. Let X be a transition system with independence and suppose $\bar{t}, \bar{r} \in Seqs(X)$. Define

$$\bar{r} \xrightarrow{a} \bar{t} \quad \text{iff} \quad \bar{r}(s \xrightarrow{a} s_1) = \bar{t}$$
$$\bar{r} \overset{a}{\rightsquigarrow} \bar{t} \quad \text{iff} \quad \exists i.\, (t_i \in BEn(\bar{t})\ \&\ \ell(t_i) = a\ \&\ \bar{r} = \delta(i, \bar{t}))$$

$\qquad\square$

In ordinary transition systems, $@A$ is interpreted as "it was the case at the last moment – just before a – that A". It seems natural for transition systems with independence to interpret $@A$ as "a could have been the last action, and at the moment before a it was the case that A".

Formally, let X be a transition system with independence and define the *satisfaction* relation $\models_X \subseteq Seqs(X) \times \mathbf{Assn}$ by structural induction on assertions:

$$\bar{\imath} \models_X \neg A \quad \text{iff} \quad \bar{\imath} \not\models_X A$$
$$\bar{\imath} \models_X \bigwedge_{j \in J} A_j \quad \text{iff} \quad \forall j \in J. \bar{\imath} \models_X A_j$$
$$\bar{\imath} \models_X \langle a \rangle A \quad \text{iff} \quad \exists \bar{r}. (\bar{\imath} \xrightarrow{a} \bar{r} \;\&\; \bar{r} \models_X A)$$
$$\bar{\imath} \models_X @A \quad \text{iff} \quad \exists \bar{r}. (\bar{r} \xrightarrow{a} \bar{\imath} \;\&\; \bar{r} \models_X A)$$

An assertion is *satisfied by* X, written $\models_X A$, iff $\varepsilon \models_X A$.

Definition 14. Two transition systems with independence X and X' are **Assn-**equivalent iff they satisfy the same assertions, i.e. iff

$$\forall A \in \mathbf{Assn}. (\models_X A \Leftrightarrow \models_{X'} A).$$

$\square$

For ordinary transition systems (without independence) this logic is characteristic for bisimulation.

Theorem 15. *Two transition systems are bisimilar iff they are **Assn**-equivalent.*

Proof. See [HS85]. $\square$

Example 3. To see the logic in action on transition systems with independence, let us return to Example 1. An assertion distinguishing the two systems is $\langle a \rangle (\langle c \rangle true \wedge \langle b \rangle @ \langle d \rangle)$. This assertion is satisfied by the right-hand system, but not by the left-hand system. $\square$

As usual, the soundness proof is straightforward.

Proposition 16. *If two transition systems with independence are* $\mathbf{Pom}_L$*-bisimilar, then they are also **Assn**-equivalent.*

Proof. Let T be a δ-bisimulation between X and X'. By structural induction on assertions it can be shown that for all $A \in \mathbf{Assn}$, $\bar{\imath} \in Seqs(X)$, and $\bar{\imath}' \in Seqs(X')$,

$$\bar{\imath} \, T \, \bar{\imath}' \Rightarrow (\bar{\imath} \models_X A \Leftrightarrow \bar{\imath}' \models_{X'} A). \tag{1}$$

The proposition follows by taking $\bar{\imath} = \bar{\imath}' = \varepsilon$. $\square$

Restriction to systems without auto-concurrency is essential for completeness.

Example 4. Consider two systems X and X'

which are identical except that the square in X is an independence square, whereas the square in X' is not. These systems satisfy the same assertions, but are certainly *not* **Pom**$_L$-bisimilar. □

For non-auto-concurrent systems, there is a simpler game, Γ', characterizing **Pom**$_L$-bisimilarity [NC94]. Backtracking on indices can be substituted by backtracking on *labels*, yielding rules like

$$(\bar{t},\bar{t}') \rhd (a,\bar{r},\bar{t}') \text{ if } \bar{r} \overset{a}{\leadsto} \bar{t},$$

where the a is a directive to Player to play backwards with an a-move in the longer of the sequences. More concretely, Player must reply with an application of the rule

$$(a,\bar{r},\bar{t}') \rhd (\bar{r},\bar{r}') \text{ if } \bar{r}' \overset{a}{\leadsto} \bar{t}'.$$

Proposition 17. *If two non-auto-concurrent transition systems with independence are* **Assn***-equivalent, then they are also* **Pom**$_L$*-bisimilar.*

Proof. Assume towards contradiction that X and X' are **Assn**-equivalent but not **Pom**$_L$-bisimilar. Then there can be no winning strategy in the modified game $\Gamma'(X,X')$. Hence, by Proposition 5, there is a winning counter-strategy τ in $\Gamma'(X,X')$. Using τ, we construct an assertion $\mathcal{A}(p)$ for any play p such that

- p respects τ, and
- $\lambda(p) = O$.

Define the following partial order on such plays:

$$p' \prec p \text{ iff } \exists c,c'. (p' = p \cdot c \cdot c').$$

As τ is winning, there can be no infinite plays respecting τ. Hence, $\prec$ is well-founded. We now define $\mathcal{A}(p)$ by well-founded recursion on p. Let p be a play of the above kind and suppose $\mathcal{A}(p')$ is defined for all $p' \prec p$. Since p respects τ, and $\lambda(p) = O$, $\tau(p)$ must be defined – otherwise τ would not be winning. Assuming the last configuration of p is $(\bar{t},\bar{t}')$, consider now the following cases of $\tau(p)$:

$\tau(p) = (\bar{r},\bar{t}')$ **where** $\bar{t} \overset{a}{\rightarrow} \bar{r}$:

$$\mathcal{A}(p) = \langle a \rangle \bigwedge \{\mathcal{A}(p') \mid \exists \bar{r}'. (p' = p \cdot \tau(p) \cdot (\bar{r},\bar{r}') \prec p)\}$$

$\tau(p) = (\bar{t}, \bar{r}')$ **where** $\bar{t}' \xrightarrow{a} \bar{r}'$:

$$\mathcal{A}(p) = \neg\langle a\rangle \bigwedge\{\neg\mathcal{A}(p') \mid \exists\bar{r}.\,(p' = p \cdot \tau(p) \cdot (\bar{r}, \bar{r}') \prec p)\}$$

$\tau(p) = (a, \bar{r}, \bar{t}')$ **where** $\bar{r} \overset{a}{\leadsto} \bar{t}$:

$$\mathcal{A}(p) = @ \bigwedge\{\mathcal{A}(p') \mid \exists\bar{r}'.\,(p' = p \cdot \tau(p) \cdot (\bar{r}, \bar{r}') \prec p)\}$$

$\tau(p) = (a, \bar{t}, \bar{r}')$ **where** $\bar{r}' \overset{a}{\leadsto} \bar{t}'$:

$$\mathcal{A}(p) = \neg@ \bigwedge\{\neg\mathcal{A}(p') \mid \exists\bar{r}.\,(p' = p \cdot \tau(p) \cdot (\bar{r}, \bar{r}') \prec p)\}$$

By well-founded induction on p, it can now be shown that if p is a play of the above kind, and the last configuration of p is $(\bar{t}, \bar{t}')$, then

$$\bar{t} \models_X \mathcal{A}(p) \ \& \ \bar{t}' \models_{X'} \neg\mathcal{A}(p). \tag{2}$$

Instantiating p to $(\varepsilon, \varepsilon)$ yields $\models_X \mathcal{A}(\varepsilon, \varepsilon)$ and $\models_{X'} \neg\mathcal{A}(\varepsilon, \varepsilon)$ which contradicts the assumption $X \sim_{\mathbf{Assn}} X'$. $\qquad\qquad\Box$

As mentioned in the introduction, the restriction to systems without auto-concurrency has to do with the logic being based on labels. Replacing the backwards modalities @, where a is label, with modalities ⓘ, where i is an *index*, and defining

$$\bar{t} \models_X \text{ⓘ}A \text{ iff } t_i \in BEn(\bar{t}) \ \& \ \delta(i, \bar{t}) \models_X A,$$

we obtain a logic which is complete for $\mathbf{Pom}_L$-bisimilarity without restrictions.

5 Conclusion

We have given concrete characterizations of $\mathbf{Pom}_L$-bisimilarity on transition systems with independence. Our characterizations are easy to understand and appear as conservative extensions of the corresponding characterizations of interleaving bisimulation.

The present work leaves open the decidability of $\mathbf{Pom}_L$-bisimilarity for finite state systems. One approach would be to look for set W of winning positions, generalizing the notion of duplicates in our argument for decidability of bisimulation for ordinary transition systems. However, it is not quite clear what the appropriate generalization should be in the setting of transition systems with independence.

References

[AJ92]   S. Abramsky and R. Jagadeesan. Games and Full Completeness for Multiplicative Linear Logic. DoC 92/24, Imperial College of Science, Technology and Medicine, 1992.

[Bed88] M. A. Bednarczyk. *Categories of asynchronous systems*. PhD thesis, University of Sussex, 1988. Technical report no. 1/88.

[Bed91] M. A. Bednarczyk. Heredity History Preserving Bisimulations. Unpublished, Draft of 1991.

[Ben84] J. Van Bentham. Correspondence theory. In D. Gabbay and F. Guenthner, editors, *Handbook of Philosophical Logic*, volume 2. Reidel, 1984.

[GG89]   R. van Glaabek and U. Goltz. Equivalence Notions for Concurrent Systems and Refinement of Actions. In *MFCS '89*. Springer-Verlag *LNCS* 379, 1989.

[GKP92] U. Goltz, R. Kuiper, and W. Penczek. Propositional Temporal Logics and Equivalences. In *Concur '92*. Springer-Verlag *LNCS* 630, 1992.

[HM85]   M. C. Hennessy and A. J. R. G. Milner. Algebraic Laws for Non-determinism and Concurrency. *Journal of ACM*, 32(1), 1985.

[HS85]   M. Hennessy and C. P. Stirling. The power of the future perfect in program logics. In A. R. Meyer, editor, *Information and Control*, volume 67. Academic Press, Inc. , 1985.

[JNW93] A. Joyal, M. Nielsen, and G. Winskel. Bisimulation and open maps. In *LICS '93*, 1993. To appear in *Information and Computation*.

[Mil89] A. J. R. G. Milner. *Communication and Concurrency*. Prentice Hall, 1989.

[NC94]   M. Nielsen and C. Clausen. Bisimulation, Games, and Logic. DAIMI-PB 467, Aarhus University, 1994.

[Old91] E.-R. Olderog. *Nets, Terms and Formulas*. Cambridge University Press, 1991.

[Par81] D. M. R. Park. Concurrency and Automata on Infinite Sequences. In *Theoretical Computer Science, 5th GL-conference*. Springer-Verlag *LNCS* 104, 1981.

[Pra86] V. R. Pratt. Modelling concurrency with partial orders. *International Journal of Parallel Programming*, 15(1), 1986.

[RT88]   A. Rabinoritch and B. Traktenbrot. Behaviour structures and nets. *Fundamenta Informatica*, 11(4), 1988.

[Shi85] M. W. Shields. Concurrent machines. *Computer Journal*, 88, 1985.

[Sti93] C. Stirling. Modal and Temporal Logics for Processes, 1993. Notes for Summer School in Logic Methods in Concurrency, Department of Computer Science, Aarhus University.

[WN94]   G. Winskel and M. Nielsen. Models for Cuncurrency. In S. Abramsky and D. Gabbay, editors, *Handbook of Logic in Computer Science*, volume 3. Oxford University Press, 1994.

Cryptographic protocols and voting

Valtteri Niemi*
Department of Mathematics and Statistics
University of Vaasa, 65101 Vaasa, Finland

Ari Renvall**
Department of Mathematics
University of Turku, 20500 Turku, Finland

Abstract. Three protocols related to computer voting are presented. First protocol is an efficient ANDOS protocol which is based on a natural cryptographic assumption. The other two protocols attack a difficult problem in computer voting: buying of votes. We manage to solve this problem but our protocols are impractical in large-scale elections.

1 Introduction

Computer voting is one of the main application areas of cryptographic protocols. Many authors have attacked the problem of arranging secure votings in computer networks, [1], [4], [8], [9], [10]. Practical signifigance of this problem is obvious but it seems to be difficult to find a totally satisfactory solution because of many strict requirements of secure and fair voting. Typically, we want that cheating is prevented from voters, organizers of the voting and outsiders. Also, individual votes are often wanted to be kept secret and, of course, it should be easy to participate in the voting process for anybody.

Voting protocols are usually built up from smaller protocols, each of which performs some non-trivial communication task where information flow is somehow controlled and restricted. One example of such subprotocol is ANDOS, i.e. *all-or-nothing disclosure of secrets*. The basic idea of ANDOS can be described by the following example:

Susan (S, the seller) possesses a number of secrets. Bob (B, the buyer) wants to learn one of these secrets. Susan is willing to disclose any one of her secrets but absolutely no more, not even partial information of two secrets. On the other hand, Bob does not want to reveal Susan which secret he wants.

In [3] a *computationally secure* ANDOS protocol is given. It uses the probabilistic encryption system based on quadratic residues. Thus the security of the protocol is based on the *quadratic residuosity assumption* (quadratic residues modulo n are polynomially indistinguishable from quadratic non-residues with the Jacobi symbol $+1$, unless the factorization of n is known). Essentially, the protocol consists of repeated calls to a simple protocol, where the buyer B asks only one bit of the desired secret from the seller S. To avoid the possibility that B gets information on

---

* email: vni@brando.uwasa.fi
** email: ariren@sara.utu.fi

more than one secret, B must prove to S that all his questions concern the same secret. Similarly, after S has constructed the encryption system she must prove to B that it really is honestly constructed. These difficulties are solved by using probabilistic interactive zero-knowledge protocols. These protocols, however, make the whole ANDOS protocol quite complex.

In [12] a pretty simple ANDOS protocol is given in the case of more than one buyer. The protocol uses bits that are left invariant when a *one-way function* is applied to a binary number. The idea is that S reveals her secrets s_i (binary numbers) hashed with some numbers r_i . If a buyer B wants to buy the secret s_u, he must know r_u but not any other r_i. This is handled using the other buyers and one-way functions. To make the protocol safe it is required that at least one of the buyers is honest. Otherwise the buyers could learn all of S's secrets. Thus the problem with this protocol - as with every multiparty protocol - is the possibility of coalitions.

In [9] ANDOS was used as an essential part of a computer voting protocol. First protocol of our paper is a new ANDOS-protocol which can be based on any such *trapdoor permutation* that satisfies a natural condition introduced in next section. The biggest advantage of our protocol is that it is extremely simple and easy to implement. Only two interactive rounds are needed, and the messages to be sent are very short. In addition, the protocol is *unconditionally secure* for the buyer: S can never find out which secret B wants. The security of the seller is computational: B cannot learn more than one of S's secrets unless he can invert a trapdoor permutation.

The other two protocols presented in this paper deal with a severe problem in computer voting: buying and selling of votes is easy. Indeed, any voter can prove that she obeys agreed voting strategy simply by inviting buyer to watch how she casts the vote. Moreover, a voter can even allow anybody to substitute her in the protocol. At first, it might even seem that this drawback is intrinsic in every computer protocol. However, we show that the state of affairs is not quite so bad.

The basic idea in our protocols is to add a preliminary registration phase. Before a computer voting environment is set up, each voter must visit a controlled place like an ordinary polling station where her identity is physically checked and where she gets some secret information needed later in the actual voting phases. The key point is that this secret information is not easy to sell because it cannot be proven to be genuine after the voter has left the registration booth! One might argue that the new registration phase destroys the whole idea of computer voting, since the voting itself could be arranged during that phase and we are back in traditional voting. However, this is not true, since the registration is needed only once for many different voting processes and, on the other hand, it seems that some kind of registration is needed in any computer voting system.

Our second protocol solves the problem of possible buyers by introducing a trusted party. We do not assume that this party is completely trustworthy, all we want is that it does not take part in any action that concerns buying of votes. For instance, the trusted party has no way of finding out single voting strategies of individual voters.

The third protocol attacks the same problem as the second one. In it we drop the assumption of a trusted party. On the other hand, the protocol uses quite costly subprotocols quite a many times, hence it seems to be worse than the second one from practical point of view.

The paper is structured as follows. In section 2 we discuss some natural assumptions on trapdoor permutations while our first protocol is presented and analyzed in section 3. The two voting protocols are given and discussed in sections 4 and 5.

2. Some basic notions

There are two alternative ways that are used to define one-way functions. The standard requirement (or, more precisely, its essential part) is the following:

(1) Given y, it is computationally infeasible for an adversary to find any x such that $f(x) = y$.

Another requirement that is used especially in the context of *hash* functions is the following:

(2) Given f, it is computationally infeasible for the adversary to find any pair (x, x') such that $f(x) = f(x')$ but $x \neq x'$.

If the second requirement is used the function is called *claw-free* (see [11]).

In the case of permutations (2) does not make any sense. However, if some operation $\star$ is defined in the underlying set (for instance, $\star$ might be xor or ordinary addition) then a third requirement could be given as follows.

(3) Given f and some z it is computationally infeasible for the adversary to find any pair (x, x') such that $x \neq x'$ and $f(x) = f(x') \star z$.

Note that if $\star$ is addition and z is zero then (3) equals (2). Hence, (3) is stronger than (2) and, also, it can be seen as a generalization of claw-freeness to the case of permutations.

Our basic assumption in next section is that there exist trapdoor permutations that satisfy requirement (3). The principal candidate we have in mind is RSA with $+$ as $\star$. Condition (3) means in this case that it should be computationally infeasible for any adversary, given an integer z, to find integers x and x' such that $x \neq x'$ (mod n) but $x^e \equiv (x')^e + z$ (mod n) (where e is the encryption exponent and n is the public modulus, as usual).

In section 3 we assume that f is a trapdoor permutation that satisfies (3). Also we assume that the domain (and image) of f is a *group* w.r.t the operation $\star$. In the case of RSA this is not quite true, since Z_n^* is not a group w.r.t $+$ but this causes only negligible complications which are discussed later. In order to emphasize practical aspects of our protocol we use the sign "$+$" instead of "$\star$" in next section.

3 First protocol: ANDOS

Let $\mathcal{F} = \{f_e \mid e \in E\}$ be a family of such trapdoor permutations in a group $(\Sigma, +)$ that satisfy condition (3). (The index set E consists of, e.g., all possible secret keys). Assume that S possesses secrets $s_1, \ldots, s_n$, where $s_i \in \Sigma$ for each i. B wants to buy the secret s_u and S should give it to him without learning the index u and without revealing any information about the other secrets.

(0) B informs S that he is interested in one of her secrets.

(1) S randomly chooses an index e such that $f_e \in \mathcal{F}$. She sends B the permutation f_e but keeps the index e secret. S also chooses a random element $r_i \in \Sigma$ for each secret s_i and sends these to B.

(2) B randomly selects an element $x \in \Sigma$ and computes the value $\alpha = r_u + f_e(x)$. He sends the element α to S and keeps x secret.

(3) For each $i = 1, \ldots, n$ S computes $z_i = s_i + f_e^{-1}(\alpha - r_i)$ and sends these values to Bob.

(4) Bob computes $s_u = z_u - x$.

It is easy to check that Bob really gets the secret s_u in step 4:

$$z_u - x = s_u + f_e^{-1}(\alpha - r_u) - x = s_u + f_e^{-1}(r_u + f_e(x) - r_u) - x = s_u.$$

It is clear that the protocol is unconditionally secure for the buyer if we operate in a group. In the case of RSA Susan can subtract each random integer r_i (which she herself generated in the beginning of the protocol) from the integer α that is sent her by Bob in step (2). If some of the resulting integers, say $\alpha - r_k$, lies outside Z_n^* then Susan knows for sure that Bob didn't want the kth secret. However, the probability of this event is negligible.

From the point of view of the seller security relies on the fact that the buyer can't invert f, hence only computational security is possible.

Let us assume that Bob gets two secrets, say s_k and s_l, instead of only one. This implies that Bob has found preimages of both $\alpha - r_k$ and $\alpha - r_l$, since the elements z_i are given to him by Susan. It follows that Bob violates the condition (3) (see section 2) with $z = r_k - r_l$. Since the elements r_i are not chosen by Bob we may conclude that we have a contradiction with the assumption that f is a trapdoor permutation in the strong sense of (3).

This argument is valid whether Bob follows the protocol correctly or tries something else (which might imply he doesn't get even a single secret). On the other hand, the idea of an ANDOS protocol does not rule out the possibility that Susan deliberately sells Bob false secrets but we assume Bob has an independent method for checking correctness of secrets. In the international spy interpretation (see [3]) this would mean, for example, sending agents to claimed hiding places of some terrorists.

So far we have not considered Bob's chances to get partial information of two or more secrets. In this case a similar reduction from the ability of breaking our protocol to violating the corresponding property of trapdoor permutations can be given. Of course, we must modify requirement (3): it should be computationally infeasible for the adversary to get any non-negligible advantage in guessing any bits of both x and x' such that $x \neq x'$ and $f(x) = f(x') \star z$.

As regards the number of secrets, it is clear that Bob's chances to get two secrets grow proportionally to the square of it. Indeed, between n random integers r_i there are $\frac{n(n-1)}{2}$ differences $r_i - r_j$. In practical applications with RSA involved this rate of growth is absolutely harmless.

Similar growth is obtained when Bob tries the birthday attack and calculates a table of values $f(x_i)$, $i = 1, \ldots, m$. There are $\frac{m(m-1)}{2}$ pairs $f(x_i) - f(x_j)$ and Bob looks for a match with differences $r_k - r_l$. A rough calculation gives us the following lower bound for the size of the underlying set Σ in order to prevent birthday attacks:

$$\log K > t + 2(\log m + \log n)$$

where K is the size of Σ, t is a *security parameter* (defined as usual), m is the size of the table containing values $f(x_i)$ and n is the number of secrets.

It is quite clear that in any practical case with RSA this inequality holds easily.

Our protocol has one drawback. Information-theoretically S reveals all her secrets, when she in step (3) gives B the values $z_i = s_i + f_e^{-1}(\alpha - r_i)$. If B somehow finds out the values $f_e^{-1}(\alpha - r_i)$, maybe after many years of hard work, he also learns the secrets s_i. This is, however, not very serious because in most cases the secrets have lost their value.

As already mentioned in the introduction, apart from the obvious applications ANDOS is useful as a building block in more complex protocols. One very interesting application is to use it in secret balloting schemes. The problem of organizing secret ballot elections in a computer network is widely studied and requires a complex protocol to solve it. One of the main problems is that the unit collecting the votes must check that every ballot has been cast by an eligible voter while it should not be able to learn the identity of the voter. In [8] and [9] this is solved by using so-called *eligibility tokens*.

Each voter sends her (or his) vote together with an eligibility token. The latter is sent to assure the center that (a) the voter has the right to cast a vote and (b) he or she does not try to cast multiple votes. It is of course important that the center can not recover the identity of the voter from the token.

The crucial phase of purchasing an eligibility token can be implemented by an ANDOS protocol. The voter 'buys' one secret number from the center. On the other hand, the center does not get any clue on tokens of individual voters.

4 Second protocol: voting

We introduce now a protocol for secret ballot elections, where the possibility of buying and selling votes is greatly reduced. To achieve this goal we need a trusted party T (for example, this could be Tarzan). A voter can convince only T that she adopted a certain voting strategy. Therefore, only T can buy votes since only he can be sure that he gets what he is paying for. However, not even T can find out the actual vote of an honest voter.

First we discuss and define some concepts which we use in our protocol.

We adopt the following notation: V_i - the voters, T - the trusted party, C - the unit computing the votes, $\mathcal{A}$ - the set of possible voting srategies.

In the protocol the actual votes are probabilistically encrypted by elements from a large set X. This means that there are many elements $x \in X$ representing a single voting strategy $a \in \mathcal{A}$. To compute the strategy one has to apply a certain function $v : X \to \mathcal{A}$. The function v should satisfy the following requirements:

1. It is computationally infeasible to compute $v(x)$ without some trapdoor information.

2. It is easy to choose random elements from $v^{-1}(a)$ for a given element $a \in \mathcal{A}$.
3. It is easy to choose random elements from $v^{-1}(v(x))$ for a given element $x \in X$.

In the following we call such functions *vote functions*. For instance, they can be based on prime residuosity [1] or discrete logarithm [8].

Our voting protocol is heavily based on a permutation with a special property. In this paper we call $f : X \rightarrow X$ a *zero-way permutation*, if there exists a piece of information s such that

1. If one knows s, it is easy to compute both $f(x)$ and $f^{-1}(x)$, when $x \in X$ is given.
2. If one does not know s, it is computationally infeasible even to verify whether $f(x) = y$, when x and y are given.

Although we cannot give a proof for the existence of zero-way permutations, it seems plausible that they exist if trapdoor permutations exist. For instance, it seems that $f_1 \circ f_2^{-1}$ is a zero-way permutation, if f_1 and f_2 are trapdoor permutations. Thus we could give a candidate zero-way permutation in terms of the RSA encryption function. An alternative way to gain such a permutation is to define it in terms of some constant, when only the image of the constant in some one-way function is revealed. (This method enables several parties to establish their own zero-way permutation operating in a common domain.)

By an *anonymous channel* we mean a channel for transmitting messages in such a way that the correspondence between a sender and her message is broken. More precisely, assume that senders $S_i (i \in I)$ send messages m_i through an anonymous channel to a receiver R during a given period of time. Then R receives messages m'_j such that $m'_j = m_{\sigma(i)}$ for some random permutation σ of I. Even if R knows the set I, he cannot figure out σ. Thus, an anonymous channel is actually a scrambler of messages. The applicability of anonymous channels to election schemes is obvious. Some implementations can be found in [4] and [10].

Now we are ready to describe our protocol. It consists of four phases:

– system construction (steps 1 – 3)
– registration (steps 4 – 5)
– voting (steps 6 – 8)
– computing the results (step 9)

1. C chooses a vote function v and publishes it.
2. T chooses a zero-way permutation f_T over a set Y larger than X and an easily computable surjective mapping $h : Y \rightarrow X$. T publishes both f_T and h.
3. C and T construct an anonymous channel for the messages to be sent later by the voters to T.
4. The voter V_i chooses the desired $a_i \in \mathcal{A}$ and selects a random $x_i \in v^{-1}(a_i)$.
5. V_i and T go through a zero-knowledge protocol, where V_i learns the value $z_i = f_T^{-1}(y_i)$ where y_i is some element in $h^{-1}(x_i)$ chosen by V_i. T will not learn any of the values x_i, y_i, z_i.
6. The voter V_i sends the element z_i to T through the anonymous channel. C and T make sure that each legitimate voter sends at most one element.

7. T receives a list of elements z_j - one from every voter. For each z_j he computes $\alpha_j = f_T(z_j)$ and chooses a random element $\beta_j \in v^{-1}(v(h(\alpha_j)))$. T publishes the elements β_j in a random order.

8. T proves in zero-knowledge that the elements β_j are honestly computed.

9. C computes and publishes the elements $v(\beta_i)$. The tally of the election can now be computed by everyone.

Next we briefly examine why a corrupted voter cannot prove her true voting strategy. It seems that such a voter has two possible ways to try to do it. One alternative would be to show that a certain element β_j (step 7) corresponds to her vote. But this is not possible, since she doesn't even know which one is the right β_j (and, even if she knew it she would still have no way to prove that β_j corresponds to a_i). The other possibility is, that the voter is able to show that the element z_i she sent to the anonymous channel (step 6) will result to a certain strategy $a \in \mathcal{A}$. Although the voter knows this a by herself, her knowledge about the connection between a_i and z_i is based on T's zero-knowledge proof (step 5). Thus she can not transfer her confidence to any third person.

In fact, in our protocol the voters have to decide their voting strategy already in the registration phase (step 4). This can be avoided by modifying the protocol. Differing from our previous assumptions, let each *permutation* of $\mathcal{A}$ correspond to one voting strategy. Now the elements to be sent to the anonymous channel should be k-tuples $(z_{i1}, \ldots, z_{ik})$, where k is the cardinality of $\mathcal{A}$. Each element z_{ij} is processed as indicated in the protocol, and as a result T produces a k-tuple $(\beta_{i1}, \ldots, \beta_{ik})$. The actual vote is now $(v(\beta_{i1}), \ldots, v(\beta_{ik}))$. (It is assumed that the voters perform steps 4 and 5 once for every element $a \in \mathcal{A}$.)

Finally, we give some tools that are needed in implementation of our protocol. Assume that $\mathcal{A} = \{0, \ldots, r-1\}$, where r is a prime. Assume further that $\gcd(r^2, \varphi(n)) = r$, where n is a product of two large primes and φ is the Euler function. If $y \notin Z_n^r$ is fixed then we can show that the function

$$v : Z_n^* \to \mathcal{A}, v(x) = i \text{ , if } x = y^i \cdot u^r \text{ for some } u \in Z^r$$

is a vote function. For details, consult [1].

The zero-way permutation of T could be constructed from two trapdoor permutations, as we suggested. However, then it is not clear how to implement step 5 of the protocol. Instead, T can use an alternative method and define a function

$$f : Z_p^* \to Z_p^*, f(x) = x^{\log_g u},$$

where p is a large prime, g is a generator of the group Z_p^* and $u \in Z_p^*$ is a constant chosen by T. In [5] Chaum used this function in order to achieve zero-knowledge signatures. He gave a zero-knowledge protocol to show that $f(x) = y$. If we use the fact that $f(x_1 x_2) = f(x_1)f(x_2)$, his protocol can with slight modifications be used in step 5.

It is known that everything that can be effectively proved in traditional methods, can also be proved in zero-knowledge. Therefore we know that step 8 of the protocol can also be implemented. However, we have not found any straight-forward method to do it. Of course we can always construct a suitable boolean circuit and use the protocol of [2]. However, these circuits are likely to be enormous, which drops the efficiency of the protocol considerably.

5 Third protocol: voting

Our third protocol is also a voting protocol. Again, main idea is to prevent buying and selling of votes. A total conspiracy of all parties is needed to be able to find out the true voting strategy of any voter. This means the voter cannot prove anything of her voting strategy to any smaller coalition of parties involved in voting process. (Following [8], we assume in the sequel that *the candidates* are the active parties participating in the protocol. In practice, it suffices if there is no doubt of total conspiracy of all those parties who communicate with the voter.)

The protocol is heavily based on multiparty computations ensuring privacy of each party's input and correctness of the result. We use protocols of [6] as subroutines but any other protocols satisfying same requirements would do as well. Heavy use of these multiparty computations makes our third protocol even more impractical for large-scale elections than the second one. Hence, the main challenge for future research is to make our protocols more efficient. In this paper, we do not give any calculations of the complexity of our voting protocols. Also, we do not discuss subroutine protocols but details can be filled in by consulting, e.g. [6]. Furthermore, the third protocol itself is described in an informal level. This style of presentation is chosen because our main objective is to show how preventing of buying is actually possible.

Let us now present the main phases of the protocol. First phase is a preliminary registration phase which is needed only once for many votings (in practice, maybe once in a year). The other two phases occur in each separate voting process.

1. As in the previous protocol, the first phase is performed in controlled circumstances where the voter is identified physically.
   The voter and all candidates execute a multiparty computation which gives a private output for the voter and no output for candidates. The output is essentially a single collective signature of all candidates. There is only a negligible chance for anybody except a full coalition of all candidates to compute or check any signature of this kind. The voter gets one specific signature for each future voting.

2. A "normal" voting procedure, see e.g. [9], [8], [1], is used in order to give anybody a chance to send pairs of the form (a voting strategy, a signature) to a public file.

3. Candidates execute a multiparty computation which counts *how many* valid signatures are associated to each voting strategy. The key point is that the output of the protocol does not give any information about the validity of *single* signatures apart from the information that can be derived from the number of *all* valid signatures. (Of course, if the number of valid signatures is zero, then we know that all single signatures are false!)

This concludes our protocol.

We do not give a detailed description of each phase of the protocol. However, several remarks are surely needed.

Multiparty computations exist for any boolean circuits. The collective signature of candidates may be defined in many different ways. For instance, we might begin with some zero-way permutation f. A secret trapdoor information possessed (and constructed) by each candidate is needed to compute f and f^{-1}. That means the trapdoor information is shared by all candidates. This can be done either by introducing some secret sharing scheme, see [13], or by constructing a special type of zero-way permutation. If x is chosen from a small enough set, then there is only a negligible chance for anyone except the whole collection of candidates to find y such that $y = f(x)$ for some x. Also, given y, all candidates are needed to invert f and to decide whether there exists x in the proper set with $f(x) = y$.

In the second phase, it is important that it is not found out *who* sent pairs to the public file. Anonymous channels may be used but perhaps the easiest way to take care of this is to skip all checking of identities. Of course, this means in practice that there surely could be plenty of false votes. In fact, this is even desirable, since in the case where all signatures associated to some voting strategy are qualified, the voter may have been able to prove her strategy to a possible buyer.

Another minor problem is multiple use of some valid signature. One solution is to qualify only the first appearance of every signature. This might not be quite simple in practice but we do not discuss this matter in detail.

As the number of pairs in the public file increases, the computation in phase 3 becomes slower. Fortunately, increase of complexity is basically linear in the number of gates in the circuit, [6]. On the other hand, the complexity is hardly low enough to lead to a practical solution in large-scale elections.

References

1. J. Benaloh: Verifiable secret-ballot elections, Ph.D. thesis, Yale university, Technical report 561, (1987).
2. G. Brassard, C. Crepeau: Zero-knowledge simulation of boolean circuits, *Proc. CRYPTO '86, Springer LNCS 263* (1987), pp. 223-233.
3. G. Brassard, C. Crepeau, J.-M. Robert: All-or-nothing disclosure of secrets, *Proc. CRYPTO '86, Springer LNCS 263* (1987), pp. 234-238.
4. D. Chaum: Untraceable electronic mail, return address, and digital pseudonyms, *Comm. of ACM*, 24 (1981), pp. 84-88.
5. D. Chaum: Zero-knowledge undeniable signatures, *Proc. EUROCRYPT '90, Springer LNCS 473*, (1991), pp. 458-464.
6. D. Chaum, I. Damgård, J. van de Graaf: Multiparty computations ensuring privacy of each party's input and correctness of the result, *Proc. CRYPTO '87, Springer LNCS 293* (1988), pp. 87-119.
7. C. Crepeau: A zero-knowledge poker protocol that achieves confidentiality of the players' strategy or how to achieve an electronic poker face, *Proc. CRYPTO '86, Springer LNCS 263* (1987), pp. 239-250.
8. K. Iversen: A cryptographic scheme for computerized general elections, *Proc. CRYPTO '91, Springer LNCS 576* (1992), pp. 405-419.
9. H. Nurmi, A. Salomaa, L. Santean: Secret ballot elections in computer networks, *Computers and Security* 10 (1991), pp. 553-560.

10. C. Park, K. Itoh, K. Kurosawa: All/nothing election scheme and anonymous channel, to appear in *Proc. EUROCRYPT '93.*

11. R. Rivest: Cryptography, in J. van Leeuwen (ed.): *Handbook of Theoretical Computer Science: Algorithms and complexity,* Elsevier (1990), pp. 719-755.

12. A. Salomaa, L. Santean: Secret selling of secrets with several buyers, *Bulletin of EATCS* **42** (1990), pp. 178-186.

13. G. Simmons: An introduction to shared secret and/or shared control schemes and their application, in G. Simmons (ed.): *Contemporary cryptology: the science of information integrity,* IEEE Press (1992), pp. 441-497.

Cryptographic Protocols for Auctions and Bargaining

Hannu Nurmi

Department of Philosophy
University of Turku
FIN-20500 TURKU
Finland

Abstract

Modern mathematical cryptography provides many protocols for designing social and economic institutions. This article deals with cryptographic protocols for auctions, bargaining and arbitration. The main contribution of the protocols is in the elimination of specific types of behaviour which otherwise might undermine the desirable properties of the institutions.

1 Introduction

The role of information is quite crucial in many important social institutions. Special precautions are often taken in order to give others no access to one's private information. A number of social institutions have the aim of guaranteeing the privacy of certain kind of information. In banking, for example, the privacy of the information given to the lender (a bank) is a necessary – albeit not sufficient – condition for the trustworthiness of the information given by the borrower (a firm).

There are other institutions where the aim is to encourage the interacting parties to reveal their private information. For example, the institution of secret ballot is specifically designed to enable the voters to express their views without a fear of being persecuted, ridiculed or ostracized because of them. The ballot secrecy is again a necessary, although *per se* insufficient condition, for what is called sincere voting, i.e. voting according to one's preferences.

The fact that we have these kinds of precautions and similar arrangements is, of course, justified by the intuition that the outcomes reached when acting within an institutional framework would be different and in fact worse if the informational aspects were given no attention. Thus, removing the ballot secrecy could easily lead to a distorted view of the preferences of the electorate. Similarly, if confidentiality were not guaranteed, the lending institutions would in many cases obtain very cursory and "harmless" information about the financial facts of their customer firms.

The design of social institutions starts from a characterization of desirable outcomes. Usually, the desirability is defined by means of some social welfare criterion, e.g. Pareto optimality or equity. The task is then to devise an interaction setting in which the desired social states are reached as stable outcomes. The latter, in turn, are defined as game-theoretic equilibria of some sort. The welfare criterion is called implementable if an arrangement exists which produces outcomes satisfying that criterion as game-theoretic equilibria.

In the following I shall discuss this general implementation problematique in the context of specific institutions, viz. auctions and bargaining. The problem I am going to deal with is how the methods of modern mathematical cryptography could be used in improving the implementability properties of the existing procedures for conducting auctions and bargaining. I shall draw heavily on the results of my scientific cooperation with Arto Salomaa (Nurmi and Salomaa 1993a; Nurmi and Salomaa 1993b; Nurmi and Salomaa 1993c; see also Nurmi 1989).

2 The Basic Cryptographic Protocol

Our primary focus is on methods or protocols based on public-key cryptography, i.e. on systems of secret writing where each participant is endowed with a public encryption and private decryption key (see Diffie and Hellman 1976 for the original idea and Salomaa 1990 for an over-view). Over the past years several cryptosystems have been developed. Perhaps the best-known one is the RSA cryptosystem designed by Rivest *et al.* (1978). It is based on the idea that factoring large numbers is computationally difficult. When RSA is used the plaintext is first encoded into numbers in a publicly known way (e.g. A = 0,..., Z=25). The number sequences are then divided into blocks of commonly known size. The public encryption method of a person consists of numbers n and t. Each textblock sent to the person is first raised to t and the result reduced modulo n. The private "trapdoor" information in the possession of the receiver of the message is the factorization of n. This information enables him/her (hereafter him) to decrypt the messages obtained by performing a computationally easy task. Thus in devising his public encryption key the person starts from two large numbers and announces their product n.

One of the basic protocols needed in this presentation concerns sending of messages from one party A to another party B in a public network. We need an arrangement that satisfies the following properties:

(1) A knows that B and only B can decrypt the message,
(2) B can be assured that the sender is A, and
(3) B knows that A cannot afterwards disclaim having sent B the message.

It can easily be seen that the following protocol satisfies these three requirements (Salomaa 1985). We denote A's (B's, respectively) public encryption key by e_A (e_B) and A's (B's) private decryption key by d_A (d_B). Moreover, we assume that for all numerical encodings of message blocks w and all parties i: $d_i(e_i(w)) = e_i(d_i(w)) = w$.

Step 1. A decrypts w using his private decryption key d_A to obtain $d_A(w)$.
Step 2. A uses B's public encryption key e_B to get $e_B(d_A(w))$ and sends this message to B.
Step 3. B first decrypts the message received using his private decryption key. Thus $d_A(w)$ is obtained.
Step 4. B then encrypts the result of the previous step by A's public encryption key. Hence, w is recovered.

For practical purposes it is useful to attach a plaintext message, like "this is A approaching B", to the message sent by A to B in *Step 2* to speed up the computations by B is *Step 4*. This is by no means necessary, though. By applying all public encryption keys to messages decrypted in *Step 3* B finds out the sender of the message since only one encryption key produces a meaningful message in *Step 4*.

3 Auctions

3.1 Basic Auction Types

In the ordinary English auctions (so-called English open outcry auctions) the bidders announce their offers in increasing order to the bid-taker who then awards the object of auction (good, property, right etc.) to the bidder whose offer is highest. The price to be charged equals his bid. In Dutch auctions, in turn, the bid-taker announces the prices of the object in a descending order. The first bidder who accepts the current price is awarded the object at that price.

Both English and Dutch auctions are conducted orally. In a paper that in many ways underlies most current works in the theory of auctions, Vickrey (1961) demonstrated that these oral auction types could also be conducted in sealed forms. The sealed counterpart of the English auction is the second-price auction, nowadays also known as Vickrey auction, whereas the sealed first-price auction corresponds the Dutch auction.

In what sense these sealed bid auctions correspond the oral ones? In the sense that the problem which has to be solved by a bidder in, say, Dutch auction who wants to plan his actions beforehand is essentially the same as the one facing a bidder planning to submit a bid is sealed first-price auction. In both cases the bidder has to decide which is the highest price at which he wants to claim the object of auction. Similarly, in English auction the bidder planning his actions beforehand finds it his dominant strategy to continue bidding until the price exceeds the value he has assigned to the object. When the current price is at his value he quits since the draws exactly zero surplus from the object at that price. Suppose that only two bidders are left and one of them quits. Then the other gets the object for the current price, i.e. the price at which his contestant withdraws which equals the latter's value. Thus, in English auction the object is awarded to the highest bidder for a price that equals the valuation of the second-highest bidder. Now, precisely the same outcome can be reached in sealed auction if it is made known to the bidders that the highest bidder wins and has to the pay the amount equal to the second-highest bid.

3.2 Some Results on Auctions

Although the problem faced by a bidder planning his bid is the same in some auction types, as was just argued, it does not follow that the revenue of the bid-taker would be the same in those auctions with similar bid-planning problems. Indeed, the fact that different types of auctions are resorted to in different contexts would seem to suggest that the party who decides the auction type, usually the bid-taker, considers certain types preferable to others. For example, many European auction houses selling antiques and works of art are resorting to English auctions. On the other hand, fresh fish and tulip auctions are often conducted as Dutch auction. The mineral rights to land owned by the United States government, in turn, are sold by first-price sealed-bid auctions as are the bills of the U.S. treasury (McAfee and McMillan 1987, 702). Most industrial procurement auctions are also first-price sealed-bid ones (Milgrom 1989, 11). Examples of the use of Vickrey auctions are essentially more difficult to come by. On some occasions the autograph and stamp sales make use of the Vickrey auctions (see Rothkopf et al. 1990, 97-98).

Despite this variety of auction types, a remarkable result of Vickrey (1961) states that under certain conditions each one of them yields an identical revenue for the bid-taker and, moreover, is efficient. The efficiency in this context means that the object is awarded to the bidder with the highest valuation. The conditions under which this revenue equivalence result holds are the following:
1. the bidders are risk-neutral,
2. the values that the bidders assign to the object are private and statistically independent,
3. the bidders are symmetric, i.e.indistinguishable from each other, and
4. the payment depends on the bids only (McAfee and McMillan 1987, 706).

Apart from the last and perhaps the first one, these conditions seldom characterize real world auctions. Hence, under more realistic conditions one is not entitled to expect the revenue equivalence to hold. The reasons for the existence of different auction forms are thus attributable to facts contradicting assumptions 2 and 3 or to characteristics not mentioned in the list.

Quite often the private value assumption of condition 2 does not hold because the object or right can be re-sold at a price which is not precisely known. Anyway, the possibility of further transactions undermines the privacy of valuations. Similarly, the object or right may have a common although not exactly known value to all bidders. In this case, one is not entitled to assume that the valuations are statistically independent.

The revenue-equivalence result holds for auctions where one unit (i.e. object, right etc.) is being sold. It does not necessarily hold in cases where the object of auction is sold in varying quantities. For example in industrial procurement where the bidders are suppliers of a good endowed with a supply function and the bid-taker is the buyer who has an elastic demand function, the winning bid determines both the quantity and price of the good purchased. In this kind of setting of endogenously determined quantity, it has been shown by Hansen (1988) that the first-price auction leads to lower price (and thus to a larger quantity sold) and higher bidder profit than the second-price auction (see also Milgrom 1989, 11-13). Thus, the revenue-equivalence breaks down in this setting; both the bidders and the bid-taker are better off in this model if the first-price auction is resorted to rather than the Vickrey auction.

Consider now the possibility that, in contradiction with assumption 2 above, the values that the bidders assign to the object of auction are correlated so that with the increase of a valuation of one bidder also the increase of other bidders' valuations becomes more likely. This is quite often a plausible assumption when the bidders are in agreement about the basic uncertainties determining the value of the object or right being auctioned. In selling the works of art the re-selling value may be such an uncertainty. Another example is provided by the mineral rights auctions where the amount of recoverable minerals, transportation costs etc. are crucial common uncertainties.

In auctions with common uncertainties or common value auctions it can be shown that the English auctions lead to higher expected revenues to the bid-taker than the first-bid sealed ones (Milgrom 1989). In fact, when the bidder's beliefs concerning the underlying uncertainties are correlated, it is in the interest of the bid-taker to resort to open rather sealed bidding. The bidders, on the other hand, are better off with sealed than open auctions (Riley 1989). These results would seem to explain the prevalence of English auctions in antiques and art auctions where normally the bid-taker determines the auction type.

3.3 Cryptographic First-Price and Vickrey Auctions

Existing cryptographic protocols can be modified for the implementation of sealed first- and second-price auctions. Not only are the desirable properties of these auction types preserved under the transformation into the cryptographic forms, but the latter contain clear improvements vis-a-vis the traditional versions. One obvious improvement is minimal bid-revelation, i.e. as few bids as possible are made known to the bid-taker and the bidders. Second improvement is the possibility of conducting the auctions in a computer network. Thereby one can do away with the necessity to rely on outside parties (mail or courier service). Third improvement is related to the first one and pertains to opening of the bids. In traditional versions all the bids are supposed to be opened simultaneously. In cryptographic auctions the bids may arrive at any time over a predetermined interval. Most of them will never be opened and, yet, the resulting allocation is the same as in the traditional versions.

These improvements have their price. To wit, the cryptographic auctions require relatively sophisticated computational equipment since the computations performed by the parties involved are demanding albeit theoretically straight-forward. The precise nature of the equipment depends on the cryptosystems used. In the following I shall assume that the well-known RSA system is resorted to (Rivest, Shamir and Adleman 1978).

Consider now the sealed first-price auction, i.e. the sealed equivalent of the Dutch auction. Let the bid-taker be denoted by A and the bidders by B_1, B_2,...,B_n. The corresponding encryption (decryption, respectively) functions are denoted by e_A, e_1,..., e_n (d_A, d_1,...,d_n). The bid of bidder B_i is denoted by p_i. This type of auction can be implemented utilizing Yao's (1982) age protocol in the following way (see also Nurmi and Salomaa 1993b).

Step 1. The bidders report to A who then arranges them in the order which without a loss of generality can be assumed to be B_1,...,B_n. A informs each bidder B_i the following bidder B_{i+1}. The possible bids are represented by integers in some interval. We assume that the interval is [1,100]. Smaller values in the interval denote smaller bids. Consider now B_1 and B_2 whose bids are i'th and j'th value in the [1,100] interval, respectively.

Step 2. B_2 chooses randomly a large number x and computes $e_1(x)=k$. B_1 and B_2 submit their bids to A by sending him the message

$<e_A(e_1(p_1s_1))$, $e_Ae_1(s_1)>$ and $<e_A(e_2(p_2s_2))$, $e_Ae_2(s_2)>$, respectively. Here s_1 (s_2, resp.) denotes a number privately chosen by B_1 (B_2).

Step 3. B_2 informs B_1 of the value k-j.

Step 4. B_1 computes the following sequence of numbers:

$y_u = d_1(k-j+u)$, where u = 1,...,100 and keeps it to himself.

B_1, moreover, computes the following sequence:

$z_u = y_u$ (mod q) where q is a prime number chosen by B_1. The value of q must be such that two conditions are met: (i) the difference between any two z- values is at least 2, and (ii) $z_u < q-1$ for all u.

Step 5. B_1 gives B_2 the following sequence:

z_1, z_2,..., z_i, $z_{i+1}+1$, $z_{i+2}+1$,..., $z_{100}+1$, q.

The conditions (i) and (ii) in Step 4 guarantee that no number appears twice in this sequence.

Step 6. B_2 now finds out if the following condition is met:

$z_j = x$ (mod q).

If it is not met, then B_2's bid is strictly larger than B_1's. Otherwise, B_1's bid is at least as large as B_2's.

Step 7. B_2 reports his conclusion from *Step 6* to B_1.

Step 8. If the condition of *Step 6* is met, then B_1 takes on B_3, i.e. the above steps are repeated with B_3 replacing B_2. If the condition of *Step 6* is not met, then B_2 confronts B_3, i.e. the steps are repeated with B_3 replacing B_1.

With n bidders we need n-1 repetitions of the above steps to determine which bid is highest. A tie can possibly emerge in the n-1'th comparison of bids. There are several ways of handling it, *e.g.* by choosing randomly one of the bidders or by choosing the bidder whose bid "survived" the n-2'th comparison.

Once the highest bid has been found the corresponding bidder identifies himself to the bid-taker who then asks him to reveal his private encryption function. Thereupon the price of the object can be determined.

Do the parties in this protocol have the right incentives? This question is pertinent to *Step 7* where one of the parties informs the other about the conclusion reached in the preceding step. Surely, there is no way to stop the informing party from cheating, *i.e.* from reporting that his own bid is smaller than that of the other bidder even though this is not the case. But there is no way such a report could benefit the informing party. Another stage in the protocol where incentive problems might emerge is the one in which the winning bidder is to reveal his bid to the bid-taker. Of course, the bidder wants to pay as low price as possible for the object of auction and, therefore, has an incentive not to reveal his true bid. However, he has no way of changing his bid as it has already been submitted – albeit in encrypted form – to the bid-taker.

Sometimes reserve prices are used by the bid-takers in first-price auctions. Thereby the effects of bidder collusion can to some extent be counteracted (Milgrom 1989). Moreover, resorting to sealed rather than open outcry bidding is one way to make rings of bidders less effective in driving down the price of the object of auction. In cryptographic auctions the fact that only the winning bid will be revealed to the bid-taker gives the eventual ring members incentives to violate ring agreements. Reserve prices may be regarded as additional bids and handled as such in the above protocol. Obviously, if the reserve price bid becomes the winner, no transaction will take place. Regarding the reservation price as one of the bids has the additional advantage of eliminating the possibility of the bid-taker driving up his reservation price upon learning some of the submitted bids or the identity of some of the bidders. The bid-taker can thus commit himself in a verifiable way to the reserve price and yet no bidder is able to find out this price.

Using Yao's age protocol the implementation of Vickrey auctions is rather straight-forward (see Nurmi and Salomaa 1993b). One simply conducts two rounds of the above protocol: one to find out the highest bidder, and second to find out the second-highest bid. The fact that the bids have been submitted to the bid-taker in encrypted forms at the outset eliminates the possibility of the second-highest bidder's driving up (or down, for that matter) the price for which the winning bidder is awarded the object of auction. An additional advantage of the cryptographic Vickrey auctions is the impossibility of the bid-taker to submit false bids once the other bids have arrived. This possibility is present in ordinary sealed second-price auctions. By requiring that the bids be publicized in encrypted forms once they have all arrived and before the above protocol has been conducted, one is able to counteract this type of fraud.

3.4 Cryptographic Multidimensional Auctions

Although auctions typically involve trade of fixed objects, they are by no means excluded in circumstances where what is being offered for bidding is a project or task characterizable by several properties with partial tradeoffs. Thus, for example in procurement contracts the price is often not the only relevant consideration. Things like time of delivery, quality of service *etc.* may also be relevant considerations for the bid-taker. The question, thus, arises as to whether it is possible to conduct auctions in these kinds of multidimensional situations (Johnson 1990; Nurmi and Salomaa 1993c).

Let us consider the setting characterized by the following assumptions. (i) Each characteristic of interest is representable by a real-valued variable. (ii) The utility functions of the bidders and the bid-taker are smooth. (iii) The indifference curves of both the bidders and the bid-taker are strictly convex. (iv) The partial derivative of the bid-taker utility function with respect to any dimension variable is less than zero, while the corresponding derivatives of the bidders are more than zero (Johnson 1990). A simple example is a procurement contract where bids are characterized by cost and time variables. The bid-taker thus prefers bids as close to the origin as possible, whereas the bidders prefer contracts allowing longer time periods and/or higher costs.

Suppose now that the auctions are conducted so that each bidder submits a bid fully cognizant of the bid-taker's evaluation function V defined in R^m, assuming that there are m characteristics of interest in each bid. The function V assigns a score to each bid and the bid with the highest score wins. In case of a tie, the winner is determined randomly. Supposing that the auction is first-price one, it can be conducted using a slight modification of the protocol of section 3.3. The modification consists of asking the bidders to submit their bids in the following form:

$<e_A e_i(c_i s_i),\ e_A e_i(s_i),\ e_A(s_i t_1),\ e_A(s_i t_2),...,e_A(s_i t_m)>,$

where $c_i = 1,..., n$ is the score of bidder B_i's bid and t_j, j=1,...m, the value of his bid in j'th dimension. The pairwise comparisons are conducted in accordance with Yao's protocol using the scores. Thus the winning bidder is identified as the bidder with the highest score. The t_j values enable to bid-taker to determine the precise content of the winning bid simultaneously with the identification of the winner.

It is worth pointing out again that one of the bids subjected to Yao's protocol may be the bid-taker's reservation level bid. If this bid becomes the winner, then no transaction will take place. In contrast to ordinary sealed bidding procedures, the cryptographic version of the first-price auction enables the bid-taker to commit himself to the reservation level in a verifiable way. To wit, he may reveal his bid once the protocol has been conducted by disclosing the private decyption key d_A.

The Vickrey auctions pose some new problems in multidimensional settings (see Nurmi and Salomaa 1993b). The identification of the winning bidder proceeds according to Yao's protocol, but the precise content of the contract that the winner is allowed to sign requires additional specifications which have to be made public before the bidding period. Easiest to handle is the version of multidimensional Vickrey auctions in which the winning bidder is allowed to choose any contract which has the same score as the second-highest bid. The latter, in turn, is found by applying Yao's protocol twice. For other Vickrey mechanisms and their cryptographic versions, the reader is referred to Nurmi and Salomaa (1993c).

4 Cryptographic Techniques in Bargaining

Auctions are but one specific method of transferring goods or rights from one party to another. Auctions are primarily used in circumstances where the value of the object of transaction is uncertain and the number of interested parties is relatively small. In most of the cases where auctions are resorted to one could also use bargaining whereby the parties make offers and counteroffers until mutually satisfactory terms of transaction are reached. With many parties bargaining is obviously very inefficient procedure. From this point of view auctions can be viewed as a way to improve the efficiency of bargaining. Yet there are situations in which bargaining seems to be the only way to conduct the transaction. For example, if a seller finds just one interested buyer for a property or if two parties try to sound about the possibilities of resolving a conflict by making concessions in some issues of the conflict.

Suppose that a property is being offered for sale by S and that the only possibly interested buyer is B. Will there be a trade? It obviously depends on the reservation prices of S and B, denoted by s and b. The former means the minimum price for which S is willing to sell the property, whereas the latter is the maximum price B is willing to pay for it. If $b > s$, a zone of agreement exists and equals the difference $b-s$ (see Raiffa 1982, 44–51). Typically, the parties know their own reservation price, but have at most probabilistic knowledge of that of the other party.

The use of Yao's (1982) age protocol could in this case be quite helpful. B and S would, accordingly, resort to this protocol in determining whether a zone of agreement exists. Upon concluding the steps of the protocol they would find out if possibilities for a transaction exist and yet all information the parties would have on the other's reservation price is of ordinal nature. No third party is needed. But what about the incentives? After all, in *Step 6* one of the parties knows something that the other does not yet know, *viz.* whether the congruence holds or does not hold (see section 3.3. above). Suppose that B_2 is the seller and B_1 the byer. In *Step 7* the seller informs the buyer about the conclusion reached in the previous step. If the congruence holds, then the seller's reservation price is strictly larger than the buyer's reservation price. Obviously, the seller does not have an incentive to hide this state of affairs. If, on the other hand, the congruence does not hold, it means that a zone of agreement exists. Surely, the seller has no incentive not to reveal this finding, either. Same conclusion can be made if B_2 is assumed to be the buyer and B_1 the seller. This time, of course, the conclusion that the congruence condition is met means that a zone of agreement exists.

In addition to facilitating the parties to find out whether a zone of agreement exists, cryptographic protocols can be used in situations where the parties have committed themselves to a simultaneous revelation of their respective reservation prices and then to the transaction based on, say, split-the-difference principle (see e.g. Raiffa 1982, 58–63). When cryptographic methods are used, no strict simultaneity is required since the prices can be submitted in encrypted forms. To ensure security the prices have to be submitted after private hashing as in *Step 2* of the protocol of section 3.3. It is also possible to use private encryption which is disclosed once both prices have been submitted.

5 Cryptographic Arbitration

Arbitration differs from bargaining is one crucial respect: the parties commit themselves to the outcome of the arbitration. In bargaining there is always the no trade option or BATNA, i.e. best alternative to negotiated agreement (Fisher and Ury 1981). Arbitration is often the last step of a bargaining process or, rather, a recognition by the bargaining parties that a negotiated agreement cannot be reached without outside help. Cryptographic methods can improve the properties of some existing and suggested arbitration methods. I shall here consider the final-offer arbitration (FOA, for brevity) and its modifications suggested by Brams, Kilgour and Merrill (1991; see also Brams and Merrill 1986; Brams and Merrill 1991).

In FOA the negotiating parties, realizing that a mutually acceptable solution cannot be found, submit their final offers to a third party who then accepts one of the offers as settlement of the dispute. The parties commit themselves to the settlement thus reached. FOA is sometimes used in settling wage disputes between employers and employees in cases where a downright labour conflict is considered to be particularly costly for the community at large. Thus, this method is in use e.g. in settling wage disputes of policemen and public employers in the some parts of the United States. It is also used in settling salary disputes between the major league baseball players and teams in the U.S.

The main motivation of FOA is that it gives the arbitrator somewhat less power than the conventional or binding arbitration where the arbitrator is free to choose any settlement and the parties are bound by it. *Prima facie*, FOA would also seem to provide the parties incentives to avoid extreme positions since the latter are unlikely to be accepted by the arbitrator. Upon closer inspection this turns out to be the case only in the sense that it encourages the parties to settle their dispute without the help of the arbitrator (see Brams, Kilgour and Merrill 1991, 48). In fact, the extreme positions may be the dominant strategies of the parties in some FOA situations. Consider the case of wage negotiations between a union and an employer's representative. Suppose that the union is demanding an hourly rate of b dollars, while the employer regards a as the right hourly compensation. Assuming that the parties regard all settlements in interval [a,b] equiprobable, a (b, respectively) is the dominant strategy for the employer (union). Thus, FOA by no means guarantees a convergence of settlements to the mean or median of the best positions of the parties (see Brams, Kilgour and Merrill 1991).

Despite this drawback, the fact that FOA "deters" parties towards negotiated solutions is certainly a desirable feature in many conflicts. The following simple cryptographic protocol enables the parties to achieve the same outcomes as in the ordinary FOA.

Step 1. The parties, denoted by A and B, publicly announce their final offers a and b, respectively, in the following form:
$<(e_A(as_A), e_A(s_A))>$, $<(e_B(bs_B), e_B(s_B))>$, where s_A (s_B, respectively) is a number privately chosen by A (B). The arbitrator C also announces his most preferred value c in the following form:
$<(e_C(cs_C), e_C(s_C))>$, where s_C is C's privately chosen number.
Step 2. Once these three announcements have been made, all parties A, B and C are requested to reveal their private decryption keys, d_A, d_B and d_C, whereupon their offers can be recovered.
Step 3. The winning offer is the one which is closest to c.

The above protocol can also be used in combined arbitration (CA, for short) which provides more incentives than FOA for submitting "centrist" offers (Brams and Merrill 1986). In CA the parties submit their final offers knowing that the arbitrator has his own ideal position c. If c is between the final offers of the parties, then the winning offer is the one which is closest to c as in ordinary FOA. However, if c happens lie outside the interval defined by the final offers, then c becomes the settlement. This feature makes it safer for the parties to move towards each other's positions in their final offers, since if by such a move a party passes c so that the latter becomes the extreme position, then c is the solution. The above protocol can accommodate CA as well as FOA.

Also more complicated arbitration procedures can easily be handled by the above protocol, *e.g.* two- or multi-stage FOA (see Brams, Kilgour and Weber 1991). The two-stage FOA allows the loser of the FOA to submit a new offer which – if closer to the arbitrator's ideal position than the winner's offer – is averaged with the winner's position to produce a settlement point. Otherwise, the previous winning position remains the settlement outcome. In multi-stage FOA the parties are allowed to respond to each other's winning offers until one party submits two consecutive offers which are closer to the arbitrator's ideal point than the offer of the opposite party.

In two- and multi-stage FOA the arbitrator announces the winning offer in each round. By conducting the above protocol anew for each round of offers and requiring that the arbitrator's ideal position be announced – albeit in encrypted form – at the outset, we can diminish the possibilities for fraudulent behaviour by the arbitrator. For each round one must, of course, insist on new values for the privately chosen numbers.

6 Concluding Remarks

We have discussed several applications of cryptographic protocols in auctions, negotiations and arbitration. Our basic instrument has been Yao's age protocol which makes it possible to determine which one of two numbers is larger without disclosing the numbers. Other interesting cryptographic protocols which have not been touched upon in the preceding are *e.g.* the secret-selling-of-secrets protocol which enables a seller to sell one of a set of secrets to a buyer so that, once the transaction has been completed, the byuer has obtained one and only one secret, but the seller does not know which secret has been sold. This and other similar protocols have application possibilities *e.g.* in secret balloting.

The most obvious advantage of the cryptographic procotols is in making commitments verifiable and yet confidential. In other words, the protocols enable the parties to commit themselves to certain acts without disclosing the precise content of those acts, e.g. payment offers. Similarly, the protocols can be used in diminishing the possibilities of certain types of fraudulent behaviour, like using accomplices to drive up the price of the object or right in Vickrey auctions.

References:

Brams, S.J., D.M. Kilgour, and S. Merrill III. 1991. "Arbitration Procedures." In *Negotiation Analysis*, ed. H.P.Young. Ann Arbor: The University of Michigan Press.

Brams, S.J., D.M. Kilgour, and S. Weber. 1991. "Sequential Arbitration Procedures." In *Systematic Analysis in Dispute Resolution*, ed. S.S. Nagel and M.K. Mills. Westport: Quorum.

Brams, S.J., and S. Merrill III. 1986. "Binding versus Final-Offer Arbitration: A Combination Is Best." *Management Science* 32: 1346-1355.

Brams, S.J., and S. Merrill III. 1991. "Final-Offer Arbitration with a Bonus." *European Journal of Political Economy* 7: 79-92.

Diffie, W., and M. Hellman. 1976. "New Directions in Cryptography." *IEEE Transactions on Information Theory* IT - 22: 644-654.

Fisher, R., and W. Ury. 1981. *Getting to Yes: Negotiating Agreement Without Giving In*. Boston: Houghton Mifflin.

Hansen, R. G.1988. "Auctions with Endogenous Quantity." *Rand Journal of Economics* 19: 44-58.

Johnson, M.R. 1990. "A Multidimensional Incentive-Compatible Mechanism for Contract Specification and Award." Department of Economics, Finance and Legal Studies, University of Alabama, April 26.

McAfee, R.P., and J. McMillan. 1987. "Auctions and Bidding." *Journal of Economic Literature* 25: 699-738.

Milgrom, P. 1989. "Auctions and Bidding: A Primer." *Journal of Economic Perspectives* 3: 3-22.

Nurmi, H. 1989. "Computational Approaches to Bargaining and Choice." *Journal of Theoretical Politics* 1: 407-426.

Nurmi, H., and A.Salomaa. 1993a. " Cancellation and Reassignment of Votes in Secret Ballot Elections." *European Journal of Political Economy* 9: 427-435.

Nurmi, H., and A. Salomaa. 1993b. "Cryptographic Protocols for Vickrey Auctions." *Group Decision and Negotiation* 2: 363-373.

Nurmi, H., and A. Salomaa. 1993c. "The Nearly Perfect Auctioneer: Cryptographic Protocols for Auctions and Bidding." Prepared for delivery at Conference on Decision Making: Towards 21st Century, Madrid, Spain, June 2-5.

Raiffa, H. 1982. *The Art and Science of Negotiation*. Cambridge, MA: Harvard University Press.

Riley, J.G. 1989. "Expected Revenue from Open and Sealed Bid Auctions." *Journal of Economic Perspectives* 3: 41-50.

Rivest, R., A. Shamir, and L. Adleman. 1978. "A Method for Obtaining Digital Signatures and Public-Key Cryptosystems." *ACM Communications* 21: 120-126.

Rothkopf, M.H., Th.J. Teisberg, and E.P.Kahn. 1990. "Why Are Vickrey Auctions Rare?" *Journal of Political Economy* 98: 94-109.

Salomaa, A. 1985. *Computation and Automata*. Cambridge: Cambridge University Press.

Salomaa, A. 1990. *Public-Key Cryptography*. Berlin-Heidelberg-New York: Springer-Verlag.

Vickrey, W. 1961. "Counter Speculation, Auctions and Competitive Sealed Tenders." *Journal of Finance* 16: 8-37.

Yao, A. C. 1982."Protocols for Secure Computation." *23rd Annual Symposium on Foundations of Computer Science* . IEEE Computer Society Press.

On the Size of Components of Cooperating Grammar Systems

Gheorghe Păun[1]

Institute of Mathematics of the Romanian Academy of Sciences
Str. Academiei 14, R-70109 Bucuresti, Romania

Jürgen Dassow and Stefan Skalla

Otto-von-Guericke-University Magdeburg, Faculty of Computer Science
PSF 4120, D-39016 Magdeburg, Germany

Abstract. We investigate the hierarchy induced by the number of components of cooperating/distributed grammar systems and by the number of production rules in these components. If one of these parameters is bounded, then the other induces an infinite hierarchy of languages (for the $*$ and t modes of derivation). If λ-rules are allowed, then for every CD grammar system an equivalent one (in the t mode of derivation) can be constructed, containing components with at most five productions. In this framework, deterministic systems are introduced and investigated; for them, four rules in each component are enough.

1. Introduction

The theory of grammar systems has been started in [3] with motivations related to the blackboard architecture in problem solving in the sense of [12]. In short, a blackboard model consists of some knowledge sources working together according to a well defined protocol in order to solve a problem whose current state is written on a "blackboard"; in every moment only one knowledge source is active, it modifies the content of the blackboard, then it becomes inactive and another component of the system comes to the blackboard and modifies the partial solution written on it; the process continues in this manner until an acceptable solution is obtained.

Exactly this is the architecture and the way of working of cooperating/distributed grammar system (we shall say shortly CD grammar system), as introduced in [3]: more usual grammars share a common sentential form, which is modified, in turn, until obtaining a terminal string.

It is quite interesting to note that the idea of grammar systems appeared already in [10], motivated by questions related to two-level grammars, and that a similar

---

[1]Research supported by Alexander von Humboldt Foundation

generative machinery is introduced in [2] (under the name of *modular grammar*), suggested by questions in regulated rewriting area (time-varying grammars).

Clearly, in all these contexts, a basic problem ("practically" important and mathematically natural) concerns the number of components in a grammar system and their complexity. Are systems with $n + 1$ components more powerful than those with n components ? Can we bound the number of rewriting rules in the components ? Intuitively, the former question should have an affirmative answer, the latter one should have a negative answer.

However, the results are exactly the opposite (at least for the main mode of derivation, considered in all quoted papers [2], [3], [10], the so-called t-mode). Namely, three components are enough (the result is proved in [2] and [3]), components consisting of at most five rules are sufficient (Theorem 3 below).

A more close look to the proofs of these results shows however that the limiting of one of the discussed parameters increases the other one, which suggests a trade-off must exist between them. This is confirmed by the second main result of this paper (Theorem 9): bounding either the number of components or their size, an infinite hierarchy is defined by the other parameter.

It is an open problem whether the bound five in Theorem 3 is optimal; for *deterministic* CD grammar systems (no component has two rules with the same nonterminal in their left-hand sides) this bound can be decreased to four. This makes interesting the study of deterministic CD grammar systems.

2. Definitions

We denote by V^* the free monoid generated by V under the operation of concatenation; the empty string will be denoted by λ and the length of a string $x \in V^*$ by $|x|$. For general elements of formal language theory we refer the reader to [9], [15] [4].

Definition 1. A *CD grammar system* (of degree $n, n \geq 1$) is a construct

$$\Gamma = (T, G_1, G_2, \ldots, G_n, S),$$

where T is an alphabet, $G_i = (N_i, T_i, P_i)$, $1 \leq i \leq n$, are Chomsky grammars without axioms, such that $T \subseteq \bigcup_{i=1}^{n} T_i$ and $S \in \bigcup_{i=1}^{n} N_i$.

Denote $V_\Gamma = \bigcup_{i=1}^{n}(N_i \cup T_i)$ and $dom(P_i) = \{A \in N_i \mid A \to x \in P_i\}$, $1 \leq i \leq n$.

A k step derivation, $k \geq 1$, in a component G_i, $1 \leq i \leq n$, as above is denoted by $\Longrightarrow_{G_i}^{=k}$. Similarly, we denote by $\Longrightarrow_{G_i}^{\leq k}, \Longrightarrow_{G_i}^{\geq k}$ a derivation consisting of at most k, and of at least k steps, respectively. As usual, $\Longrightarrow_{G_i}^*$ denotes an arbitrary derivation. If $x \Longrightarrow_{G_i}^* y$ and there is no $z \in V_\Gamma^*$, $z \neq y$, such that $y \Longrightarrow_{G_i}^* z$, then we write $x \Longrightarrow_{G_i}^t y$ (the grammar G_i rewrites the sentential form as long as it can).

The language generated by a CD grammar system Γ according to a *mode of derivation*, f, as above, $f \in \{*, t\} \cup \{\leq k, = k, \geq k \mid k \geq 1\}$, is

$$L_f(\Gamma) = \{x \in T^* \mid S = x_0 \Longrightarrow_{G_{i_1}}^f x_1 \Longrightarrow_{G_{i_2}}^f x_2 \Longrightarrow \ldots \Longrightarrow_{G_{i_m}}^f x_m = x,$$
$$m \geq 1, 1 \leq i_j \leq n, 1 \leq j \leq m\}.$$

We have denoted by V^* the free monoid generated by V under the operation of concatenation; the empty string will be denoted by λ and the lenght of strings $x \in V^*$ by $|x|$. For general elements of formal language theory we refer the reader to [9], [15].

Some **examples** could be useful here (we shall refer to them also later): take

$$\Gamma_1 = (\{a, b, c\}, G_1, G_2, G_3, S),$$

with

$$G_1 = (\{S, S'\}, \{A, B\}, \{S \to S', S' \to AB\}),$$
$$G_2 = (\{A, B\}, \{A', B', a, b, c\}, \{A \to ab, B \to c, A \to aA'b, B \to cB'\}),$$
$$G_3 = (\{A', B'\}, \{A, B\}, \{A' \to A, B' \to B\}).$$

We obtain

$$L_{=2}(\Gamma_1) = L_{\geq 2}(\Gamma_1) = \{a^n b^n c^n \mid n \geq 1\},$$
$$L_t(\Gamma_1) = L_*(\Gamma_1) = L_{\leq k}(\Gamma_1) = \{a^n b^n c^m \mid n, m \geq 1\}, k \geq 1,$$
$$L_{=k}(\Gamma_1) = L_{\geq k}(\Gamma_1) = \emptyset, k \geq 3.$$

However, for

$$\Gamma_2 = (\{a\}, G_1, G_2, G_3, S),$$

with

$$G_1 = (\{S, A\}, \{a\}, \{S \to AA\}),$$
$$G_2 = (\{S, A\}, \{a\}, \{A \to S\}),$$
$$G_3 = (\{S, A\}, \{a\}, \{A \to a\}),$$

we obtain

$$L_t(\Gamma_2) = \{a^{2^n} \mid n \geq 1\}.$$

These examples are not only intended to illustrate the way of working of CD grammar systems and their generative capacity, but also to point out the following features: the terminals of one component can be rewritten in other components, and there is a relatively large liberty in choosing the nonterminal and the terminal alphabets of system components. For instance, we can ensure T, the terminal alphabet of Γ, to be equal to the terminal alphabet of one component, or included in all these terminal alphabets and so on. We do not distinguish here such variants, but continue in the frame of Definition 1. However, occasionally we shall refer to systems where terminals cannot be rewritten.

Definition 2. A CD grammar systems $\Gamma = (T, G_1, \ldots, G_n, S)$ is called *restricted* if $G_i = (N, T, P_i)$, for all $1 \leq i \leq n$. (We can then write the system in the simpler form $\Gamma = (N, T, P_1, \ldots, P_n, S)$.)

The (descriptional) complexity of CD grammar systems is basically expressed by the next two measures.

Definition 3. For a CD grammar system $\Gamma = (T, G_1, \ldots, G_n, S)$ with $G_i = (N_i, T_i, P_i)$ for $1 \leq i \leq n$, let

$$Deg(\Gamma) = n,$$
$$CProd(\Gamma) = max\{card(P_i) \mid 1 \leq i \leq n\}.$$

(For restricted CD grammar systems the modifications are obvious.)

Then, for $n \geq 1, m \geq 1$ (including $n = \infty$, $m = \infty$), we denote by $CD_{n,m}CF$ the class of CD grammar systems Γ with $Deg(\Gamma) \leq n$, $CProd(\Gamma) \leq m$, and context-free rules, and by $CD'_{n,m}CF$ the class of corresponding restricted CD grammar systems. For a class X of CD grammar systems and a derivation mode f, $f \in \{*, t\} \cup \{\leq k, = k, \geq k \mid k \geq 1\}$, we define by

$$\mathcal{L}_f(X) = \{L_f(\Gamma) \mid \Gamma \in X\}$$

the family of corresponding generated languages.

Moreover, we denote by $\mathcal{L}(CF), \mathcal{L}(ET0L), \mathcal{L}(EDT0L)$ the families of context-free languages, of languages generated by ET0L and by deterministic ET0L systems, respectively.

3. Limiting the Number of Productions

The following relations either directly follow from definitions or can be easily proved:

$$\mathcal{L}_*(X) = \mathcal{L}_{\leq k}(X) = \mathcal{L}_{=1}(X) = \mathcal{L}_{\geq 1}(X) = \mathcal{L}(CF)$$

for all X (hence these derivation modes need no further investigation);

$$\mathcal{L}_f(CD_{n,m}CF) \subseteq \mathcal{L}_f(CD_{n+1,m}CF),$$
$$\mathcal{L}_f(CD_{n,m}CF) \subseteq \mathcal{L}_f(CD_{n,m+1}CF)$$

for all f, n, m and similarly for restricted CD grammar systems;

$$\mathcal{L}_f(CD'_{n,m}CF) \subseteq \mathcal{L}_f(CD_{n,m}CF)$$

for all f, n, m.

The difference between CD grammar systems and restricted CD grammar systems is essential when we distinguish systems with right-linear production rules in components: for example, $\mathcal{L}_t(CD_{n,m}CF) = \mathcal{L}_t(CD_{n,m}REG)$, (all rules can be arranged to be terminal), but $\mathcal{L}_t(CD'_{\infty,\infty}REG) = \mathcal{L}(REG)$ (we have put REG instead of CF, when right-linear rules are used).

On the other hand, $\mathcal{L}_t(CD'_{\infty,\infty}CF) = \mathcal{L}_t(CD_{\infty,\infty}CF)$ (for $\Gamma = (T, (N_1, T_1, P_1), \ldots, (N_n, T_n, P_n), S)$ construct $\Gamma' = (\{X' \mid X \in T \cup \bigcup_{i=1}^n N_i\}, T, P'_1, \ldots, P'_n, P_{n+1}, S)$, where P'_i contains the rules obtained by replacing each symbol in rules of P_i by its primed version, $1 \leq i \leq n$, and $P_{n+1} = \{a' \to a \mid a \in T\}$. Thus, for Γ with

$Deg(\Gamma) = n$, $CProd(\Gamma) = m$ we have obtained $L_t(\Gamma) \in \mathcal{L}_t(CD'_{n+1,m'}CF)$, for $m' = max\{m, card(T)\}$.) When we refer to parameters n, m in $\mathcal{L}_t(CD_{n,m}CF)$, the difference between CD and CD' grammar systems is however relevant. Similar results are obtained for modes $= k$ and $\geq k$ of derivation.

Moreover, in [2] and [3] it is proved that

Lemma 1. $\mathcal{L}_t(CD_{\infty,\infty}CF) = \mathcal{L}_t(CD_{3,\infty}CF)$ (and this family is equal to $\mathcal{L}(ET0L)$).
□

It might be of interest to note that similar limitations of the number of components were obtained for other types of CD grammar systems too. For instance, two components are sufficient in the case of regular CD grammar systems with an additive or multiplicative register and for context-free CD grammar systems with a multiplicative register, in the sense of [5] (see [17]), whereas for *hybrid* CD grammar systems (where different components can work in different modes) four components are sufficient (see [11]).

No such results were obtained so far for the $= k$ and $\geq k$ modes of derivation.

On the other hand, the proof of these results increases arbitrarily the number of productions. What about limiting the parameter $CProd$?

Obviously, in the case of modes of derivation $*, \leq k, = 1, \geq 1$, for every system Γ we can find an equivalent system Γ' with $CProd(\Gamma') = 1$: take a context-free grammar $G = (N, T, P, S)$ equivalent with Γ and write it in the form $\Gamma' = (N, T, \{p_1\}, \ldots, \{p_n\}, S)$, for $P = \{p_1, \ldots, p_n\}$. For the specified modes of derivation we have $L_f(\Gamma) = L(G)$. Therefore we obtain the following theorem.

Theorem 1. $\mathcal{L}_f(CD_{\infty,\infty}CF) = \mathcal{L}_f(CD_{\infty,1}CF)$ for $f \in \{*, = 1, \geq 1\} \cup \{\leq k \mid k \geq 1\}$.
□

Some rough limitations can be obtained also for the derivation modes $= k, \geq k$.

Theorem 2. $\mathcal{L}_{=k}(CD_{\infty,\infty}CF) = \mathcal{L}_{=k}(CD_{\infty,k}CF)$ for $k \geq 2$,

$\mathcal{L}_{\geq k}(CD_{\infty,\infty}CF) = \mathcal{L}_{\geq k}(CD_{\infty,2k-1}CF)$ for $k \geq 2$.

Proof. Given a CD grammar system $\Gamma = (T, G_1, \ldots, G_n, S)$, construct the systems Γ', Γ'', both having T as terminal alphabet and S as axiom; Γ' has the components

- $G_i = (N_i, T_i, P_i)$, if $card(P_i) \leq k$, and

- all $G_{i,s} = (N_i, T_i, P_{i,s})$ with $P_{i,s} \subseteq P_i$ and $card(P_{i,s}) = k$, if $card(P_i) > k$,

whereas Γ'' has the components

- $G_i = (N_i, T_i, P_i)$, if $card(P_i) \leq 2k - 1$, and

- all $G_{i,s} = (N_i, T_i, P_{i,s})$ with $P_{i,s} \subseteq P_i$ and $k \leq card(P_{i,s}) \leq 2k-1$, if $card(P_i) \geq 2k$.

The equality $L_{=k}(\Gamma) = L_{=k}(\Gamma')$ is obvious, as well as the inclusion $L_{\geq k}(\Gamma'') \subseteq L_{\geq k}(\Gamma)$. Also the converse inclusion is true: all derivations in Γ using at most $2k - 1$ rules are already derivations in Γ''; a derivation in Γ using $rk + q$ distinct rules in a component P_i, $r \geq 2$, $0 \leq q \leq k - 1$, can be reproduced in Γ'' using $r - 1$ times components $P_{i,s}$ with $card(P_{i,s}) = k$, plus one component $P_{i,s}$ with $card(P_{i,s}) = k + q$. Consequently, $L_{\geq k}(\Gamma'') = L_{\geq k}(\Gamma)$, which completes the proof. □

A surprising limitation of the parameter $CProd$ can be found for the t-mode of derivation, providing λ-rules are allowed. (We shall replace CF by CF^λ in order to indicate this.)

Theorem 3. $\mathcal{L}_t(CD_{\infty,\infty}CF^\lambda) = \mathcal{L}_t(CD_{\infty,5}CF^\lambda)$.

Proof. The inclusion $\supseteq$ is obvious.

Conversely, take a language $L \in \mathcal{L}_t(CD_{\infty,\infty}CF^\lambda)$. Lemma 1 is clearly true also for the case of using λ-rules, hence there is a CD grammar system with (at most) three components,

$$\Gamma = (T, (N_1, T_1, P_1), (N_2, T_2, P_2), (N_3, T_3, P_3), S),$$

such that $L = L_t(\Gamma)$.

Assume $dom(P_i)$, $1 \leq i \leq 3$, and $V_\Gamma \setminus T$ ordered as follows

$$dom(P_i) = \{A_{i,1}, A_{i,2}, \ldots, A_{i,m_i}\}, 1 \leq i \leq 3,$$
$$V_\Gamma \setminus T = \{A_{4,1}, A_{4,2}, \ldots, A_{4,m_4}\},$$

and for each such symbol $A_{i,j}$, $1 \leq i \leq 3$, $1 \leq j \leq m_i$, consider the new symbols

$$[A_{i,j}], [A'_{i,j}],$$

mutually different and different from all symbols in V_Γ.

We construct a CD grammar system Γ' with T as terminal alphabet, S_0 as axiom and with components (N_s, T_s, Q_s) with the production sets Q_s constructed as follows; the sets N_s, T_s depend on N_i, T_i, $1 \leq i \leq 3$, in Γ and N_s include all the new nonterminal symbols, hence we do not explicitly write them.

We proceed to constructing the sets Q_s, giving also explanations about the way of using them.

$$(1) \quad Q_0 = \{S_0 \to SE_iD[A_{4,1}, 4][A'_{4,1}, 4] \ldots [A_{4,m_4}, 4][A'_{4,m_4}, 4] \mid 1 \leq i \leq 3\}.$$

One starts by introducing the axiom of Γ and a series of new nonterminals having the following roles: In the presence of E_i we simulate a derivation in P_i, $1 \leq i \leq 3$; D indicates the phase of working in Γ' when we *derive* (as in Γ), in order to make difference with a *final* phase – indicated by the nonterminal symbol F – when we close the derivation. The nonterminals $[A, 4], [A', 4]$, $A \in V_\Gamma \setminus T$, will be present all the D phase and they can be eliminated only when the string generated from S is terminal. The control symbols E_i can be removed only after eliminating the symbols $[A, 4], [A', 4]$.

$$(2) \quad \begin{aligned} Q_{1,p} &= \{E_2 \to Z, E_3 \to Z, C \to Z, X \to x, X \to X'\} \text{ for } p = X \to x \in P_1, \\ Q_{2,p} &= \{E_1 \to Z, E_3 \to Z, C \to Z, X \to x, X \to X'\} \text{ for } p = X \to x \in P_2, \\ Q_{3,p} &= \{E_1 \to Z, E_2 \to Z, C \to Z, X \to x, X \to X'\} \text{ for } p = X \to x \in P_3, \\ Q_x &= \{C \to Z, F \to Z, X' \to X\} \text{ for } X \in dom(P_1) \cup dom(P_2) \cup dom(P_3). \end{aligned}$$

One simulates the derivation in the components of Γ. Z is a trap-symbol, C is a symbol which appears in the moment when we want to change the component P_i we simulate. When at most one of E_1, E_2, E_3 is present, say E_i (if any), we can use the rules in P_i. Initially we introduce one E_i; no E_i will appear when C is present, but in the presence of C the components $Q_{j,p}$ cannot be used.

If P_i has only one rule $X \to x$ with X in the left-hand side, then the rule $X \to X'$ is not necessary. If more rules $X \to x_1, \ldots, X \to x_r$ appear in P_i, then any combination of their applications can be simulated in Γ' by blocking some X by X', using some rules $X \to x_j$ and then reintroducing X by Q_X.

For $1 \leq i \leq 3$, let

$$
\begin{align}
(3) \qquad Q_{i,ch} &= \{F \to Z, E_i \to C[A_{i,1}, i][A'_{i,1}, i] \ldots [A_{i,m_i}, i][A'_{i,m_i}, i]\}, \\
Q_{i,ch,1} &= \{[A_{i,1}, i] \to \lambda, A_{i,1} \to Z\}, \\
Q_{i,ch,2} &= \{[A_{i,1}, i] \to Z, [A_{i,2}, i] \to \lambda, A_{i,2} \to Z\}, \\
&\qquad \cdots \cdots \cdots \\
Q_{i,ch,m_i} &= \{[A_{i,m_i-1}, i] \to Z, [A_{i,m_i}, i] \to \lambda, A_{i,m_i} \to Z\}, \\
Q'_{i,ch,1} &= \{[A_{i,m_i}, i] \to Z, [A'_{i,1}, i] \to \lambda, A'_{i,1} \to Z\}, \\
Q'_{i,ch,2} &= \{[A'_{i,1}, i] \to Z, [A'_{i,2}, i] \to \lambda, A'_{i,2} \to Z\}, \\
&\qquad \cdots \cdots \cdots \\
Q'_{i,ch,m_i} &= \{[A'_{i,m_i-1}, i] \to Z, [A'_{i,m_i}, i] \to \lambda, A_{i,m_i} \to Z\}, \\
Q'_{i,ch} &= \{[A'_{1,m_1}, 1] \to Z, [A'_{2,m_2}, 2] \to Z, [A'_{3,m_3}, 3] \to Z, C \to E_i\}.
\end{align}
$$

In any moment the derivation phase – hence not in the presence of F, which indicates the final phase – the current E_i can introduce the symbol C, for entailing a change of the simulated component, as well as the nonterminals $[A, i], [A', i], A \in dom(P_i)$. The components $Q_{i,ch,t}$ can be used only after using $Q_{i,ch}$, because the non-blocking rules are of the form $[A, i] \to \lambda$ and such nonterminals appear only in the presence of C, introduced by $Q_{i,ch}$. In order to remove C, no one of $[A'_{i,m_i}, i], i = 1, 2, 3$, must be present. But, for removing $[A'_{i,m_i}, i]$, using Q'_{i,ch,m_i}, the current string has to not contain $[A'_{i,m_i-1}, i]$, and so on until $[A'_{i,1}, i]$, which can be removed only if $[A_{i,m_i}, i]$ is not present (component $Q'_{i,ch,1}$), which implies $[A_{i,m_i-1}, i]$ has been removed, and so on until $[A_{i,1}, i]$. In conclusion, C can be removed only when all symbols $[A, i], [A', i]$, $A \in dom(P_i)$, are removed, hence no symbol A, A' is present in the sentential form. This means the derivation in P_i is terminal (with respect to P_i), hence we can change the component. This is done by the rule $C \to E_j$ in $Q'_{j,ch}$. If P_j called for in this way is the already simulated component, the derivation can continue either by changing again the component (starting with $Q_{j,ch}$), or passing to the final stage.

Anyway, after using the above components, exactly one E_i is again present, and in the steps when no E_i is present, we have the symbol C. Thus, no component $Q_{i,p}$, $p \in P_i$, can be intercalated with the previous components. Similarly, no component Q_X can be used in the presence of C, hence the string generated from S remains unchanged after using $Q_{i,ch}$ until using $Q'_{j,ch}$.

$$
(4) \qquad Q_{fin} = \{C \to Z, D \to FE_1E_2E_3\},
$$

$$Q_{fin,1} = \{D \to Z, [A_{4,1}, 4] \to \lambda, A_{4,1} \to Z\},$$
$$Q_{fin,2} = \{[A_{4,1}, 4] \to Z, [A_{4,2}, 4] \to \lambda, A_{4,2} \to Z\},$$
$$\cdots\cdots\cdots\cdots$$
$$Q_{fin,m_4} = \{[A_{4,m_4-1}, 4] \to Z, [A_{4,m_4}, 4] \to \lambda, A_{4,m_4} \to Z\},$$
$$Q'_{fin,1} = \{[A_{4,m_4}, 4] \to Z, [A'_{4,1}, 4] \to \lambda, A'_{4,1} \to Z\},$$
$$Q'_{fin,2} = \{[A'_{4,1}, 4] \to Z, [A'_{4,2}, 4] \to \lambda, A'_{4,2} \to Z\},$$
$$\cdots\cdots\cdots\cdots$$
$$Q'_{fin,m_4} = \{[A'_{4,m_4-1}, 4] \to Z, [A'_{4,m_4}, 4] \to \lambda, A'_{4,m_4} \to Z\},$$
$$Q_{0,ter} = \{[A'_{4,m_4}, 4] \to Z, F \to \lambda\},$$
$$Q_{i,ter} = \{D \to Z, F \to Z, E_i \to \lambda\}, \quad i = 1, 2, 3.$$

In any moment of the derivation phase, but not in the presence of C, we can use Q_{fin}; the symbol F is introduced, as well as the symbols E_1, E_2, E_3. From now on, no component in groups (2) and (3) can be used: $Q_{i,p}$, $p \in P_i$, $i = 1, 2, 3$, because all E_1, E_2, E_3 are present, Q_X, $X \in dom(P_i)$ and $Q_{i,ch}$, $i = 1, 2, 3$, because F is present, the other components in group (3) because the nonterminals $[A, i], [A', i]$, $i = 1, 2, 3$, are introduced by $Q_{i,ch}$, and this component cannot be applied.

Now, F can be eliminated only after removing all symbols $[A, 4], [A', 4]$, one by one, starting with $[A_{4,1}, 4]$. This implies, on the one hand, that no symbol A, A', $A \in V_\Gamma \setminus T$, is present in the sentential form and, on the other hand, that D is not present: only in such a case we can use $Q_{fin,1}$. Therefore, $Q_{fin,1}$ (and hence all other subsequent components in group(4)) cannot be used in the derivation phase – remember, all symbols $[A, 4], [A', 4]$ are introduced, together with D, in the first step of the derivation. The elimination of F means also D is not present; in such circumstances we can use $Q_{i,ter}$, for removing the symbols E_i, $i = 1, 2, 3$, too and the derivation is finished.

In conclusion, $L_t(\Gamma) = L_t(\Gamma')$, which completes the proof. $\square$

As Lemma 1 is also valid for restricted CD grammar systems, the above result is true for this case, too.

In conclusion, the number of production rules in components leads to the following hierarchy with at most five levels

$$\mathcal{L}_t(CD_{\infty,1}CF^\lambda) \subseteq \mathcal{L}_t(CD_{\infty,2}CF^\lambda) \subseteq \mathcal{L}_t(CD_{\infty,3}CF^\lambda) \subseteq$$
$$\subseteq \mathcal{L}_t(CD_{\infty,4}CF^\lambda) \subseteq \mathcal{L}_t(CD_{\infty,5}CF^\lambda) = \mathcal{L}_t(CD_{\infty,\infty}CF^\lambda) = \mathcal{L}(ET0L).$$

In the next section we shall prove that the first inclusion is proper. The following relations will be used in this aim.

Lemma 2. (i) $\mathcal{L}(CF) \subset \mathcal{L}_t(CD_{\infty,2}CF)$,

(ii) $\mathcal{L}_t(CD_{\infty,1}CF) \setminus \mathcal{L}(CF) \neq \emptyset$.

Proof. The system Γ_2 considered in Section 2 proves the second assertion and thus the properness of the inclusion (i) too.

For a context-free grammar $G = (N, T, P, S)$, consider the (restricted) CD grammar system Γ with the nonterminal alphabet

$$N' = N \cup \{A' \mid A \in N\},$$

the terminal alphabet T, the axiom S and all the components of the form

$$\{A \to A', A \to x\}, \text{ for } A \to x \in P,$$
$$\{A' \to A\}, \text{ for } A \in N.$$

The equality $L(G) = L_t(\Gamma)$ is obvious (every derivation in G can be reproduced in Γ by appropriately using the rules $A \to A'$, $A \to x$ for $A \to x \in P$ and, conversely, each derivation in Γ is a derivation in G, modulo using some rules $A \to A'$, $A' \to A$).

4. Deterministic CD Grammar Systems

We note that in the proof of Theorem 3 only the components $Q_{i,p}$ have five rules each, and this depends on the components of Γ. This leads to the following definition.

Definition 4. A CD grammar system $\Gamma = (T, G_1, \ldots, G_n, S)$ is called *deterministic* if for each component $G_i = (N_i, T_i, P_i)$, $A \to x_1 \in P_i$, $A \to x_2 \in P_i$, $A \in N_i$, implies $x_1 = x_2$.

Denote by $DCD_{n,m}CF$ the class of deterministic CD grammar systems corresponding to $CD_{n,m}CF$.

The following relations are obvious.

Lemma 3. *(i)* $L_t(DCD_{n,m}CF) \subseteq L_t(CD_{n,m}CF)$ *for* $n, m \geq 1$;

(ii) $L_t(DCD_{n,1}CF) = L_f(CD_{n,1}CF)$ *for* $n \geq 1$ *and any* f. $\qquad\square$

Theorems 1 and 2 are valid also for the deterministic case as one can be easily seen. Moreover, we obtain the following result.

Theorem 4. $L_t(DCD_{\infty,\infty}CF^\lambda) = L_t(DCD_{\infty,4}CF^\lambda)$.

Proof. The proof of Lemma 1 in [3] starts from an arbitrary CD grammar system Γ_0 and construct a CD grammar system Γ with three components, equivalent with Γ_0. If Γ_0 is deterministic, then also Γ is deterministic. Starting from a deterministic CD grammar system Γ, in the construction in the proof of Theorem 3 the primed symbols are no more necessary, hence these symbols can be eliminated (from components Q_0 and $Q_{i,ch}$), as well as the rules $X \to X'$ from the components $Q_{i,p}, i = 1, 2, 3$; the components $Q_X, Q'_{i,ch,j}, 1 \leq j \leq m_i, 1 \leq i \leq 3$, and $Q'_{fin,j}, 1 \leq j \leq m_4$, are also eliminated, whereas $Q'_{j,ch}, j = 1, 2, 3$, and $Q_{0,ter}$ are replaced by

$$Q_{j,ch} = \{[A_{1,m_1}, 1] \to Z, [A_{2,m_2}, 2] \to Z, [A_{3,m_3}, 3] \to Z, C \to E_j\},$$
$$Q_{0,ter} = \{[A_{4,m_4}, 4] \to Z, F \to \lambda\},$$

respectively. Thus, a system Γ' is obtained, deterministic too, with $CProd(\Gamma') = 4$, which proves the assertion in the theorem. $\qquad\square$

We shall investigate in more details the families $\mathcal{L}_t(DCD_{\infty,i}CF^\lambda)$, $1 \le i \le 4$.

Lemma 4. $\mathcal{L}_t(DCD_{\infty,\infty}CF^\lambda) = \mathcal{L}(EDTOL)$.

Proof. Consider again the proof of Theorem 4, based on the proof of Theorem 3. If we start from Γ deterministic, then we obtain Γ' deterministic too. Moreover, no rule of the form $X \to x$, $x = x_1 X x_2$, $x_1 x_2 \ne \lambda$, can appear in Γ (hence in Γ' either), otherwise the derivation never terminates. This means each derivation in Γ' is done in the L sense: no two rules of the form $A \to uBv$, $B \to x$ there exists, hence one replaces only symbols appearing in the current sentential form, not introduced by preceeding rules at the same step. If we add to the components of Γ' completion rules $Y \to Y$ for symbols Y for which no rule $Y \to w$ there already exists, we obtain an EDT0L system generating $L_t(\Gamma')$.

Conversely, given an EDT0L system $G = (V, T, P_1, \ldots, P_n, w)$, we construct the (restricted) CD grammar system

$$\Gamma = (N, T, P_0, P_1', \ldots, P_n', P_{n+1}, P_{n+2}, S),$$

with

$$
\begin{aligned}
N &= \{a', a'' \mid a \in V\} \cup \{S\}, \\
P_0 &= \{S \to w'\}, \\
P_i' &= \{a' \to x'' \mid a \to x \in P\}, 1 \le i \le n, \\
P_{n+1} &= \{a'' \to a' \mid a \in V\}, \\
P_{n+2} &= \{a'' \to a \mid a \in T\},
\end{aligned}
$$

where w', x'' are obtained by replacing each $a \in V$ appearing in w, x, by a', a'', respectively.

A derivation in Γ starts by P_0, consists of alternate using of components P_i', $1 \le i \le n$, and P_{n+1}, and ends by using P_{n+2}. The use of primed symbols ensures the fact that the derivation in Γ is done in the L style, that is replacing only symbols existing in the current sentential form. In conclusion, $L(G) = L_t(\Gamma)$, which concludes the proof. $\square$

For the deterministic case, a result like Lemma 2 (i) is not true, but we have the next result, where $\mathcal{L}(CF_{fin})$ denotes the family of context-free languages of finite index.

Lemma 5. $\mathcal{L}(CF_{fin}) \subset \mathcal{L}_t(DCD_{\infty,1}CF)$.

Proof. Let $G = (N, T, P, S)$ be a context-free grammar of index k and construct the grammar

$$G' = (N', T, P', (S, 1)),$$

with

$$N' = \{(A, i) \mid A \in N, 1 \le i \le k + 1\},$$

and P' containing all terminal rules in P, plus all rules

$$(A, t) \to x_1(B_1, j_1)x_2(B_2, j_2)\ldots x_r(B_r, j_r)x_{r+1},$$

for $1 \le t \le k+1$, $A \to x_1 B_1 x_2 B_2 \ldots x_r B_r x_{r+1} \in P$, $x_i \in T^*$, $B_i \in N$, for all i, and

- $1 \leq j_i \leq k+1, 1 \leq i \leq r,$

- $j_i \neq j_s,$ for $i \neq s,$

- $j_i \neq t,$ for all $1 \leq i \leq r.$

The equality $L(G) = L(G')$ is obvious: the only difference between derivations in G and in G' is that the nonterminals $A \in N$ are replaced by (A, i), for various $i, 1 \leq i \leq k+1$.

Take now Γ consisting of N', T as alphabets, $(S, 1)$ as axiom and all the components

$$\{(A, t) \to x'\},$$

for $(A, t) \to x' \in P'$ (corresponding to $A \to x \in P$).

We have $L(G') = L_t(\Gamma)$. Indeed, the rules in G' are not of the form $(A, t) \to u(A, t)v$; moreover, the existence of nonterminals (A, t) with enough values for t, $1 \leq t \leq k+1$, for each $A \in N$, ensures the possibility that, starting from any derivation in G (with at most k nonterminal occurrences in its sentential forms), to construct a derivation in G' having only sentential forms in which no nonterminal appears twice. Such a derivation can be considered a derivation in Γ, hence $L(G) = L(G') \subseteq L_t(\Gamma)$. The converse inclusion is obvious, as Γ contains only rules of G'.

In conclusion, $L(G) = L_t(\Gamma), L(G) \in \mathcal{L}_t(DCD_{\infty,1}CF)$.

The inclusion is proper: take again the system Γ_2 in Section 2, which is deterministic and generates a non-context-free language. □

We summarize now the results obtained hitherto.

Theorem 5. *The relations in the diagram on the following page hold; the arrows indicate strict inclusions, the dotted arrows indicate inclusions, whereas the families linked by dotted lines are incomparable.*

Proof. All the inclusions (for most of them also the properness) and the equalities are already proved. In order to obtain the other relations it is enough to mention that $\mathcal{L}(CF) \setminus \mathcal{L}(EDT0L) \neq \emptyset$ [8]. This implies $\mathcal{L}(CF)$ is incomparable with all families $\mathcal{L}_t(DCD_{\infty,i}CF^\lambda)$, $i = 1, 2, 3, 4$ (we also have $\mathcal{L}_t(DCD_{\infty,1}CF) \setminus \mathcal{L}(CF) \neq \emptyset$) and that $\mathcal{L}_t(DCD_{\infty,i}CF^\lambda) \subset \mathcal{L}_t(CD_{\infty,i}CF^\lambda)$, $i = 2, 3, 4$, are proper inclusions. The relations between $\mathcal{L}(CF_{fin})$ and $\mathcal{L}(CF)$, and between $\mathcal{L}(EDT0L)$ and $\mathcal{L}(ET0L)$ are classic. □

Theorem 6. *All the relations in the previous diagram are also true for restricted CD grammar systems. Moreover, the inclusion*

$$\mathcal{L}_t(DCD'_{\infty,1}CF^\lambda) \subset \mathcal{L}_t(DCD'_{\infty,2}CF^\lambda)$$

is proper.

Proof. All the previous proofs remain the same (some are simpler) for restricted CD grammar systems, including the examples (Γ_2 in Section 2 is restricted and deterministic).

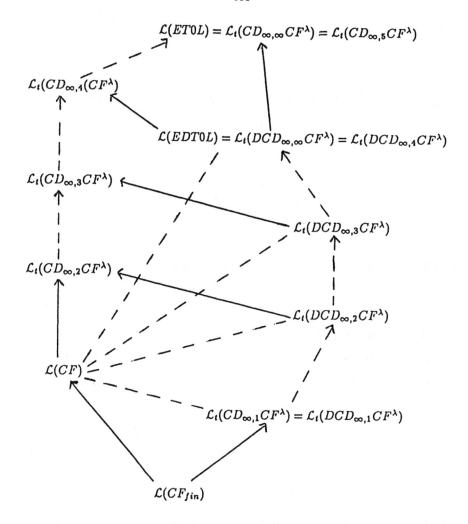

Moreover, $\mathcal{L}_t(DCD'_{\infty,1}CF^\lambda)$ is included into the family of languages generated by Indian parallel grammars (context-free grammars where one rule is used in parallel in a derivation step, [4]). Indeed, if $\Gamma = (N, T, P_1, \ldots, P_n, S)$ is a restricted deterministic CD grammar system, with $P_i = \{A_i \to x_i\}$, $1 \le i \le n$, then we can assume that in such rules x_i does not contain the symbol A_i (if $x_i = A_i$, then such a rule is useless, it can be eliminated, if $x_i = u_i A_i v_i$, $u_i v_i \neq \lambda$, then the derivation in Γ using P_i never ends, hence again such a component can be eliminated). This ensures the equality $L_t(\Gamma) = L(G)$, for G the Indian parallel grammar

$$G = (N, T, \{A_i \to x_i \mid 1 \le i \le n\}, S).$$

On the other hand, the language

$$L = \{a^n b^n c^n \mid n \geq 1\}$$

cannot be generated by an Indian parallel grammar ([16]; Example 2.4.3 in [4]), but it can be generated by the deterministic restricted CD grammar system

$$\Gamma = (\{S, A, B, A', B'\}, \{a, b, c\}, P_1, P_2, P_3, P_4, S),$$

with

$$P_1 = \{S \to AB\},$$
$$P_2 = \{A \to aA'b, B \to cB'\},$$
$$P_3 = \{A' \to A, B' \to B\},$$
$$P_4 = \{A \to ab, B \to c\}$$

(a modification of the system Γ_1 in Section 2). Therefore we obtain $\mathcal{L}_t(DCD'_{\infty,2}CF^\lambda)$ $\backslash \mathcal{L}_t(DCD'_{\infty,1}CF^\lambda) \neq \emptyset$. □

5. Infinite Hierarchies

We discuss now the families $\mathcal{L}_t(CD_{n,m}CF)$ with finite n and finite m for $f \in \{*, t\}$.

Theorem 7. *For all finite* $n, m \geq 1$ *we have*

$$\mathcal{L}_*(CD_{n,m}CF) \subset \mathcal{L}_*(CD_{n+1,m}CF),$$
$$\mathcal{L}_*(CD_{n,m}CF) \subset \mathcal{L}_*(CD_{n,m+1}CF).$$

Proof. The inclusions are obvious. We have to prove only their properness. For, consider the finite languages

$$L_n = \{a^{2^i} \mid 1 \leq i \leq n\}.$$

In [7] it is proved that $Prod(G) \geq n$ for all context-free grammar G generating L_n. Obviously, $L_{(n+1)m} \in \mathcal{L}_*(CD_{n+1,m}CF)$, since $L_{(n+1)m}$ can be generated by the CD grammar systems with the components

$$G_i = (\{S\}, \{a\}, \{S \to a^{2^j} \mid (i-1)m \leq j \leq im\}),$$

for $1 \leq i \leq n+1$.

Now assume that $L_{(n+1)m}$ is generated by some CD grammar system Γ with at most n components and at most m productions in any component. Clearly $T = \{a\}$ has to hold. Moreover, we can remove all productions of the form $a \to xAy$ when no derivation $A \Longrightarrow^* z, z \in \{a\}^*$, exists. Thus, if there is a production with the left side a, then there is a derivation $a \Longrightarrow^* a^i$ for some $i \geq 0$. If $i = 0$ or $i > 1$, then the application of this derivation to a^{2^n} yields a string which is not in $L_{(n+1)m}$. If $i = 1$ holds for any such derivation, then we can omit all the productions with left side a without changing the generated language. Thus we can assume without loss of generality that there is no production with the left side a in any component of Γ and hence $a \notin N_i$, for all $1 \leq i \leq n$. Therefore, the context-free grammar

$$G = (\bigcup_{i=1}^{n} N_i, \{a\}, \bigcup_{i=1}^{n} P_i, S),$$

generates the same language as Γ, $L(G) = L_{(n+1)m}$. However, $Prod(G) \leq n \cdot m$, which contradicts the result in [7]. Therefore, $L_{(n+1)m} \notin \mathcal{L}_*(CD_{n,m}CF)$, which proves the first inclusion in the theorem is proper.

The properness of the second inclusion can be proved in the same way.

Theorem 8. *For all finite $n, m \geq 1$ we have*

$$\mathcal{L}_t(CD_{n,m}CF) \subset \mathcal{L}_t(CD_{n+1,m}CF),$$
$$\mathcal{L}_t(CD_{n,m}CF) \subset \mathcal{L}_t(CD_{n,m+1}CF).$$

Proof. We give the proof for the first relation; the proof of the second statement is analogous.

The inclusion is obvious. We show the properness by the following example. Let $T = \{a_1, a_2, \ldots, a_{(n+1) \cdot m}\}$ be an alphabet with $(n+1) \cdot m$ different letters. Let $L = T$.

Since L is generated by the CD grammar system $\Gamma = (T, G_1, G_2, \ldots, G_{n+1}, S)$ with

$$G_i = (\{S\}, T, \{S \to a_{m(i_1)+1}, S \to a_{m(i-1)+2}, \ldots, S \to a_{mi})$$

for $1 \leq i \leq n+1$, we obtain $L \in \mathcal{L}_t(CD_{n+1,m}CF)$.

On the other hand, for $1 \leq i \leq (n+1)m$, the generation of $a_i \in T$ requires a rule with right side a_i. Thus any grammar system Γ' with $L = L(\Gamma')$ has at least $(n+1)m$ different rules in the union of the production sets of its components. Since any grammar system with at most n components and at most m productions in each component has at most nm different productions, $L \notin \mathcal{L}_t(CD_{n,m}CF)$. $\quad\square$

Obviously, Theorem 7 and Theorem 8 are also valid for restricted CD grammar systems.

Between Theorem 7 and Theorem 8 is a difference which cannot be seen from the formulation of the theorems but by their proofs. Whereas Theorem 7 also holds if we restrict to languages over a fixed alphabet (since the languages used in the proof are languages over a unary alphabet), the proof of Theorem 8 uses languages over alphabets of larger size for larger parameters.

With respect to alphabets of fixed size we only know that infinite hierarchies (with an proper inclusion at each step) are obtained for

- the families of languages generated by CD grammar systems with at most one component and an arbitrary fixed alphabet and

- the families of languages generated by restricted CD grammar systems where each component has only one rule and the alphabet contains at least two letters.

The first assertion follows by the languages used in the proof of Theorem 7 since CD grammar systems with only one component work as context-free grammars.

The second statement can be seen as follows: We recall that restricted CD grammar systems with only one rule in each component correspond to Indian parallel grammars where the symbol of the left side of a production is not contained in the right side (see the proof of Theorem 6). Now, in [13] it is shown that the language

$$L = \{aba^2b\ldots a^ib \mid 1 \leq i \leq n\}$$

has exactly one minimal Indian parallel grammar

$$G = \{\{S\}, \{a, b\}, \{S \rightarrow aba^2b\ldots a^ib \mid 1 \leq i \leq n\}$$

with $L = L(G)$. This implies that n components with only one rule are necessary in order to generate L.

We now discuss the situation with respect to deterministic systems.

Theorem 9 *(i) For $m \geq 1$,*

$$\mathcal{L}_t(CD_{1,m}CF) = \mathcal{L}_t(CD_{1,1}CF).$$

(ii) For finite $n \geq 1$ and $m \geq 1$,

$$\mathcal{L}_t(CD_{n,m}CF) \subset \mathcal{L}_t(CD_{n+1,m}CF).$$

(iii) For finite $n \geq 2$ and $m \geq 1$,

$$\mathcal{L}_t(CD_{n,m}CF) \subset \mathcal{L}_t(CD_{n,m+1}CF).$$

Proof. (i) Deterministic CD grammar systems with only one component are deterministic context-free grammars in the sense of [1]. There it is shown that such grammars only generate the empty languages and languages consisting of a single word. Obviously, all these languages can be generated by CD grammar systems with exactly one component which has one rule.

(ii) Let $m = 1$. We repeat the above considerations on CD grammar systems with one rule in each component with a fixed terminal alphabet and obtain the desired result. Let $m \geq 2$. We consider the alphabet $T = \{a_1, a_2, \ldots, a_{nm}\}$ and $L = T$. Then, for $1 \leq i \leq nm$, we need productions $X_i \rightarrow a_i$. This requires at least nm productions. If we have less then nm components, at least one component contains two productions $X_i \rightarrow a_i$ and $X_j \rightarrow a_j$, $i \neq j$. By the determinism, $X_i \neq X_j$. Hence - without loss of generality - $X_1 \neq S$. Therefore we need at least one additional rule in order to realize $S \Longrightarrow^* X_1$. If we restrict to CD grammar systems with at most m rules in any component, at least $n + 1$ components are necessary. This proves $L \notin \mathcal{L}_t(DCD_{n,m}CF)$.

If $m \geq n$, $L = L_t(\Gamma)$ for the restricted deterministic grammar system

$$\Gamma = (T, (N, T, P_1), (N, T, P_2), \ldots, (N, T, P_{n+1}), S)$$

with

$$N = \{S, A_1, A_2, \ldots A_m\},$$
$$P_i = \{S \rightarrow A_i\} \cup \{A_j \rightarrow a_{(m-1)(i-1)+j} \mid 1 \leq j \leq i-1\}$$
$$\cup \{A_j \rightarrow a_{(m-1)(i-1)+j-1} \mid i+1 \leq j \leq m\} \quad \text{for} \quad 1 \leq i \leq n,$$
$$P_{n+1} = \{A_j \rightarrow a_{(m-1)n+j} \mid 1 \leq j \leq n\}.$$

If $m < n$, we modify the construction of Γ by choosing

$$P_i = \{S \rightarrow A_i\} \cup \{A_j \rightarrow a_{(m-1)(i-1)+j} \mid 1 \leq j \leq i-1\}$$
$$\cup \{A_j \rightarrow a_{(m-1)(i-1)+j-1} \mid i+1 \leq j \leq m\}) \quad \text{for} \quad 1 \leq i \leq m,$$
$$P_{m+i} = (N, T, \{A_j \rightarrow a_{(m-1)m+m(i-1)+j} \mid 1 \leq j \leq m\}$$
$$\text{for} \quad 1 \leq i \leq n+1-m.$$

(iii) can be proved analogously.

6. Algorithmic questions

In this section we present undecidability results (of the type usual in descriptional complexity area [8]).
First we extend the parameters Deg and $CProd$ to languages by

$$M(L) = inf\{M(\Gamma) \mid L = L_t(\Gamma)\}$$

for $M \in \{Deg, CProd\}$.

Theorem 10. *(i) $CProd(L_t(\Gamma))$ is not algorithmically computable for an arbitrarily given CD grammar system Γ.*
(ii) The equality $CProd(\Gamma) = CProd(L_t(\Gamma))$ is undecidable for arbitrarily given Γ.

Proof. According to [6], there are context-free languages not in $\mathcal{L}(EDT0L)$. Take such a language $L \subseteq \{a, b\}^*$ and, for an arbitrarily given context-free grammar G, with $L(G) \subseteq \{c, d\}^*$, consider the language

$$L' = L\{c, d\}^* \cup \{a, b\}L(G).$$

The language L' is context-free, hence $L' \in \mathcal{L}_t(CD_{\infty,2}CF)$ (Lemma 2 (i)), that is $CProd(L') \leq 2$.
If $L(G) = \{c, d\}^*$, then $L' = \{a, b\}^*\{c, d\}^*$. Hence it is regular, therefore in $\mathcal{L}(CF_{fin})$ and in $\mathcal{L}_t(CD_{\infty,1}CF)$ by Lemma 5.
If $L(G) \neq \{c, d\}^*$, then $L' \notin \mathcal{L}(EDT0L)$: for $w \in \{c, d\}^* \setminus L(G)$, we have

$$L = h(L' \cap \{a, b\}^*\{w\}),$$

where h is the homomorphism which erases the symbols c, d and leaves a, b unchanged. As the family $\mathcal{L}(EDT0L)$ is closed under intersection by regular sets and arbitrary homomorphisms [14], if $L' \in \mathcal{L}(EDT0L)$, then $L \in \mathcal{L}(EDT0L)$, which is not true. On the other hand, if $L' \notin \mathcal{L}(EDT0L)$, then $L' \notin \mathcal{L}_t(CD_{\infty,1}CF)$, which implies $CProd(L') \geq 2$.

In conclusion, $CProd(L') = 1$ if and only if $L(G) = \{c, d\}^*$ (otherwise, $CProd(L') = 2$), which is undecidable.

Taking for L' a CD grammar system Γ with $CProd(\Gamma) = 2$ we have $CProd(\Gamma) = CProd(L_t(\Gamma))$ if and only if $L(G) \notin \{c, d\}^*$, hence also point (ii) follows. □

In [3] it is proved that $\mathcal{L}_t(CD_{2,\infty}CF) = \mathcal{L}(CF)$. By Lemma 1 and the known undecidability of the context-freeness of an ETOL language, we obtain the following statements.

Theorem 11. *(i) $Deg(L_t(\Gamma))$ is not algorithmically computable for an arbitrarily given restricted CD grammar system Γ.*
(ii) The equality $Deg(\Gamma) = Deg(L_t(\Gamma))$ is undecidable for arbitrarily given restricted CD grammar system Γ.

From the latter two results easily further undecidability results can be obtained, e.g. that there is no algorithm for determining minimal CD grammar systems with respect to $CProd$ or Deg.

7. Final Remarks

First we mention some problems which are left open in this paper.
Are the bounds given in Theorem 3 and Theorem 4 optimal ?
Do there exist results analogous to Theorem 3 and Theorem 4 for λ-free CD grammar systems ?
Are there results similar to Theorem 7 or Theorem 8 for the modes $= k$ and $\geq k$ with $k \geq 2$?

Other two well-known measures of syntactic complexity of context-free grammars and languages (see [8]) are Var - the number of nonterminals - and $Symb$ - the total number of symbols necessary for writing the production rules.
The parameter Var seems to be interesting for restricted CD grammar systems only, but $Symb$ is also natural for general CD grammar systems (and has a clear relevance for "applications" in the blackboard systems area). Define

$$CSymb(\Gamma) = max\{Symb(G_i) \mid 1 \leq i \leq n\}$$

for $\Gamma = (T, G_1, \ldots, G_n, S)$ where

$$Symb(G_i) = \sum_{A \to x \in P_i} (|x| + 2).$$

The proof of Theorem 3 increases arbitrarily this measure:

$$CSymb(\Gamma') = Symb(Q_{i,ch}) = 6 + 2 \cdot card(V_\Gamma).$$

(For the deterministic case we have $CSymb(\Gamma') = 6 + card(V_\Gamma)$.)
The existence of bounds as in Theorem 3 and of hierarchies as in Theorems 7 and 8 for the measure Var and $CSymb$ remains to be investigated.

References

[1] H. Bordihn and J. Dassow, A note on the degree of nondeterminism. In: Developments in Language Theory (Eds. G. Rozenberg and A. Salomaa), World Scientific Publ., 1993.

[2] A. Atanasiu and V. Mitrana, The modular grammars. *Intern. J. Computer Math.* 30 (1989) 101-122.

[3] E. Csuhaj-Varju and J. Dassow, On cooperating/distributed grammar systems. *J Inf. Process. Cybern. EIK* 26 (1990) 49-63.

[4] J. Dassow and Gh. Păun, *Regulated Rewriting in Formal Language Theory.* Springer-Verlag, Berlin, Heidelberg, 1989.

[5] J. Dassow and Gh. Păun, Cooperating/distributed grammar systems with registers. *Found. Control Eng.* 15 (1990) 19-38.

[6] A. Ehrenfeucht and G. Rozenberg, On some context-free languages that are not deterministic ET0L languages. *RAIRO* 11 (1977) 273-291.

[7] J. Gruska, Some classifications of context-free languages. *Inform. Control* 14 (1969) 152-179.

[8] J. Gruska, Descriptional complexity of context-free languages. *Proc. MFCS '73 Symp.* (1973) 71-84.

[9] J.E. Hopcroft and J.D. Ullman, *Introduction to Automata Theory, Languages and Computation.* Addison-Wesley, Reading, Mass., 1979.

[10] R. Meersman and G. Rozenberg, Cooperating grammar systems. *Proc MFCS '78 Symp.*, LNCS 64, Springer-Verlag, Berlin (1978), 364-374.

[11] V. Mitrana, Hybrid cooperating/distributed grammar systems. *Computers and AI* 12, 1992.

[12] P.H. Nii, Blackboard systems. In *The Handbook of AI*, vol. 4 (A. Barr, P. R. Cohen, E. A. Feigenbaum, Eds.), Addison-Wesley, Reading, Mass., 1989.

[13] B. Reichel, Some classifications of Indian parallel languages. *J. Inf. Process. Cybern. EIK* 26 (1990) 85-99.

[14] G. Rozenberg and A. Salomaa, *The Mathematical Theory of L Systems.* Academic Press, New York, 1980.

[15] A. Salomaa, *Formal Languages.* Academic Press, New York, London, 1973.

[16] E.D. Stotskij, Remark on the paper by M. K. Levitina. *NTI*, Ser. 2, 4 (1972), 40-45 (in Russ.).

[17] S. Vicolov, Cooperating/distributed grammar systems with registers: the regular case. *Computers and AI* 1992.

An Elementary Algorithmic Problem from an Advanced Standpoint

Azaria Paz *

Technion - Israel Institute of Technology, Haifa

Abstract

An optimal algorithm which finds all the solutions, over the nonnegative integers of an equation of the form $ax_1 + bx_2 + cx_3 = m$, a, b, c, m positive integers, is given. The algorithm is polynomial in the length of the input and is based on advanced concepts and methods. The algorithm is not based on Lenstra's integer programming algorithm.

1   Introduction

Consider the problem of constructing an optimal algorithm which finds all the solutions, over the nonnegative integers, of the 3-dimensional linear diophantine equation $ax_1 + bx_2 + cx_3 = m$ with a, b, c, m positive integers. An algorithm based on exhaustive search may require $m^2/2bc$ probes which is exponential in the length of the input. On the other hand, it is clear that this problem can be considered as an integer programming problem and solved as such by the method developed by Lenstra [L]. Using Lenstra's method for this problem, however, does not allow for fine tuning and is not optimal, since Lenstra's method is a general method, and, as such, relies on several nonoptimal procedures.

We present in this paper an algorithms which is not based on Lenstra's method and which is made to fit exactly the particular problem it solves. The algorithm is polynomial in the length of its input (counting the number of arithmetical operations involved) and is based on advanced concepts. The methods used in the construction of the algorithm suggest an open problem connected to integer programming and related problems (section 6). It is interesting to note that the solving of 3-dimensional linear diophantine equations is related to several nontrivial problems, see [S].

2   The 2-Dimensional Equation

Finding the solutions of the 3-dimensional equation $ax + by + cz = m$ is based on an optimal algorithm for finding the solutions (over the nonnegative integers) of a 2-dimensional equation $ax + by = m$. We shall deal therefore with this problem first. While such algorithms can be found in high-school algebra books (e.g., [HN], chapter XXVI) we prefer to introduce here a more general algorithm, set in a compact form.

---

*This research was supported by the Fund for the Promotion of Research at the Technion.

Problem: Find all the solutions over the integers of a given equation $ax + by = m$ constrained by $x_0 \leq x \leq x_1$ where a, b, m are positive integers and x_0, x_1 are rational numbers. W.l.o.g., we may assume that $a \neq b$; that $a, b, m > 1$ (otherwise the problem is trivial) and that $\gcd(a, b) = 1$ (otherwise the gcd of a, b must divide m if solutions exist, and we can divide both sides of the equation by $\gcd(a, b)$).

Remark: For $x_0 = 0$ and $x_1 = m/a$ we get all solutions over the nonnegative integers as is easy to see.

The following algorithm solves the above problem.

Algorithm LI-2

Input: Linear equation

$$ax + by = m \tag{1}$$

constrained by $x_0 \leq x \leq x_1$. a, b, m integers, $a, b, m > 1; a \neq b; \gcd(a, b) = 1; x_0, x_1$ rational numbers.

1. Using the extended Euclidean algorithm, find integers $u, v > 0$ satisfying the equation.

$$au - bv = 1. \tag{2}$$

2. Find all integers z satisfying

$$\frac{mu - x_1}{b} \leq z \leq \frac{mu - x_0}{b} \tag{3}$$

if no such integers exist then the constrained equation at input has no solution. Otherwise, let $Z(a, b, m, x_0, x_1)$ be the set of solutions of (3) over the integers.

3. Return $\{(\hat{x}, \hat{y}) : \hat{x} = mu - b\hat{z}, \hat{y} = a\hat{z} - mv, \hat{z} \in Z(a, b, m, x_0, x_1)\}$.

end of algorithm. $\square$

Remark 1: Assume that $Z(a, b, m, x_0, x_1) = \{z_0 + i : 0 \leq i \leq k\}$, then the set of all solutions of (1) can be defined as below:

$$\{(\hat{x}, \hat{y}) : \hat{x} = mu - bz_0 - ib, \hat{y} = az_0 - mv + ia, 0 \leq i \leq k\}.$$

To show that the algorithm is correct, we must prove that $z = vx + uy$ and $\{x = mu - bz, y = az - mv\}$ where u, v are defined as in (2), are inverse transformations such that z is an integer iff (x, y) is a pair of integers and z satisfies (3) iff (x, y) satisfy (1) with $x_0 \leq x \leq x_1$.

The proof is easy and is left to the reader.

The complexity of the algorithm is determined by step 1 which is logarithmic in the magnitude of $\min(a, b)$ or linear in the length of $\min(a, b)$ - see [Kn], Vol. 2.

Remark 2: If we substitute in (3) $x_0 = 0$ and $x_1 = \frac{m}{a}$, i.e., we restrict ourselves to the solutions over the nonnegative integers, we get (by (2) the condition

$$\frac{mv}{a} \leq z \leq \frac{mu}{b} \tag{3'}$$

since

$$\frac{mu - \dfrac{m}{a}}{b} = m\frac{\dfrac{au - 1}{a}}{b} = m\frac{\dfrac{bv}{a}}{b} = \frac{mv}{a}.$$

Now

$$\frac{mu}{b} - \frac{mv}{a} = \frac{m(au - bv)}{ab} = \frac{m}{ab}$$

It follows that if $m \geq nab$ then the number of integers in the interval $[\frac{mv}{a}, \frac{mu}{b}]$ is at least n implying that the equation (1) has at least n solutions over the nonnegative integers if this is the case.

It is worth noticing than an old theorem due to Sylvester [Syl] states that the set of solutions of (1) over the nonnegative integers is not empty if $m \geq (a - 1)(b - 1)$.

3 The 3-dimensional equation

We consider below the 3-dimensional problem:

Find all the solutions, over the nonnegative integers, of the equation

$$ax + by + cz = m$$

where a, b, c, m are positive integers. W.l.o.g. and in order to avoid trivial cases we may assume here too that:

no two of a, b, c are equal; that $a, b, c, m \geq 2$; that $\gcd(a, b, c) = 1$ and we shall assume also that $a < b < c$. The algorithm is split into two parts.

In the first part the 3-dimensional problem is reduced to an equivalent 2-dimensional problem and in the second part we solve the equivalent 2-dimensional problem which is incorporated in the first part as a procedure, the procedure $SI(\alpha, \beta, \gamma)$.

3.1 Algorithm LI-3

Input: Linear equation

$$ax_1 + bx_2 + cx_3 = m \tag{4}$$

a, b, c, m integers; $a, b, c, m \geq 2; \gcd(a, b, c) = 1; a < b < c$.

1. Using the extended Euclidean algorithm find integers $u, v, > 0$ s.t. $au - bv = \gcd(a, b) = d$, then find integers $w, r \geq 0$ s.t. $dw - cr = 1$.

2. Compute $um/b, vm/a, rm/d, wm/c$ (rational numbers) and define the vectors
$\alpha = (um/b, rm/d), \beta = (vm/a, rm/d), \gamma = (0, wm/c)$.

   { Consider the triangle in 2-dimensional space (y_1, y_2) whose vertices are the point vectors α, β and γ defined in step 2. It will be shown in the sequel that a 1-1 correspondence exists between the nonnegative solutions of (4) over the integers, and the point vectors with integer coordinates inside or on the border of this triangle. Step 3 of the algorithm calls a procedure that finds the integral points, in (y_1, y_2) space, inside or on the sides of the triangle. Step 4 finds the corresponding solutions of the original equation (4) }.

3. Call the procedure $ST(\alpha, \beta, \gamma)$ { outputs all integral points inside or on the sides of the triangle $\Delta(\alpha, \beta, \gamma)$ }.

4. If the output of $ST(\alpha, \beta, \gamma)$ is "no points", the return "no solutions", else for every $(\hat{y}_1, \hat{y}_2)$ output by $ST(\alpha, \beta, \gamma)$ derive the solution $\hat{x}_1, \hat{x}_2, \hat{x}_3$ of (4) as defined below:

$$
\begin{aligned}
\hat{x}_1 &= uwm - b\hat{y}_1/d - uc\hat{y}_2 \qquad (5)\\
\hat{x}_2 &= -vwm + a\hat{y}_1/d + vc\hat{y}_2\\
\hat{x}_3 &= -rm + d\hat{y}_2
\end{aligned}
$$

end of algorithm. □

We show now that a 1-1 correspondence exists between the solutions of (1) over the nonnegative integers and the points with integral coordinates in 2-dimensional space (y_1, y_2), inside or on the sides of the triangle whose vertices are α, β, γ.

Consider the matrix below

$$
A = \begin{bmatrix}
uwm & -vwm & -rm \\
-b/d & a/d & 0 \\
-uc & vc & d
\end{bmatrix}
\qquad (6)
$$

If we multiply the first row of A by the vector $(a/m, b/m, c/m)$ we get (by step 1) that $uwa - vwb - rc = w(ua - vb) - rc = wd - rc = 1$. It follows that $(a/m, b/m, c/m)^T$ is the first column of A^{-1}. The equations (5) can be rewritten then as

$$
(\hat{x}_1, \hat{x}_2, \hat{x}_3) = (1, \hat{y}_1, \hat{y}_2)A
\qquad (7)
$$

multiplying both sides by $(a/m, b/m, c/m)^T$ we get

$$
a\hat{x}_1/m + b\hat{x}_2/m + c\hat{x}_3/m = (1, \hat{y}_1, \hat{y}_2)(1, 0, 0)^T = 1
$$

or

$$a\hat{x}_1 + b\hat{x}_2 + c\hat{x}_3 = m.$$

Moreover, the entries of $(\hat{x}_1, \hat{x}_2, \hat{x}_3)$ are nonnegative if and only if the entries of $(1, \hat{y}_1, \hat{y}_2)A$ are nonnegative or

$$b\hat{y}_1/d + uc\hat{y}_2 \quad \leq \quad uwm \qquad (8)$$

$$a\hat{y}_1/d + vc\hat{y}_2 \quad \geq \quad vwm$$

$$d\hat{y}_2 \quad \geq \quad rm$$

but the inequalities (8) define a triangle in (y_1, y_2)-space whose vertices are the point vectors defined in step 2 of the algorithm (this is easy to verify by substitution).

We have thus shown that the 1-1 correspondence between the (x_1, x_2, x_3)-space and the (y_1, y_2) space given by the transformations

$$(x_1, x_2, x_3) = (1, y_1, y_2)A \qquad (9)$$

$$(x_1, x_2, x_3)A^{-1} = (1, y_1, y_2)$$

has the required property, i.e., (x_1, x_2, x_3) satisfies (4) and has nonnegative integer entries iff (y_1, y_2) has integer entries and satisfies (8). $\square$

3.2 The procedure $ST(\alpha, \beta, \gamma)$

Consider the figure below

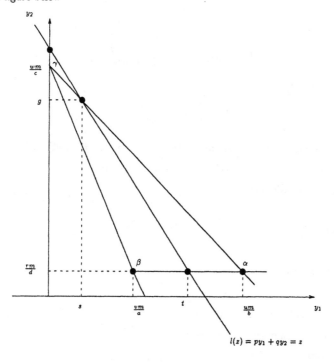

Figure 1: The triangle $\Delta(\alpha, \beta, \gamma)$

In step 2 of the $LI-3$ algorithm the vertices α, β, γ of a triangle $\Delta(\alpha, \beta, \gamma)$ in (y_1, y_2)-space are provided such that every integral point inside or on the sides of this triangle correspond to a solution of the original problem (step 3 of the algorithm). This triangle is shown in the figure.

Let $l(z): py_1 + qy_2 = z$, p, q and z integers, be a line intersecting $\Delta(\alpha, \beta, \gamma)$ at the points (s, g) and $(t, \frac{rm}{d})$. Then all points with integer coordinates such that $s \le y_1 \le t$ can be found by the $LI-2$ algorithm in section 2. An optimal $ST(\alpha, \beta, \gamma)$ procedure will result if we can find two integers p and q such that the number of translates of $l(z)$ intersecting $\Delta(\alpha, \beta, \gamma)$ is minimal.

Let p and q be any two integers.

For $(y_1, y_2) = \alpha, \beta, \gamma$, correspondingly, the corresponding value of z is

$$z(\alpha) = p\frac{um}{b} + q\frac{rm}{d} \tag{10}$$
$$z(\beta) = p\frac{vm}{a} + q\frac{rm}{d}$$
$$z(\gamma) = q\frac{wm}{c}$$

Define d_1, d_2 and d_3 as below:

$$d_1 = |z(\alpha) - z(\gamma)| = m|p\frac{u}{b} + q\frac{rc - wd}{cd}| =$$
$$= m|p\frac{u}{b} - q\frac{1}{cd}| = \frac{m}{cd}|p\frac{cu}{b/d} - q|$$

similarly

$$d_2 = |z(\beta) - z(\gamma)| = \frac{m}{cd}|p\frac{cv}{a/d} - q|$$
$$d_3 = |z(\alpha) - z(\beta)| = \frac{m}{cd}\frac{pc}{(a/d)(b/d)}.$$

Set $a' = a/d, b' = b/d$ and set

$$d'_1 = |p\frac{cu}{b'} - q|, d'_2 = |p\frac{cv}{a'} - q|, d'_3 = p\frac{c}{a'b'} \tag{11}$$

The required integers p and q are the integers that minimize $\max(d'_1, d'_2, d'_3)$, and one can find such p and q using techniques from the theory of continued fractions.

We shall need the following

Procedure $AS(N, M)$

Input N, M, positive integers.

begin

1. Set $(p', q') := (1, \lfloor\frac{M}{N}\rfloor); (p'', q'') := (0, 1)$;

   output (p', q'); return or continue on request;

2. If $M = 0$ return;

3. Reset $M := M \bmod N$;

Repeat forever

    3.1 While $N \geq M$ do

        begin $N := N - M; (p'', q'') := (p'', q'') + (p', q')$;

        output (p'', q''); return or continue on request end;

    3.2 if $N = 0$ return

    3.3 While $M \geq N$ do

        begin $M := M - N; (p', q') := (p', q') + (p'', q'')$

        output (p', q'); return or continue on request end;

    3.4 if $M := 0$ return

end

The procedure outputs a sequence of pairs $(p_i q_i)$ with increasing p_i, q_i and such that q_i/p_i is an approximation of M/N, e.g., for $M_0 = 25$ and $N_0 = 7, AS(7, 25)$ produces the following sequences of outputs where i denotes the itteration number.

i	N_i	M_i	(p', q')	(p'', q'')	$(p_i q_i)$-output	$\left\|\frac{M_0}{N_0} - \frac{q_i}{p_i}\right\| = \delta_i$
0	7	25	(1,3)	(0,1)	(1,3)	4/7
1	3	4	(1,3)	(1,4)	(1,4)	3/7
2	3	1	(2,7)	(1,4)	(2,7)	1/14
3	2	1	(2,7)	(3,11)	(3,11)	2/21
4	1	1	(2,7)	(5,18)	(5,18)	1/35
5	0	1	(2,7)	(7,25)	(7,25)	0

Table 2

Claim 1: The procedure $AS(N, M)$ has the following properties:

(a.) The average number of itterations of the procedure is $O(\log^2 \min(M, N))$.

(b.) Let (p_i, q_i) and (p_{i+1}, q_{i+1}) be two consecutive outputs, let (p, q) be any pair of integers with $p_i < p < p_{i+1}$ and denote by $\delta(p)$ the 'error' $\delta(p) = |\frac{M_0}{N_0} - \frac{p}{q}|$. Then $\delta(p) \geq \delta_i$.

Remark 1: Notice that part b of the claim does not imply that $\delta_{i+1} < \delta_i$ necessarily but leaves this strict inequality as a possibility only.

Remark 2: Given $M, N > 0$ let (p'_j, q'_j) $j = 1, 2, \ldots$ be a sequence of pairs of integers such that for all j $p'_{j+1} > p'_j$, $\delta(p'_{j+1}) < \delta(p'_j)$ and for any integer p, such that $p'_j < p < p'_{j+1}$, $\delta(p) \geq \delta(p'_j)$. It follows from part b of the claim that the (p'_j, q'_j) sequence is a subsequence of the sequence of the (p_i, q_i) sequence generated by the $AS(N, M)$ algorithm.

Proof of Claim 1: The proof of part a of the claim follows from the fact that the number of itterations of the procedure equals the number of itterations of the subtractive Euclidean algorithm when applied to the pair $(N, M \bmod N)$ (see the M and N columns in Table 2), and the average complexity of the subtractive Euclidean algorithm has been shown to be $O(\log^2 N)$ by Yao and Knuth [YK].

The proof of part b of the claim follows from the theory of best approximations of real numbers by continued fractions, see e.g., [K] or [HW].

We return now to the task of finding p, q which minimize $\max(d_1', d_2', d_3')$ defined as in (11).

Dividing (d_1', d_2', d_3') by p we set

$$(d_1'', d_2'', d_3'') = \left(\left| \frac{cu}{b'} - \frac{q}{p} \right|, \left| \frac{cv}{a'} - \frac{q}{p} \right|, \frac{c}{a'b'} \right) \tag{12}$$

Now

$$\frac{cu}{b'} - \frac{cv}{a'} = \frac{cua' - cvb'}{a'b'} = \frac{c}{a'b'} \tag{13}$$

since $ua' - vb' = 1$, by the definitions of u and v, implying that $\frac{cu}{b'} > \frac{cv}{a'}$.

It follows that for any rational number q/p satisfying $\frac{cu}{b'} > \frac{q}{p} > \frac{cv}{a'}$ we have that $d_3'' > d_1'', d_2''$ implying that $d_3' = p d_3'' > p d_1'', p d_2'' = d_1', d_2'$.

Moreover, if for some $\bar{p}, \bar{q}$ we get that $d_3(\bar{p}, \bar{q}) > d_1'(\bar{p}, \bar{q}), d_2'(\bar{p}, \bar{q})$ then for any p, q such that $\max(d_1'(p, q), d_2'(p, q)) \leq \max(d_1'(\bar{p}, \bar{q}), d_2'(\bar{p}, \bar{q}))$ and $p > \bar{p}$, we must have that $d_3'(p, q) = p \frac{c}{a'b'} > \bar{p} \frac{c}{a'b'} = d_3'(\bar{p}, \bar{q}) > \max(d_1'(\bar{p}, \bar{q}), d_2'(\bar{p}, \bar{q})) \geq \max(d_1'(p, q), d_2'(p, q))$. The following claim ensues.

Claim 2: If $\frac{cu}{b'} > \frac{q}{p} > \frac{cv}{a'}$ then

$$\max(d_1'(\bar{p}, \bar{q}), d_2'(\bar{p}, \bar{q}), d_3'(\bar{p}, \bar{q})) = d_3'(\bar{p}, \bar{q}). \tag{14}$$

If $\bar{p}, \bar{q}$ satisfy (14) then, for any p, q with $p > \bar{p}$ and such that $\max(d_1'(\bar{p}, \bar{q}), d_2'(\bar{p}, \bar{q})) \geq \max(d_1'(p, q), d_2'(p, q))$ the equality $\max(d_1'(p, q), d_2'(p, q), d_3'(p, q)) = d_3'(p, q)$ holds with $d_3'(p, q) > d_3'(\bar{p}, \bar{q})$.

We are now ready to define a procedure which finds the integers p, q minimizing $\max(d_1', d_2', d_3')$.

Procedure Min Max (p, q)

1. Compute $\frac{cu}{b'} > \frac{cv}{a'}$ and $\frac{c}{a'b'}$.

2. If $\frac{c}{a'b'} > 1$ then return $(p, q) := (0, 1)$.

3. If there is an integer k s.t. $\frac{cu}{b'} \geq k \geq \frac{cv}{a'}$ (at least one inequality is strict) then return $(p, q) := (1, \lceil \frac{cv}{a'} \rceil)$.

4. Compute $\frac{cu + cv}{b' + a'} = \frac{M}{N}$.

5. Call $AS(N, M)$; generate (p_0, q_0);
   Compute $\delta_0 = \max(d_1'(p_0, q_0), d_2'(p_0, q_0), d_3'(p_0, q_0))$;
   Set $\delta := \delta_0; j := 0; i := 0;$

6. While $d'_3(p_i, q_i) < \max(d'_1(p_i, q_i), d'_2(p_i, q_i))$

   do begin

   $i := i + 1$; generate (p_i, q_i) through $AS(N, M)$;

   Compute $\delta_i = \max(d'_1(p_i, q_i), d'_2(p_i, q_i), d'_3(p_i, q_i))$;

   If $\delta_i < \delta$ reset $\delta := \delta_i, j := i$

   end.

7. Return $(p, q) = (p_j, q_j)$;

   end of procedure. $\square$

Claim 3: The average number of itterations of the minmax procedure is $O(\log^2(a' + b'))$.

Proof: By Claim 2 the average number of itteration of the while loop at step 6 is $O(\log^2 \min(N, M))$ where $N = a' + b'$. $\square$

Notice that if step 4 of the procedure applies, then $c \leq a'b'$.

Claim 4: The procedure Min Max is correct.

Step 2. Assume that $\frac{c}{a'b'} > 1$.

If we choose positive integers p, q such that $\frac{q}{p} \geq \frac{cu}{b'}$ or $\frac{cu}{a'} \geq \frac{q}{p}$ then $\max(d''_1, d''_2, d''_3) \geq d''_3$ (see 13) implying that $\max(d'_1, d'_2, d'_3) \geq d''_3 > 1$. On the other hand, if we choose p, q such that $\frac{cu}{b'} \geq \frac{q}{p} \geq \frac{cu}{a'}$ then, by Claim 2, $\max(d'_1, d'_2, d'_3) = d'_3 = p \frac{c}{a'b'} > 1$.

But, if we choose $(p, q) = (0, 1)$ then $\max(d'_1, d'_2, d'_3) = \max(1, 1, 0) = 1$. Therefore $\max(d'_1, d'_2, d'_3)$ is minimized when $(p, q) = (0, 1)$.

Step 3. Given that there is an integer k s.t. $\frac{cu}{b'} \geq k \geq \frac{cv}{a'}$, but $\frac{c}{a'b'} \leq 1$.

As in the previous case, if we choose $p; q$ s.t. $\frac{q}{p} > \frac{cu}{b'}$ or $\frac{cu}{a'} > \frac{q}{p}$ then $\max(d'_1, d'_2, d'_3) > \frac{c}{a'b'}$.

If we choose p, q s.t. $\frac{cu}{b'} \geq \frac{q}{p} \geq \frac{cu}{a'}$ then $\max(d'_1, d'_2, d'_3) = d'_3 = \frac{pc}{a'b'}$ and, in order to minimize this value, we can choose $p = 1, q = \lceil \frac{cv}{a'} \rceil \leq k \leq \frac{cu}{b'}$ (such an integer k exists by assumption).

If we choose $(p, q) = (0, 1)$ then $\max(d'_1, d'_2, d'_3) = 1$ (as in the previous case) with $1 \geq \frac{c}{a'b'}$.

Minimization is therefore achieved with $(p, q) = (1, \lceil \frac{cv}{a'} \rceil)$ although this choice of $(p. q)$ may not be unique in this case.

Steps 5 and 6. By definition $\frac{M}{N}$ is inside the interval $[\frac{cu}{b'}, \frac{cv}{a'}]$. As the algorithm proceeds, the values of q_i/p_i get closer and closer to $\frac{M}{N}$. There is a minimal integer i_0 such that q_{i_0}/p_{i_0} is inside the interval $[\frac{cu}{b'}, \frac{cv}{a'}]$. It follows, by Claim 2, that for all $i \geq i_0$ $\delta_i = \delta'_3(p_i, q_i)$ and $\delta_i > \delta_{i_0}$ for all

$i > i_0$. Therefore, the minimal value of δ_i is to be found in the range $o \leq i \leq i_0$, and the procedure searches for this minimal value precisely in that range. $\square$

Remark: It follows from the theory of continued fractions that the integers p, q output by the procedure min max have the property that $\gcd(p, q) = 1$.

We are now ready to define the main procedure.

Procedure $ST(\alpha, \beta, \gamma)$

Input: a, b, c, m, integers defining the equation (4) and u, v, d, w, r, integers computed in Step 1 of the LI-3 algorithm.

1. Set $a' := a/d$; $b' := b/d$;

2. Call minmax (p, q);

3. Let (p, q) be the integer output at Step 2. Compute $Z(\alpha), Z(\beta), Z(\gamma)$ as defined in (10) and set $Z_l = \min(Z(\alpha), Z(\beta), Z(\gamma))$, $Z_h = \max(Z(\alpha), Z(\beta), Z(\gamma))$.

4. If $\lceil Z_l \rceil > \lfloor Z_h \rfloor$, then return "no points";

5. For every j in the range $\lceil Z_l \rceil \leq j \leq \lfloor Z_h \rfloor$ find the y_1 coordinates s_j and t_j of the points of intersection of $py_1 + qy_2 = j$ with the triangle $\Delta(\alpha, \beta, \gamma)$.

6. For every j, s_j, t_j found in Step 5, return LI-2 $(py_1 + qy_2 = j; s_j \leq y_1 \leq t_j)$.

7. If step 6 produces no solutions for all the j's considered, then return "no points".
   End of procedure. $\square$

As is easy to see, the procedure finds a line $py_1 + qy_2 = z$, p and q integers, whose number of translates, with integer z, cutting the triangle $\Delta(\alpha, \beta, \gamma)$ is minimal (Step 2). For every such translate, $py_1 + qy_2 = j$ it outputs the points with integer coordinates on the line, and inside or on the sides of $\Delta(\alpha, \beta, \gamma)$.

4   An Example

Consider the equation

$$ax_1 + bx_2 + cx_3 = 271x_1 + 281x_2 + 283x_3 = 30,000 = m$$

over the nonnegative integers.

Using the extended Euclidean algorithm (Step 1 of Algorithm LI-3) we find

$$ua - vb = 28 * 271 - 27 * 281 = 1 = d$$

Thus $d = 1 = w, r = 0, \ u = 28, v = 27$.

The points α, β and γ as defined in Step 2 of the algorithm, in $(y_1 y_2)$ space, are found to be

$$\alpha = (28m/281, 0), \beta = (27m/271, 0)$$

$$\gamma = (0, 30, 000/283)$$

We now turn to the procedure $ST(\alpha, \beta, \gamma)$, which calls the procedure minmax (p, q).
With $a' = a, b' = b$, we get

$$\frac{cu}{b'} = \frac{283 * 28}{281} = \frac{7,924}{281} \cong 28.199$$

$$\frac{cv}{a'} = \frac{283 * 27}{271} = \frac{7,641}{271} \cong 28.195$$

$$\frac{c}{a'b'} = \frac{283}{76,151} < 1$$

Steps 2 and 3 of the minmax procedure do not apply, so we move to Step 4:

$$\frac{7,924 + 7,641}{281 + 271} = \frac{15,565}{552} \cong 28.197$$

$AS(552, 15, 565)$ is now called:

$$(p_0, q_0) = (1, \lfloor \frac{M}{N} \rfloor) = (1, 28) \text{ with } \delta \cong 0.199$$

The next 4 itterations of the AS procedure do not reduce δ but the fifth itteration produces the pair $(p_5, q_5) = (5, 141)$ with a smaller $\delta \cong 0.0221$. The next 9 itterations do not reduce δ but after those 9 itterations we get $(p_{14}, q_{14}) = (46, 1297)$ having the property that $\delta_{14} = d'_3(p_{14}, q_{14}) \cong 0.170$, i.e., the value $1297/46$ is inside the interval $[\frac{cu}{b'}, \frac{cv}{a'}] = [\frac{cu}{b'}, \frac{cv}{a'}]$ so that it's distance from the endpoints of the interval is less than the size of the interval which equals d'_3. The procedure minmax is therefore exited at this point with output $(p, q) = (5, 141)$ and we enter Step 3 of the $ST(\alpha, \beta, \gamma)$ procedure: For $(p, q) = (5, 141)$ we compute

$$Z(\alpha) = \frac{5 * 28 * 30,000}{281} \cong 14, 946.61$$

Similarly,

$$Z(\beta) \cong 14, 944.64, Z(\gamma) \cong 14, 946.99$$

with $Z_l = Z_\beta$ and $Z_h = Z(\gamma)$.

Step 4 of the ST procedure does not apply. The range of j at Step 5 us found to be $\lceil Z_l \rceil = 14, 945 \le j \le \lfloor Z_h \rfloor = 14, 946$, i.e., j can assume only 2 values, $j_1 = 14, 945$ and $j_2 = 14, 946$.

For $j_1 = 14, 945$ we find the y_1 coordinates of the points of intersection of the line $5y_1 + 141y_2 = 14, 945$ with $\Delta(\alpha, \beta, \gamma)$ to be $y_{11} = s_{j_1} = 2, 542.5, y_{12} = t_{j_1} = 2, 989$. Similarly for $j_2 = 14, 946$ we find $s_{j_2} = 1, 269, t_{j_2} = 2, 989.2$.

We apply now the LI-2 algorithm (Step 6) to $5y_1 + 141y_2 = 14,945, s_{j_1} \leq y_1 \leq t_{j_1}$ and $5y_1 + 141y_2 = 14,946, s_{j_2} \leq y_1 \leq t_{j_2}$, resulting in the following points

$$\hat{y}_{1i} = 2,989 - 141i, \hat{y}_{2i} = 5i : 0 \leq i \leq 3$$

$$\hat{y}_{1j} = 2,961 - 141j, \hat{y}_{2j} = 1 + 5j : 0 \leq j \leq 12$$

17 points in (y_1, y_2) space.

We return now to the LI-3 algorithm Step 3, and find, by formula (5), the solutions of the given equation to be:

$$\left. \begin{array}{l} \hat{x}_{1i} = 91 + i \\ \hat{x}_{2i} = 19 - 6i \\ \hat{x}_3 = 5i \end{array} \right\} 0 \leq i \leq 3$$

and

$$\left. \begin{array}{l} \hat{x}_{1j} = 35 + j \\ \hat{x}_{2j} = 72 - 6j \\ \hat{x}_{3j} = 1 + 5j \end{array} \right\} 0 \leq j \leq 12$$

The above set of 17 points is the set of all solutions of the given equation.

Some of the computations involved in the above example have been omitted but are straightforward and can be verified easily by the reader.

Remark: The area of the projection of the plane defined by the given equation, constrained by $x_1, x_2, x_3 \geq 0$ over the (x_1, x_2) plane is $\frac{30,000^2}{281 \cdot 283 \cdot 2} \cong 5,658$.

Thus, finding the above 17 solutions by exhaustive search involves the probing of about 5658 points.

5 Complexity Issues

Finding all the solutions of an equation $ax_1 + bx_2 + cx_3 = m$ over the nonnegative integers by exhaustive search may require about $m/(2bc)$ probes and this number is exponential in the length of the input. Some saving my be gained if one uses the fact that the set of solutions is embedded in a lattice.

Still, finding a basis for this lattice by exhaustive search may not be an easy task. We shall analyze now the complexity of the Algorithm LI-3, with the equation $ax_1 + bx_2 + cx_3 = m$ at input; $a < b < c$ and m positive integers; counting the number of arithmetical operations involved.

Step 1 is $O(\log a)$

Step 2 is Constant

Step 3 depends on the procedure ST.

Analyzing the ST procedure we see that all its steps are constant except Step 2 which depends on the minmax procedure.

The minmax procedure depends on the AS procedure which is $O(\log^2(a' + b'))$ on the average. All in all, the algorithm LI-3 is therefore $O(\log^2(a + b))$ on the average.

We would like, however, to make the following remarks.

Remark 1: Notice the fact that the complexity of the algorithm does not depend on m. If $m \geq nab$, then we should expect at least n solutions (with $x_3 = 0$), see Remark 2 in Section 2, but, due to the lattice structure of the solutions, all the solutions can be expressed in a single formula as a 2-parametric set.

Remark 2: Consider the procedure minmax, which determines the complexity of Step 3 of the algorithm.

If Step 2 or Step 3 of the minmax procedure applies, which happens for example when $c > a'b'$, then the complexity of this procedure becomes constant. If this is the case, then the worst case complexity of the LI-3 reduces to $O(\log a)$.

Moreover, the average complexity of the minmax procedure, when its 2nd and 3rd steps do not apply, is actually much lower than $O(\log^2(a + b))$ since the procedure AS used by the minmax procedure is not carried through to its end but is abandoned when the pair (p_i, q_i) generated at itteration i has the property that

$$\frac{cu}{b'} \leq \frac{q_i}{p_i} \leq \frac{cv}{a'}.$$

Remark 3: It is easy to see that all the procedures and algorithms involved in the paper do not produce intermediary values whose bit size is larger than the bit size of the input.

6   Open Problem

Let $v_1, v_2 \cdots v_m$ be m points in an n-dimensional Euclidean space with $m \geq n + 1$. Provide a polynomial algorithm (in the length of the input) which finds a vector of integers $p = (p_1, ..., p_n)$ such that $\max_{1 \leq i \leq m} \lfloor p(v_i) \rfloor - \min_{1 \leq i \leq m} \lceil p(v_i) \rceil$ is minimal, where $p(v_i)$ is the value of $p_1 x_1 + p_2 x_2 + \cdots + p_n x_n$ at $(x_1 \cdots x_n) = v_i$.

The procedure minmax given in this paper solves the above problem for $n = 2$ and v_1, v_2, v_3 of a particular form. For $n = 2$ this procedure can be extended so as to solve the problem for any v_1, v_2, v_3.

A general and efficient solution to the above problem may provide an alternative algorithm for solving integer programming and related problems.

References

[HW] G.H. Hardy, F.M. Wright, "An Introduction to the Theory of Numbers". Oxford, Clarendon Press, 1962.

[HN] H.S. Hall, S.R. Knight, "Higher Algebra". Third edition, Macmillan, 1957.

[K] A. Ya. Khintchine, "Continued Fractions". Noordhoff, Groningen, 1963, or Univ. of Chicago Press, 1964.

[Kn] D.E. Knuth, "The Art of Computer Programming". Second edition, Addison-Wesley, 1981, Vol.2, Ch.4.

[L] H.W. Lenstra, "Integer programming with a Fixed Number of Variables", *Math. of Oper. Res.*, Vol. 8, 1983, pp. 583-548.

[S] E.S. Selmer, "On the Linear Diophantine Problem of Frobenius in Three Variables", *J. reine. angew. Math.*, Vol. 293-294, 1977, pp. 1-17.

[Syl] J.J. Sylvester, "Mathematical Questions with their Solutions", *Educational Times*, Vol. 41, 1884, p. 21.

[YK] A.C. Yao, D.E. Knuth, "Analysis of the Substractive Algorithm for Greatest Common Divisors", Stanford C-S-75-510 Report, September 1975.

EVENT DETECTION FOR ODES AND NONRECURSIVE HIERARCHIES

KEIJO RUOHONEN
Department of Mathematics
Tampere University of Technology
33101 Tampere, FINLAND

1. Introduction

Numerical solution of initial value problems for normal form nonlinear ODEs can be a demanding task, even when the ODE is of a relatively simple form. The phenomena around strange attractors and chaos indicate that this is an inherent property of these initial value problems, which cannot be avoided. For some poignant examples see e.g. [13]. The solution $y(t;c)$ of the initial value problem

$$y' = f(y,t), \qquad y(0) = c$$

is however globally computable when some mild assumptions are satisfied (the chief among them being computability of f and uniqueness of the solution). Indeed, as pointed out in [4], this follows easily from the standard proof of Osgood's existence theorem. (The main result of [4] is the spectacular loss of computability when the solution is not unique, see also [3].) A similar result can be obtained for s y s t e m s of differential equations but the proof is more complicated, see [11].

Numerical solution of event detection problems for normal form ODEs can also be a demanding task, see [12]. An *event* of an ODE $y' = f(y,t)$, with the initial value $y(0) = c$, occurs whenever at least one of the given equations

$$g_j(t,y(t;c),y'(t;c)) = 0 \qquad (j = 1,\dots,k)$$

is satisfied for some t in a given interval I. (In case the solution is not unique it is required that each solution satisfies at least one of the equations.) Now, obviously event detection is undecidable in the sense that detection of an event $y(t;c) = 0$ for a given computable real c and the initial value problem $y' = 0$, $y(0) = c$, is undecidable, because $c = 0$ is undecidable. (In a similar vein event detection is symbolically undecidable, see [9].) Thus decidability questions concerning event detection would not seem to be very interesting.

Event detection is however also d y n a m i c a l l y undecidable for time intervals of the form $[0,T)$ and $[0,\infty)$, as was shown in [9] through dynamical simulation of a universal Turing machine by an ODE. Indeed, in [9] initial values c are n-tuples of nonnegative integers, f is a f i x e d explicitly given function and the event to be detected is of the simple form $y_i(t;c) = 0.5$. (And no reference to computability of reals or functions actually appears.) Even a smooth choice for f is possible. A similar result can be obtained for a closed finite time interval $[0,T]$ but only at the expense of allowing f to be unbounded on $[0,T]$ and discontinuous at $t = T$. (The case of a c o n t i n u o u s f on a closed finite time interval remains open.)

The first theme of this paper is to investigate how high a "dynamical" undecidability can be obtained by allowing f to be noncomputable using oracle sets in its definition, or by allowing nonuniqueness of solutions. In a way this investigation was already began in [9]. Successive embedding of oracle machines and simulation by ODEs were used there to get event detection problems "dynamically" hard for any level Σ_n in the arithmetical hierarchy, but only at the expense of allowing f to be discontinuous and unbounded. Whatever precise meaning of "dynamical" one may use, it will of course be quite stretched when oracles, nonuniqueness of solutions or discontinuities are introduced.

As another theme it is shown that quite natural parametric event detection problems lead to very high undecidabilities, in fact the whole analytical hierarchy can be reached by quantified parameters. The simplest of these may be considered as a "disturbed" event detection problem where it is required that the occurrence of an event does not depend on "small" variations in the value of a parameter appearing in f. All ODEs appearing in this paper are very unstable numerically. What the undecidabilities obtained here indicate is that even assuming perfect numerical accuracy another kind of instability remains, which could be called "computational instability".

Only some rather basic results in automata theory, recursive function theory and ODE theory are needed, they can be found e.g. in [2], [6], [7] and [1]. Basics on computability of reals and functions can be obtained in [5].

2. Preliminaries

The central tool of [9] is simulation of a counter machine $\mathcal{M}$ with m counters and counter input (and no internal states) by a $2m + 1$-dimensional autonomous ODE

$$\frac{dq}{dt} = Q(q(t))$$

with an initial value at $t = 0$. As is well known, counter machines have a universal computing power. The following characteristics of this simulation will be needed:

   (A) The simulation of the i-th step of the computation of $\mathcal{M}$ takes place in two stages, the first stage in the time interval $2i - 2 < t < 2i - 1$ and the second in $2i - 1 < t < 2i$.
   (B) Two copies of counters of $\mathcal{M}$ are kept, the first in $q_1,...,q_m$ and the second in $q_{m+1},...,q_{2m}$, giving the counts of symbols in the counters. The state q_{2m+1} is the time t (whence $Q_{2m+1} = 1$).
   (C) During the first stage of simulation counter transition of $\mathcal{M}$ is performed on $q_1,...,q_m$ using $q_{m+1},...,q_{2m+1}$, and $q_{m+1},...,q_{2m}$ will remain unchanged. During the second stage the states $q_{m+1},...,q_{2m}$ are updated using $q_1,...,q_m,q_{2m+1}$, and $q_1,...,q_m$ remain unchanged.

(D) If the input count of $\mathcal{M}$ is n then the initial value is $c = (n,0,\ldots,0,n,0,\ldots,0)$ where the n's are at the first and the $m + 1$-th position.

(E) When $\mathcal{M}$ halts at the ith step, then the value of q_m, which hitherto has been 0, is raised to 1 during $2i - 2 < t < 2i - 1$, and will stay there for $t \geq 2i - 1$. The ODE does not "halt". Halting of $\mathcal{M}$ is thus signalled by the event $q_m(t) = 0.5$.

Structural properties and explicit construction of Q are given in [9] (Theorem 1 and its proof).

A *counter machine with oracle L* is like a usual counter machine, except that certain counters, say the $m - 2$-th and the $m - 1$-th counters, are reserved for oracle calls. L is a set of positive integers and an oracle call is the query "$j \in L$?". It will be assumed here that the oracle calls are done in order, that is, the call previous to "$j + 1 \in L$?" is always the call "$j \in L$?" This obviously does not detract from the generality of oracle computations. An oracle call is indicated by raising the count of the $m - 2$-th counter from 0 to 1 the count of the $m - 1$-th counter remaining 0. During the jth oracle query step the $m - 2$-th counter is popped and the count of the $m - 1$-th counter is raised to 1 if $j \in L$ (but not otherwise), other counters remaining as they are. The $m - 1$-th counter is then immediately popped, i.e., the oracle answer is either "used" immediately or stored elsewhere. The $m - 2$-th and the $m - 1$-th counters remain empty until the next oracle call. (For technical reasons the oracle counter machine model here is somewhat different from the one used in [9].)

Simulation of an oracle query step by an ODE, whichever way it is done, all takes place during a time interval $2i - 2 < t < 2i - 1$. In [9] the trick was to simulate the whole computation sequence of another (oracle) counter machine during this time interval. Here oracle sets are used in the definition of the ODE thus making it noncomputable, but still computable relative to the oracle.

For the sake of definiteness the form of the *event detection problem* (*EDP* in short) considered in this paper is now fixed as follows:

(EDP) *For an ODE* $y' = f(y)$, *components* $y_{i_1},\ldots,y_{i_k}$ *of* y, *rational numbers* $w_1,\ldots,w_k$ *and a time interval* I, *decide whether or not for a given initial value* $y(0) = c$ *with nonnegative integer components the event defined by*

$$y_{i_1}(t) = w_1 ,\ldots, y_{i_k}(t) = w_k$$

occurs for some $t \in I$.

For a p a r a m e t r i c O D E $y' = f(y,p)$, where p is a parameter vector in a given parameter domain, EDP is defined analogously: EDP has a positive solution if e a c h of the "usual" EDPs obtained by fixing a parameter value has a positive solution.

As noted, in the case of time intervals $[0,T)$ and $[0,\infty)$, EDP is undecidable for an ODE with a computable—in fact, explicitly given—effectively bounded f and unique solutions. Furthermore, for time intervals of the form $[0,T]$ EDP is undecidable for an

ODE with a computable—in a properly extended sense, but in fact explicitly given—f and unique solutions.

3. Undecidability Relative to an Oracle

Take a set L of positive integers which is Σ_{k-1}-complete ($k \geq 2$) and code it as a binary $\omega = 0.b_1 b_2 b_3 \cdots$, say, as follows:

$$b_i = \begin{cases} 1 & \text{if } i \in L \\ 0 & \text{if } i \notin L. \end{cases}$$

Such an ω is computable relative to the oracle L. Obviously ω contains infinitely many 1's and infinitely many 0's.

A counter machine $\mathscr{M}$ with oracle L can now be simulated by an ODE

$$\frac{dr}{dt} = R(r(t))$$

as follows. First take an ODE

$$\frac{dq}{dt} = Q(q(t))$$

of dimension $2m + 1$ which simulates $\mathscr{M}$ without the oracle call steps, as described above in (A)–(E). Note that also transitions other than oracle call steps may involve the $m - 2$-th and the $m - 1$-th counters specifically dedicated to oracle calls (the flag indicating oracle queries must be set and the oracle answers are used later). Thus q_{m-2} and q_{m-1} will not change during the second stage.

The new ODE will be of dimension $2m + 3$ and its initial value is of the form $c = (n,0,\ldots,0,n,0,\ldots,0)$ where the n's are at the first and the $m + 1$-th position. Denote

$$h(x) = \begin{cases} e^{1-1/x} & \text{if } x > 0 \\ 0 & \text{if } x \leq 0 \end{cases}$$

and

$$l(q) = 1 - h(1 - h(q))$$

(note that $h(1) = 1$). Thus $l(q)$ is a smooth sigmoid, equal to 0 for $q \leq 0$ and equal to 1 for $q \geq 1$. Take then

$$R_i = Q_i(r_1,\ldots,r_{2m+1})(1 - r_{2m-2}) \quad (i = 1,\ldots,m-3 \text{ and } i = m)$$

which makes the first $m - 3$ components and the mth component of the new ODE behave exactly as those of the old one when oracle calls are not simulated, and forces these components to remain as they are during simulation of an oracle call. Further take

$$R_{m-2} = Q_{m-2}(r_1,...,r_{2m+1})(1 - r_{2m-2}) - r_{2m-2}s(r_{2m+1})$$

where $s(t) = ah(\sin \pi t)$ and the (computable) constant a is chosen to satisfy

$$\int_{2i-2}^{2i-1} s(t)\, dt = 1.$$

This in turn makes the $m - 2$-th component of the new ODE behave exactly as that of the old one when oracle calls are not simulated, and removes the oracle call flag during simulation of an oracle call. (From [9] it may be recalled that $s(q_{2m+1})$ is used to separate the working of the ODE into the two stages and hence it appears as a multiplier in $Q_1,...,Q_m$.)

For the new ODE the second stage is always exactly the same as that of the old one, as is the flow of time, so

$$R_i = Q_i(r_1,...,r_{2m+1}) \qquad (i = m + 1,...,2m + 1).$$

The $2m + 2$-th and the $2m + 3$-th components of the new ODE are used to generate the bits $b_1,b_2,...$ of ω one by one to be used as oracle answers. After the jth oracle call r_{2m+2} has the value $b_{j+1}.b_{j+2}b_{j+3}\cdots$. At the time of the jth oracle call r_{2m+3} contains $2b_j$, so

$$R_{m-1} = Q_{m-1}(r_1,...,r_{2m+1})(1 - r_{2m-2}) + \frac{1}{2} r_{2m+3}r_{2m-2}s(r_{2m+1})$$

which makes r_{m-1} behave exactly as q_{m-1} when there are no oracle calls and generates the oracle answer. Finally take

$$R_{2m+2} = [\ln 2\, r_{2m-2}l(r_{2m+1} - 1)(r_{2m+2} - r_{2m+3}) + 2\omega(1 - l(r_{2m+1} - 1))]s(r_{2m+1})$$

and

$$R_{2m+3} = [d(r_{2m+2},r_{2m+3})(1 - r_{m-2}) + g(r_{2m+3})r_{m-2}]s(r_{2m+1} + 1)$$

where

$$d(c,r) = (c - r)(\ln(|c - r|/2) - 1)^2 \quad \text{and} \quad g(r) = -\sin \pi r\, (\ln |\sin \pi r| - 1)^2.$$

The first part of R_{2m+2} doubles the value of r_{2m+2} and then subtracts r_{2m+3} from it during an oracle call, the second part raises the value of r_{2m+2} to 2ω during $0 \le t \le 1$ (first stage). During the second stage $R_{2m+2} = 0$. While there are no oracle calls the value of r_{2m+3} remains in r_{2m+2}, during an oracle call R_{2m+3} acts by replacing r_{2m+3} with twice its integer part which gives the oracle answer (second stage), then remaining the same (first stage) and finally updating the value of r_{2m+3} to the new value of r_{2m+2} (second stage).

The detailed working of R_{2m+2} and R_{2m+3} is best explained by the table below and the following simple initial value problems and their solutions:

(1) The solution of the initial value problem

$$\frac{dr}{dt} = \ln 2 \, (r - c), \qquad r(0) = r_0,$$

is $r(t) = c + (r_0 - c)2^t$, and so $r(1) = 2r_0 - c$.
(2) The solution of the initial value problem

$$\frac{dr}{dt} = (c - r)(\ln(|c - r|/2) - 1)^2, \qquad r(0) = r_0,$$

where $0 \le r_0 \le 2$ and $0 \le c \le 2$, is

$$r(t) = c \pm 2h(T - t),$$

where

$$T = \frac{1}{1 - \ln(\pm(r_0 - c)/2)}.$$

Thus $r(1) = c$.
(3) The solutions of the initial value problems

$$\frac{dr}{dt} = -\sin \pi r \, (\ln |\sin \pi r| - 1)^2, \qquad r(0) = r_0 \text{ and } r(0) = r_1,$$

where $0 < r_0 < 1$ and $1 < r_1 < 2$, are respectively given by

$$-\int_{r_0}^{r(t)} \frac{du}{\sin \pi u \, (\ln(\sin \pi u) - 1)^2} = t$$

while $r(t) > 0$ and $r(t) = 0$ afterwards, and

$$-\int_{r_1}^{r(t)} \frac{du}{\sin \pi u \, (\ln(-\sin \pi u) - 1)^2} = t$$

while $r(t) < 2$ and $r(t) = 2$ afterwards. It is easily verified that then $r(1) = 0$ for any initial value $r(0) = r_0$, and $r(1) = 2$ for any initial value $r(0) = r_1$.

The table below contains the values of various components of the new ODE during ordinary steps and oracle calls after $t = 1$. Printing in boldface indicates a (possibly) new value.

flag		oracle answer		stage	oracle answer generation	
r_{m-2}	r_{2m-2}	r_{m-1}	r_{2m-1}		r_{2m+2}	r_{2m+3}
0	0	0	0	I	r_{2m+2}	r_{2m+3}
0	0	0	0	II	r_{2m+2}	r_{2m+3}
1	0	0	0	I	r_{2m+2}	r_{2m+3}
1	1	0	0	II	r_{2m+2}	$2\lfloor r_{2m+3}\rfloor$
0	1	$r_{2m+3}/2$	0	I	$2r_{2m+2}-r_{2m+3}$	r_{2m+3}
0	0	r_{m-1}	r_{m-1}	II	r_{2m+2}	$\to r_{2m+2}$
0	0	0	r_{2m-1}	I	r_{2m+2}	r_{2m+3}
0	0	0	0	II	r_{2m+2}	r_{2m+3}

It is not difficult to see that the solution $r(t)$ will be a smooth function (as mentioned in [9], $q(t)$ is smooth).

The choice of d and g is, of course, somewhat arbitrary. Another choice is e.g.

$$d(c,r) = 3\sqrt[3]{(c-r)/2} \quad \text{and} \quad g(r) = -2\sqrt[3]{\sin \pi r}$$

but then r_{2m+3} is not smooth. A discontinuous choice is

$$d(c,r) = 2\,\mathrm{sgn}(c-r) \quad \text{and} \quad g(r) = -\mathrm{sgn}(\sin \pi r).$$

For all these choices the solution is forward unique (the trouble point $r_{2m+3} = 1$ cannot occur because ω contains infinitely many 1's and infinitely many 0's), but not backward unique. A solution which is forward unique even for $r_{2m+3} = 1$ is obtained by taking $g(r) = \ln 2\,(r - 2b)$ where $b = r_{2m+2} - \lfloor r_{2m+2}\rfloor$ which however makes R discontinuous.

Denote then by G_1 the family of multivariable functions obtained from the rationals, the constants π and $\ln 2$, variables, the (left continuous) unit step $u(x)$ and the trigonometric functions by closure under $+$, $-$, $\cdot$ and composition of mappings. The family G_2 is defined similarly: in addition to π the real constant a is needed as well as closure under h and logarithm. Note that G_1 contains the functions $u(x)x^n$ ($n = 0,1,2,\ldots$) which can be used in place of $h(x)$. (The construction of Q is explained in [9], and there G_2 was closed under cube root, but closure under logarithm works equally well.)

An infinite acceleration ($+$ downscaling), as explained in [9], squeezes the computation to the finite time interval $[0,1)$ and keeps the solution bounded.

The following theorem is then proved above. (The time interval $[0,1)$ may of course be replaced by any interval $[0,T)$ where T is a positive rational, say.)

THEOREM 1. *Let ω be a Σ_{k-1}-complete real $(k \geq 2)$ in $(0,1)$ and I be $[0,\infty)$ or $[0,1)$. Then there exists an explicitly given ODE $y' = f(y,\omega)$ where f belongs to G_1 (resp. G_2 and is continuous) for which EDP is Σ_k-hard in the interval I. The solution $y(t)$ is continuous (resp. smooth), and bounded for $I = [0,1)$.* ∎

Of course, only a fraction of the functions in the families G_1 and G_2 will be needed for the ODE in Theorem 1, and countless other choices, perhaps more natural than G_1 and G_2, are possible. The present G_1 and G_2 are chosen for the sake of definiteness only. The choice of G_1 shows that some very simple functions suffice to get the result, and the choice of G_2 that discontinuities are not necessary and that a smooth solution is also possible.

It may be noted that, instead of passing ω as a parameter in $f(y,\omega)$ in the above theorem, it may be passed alternatively as a fixed initial value. Only some small changes in R_{2m+2} and R_{2m+3} are needed.

It is perhaps worthwhile to describe another way of embedding oracles in ODEs (used in [8]). Define the function $\omega(x)$ on $[j - 0.5, j + 0.5)$ by

$$\omega(x) = \begin{cases} h(\cos^2 \pi x) = e^{-\tan^2 \pi x} & \text{if } j \in L \\ 0 & \text{if } j \notin L \end{cases} \qquad (j = 1,2,\ldots).$$

$\omega(x)$ is smooth but computable only relative to L. Take the ODE

$$\frac{dq}{dt} = Q(q(t))$$

as above. Now the new ODE

$$\frac{dv}{dt} = V(v(t))$$

will be of dimension $2m + 2$ and its initial value is of the form $c = (n,0,\ldots,0,n,0,\ldots,0)$ where the n's are at the first and the $m + 1$-th position, as before. V is given by

$$V_i = Q_i(v_1,\ldots,v_{2m+1})(1 - v_{2m-2}) \qquad (i = 1,\ldots,m - 3 \text{ and } i = m),$$

$$V_{m-2} = Q_{m-2}(v_1,\ldots,v_{2m+1})(1 - v_{2m-2}) - v_{2m-2}s(v_{2m+1}),$$

$$V_i = Q_i(v_1,\ldots,v_{2m+1}) \qquad (i = m + 1,\ldots,2m + 1),$$

$$V_{m-1} = Q_{m-1}(v_1,\ldots,v_{2m+1})(1 - v_{2m-2}) + \omega(v_{2m+2})v_{2m-2}s(v_{2m+1})$$

and

$$V_{2m+2} = v_{m-2} \, s(v_{2m+1} + 1).$$

The working of V is similar to that of R and is given by the table below. Printing in boldface indicates a (possibly) new value.

flag		oracle answer		stage	oracle answer generation
v_{m-2}	v_{2m-2}	v_{m-1}	v_{2m-1}		v_{2m+2}
0	0	0	0	I	n
0	0	0	0	II	n
1	0	0	0	I	n
1	1	0	0	II	$n+1$
0	1	$\omega(n+1)$	0	I	$n+1$
0	0	$\omega(n+1)$	$\omega(n+1)$	II	$n+1$
0	0	0	$\omega(n+1)$	I	$n+1$
0	0	0	0	II	$n+1$

If this ODE is used, then the ODE in Theorem 1 will be of the form $y' = f(y, \omega(y_i))$ where ω acts as a "plugged-in" real function.

The advantage of this latter construct is that now the oracle answer generating process is completely reversible, because all the answers are conveniently preserved in ω, and V is continuous (assuming Q is in G_2). It remains an open problem whether or not one could use a smooth f in Theorem 1. For this one would probably need a reversible counter machine with oracle—based on a reversible Turing machine model, the one described in [10], say—and its simulation by a smooth ODE (see [9] and [8]). The latter ODE would seem to be more amenable to such a simulation. Nevertheless, the whole construct is likely to be quite elaborate and is not pursued any further here.

4. The Parametric EDP

An oracle L may be used to define a mapping ϕ from positive integers to positive integers, say, as follows. The binary expansion of ω (the real number ω obtained from L) is of the form

$$\omega = 0.1^{(n_1-1)}01^{(n_2-1)}01^{(n_3-1)}...,$$

where $1^{(n)}$ denotes a sequence of n ones, and defines the mapping $\phi(k) = n_k$. It will be assumed that the binary expansion of a real cannot contain only finitely many zeros and hence is unique. Thus cofinite oracles are not allowed. Values of ω with binary expansions containing only finitely many ones (i.e., finite oracles) will be allowed. The ODE $r' = R(r)$ in Theorem 1 may then actually be considered as having an additional function plug-in, i.e., a counter machine (and thus a Turing machine) with a function input ϕ (in addition to the usual counter input) can be simulated by the ODE. Two possibilities for such a simulation are now described.

(I) As mentioned, values of ω with binary expansions containing only finitely many ones are now allowed. If in R the definition $g(r) = \ln 2 \ (r - 2b)$, where $b = r_{2m+2} - \lfloor r_{2m+2} \rfloor$, is chosen then these values cause no trouble. Unfortunately R is then discontinuous.

(II) Choices of $g(r)$ given in Section 3, other than the one in (I), lead to a continuous R, but values of ω with binary expansions the form $\omega = 0.b_1 \cdots b_l 1^{(n)} 0 \cdots$ $(n > 0)$ will cause trouble. Eventually r_{2m+2} will have the value 1 prior to an oracle call. Truncation to the nearest even integer will not then necessarily lead to the correct value $r_{2m+3} = 2$, in fact, due to forward nonuniqueness, the result can be any number in [0,2]. The value $r_{2m+3} = 0$ in effect replaces the binary expansion of ω by the equivalent forbidden expansion $0.b_1 \cdots b_l 1^{(n-1)} 01 \cdots$. Since cofinite oracles were not allowed the machine $\mathcal{M}$ to be simulated then does not halt. This situation is however signalled by the event $r_{2m+2} = 2$, which does not happen for other values of ω, and is thus caught. Values of r_{2m+3} in (0,2) obtained after the truncation lead to profoundly wrong behaviour, which also must be caught. For this purpose a new component r_{2m+4} is added to the ODE the working of which is given by

$$R_{2m+4} = r_{2m-2}^2 h(r_{2m+3}) h(2 - r_{2m+3}) s(r_{2m+1}) + r_{2m+4}, \qquad r_{2m+4}(0) = 0.$$

Thus a "truncated" value of r_{2m+3} in (0,2) leads to a positive value of r_{2m+4} which immediately starts growing indefinitely, and is eventually signalled by the event $r_{2m+4} = 1$. This event does not happen when an ω with infinitely many 1's in its binary expansion is used.

For a counter machine $\mathcal{M}$ with function input the set

$$P(\mathcal{M}) = \{ \ n \ | \ \text{There is a function input } \phi \text{ such that}$$
$$\mathcal{M} \text{ does not halt when receiving } \phi \text{ and } n. \ \}$$

and its complement $Q(\mathcal{M})$ can be defined. The family of all sets of the form $P(\mathcal{M})$ is the family Σ_1^1, and the family of all sets of the form $Q(\mathcal{M})$ is the family Π_1^1, the first two families in the analytical hierarchy of sets of positive integers, see e.g. [6].

Taking a Π_1^1-complete $Q(\mathcal{M})$ one gets the following theorem where G_3 is defined as G_1, except that in addition to the unit step the floor function is included, too.

THEOREM 2. Let I be $[0,\infty)$ or $[0,1)$. Then there exists an explicitly given parametric ODE $y' = f(y,p), p \in [0,1)$, where f belongs to G_1 (resp. G_2 and is continuous) such that the corresponding parametric EDP in the interval I is Π_1^1-hard. Nonuniqueness in the forward direction appears for some values of p but each extra solution is sig-

nalled by an event. However, if $f \in G_3$ is allowed, then the solution is forward unique. ∎

It remains an open problem whether or not the theorem holds true for a continuous $f(y,p)$ and forward unique (or unique) solutions.

Note. Of course, it may be assumed that only reals ω with binary expansions containing infinitely many 1's (and infinitely many 0's) are used to code the mappings ϕ. The exact correspondence might be, say,

$$\omega = 0.0^{(\phi(1)-1)}1^{(\phi(2))}0^{(\phi(3))}...,$$

where $1^{(n)}$ denotes a sequence of n ones and $0^{(n)}$ a sequence of n zeros. Thus Theorem 2 holds true also if, instead of requiring an event to occur for each solution of the initial value problem, as was done above, an event is required to occur for a t l e a s t   o n e of the solutions.

Since the set

$\{ n \mid$ There is a function input ϕ such that $\mathcal{M}$ halts when receiving ϕ and n. $\}$

is always recursively enumerable it would appear that the "existential version" of parametric EDP, where it is required that an event occurs for at least one parameter value in the parameter domain, is not very interesting. The following simple observation is of interest, however. Taking the basic (universal) counter machine simulating ODE

$$\frac{dq}{dt} = Q(q(t))$$

(cf. Section 2) and introducing the parameter $p \in [0,1)$ by $w(t) = q(t/(1-p))$ one gets the parametric initial value problem

$$\frac{dw}{dt} = \frac{1}{1-p}Q(w(t)), \qquad w(0) = c$$

for which the existential parametric EDP is undecidable (Σ_1-hard) in any c l o s e d interval $[0,T]$.

Returning now to the construct in Section 3 it should be obvious how it could be modified to include several parameters, say $p_1,...,p_k$, each in the interval $[0,1)$. In addition to k oracle call flags, say $r_{m-2k},...,r_{m-k-1}$, and k oracle answer components, say $r_{m-k},...,r_{m-1}$, $2k$ "bit generating" components $r_{2m+2},r_{2m+3},...,r_{2m+2k},r_{2m+2k+1}$ are introduced (and, should alternative *(II)* above be adopted, also an "unsuccessful truncation detecting" component $r_{2m+2k+2}$, shared by all oracles). These parameters code k oracles and the corresponding mappings $\phi_1,...,\phi_k$. To make matters more simple, it may be assumed that only one oracle at a time may answer a query.

Suppose the parameters are then quantified by the alternating quantifier sequence

$$\begin{cases} (\exists p_k)(\forall p_{k-1})\cdots(\exists p_2)(\forall p_1), & \text{if } k \text{ is even} \\ (\forall p_k)(\exists p_{k-1})\cdots(\exists p_2)(\forall p_1), & \text{if } k \text{ is odd,} \end{cases}$$

with the obvious interpretation in event detection. The resulting EDP is called the k-∀EDP. (Obviously 1-∀EDP is the usual parametric EDP.) If alternative (I) above is used then the following theorem is obtained.

THEOREM 3. *Let I be $[0,\infty)$ or $[0,1)$. Then, for any $k \geq 1$, there exists an explicitly given parametric ODE $y' = f(y,p)$, $p \in [0,1)^k$, where f belongs to G_3, such that the corresponding k-∀EDP in the interval I is Σ^1_k-hard if k is even and Π^1_k-hard if k is odd. The solution is forward unique.* ∎

The parameters can be quantified by a sequence

$$\begin{cases} (\forall p_k)(\exists p_{k-1})\cdots(\forall p_2)(\exists p_1), & \text{if } k \text{ is even} \\ (\exists p_k)(\forall p_{k-1})\cdots(\forall p_2)(\exists p_1), & \text{if } k \text{ is odd} \end{cases}$$

as well, and the resulting EDP is called the k-∃EDP. As noted above, 1-∃EDP is Σ_1-hard, so a somewhat weaker undecidability is obtained for the k-∃EDP, which however holds for a closed finite time interval.

THEOREM 4. *For any $k \geq 2$, there exists an explicitly given parametric ODE $y' = f(y,p)$, $p \in [0,1)^k$, where f belongs to G_3, such that the corresponding k-∃EDP in the interval $[0,1]$ is Π^1_{k-1}-hard if k is even and Σ^1_{k-1}-hard if k is odd. The solution is forward unique.* ∎

5. Nonuniqueness of Solutions

So far nonuniqueness of solutions in the forward direction has been more a nuisance to be avoided than a boon. It can be used to "generate" a real value in a given interval, however, which leads to a situation very similar to the one in Theorem 2. Indeed one only needs to take

$$R_{2m+2} = [\ln 2 \, r_{2m-2} l(r_{2m+1} - 1)(r_{2m+2} - r_{2m+3})$$

$$+ e(r_{2m+2})(1 - l(r_{2m+1} - 1))]s(r_{2m+1}),$$

say, where

$$e(r) = |r|(\ln |r| - 1)^2.$$

(Another continuous choice would be $e(r) = 3r^{2/3}$ which however does not make r_{2m+2} smooth, and a discontinuous choice would be simply $e(r) = u(r)$.) The maximum solution of the initial value problem

$$\frac{dr}{dt} = |r|(\ln |r| - 1)^2, \qquad r(0) = 0,$$

is $r(t) = h(t)$, and its minimum solution is $r(t) = 0$. Thus the value of $r_{2m+2}(1)$ can be any number in $[0,1]$ which is quite sufficient. Since nonuniqueness occurs anyway, alternative *(II)* given in the previous section is a natural choice and leads to the following theorem.

THEOREM 5. *Let I be* $[0,\infty)$ *or* $[0,1)$. *Then there exists an explicitly given ODE* $y' = f(y)$, *where f belongs to* G_2 *and is continuous, such that the corresponding EDP in the interval I is* Π_1^1-*hard. The solution is not unique in the forward direction.* ∎

Parameters $p_1, \ldots, p_k$ may be added, each in the interval $[0,1)$, and the k-∃EDP considered. This implies that alternative *(I)* in the previous section should be chosen (and also the discontinuous $e(r)$ above). Now, thinking of the real value $r_{2m+2}(1)$ as if it were a universally quantified $k + 1$-th parameter one gets a more general result.

THEOREM 6. *Let I be* $[0,\infty)$ *or* $[0,1)$. *Then there exists an explicitly given parametric ODE* $y' = f(y,p)$, $p \in [0,1)^k$, *where f belongs to* G_3, *such that the corresponding* k-∃EDP *in the interval I is* Π_{k+1}^1-*hard if k is even and* Σ_{k+1}^1-*hard if k is odd. The solution is not unique in the forward direction.* ∎

References

[1]   HARTMAN, P.: *Ordinary Differential Equations.* Birkhäuser (1982)
[2]   HOPCROFT, J.E. & ULLMAN, J.D.: *Introduction to Automata Theory, Languages and Computation.* Addison–Wesley (1979)
[3]   KO, KER-I: On the Computational Complexity of Ordinary Differential Equations. *Inform. and Control 58* (1983), 157–194
[4]   POUR-EL, M.B. & RICHARDS, I.: A Computable Ordinary Differential Equation which Possesses No Computable Solutions. *Ann. Math. Logic 17* (1979), 61–90
[5]   POUR-EL, M.B. & RICHARDS, I.: *Computability in Analysis and Physics.* Springer–Verlag (1989)
[6]   ROGERS, H.: *Theory of Recursive Functions and Effective Computability.* McGraw–Hill (1967)
[7]   ROXIN, E.O.: *Ordinary Differential Equations.* Wadsworth (1972)
[8]   RUOHONEN, K.: Turing Machine Simulation by ODEs. *Report 59,* Tampere University of Technology, Department of Electrical Engineering, Mathematics. Tampere (1991)
[9]   RUOHONEN, K.: Undecidability of Event Detection for ODEs. *J. Inform. Proc. Cybern. EIK 29* (1993), 101–113

[10]   RUOHONEN, K.: Reversible Machines and Post's Correspondence Problem for Biprefix Morphisms. *Elektron. Inf.verarb. Kybern. EIK 21* (1985), 579–595

[11]   RUOHONEN, K.: An Effective Cauchy–Peano Existence Theorem for Unique Solutions. *Report 63*, Tampere University of Technology, Department of Information Technology, Mathematics. Tampere (1993)

[12]   SHAMPINE, L.F. & GLADWELL, I. & BRANKIN, R.W.: Reliable Solution of Special Event Location Problems for ODEs. *ACM Trans. on Math. Software 17* (1991), 11–25

[13]   VICHNIAC, G.Y.: Instability in Discrete Algorithms and Exact Reversibility. *SIAM J. Alg. Disc. Math. 5* (1984), 596–602

Rediscovering Pushdown Machines

Kai Salomaa, Derick Wood, and Sheng Yu

Department of Computer Science, University of Western Ontario, London, Ontario
N6A 5B7, Canada.

Abstract. We reexamine pushdown machines from the device-oriented viewpoint, promulgated by Floyd, and by adding lookahead. We reprove some well-known results and prove some new results. First, we prove that every pushdown language is context free using two related yet different proof techniques. Second, we prove that every pushdown transduction is context free and, third, we prove that the language $\{a^i b^i, a^i b^{2i} : i \geq 1\}$ is not a deterministic context-free language. In addition, we investigate lookahead deterministic pushdown machines that have only one state and that accept by empty pushdown. We examine their relationship with LL languages and prove that every LL language is a lookahead deterministic pushdown language, the language $\{a^i b^i, a^i c^i : i \geq 0\}$ is a 1-lookahead deterministic pushdown language that is not $LL(k)$, for any $k \geq 1$, and the language $\{a^i 0 a^i 0, a^i 1 a^i 1 : i \geq 0\}$ is not a k-lookahead deterministic pushdown language, for any $k \geq 1$. The latter result provides an alternative proof that the corresponding language is not $LL(k)$, for any $k \geq 1$.

1 Introduction

There are beautiful ideas that are kept alive by a few disciples, but are unknown to most practitioners. We explore one such beautiful idea originated by Bob Floyd about 20 years ago; namely, treating machines, in particular pushdown machines, as a finite number of devices that form transition systems, and treating instruction (or transition) sequences as first-class objects. The idea has resurfaced twice since Kurki-Suonio [10] investigated their basic properties in 1975. First, Jonathan Goldstine, in a sequence of three articles [3,4,5] rediscovered Floyd's idea and he applied it to AFA theory and to the theory of pushdown and Turing machines. Second, Floyd and Beigel have written a text [2] on the language of machines that develops the ideas rigorously and also applies them consistently to the standard collection of machines that are studied in a first theory of computation course. Wood [15] is also using this approach in the second edition of his text.

We explore the Floydian view by reproving the well-known result that pushdown-machine languages and transductions are context-free, by establishing and applying machine-specific pumping lemmas, and by investigating lookahead pushdown machines.

2 Preliminaries

We give a nonstandard definition of a pushdown machine that is similar to the definition of Floyd (see the report of Kurki-Suonio [10] and the text of Floyd and Beigel [2]).

Given an alphabet Σ, we let Σ_λ denote $\Sigma \cup \{\lambda\}$ and Σ^{-1} denote $\{a^{-1} : a \in \Sigma\}$. We treat a^{-1} as the right inverse of a; thus, $aa^{-1} \equiv \lambda$. Given the identities $aa^{-1} \equiv \lambda$, for all $a \in \Sigma$, a string $x \in (\Sigma \cup \Sigma^{-1})^*$ is **well formed** with **content** $y \in \Sigma^*$ if either $x \in \Sigma^*$ and $x = y$, or $x = uaa^{-1}v$, for some u and v in $(\Sigma \cup \Sigma^{-1})^*$, and uv is well formed with content y. Each well-formed string in $(\Sigma \cup \Sigma^{-1})^*$ corresponds to exactly one content string; thus, we denote the content of a well-formed string $x \in (\Sigma \cup \Sigma^{-1})^*$ by content(x).

When the content of a string x is λ, we say that the string is **balanced**.

We need the notion of a restricted morphism, called a **projection**. Given two alphabets Σ and Γ such that $\Sigma \subseteq \Gamma$, a function π_Σ is a projection with respect to Γ if, for all $a \in \Sigma$, $\pi_\Sigma(a) = a$ and, for all $a \notin \Sigma$, $\pi_\Sigma(a) = \lambda$. Clearly, a projection is a morphism that preserves some symbols and erases others; thus, it has a natural inverse. An **inverse projection** $\pi_\Sigma^{-1} : \Sigma^* \to 2^{\Gamma^*}$ is defined by, for all $x \in \Sigma^*$,

$$\pi_\Sigma^{-1}(x) = \{y : y \in \Gamma^* \text{ and } \pi_\Sigma(y) = x\}.$$

It is well known that the families of regular languages and context-free languages are closed under projection and inverse projection.

We specify a **pushdown machine** M with a tuple $(Q, \Sigma, \Gamma, \delta, s, F, Z)$, where Q is a **state alphabet**, Σ is an **input alphabet**, Γ is a **pushdown alphabet**, $\delta \subseteq Q \times \Sigma_\lambda \Gamma^{-1} \Gamma^* \times Q$ is a **program**, where $\Gamma^{-1} = \{a^{-1} : a \in \Gamma\}$, s is a **start state**, $F \subseteq Q$ is a set of **final states**, and $Z \in \Gamma$ is the **initial pushdown symbol**. The inverse pushdown symbol a^{-1} denotes the **pop operation** that pops the symbol a from the top of the pushdown, whereas a string $x \in \Gamma^*$ denotes the **push operation** that pushes the string x onto the top of the pushdown. Observe that we view M as a finite-state machine (or transition system) with input alphabet $\{x : (p, x, q) \in \delta\}$.

Given a pushdown machine $M = (Q, \Sigma, \Gamma, \delta, s, F, Z)$, we consider a tuple in δ to be an **instruction** and we define an instruction sequence as follows. A sequence $Zp_0x_1p_1 \cdots x_mp_m$ is an **instruction sequence** if $p_0 = s$ and $(p_i, x_{i+1}, p_{i+1}) \in \delta$, $0 \leq i < m$. It is a **well-formed instruction sequence** if, in addition, $\pi_{\Gamma \cup \Gamma^{-1}}(Zp_0x_1p_1 \cdots x_mp_m)$ is well formed.

We associate three languages with a pushdown machine $M = (Q, \Sigma, \Gamma, \delta, s, F, Z)$. First, we have the **instruction sequence language**, ISL(M), that is defined by

$$\text{ISL}(M) = \{Zp_0x_1p_1 \cdots x_mp_m : Zp_0x_1p_1 \cdots x_mp_m \text{ is}$$
$$\text{an instruction sequence and } p_m \in F\}.$$

Second, we have the **well-formed instruction sequence language**, WFL(M), that is defined by

$$\text{WFL}(M) = \{Zp_0x_1p_1 \cdots x_mp_m : Zp_0x_1p_1 \cdots x_mp_m \text{ is a well-formed}$$

instruction sequence and $p_m \in F\}$.

Lastly, we have the **(input) language**, $L(M)$, that is defined by

$$L(M) = \{x : Zp_0x_1p_1 \cdots x_mp_m \text{ is a well-formed instruction}$$
$$\text{sequence, } p_m \in F, \text{ and } \pi_\Sigma(Zp_0x_1p_1 \cdots x_mp_m) = x\}.$$

If we want to accept by final state and empty pushdown, then we must use balanced instruction sequences, based on balanced pushdown-action strings, rather than on well-formed instruction sequences.

We define a **pushdown transducer** in a similar way. Recall that a projection π_i for an n-tuple $(x_1, \ldots, x_n)$ gives x_i, if $1 \leq i \leq n$, and is undefined otherwise. We use the notation $\pi_{\{1,\ldots,k\}}$ to mean the projection from positions 1 to k of an n-tuple that gives a k-tuple.

For $n \geq 1$, a pushdown n-transducer M is a tuple $(Q, \Sigma_1, \ldots, \Sigma_n, \Gamma, \delta, s, F, Z)$, where Q is a state alphabet, the Σ_i are alphabets, $1 \leq i \leq n$, Γ is a pushdown alphabet, $\delta \subseteq Q \times \Sigma_{1,\lambda} \times \cdots \times \Sigma_{n,\lambda} \times \Gamma^{-1}\Gamma^* \times Q$ is a program, where $\Gamma^{-1} = \{a^{-1} : a \in \Gamma\}$, s is a start state, $F \subseteq Q$ is a set of final states, and $Z \in \Gamma$ is the initial pushdown symbol.

A tuple sequence $(p_0x_{1,1}p_1 \cdots x_{1,m}p_m, \ldots, Zp_0x_{n+1,1}p_1 \cdots x_{n+1,m}p_m)$ is a **tuple instruction sequence** if $p_0 = s$ and $(p_i, x_{1,i+1}, \ldots, x_{n+1,i+1}, p_{i+1}) \in \delta$, $0 \leq i < m$. It is a **well-formed tuple instruction sequence** if, in addition,

$$\pi_{\Gamma \cup \Gamma^{-1}}(\pi_{n+1}((p_0x_{1,1}p_1 \cdots x_{1,m}p_m, \ldots, Zp_0x_{n+1,1}p_1 \cdots x_{n+1,m}p_m)))$$

is well formed.

We associate three transductions with a pushdown n-transduction $M = (Q, \Sigma_1, \ldots, \Sigma_n, \Gamma, \delta, s, F, Z)$. First, we have the **(tuple) instruction sequence transduction**, $\text{IST}(M)$, that is defined by

$$\text{IST}(M) = \{z : z = (p_0x_{1,1}p_1 \cdots x_{1,m}p_m, \ldots, Zp_0x_{n+1,1}p_1 \cdots x_{n+1,m}p_m)$$
$$\text{is a tuple instruction sequence and } p_m \in F\}.$$

Second, we have the **well-formed (tuple) instruction sequence transduction**, $\text{WFT}(M)$, that is defined by

$$\text{WFT}(M) = \{z : z = (p_0x_{1,1}p_1 \cdots x_{1,m}p_m, \ldots, Zp_0x_{n+1,1}p_1 \cdots x_{n+1,m}p_m)$$
$$\text{is a well-formed tuple instruction sequence and } p_m \in F\}.$$

Lastly, we have the **transduction**, $T(M)$, that is defined by

$$T(M) = \{x : (p_0x_{1,1}p_1 \cdots x_{1,m}p_m, \ldots, Zp_0x_{n+1,1}p_1 \cdots x_{n+1,m}p_m)$$
$$\text{is a well-formed tuple instruction sequence, } p_m \in F, \text{ and}$$
$$\pi_{\Sigma_1 \cup \cdots \cup \Sigma_n}(\pi_{\{1,\ldots,n\}}((p_0x_{1,1}p_1 \cdots x_{1,m}p_m, \ldots, Zp_0x_{n+1,1}p_1 \cdots x_{n+1,m}p_m)))$$
$$= x\}.$$

Observe that when M is a pushdown machine that $\text{WFT}(M)$ is a set of ordered pairs of strings, the first string contains the input string and the second the pushdown-action string.

3 Context-Freeness

We consider two different, yet similar, approaches to proving that pushdown languages and transductions are context-free. The idea in each case is to consider the instruction sequences of a pushdown machine. In the first approach we treat the sequences as strings and in the second we treat them as tuples of strings. We view the sets of instruction sequences as languages in the first case and as transductions in the second case.

We express WFL(M) and $L(M)$ in terms of ISL(M) using the **Dyck language**, $D_{\Gamma \cup \Gamma^{-1}}$, over the alphabet $\Gamma \cup \Gamma^{-1}$, and the language $P_{\Gamma \cup \Gamma^{-1}}$ of prefixes of all strings in $D_{\Gamma \cup \Gamma^{-1}}$. The Dyck language, $D_{\Gamma \cup \Gamma^{-1}}$, is defined as the set of all balanced strings over $(\Gamma \cup \Gamma^{-1})^*$, whereas $P_{\Gamma \cup \Gamma^{-1}}$ is the set of all well-formed strings over $(\Gamma \cup \Gamma^{-1})^*$. We interpret a symbol in Γ as a left-labeled bracket and an inverse symbol in Γ^{-1} as a right-labeled bracket. A valid sequence of pushes and pops must be the prefix of an appropriate Dyck string; otherwise, it must have either a pop when the pushdown is empty or a pop of a symbol that is not on the top of the pushdown.

We can express WFL(M), for a pushdown machine M, in terms of ISL(M) as follows:

$$\mathrm{WFL}(M) = \mathrm{ISL}(M) \cap \pi_{\Gamma \cup \Gamma^{-1}}^{-1}(P_{\Gamma \cup \Gamma^{-1}}).$$

Similarly, we can express WFT(M), for a pushdown machine M, in terms of IST(M) as follows:

$$\mathrm{WFT}(M) = \mathrm{IST}(M) \cap [(\Sigma \cup Q)^* \times \pi_Q^{-1}(P_{\Gamma \cup \Gamma^{-1}})].$$

In addition, we can express $L(M)$ in terms of WFL(M) and WFT(M) as follows:

$$L(M) = \pi_\Sigma(\mathrm{WFL}(M))$$

and

$$L(M) = \pi_\Sigma(\pi_1(\mathrm{WFT}(M))).$$

Since π_Σ and $\pi_{\Gamma \cup \Gamma^{-1}}$ are string morphisms, $P_{\Gamma \cup \Gamma^{-1}}$ is a context-free language, and the family of context-free languages is closed under intersection with regular sets, morphism, and inverse morphism, expressing $L(M)$ in terms of WFL(M) and ISL(M) implies that $L(M)$ is context-free. Note that if we prefer acceptance by both final state and empty pushdown, then we must replace the Dyck prefix language with the Dyck language in the equation that expresses WFL(M) in terms of ISL(M).

Alternatively, we can use the equation that expresses $L(M)$ in terms of WFT(M) and IST(M) to establish the context-freeness of $L(M)$, once we have established the following results for context-free transductions:

- Every projection of a context-free transduction is a context-free language
- The Cartesian product of two or more context-free languages is a context-free transduction
- The intersection of a regular transduction and a context-free transduction is a context-free transduction

We argue that these three results hold. Observe that we must base our proofs on specification mechanisms for context-free languages and transductions that are not pushdown machines. We base them on context-free grammars and **context-free transduction grammars** (also called tuple grammars [8,9]).

For an integer $n \geq 1$, a **context-free n-transduction grammar** $G = (N, \Sigma_1, \ldots, \Sigma_n, P, S)$ has a finite set P of productions, where each production $A \to \alpha$ satisfies the requirement that

$$\alpha \in (N \cup (\Sigma_1^* \times \Sigma_n^*))^*.$$

[Note that $(\lambda, \ldots, \lambda)$ is treated identically to the empty string λ.] We can define derivation sequences in the usual way and define the **n-transduction**, $T(G)$, of G as

$$T(G) = \{(x_1, \ldots, x_n) \in \Sigma_1^* \times \cdots \times \Sigma_n^* : S \Longrightarrow^* (x_1, \ldots, x_n) \text{ in } G\}.$$

A projection π_i, $1 \leq i \leq n$, of a context-free n-transduction clearly yields a context-free language. We simply replace all n-tuples on the right-hand sides of productions in G with their ith projections.

Conversely, for each $n \geq 2$ and for n context-free languages $L_i \subseteq \Sigma_i^*$, $1 \leq i \leq n$, the transduction $L_1 \times \cdots \times L_n$ is context-free. The idea behind a formal proof is constructive. For each i, $1 \leq i \leq n$, since L_i is context-free, there is a context-free grammar $G_i = (N_i, \Sigma_i, P_i, S_i)$ such that $L(G_i) = L_i$. First, we modify each context-free grammar G_i such that it defines the transduction $\{\lambda\} \times \cdots \times L_i \times \cdots \times \{\lambda\}$, where $\pi_i(L(G_i)) = L_i$. We replace each terminal string appearance on the right-hand side of a production with its "λ extension." Second, construct a new transduction grammar H that has a new sentence symbol Z, a new production $Z \to S_1 \cdots S_n$, and all the productions from $P_1, \ldots, P_n$. Now $T(H) = L(G_1) \cdots L(G_n)$; therefore, $T(H)$ is context-free.

Finally, we need to establish the regular intersection result. Let T be a context-free n-transduction, for some $n \geq 1$, and R be a regular n-transduction. We claim that $T \cap R$ is a context-free transduction. We prove this result by generalizing the triple construction; see the texts of Salomaa [12] and Wood [15]. We need two preliminary results that are of independent interest. First, a context-free n-transduction grammar is in **Chomsky normal form** if there are only the following $n + 1$ types of productions:

$$A \to BC,$$

where A, B, and C are nonterminals,

$$A \to (a, \lambda, \ldots, \lambda),$$

where a is in $\Sigma_1, \ldots$, and

$$A \to (\lambda, \ldots, \lambda, a),$$

where a is in Σ_n. With a Chomsky normal form grammar, each terminating production can deposit exactly one terminal symbol in only one of the n positions. Similarly, a finite-state n-transducer $M = (Q, \Sigma_1, \ldots, \Sigma_n, \delta, s, F)$ is in **factored**

form if each instruction in δ reads only one symbol from one of the n input devices. We say that a finite-state n-transducer $M = (Q, \Sigma_1, \ldots, \Sigma_n, \delta, s, F)$ is in **commutative normal form** if the transducer is factored and whenever there are two instructions $(p, A_1, \ldots, A_n, q)$ with A_i nonnull and $(q, B_1, \ldots, B_n, r)$ with B_j nonnull in δ such that $i \neq j$, then the instructions $(p, B_1, \ldots, B_n, t)$ and $(t, A_1, \ldots, A_n, r)$ are in δ, for some t in Q. Because only one A_i is nonnull and only one B_i is nonnull, commutative normal form allows the two nonnull actions to be performed in either order if they act on different components or devices.

Given a context-free transduction grammar, we can effectively construct a transduction grammar in Chomsky normal form from it. Similarly, given a finite-state transducer, we can effectively construct a transducer in commutative normal form from it.

We are now ready for the demonstration of the third result. Assume that we have a context-free n-transduction grammar $G = (N, \Sigma_1, \ldots, \Sigma_n, P, S)$ in Chomsky normal form and a finite-state n-transducer $M = (Q, \Sigma_1, \ldots, \Sigma_n, \delta, s, F)$ in commutative normal form. Then we can construct a new context-free n-transduction grammar H as follows. The nonterminal set $N_H = \{Z\} \cup \{[p, A, q] : p, q \in Q$ and $A \in N\}$ and the set P_H of productions contains all productions of the following three kinds:

1. $[p, A, q] \rightarrow [p, B, r][r, C, q]$, for all $p, q, r \in Q$ and for all $A, B, C \in N$ such that $A \rightarrow BC$ is in P.
2. $[p, A, q] \rightarrow (\lambda, \ldots, a, \ldots, \lambda)$, for all $p, q \in Q$ such that $(p, \lambda, \ldots, a, \ldots, \lambda, q)$ is in δ and for all $A \in N$ such that $A \rightarrow (\lambda, \ldots, a, \ldots, \lambda)$ is in P.
3. $Z \rightarrow [s, S, f]$, for all $f \in F$.

The construction is a generalization of the standard grammatical construction. It is more complex because we need to ensure that whenever a string n-tuple is generated by the grammar G and by the machine M, it is also generated by the new grammar H. The commutative normal form for transducers and the generalized Chomsky normal form for grammars ensures that this property does indeed hold.

We conclude that the n-transduction defined by a pushdown n-transducer is context-free.

4 Pushdown machines and pumping

There are two varieties of pumping lemmas for language families. First, we have the system-dependent pumping lemmas that present a pumping lemma in terms of a class of language-description systems. For example, we can give a pumping lemma for context-free grammars that describes pumping for syntax trees, which are sufficiently tall. Similarly, we can give a pumping lemma for deterministic finite-state machines that describes pumping for computations that are sufficiently long.

Second, we have system-independent pumping lemmas that present pumping lemmas without any reference to a language-description system. The following pumping lemma for context-free languages has this form.

Lemma 1. *For each context-free language L there is a constant $p \geq 0$ such that, for all strings z in L of length at least p, there are strings u, v, w, x, and y such that the following four conditions hold:*

1. $z = uvwxy$.
2. $|vx| \geq 1$.
3. $|vwx| \leq p$.
4. *For all $i \geq 0$, $uv^i wx^i y \in L$.*

We also recall the following pumping lemma for context-free languages (see Harrison's text [6] for more details). We use it in Section 5.

Lemma 2. *For each context-free language L there is a constant $p \geq 0$ such that, for all z in L and for any set S of distinguished positions in z, if $\#S \geq p$, then there are strings $v_1, \ldots, v_5$ such that the following four conditions hold (where S_i is the set of distinguished positions that corresponds to the substring v_i, $1 \leq i \leq 5$):*

1. $z = v_1 v_2 v_3 v_4 v_5$.
2. *Either $S_1, S_2, S_3 \neq \emptyset$ or $S_3, S_4, S_5 \neq \emptyset$.*
3. $\#(S_2 \cup S_3 \cup S_4) \leq p$.
4. *For all $i \geq 0$, $v_1 v_2^i v_3 v_4^i v_5 \in L$.*

Since we can always transform system-dependent pumping lemmas into system-independent pumping lemmas, why do we make the distinction? The reason is simple. We can use system-dependent pumping lemmas to provide system-dependent information about sentences and their generation or acceptance. We will now demonstrate this idea with two examples. We have also proved a new result by this technique [13].

We reprove the well-known results that the languages

$$L_1 = \{a^i b^i, a^i b^{2i} : i \geq 1\}$$

and

$$L_2 = \{a^i b^j c^k : i, j, k \geq 0 \text{ and either } i = j \text{ or } j = k\}$$

are not deterministic context-free languages. Since the family of deterministic context-free languages is defined by the class of deterministic pushdown machines that accept by final state, it is exactly the set of languages $L(M)$, where M is a deterministic pushdown machine. We begin by defining this subclass of pushdown machines.

A pushdown machine $(Q, \Sigma, \Gamma, \delta, s, F, Z)$ is **deterministic** if it satisfies the following two conditions.

1. For all $p \in Q$, for all $A \in \Sigma_\lambda$, and for all $B \in \Gamma$, there is at most one instruction of the form $(p, AB^{-1}x, q)$ in δ.
2. For all $p \in Q$ and for all $B \in \Gamma$, if there is an instruction of the form $(p, B^{-1}x, q)$ in δ, then, for all $a \in \Sigma$, there is no instruction of the form $(p, aB^{-1}y, r)$ in δ.

Without more ado we reprove the following theorem using our new technique.

Theorem 3. $L_1 = \{a^i b^i, a^i b^{2i} : i \geq 1\}$ is not a deterministic context-free language.

Proof. We argue by contradiction. Assume that $L_1 = L(M)$ for some deterministic pushdown machine $M = (Q, \Sigma, \Gamma, \delta, s, F, Z)$, where $\Sigma = \{a, b\}$. Since WFL(M) is context-free and infinite, we can apply the context-free pumping lemma (Lemma 1) to it. Thus, there is a constant $p > 0$ such that, for all strings W in WFL(M) of length at least p, we can decompose W into $uvxyz$, where $|vy| \geq 1$ and $|vxy| \leq p$, and, for all $i \geq 0$, $uv^i xy^i z \in$ WFL(M).

We consider the pumping of the well-formed instruction sequence W whose input string is $w = \pi_\Sigma(W) = a^{2p} b^{4p}$. Now if v is empty, then y must be nonempty. Thus, y can have one of four forms $\pi_\Sigma(y) = \lambda$, $\pi_\Sigma(y) \in a^+$, $\pi_\Sigma(y) \in b^+$, or $\pi_\Sigma(y) \in a^+ b^+$. The last three forms lead to an immediate contradiction when we consider the string $uv^2 xy^2 z$. The first possibility implies that y corresponds to a sequence of null-input instructions; therefore, $uv^2 xy^2 z$ is well-formed and is an accepting sequence for w. Since M is deterministic and we have two distinct accepting sequences, we have obtained a contradiction. We can argue in a similar manner if y is empty and v is nonempty. Hence both v and y must be nonempty.

If v and y are both nonempty, then by similar arguments we can deduce that $\pi_\Sigma(v)$ and $\pi_\Sigma(y)$ are nonempty. If $\pi_\Sigma(vy) \in \lambda + a^+ + b^+, \pi_\Sigma(v) \in a^+ b^+$, or $\pi_\Sigma(y) \in a^+ b^+$, then $uv^2 xy^2 z$ provides a contradiction. Therefore, $\pi_\Sigma(v) \in a^+$ and $\pi_\Sigma(y) \in b^+$ is the only remaining possibility (the reverse assignment is impossible).

Now, letting $|v|_a = l$, we must have that $|y|_b = 2l$; otherwise, the input string uxz is outside L_1. Since $|vxy| \leq p$, the number of b's in xy is at most p; therefore, the decomposition does not affect the rightmost $3p$ b's.

We now use this analysis in conjunction with the determinism of M to obtain a contradiction. Since M is deterministic, the well-formed instruction sequence W' of the string $w' = \pi_\Sigma(W') = a^{2p} b^{2p}$ must be a prefix of the well-formed instruction sequence W for w. Moreover, a corresponding decomposition of W' is $uvxyz'$, where z' is a prefix of z. Lastly, observe that uxz' is in WFL(M), yet $|uxz'|_a \neq |uxz'|_b$ and $2|uxz'|_a \neq |uxz'|_b$. Thus, we have obtained a contradiction and L_1 is not a deterministic context-free language.

Theorem 4. $L_2 = \{a^i b^j c^k : i, j, k \geq 0 \text{ and either } i = j \text{ or } j = k\}$ is not a deterministic context-free language.

Proof. We argue by contradiction using the positional pumping lemma, Lemma 2. Assume that L_2 is deterministic context-free, then $L_2 = L(M)$, for some deterministic pushdown machine $M = (Q, \Sigma, \Gamma, \delta, s, F, Z)$, where $\Sigma = \{a, b, c\}$. Since

WFL(M) is context-free and infinite, we can apply the context-free pumping lemma (Lemma 2) to it. Thus, there is a constant $p > 0$ such that, for all strings W in WFL(M) of length at least p, we can decompose W into $V_1 V_2 V_3 V_4 V_5$, where $|V_2 V_4| \geq 1$ and $|V_2 V_3 V_4| \leq p$, and, for all $i \geq 0$, $V_1 V_2^i V_3 V_4^i V_5 \in$ WFL(M).

We consider the computations of two strings; namely, $w_1 = a^p b^{p!} c^{p!}$ and $w_2 = a^{p!} b^{p!} c^p$. Since M is deterministic and $w_i \in L_2$, there is exactly one accepting instruction sequence W_i for w_i, for $i = 1, 2$.

We designate the as in W_1 as the distinguished positions, in which case, by Lemma 2, we can decompose W_1 into $V_1 V_2 V_3 V_4 V_5$, where $V_2 V_4$ contains only as and $V_1 V_2^i V_3 V_4^i V_5$ is a well-formed instruction sequence, for all $i \geq 0$. The number of as in $V_2 V_4$ is at least one and at most p; thus, we can choose an $i \geq 1$ such that $W_1' = V_1 V_2^i V_3 V_4^i V_5$ contains exactly $p!$ as. We can argue similarly for W_2 for which we choose the cs as distinguished positions and obtain $W_2' = U_1 U_2^j U_3 U_4^j U_5$ that contains exactly $p!$ cs, for some $j \geq 1$.

Now, either $W_1' = W_2'$, in which case we can deduce that the string $a^p b^{p!} c^p$ is in $L(M)$ or $W_1' \neq W_2'$, in which case the string $a^{p!} b^{p!} c^{p!}$ has two distinct computations. We have obtained a contradiction in both cases.

Hence L_2 is not a deterministic context-free language.

Note that the proof of Theorem 4 can be used, without change, to demonstrate that L_2 is an ambiguous pushdown machine language.

5 Lookahead Pushdown Machines

It is a truism that when we have different, yet equivalent, models available, we normally use the model that is more appropriate for the task in hand. For example, we express substring searches with regular expressions; we do not use finite-state machines. In contrast we use deterministic finite-state machines when we want to tokenize a string; we do not use regular expressions.

Traditionally, proving that a language is not the language of any grammar from a given class uses either an *ad hoc* approach or class-specific pumping lemma. For example, Beatty [1] developed two pumping lemmas for $LL(k)$ grammars that can be used to establish that certain languages are not LL languages, whereas van Leeuwen [14] used a powerful and generalizable *ad hoc* approach to the same problem. Unfortunately, we have no characterization of the $LL(k)$ languages other than their defining model, the $LL(k)$ grammars. Rosenkrantz and Stearns [11], however, introduced a parsing model for $LL(k)$ grammars that, as we shall demonstrate, leads to a machine model that has greater expressive power than $LL(k)$ grammars yet is, at the same time, weak enough that we can use it to establish the non-LL-ness of certain languages.

The new model is the **k-lookahead pushdown machine**. We are particularly interested in its deterministic version. The lookahead pushdown machines have a single state, may use null-input instructions, and accept by empty pushdown; they are deterministic with respect to the k-lookahead and the top symbol of the pushdown. We demonstrate that k-lookahead deterministic pushdown machines provide a parsing model for $LL(k)$ grammars, for all $k \geq 1$.

Since the simple deterministic pushdown machines of Korenjak and Hopcroft [7] are a restricted version of the 1-lookahead deterministic pushdown machines, it is surprising that the language $\{a^i b^i, a^i c^i : i \geq 1\}$ is the language of a 1-lookahead deterministic pushdown machine. Korenjak and Hopcroft [7] proved that it is not simple deterministic and Beatty [1] proved that it is not $LL(k)$ for any $k \geq 1$. Thus, these results demonstrate that the family of k-lookahead deterministic pushdown languages are a proper superset of the family of $LL(k)$ languages and that 1-lookahead deterministic machines are quite powerful. We then prove that the language $\{a^i 0 a^i 0, a^i 1 a^i 1 : i \geq 0\}$ is not a k-lookahead deterministic pushdown language, for any $k \geq 1$.

We begin by defining the new model. Δ

Definition 5. For $k \geq 1$, a k-lookahead pushdown machine $M = (s, \Sigma, \Gamma, \delta, Z)$ has a program that consists of instructions of the form $(s, A\#x, g, s)$, where $A \in \Sigma_\lambda$, $x \in \Sigma^{\leq k}$ and A is a prefix of x, and $g \in \Gamma^{-1}\Gamma^*$. The symbol "#" is a separating symbol that is not in any alphabet. The machine can execute an instruction $(s, A\#x, g, s)$ if x is a prefix of the remaining input string and the top symbol of the pushdown is the first symbol of g. If x is shorter than k, then we also require that it match the remaining input exactly.

Letting $s(x\underline{y}, gB)$ be a configuration of M, where the underscore indicates the position of the read head in the input string, we can execute the instruction $(s, A\#z, B^{-1}\alpha, s)$ if either z is of length k and it is a prefix of y or z is shorter than k and $z = y$. In both cases, the new configuration is $s(xA\underline{y'}, g\alpha)$, where $y = Ay'$.

We define computations as sequences of configurations in which each successor configuration is obtained from its predecessor according to the method we have outlined. It is an accepting computation if the initial configuration has the form $s(\underline{x}, Z)$ and the final configuration has the form $(s, x\underline{\,}, \lambda)$ (that is, the pushdown is empty and the input has been completely read).

We are now ready to begin. A k-lookahead pushdown machine is **deterministic** if the remaining input and the current top symbol of the pushdown determine at most one applicable instruction.

We provide only sketches of the results. For each $k \geq 1$, we define an $LL(k)$ grammar $G = (N, \Sigma, P, S)$ to be a context-free grammar in which, for all $A \in N$ and for all $x \in \Sigma^{\leq k}$, there is at most one production $A \to \alpha \in P$ such that $x \in FF_k(A \to \alpha)$, where $FF_k(A \to \alpha)$ is the first-follow set of α with respect to A and k. (Strictly speaking, we have defined strong $LL(k)$ grammars.)

Theorem 6. We can construct a k-lookahead deterministic pushdown machine $M = (s, \Sigma, N, \delta, S)$ from an $LL(k)$ grammar $G = (N, \Sigma, P, S)$ that accepts exactly the sentences of the grammar. Thus, every LL language is a lookahead deterministic pushdown machine language.

Proof. Without loss of generality we can assume that each $LL(k)$ grammar G has productions of only the forms $A \to BC$, $B, C \in N$, $A \to a$, $a \in \Sigma$, and $A \to \lambda$. We include the following instructions in δ:

1. For every production of the form $A \to BC \in P$ and every lookahead x such that $x \in FF_k(A \to BC)$, $(s, \#x, A^{-1}CB, s)$.
2. For every production of the form $A \to a \in P$ and every lookahead x such that $x \in FF_k(A \to a)$, $(s, a\#x, A^{-1}, s)$.
3. For every production of the form $A \to \lambda \in P$ and every lookahead x such that $x \in FF_k(A \to \lambda)$, $(s, \#x, A^{-1}, s)$.

By the definition of $LL(k)$ grammars we are guaranteed that the machine that we have constructed is deterministic and that its accepted strings are exactly the sentences of the given grammar.

Theorem 7. *The non-LL-language $L_3 = \{a^i b^i, a^i c^i : i \geq 1\}$ is a 1-lookahead deterministic pushdown machine language. Thus, the family of lookahead deterministic pushdown languages properly contains the family of LL languages.*

Proof. At first glance it does not seem possible because we must, with one state, not only separate the as from the bs and cs, we must also not allow the bs and cs to mix. We solve the first problem by maintaining a top-o- pushdown marker that is changed as soon as the machine reads the first b or c. We solve the second problem by using different top-of-pushdown markers for the bs and cs and deleting them when we know that the next input symbol is the same as the one we just read. We assume that Z is the initial pushdown symbol. The instructions are

$$(s, a\#a, Z^{-1}\bar{B}, s)$$
$$(s, a\#a, \bar{B}^{-1}B\bar{a}, s)$$
$$(s, a\#a, \bar{a}^{-1}a\bar{a}, s)$$
$$(s, b\#b, \bar{B}^{-1}, s)$$
$$(s, b\#b, \bar{a}^{-1}b, s)$$
$$(s, b\#b, a^{-1}b, s)$$
$$(s, \#b, b^{-1}, s)$$
$$(s, b\#b, B^{-1}, s)$$
$$(s, c\#c, \bar{B}^{-1}, s)$$
$$(s, c\#c, \bar{a}^{-1}c, s)$$
$$(s, c\#c, a^{-1}c, s)$$
$$(s, \#c, c^{-1}, s)$$
$$(s, c\#c, B^{-1}, s)$$

The symbols B and $\bar{B}$ are used to ensure correct termination.

Theorem 8. *The language $L_4 = \{a^i0a^i0, a^i1a^i1 : i \geq 1\}$ is not a k-lookahead deterministic pushdown language, for any $k \geq 1$. Therefore, L_4 is not an LL language.*

Proof. We assume that L_4 is the language of a k-lookahead deterministic pushdown machine $M = (s, \Sigma, \Gamma, \delta, Z)$, where $\Sigma = \{a, 0, 1\}$. We first argue that there is a symbol A in Γ that has certain properties. For each $A \in \Gamma$ and each $z \in \Sigma^{\leq k}$, define the set $P(A, z) \subseteq \{a\}^*$ of prefixes of strings that, in accepting computations, leave A on top of the pushdown exactly when the lookahead is z. In addition, define the set $D(A)$ of those substrings that, in accepting computations, remove A and subsequently pushed symbols from the top of the pushdown and do not disturb the underlying pushdown contents. Formally, we have

$$P(A, z) = \{w : s(\underline{w}xy, Z), \ldots, s(w\underline{x}y, \alpha A), \ldots, s(wxy_-, \lambda)$$
$$\text{such that } First_k(xy) = z\}$$

and

$$D(A) = \{x : s(\underline{w}xy, Z), \ldots, s(w\underline{x}y, \alpha A), \ldots, s(wx\underline{y}, \alpha), \ldots, s(wxy_-, \lambda)\}.$$

Now, there must be an $A \in \Gamma$ such that $P(A, a^k)$ is infinite. Moreover, there is a $B \in \Gamma$ such that $D(B)$ is infinite. We can deduce that there is an $A \in \Gamma$ that satisfies both conditions; otherwise, $L(M)$ would be finite.

Consider such a symbol $A \in \Gamma$. There are six cases to consider, each of which leads to a contradiction. The cases are:

1. $D(A) \cap a^*$ is infinite.
2. $D(A) \cap a^*0a^*0$ is infinite.
3. $D(A) \cap a^*1a^*1$ is infinite.
4. $D(A) \cap a^*0a^*$ is infinite and $D(A) \cap a^*1a^*$ is finite.
5. $D(A) \cap a^*0a^*$ is finite and $D(A) \cap a^*1a^*$ is infinite.
6. $D(A) \cap a^*0a^*$ and $D(A) \cap a^*1a^*$ are both infinite.

We examine one of these cases in more detail.
Case 1: $D(A) \cap a^*$ is infinite. There are a^l and a^m in $D(A)$ such that $m > l > k$,

$$s(\underline{a}^p a^l u, Z), \ldots, s(a^p \underline{a}^l u, \alpha A), \ldots, s(a^p a^l \underline{u}, \alpha), \ldots, s(a^p a^l u_-, \lambda),$$

$$s(\underline{a}^q a^m v, Z), \ldots, s(a^q \underline{a}^m v, \beta A), \ldots, s(a^q a^m \underline{v}, \beta), \ldots, s(a^q a^m v_-, \lambda),$$

and $First_k(u) = First_k(v)$. We can construct the computation

$$s(\underline{a}^p a^m u, Z), \ldots, s(a^p \underline{a}^m u, \alpha A), \ldots, s(a^p a^m \underline{u}, \alpha), \ldots, s(a^p a^m u_-, \lambda).$$

Thus, $a^p a^m u \in L(M)$. Since $a^p a^l u \in L(M)$ and $l < m$, $a^p a^m u \notin L$ and it is not in $L(M)$. We have obtained a contradiction; thus, $D(A) \cap a^*$ is finite.
The other cases lead to contradictions in similar ways.

6 Conclusions

We have described new research directions for pushdown machines. The results that we have obtained are encouraging. For example, the proof that pushdown transductions are context free is a fundamental result; however, previous proofs of context-freeness are laborious and unintuitive. The synthesis of context-free pumping lemmas and the Floydian view of pushdown machines yields an elegant proof that $\{a^i b^i, a^i b^{2i} : i \geq 0\}$ is not deterministic context free. Lastly, using lookahead deterministic pushdown machines to establish results about LL languages is novel and promising; we have only scratched the surface of possibilities in this paper.

7 Acknowledgements

This research was supported by grants from the Natural Sciences and Engineering Research Council of Canada and from the Information Technology Research Centre of Ontario.

References

1. J.C. Beatty. Two iteration theorems for the $LL(k)$ languages. *Theoretical Computer Science*, 12:193–228, 1980.
2. R.W. Floyd and R. Beigel. *The Language of Machines: An Introduction to Computability and Formal Language Theory*. Computer Science Press, San Francisco, CA, 1994.
3. J. Goldstine. Automata with data storage. In *Proceedings of the Conference on Theoretical Computer Science*, pages 239–246, Waterloo, Canada, 1977. University of Waterloo.
4. J. Goldstine. A rational theory of AFLs. In *Proceedings of the Sixth Colloquium on Automata, Languages, and Programming*, volume 71 of *Lecture Notes in Computer Science*, pages 271–281, New York, NY, 1979. Springer-Verlag.
5. J. Goldstine. Formal languages and their relation to automata: What Hopcroft & Ullman didn't tell us. In R.V. Book, editor, *Formal Language Theory: Perspectives and Open Problems*, pages 109–140, New York, NY, 1980. Academic Press.
6. M.A. Harrison. *Introduction to Formal Language Theory*. Addison-Wesley, Reading, MA, 1978.
7. A.J. Korenjak and J.E. Hopcroft. Simple deterministic languages. In *Proceedings of the Seventh Annual IEEE Symposium on Switching and Automata Theory*, pages 36–46, 1966.
8. W. Kuich and H.A. Maurer. On the inherent ambiguity of tuple languages. *Computing*, 7:194–203, 1971.
9. W. Kuich and H.A. Maurer. The structure generating function and entropy of tuple languages. *Information and Control*, 19:195–203, 1971.

10. R. Kurki-Suonio. Describing automata in terms of languages associated with their peripheral devices. Technical Report STAN-CS-75-493, Computer Science Department, Stanford University, Stanford, CA, 1975.

11. D.J. Rosenkrantz and R.E. Stearns. Properties of deterministic top-down grammars. *Information and Control*, 17:226–256, 1970.

12. A. Salomaa. *Formal Languages*. Academic Press, New York, NY, 1973.

13. K. Salomaa, D. Wood, and S. Yu. Pumping and pushdown machines. *RAIRO Informatique théoretique*, to appear, 1994.

14. J. van Leeuwen. An elementary proof that a certain context-free language is not $LL(k)$, and a generalization. Unpublished manuscript, University of California, Berkeley, 1972.

15. D. Wood. *Theory of Computation*. John Wiley & Sons, Inc., New York, NY, second edition, 1994. In preparation.

String Matching Algorithms and Automata

Imre Simon*

Instituto de Matemática e Estatística
Universidade de São Paulo
05508-900 São Paulo, SP, Brasil
<is@ime.usp.br>

Abstract. In this paper we study the structure of finite automata recognizing sets of the form A^*p, for some word p, and use the results obtained to improve the Knuth-Morris-Pratt string searching algorithm. We also determine the average number of nontrivial edges of the above automata.

1   Introduction

It has been known for a long time that sequential string matching algorithms, such as the Morris and Pratt [15] or the Knuth, Morris and Pratt [14] algorithms are intimately related to finite automata recognizing sets of the form A^*p, where $p \in A^*$ is the pattern to be found. This approach, found in [1, 8, 18, 7, 2], was not further developed probably because such an automaton has $|A||p|$ edges while the before mentioned algorithms work in time $O(|p| + |t|)$, for a text t and pattern p, with a proportionality constant independent of the alphabet size.

In the next section we shall show that most edges of the automaton for A^*p are not essential. More precisely, we shall classify the edges of $\mathcal{A}$ as either forward, backward or trivial and shall show that $\mathcal{A}$ has exactly $|p|$ forward edges and at most $|p|$ backward edges. Furthermore, knowledge of these edges is sufficient to simulate the automaton in linear time, without dependence of the alphabet size.

Using these ideas we show an implementation of automaton $\mathcal{A}$ which leads to an improvement of the Knuth, Morris and Pratt algorithm, in the sense that for any pattern p and text t the set of character comparisons of our algorithm is a (usually proper) subset of the set of character comparisons of the Knuth, Morris and Pratt algorithm. Besides, our algorithm is a real-time string matching algorithm, with delay bounded by $|A|$. Using techniques of Galil [10] this delay can be reduced to be bounded by a constant independent of the alphabet size.

We remark that Hancart [12, 13] has shown the surprising result that any "reasonable" implementation of our automaton leads to a linear pattern matching algorithm.

In section 4 we make a detailed study of the automaton $\mathcal{A}$ and compute the average number of its nontrivial edges. This is achieved by using an easy and elementary method to count the number of un-bordered words of a given length over a fixed alphabet.

---

* This work was done with partial support from FAPESP, CNPq and the Fibonacci Institute.

2   Finite automata recognizing sets of the form A^*p

Let p be a nonempty word in A^* and let $\mathcal{A}$ be the reduced finite automaton recognizing the set A^*p. Assume that p has length m and let us denote by $p[i]$ the i-th letter of p, i.e. $p = p[1]p[2]\ldots p[m]$. The factor $p[i]\ldots p[j]$ of p will be denoted by $p[i..j]$.

Initially we present a construction of $\mathcal{A}$ done purely in syntactic terms. Recall that any set $X \subseteq A^*$ defines a coarsest right congruence on A^*, its *syntactical right congruence*, for which X is a union of congruence classes. These congruence classes can be considered the states of the reduced automaton accepting X, the initial state being the class containing the empty word 1 and the final states being the classes which contain some word of X. Furthermore, for words u and v the congruence is defined by

$$u \equiv v \ (\mathrm{mod}\, X) \text{ iff } \forall x \in A^* \ : \ ux \in X \text{ iff } vx \in X.$$

In the sequel we apply these concepts to the set $X = A^*p$.

For a word u we denote by $\mathrm{pre}(u), \mathrm{suf}(u), \mathrm{fat}(u)$ the set of prefixes, suffixes and factors of u; in other words, $\mathrm{pre}(u) = uA^{*-1}$, $\mathrm{suf}(u) = A^{*-1}u$ and $\mathrm{fat}(u) = A^{*-1}uA^{*-1}$, where we use the quotient notation developed by Eilenberg [9]. For words u, v the *overlap of u and v* (in that order) is the longest word in $\mathrm{suf}(u) \cap \mathrm{pre}(v)$. It is denoted by $u \rightleftharpoons v$. The *borders of u* are the nonempty words in $\mathrm{suf}(A^{-1}u) \cap \mathrm{pre}(uA^{-1})$. In other words, v is a border of u if $0 < |v| < |u|$ and $u \in vA^* \cap A^*v$. A word is *un-bordered* if the set of its borders is empty. Note that the empty word is un-bordered. We denote by $\mathrm{alpha}(u)$ the set of letters which appear in the word u.

The reader will verify without difficulty that

$$u \equiv v \ (\mathrm{mod}\, X) \text{ iff } u \rightleftharpoons p = v \rightleftharpoons p.$$

Clearly p has $m + 1$ prefixes and no two of them are congruent $\mathrm{mod}\, X$, hence we can denote the states of $\mathcal{A}$ by $0, 1, \ldots m$ with 0 the initial state, with m the final state and satisfying the property that $0p[1..i] = i$, that is to say, the prefix of length i of p takes automaton $\mathcal{A}$ from state 0 to state i. Figure 1 represents automaton $\mathcal{A}$ for the word $p = abacabadabacaba$.

Clearly A^*p is a definite language, in the sense of [5, 16]; hence $\mathcal{A}$ is a definite automaton, i.e. for every sufficiently long word $w \in A^*$ the map defined by w on the states of $\mathcal{A}$ is a constant function.

Besides, automaton $\mathcal{A}$ has the following basic properties. For every word w, $0w = |w \rightleftharpoons p|$, i.e. w takes the initial state to the state corresponding to the length of the longest suffix of w which is also a prefix of p. Furthermore, the triple (i, a, j) is an edge of $\mathcal{A}$, i.e. state i goes to state j under letter a, iff $p[1..i]a \rightleftharpoons p = p[1..j]$.

Notice next that most edges of the automaton $\mathcal{A}$ end at the initial state 0; we shall call such edges *trivial*. The non-trivial edges of $\mathcal{A}$, (i, a, j), with $j \neq 0$, will be called *forward* or *backward* according $j = i + 1$ or $j \leq i$, respectively. Clearly, all edges of $\mathcal{A}$ have been classified. We need another definition: the *length* of the

q	0	1	2	3	4	5	6	7	8	9	10	11	12	13	14	15
qa	1	1	3	1	5	1	7	1	9	1	11	1	13	1	15	1
qb	0	2	0	2	0	6	0	2	0	10	0	2	0	14	0	2
qc	0	0	0	4	0	0	0	4	0	0	0	12	0	0	0	4
qd	0	0	0	0	0	0	0	8	0	0	0	0	0	0	0	8

Fig. 1. The reduced automaton $\mathcal{A}$ recognizing A^*p, for $p = abacabadabacaba$.

backward edge (i, a, j) is the integer $i - j$. We state now one of the main results of the paper.

Theorem 1 *For every $p \in A^*$, of length m, the reduced automaton $\mathcal{A}$ recognizing A^*p has exactly m forward edges, its number of backward edges is at least $|alpha(p)|$ and at most m.*

The extreme values in theorem 1 are actually obtained. To see this, consider the word $p = a_1^{q_2} a_2 a_1^{q_3} a_3 \cdots a_1^{q_k} a_k$, with $0 \leq q_3, q_4, \ldots, q_k < q_2$. It is not difficult to see that $\mathcal{A}$ has exactly k backward edges. On the other hand, a very interesting sequence of words is given by the so called *sesquipowers*, of which the word of figure 1 is an example. Consider a sequence of letters $(a_1, a_2, \ldots)$ and construct the words $p_1 = a_1$ and $p_{n+1} = p_n a_{n+1} p_n$, for $n \geq 1$. The reader will verify that, unless $a_i = a_{i+1}$ for some $i \leq n$, the automaton $\mathcal{A}_n$ has exactly $|p_n|$ backward edges.

Actually, we can characterize an even more precise set which contains always m elements, which is easily constructed, and from which the set of edges of $\mathcal{A}$ can be obtained. The *return set* of a word p, denoted $\text{Ret}(p)$ is a subset of $[1..m] \times A \times [1..m]$ which contains an element for every $k \in [1, m]$. The element corresponding to k is $(k + j, p[j + 1], j + 1)$, where $j \in [0..m - 1]$ is the unique value given by

$$p[k + 1..k + j] = p[1..j] \text{ and } p[k + j + 1] \neq p[j + 1] \text{ or } k + j = m.$$

The element corresponding to k can be obtained as follows. Let us spell word p in p itself, as far as possible, beginning to match $p[1]$ with $p[k + 1]$; assume that we succeed to match j letters but not more. Then the triple $(k + j, p[j + 1], j + 1)$ belongs to the return set of p. Notice that whatever the resulting value of j, the length of the triple corresponding to k is always $k - 1$. It follows that $\text{Ret}(p)$ has exactly one triple of each length $0, 1, \ldots, m - 1$. Hence, $|\text{Ret}(p)| = m$.

We have now:

Theorem 2 *The triple (i, a, j) is a backward edge of $\mathcal{A}$ iff it belongs to the return set of p and no other triple (i, a, k), with $k > j$, belongs to $\text{Ret}(p)$.*

3 Application to string matching

In this section we informally explore the consequences of our study of the automaton $\mathcal{A}$ recognizing A^*p for string matching algorithms.

Let us first note that the Knuth-Morris-Pratt algorithm can be easily described in terms of the automaton $\mathcal{A}$. Indeed, that algorithm, based on character comparisons, computes a failure function which is to be used whenever the matching of p with the text t comes to a mismatch or reaches an occurrence of p in t. More precisely, assume that comparison of $t[i]$ with $p[j]$ resulted in a mismatch. Then we substitute j by fail(j) and repeat the algorithm. Unless fail(j) = 0, in which case we abandon the current value of i and re-initialize everything with $i + 1$ for i and 1 for j.

But what is fail(j)? It is defined, for $1 \leq j \leq m$, as being the greatest k for which $p[1..k - 1]$ is a border of $p[1..j - 1]$ and for which $p[k] \neq p[j]$ or is 0 if no such k exists. By analogy, we also define fail($m + 1$), to be used after a complete match of p has been found, as being 1 plus the length of the longest border of p. One can verify that fail(j) = 0 if there are no backward edges issuing from state $j - 1$ or is the terminus of the shortest return edge issuing from $j - 1$. Besides, the label of such edge is always $p[\text{fail}(j)]$ in consequence of the definiteness of our automaton, hence comparing $t[i]$ with that label nothing else is but comparing $t[i]$ with $p[\text{fail}(j)]$.

As an illustration, we show on figure 2 the failure function of the word of figure 1.

j	1	2	3	4	5	6	7	8	9	10	11	12	13	14	15	16
fail(j)	0	1	0	2	0	1	0	4	0	1	0	2	0	1	0	8

Fig. 2. The failure function of $p = abacabadabacaba$.

Thus, the Knuth-Morris-Pratt algorithm can be seen as being based on a representation of the automaton $\mathcal{A}$. Such representation is achieved through the failure function. This strategy succeeds because of the following two properties of the definite automaton $\mathcal{A}$.

- every edge terminating at state j has label $p[j]$,
- if $0 \neq \text{fail}(j) = k$ then for every edge $(k - 1, a, l)$, $\mathcal{A}$ also has the edge $(j - 1, a, l)$.

In other words, iterating successively the failure function one recovers all the edges of $\mathcal{A}$ but some of them might be recovered more than once.

The foregoing discussion illustrates why is the use of the automaton $\mathcal{A}$ possibly more efficient than its simulation by the failure function? We realize a gain whenever we are looking for an edge with label c and the successive values of the failure function lead to letters alternating between, say, a and b, before hitting a c. In this situation the automaton simulation examines only once the transition a and only once the transition b, while the Knuth-Morris-Pratt algorithm can spend up to $\Omega(\log m)$ consecutive jumps of the failure function before finding the correct transition labeled by c. Examples when this behavior arises can be constructed by suitable sesquipowers. Take, for instance, the sesquipower u defined by the sequence (c, a, b, a, b, a, b) and then search for the pattern $p = udu$ in the text $t = (uc)^n$.

This analysis can be resumed by saying that our string matching algorithm simulating the automaton $\mathcal{A}$ is a real-time algorithm with delay bounded by $|A|$, while the Knuth-Morris-Pratt algorithm does not work in real-time.

It remains to be seen whether the automaton $\mathcal{A}$ can be constructed and simulated in linear time. This is indeed the case and this also leads to some interesting considerations.

First, we shall describe a data structure to store and search the edges which corresponds to the Knuth-Morris-Pratt algorithm. This is achieved by storing, for every state j the number back(j) of backward edges with origin in j and storing the set of backward edges with origin in j in a vector or list edge(j) in increasing order of length. With this data structure and exploiting the properties of automaton $\mathcal{A}$ one obtains:

Theorem 3 *The automaton $\mathcal{A}$ can be constructed for a pattern p and simulated for any text t using a set of letter comparisons which is a (proper) subset of the letter comparisons performed by the Knuth-Morris-Pratt algorithm. It follows that the construction and the simulation of automaton $\mathcal{A}$ can be done in time and space proportional to $|p| + |t|$, where the constant of proportionality does not depend on the size of the alphabet.*

We mention now a surprising property discovered by Christophe Hancart [12, 13]. He proved that the time to spell a text t in the automaton $\mathcal{A}$ is bounded by at most $2|t| - 1$ comparisons even if *all* the edges issuing from the current state are consulted while computing each transition. Note that the bound $2|t| - 1$ is the same as the one obtained in the Knuth-Morris-Pratt algorithm! This intuitively means that the edges in the automaton are arranged so sparsely that one never "crosses" with more than $2|t| - 1$ edges when spelling a word t. It also implies that the edges in the lists edge(j) can be stored in any order whatsoever without compromising the time bound $2|t| - 1$ necessary to spell the word t. Actually, the edges in edge(j) can even be randomly permuted *before* consulting each list.

We conclude this section with an interesting problem. Does there exist some representation, comparable to the ones we have seen for the automaton of A^*p, for the suffix automaton of a word, as described by Blumer et. al. [4]? Such a structure would be especially interesting if it provided a representation of the suffix automaton in linear space which could be traversed in linear time with constants independent of the alphabet size. As far as we know the existence of such a representation is an open question.

4 The Average Number of Backward Edges

In this section we will deepen our analysis of the return set of a word p in order to obtain the average number of backward edges of automata $\mathcal{A}$ recognizing A^*p, when p runs over the set of words of length m. We shall show that as m goes to infinity the limit of the average number of edges divided by m tends to a constant depending only on $|A|$ and whose value is always less than 1. To achieve our objectives we introduce an easy and elementary method for counting the un-bordered words of a given length over a finite alphabet.

We begin with an alternate characterization of the return set of p. We call the *neighbor set* of p the set $\text{nb}(p) = \text{pre}(p)A - \text{pre}(p)$. The reason behind the terminology is that if we represent the words of A^* in a regular tree then the vertices corresponding to $\text{nb}(p)$ are exactly those (graph-theoretic) neighbors of the path spelling p which do not belong to the path itself.

Theorem 4 *For every word $p \in A^*$ of length m,*

$$\text{Ret}(u) = \{\, (|u|, a, |v|) \mid a \in A,\ ua \in \text{nb}(p) \text{ and } v \text{ is a border of } ua \,\}.$$

It follows that for any p the total number of borders of the neighbor set of p is exactly m.

Note that theorems 2 and 4 show that the values of the function $f(u)$, the number of borders of word u, considered on the neighbor set of p give important information on $\mathcal{A}$. Indeed, state j has a backward edge with label a iff the a-neighbor of $p[1..j]$ has a non-null f-value. Hence, the number of backward edges is exactly the number of neighbors whose f-value is non-null. Since the sum of the f-values on all neighbors is exactly m, the more neighbors with f-values greater than 1 we have and the greater those f-values are the less backward edges we have in $\mathcal{A}$.

In the sequel we shall denote by q the cardinality of the nonempty alphabet A. Let us denote by $U(r, q)$ the number of un-bordered words of length r over a q-letter alphabet, i.e.

$$U(r, q) = |\{\, u \in A^r \mid A^{-1}u \rightleftharpoons uA^{-1} = 1 \,\}|.$$

Let us denote by $T(r, q)$ the total number of borders of words of length r over a q-letter alphabet, i.e.

$$T(r, q) = |\{\, (u, v) \mid u \in A^r,\ \ 0 < |v| < r,\ \ u \in vA^* \cap A^*v \,\}|.$$

We shall also need the values of $U(r, q)$ and $T(r, q)$ relative to q^r, the total number of words of length r over A, i.e.

$$u(r, q) = U(r, q)/q^r \quad \text{and} \quad t(r, q) = T(r, q)/q^r.$$

We have now a consequence of theorem 4 and the analysis following it.

Proposition 5 *The average number $E(m, q)$ of backward edges of reduced automata recognizing A^*p, for words p of length m over a q-letter alphabet is*

$$E(m, q) = 2m + q + 1 - q(t(m+1, q) + u(m+1, q)) - \sum_{r=0}^{m}(t(r, q) + u(r, q)).$$

Now we make an excursion in order to compute the numbers $t(r, q)$ and $u(r, q)$. Initially we state an easy lemma.

Lemma 6 *Let v be the shortest border of u or 1 if u is un-bordered. Then, $u \in vA^*v$, i.e. v is a non-overlapping border of u.*

Our initial aim is to determine the number $U(r, q)$ of un-bordered words of length $r \geq 0$ over an alphabet of $q \geq 1$ symbols. These values can be computed using results in [11, 17], but our arguments are simpler then the previous ones.

Theorem 7 *Let $q \geq 1$. The numbers $U(r, q)$ satisfy the following recurrence:*

$$U(r, q) = \begin{cases} 1 & \text{if } r = 0, \\ qU(r-1, q) & \text{if } r \text{ is odd}, \\ q^2U(r-2, q) - U(r/2, q) & \text{if } r \text{ is even}. \end{cases}$$

Proof. Assume first that $r > 0$ is odd, say $r = 2n + 1$. Then every $u \in A^{2n+1}$ has a factorization $u = v_1 a v_2$ for appropriate words $v_1, v_2 \in A^n$ and a letter $a \in A$. Due to lemma 6 u is un-bordered iff $v_1 v_2$ is un-bordered. It follows that $U(2n+1, q) = qU(2n, q)$.

Assume now that $r > 0$ is even, say $r = 2n + 2$. Then every $u \in A^{2n+2}$ has a factorization $u = v_1 ab v_2$ for appropriate words $v_1, v_2 \in A^n$ and letters $a, b \in A$. Due to lemma 6 u is un-bordered iff $v_1 v_2$ is un-bordered and $v_1 a \neq b v_2$. Further, let $u = v_1 ab v_2$ be such that $|v_1| = |v_2|$ and $a, b \in A$. Then $v_1 v_2$ is un-bordered iff $v_1 a$ is un-bordered. It follows that $U(2n+2, q) = q^2U(2n, q) - U(n+1, q)$. The proof is complete. ∎

An immediate consequence of theorem 7 is that the function $U(r, q)$ is a polynomial of degree r in q. Further, $U(r, 1)$ is 1 for $r = 1$ and is zero otherwise. It follows that $u(r, q)$ is a polynomial in q^{-1}; further, we have the following result.

Theorem 8 *For every $q > 0$ the limit*

$$u(q) = \lim_{r \to \infty} u(r, q)$$

exists and is a series in q^{-1}. Besides, the terms of degree at most n in q^{-1} of $u(q)$ and $u(2n, q)$ are the same. Finally, for every $q \geq 2$, $(q-2)/(q-1) < u(q) < (q-1)/q$, .

Proof. The second sentence follows from the fact that the recurrence in theorem 7 implies that for every $m \geq n$, $u(n,q)$ and $u(m,q)$ have the same terms of degree at most $n/2$ in q^{-1}. This implies the first sentence. To see the last sentence it suffices to observe that, for $r \geq 4$, $U(r,q) \leq q^r - q^{r-1} - q^{r-3}(q-1)$, since (a) every word in $aA^{r-2}a$, for $a \in A$, has a border and there are q^{r-1} such words, (b) every word in $abA^{r-4}ab$, for $a, b \in A$, $a \neq b$, has a border and there are $q^{r-3}(q-1)$ such words, and (c) the sets in (a) and (b) are disjoint and nonempty. It follows that $u(r,q) < 1 - 1/q = (q-1)/q$. The proof of the lower bound is a bit more elaborate. It is based on the fact that $u(r,q) \leq 1$ and this allows to obtain a recursive sequence, say $l(r,q)$, whose value is at most $u(r,q)$ and which tends to a value strictly greater than $(q-2)/(q-1)$ when r tends to ∞. ∎

The initial terms of $u(q)$ can be easily computed with Maple [6]. The series begins as follows:

$$u(q) = 1 - q^{-1} - q^{-2} + q^{-6} + q^{-9} + q^{-12} - q^{-14} + q^{-15} - q^{-17} + q^{-18} - q^{-20} - q^{-23} - q^{-26} - q^{-28} - q^{-29} + q^{-30} - q^{-31} - q^{-32} + q^{-33} - q^{-34} - 2q^{-35} + q^{-36} + \cdots.$$

Table 1 shows the values of $u(q)$ for small values of q.

q	2	3	4	5	6	7	8
$u(q)$	.267787	.556980	.687748	.760065	.805577	.836743	.859379

Table 1. Values of $u(q)$ for small q.

The value of $t(r,q)$ is easier to obtain.

Proposition 9 *For every $q, r > 0$, $t(r,q) = \sum_{p=1}^{r-1} 1/q^p$. Consequently, for $q > 1$, $t(q) = \lim_{r \to \infty} t(r,q) = 1/(q-1)$.*

The above results and proposition 5 can be used to compute $E(m,q)$ which is a polinomial in q for every m. In view of theorem 1 it is interesting to compare $E(m,q)$ to m. The next result shows that the sequence $E(m,q)/m$, $m = 1, 2, \ldots$, converges to a value strictly less than one, which is dependent on q.

Theorem 10 *For every $q \geq 2$, the limit $e(q)$,*

$$e(q) = \lim_{m \to \infty} E(m,q)/m = 2 - t(q) - u(q),$$

hence $e(q)$ is a series in q^{-1}. Further, for every $q \geq 2$, $e(q) < 1$.

Again, the initial terms of the series $e(q)$ can be easily computed. They are as follows and were used to compute the first few numerical values of $e(q)$ shown in table 2.

$$e(q) = 1 - q^{-3} - q^{-4} - q^{-5} - 2q^{-6} - q^{-7} - q^{-8} - 2q^{-9} - q^{-10} - q^{-11} - 2q^{-12} - q^{-13} - 2q^{-15} - q^{-16} - 2q^{-18} - q^{-19} - q^{-21} - q^{-22} - q^{-24} - q^{-25} - q^{-27} - 2q^{-30} - 2q^{-33} + q^{-35} - 2q^{-36} + \cdots.$$

q	2	3	4	5	6	7	8
$e(q)$	.732213	.943020	.978916	.989935	.994423	.996590	.997764

Table 2. Values of $e(q)$ for small q.

TEMPORAL NOTES The main property of this paper, namely that the automaton $\mathcal{A}$ has at most $|p|$ backward edges was discovered by the author in 1989, based on the work of Knuth, Morris and Pratt [14] and especially Duval [8], while trying to prepare a text covering the most important algorithms on words in everyday use. Unfortunately he was unable to conclude that text, actually he was even unable to publish these results in due time. In the meanwhile, some renderings of the ideas of the first three sections appeared, based on lectures he gave in Paris, Naples and São Paulo. These include the book of Beauquier, Berstel and Chrétienne [3], an examination problem in the Concourse 1990 to the École Normale Superieure and the Doctoral Dissertation of Hancart [12, 13]. He sincerely hopes that he will be able to publish the complete proofs of the results here reported before such a long time passes again!

References

1. A. V. Aho, J. E. Hopcroft, and J. D. Ullman. *The Design and Analysis of Computer Algorithms*. Addison-Wesley, Reading, MA, 1974.
2. M. V. A. Andrade. Métodos eficientes para reconhecimento de padrões em texto (in portuguese). Master's thesis, UNICAMP, Campinas, Brazil, 1993.
3. D. Beauquier, J. Berstel, and P. Chrétienne. *Éléments d'algorithmique*. Manuels Informatiques Masson. Masson, Paris, 1992.
4. A. C. Blumer, J. A. Blumer, D. Haussler, A. Ehrenfeucht, M. T. Chen, and J. Seiferas. The smallest automaton recognizing the subwords of a text. *Theoretical Comput. Sci.*, 40:31–55, 1985.
5. J. A. Brzozowski. Canonical regular expressions and minimal state grahps for definite events. In *Proc. of the Symp. of Math. Theory of Automata*, pages 529–561, New York, 1962. Polytechnic Institute of Brooklyn.
6. B. W. Char, K. O. Geddes, G. H. Gonnet, B. L. Leong, M. B. Monagan, and S. M. Watt. *Maple V Language Reference Manual*. Springer-Verlag, New York, 1991.
7. T. H. Cormen, C. E. Leiserson, and R. L. Rivest. *Introduction to Algorithms*. The M.I.T. Press, Cambridge, Mass., 1990.
8. J.-P. Duval. Contribution a la combinatoire du monoïde libre. Thèse, Faculté des Sciences de L'Université de Rouen, 1980.

9. S. Eilenberg. *Automata, Languages, and Machines, Volume A*. Academic Press, New York, 1974.

10. Z. Galil. String matching in real time. *J. ACM*, 28:134–149, 1981.

11. L. J. Guibas and A. M. Odlyzko. Periods in strings. *J. Comb. Th. A*, 30:19–42, 1981.

12. C. Hancart. *Analyse Exacte et en Moyenne d'Algorithmes de Recherche d'un Motif dans un Texte*. PhD thesis, Université Paris 7, Paris, 1993.

13. C. Hancart. On Simon's string searching algorithm. *Inf. Process. Lett.*, 47:95–99, 1993.

14. D. E. Knuth, J. H. Morris, Jr., and V. R. Pratt. Fast pattern matching in strings. *SIAM J. Comput.*, 6:323–350, 1977.

15. J. H. Morris, Jr. and V. R. Pratt. A linear pattern–matching algorithm. Research report 40, University of California, Berkeley, 1970.

16. M. Perles, M. O. Rabin, and E. Shamir. The theory of definite automata. *IEEE Trans. Electronic Computers*, EC-12:233–243, 1963.

17. M. Regnier. Enumeration of bordered words, le langage de la Vache-Que-Rit. *R.A.I.R.O. Informatique Théorique*, 26:303–317, 1992.

18. R. Sedgewick. *Algorithms*. Addison-Wesley, Reading, MA, 1983.

Classifying Regular Languages by Their Syntactic Algebras

Magnus Steinby
Department of Mathematics
University of Turku

1. Introduction

M.P. Schützenberger's discovery that the star-free languages can be characterized by their syntactic monoids was followed by similar descriptions of many other families of regular languages, and now S. Eilenberg's Variety Theory serves as a common setting for such characterizations (cf. [Ei76, Ho91, La79, Pi86], for example).

Syntactic monoids of tree languages can also be defined and they have been used with some success. However, one could argue that the syntactic monoid of a string language is a monoid just because the language is treated as a subset of a free monoid. Therefore, if we regard a Σ-tree language T as a subset of a Σ-term algebra, the corresponding syntactic invariant of T should not be a monoid but a Σ-algebra. This leads to a variety theory of tree languages in which the central notion is the *syntactic algebra* of a tree language (cf. [Al91, St79, St92]). When finite automata are viewed as unary algebras, as J.R. Büchi and J.B. Wright proposed already in the early sixties, strings become unary trees (cf. [Bü89, St81]). This 'unary interpretation' naturally suggests the syntactic algebra of a language as an alternative to the syntactic monoid. The syntactic algebra of a regular language is a finite unary algebra, the algebra of the minimal recognizer of the language. Our goal here is to describe the families of regular languages characterizable by their syntactic algebras. We shall also consider the classes of algebras which correspond to these families of languages.

A direct specialization of the theory of tree varieties presented in [St92], or of the more general versions considered in [Al91, St79], to the unary case does not suffice since the syntactic algebras of string languages are always monogenic. Hence we shall consider varieties of monogenic finite algebras. These can be obtained from the usual varieties of finite algebras by counting their monogenic members only. However, this correspondence between the two types of varieties is not bijective, and we shall define varieties of monogenic finite algebras directly by modifying the subalgebra operator S and the finite direct product operator P_f so that they yield monogenic algebras only. For any alphabet Σ, there is then an Eilenberg-type correspondence between certain sets of regular Σ-languages, called here Σ-varieties of languages, and varieties of monogenic finite Σ-algebras. Any *-variety restricted to a given alphabet Σ yields a Σ-variety of languages, but not all Σ-varieties of languages are obtained this way. We shall also show that Σ-varieties of languages can also be defined by certain systems of congruences of the Σ-term algebra.

2. Preliminaries

In what follows, Σ is always a finite alphabet, Σ^* denotes the set of all (finite) words over Σ, and e denotes the empty word. Elements and subsets of Σ^* are also called Σ-*words* and Σ-*languages*, respectively.

A Σ-*automaton* $\mathfrak{A} = (A,\Sigma,\delta)$ consists of a non-empty set A of *states*, the *input alphabet* Σ, and a *transition function* $\delta: A \times \Sigma \rightarrow A$. Any input letter $f (\in \Sigma)$ defines a unary operation

$$f^{\mathfrak{A}}: A \rightarrow A, \quad a \mapsto \delta(a,f)$$

on the state set. The family $(f^{\mathfrak{A}}: f \in \Sigma)$ determines δ completely and thus one may regard Σ as a set of unary operation symbols and Σ-automata as Σ-algebras. This is the starting point of Büchi's and Wright's 'unary interpretation' of automaton theory (cf. [Bü89, St81]). We shall recall a few general algebraic notions applying them directly to the special case at hand. General expositions of the basic universal algebra needed here can be found conveniently in [BS81], [Co81] or [We92], for example.

Hereafter the alphabet Σ is treated also as a finite set of unary operation symbols. A Σ-*algebra* consists of a non-empty set A of elements and a Σ-indexed family of unary operations $f^{\mathfrak{A}}: A \rightarrow A$ $(f \in \Sigma)$. We shall write simply $\mathfrak{A} = (A,\Sigma)$. The Σ-algebra $\mathfrak{A} = (A,\Sigma)$ is *finite* if A is a finite set. If $f \in \Sigma$ and $a \in A$, we write $af^{\mathfrak{A}}$, or simply af, instead of $f^{\mathfrak{A}}(a)$. Accordingly, we also compose these mappings and morphisms from left to right.

A Σ-algebra $\mathfrak{B} = (B,\Sigma)$ is a *subalgebra* of $\mathfrak{A} = (A, \Sigma)$, if $B \subseteq A$ and $f^{\mathfrak{B}} = f^{\mathfrak{A}} | B$ for every f in Σ. As usual, the corresponding closed subset B is also called a subalgebra of $\mathfrak{A}$. The set of all subalgebras of $\mathfrak{A}$ is denoted by $\mathrm{Sub}(\mathfrak{A})$. If $\varnothing \neq H \subseteq A$, the *subalgebra generated* by H is $[H] = \cap\{B \in \mathrm{Sub}(\mathfrak{A}): H \subseteq B\}$. For $H = \{a\}$, we write $[a]$ instead of $[\{a\}]$. The subalgebras $[a]$ are called *monogenic*, and the algebra $\mathfrak{A}$ itself is *monogenic* if $A = [a]$ for some a.

A mapping $\varphi: A \rightarrow B$ is a *morphism* from $\mathfrak{A} = (A, \Sigma)$ to $\mathfrak{B} = (B,\Sigma)$, and we write $\varphi: \mathfrak{A} \rightarrow \mathfrak{B}$, if $af^{\mathfrak{A}}\varphi = a\varphi f^{\mathfrak{B}}$ for all $a \in A$, $f \in \Sigma$. Surjective, injective and bijective morphisms are, respectively, *epimorphisms*, *monomorphisms* and *isomorphisms*. If there is an epimorphism $\varphi: \mathfrak{A} \rightarrow \mathfrak{B}$, then $\mathfrak{B}$ is an *image* of $\mathfrak{A}$. The algebras $\mathfrak{A}$ and $\mathfrak{B}$ are *isomorphic*, which is expressed by writing $\mathfrak{A} \cong \mathfrak{B}$, if there is an isomorphism from $\mathfrak{A}$ to $\mathfrak{B}$. We write $\mathfrak{A} < \mathfrak{B}$ and say that $\mathfrak{B}$ *covers* $\mathfrak{A}$, if $\mathfrak{A}$ is an image of a subalgebra of $\mathfrak{B}$.

The *direct product* $\mathfrak{A}_1 \times \cdots \times \mathfrak{A}_n = (A_1 \times \cdots \times A_n, \Sigma)$ of the algebras $\mathfrak{A}_i = (A_i, \Sigma)$ $(i = 1,...,n; n \geq 0)$ is defined so that

$$(a_1,...,a_n)f^{\mathfrak{A}_1 \times \cdots \times \mathfrak{A}_n} = (a_1 f^{\mathfrak{A}_1},...,a_n f^{\mathfrak{A}_n}),$$

whenever $a_1 \in A_1,...,a_n \in A_n$ and $f \in \Sigma$. The case $n = 0$ yields the trivial Σ-algebra. For every i, $1 \leq i \leq n$, the ith *projection*

$$\pi_i : A_1 \times \cdots \times A_n \to A_i, \quad (a_1, \ldots, a_n) \mapsto a_i,$$

is an epimorphism from the direct product onto $\mathfrak{A}_i$. A finite Σ-algebra $\mathfrak{A}$ is called *subdirectly irreducible*, if there is no monomorphism $\varphi : \mathfrak{A} \to \mathfrak{A}_1 \times \cdots \times \mathfrak{A}_n$ into a direct product such that the morphisms $\varphi \pi_i : \mathfrak{A} \to \mathfrak{A}_i$ are surjective but none of them is an isomorphism.

Let ε $(\notin \Sigma)$ be a new symbol. The set $T(\Sigma, \varepsilon)$ of $\Sigma\varepsilon$-*terms* is the smallest set T of words over $\Sigma \cup \{\varepsilon\}$ such that (1) $\varepsilon \in T$, and (2) $sf \in T$ whenever $s \in T$ and $f \in \Sigma$. The reverse Polish notation makes the natural bijection

$$\varepsilon f_1 \ldots f_n \quad \leftrightarrow \quad f_1 \ldots f_n \qquad (n \geq 0, \, f_1, \ldots, f_n \in \Sigma)$$

between $T(\Sigma, \varepsilon)$ and Σ^* obvious. One may identify $\Sigma\varepsilon$-terms with Σ-words, and we shall denote $T(\Sigma, \varepsilon)$ also by Σ^* and use the word notation for terms.

The *term algebra* $\mathcal{T}(\Sigma, \varepsilon) = (\Sigma^*, \Sigma)$, which we usually denote by $\mathcal{T}$, is defined so that $sf^{\mathcal{T}} = sf$, for all $s \in \Sigma^*$ and $f \in \Sigma$. The algebra $\mathcal{T}$ is *freely generated* by ε over the class of all Σ-algebras, i.e.

(1) $[\varepsilon] = \Sigma^*$, and

(2) any mapping φ_0 of $\{\varepsilon\}$ into any Σ-algebra $\mathfrak{A}$ can be (uniquely) extended to a morphism $\varphi : \mathcal{T} \to \mathfrak{A}$.

The *term operations* $s^{\mathfrak{A}} : A \to A$ $(s \in \Sigma^*)$ of a Σ-algebra $\mathfrak{A}$ are defined so that

(1) $a\varepsilon^{\mathfrak{A}} = a$ for every $a \in A$, and

(2) $a(tf)^{\mathfrak{A}} = (at^{\mathfrak{A}})f^{\mathfrak{A}}$ for all $a \in A$, $t \in \Sigma^*$ and $f \in \Sigma$.

If $\mathfrak{A} = (A, \Sigma)$ is now the Σ-algebra corresponding to a Σ-automaton (A, Σ, δ) and

$$\delta^* : A \times \Sigma^* \to A$$

is the extended transition function, then $\delta^*(a, s) = as^{\mathfrak{A}}$, for all $a \in A$ and $s \in \Sigma^*$.

A Σ-*recognizer* $\mathbf{A} = (\mathfrak{A}, a_0, F)$ consists of a finite Σ-algebra $\mathfrak{A} = (A, \Sigma)$, an *initial state* a_0 $(\in A)$, and a set of *final states* F $(\subseteq A)$. The *language recognized* by $\mathbf{A}$ is the set $L(\mathbf{A}) = \{s \in \Sigma^* : a_0 s^{\mathfrak{A}} \in F\}$. A Σ-language is *regular* or *recognizable*, if it is recognized by some Σ-recognizer. The set of all recognizable Σ-languages is denoted by $\mathrm{Rec}(\Sigma)$.

For any Σ-recognizer $\mathbf{A} = (\mathfrak{A}, a_0, F)$, there is a unique morphism $\varphi : \mathcal{T} \to \mathfrak{A}$ such that $\varepsilon \varphi = a_0$. For every $s \in \Sigma^*$, $a_0 s^{\mathfrak{A}} = s\varphi$, and hence $L(\mathbf{A}) = F\varphi^{-1}$. More generally, any Σ-algebra $\mathfrak{A}$ is said to *recognize* a Σ-language L, if $L = F\varphi^{-1}$ for some morphism $\varphi : \mathcal{T} \to \mathfrak{A}$ and some F $(\subseteq A)$. A Σ-language is regular iff it is recognized by a finite Σ-algebra.

An equivalence relation θ on A is a *congruence* of the Σ-algebra $\mathfrak{A} = (A, \Sigma)$ if for all $a, b \in A$ and $f \in \Sigma$, $a \theta b$ implies $af \theta bf$. We denote the set congruences of $\mathfrak{A}$ by $\mathrm{Con}(\mathfrak{A})$. If $\theta \in \mathrm{Con}(\mathfrak{A})$, the *quotient algebra* $\mathfrak{A}/\theta = (A/\theta, \Sigma)$ is defined so that

$$(a/\theta)^{\mathfrak{A}/\theta} = af^{\mathfrak{A}}/\theta \qquad (a \in A, \, f \in \Sigma).$$

An equivalence relation θ on a set A *saturates* a subset P of A, if P is the union of some θ-classes.

3. Syntactic Algebras

The following theory of syntactic unary algebras is obtained as a specialization by obvious adaptations from the theory of syntactic algebras of subsets of general algebras (cf. [Al91, St79, St92]) which is an abstraction of the original theory of syntactic monoids (cf. [Ei76, Ho91, La79, Pi86], for example. Hence, we can omit the proofs.

The syntactic congruence of a subset of any algebra can be defined by using unary polynomial functions or translations as abstract substitutes for 'contexts'. In unary algebras both of these coincide with unary term functions. Therefore the *syntactic congruence* $\approx_P$ of a subset P of a Σ-algebra $\mathfrak{A} = (A, \Sigma)$ is a relation in A defined by

$$a \approx_P b \quad \text{iff} \quad (\forall s \in \Sigma^*)[as^{\mathfrak{A}} \in P \Leftrightarrow bs^{\mathfrak{A}} \in P].$$

This $\approx_P$ is the greatest congruence of $\mathfrak{A}$ which saturates P. The $\approx_P$-class of an element $a \, (\in A)$ is denoted by a/P, and the quotient set $A/\approx_P$ by A/P. The corresponding quotient algebra, denoted by $\mathfrak{A}/P$, is called the *syntactic algebra* of P, and the canonical morphism

$$\varphi_P : \mathfrak{A} \to \mathfrak{A}/P, \quad a \mapsto a/P,$$

is the *syntactic morphism* of P. A Σ-algebra is said to be *syntactic* if it is isomorphic to the syntactic algebra of a subset of some Σ-algebra. A subset P of a Σ-algebra $\mathfrak{A}$ is *disjunctive* if $\approx_P$ is the diagonal relation $\delta_A = \{(a,a): a \in A\}$.

Lemma 3.1
  (a) A Σ-algebra is syntactic iff it has a disjunctive subset.
  (b) Every subdirectly irreducible Σ-algebra is syntactic.

In a Σ-recognizer $\mathbf{A} = (\mathfrak{A}, a_0, F)$ the congruence $\approx_F$ is the state-equivalence relation and $\mathfrak{A}/F$ is the algebra of the reduced form of $\mathbf{A}$. Thus $\mathbf{A}$ is minimal iff it is connected (i.e. $[a_0] = A$) and F is a disjunctive subset of $\mathfrak{A}$.

If a Σ-language L is regarded as a subset of the term algebra $\mathfrak{T} = (\Sigma^*, \Sigma)$, then $\approx_L$ is the *Nerode congruence* of L which is the greatest right congruence of the monoid Σ^* saturating L. However, the syntactic algebra $\mathfrak{T}/L$ is now a Σ-algebra.

Lemma 3.2
  (a) A Σ-language L is regular iff its syntactic algebra $\mathfrak{T}/L$ is finite. In any case, $\mathbf{A}_L = (\mathfrak{T}/L, e/L, \{s/L: s \in L\})$ is a minimal recognizer of L.
  (b) A Σ-algebra $\mathfrak{A}$ recognizes a given Σ-language L iff $\mathfrak{T}/L < \mathfrak{A}$.
  (c) A monogenic finite Σ-algebra $\mathfrak{A}$ is syntactic iff $\mathfrak{A} \cong \mathfrak{T}/L$ for some regular Σ-language L.

For $L \subseteq \Sigma^*$ and $s \in \Sigma^*$, the languages

$$s^{-1}L = \{u \in \Sigma^*: su \in L\} \quad \text{and} \quad Ls^{-1} = \{u \in \Sigma^*: us \in L\}$$

are, respectively, the *left* and *right quotient* of L with respect to s.

Lemma 3.3 For any Σ-languages K and L, and any Σ-word s,

(a) $\mathcal{J}/\Sigma^*-L = \mathcal{J}/L$,

(b) $\mathcal{J}/K \cap L < \mathcal{J}/K \times \mathcal{J}/L$, and

(c) $\mathcal{J}/s^{-1}L < \mathcal{J}/L$ and $\mathcal{J}/Ls^{-1} < \mathcal{J}/L$.

4. Varieties of Monogenic Finite Unary Algebras

For any class $\mathbf{K}$ of Σ-algebras,
- $S(\mathbf{K})$ consists of all subalgebras of members of $\mathbf{K}$,
- $H(\mathbf{K})$ consists of all images of members of $\mathbf{K}$, and
- $P_f(\mathbf{K})$ consists of all algebras isomorphic to the direct products of finite sequences of members of $\mathbf{K}$.

The compositions of such class operators are denoted as usual: $OO'(\mathbf{K}) = O(O'(\mathbf{K}))$. If $O(\mathbf{K}) \subseteq O'(\mathbf{K})$ for every class $\mathbf{K}$, we write $O \subseteq O'$.

The following facts are well-known.

Lemma 4.1
(a) $\mathbf{K} \subseteq S(\mathbf{K}), H(\mathbf{K}), P_f(\mathbf{K})$, for every class $\mathbf{K}$ of Σ-algebras.
(b) $SS = S$, $HH = H$ and $P_f P_f = P_f$.
(c) $SH \subseteq HS$, $P_f S \subseteq SP_f$ and $P_f H \subseteq HP_f$.

A class $\mathbf{K}$ is a *variety of finite Σ-algebras*, or a Σ-VFA for short, if $S(\mathbf{K})$, $H(\mathbf{K})$, $P_f(\mathbf{K}) \subseteq \mathbf{K}$. The class of all Σ-VFAs is denoted by $VFA(\Sigma)$. Since this class is closed under arbitrary intersections, $(VFA(\Sigma), \subseteq)$ is a complete lattice.

The Σ-VFA *generated* by a class $\mathbf{K}$ of finite Σ-algebras is the Σ-VFA

$$V_f(\mathbf{K}) = \cap \{\mathbf{V}: \mathbf{K} \subseteq \mathbf{V}, \mathbf{V} \in VFA(\Sigma)\}.$$

Lemma 4.1 yields the representation $V_f(\mathbf{K}) = HSP_f(\mathbf{K})$.

The syntactic algebras of Σ-languages are monogenic and only the monogenic subalgebras of a Σ-algebra can be used for recognizing languages. This means that the Σ-VFAs will not directly correspond to the families of Σ-languages characterized by syntactic algebras. We shall modify the operators S and P_f which may produce non-monogenic algebras from monogenic algebras. In terms of the new operators we define varieties of monogenic finite Σ-algebras. It turns out that these varieties can be obtained also simply by taking the monogenic members of a Σ-VFA, but it seems that the modified operators are useful also for computing varieties of monogenic finite Σ-algebras generated by a given class of monogenic finite Σ-algebras. The operators S_m and P_{mf} are defined so that for any class $\mathbf{K}$ of algebras,
- $S_m(\mathbf{K})$ is the class of monogenic subalgebras of members of $\mathbf{K}$, and
- $P_{mf}(\mathbf{K}) = S_m P_f(\mathbf{K})$.

For a Σ-algebra $\mathfrak{A}$, $S_m(\mathfrak{A})$ denotes the set of all monogenic subalgebras of $\mathfrak{A}$.

Lemma 4.2

    (a) If **K** is a class of monogenic Σ-algebras, then $\mathbf{K} \subseteq S_m(\mathbf{K})$ and $\mathbf{K} \subseteq P_{mf}(\mathbf{K})$.

    (b) $S_m S_m = S_m$ and $P_{mf} P_{mf} = P_{mf}$.

    (c) $S_m P_{mf} = P_{mf} S_m = S_m P_f = P_{mf}$.

    (d) $S_m H \subseteq H S_m$ and $P_{mf} H \subseteq H P_{mf}$.

    (e) $S_m \subseteq S$ and $P_{mf} \subseteq P_f$.

    (f) $S_m S = S_m$ and $S S_m \subseteq S$.

    (g) $P_{mf} S = P_{mf} P_f = P_{mf}$.

Proof. The claims (a), (b), (e), (f) and (g) are quite obvious. The identity $S_m P_f = P_{mf}$ is the definition of P_{mf} and it also implies $S_m P_{mf} = P_{mf}$. Clearly, $P_{mf} S_m \supseteq P_{mf}$. The converse inclusion follows from Lemma 4.1 and the definition of P_{mf}:

$$P_{mf} S_m = S_m P_f S_m \subseteq S_m P_f S \subseteq S_m S P_f = S_m P_f = P_{mf}.$$

This completes the proof of (c). The first inclusion of (d) is quite obvious. It remains to prove the inclusion $P_{mf} H \subseteq H P_{mf}$.

If $\mathfrak{B} \in P_{mf} H(\mathbf{K})$, then $\mathfrak{B} \in S_m(\mathfrak{B}_1 \times \cdots \times \mathfrak{B}_n)$, where $\mathfrak{B}_1, \ldots, \mathfrak{B}_n$ are Σ-algebras for which there exist epimorphims $\varphi_i: \mathfrak{A}_i \to \mathfrak{B}_i$ from some algebras $\mathfrak{A}_1, \ldots, \mathfrak{A}_n \in \mathbf{K}$. From the φ_i's we get the epimorphism

$$\varphi: \mathfrak{A}_1 \times \cdots \times \mathfrak{A}_n \to \mathfrak{B}_1 \times \cdots \times \mathfrak{B}_n, \quad (a_1, \ldots, a_n) \mapsto (a_1 \varphi_1, \ldots, a_n \varphi_n).$$

Suppose $\mathfrak{B}$ is generated by $\mathbf{b}$ ($\in B_1 \times \cdots \times B_n$). For any $\mathbf{a}$ ($\in A_1 \times \cdots \times A_n$) such that $\mathbf{a}\varphi = \mathbf{b}$, the restriction of φ to $[\mathbf{a}]$ is an epimorphism from $[\mathbf{a}]$ onto $[\mathbf{b}]$. Since $[\mathbf{a}] \in P_{mf}(\mathbf{K})$, this proves $\mathfrak{B} \in H P_{mf}(\mathbf{K})$..

Let us call a class **K** of monogenic finite Σ-algebras a *variety of monogenic finite Σ-algebras*, a Σ-VMFA for short, if $S_m(\mathbf{K}) \subseteq \mathbf{K}$, $H(\mathbf{K}) \subseteq \mathbf{K}$ and $P_{mf}(\mathbf{K}) \subseteq \mathbf{K}$. The class of all Σ-VMFAs is denoted by VMFA(Σ).

Every Σ-VMFA is nonempty since $P_{mf}(\mathbf{K})$ gives at least the trivial Σ-algebras. The intersection of any Σ-VMFAs is a Σ-VMFA, and we have a complete lattice (VMFA(Σ), $\subseteq$) of all Σ-VMFAs. Also, the Σ-VMFA *generated* by a class **K** of monogenic finite Σ-algebras, denoted by $V_{mf}(\mathbf{K})$, can be defined as the intersection of all Σ-VMFAs which contain **K** as a subclass. Lemma 4.2 gives the following decompositions of the V_{mf}-operator.

Proposition 4.3 $V_{mf} = H S_m P_{mf} = H S_m P_f = H P_{mf}$.

The following description of $V_{mf}(\mathbf{K})$ is also useful.

Proposition 4.4 If **K** is a class of monogenic finite Σ-algebras and $\mathfrak{A}$ is a monogenic finite Σ-algebra, then

$$\mathfrak{A} \in V_{mf}(\mathbf{K}) \text{ iff } \mathfrak{A} < \mathfrak{A}_1 \times \ldots \times \mathfrak{A}_n \text{ for some } n \geq 0 \text{ and } \mathfrak{A}_1, \ldots, \mathfrak{A}_n \in \mathbf{K}.$$

Proof. The necessity of the condition follows from $V_{mf}(K) = HS_m P_f(K)$. On the other hand, $\mathfrak{A} < \mathfrak{A}_1 \times \ldots \times \mathfrak{A}_n$ with $\mathfrak{A}_1, \ldots, \mathfrak{A}_n \in K$, implies $\mathfrak{A} \in HSP_f(K)$. Since $\mathfrak{A}$ is monogenic, this together with Lemma 4.2 yields

$$\mathfrak{A} \in S_m HSP_f(K) \subseteq HS_m SP_f(K) = HS_m P_f(K) = V_{mf}(K).$$

The factors in a subdirect decomposition of a monogenic finite Σ-algebra $\mathfrak{A}$ are in any Σ-VMFA in which $\mathfrak{A}$ is. Since they are also syntactic by Lemma 3.1, we get the following result.

Proposition 4.5 Every Σ-VMFA is generated by the syntactic algebras it contains.

From the previous two propositions we get the following conclusion.

Corollary 4.6 If V is a Σ-VMFA and $\mathfrak{A}$ a monogenic finite Σ-algebra, then $\mathfrak{A} \in V$ iff $\mathfrak{A} < \mathfrak{A}_1 \times \ldots \times \mathfrak{A}_n$ for some $n \geq 0$ and some syntactic algebras $\mathfrak{A}_1, \ldots, \mathfrak{A}_n \in V$.

For any class K of Σ-algebras, let μK denote the class of all monogenic algebras in K. The most immediate connections between Σ-VMFAs and Σ-VFAs can be expressed in terms of this operator μ.

Proposition 4.7
(a) If V is a Σ-VFA, then μV is a Σ-VMFA.
(b) For any class K of monogenic finite Σ-algebras, $V_{mf}(K) = \mu V_f(K)$.
(c) If K is a Σ-VMFA, then $\mu V_f(K) = K$.

Proof. (a) The inclusions $S(V) \subseteq V$, $H(V) \subseteq V$ and $P_f(V) \subseteq V$ imply immediately the required inclusions $S_m(\mu V) \subseteq \mu V$, $H(\mu V) \subseteq \mu V$ and $P_{mf}(\mu V) \subseteq \mu V$. For example, if $\mathfrak{A} \in P_{mf}(\mu V)$, then $\mathfrak{A} \in \mu V$ follows since $\mathfrak{A} \in S_m P_f(\mu V) \subseteq S_m P_f(V) \subseteq V$ and $\mathfrak{A}$ is monogenic.
(b) Obviously, $V_{mf}(K) = \mu V_{mf}(K) \subseteq \mu V_f(K)$. The converse inclusion follows from Lemma 4.2 and Proposition 4.3:

$$\mu V_f(K) \subseteq S_m HSP_f(K) \subseteq HS_m SP_f(K) \subseteq HS_m P_f(K) = V_{mf}(K).$$

(c) follows immediately from (b).

Proposition 4.7 shows that the two types of varieties are closely connected, but there is no isomorphism between the lattices $(VFA(\Sigma), \subseteq)$ and $(VMFA(\Sigma), \subseteq)$: the same Σ-VMFA can be obtained as the μ-image of several Σ-VFAs. We shall single out the two extreme Σ-VFAs which yield a given Σ-VMFA.

For any class K of monogenic finite Σ-algebras, let $L(K)$ be the class of all finite Σ-algebras $\mathfrak{A}$ such that $S_m(K) \subseteq K$, i.e. the class of finite Σ-algebras 'locally in K'.

Proposition 4.8 If **K** is a Σ-VMFA, then

    (a) L(**K**) is a Σ-VFA,

    (b) μL(**K**) = **K**, and

    (c) if **V** is any Σ-VFA such that μ**V** = **K**, then **V** $\subseteq$ L(**K**).

Proof. The first assertion follows directly from the definitions of L(**K**), Σ-VFAs and Σ-VMFAs. In order to prove (b), we suppose first that $\mathfrak{A} \in$ **K**. Then $S_m(\mathfrak{A}) \subseteq$ **K** which implies $\mathfrak{A} \in$ L(**K**). Since $\mathfrak{A}$ is monogenic, this proves that $\mathfrak{A} \in \mu$L(**K**). Conversely, if $\mathfrak{A} \in \mu$L(**K**), then $\mathfrak{A} \in S_m(\mathfrak{A}) \subseteq$ **K**. For proving (c), let **V** be a Σ-VFA such that μ**V** = **K**. If $\mathfrak{A} \in$ **V** and $a \in A$, then $[a] \in S_m(\textbf{V}) \subseteq$ **V** and hence $[a] \in \mu$**V** = **K**. This shows that $\mathfrak{A} \in$ L(**K**).

Proposition 4.8 means that for any Σ-VMFA **K**, L(**K**) is greatest Σ-VFA **V** such that μ**V** = **K**. Proposition 4.7 shows that the smallest Σ-VFA for which this holds, is $V_f(\textbf{K})$.

5. Σ-varieties of Languages and the Correspondence Theorem

Let us call a set $\mathcal{L}$ of Σ-languages a Σ-*variety of languages*, briefly a Σ-VL, if

    (L1) $\varnothing \neq \mathcal{L} \subseteq \text{Rec}(\Sigma)$,

    (L2) $R \in \mathcal{L}$ implies $\Sigma^* - R \in \mathcal{L}$,

    (L3) $R, S \in \mathcal{L}$ implies $R \cap S \in \mathcal{L}$, and

    (L4) $s^{-1}R, Rs^{-1} \in \mathcal{L}$ whenever $R \in \mathcal{L}$ and $s \in \Sigma^*$.

The set of all Σ-varieties of languages is denoted by VL(Σ).

If we disregard the restriction to one alphabet, these Σ-VLs differ from $*$-varieties mainly in that they are not required to be closed under inverse endomorphisms of the monoid Σ^*. However, the corresponding requirement consistent with the 'unary interpretation' is a part of (L4): for each endomorphism φ of the term algebra $\mathcal{T}$ and any Σ-language R, $R\varphi^{-1} = s^{-1}R$, where $s = e\varphi$ (cf. [St81]). Similarly, the requirement concerning Rs^{-1} reflects the fact that in the general case a variety of subsets of algebras should be closed under inverse translations (cf. [Al91, St79, St92]). Note also that a Σ-VL is always nonempty.

The intersection of any family of Σ-VLs is a Σ-VL, and the Σ-VL *generated* by any set $\mathcal{S}$ of regular Σ-languages can be defined as the Σ-VL

$$\text{VL}(\mathcal{S}) = \bigcap \{\mathcal{L} : \mathcal{S} \subseteq \mathcal{L}, \mathcal{L} \in \text{VL}(\Sigma)\}.$$

The union of any directed family of Σ-VLs is a Σ-VL, and hence (VL(Σ), $\subseteq$) is an algebraic lattice in which,

$$\inf(\mathcal{F}) = \bigcap \mathcal{F} \quad \text{and} \quad \sup(\mathcal{F}) = \text{VL}(\bigcup \mathcal{F}),$$

for any $\mathcal{F} \subseteq \text{VL}(\Sigma)$.

With each class **K** of monogenic finite Σ-algebras we associate the set

$$\mathbf{K}^\lambda = \{R \subseteq \Sigma^*\colon \mathcal{T}/R \in \mathbf{K}\}$$

of regular Σ-languages, and with each set $\mathscr{L}$ of regular Σ-languages we associate the Σ-VMFA

$$\mathscr{L}^\alpha = V_{mf}(\{\mathcal{T}/R\colon R \in \mathscr{L}\}).$$

We shall show that $\mathbf{K} \mapsto \mathbf{K}^\lambda$ and $\mathscr{L} \mapsto \mathscr{L}^\alpha$ define a pair of mutually inverse isomorphisms between the lattices (VMFA(Σ), $\subseteq$) and (VL(Σ), $\subseteq$). The basic strategy is the same as in the corresponding proofs in [Ei76], [Pi86] or [St79, St92], but the present situation has its special features, too.

It is obvious that the two mappings are isotonic, i.e.

$$\mathbf{K} \subseteq \mathbf{L} \quad \text{implies} \quad \mathbf{K}^\lambda \subseteq \mathbf{L}^\lambda \quad \text{and} \quad \mathscr{F} \subseteq \mathscr{L} \quad \text{implies} \quad \mathscr{F}^\alpha \subseteq \mathscr{L}^\alpha.$$

The rest will follow from Lemma 5.1 and Propositions 5.2 and 5.4. It is easy to see that Lemma 5.1 follows from Lemma 3.3 and the definition of the λ-operator.

Lemma 5.1 If **V** is a Σ-VMFA, then $\mathbf{V}^\lambda$ is a Σ-VL.

The following proposition can be proved similarly as the corresponding facts are shown in [Ei76], [Pi86] or [St79, St92]. It holds basically because both Σ-VMFAs are generated by the syntactic algebras of the languages in $\mathbf{V}^\lambda$.

Proposition 5.2 If **V** is a Σ-VMFA, then $\mathbf{V}^{\lambda\alpha} = \mathbf{V}$.

We still have to show that $\mathscr{L}^{\alpha\lambda} = \mathscr{L}$ for every Σ-VL $\mathscr{L}$. The proofs of the corresponding facts for $*$-varieties or varieties of tree languages use the closure under inverse morphisms, a property we cannot assume here. This is, however, compensated for by the following fact.

Lemma 5.3 Let $\mathfrak{A} = (A, \Sigma)$ be the syntactic algebra $\mathcal{T}/R$ of a regular Σ-language R. If $\varphi\colon \mathcal{T} \to \mathfrak{A}$ is a morphism and $a \in A$, then $a\varphi^{-1}$ can be expressed as a Boolean combination of finitely many quotient languages $u^{-1}Rv^{-1}$ $(u, v \in \Sigma^*)$.

Proof. Let $\mathbf{A} = (\mathfrak{A}, a_0, F)$ be a minimal recognizer of R. Suppose $e\varphi = b$ $(\in A)$. Since **A** is connected, $b = a_0 t$ for some $t \in \Sigma^*$. For any $s \in \Sigma^*$

$$s\varphi = es^{\mathcal{T}}\varphi = bs^{\mathfrak{A}}.$$

Hence, $s \in a\varphi^{-1}$ iff $bs^{\mathfrak{A}} = a$. Since **A** is reduced, there are Σ-words u_i and v_j such that, for any $c \in A$,

$$c = a \quad \text{iff} \quad cu_1^{\mathfrak{A}}, \ldots, cu_m^{\mathfrak{A}} \in F \quad \text{and} \quad cv_1^{\mathfrak{A}}, \ldots, cv_n^{\mathfrak{A}} \notin F.$$

Hence,

$$s \in a\varphi^{-1} \quad \text{iff} \quad (\forall i)\, a_0(tsu_i)^{\mathfrak{A}} \in F \quad \text{and} \quad (\forall j)\, a_0(tsv_j)^{\mathfrak{A}} \notin F,$$

which yields the representation

$$a\varphi^{-1} = (t^{-1}Ru_1^{-1} \cap \ldots \cap t^{-1}Ru_m^{-1}) \setminus (t^{-1}Rv_1^{-1} \cup \ldots \cup t^{-1}Rv_n^{-1})$$

of the required form.

Proposition 5.4 If $\mathscr{L}$ is a Σ-VL, then $\mathscr{L}^{\alpha\lambda} = \mathscr{L}$.

Proof. The inclusion $\mathscr{L} \subseteq \mathscr{L}^{\alpha\lambda}$ is obvious since $R \in \mathscr{L}$ implies $\mathscr{T}/R \in \mathscr{L}^{\alpha}$ which means that $R \in \mathscr{L}^{\alpha\lambda}$. For the converse inclusion, suppose $R \in \mathscr{L}^{\alpha\lambda}$. Proposition 4.4 shows that

$$\mathscr{T}/R < \mathscr{T}/R_1 \times \cdots \times \mathscr{T}/R_n, \text{ for some } n \geq 0 \text{ and } R_1, \ldots, R_n \in \mathscr{L}.$$

By Lemma 3.2(b), we have a morphism

$$\varphi : \mathscr{T} \to \mathscr{T}/R_1 \times \cdots \times \mathscr{T}/R_n$$

and a subset H of $\Sigma^*/R_1 \times \ldots \times \Sigma^*/R_n$ such that $R = H\varphi^{-1}$. Since H is finite, $R \in \mathscr{L}$ follows if we show that $h\varphi^{-1} \in \mathscr{L}$ for every $h \in H$. But if $h = (h_1, \ldots, h_n)$ and

$$\pi_i : \mathscr{T}/R_1 \times \cdots \times \mathscr{T}/R_n \to \mathscr{T}/R_i$$

denotes the ith projection ($i = 1, \ldots, n$), then

$$h\varphi^{-1} = h_1(\varphi\pi_1)^{-1} \cap \ldots \cap h_n(\varphi\pi_n)^{-1},$$

from which $h\varphi^{-1} \in \mathscr{L}$ follows by Lemma 5.3.

6. Σ-varieties of Finite Congruences

Varietes of languages are often defined in terms of congruences, and it was shown by Thérien [Th80, Th81] that Eilenberg's Variety Theorem can be extended by a bijective correspondence between $*$-varieties and varieties of congruences of the finitely generated free monoids. A similar result holds also for tree languages and even more generally (cf. [Al91], [St92]). In our present case the relevant congruences are the finite congruences of the term algebra $\mathscr{T}$. These are also the finite right congruences of the monoid Σ^*; the missing requirement of left invariance is compensated for by a special condition satisfied by a our varieties of congruences. This condition is actually a logical consequence of regarding strings as unary trees.

A congruence is *finite* if it has finitely many congruence classes. Let $\mathrm{FCon}(\mathscr{T})$ denote the set of all finite congruences of $\mathscr{T}$. If θ is a (finite) congruence of $\mathscr{T}$ and $u \in \Sigma^*$, the relation $u{:}\theta$ on Σ^* is defined by the condition

$$s \, u{:}\theta \, t \quad \text{iff} \quad us \, \theta \, ut \quad (s, t \in \Sigma^*)$$

is a (finite) congruence of $\mathscr{T}$. A set Γ is called a Σ-*variety of finite congruences* (briefly, a Σ-VFC) if

(C1) $\varnothing \neq \Gamma \subseteq \mathrm{FCon}(\mathscr{T})$,

(C2) $\theta \subseteq \rho \in \mathrm{FCon}(\mathscr{T})$ and $\theta \in \Gamma$ imply $\rho \in \Gamma$,

(C3) $\theta, \rho \in \Gamma$ implies $\theta \cap \rho \in \Gamma$, and

(C4) $u{:}\theta \in \Gamma$ whenever $\theta \in \Gamma$ and $u \in \Sigma^*$.

The set of all Σ-VFCs is denoted by VFC(Σ).

Hence, a Σ-VFC is a filter of the lattice (FCon($\mathcal{T}$), $\subseteq$) which satisfies the further condition (C4). It is clear that $\mathscr{C} \subseteq$ VFC(Σ) implies $\bigcap \mathscr{C} \in$ VFC(Σ), which means that (VFC(Σ), $\subseteq$) is a complete lattice. The greatest element is FCon($\mathcal{T}$) and the least element is $\{\iota\}$, where $\iota = \Sigma^* \times \Sigma^*$. Since any finite congruence of $\mathcal{T}$ is the intersection of the syntactic congruences of finitely many regular Σ-languages (cf. [St79, St92]), every Σ-VFC is generated by the syntactic congruences it contains.

For any subset Γ of FCon($\mathcal{T}$), let

$$\Gamma^\alpha = V_{mf}(\{\mathcal{T}/\theta : \theta \in \Gamma\}),$$

and for any class $\mathbf{K}$ of monogenic finite Σ-algebras, let

$$\mathbf{K}^\gamma = \{\theta \in \mathrm{FCon}(\mathcal{T}): \mathcal{T}/\theta \in \mathbf{K}\}.$$

We shall now show that $\mathbf{K} \mapsto \mathbf{K}^\gamma$ and $\Gamma \mapsto \Gamma^\alpha$ define a pair of mutually inverse isomorphisms between the lattices (VMFA(Σ), $\subseteq$) and (VFC(Σ), $\subseteq$). This will follow from Lemma 6.1 and Proposition 6.3.

Lemma 6.1

    (a) For any classes of monogenic finite Σ-algebras, $\mathbf{K} \subseteq \mathbf{L}$ implies $\mathbf{K}^\gamma \subseteq \mathbf{L}^\gamma$.

    (b) If $\mathbf{V} \in$ VMFA(Σ), then $\mathbf{V}^\gamma \in$ VFC(Σ).

    (c) For any $\Gamma, \Delta \subseteq$ FCon($\mathcal{T}$), $\Gamma \subseteq \Delta$ implies $\Gamma^\alpha \subseteq \Delta^\alpha$.

    (d) If $\Gamma \in$ VFC(Σ), then $\Gamma^\alpha \in$ VMFA(Σ).

Proof. The assertions (a), (c) and (d) are completely obvious. For proving (b) we suppose that $\mathbf{V}$ is a Σ-VMFA and verify that $\mathbf{V}^\gamma$ satisfies conditions (C1)-(C4). First of all, (C1) holds since $\mathbf{V}$ is a nonempty class of finite Σ-algebras. For (C2) it suffices to notice that if $\theta \subseteq \rho \in$ FCon($\mathcal{T}$) and $\theta \in \mathbf{V}^\gamma$, then $\mathcal{T}/\rho$ is an image of the algebra $\mathcal{T}/\theta$ which belongs to $\mathbf{V}$. (C3) follows from the fact that $\mathcal{T}/\rho \cap \theta \prec \mathcal{T}/\theta \times \mathcal{T}/\rho$, for any $\theta, \rho \in$ Con($\mathcal{T}$). To prove (C4), we assume that $\theta \in \mathbf{V}^\gamma$ and $u \in \Sigma^*$. Let $\mathfrak{A}$ be the subalgebra of $\mathcal{T}/\theta$ generated by the element u/θ. It is easy to show that $u{:}\theta = \ker \varphi$ for the epimorphism $\varphi: \mathcal{T} \to \mathfrak{A}$ such that $e\varphi = u/\theta$. Since

$$\mathcal{T}/\ker\varphi \cong \mathfrak{A} \in \mathbf{V},$$

this implies $u{:}\theta \in \mathbf{V}^\gamma$.

Lemma 6.2 If Γ is a Σ-VFC and $\mathfrak{A}$ is any Σ-algebra, then $\mathfrak{A} \in \Gamma^\alpha$ iff there exists an epimorphism $\varphi: \mathcal{T} \to \mathfrak{A}$ such that $\ker \varphi \in \Gamma$.

Proof. If $\varphi: \mathcal{T} \to \mathfrak{A}$ is an epimorphism such that $\ker \varphi \in \Gamma$, then $\mathfrak{A} \cong \mathcal{T}/\ker \varphi \in \Gamma^\alpha$. Suppose now that $\mathfrak{A} \in \Gamma^\alpha$. By the definition of Γ^α and Proposition 4.3 this implies that for some $\theta_1, ..., \theta_k \in \Gamma$, there exist a monogenic Σ-algebra $\mathfrak{B}$, a monomorphism

$$\psi: \mathfrak{B} \to \mathcal{T}/\theta_1 \times \cdots \times \mathcal{T}/\theta_k$$

and an epimorphism $\eta: \mathfrak{B} \to \mathfrak{A}$. There is an epimorphism

$$\tau: \mathcal{T} \to \mathcal{B}, \quad e \mapsto b,$$

where b is an element which generates $\mathcal{B}$. We also have the epimorphism

$$\chi: \mathcal{T}^k \to \mathcal{T}/\theta_1 \times \cdots \times \mathcal{T}/\theta_k, \quad (t_1,...,t_k) \mapsto (t_1/\theta_1,...,t_k/\theta_k).$$

Suppose $b\psi = (u_1/\theta_1,...,u_k/\theta_k)$. For the morphism

$$\sigma: \mathcal{T} \to \mathcal{T}^k, \quad e \mapsto (u_1,...,u_k)$$

we have $\tau\psi = \sigma\chi$. Now $\tau\eta: \mathcal{T} \to \mathfrak{A}$ is an epimorphism and we prove that $\ker \tau\eta \in \Gamma$. If for some Σ-words s and t,

$$(s,t) \in u_1{:}\theta_1 \cap ... \cap u_k{:}\theta_k,$$

then

$$s\sigma\chi = es^{\mathcal{T}}\sigma\chi = (u_1,...,u_k)s^{\mathcal{T}^k}\chi = (u_1s/\theta_1,...,u_ks/\theta_k) = (u_1t/\theta_1,...,u_kt/\theta_k) = t\sigma\chi,$$

i.e. $(s,t) \in \ker \sigma\chi$. Hence

$$u_1{:}\theta_1 \cap ... \cap u_k{:}\theta_k \subseteq \ker \sigma\chi.$$

Conditions (C4), (C3) and (C2) now imply that $\ker \sigma\chi \in \Gamma$. Since

$$\ker \tau\eta \supseteq \ker \tau = \ker \tau\psi = \ker \sigma\chi,$$

this shows $\ker \tau\eta \in \Gamma$, and we may conclude that $\tau\eta$ is the required epimorphism.

Proposition 6.3
  (a) If $\mathbf{V}$ is a Σ-VMFA, then $\mathbf{V}^{\gamma\alpha} = \mathbf{V}$.
  (b) If Γ is a Σ-VFC, then $\Gamma^{\alpha\gamma} = \Gamma$.

Proof. Assertion (a) follows from Lemma 6.2. If $\mathfrak{A} \in \mathbf{V}^{\gamma\alpha}$, there is an epimorphism $\varphi: \mathcal{T} \to \mathfrak{A}$ such that $\ker \varphi \in \mathbf{V}^{\gamma}$. Since $\mathfrak{A} \cong \mathcal{T}/\ker \varphi$, this implies $\mathfrak{A} \in \mathbf{V}$. On the other hand, if $\mathfrak{A} \in \mathbf{V}$ and $\varphi: \mathcal{T} \to \mathfrak{A}$ is any epimorphism such that $e\varphi$ is an element generating $\mathfrak{A}$, then $\ker \varphi \in \mathbf{V}^{\gamma}$ and $\mathfrak{A} \cong \mathcal{T}/\ker \varphi$ imply $\mathfrak{A} \in \mathbf{V}^{\gamma\alpha}$.
Let us now prove (b). Suppose $\Gamma \in \mathrm{VFC}(\Sigma)$ and let $\theta \in \mathrm{FCon}(\mathcal{T})$. If $\theta \in \Gamma$, then $\mathcal{T}/\theta$ is in Γ^{α} and therefore $\theta \in \Gamma^{\alpha\gamma}$. Assume now that $\theta \in \Gamma^{\alpha\gamma}$. Then $\mathcal{T}/\theta \in \Gamma^{\alpha}$ and, by Lemma 6.2, there is an epimorphism $\varphi: \mathcal{T} \to \mathcal{T}/\theta$ such that $\ker \varphi \in \Gamma$. Since φ is surjective, there is a Σ-word u such that $u\varphi = e/\theta$. Let $\psi: \mathcal{T} \to \mathcal{T}$ be the endomorphism for which $e\psi = u$. Then $\psi\varphi$ is the canonical morphism $\theta^*: \mathcal{T} \to \mathcal{T}/\theta$, $t \mapsto t/\theta$, and

$$\theta = \ker \theta^* = \ker \psi\varphi = u{:}\ker \varphi \in \Gamma,$$

which proves that completes the proof of (b).

The results of this and the previous section show that the lattices $(\mathrm{VMFA}(\Sigma), \subseteq)$, $(\mathrm{VL}(\Sigma), \subseteq)$ and $(\mathrm{VFC}(\Sigma), \subseteq)$ are all isomorphic. Without presenting any proofs, we note that the direct isomorphisms between the two last-mentioned lattices are given by $\mathcal{L} \mapsto \mathcal{L}^{\gamma}$ and $\Gamma \mapsto \Gamma^{\lambda}$, where $\mathcal{L}^{\gamma}$ is Σ-VFC generated by the syntactic congruences of the languages in $\mathcal{L}$ and Γ^{λ} is the set of all Σ-languages R such that $\approx_R \in \Gamma$.

7. Some Concluding Remarks

In spite of their rather technical appearance, most of the results presented above are intuitively quite natural. In particular, the defining closure properties a Σ-VL are easily recognized as necessary: the Boolean operations reflect the ways of combining sets of final states and the quotient operations correspond to the possibilities of changing the initial state or choosing a new set of final states. That these closure properties already give the correspondence with Σ-VMFAs is perhaps less obvious.

It is clear that the set $\mathcal{L}(\Sigma)$ of all Σ-languages belonging any given *-variety $\mathcal{L} = \{\mathcal{L}(\Sigma)\}$ is a Σ-VL. Let us now consider an example of a Σ-VL which does not arise from a *-variety in this way.

A Σ-language L is *directable* if there exists a *directing word d* $(\in \Sigma^*)$ such that

$$(\forall u,v,t \in \Sigma^*)(udt \in L \Leftrightarrow vdt \in L).$$

Let $\mathrm{Dir}(\Sigma)$ the set of all directable regular Σ-languages. It is easy to see that $\mathrm{Dir}(\Sigma)$ is a Σ-VL. For example, if d and d' are directing words for the Σ-languages R and R', respectively, then dd' is a directing word for $R \cap R'$. On the other hand, if Σ contains at least two symbols, then $\mathrm{Dir}(\Sigma)$ is not closed under inverse endomorphisms of Σ^*. For example, the $\{0,1\}$-language R denoted by the regular expression

$$(00)^* + (0+1)^*1(0+1)^*$$

is directable with 1 as a directing word. However, for the endomorphism

$$\varphi : \Sigma^* \to \Sigma^*, \quad 0 \mapsto 0, 1 \mapsto 0,$$

the set $R\varphi^{-1}$, which consists of all $\{0,1\}$-words of even length, is not directable. The Σ-VMFA corresponding to $\mathrm{Dir}(\Sigma)$ is the class of all monogenic finite *directable Σ-algebras*, i.e. the finite Σ-algebras $\mathfrak{A} = (A, \Sigma)$ which have a *directing word d* such that for all $a,b \in A$, $ad^{\mathfrak{A}} = bd^{\mathfrak{A}}$ (cf. [ČPR71], for example).

Of course, these remarks do not describe fully the connections between *-varieties and Σ-varieties. Also the relationship between Σ-VMFAs and Σ-VFAs should be studied in depth. Some of the results of Section 4 might be interpreted so that we could do without Σ-VMFAs altogether by replacing each Σ-VMFA **V** by some canonical Σ-VFA **K** such that $\mu\mathbf{K} = \mathbf{V}$. However, at least it seems clear that using the modified operators S_m and P_{mf} when constructing the Σ-MVFA generated by a class **K** of monogenic finite Σ-algebras is more convenient than finding first $V_f(\mathbf{K})$.

Finally, let us note that although the approach proposed here is very Büchian in spirit, a more faithful adherence to Büchi's formulation of the theory of finite automata would have lead to a slightly different theory since in [Bü89] each algebra has a fixed initial state.

References

[Al91]

J. Almeida: *On pseudovarieties, varieties of languages, filters of congruences, pseudoidentities and related topics.* Algebra Universalis 27 (1990), 333-350.

[Bü89]
J.R. Büchi: *Finite automata, their algebras and grammars. Towards a theory of formal expressions* (ed. D. Siefkes). Springer-Verlag, New York 1989.

[BS81]
S. Burris and H.P. Sankappanavar: *A course in universal algebra.* Springer-Verlag, New York 1981.

[ČPR71]
J. Černý, A. Pirická and B. Rosenauerová: *On directable automata.* Kybernetika (Praha) 7(1971), 289-297.

[Co81]
P.M. Cohn: *Universal algebra* (2. ed.). D. Reidel Publ. Company, Dordrecht 1981.

[Ei76]
S. Eilenberg: *Automata, languages, and machines. Volume B.* Academic Press, New York 1976.

[Ho91]
J.M. Howie: *Automata and languages.* Clarendon Press, Oxford 1991.

[La79]
G. Lallement: *Semigroups and combinatorial applications.* John Wiley & Sons, New York 1979.

[Pi86]
J.E. Pin: *Varieties of formal languages.* North Oxford Academic Publ., London 1986.

[St79]
M. Steinby: *Syntactic algebras and varieties of recognizable sets.* Les arbres en algèbre et en programmation, 4éme Colloque de Lille (Proc. Colloq., Lille 1979), University of Lille, Lille 1979, 226-240.

[St81]
M. Steinby: *Some algebraic aspects of recognizability.* Fundamentals of computation theory (Proc. Conf., Szeged 1981). Lect. Notes in Comput. Sci. 117, Springer-Verlag, Berlin 1981, 360-372.

[St92]
M. Steinby: *A theory of tree language varieties.* Tree automata and languages (eds. M. Nivat and A. Podelski), Elsevier Science Publishers B.V., Amsterdam 1992, 57-81.

[Th80]
D. Thérien: *Classification of regular languages by congruences.* Rep. CS-80-19, University of Waterloo, Dept. Comput. Sci., Waterloo, Ontario 1980.

[Th81]
D. Thérien: *Recognizable languages and congruences.* Semigroup Forum 23 (1981), 371-373.

[We92]
W. Wechler: *Universal algebra for computer scientists.* EATCS Monographs on theoretical computer science, Vol. 25, Springer-Verlag, Berlin 1992.

On Polynomial Matrix Equations
$X^T = p(X)$ and $X = p(X)$
Where all Parameters are Nonnegative

Paavo Turakainen

Department of Mathematics
University of Oulu
SF-90570 Oulu, Finland

Abstract

It is shown that the polynomial matrix equation $A^T = p(A)$ does not have any nonnegative nonsymmetric solution if the coefficients of $p(\lambda)$ are nonnegative and the constant term $p(0)$ is positive. The equation is studied in [4] where some necessary conditions for the existence of such solutions are presented. Then a structural characterization is given for nonnegative square matrices A such that $A = A^T = p(A)$ or $A = p(A)$ where $p(0) > 0$. Finally, equations $A^T = p(A)$ and $A = p(A)$ where $p(0) = 0$ are reduced to equations $A^T = aA^k$ and $A = aA^k$ supplemented by some divisibility conditions on the exponents occurring in $p(\lambda)$. The solutions of these monomial equations have been characterized earlier.

1 Introduction

It is well known that, for any complex square matrix A, its conjugate transpose A^* is a polynomial in A if and only if A is normal. The problem is more involved if A is nonnegative and the coefficients of $p(\lambda)$ are required to be nonnegative.

Stochastic matrices satisfying the equation $A^T = A^k$ for some integer $k > 0$ were characterized by Sinkhorn [6]. We characterized in [7] all nonnegative matrices satisfying $A^T = A^k$. The more general equation $A^T = aA^k$ with $a > 0$ can be reduced to the previous one, since $A^T = aA^k$ if and only if $(bA)^T = (bA)^k$ where $b^{k-1} = a$. But we can go further.

The matrix equation $X^T = p(X)$ where $p(\lambda)$ is any polynomial whose coefficients are nonnegative and $p(0) = 0$ can be reduced to an equation of the above form $X^T = aX^k$ (Theorem 4). Another approach based on the theory of nonnegative generalized inverses is presented by Jain and Snyder in [4].

The matrix equation $X = p(X)$ where $p(0) = 0$ can also be reduced to a monomial equation $X = aX^k$ where a and k are the same as in the case of $X^T = p(X)$ but the divisibility conditions are different (Theorem 5).

The equation $X^T = p(X)$ where $p(0) > 0$ is studied in [4] where, for instance, it is shown that if a nonnegative nonsymmetric solution exists, then $\deg p(\lambda) > 2$. We prove in Theorem 1 that no nonnegative nonsymmetric solution exists. On the other hand, symmetric nonnegative solutions exist and are characterized in Theorem 3 as a corollary of a structural characterization of the nonnegative solutions of $X = p(X)$ (Theorem 2).

2 Preliminaries

A real matrix A is *nonnegative* if all its entries are nonnegative. It is called *positive* if all its entries are positive. It is an *M-matrix* if it is square and there exist a nonnegative matrix B and a constant $s \geq \varrho(B)$, where $\varrho(B)$ is the spectral radius of B, such that $A = sI - B$. Here and in what follows, I denotes an identity matrix of appropriate order.

A square matrix A is *cogredient* to a matrix E if for some permutation matrix P, $PAP^T = E$. A is *reducible* if it is the 1×1 zero matrix or is cogredient to a matrix

$$\begin{pmatrix} B & 0 \\ C & D \end{pmatrix}$$

where B and D are square matrices. Otherwise A is *irreducible*. Every square matrix is cogredient to a lower block triangular matrix

$$\begin{pmatrix} A_{11} & 0 & \cdots & 0 \\ A_{21} & A_{22} & \cdots & 0 \\ \vdots & \vdots & \ddots & \vdots \\ A_{\alpha 1} & A_{\alpha 2} & \cdots & A_{\alpha \alpha} \end{pmatrix} \tag{1}$$

where $\alpha \geq 1$, each block A_{ii} is square and is either irreducible or the 1×1 zero matrix (see [1, p.39]).

If A is irreducible and has h eigenvalues of modulus $\varrho(A)$, then by the Perron-Frobenius theorem, they are all distinct and are the roots of the equation $\lambda^h = \varrho(A)^h$. The number h is called the *index of imprimitivity* of A. If $h = 1$, A is called *primitive*.

A square matrix is called *strictly lower triangular* if it is lower triangular and its diagonal consists of zeros.

The transpose of A is denoted by A^T and the conjugate transpose by A^*. A is called *normal* if $AA^* = A^*A$.

Finally, we recall the Harriot-Descartes rule. It says that the equation

$$\alpha_0 + \alpha_1 \lambda + \cdots + \alpha_k \lambda^k = 0$$

cannot have more positive roots than the number of sign changes in the sequence $\alpha_0, \alpha_1, \ldots, \alpha_k$ (ignoring zeros) and it differs from the number of these changes by an even number.

3 Matrix Equation $X^T = p(X)$ Where $p(0) > 0$

The following simple result will be used frequently in the sequel.

Lemma 1 Let A be any real square matrix and $p(\lambda)$ any polynomial with real coefficients. Then $A^T = p(A)$ if and only if A is normal and $p(\lambda_j) = \bar{\lambda}_j$ for each eigenvalue of A. If $A^T = p(A)$ and every eigenvalue of A is real, then A is symmetric.

Proof Let A be normal. Thus $A = UDU^*$ where $U^{-1} = U^*$ and $D = \operatorname{diag}(\lambda_1, \lambda_2, \ldots, \lambda_n)$ with the eigenvalues of A on the diagonal. Hence $p(A) = Up(D)U^*$ and $A^T = A^* = U\bar{D}U^*$ where $\bar{D} = \operatorname{diag}(\bar{\lambda}_1, \bar{\lambda}_2, \ldots, \bar{\lambda}_n)$. Therefore, $A^T = p(A)$ if and only if $p(\lambda_j) = \bar{\lambda}_j$ for each eigenvalue. Since A is normal if $A^T = p(A)$, the first claim follows. The rest of the lemma is obvious. $\square$

The following result will be used in Theorems 1 and 2.

Lemma 2 Let $p(\lambda)$ be any polynomial

$$p(\lambda) = a_0 + a_1\lambda^{k_1} + \cdots + a_s\lambda^{k_s},$$

where $s \geq 1, 1 \leq k_1 < k_2 < \cdots < k_s$, and each coefficient is positive. If A is a nonnegative square matrix such that $A = p(A)$ or $A^T = p(A)$, then every eigenvalue of A is a positive fixed point of $p(\lambda)$.

Proof Assume first that $A = p(A)$. Since now

$$A(I - a_1 A^{k_1 - 1} - \cdots - a_s A^{k_s - 1}) = a_0 I$$

and $a_0 > 0$, A is nonsingular and A^{-1} is a Z-matrix, i.e., its nondiagonal entries are nonpositive. By condition N_{38} in [1, p.137], A^{-1} is an M-matrix. Therefore, condition G_{20} in [1, p.135] implies that the real parts of the eigenvalues of A are positive. Since $A = p(A)$, the eigenvalues of A satisfy the equation $p(\lambda) = \lambda$, so that each of the real eigenvalues is a positive fixed point of $p(\lambda)$. Consequently, it suffices to prove that A has no nonreal eigenvalues.

On the contrary, assume $\lambda_0 = c + di = |\lambda_0|e^{i\varphi}$ is an eigenvalue of A with $d \neq 0$. Since $c - di$ also is an eigenvalue of A, we may assume that $d > 0$. Since $c > 0$, we have $0 < \varphi < \pi/2$. Let K be a positive integer for which $\sin\varphi > 1/K$. We derive a contradiction by showing that $\sin\varphi < 1/K$.

If $k_1 = 1$, then $s > 1$, because otherwise the fact $p(\lambda_0) = \lambda_0$ implies $a_1 = 1$ and $a_0 = 0$. Hence, raising both sides of $A = p(A)$ to the power k_1 we get

$$A^{k_1} = a_0^{k_1} I + k_1 a_0^{k_1 - 1} a_1 A^{k_1} + A^k q(A)$$

where $k > k_1$, $q(\lambda)$ is a polynomial with nonnegative coefficients, and $q(0) > 0$. Since $a_0 > 0$, we have $k_1 a_0^{k_1 - 1} a_1 < 1$. Therefore A^{k_1} has the form $b_0 I + b_1 A^k q(A)$ where $b_0 > 0$ and $b_1 > 0$. Substituting this for A^{k_1} in $A = p(A)$ gives $A = c_0 I + A^m q_1(A)$ where $c_0 > 0$, $m > k_1$, and $q_1(\lambda)$ is a polynomial with nonnegative coefficients and $q_1(0) > 0$. Repeating the same process we can increase the value of m as much as we want, so that finally we get $A = p_1(A)$ where $p_1(\lambda)$ has the form

$$p_1(\lambda) = \beta_0 + \beta_1 \lambda^{t_1} + \cdots + \beta_\nu \lambda^{t_\nu} \tag{2}$$

where $\nu \geq 1$, $K < t_1 < \cdots < t_\nu$, and all coefficients are positive.

We show next that $p_1'(|\lambda_0|) \leq 1$ where $p_1'(\lambda)$ denotes the derivative of $p_1(\lambda)$. Since $p_1(\lambda_0) = \lambda_0$, we have $p_1(|\lambda_0|) \geq |p_1(\lambda_0)| = |\lambda_0|$. Since A is nonsingular, all diagonal blocks in its block triangular form (1) are irreducible. These blocks must be primitive, because the real parts of their eigenvalues are positive. Hence $|\lambda_0| < \varrho(A)$.

Let $p_2(\lambda) = p_1(\lambda) - \lambda$. Then $\deg p_2(\lambda) > 2$, since $t_1 > K \geq 2$. Now the equality $p_1(\varrho(A)) = \varrho(A) > 0$ and the Harriot-Descartes rule (see Section 2) imply that $p_1(\lambda)$ has exactly two positive fixed points. One of them is $\varrho(A)$. Denote the other by r_1 and let $r_0 = \min(r_1, \varrho(A))$. If $r_0 = r_1 = \varrho(A)$, then $(\lambda - r_0)^2$ divides $p_2(\lambda)$, that is, $p_2'(r_0) = 0$. If $r_1 \neq \varrho(A)$, then by Rolle's theorem, $p_2'(\eta) = 0$ for some $\eta > r_0$. By the Harriot-Descartes rule, η (or r_0 if $r_0 = r_1 = \varrho(A)$) is the only positive root of $p_2'(\lambda)$. Hence $p_2'(\lambda) \leq 0$ whenever $0 \leq \lambda \leq r_0$, because $p_2'(0) < 0$. Combining with the previous facts that $|\lambda_0| < \varrho(A)$ and $p_1(|\lambda_0|) - |\lambda_0| \geq 0$ we obtain $|\lambda_0| \leq r_0$ and $p_2'(|\lambda_0|) \leq 0$, that is, $p_1'(|\lambda_0|) \leq 1$.

From $p_1'(|\lambda_0|) \leq 1$ and $K < t_1 < \cdots < t_\nu$ we now conclude (see (2))

$$\beta_1 |\lambda_0|^{t_1 - 1} + \cdots + \beta_\nu |\lambda_0|^{t_\nu - 1} < 1/K. \tag{3}$$

On the other hand, the equality $p_1(\lambda_0) = \lambda_0$ gives

$$\beta_1 |\lambda_0|^{t_1} \sin t_1 \varphi + \cdots + \beta_\nu |\lambda_0|^{t_\nu} \sin t_\nu \varphi = d,$$

so that

$$\beta_1 |\lambda_0|^{t_1 - 1} + \cdots + \beta_\nu |\lambda_0|^{t_\nu - 1} \geq \sin \varphi, \tag{4}$$

because $d/|\lambda_0| = \sin \varphi$. Since $\sin \varphi > 1/K$, inequalities (3) and (4) yield a contradiction.

Finally, assume $A^T = p(A)$. Then $A = p(A^T) = p(p(A)) = p(a_0) + A^{k_1} q(A)$ for some polynomial $q(\lambda)$ with nonnegative coefficients and $q(0) > 0$. Since $p(a_0) > 0$, we find that A is as in the first part of the proof. Hence its eigenvalues are real and positive. By Lemma 1, they are fixed points of $p(\lambda)$. Hence the lemma follows. $\square$

As an immediate consequence of Lemmas 1 and 2 we get the following solution to a problem raised by Jain and Snyder [4].

Theorem 1 *Let $p(\lambda)$ be any polynomial with nonnegative coefficients and $p(0) > 0$. Then the inequality $A^T \neq p(A)$ holds for all nonnegative square matrices having a nonreal eigenvalue. Hence $A^T \neq p(A)$ for all nonnegative nonsymmetric square matrices.*

Corollary *If A is a normal nonnegative, nonsymmetric square matrix and $p(\lambda)$ is a polynomial whose coefficients are nonnegative and $p(0) > 0$, then the set $\{\lambda \in \mathbb{C} \mid p(\lambda) = \bar{\lambda}\}$ does not contain all of the eigenvalues of A.*

Proof Assuming the contrary implies $p(\lambda_j) = \bar{\lambda}_j$ for each eigenvalue of A. Then by Lemma 1, $A^T = p(A)$ contradicting Theorem 1. $\square$

4 Matrix Equation $X = p(X)$ Where $p(0) > 0$

After Theorem 1, a natural question arises as to what the structure is for nonnegative square matrices A for which $A = A^T = p(A)$ or, more generally, $A = p(A)$. We settle the latter case first. The answer to the former is obtained as a corollary by means of the well known structural characterization of nonnegative idempotent matrices.

In the following theorem, we omit the trivial equation where $\deg p(\lambda) \leq 1$. We may also assume that $k_1 \geq 2$, because otherwise the equation can be replaced by another in which this condition is satisfied. (If $k_1 = 1$ and $A = p(A)$, then $a_1 < 1$, since $p(\varrho(A)) = \varrho(A)$.) Moreover, $A = p(A)$ implies that $p(\lambda)$ has a positive fixed point.

Theorem 2 *Let $p(\lambda)$ be any polynomial*

$$p(\lambda) = a_0 + a_1 \lambda^{k_1} + \cdots + a_s \lambda^{k_s},$$

where $s \geq 1, 2 \leq k_1 < \cdots < k_s$, all coefficients are positive, and $p(\lambda)$ has at least one positive fixed point, say r. Let A be any nonnegative square matrix of order ≥ 2. Then the following assertions hold:

(i) *If r is the only positive fixed point of $p(\lambda)$, then $A = p(A)$ if and only if there exists a nonnegative matrix B such that A is cogredient to*

$$rI + \begin{pmatrix} 0 & 0 \\ B & 0 \end{pmatrix} \tag{5}$$

where the zero blocks on the diagonal are square. Moreover, $A = p(A)$ if and only if $(A - rI)^2 = 0$;

(ii) *If $p(\lambda)$ has two distinct positive fixed points, say r_0 and r with $r_0 < r$, then $A = p(A)$ if and only if there exists a nonnegative idempotent matrix B such that $A = r_0 I + (r - r_0)B$. Furthermore, $A = p(A)$ if and only if $(A - r_0 I)(A - rI) = 0$.*

Proof For the 'if' part of (i) assume that $A = Q(rI + C)Q^T$ where Q is a permutation matrix and C is the nilpotent matrix occurring in (5). It is easy to verify that

$$p(A) = Q(p(r)I + p'(r)C)Q^T.$$

Since $p(r) = r$, the Harriot-Descartes rule implies that r is a 2-fold root of $p(\lambda) - \lambda = 0$. Hence $p'(r) = 1$, so that $p(A) = A$.

To prove the 'only if' part of (i) assume $A = p(A)$. Since r is the only positive fixed point of $p(\lambda)$, Lemma 2 implies that all eigenvalues of A are equal to r. Therefore the minimal polynomial of A is $(\lambda - r)^k$ for some $k \geq 1$. Since $p(A) - A = 0$, $(\lambda - r)^k$ divides $p(\lambda) - \lambda$. Hence by the Harriot-Descartes rule, $k \leq 2$. If $k = 1$, then $A = rI$, i.e. A is of the required form where $B = 0$. If $k = 2$, $(A - rI)^2 = 0$, so that $A - rI$ is nilpotent and its degree of nilpotency is 2. Consequently (see, for instance, Corollary 4 in [7]),

$$A - rI = P \begin{pmatrix} 0 & 0 \\ B & 0 \end{pmatrix} P^T$$

for some permutation matrix P and some nonnegative matrix B. Hence A is of the type required in (i).

If $A = p(A)$, then $(A - rI)^2 = 0$ as we saw above. Conversely, if $(A - rI)^2 = 0$, then $A = q(A)$ where $q(\lambda) = r/2 + (1/2r)\lambda^2$. Since r is the only fixed point of $q(\lambda)$, we may apply the above proof and conclude that A is as in (i). Hence $A = p(A)$. This completes the proof of part (i).

To prove the 'if' part of (ii) assume that $A = r_0 I + (r - r_0)B$ where B is nonnegative and $B^2 = B$. It is easy to verify that

$$A^k = r_0^k I + (r^k - r_0^k)B$$

for all $k \geq 1$. Using this we find that

$$p(A) = p(r_0)I + (p(r) - a_0)B - (p(r_0) - a_0)B.$$

Hence $p(A) = A$.

Conversely, assume $A = p(A)$. Hence the minimal polynomial of A divides $p(\lambda) - \lambda$. Since we assumed in (ii) that $p(\lambda)$ has two distinct positive fixed points r_0 and r, the Harriot-Descartes rule and Lemma 2 imply that the minimial polynomial of A is $\lambda - r_0$, $\lambda - r$, or $(\lambda - r_0)(\lambda - r)$. In the first two cases $A = r_0 I$ or $A = rI$, i.e., A is of the required form where $B = 0$ or $B = I$. In the last case $(A - r_0 I)(A - rI) = 0$ and A is similar to a diagonal matrix. By the spectral resolution theorem (see [5], p.154 or 314), $A = r_0 B_0 + rB$ where $B_0 + B = I$ and B is idempotent. Hence $A = r_0 I + (r - r_0)B$. We have to show that B is nonnegative. This is clear for the nondiagonal entries. If some entry b_{ii} is negative, then $a_{ii} - r_0 < 0$, because $r - r_0 > 0$. Now $a_{ii} - r < 0$, so that the (i, i) entry in $(A - r_0 I)(A - rI)$ is positive, a contradiction, since the matrix is zero. Thus A has the form required in (ii).

Finally if $A = p(A)$, then $(A - r_0 I)(A - rI) = 0$ as seen above. Conversely, if the latter equality holds, then $A = q(A)$ where $q(\lambda) = (r_0 + r)^{-1} r_0 r + (r_0 + r)^{-1}\lambda^2$. Since r_0 and r are the only fixed points of $q(\lambda)$, the above proof implies that $A = r_0 I + (r - r_0)B$ for some nonnegative idempotent matrix B. Hence $A = p(A)$. This completes the proof. $\square$

Nonnegative idempotent matrices needed in part (ii) of Theorem 2 are characterized by Flor [2] (see, for instance, [1, p.65]). Especially, a nonnegative symmetric matrix is idempotent if and only if it is cogredient to a direct sum of matrices each of which is either the 1×1 zero matrix or of the form uu^T where u is a positive column vector with $u^T u = 1$. Together with Theorem 2 this gives the following result supplementing Theorem 1.

Theorem 3 *Let $p(\lambda)$ be as in Theorem 2. For any nonnegative square matrix A, the following assertions hold:*

(i) *If r is the only positive fixed point of $p(\lambda)$, then $A = A^T = p(A)$ if and only if $A = rI$;*

(ii) *If $p(\lambda)$ has two distinct positive fixed points, say r_0 and r with $r_0 < r$, then $A = A^T = p(A)$ if and only if A is cogredient to a direct sum of matrices each of which is of the form $[r_0]$, $[r]$, or $r_0I + (r - r_0)uu^T$ where u is a positive column vector with $u^Tu = 1$.*

5 Matrix Equation $\mathbf{X^T = p(X)}$ Where $\mathbf{p(0) = 0}$

In the following theorem we may assume that A is irreducible, since if $A^T = p(A)$, then each nondiagonal block A_{ij} in (1) is a zero matrix. Now, if A is irreducible and $A^T = p(A)$, then $\varrho(A) > 0$ and $p(\varrho(A)) = \varrho(A)$ by Lemma 1. Hence we observe that (a) $a_1 \leq 1$ if $k_1 = 1$, (b) $s \geq 2$ if $a_1 < 1$ and $k_1 = 1$, and (c) $s = 1$ if $k_1 = a_1 = 1$. In the last case $A^T = p(A)$ is the trivial equation $A^T = A$. Hence, we may also assume that $a_1 < 1$ and $s \geq 2$ if $k_1 = 1$. Consequently, $p(\lambda)$ has one and only one positive fixed point.

The proof of Theorem 4 will be utilized in the proof of Lemma 5.

Theorem 4 *Let $p(\lambda)$ be any polynomial*

$$p(\lambda) = a_1\lambda^{k_1} + \cdots + a_s\lambda^{k_s},$$

where all coefficients are positive, $1 \leq k_1 < k_2 < \cdots < k_s$, and if $k_1 = 1$, then $a_1 < 1$ and $s \geq 2$. Let r denote the unique positive fixed point of $p(\lambda)$. Then the following assertions hold:

(i) *If $k_1 \geq 2$, then for any irreducible nonnegative square matrix A, $A^T = p(A)$ if and only if $A^T = r^{1-k_1}A^{k_1}$ and the index of imprimitivity of A divides each of the integers $k_1 + 1, \ldots, k_s + 1$;*

(ii) *If $k_1 = 1$, then for any irreducible nonnegative square matrix A, $A^T = p(A)$ if and only if $A = A^T = r^{1-k_2}A^{k_2}$ and the index of imprimitivity of A divides each of the integers $k_2 + 1, \ldots, k_s + 1$ (Note that the index does not exceed 2 if $A = A^T$.);*

(iii) *If $\gcd(k_i + 1, k_j + 1) \leq 2$ for some $i \leq j$, then $A^T \neq p(A)$ for all nonnegative nonsymmetric matrices.*

Proof Let A be irreducible and let its eigenvalues be $\lambda_0, \lambda_1, \ldots, \lambda_{n-1}$ where $\lambda_0 \geq |\lambda_1| \geq \ldots \geq |\lambda_{n-1}|$. To prove the 'only if' part of (i) assume $A^T = p(A)$. Then by Lemma 1, $p(\lambda_j) = \bar{\lambda}_j$ for each eigenvalue, and $\lambda_0 = r$ because $\lambda_0 > 0$. Since $|\lambda_j| \leq r$ and the only nonnegative fixed points of $p(\lambda)$ are 0 and r, we conclude $p(|\lambda_j|) \leq |\lambda_j| = |p(\lambda_j)|$. On the other hand, $p(|\lambda_j|) \geq |p(\lambda_j)|$. Therefore,

$$p(|\lambda_j|) = |p(\lambda_j)| = |\lambda_j| \tag{6}$$

Since r is the only positive fixed point of $p(\lambda)$, (6) reveals the fact that $|\lambda_j| = r$ for every nonzero eigenvalue of A. Applying the Perron-Frobenius theorem we deduce that the nonzero eigenvalues of A are the roots of the equation $\lambda^h = r^h$ where h is the index of imprimitivity of A. Hence,

$$\lambda_j = re^{j(2\pi i)/h} \qquad (j = 0, 1, \ldots, h-1).$$

Since A as a normal matrix is diagonalizable and $\lambda_j^h = r^h$ for the nonzero eigenvalues of A, it follows that for all integers $m \geq 0$ and $q \geq 1$,

$$A^{mh+q} = r^{mh}A^q. \tag{7}$$

By (6), $p(|\lambda_j|) = |p(\lambda_j)|$ for each $j = 0, \ldots, h-1$. This is possible only if the arguments of the numbers $\lambda_j^{k_1}, \ldots, \lambda_j^{k_s}$ are equal. Thus, there exist nonnegative integers n_ν ($\nu = 1, \ldots, s$) such that $k_\nu = k_1 + n_\nu h$. Therefore, (7) gives

$$A^{k_\nu} = r^{n_\nu h}A^{k_1} = r^{k_\nu - k_1}A^{k_1}.$$

Hence, $r^{1-k_1}A^{k_1} = r^{-k_1}p(r)A^{k_1} = p(A)$, that is, the equality $A^T = r^{1-k_1}A^{k_1}$ follows. Consequently, if $h > 1$, then $\bar{\lambda}_1 = r^{1-k_1}\lambda_1^{k_1}$ by Lemma 1. So, h divides $k_1 + 1$. Since $k_\nu = k_1 + n_\nu h$, h divides each of the integers $k_1 + 1, \ldots, k_s + 1$. For $h = 1$ the same is trivially true. Hence, the 'only if' part of (i) follows.

To prove the 'if' part, assume $A^T = r^{1-k_1}A^{k_1}$ where $k_1 \geq 2$ and h divides $k_1 + 1, \ldots, k_s + 1$. Since $k_1 \geq 2$, r is the only positive fixed point of the monomial $r^{1-k_1}\lambda^{k_1}$. Hence, we may apply the first part of the proof with $p(\lambda)$ replaced by this monomial. Thus, we obtain equality (7). By our assumption there exist integers $n_\nu \geq 0$ such that $k_\nu = k_1 + n_\nu h$ for $\nu = 1, \ldots, s$. As in the first part, it follows that $r^{1-k_1}A^{k_1} = p(A)$, i.e., $p(A) = A^T$. Hence part (i) follows.

To prove part (ii), let $k_1 = 1$, $a_1 < 1$ and $s \geq 2$. If $A^T = p(A)$, then the equality $A^T = r^{1-k_1}A^{k_1}$ follows as in the 'only if' part of (i), because we did not use the assumption $k_1 \geq 2$ there. Hence, $A^T = p(A)$ implies $A^T = A$. Therefore, $A^T = p(A)$ if and only if $A = A^T = p(A)$. Since $a_1 < 1$ and $s \geq 2$, we find that $A^T = p(A)$ if and only if $A = A^T = p_1(A)$ where $p_1(\lambda) = b_2\lambda^{k_2} + \cdots + b_s\lambda^{k_s}$ and $b_\nu = a_\nu/(1 - a_1)$ for each ν. Clearly, r also is the unique positive fixed point of $p_1(\lambda)$. Since $k_2 \geq 2$, we can apply part (i) to the equation $A^T = p_1(A)$, so that part (ii) follows.

Hence part (iii) holds if $k_1 = 1$. For $k_1 \geq 2$ part (iii) follows from (i) and Lemma 1, because $h \leq 2$ implies that every eigenvalue of A is real. This completes the proof. $\square$

By Theorem 4, the matrix equation $X^T = p(X)$ is reduced to $(r^{-1}X)^T = (r^{-1}X)^{k_1}$ or $r^{-1}X = (r^{-1}X)^T = (r^{-1}X)^{k_2}$ which are solved in [7].

6 Matrix Equation $X = p(X)$ Where $p(0) = 0$

Our discussion will be based on the following normal form established in [7].

Lemma 3 *Let A be any real square matrix. There exists a permutation matrix P such that*

$$PAP^T = \begin{pmatrix} L & 0 & 0 \\ B & D & 0 \\ E & C & M \end{pmatrix} \tag{8}$$

where L and M are strictly lower triangular, possibly empty, and either $D = 0$ or D has no zero rows and no zero columns.

Before the next lemma we make a couple of comments on two special cases. The equation $A = a_1 A^{k_1} + \cdots + a_s A^{k_s}$ where $a_1 = k_1 = 1$ takes the form $A^{k_2} = \cdots = A^{k_s} = 0$, i.e., the question is about nilpotent matrices. Their structure is known (see, for instance, [7, p.155]). In the case where $k_1 = 1$ and $a_1 < 1$ the equation is reduced to $A = b_2 A^{k_2} + \cdots + b_s A^{k_s}$ where $b_\nu = a_\nu/(1-a_1)$. Hence we may assume in what follows that $2 \leq k_1 < k_2 < \cdots < k_s$, which implies that $p(\lambda)$ has one and only one positive fixed point.

Lemma 4 *Let $p(\lambda)$ be any polynomial*

$$p(\lambda) = a_1 \lambda^{k_1} + \cdots + a_s \lambda^{k_s}$$

where $s \geq 1$, all coefficients are positive, and $2 \leq k_1 < k_2 < \cdots < k_s$. For any nonnegative square matrix $A \neq 0$, the equality $A = p(A)$ holds if and only if the normal form (8) satisfies the following conditions:
(i) $L = 0$ and $M = 0$, possibly empty;
(ii) $D = p(D)$ and D is cogredient to a block diagonal matrix $\mathrm{diag}(A_1, \ldots, A_\alpha)$ where $\alpha \geq 1$ and each block A_ν is irreducible;
(iii) $B = p_1(D)B$, $C = Cp_1(D)$, and $E = Cp_2(D)B$ where

$$p_\nu(D) = a_1 D^{k_1-\nu} + \cdots + a_s D^{k_s-\nu}.$$

Proof Firstly, assume $A = p(A)$. Then by (8), $L = p(L)$ and $M = p(M)$. Since $k_1 \geq 2$, it follows that $L = 0$ and $M = 0$, possibly empty. Since $A \neq 0$, it also follows that $D \neq 0$. A direct calculation shows that (iii) holds, because for all $k \geq 2$,

$$PA^k P^T = \begin{pmatrix} 0 & 0 & 0 \\ D^{k-1}B & D^k & 0 \\ CD^{k-2}B & CD^{k-1} & 0 \end{pmatrix}.$$

To prove (ii) let Q be a permutation matrix such that QDQ^T assumes a lower block triangular form

$$QDQ^T = \begin{pmatrix} D_{11} & 0 & \cdots & 0 \\ D_{21} & D_{22} & \cdots & 0 \\ \vdots & \vdots & \ddots & \vdots \\ D_{\alpha 1} & D_{\alpha 2} & \cdots & D_{\alpha\alpha} \end{pmatrix}$$

where $\alpha \geq 1$, each diagonal block is square and is either irreducible or the 1×1 zero matrix. We have to verify that $D_{ij} = 0$ whenever $i \neq j$.

Assuming the converse, let t be the largest integer such that $D_{tj} \neq 0$ for some $j \neq t$. Then D_{tt} cannot have any zero columns, since D has this property. Now, consider the following upper left corner of QDQ^T:

$$G = \begin{pmatrix} H & 0 \\ F & D_{tt} \end{pmatrix}.$$

Here $F \neq 0$ by the choice of t.

For each $k \geq 1$ the lower left block in G^{k+1} is

$$FH^k + D_{tt}FH^{k-1} + \cdots + D_{tt}^k F.$$

Since $A = p(A)$, it follows that $G = p(G)$, so that $G^2 = Gp(G)$. Taking the lower left corner blocks in G^2 and $Gp(G)$ and omitting some terms, we obtain

$$FH + D_{tt}F \geq Fp(H) + a_1 D_{tt}FH^{k_1-1} + p(D_{tt})F.$$

Since $p(H) = H$ and $p(D_{tt}) = D_{tt}$, we thus have $D_{tt}FH^{k_1-1} = 0$.

Since $D \neq 0$, D and hence H have no zero rows. From $D_{tt}FH^{k_1-1} = 0$ we can now conclude that $D_{tt}FH^{k_1-2} = 0$. If $k_1 - 2 > 0$, we repeat the conclusion. Finally we get $D_{tt}F = 0$. Since $D \neq 0$, D and hence D_{tt} by the choice of t have no zero columns. It is now easy to see that $F = 0$. But we found before that $F \neq 0$, a contradiction.

Consequently, $QDQ^T = \text{diag}(D_{11}, \ldots, D_{\alpha\alpha})$ where no diagonal block can be a zero matrix, since D has no zero rows. Hence part (ii) holds. Since the 'if' part is obvious, the lemma follows. $\square$

The following lemma bears resemblance to Theorem 4.

Lemma 5 *Let $p(\lambda)$ be as in Lemma 4 and let r denote its unique positive fixed point. For any irreducible nonnegative square matrix A, the equality $A = p(A)$ holds if and only if $A = r^{1-k_1}A^{k_1}$ and each of the integers $k_1 - 1, \ldots, k_s - 1$ is divisible by h, the index of imprimitivity of A. Moreover, if $A = p(A)$, then A is similar to the diagonal matrix $\text{diag}(\lambda_0, \lambda_1, \ldots, \lambda_{h-1}, 0, \ldots, 0)$ where $\lambda_0, \ldots, \lambda_{h-1}$ are the roots of the equation $\lambda^h = r^h$, so that $r^h A = A^{h+1}$.*

Proof Assume A is an irreducible nonnegative square matrix. Let $\lambda_0, \lambda_1, \ldots, \lambda_{n-1}$ be the eigenvalues of A with $\lambda_0 \geq |\lambda_1| \geq \cdots \geq |\lambda_{n-1}|$.

To prove the 'only if' part assume $A = p(A)$. This implies the equality $p(\lambda_j) = \lambda_j$ for each j, so that $\lambda_0 = r$. As in the proof of Theorem 4 it follows that $\lambda_j = e^{j(2\pi i)/h}$ for $j = 0, 1, \ldots, h-1$. Moreover, $\lambda_h = \cdots = \lambda_{n-1} = 0$. Hence A is similar to a Jordan matrix $J = \text{diag}(\lambda_0, \ldots \lambda_{h-1}, H_1, \ldots, H_q)$ where either $H_1, \ldots, H_q$ are empty ($h = n$) or each H_j is a nilpotent matrix whose (i,j) entry is 1 if $j = i+1$ and is 0 otherwise (see [5, p.270]). Since $A = p(A)$, it is clear that $J = p(J)$ and hence $H_j = p(H_j)$. From $k_1 \geq 2$ it now follows each H_j is the 1×1 zero matrix. Consequently, A is similar to the diagonal matrix $\mathrm{diag}(\lambda_0,\ldots,\lambda_{h-1},0,\ldots,0)$ and so the last claim of the lemma is true.

From now on, we may proceed as in the proof of Theorem 4 starting from the point where equation (7) was obtained. The only difference is that A^T is replaced by A and instead of the equation $\bar\lambda_1 = r^{1-k_1}\lambda_1^{k_1}$ $(h > 1)$ we write $\lambda_1 = r^{1-k_1}\lambda_1^{k_1}$ implying that h divides $k_1 - 1$. $\square$

The right side of the equation $A = p(A)$ will now be reduced to the same monomial as in the case of $A^T = p(A)$.

Theorem 5 *Let $p(\lambda)$ be any polynomial*

$$p(\lambda) = a_1\lambda^{k_1} + \cdots + a_s\lambda^{k_s}$$

where $s \geq 1$, all coefficients are positive, and $2 \leq k_1 < k_2 < \cdots < k_s$. Let r denote the unique positive fixed point of $p(\lambda)$. Then for any nonnegative square matrix $A \neq 0$, the equality $A = p(A)$ holds if and only if $A = r^{1-k_1}A^{k_1}$ and each of the integers $k_1 - 1,\ldots,k_s - 1$ is divisible by $h = \mathrm{lcm}(h_1,\ldots,h_\alpha)$ where $h_1,\ldots,h_\alpha$ are the indices of imprimitivity of the blocks $A_1,\ldots,A_\alpha$ in Lemma 4.

Proof Firstly, assume $A = p(A)$. By Lemma 4, the normal form of A in Lemma 3 satisfies the conditions (i)-(iii). Applying Lemma 5 to the blocks A_i we obtain from $D = p(D)$ that $D = r^{1-k_1}D^{k_1}$ and $k_1 - 1,\ldots,k_s - 1$ are divisible by any of the numbers $h_1,\ldots,h_\alpha$, that is, by h. In addition,

$$DD^h = r^h D. \tag{9}$$

Consequently, there exist integers $n_\nu \geq 0$ such that $k_\nu - 1 = k_1 - 1 + n_\nu h$ for each $\nu = 1,\ldots,s$. Since $k_1 - 1 \geq 1$, (9) implies

$$D^{k_\nu-1} = r^{n_\nu h}D^{k_1-1} = r^{k_\nu-k_1}D^{k_1-1}.$$

Hence (see Lemma 4)

$$p_1(D) = r^{-k_1}p(r)D^{k_1-1} = r^{1-k_1}D^{k_1-1},$$

so that

$$
\begin{aligned}
B &= p_1(D)B = (r^{1-k_1}D^{k_1-1})B,\\
C &= Cp_1(D) = C(r^{1-k_1}D^{k_1-1}).
\end{aligned}
\tag{10}
$$

Next, consider the matrix $E = Cp_2(D)B$. If $k_1 = 2$, we use the first of the equations (10) giving $B = r^{-1}DB$ and $p_1(D)B = B$ from which ($p_2(D)D = p_1(D)$)

$$E = Cp_2(D)B = r^{-1}Cp_1(D)B = C(r^{1-k_1}D^{k_1-2})B.$$

If $k_1 \geq 3$, we get the same result

$$E = C(r^{1-k_1}D^{k_1-2})B, \tag{11}$$

because $k_\nu - 2 = k_1 - 2 + n_\nu h$ and (9) implies

$$D^{k_\nu-2} = r^{n_\nu h} D^{k_1-2} = r^{k_\nu-k_1} D^{k_1-2}$$

from which $p_2(D) = r^{1-k_1} D^{k_1-2}$. From (10), (11) and $D = r^{1-k_1} D^{k_1}$ it now follows that A and the polynomial $r^{1-k_1} \lambda^{k_1}$ satisfy the conditions of Lemma 4, so that $A = r^{1-k_1} A^{k_1}$.

To prove the 'if' part assume that $A = r^{1-k_1} A^{k_1}$ and each of the integers $k_1-1, \ldots, k_s-1$ is divisible by h . The conditions of Lemma 4 are now satisfied by A and the polynomial $q(\lambda) = r^{1-k_1} \lambda^{k_1}$. Since $D = q(D)$, Lemma 5 gives $D = p(D)$, and (9) holds. Equalities (10) and $E = Cp_2(D)B$ can be verified in the same manner as before. In the latter case, (11) is known. Consequently, $A = p(A)$ by Lemma 4. This completes the proof. $\square$

We have reduced the equation $A = p(A)$ to the monomial equation $r^{-1}A = (r^{-1}A)^{k_1}$ whose solutions are characterized in [7]. As an application we could, for instance, characterize those nonnegative square matrices A having a generalized inverse X such that $AXA = A$ and $X = q(A)$ where $q(\lambda)$ is any polynomial

$$q(\lambda) = a_1 \lambda^{k_1} + \cdots + a_s \lambda^{k_s}$$

with positive coefficients and $0 \leq k_1 < k_2 \cdots < k_s$. Namely, $Aq(A)A = A$ if and only if $r^{-1}A = (r^{-1}A)^{k_1+2}$ and h divides $k_1+1, \ldots, k_s+1$, where h is as in Theorem 5 and r is the unique positive fixed point of $\lambda^2 q(\lambda)$. The topic is studied in a more general setting by Jain and Snyder [3].

References

[1] A. Berman and R.J. Plemmons,*Nonnegative Matrices in the Mathematical Sciences*, Academic Press, New York, 1979.

[2] P. Flor, On groups of nonnegative matrices, *Compositio Math.* 21: 376-382 (1969).

[3] S.K. Jain and L.E. Snyder, Nonnegative λ -monotone matrices, *SIAM J. Algebraic Discrete Methods* 2: 66-76 (1981).

[4] S.K. Jain and L.E. Snyder, Nonnegative normal matrices, *Linear Algebra Appl.* 182: 147-155 (1993).

[5] P. Lancaster and M. Tismenetsky, *The Theory of Matrices*, Second Edition with Applications, Academic Press, Orlando, 1985.

[6] R. Sinkhorn, Power symmetric stochastic matrices, *Linear Algebra Appl.* 40: 225-228 (1981).

[7] P. Turakainen, On nonnegative matrices generating a finite multiplicative monoid, *Internat. J. Computer Math.* 39: 151-161 (1991).

Gram's Equation – A Probabilistic Proof

Emo Welzl

Institut für Informatik
Freie Universität Berlin
Takustr. 9, 14195 Berlin, Germany
e-mail: emo@inf.fu-berlin.de

If β_v are the angles at the vertices v, $v \in V$, of a convex n-gon in the plane, then $\sum_{v \in V} \beta_v = (n-2)\pi$ – known as Euclid's angle-sum equation. We normalize the full angle to 1, i.e. we set $\alpha_v = \beta_v/(2\pi)$. Then the equation reads as

$$\sum_{v \in V} \alpha_v = \frac{n}{2} - 1 . \tag{1}$$

This identity has a generalization to higher dimensions, called Gram's equation. We want to derive this identity by a probabilistic argument. Let us immediately start with the proof, the identity will emerge quite naturally.

Consider a convex polytope $\mathcal{P}$ in 3-space, with vertex set V, edge set E and face set F. For a vertex v, let α_v denote the fraction of an infinitesimally small sphere centered at v that is contained in $\mathcal{P}$. Similarly, for an edge e, let α_e denote the fraction of an infinitesimally small sphere centered at a point in the relative interior of e that is contained in $\mathcal{P}$.

Let us now investigate a random parallel orthogonal projection of $\mathcal{P}$, i.e. we choose a random point uniformly distributed on S^2, and we project $\mathcal{P}$ in the direction specified by this point into a plane orthogonal to the direction. The projection is a convex polygon. What is the expected number of vertices we get? The probability that a vertex v will not project to a vertex in the projected polygon is $2\alpha_v$. Thus the expected number of vertices is

$$\sum_{v \in V} (1 - 2\alpha_v) . \tag{2}$$

Similarly, the expected number of edges in the projection is

$$\sum_{e \in E} (1 - 2\alpha_e) . \tag{3}$$

Now, since the number of vertices equals the number of edges, (2) equals (3) and we have the equation

$$\sum_{v \in V} \alpha_v - \sum_{e \in E} \alpha_e = \frac{|V| - |E|}{2} = -\frac{|F|}{2} + 1 . \tag{4}$$

The formula was known to de Gua (1783) for the case of a tetrahedron. Hopf attributes the result for 3-polytopes to Brianchon (1837), while Grünbaum refers to Gram [4] for a first proof of the result. Grünbaum reports that Gram's paper was forgotten and that meanwhile Dehn [2] and Poincaré [8] contributed to the subject.

Hopf gave another simple proof of the identity. He uses the angle-sum equation for spherical triangles (which we somehow replaced by the probabilistic argument).

The formula generalizes to arbitrary dimensions (see e.g. [5]). For a d-polytope, let α_i, $i = 0, 1, \ldots d$, be the sum of all solid angles at i-faces (defined as above for 0- and 1-faces). In particular, $\alpha_d = 1$, and α_{d-1} is half the number f_{d-1}, where f_i, $0 \leq i \leq d$, denotes the number of i-faces of the polytope ($f_d = 1$). Then

$$\sum_{i=0}^{d}(-1)^i\alpha_i = 0 \tag{5}$$

which looks similar to Euler's formula

$$\sum_{i=0}^{d}(-1)^i f_i = 1 , \tag{6}$$

or

$$\sum_{i=0}^{d-2}(-1)^i\alpha_i = (-1)^d\left(\frac{f_{d-1}}{2} - 1\right)$$

to show the similarities to equations (1) and (4) in 2- and 3-space, respectively. The probabilistic argument readily generalizes to a proof of the higher dimensional result. Using arguments as above for the expected number of i-faces in a random projection, by the linearity of expectation and by applying Euler's formula in $d - 1$-space, we have

$$\sum_{i=0}^{d-2}(-1)^i(f_i - 2\alpha_i) + (-1)^{d-1} = 1 .$$

We rearrange sums

$$\left(\sum_{i=0}^{d}(-1)^i f_i\right) - (-1)^{d-1}f_{d-1} - (-1)^d f_d$$

$$-2\left(\sum_{i=0}^{d}\alpha_i\right) + 2(-1)^{d-1}\alpha_{d-1} + 2(-1)^d\alpha_d + (-1)^{d-1} = 1 .$$

After cancelling terms via $\alpha_{d-1} = f_{d-1}/2$, $\alpha_d = 1$ and $f_d = 1$, we invoke Euler's formula (6) in d dimensions to obtain (5).

A proof of (5) is indicated also by Edelsbrunner in [3] (Remark 3, Section 6). Barnette [1] uses very similar arguments (although in a different terminology) to prove a tight bound of

$$\alpha_i \leq \frac{1}{2}\left(f_i - \binom{d}{i+1}\right) , \qquad 0 \leq i \leq d-2 .$$

The proof exploits the fact that for every projection of a d-polytope the number of i-faces is at least $\binom{d}{i+1}$.

References

[1] D. Barnette, The sum of the solid angles of a d-polytope, *Geometriae Dedicata* **1** (1972) 100–102

[2] M. Dehn, Die Eulersche Formel in Zusammenhang mit dem Inhalt in der nicht-Euklidischen Geometrie, *Math. Ann.* **61** (1905) 561–586

[3] H. Edelsbrunner, The union of balls and its dual shape, *Proc. 9th Annual ACM Symposium on Computational Geometry* (1993) 218–231

[4] J. P. Gram, Om Rumvinklerne i et Polyeder, *Tidsskr. Math.* **4** (1874), 161–163

[5] B. Grünbaum, *Convex Polytopes*, John Wiley & Sons, Interscience, London (1967)

[6] de Gua de Malves, Propositions neuves, et non moins utiles que curieuses, sur le tétraèdre, *Hist. Acad. R. des Sci.*, Paris (1783)

[7] H. Hopf, Über Zusammenhänge zwischen Topologie und Metrik im Rahmen der elementaren Geometrie, *Math. Physik. Sem. Ber.* **3** (1953) 16–29

[8] H. Poincaré, Sur la generalization d'un theoreme élémentaire de Geometrie, *Compt. Rend. Acad. Sci. Paris* **140** (1905) 113–117

ARTO SALOMAA: CURRICULUM VITAE

Born in Turku, Finland, June 6, 1934.
Married since 1959.
Children: Kai (b. 1960), Kirsti (b. 1961)
Grandchildren: Suvi (b. 1987), Juhani (b. 1989), Daniel (b. 1991)

1. Studies

Elementary, high school and beginning university studies in Turku. MA, University of Turku, 1954.
Graduate studies at the University of California, Berkeley, 1956-57.
Ph. Lic., University of Helsinki, 1959.
Ph. D., University of Turku, 1960.

2. Positions held in Finland

Assistant, instructor and docent, University of Turku, 1957–65
Professor of Applied Mathematics, University of Oulu, 1965.
Professor of Mathematics, University of Turku, 1966–.
Research Professor at the Academy of Finland, 1975–1980.
Research Professor at the Academy of Finland, 1989–.

3. Visiting positions

Visiting Professor of Computer Science, University of Western Ontario, London, Ontario, 1966–68.
Visiting Professor of Computer Science, University of Aarhus, Denmark, 1973–75.
Visiting Professor of Computer Science, University of Waterloo, Canada, 1981–82.
Shorter visits to 150 universities in Europe, North America and Asia.

4. Invited lectures at international conferences

Invited lectures and lecture series at the following scientific conferences, work shops and summer schools.

International Colloquium on Modal and Many-Valued Logic, Helsinki, 1962.
CSA Research Seminar on Computer Science, University of Toronto, 1967.
Second Annual Princeton Conference on Information Sciences and Systems, 1968.
First Scandinavian Logic Symposium, Turku, 1968.

Work shop and summer school in formal language theory, University of Western Ontario, 1971.

Winter school in unusual automata theory, University of Aarhus, 1972.

Oberwolfach Conference in Formal Languages, 1972, 1973, 1974, 1975.

Colloquium on Parallel Rewriting Systems. McMaster University, 1973.

Third Scandinavian Logic Symposium, Uppsala, 1973.

1. Fachtagung über Automatentheorie und Formale Sprachen, Bonn, 1973.

Algebraic Automata Theory, University of Szeged, 1973.

Mathematical Foundations of Computer Science, High Tatras 1973, Marianske Lazne 1975, Gdansk 1976, Olomouc 1979.

Winter school in L systems, University of Aarhus, 1974.

Fachtagung über Automatentheorie, University of Dortmund, 1974.

Biologically Motivated Automata Theory, MITRE Corporation, Virginia, 1974.

Second ICALP Conference, Saarbrücken, 1974.

Formal Languages, Automata and Development, Noordwijkerhout, 1975.

Formal Languages and Programming, Madrid, 1975.

Second Advanced Course on the Foundations of Computer Science, University of Amsterdam, 1976.

500-Year Festival Symposium "Philosophy and Grammar", Uppsala University, 1977.

Advanced Unesco summer school on Mathematical Foundations of Computer Science, University of Turku, 1977.

Work shop on Automata Theory, Nanyang University, Singapore, 1977.

Fourth IBM Symposium on Mathematical Foundations of Computer Science, Oiso, Japan, 1979.

International Conference on Formal Language Theory, University of California, Santa Barbara, 1979.

Seventh ICALP Conference, Noordwijkerhout, 1980.

18th Scandinavian Congress of Mathematicians, Aarhus, 1980.

International Conference on Combinatorics of Words, Waterloo, 1982.

American Mathematical Society Summer Meeting, Toronto, 1982.

International Conference on Algebra, Combinatorics and Logic in Computer Science, Györ, 1983.

19th Scandinavian Congress of Mathematicians, Reykjavik, 1984.

International Conference on Theoretical Computer Science, Györ 1985.

Oberwolfach Conference in Semigroup Theory, 1986.

Latvian Computer Science Conference, Riga, 1987.

IIG Festival Conference, Graz, 1988.

5th International Meeting of Young Computer Scientists, Smolenice, 1988.

XII Österreichischer Mathematikerkongress, Wien, 1989.

300-Year Festival Congress of the Hamburg Mathematical Association, 1990.

Festival Congress "New Trends and Results in Computer Science", Graz 1991.

Conference of the Austrian and German Mathematical Associations, Wien 1992.

Conference "Salodays in Formal Languages", Bucharest 1992.

Festival conference in formal languages, Magdeburg 1992.

9th International Conference "Automata, Formal Languages", Salgotarjan 1993.

FCT-93, Szeged 1993.
MFCS-93, Gdansk 1993.
Conference "Salodays", Auckland 1994.

5. Editing scientific journals

Editor of the following scientific journals:

- Journal of Symbolic Logic 1968–
- Information and Control 1972–
- Acta Informatica 1973–
- Theoretical Computer Science 1975–
- Elektronische Informationsverarbeitung und Kybernetik 1975–
- Discrete Applied Mathematics 1978–
- Fundamenta Informaticae 1980–
- Acta Cybernetica 1988–
- Journal of Computer Science and Technology, Beijing, 1988–

6. Ph.D. Students

Supervisor of the following Ph.D. students. After the name, the year of getting
Ph.D. is indicated.

Neil Jones	1967	Mogens Nielsen	1976
Paavo Turakainen	1968	Juhani Karhumäki	1976
Magnus Steinby	1969	Paul Vitanyi	1978
Topi Urponen	1971	Raija Leipälä	1979
Andrew Szilard	1974	Tero Harju	1979
Martti Penttonen	1974	Juha Honkala	1988
Sven Skyum	1974	Valtteri Niemi	1989
Matti Linna	1975	Jarkko Kari	1990
Matti Soittola	1976	Lila Kari	1991
Keijo Ruohonen	1976		

In addition, the external examiner (or "official opponent" in Europe) of a number
of Ph.D. candidates. In 1983, such occasions took place in Leiden, Antwerp and
Darmstadt, and in 1984 in Antwerp, and again in 1986 and 1987 in Leiden.

7. Miscellaneous scientific activities

Regular reviewer for the following journals:

Zentralblatt für Mathematik und ihre Grenzgebiete 1962- .
Journal of Symbolic Logic 1968- .
Mathematical Reviews 1968- .
Computing Reviews 1970- .

Program committee member for the following conferences:

- First ICALP Conference, Paris, 1972.
- Second ICALP Conference, Saarbrücken, 1974.
- Biologically Motivated Automata Theory, MITRE, Virginia, 1974.
- Automata, Languages, Development, Noordwijkerhout, 1975.
- Uniformly Structured Automata and Logic, Tokyo, 1975.
- Third ICALP, Edinburgh, 1976.
- Fourth ICALP, Turku, 1977 (chairman of the program committee).
- Theoretical Computer Science, University of Waterloo, 1977.
- International Congress of Mathematicians, Helsinki, 1978.
- Sixth ICALP, Graz, 1979.
- Seventh ICALP, Noordwijkerhout, 1980.
- Eighth ICALP, Haifa, 1981.
- ACM Symposium on Theory of Computing (STOC), Milwaukee, 1981.
- FCT, Szeged, 1981.
- MFCS, High Tatras, 1981.
- Ninth ICALP, Aarhus, 1982.
- FCT, Linköping, 1983.
- Eleventh ICALP, Antwerp, 1984.
- Parallel Processing, Berlin, 1984.
- Twelfth ICALP, Greece, 1985.
- FCT, Berlin, 1985.
- International Congress of Mathematicians, Berkeley, 1986.
- MFCS, Bratislava, 1986.
- Parallel Processing (PARCELLA), Berlin, 1986.
- FCT, Kazan, 1987.
- MFCS, Prague, 1988.
- Fifteenth ICALP, Tampere, 1988 (chairman).
- Sixteenth ICALP, Stresa, 1989.
- FCT, Szeged, 1989.
- MFCS, Banska Bystrica, 1990.
- Nineteenth ICALP, Wien, 1992.
- MFCS, Praha, 1992.
- Developments in Language Theory, Turku, 1993 (chairman).
- MFCS, Kosice 1994.

Member of the Academy of Sciences of Finland 1970- .
Member of the Swedish Academy of Sciences of Finland 1980- .
Member of the Academia Europaea 1992- .
Referee and member of numerous selection committees for professorships in mathematics and computer science, as well as of selection committees for inviting conference speakers and awarding prizes in computer science. Chairman of a 3-man IMU committee for choosing the winner of the first Nevanlinna prize. Member of the Board of the Nevanlinna Institute 1987- and organizer of the Institute's Thematic Year for Theoretical Computer Science 1988–1989.

Member of the international committee awarding the first Gödel prize 1993.
Chairman of the committee (consisting of S. Cook, J. van Leeuwen, R. Karp,
R. Milner, M. Rabin) since summer 1993.
Occasional referee of scientific journals other than those listed in point 5).
Editor of the series of books "EATCS Monographs in Theoretical Computer
Science", Springer-Verlag 1983– .
Delivered the invited Kloosterman lectures in Leiden, May–June 1988.
Member of the international committee to evaluate research in computer science
and related areas in mathematics in Norway 1992.

8. Administrative and organizational duties

Chairman of the Mathematics Department, University of Turku, 1971–73.
Member and chairman of various committees on curriculum-planning and graduate admission at the universities of Turku, Western Ontario, Aarhus and Waterloo.
Director of the summer program in theoretical computer science at the university
of Western Ontario, 1971.
Director of the winter school in L systems, University of Aarhus, 1974.
Director of the advanced Unesco summer school on Mathematical Foundations
of Computer Science, University of Turku, 1977.
Member and chairman of the organizing committees for the Scandinavian Con-
gress of Mathematicians, Turku 1976, Fourth ICALP Conference, Turku 1977,
and the World Congress of Mathematicians, Helsinki 1978.
Council member of the European Association for Theoretical Computer Science
(EATCS) 1973– . President of EATCS 1979–1985.
Member and chairman of several committees chosen by EATCS and SIGACT.
Director of the research group "Data transmission and data security", Academy
of Finland, 1989–91.
Director of the research group "Mathematical structures in computer science",
Academy of Finland, 1992– .
Chairman of the organizing committee for the conference "Developments in Lan-
guage Theory", Turku 1993.

9. Honorary degrees and special awards

The yearly prize of Suomen Kulttuurirahasto (The Foundation for the Finnish
Culture) 1986.
Ph. D. h.c. Åbo Akademi 1988.
Ph. D. h.c., University of Oulu 1989.
Doctor Rerum Naturalium h.c., University of Szeged, Hungary, 1989.
Magnus Ehrnrooth prize of the Societas Scientiarum Fennica, 1991.
Ph. D. h.c., University of Bucharest, Romania, 1992.
Doktor-Ingenieur Ehren halber (h.c.), TU Magdeburg, Germany, 1992.
Professor of the Year 1993 in Finland.

PUBLICATIONS by ARTO SALOMAA

1959

On many-valued systems of logic. Ajatus 22, 115 -159.

1960

On the composition of functions of several variables ranging over a finite set. Ann. Univ. Turku, Ser. A I 41, 48 pp.

A theorem concerning the composition of functions of several variables ranging over a finite set. Journal of Symbolic Logic 25, 203–8.

1962

On the number of simple bases of the set of functions over a finite domain. Ann. Univ. Turku, Ser. A I 52, 4 pp.

Some completeness criteria for sets of functions over a finite domain, I. Ibid., Ser. A I 53, 10 pp.

1963

Some completeness criteria for sets of functions over a finite domain, II. Ibid., Ser. A I 63, 19 pp. (Russian translations of two previous papers in Kibernetitseskii sbornik 8 (1964), 8–32.)

On sequences of functions over an arbitrary domain. Ibid., Ser. A I 62, 5 pp.

Some analogues of Sheffer functions in infinite-valued logics. Proc. Colloq. Modal and Many-valued Logics in Helsinki 1962, 227–235.

On basic groups for the set of functions over a finite domain. Ann. Acad. Scient. Fennicae, Ser. A I 338, 15 pp.

On essential variables of functions, especially in the algebra of logic. Ibid., Ser. A I 339, 11 pp.

1964

Theorems on the representation of events in Moore automata. Ann. Univ. Turku, Ser. A I 69, 14 pp.

On infinitely generated sets of operations in finite algebras. Ibid., Ser. A I 74, 13 pp.

Axiom systems for regular expressions of finite automata. Ibid., Ser. A I 75, 29 pp.

On the reducibility of events represented in automata. Ann. Acad. Scient. Fennicae, Ser. A I 353, 16 pp.

1965

On the heights of closed sets of operations in finite algebras. Ibid., Ser. A I 363, 12 pp.

On some algebraic notions in the theory of truthfunctions. Acta Philos. Fennica 18, 193–202.

On probabilistic automata with one input letter. Ann. Univ. Turku, Ser. A I 85, 16 pp.

Automaattien teoriasta. Arkhimedes, 7–20.

1966

Two complete axiom systems for the algebra of regular events. Journal of the Association for Computing Machinery 13, 158–169.

Aksiomatizatsija algebry sobytii, realizuemyh logitseskimi setjami. Problemy Kibernetiki 17, 237–246.

1967

On m-adic probabilistic automata. Information and Control 10, 215–19.

Formal languages. Lecture Notes for the Research Seminar on Computer Science, Univ. of Toronto, 58 pp.

1968

On events represented by probabilistic automata of different types. Canadian Journal of Mathematics 20, 242–251.

On languages accepted by probabilistic and time-variant automata. Proc. II Princeton Conf. On Information Sciences and Systems 184–188.

(with V. Tixier) Two complete axiom systems for the extended language of regular expressions. IEEE Computer Trans. C-17, 700–701.

On finite automata with a time-variant structure. Information and Control 13, 85–98.

On finite time-variant automata with monitors of different types. Ann. Univ. Turku, Ser. A I 118:3, 12 pp.

On regular expressions and regular canonical systems. Mathematical Systems Theory 2, 341–355.

Matematiikka ja tietokone. Arkhimedes, 5–10.

1969

"Theory of Automata". International Series of Monographs in Pure and Applied Mathematics, Vol. 100, Pergamon Press, 276 pp. Japanese translation by Kyoritsu Shuppan in 1974.

On the index of a context-free grammar and language. Information and Control 14, 474–477.

Probabilistic and time-variant grammars and languages. Avh. Första Nordiska Logikersymposiet, 115–133.

On grammars with restricted use of productions. Ann. Acad. Scient. Fennicae, Ser. A I 454, 32 pp.

1970

On some families of formal languages obtained by regulated derivations. Ibid., Ser. A I 479, 18 pp.

Probabilistic and weighted grammars. Information and Control 15, 529–544.

Periodically time-variant context-free grammars. Ibid., 17, 294–311.

1971

The generative capacity of transformational grammars of Ginsburg and Partee. Ibid., 18, 227–232.

Theories of abstract automata (review). Ibid., 19, 476–478.

Grammars with control languages. Mathematisch Instituut, Utrecht, publ. no. 7, 8 pp.

1972

Matrix grammars with a leftmost restriction. Information and Control 20, 143–149.

On a homomorphic characterization of recursively enumerable languages. Ann. Acad. Sci. Fennicae, Ser. A I 525, 10 pp.

1973

"Formal Languages". Academic Press, New York, 335 pp.

On exponential growth in Lindenmayer systems. Indagationes Mathematicae 35, 23–30.

On sentential forms of context-free grammars. Acta Informatica 2, 40–49.

(with A. Paz) Integral sequential word functions and growth equivalence of Lindenmayer systems. Information and Control 23, 313–343.

Macros, iterated substitution and Lindenmayer AFL's. Aarhus University DAIMI Publications 18, 13 pp.

On some decidability problems concerning developmental languages. Proc. 3rd Scandinavian Logic Symposium, North-Holland Publ. Co. (1975), pp. 144–153.

Growth functions associated with some new types of grammars. Proc. Conf. on Algebraic Theory of Automata, Szeged, 27–31.

On some recent problems concerning developmental languages. Proc. 1. Fachtagung über Automatentheorie und formale Sprachen, Springer Lecture Notes in Computer Science, Vol. 2, 23–34.

L-systems: a device in biologically motivated automata theory. Proc. Conf. on Mathematical Foundations of Computer Science, Slovak Academy of Sciences, 147–151.

Developmental languages: a new type of formal languages. Ann. Univ. Turku, Ser. B 126, pp. 183–189.

1974

Solution of a decision problem concerning unary Lindenmayer systems. Discrete Mathematics 9, 71–77.

Some remarks concerning many-valued propositional logics. In: S. Stenlund (ed.), Logical Theory and Semantical Analysis, D. Reidel Publ. Co., 15–21.

(with M. Nielsen, G. Rozenberg and S. Skyum) Nonterminals, homomorphisms and codings in different variations of OL-systems, Parts I-II. Acta Informatica 3, pp. 357-364, and 4, pp. 87–106.

(with G. Rozenberg) The mathematical theory of L systems. Aarhus University DAIMI Publications 33, 67 pp., extended version appears also in: J. Tou (ed.), Advances in Information Systems Science, Vol. 6, Plenum Press (1976), pp. 161–206.

Recent results on L-systems. Proc. Conf. on Biologically Motivated Automata Theory, IEEE Publications no. 74 CH0 889-6 C, pp. 38–45.

Parallelism in rewriting systems. Proc. 2nd Colloquium on Automata, Languages and Programming, Springer Lecture Notes in Computer Science, Vol. 14, 523–533.

(edited with G. Rozenberg) "L Systems". Springer Lecture Notes in Computer Science, Vol. 15, 338 pp.

Iteration grammars and Lindenmayer AFL's. Previous Volume, pp. 250–253.

1975

Formal power series and growth functions of Lindenmayer systems. Springer Lecture Notes in Computer Science, Vol. 32, pp. 101–113.

Comparative decision problems between sequential and parallel rewriting. Proc. Intern. Symp. Uniformly Structured Automata and Logic, IEEE Publications 75 CH1 052-0 C, pp. 62–66.

Growth functions of Lindenmayer systems: some new approaches. In: Automata, Languages and Development, North-Holland (1976), pp. 271–282.

Tietokoneiden tulo. In: Luonnontieteellisen tutkimuksen historia. WSOY, Porvoo, Finland, pp. 245–256.

1976

(with G. Rozenberg) Context-free grammars with graph-controlled tables. Journal of Computer and System Sciences 13, pp. 90–99.

(with G. Rozenberg and K. Ruohonen) Developmental systems with fragmentation. International Journal of Computer Mathematics 5, pp. 177–191.

L systems: A parallel way of looking at formal languages. New ideas and recent developments. Mathematical Centre Tracts 82, Amsterdam, pp. 65–107.

Sequential and parallel rewriting. In: R. Aguilar (ed.), Formal Languages and Programming. North-Holland, pp. 111–129.

Undecidable problems concerning growth in informationless Lindenmayer systems. Elektronische Informationsverarbeitung und Kybernetik 12, pp. 331–335.

Recent results on L systems. Springer Lecture Notes in Computer Science, Vol. 45, pp. 115–123.

1977

(with G. Rozenberg) New squeezing mechanisms for L systems. Information Sciences 12, pp. 187–201.

Formal power series and language theory. Nanyang University Publications, 23 pp.

(with H. Maurer and D. Wood) EOL forms. Acta Informatica 8, pp. 75–96.

(with H. Maurer and Th. Ottman) On the form equivalence of L forms. Theoretical Computer Science 4, pp. 199–225.

(with M. Penttonen and G. Rozenberg) Bibliography of L systems. Theoretical Computer Science 5, pp. 339–354.

(ed. with M. Steinby) Automata, Languages and Programming. Proc. 4th ICALP Conference in Turku. Springer Lecture Notes in Computer Science, Vol. 52, 569 pp.

1978

(with M. Soittola) *Automata-Theoretic Aspects of Formal Power Series.* Springer-Verlag, New York, 181 pp.

(with H. Maurer and D. Wood) On good EOL forms. SIAM Journal of Computing, Vol. 7, pp. 158–166.

(with H. Maurer and D. Wood) Uniform interpretations of L forms. Information and Control 36, pp. 157–173.

(with H. Maurer and D. Wood) ETOL forms. Journal of Computer and System Sciences, Vol. 16, pp. 345–361.

(with K. Culik, H. Maurer, Th. Ottman and K. Ruohonen) Isomorphism, form equivalence and sequence equivalence of PDOL forms. Theoretical Computer Science 6, pp. 143–173.

(with H. Maurer and D. Wood) Relative goodness of EOL forms. RAIRO/Theoretical Computer Science, Vol. 12, pp. 291–304.

DOL equivalence: The problem of iterated morphisms. EATCS Bulletin 4, pp. 5–12.

L systems and L forms. Journal of the Computer Society of India, Vol. 8, pp. 23–30.

Equality sets for homomorphisms of free monoids. Acta Cybernetica Vol. 4, pp. 127–139.

(with K. Culik) On the decidability of homomorphism equivalence for languages. Journal of Computer and System Sciences 17, pp. 163–175.

1979

(with H. Maurer, M. Penttonen and D. Wood) On non context-free grammar forms. Mathematical Systems Theory 12, pp. 297–324.

Formale Sprachen. Springer-Verlag, Berlin-Heidelberg-New York, 314 pp. (Translation of *"Formal Languages"*.)

D0L language equivalence. EATCS Bulletin 8, pp. 4–12.

Power from power series. Springer-Verlag Lecture Notes in Computer Science, Vol. 74, pp. 170–181.

Language theory based on parallelism: old and new results about L systems. Proceedings of the Fourth IBM Symposium on Mathematical Foundations of Computer Science (Oiso, Japan), pp. 1–20.

(with H. Maurer, G. Rozenberg and D. Wood) Pure interpretations of E0L forms. RAIRO/Theoretical Computer Science, Vol. 13, pp. 347–362.

(with H. Maurer and D. Wood) Context-dependent L forms. Information and Control 42, pp. 97–118.

Sata vuotta matemaattista logiikkaa: päättelysäännöistä tietokoneohjelmointiin. In: Muuttuvat ajat, WSOY, Porvoo, Finland, pp. 116–130.

1980

(with G. Rozenberg) *The Mathematical Theory of L Systems.* Academic Press, New York, xvi+352 pp.

Morphisms on free monoids and language theory. In R. Book (ed.) Formal Language Theory, Academic Press, pp. 141–166.

(with H. Maurer and D. Wood) Synchronized E0L forms. Theoretical Computer Science, Vol. 12, pp. 135–159.

(with H. Maurer and D. Wood) Pure grammars. Information and Control 44, pp. 47–72.

(with H. Maurer and D. Wood) On generators and generative capacity of E0L forms. Acta Informatica 13, pp. 87–107.

(with K. Culik) Test sets and checking words for homomorphism equivalence. Journal of Computer and System Sciences, Vol. 20, pp. 379–395.

(with H. Maurer and D. Wood) Context-free grammar forms with strict interpretations. Journal of Computer and System Sciences, Vol. 21, pp. 110–135.

Grammatical families. Springer Lecture Notes in Computer Science, Vol. 85, pp. 543–554.

(with H. Maurer and D. Wood) MSW spaces. Information and Control 46, pp. 187–199.

1981

Jewels of Formal Language Theory. Computer Science Press, Potomac, Maryland, x+144 pp.

(with H. Maurer and D. Wood) Derivation languages of grammar forms, Journal of Computer Mathematics Section A, Vol. 9, pp. 117–130.

(with H. Maurer and D. Wood) Colorings and interpretations: a connection between graphs and grammar forms, Discrete Applied Mathematics 3, pp. 119–135.

(with H. Maurer and D. Wood) Decidability and density in two-symbol grammar forms, Discrete Applied Mathematics 3, pp. 289–299.

(with H. Maurer and D. Wood) Uniform interpretations of grammar forms, SIAM Journal of Computing, Vol. 10, pp. 483–502.

(with Th. Ottman and D. Wood) Sub-regular grammar forms, Information Processing Letters, Vol. 12, pp. 184–187.

Salakirjoitus ja tietosuoja — näkymiä kryptografian tutkimuksesta. Arkhimedes, Vol. 33, pp. 129–135.

What computer scientists should know about sauna? European Association for Theoretical Computer Science Bulletin, Vol. 15, pp. 8–21.

(with H. Maurer and D. Wood) Synchronized E0L forms under uniform interpretation. RAIRO/Theoretical Computer Science, Vol. 15 (1981), pp. 337–353.

(with H. Maurer and D. Wood) Completeness of context-free grammar forms, Journal of Computer and System Sciences, 23, pp. 1–10.

(with G. Rozenberg) Table systems with unconditional transfer. Discrete Applied Mathematics 3, pp. 319–322.

Formal power series in noncommuting variables. Proceedings of the 18th Scandinavian Congress for Mathematicians, Birkhäuser, 104–124.

On color-families of graphs. Annales Academiae Scientiarum Fennicae, Ser. A I, 6, 135–148.

(with J. Mäenpää and G. Rozenberg) Bibliography of L systems. Leiden University Computer Science Technical Report.

1982

(with H. Maurer and D. Wood) Dense hierarchies of grammatical families. Journal of the Association for Computing Machinery 29, 118–126.

(with K. Culik and F.E. Fich) A homomorphic characterization of regular languages. Discrete Applied Mathematics 4, 149–152.

(with K. Culik and J. Gruska) On non-regular context-free languages and pumping. Bulletin of the European Association for Theoretical Computer Science, Number 16, pp. 22–24.

(with H. Maurer and D. Wood) On predecessors of finite languages. Information and Control 50, 259–275.

(with K. Culik) On infinite words obtained by iterating morphisms. Theoretical Computer Science 19, 29–38.

(with H. Maurer and D. Wood) Finitary and infinitary interpretations of languages. Mathematical Systems Theory 15, 251–265.

1983

(with K. Culik and J. Gruska) Systolic Automata for VLSI on balanced trees. Acta Informatica 18, 335–344.

(with H. Maurer and D. Wood) L codes and number systems. Theoretical Computer Science 22, 331–346.

(with H. Maurer and D. Wood) A supernormal-form theorem for context-free grammars. Journal of the Association for Computing Machinery 30, 95–102.

(with J. Honkala) How do you define the complement of a language. EATCS Bulletin 20, 68–69.

(with H. Maurer and D. Wood) On finite grammar forms. International Journal of Computer Mathematics 12, 227–240.

(with K. Culik and J. Gruska) On a family of L languages resulting from systolic tree automata. Theoretical Computer Science 23, 231–242.

(with K. Culik) Ambiguity and decision problems concerning number systems. Springer Lecture Notes in Computer Science 154, 137–146.

1984

(with K. Culik and J. Gruska) Systolic trellis automata, I and II. International Journal of Computer Mathematics 15, 195–212 and 16, 3–22.

Trapdoors and protocols: recent trends in cryptography. In: H. Maurer (ed.) "Überblicke Informationsverarbeitung 1984". Bibliographisches Institut Mannheim-Wien-Zürich, 275–320.

(with K. Culik and D. Wood) Systolic tree acceptors. RAIRO 18, 53–69.

(with K. Culik) Ambiguity and decision problems concerning number systems. Information and Control 56, 139–153.

Julkiset salat. Tiede 2000 9-10, 46–52.

(ed. with W. Brauer and G. Rozenberg) 3 volumes of EATCS Monographs on Theoretical Computer Science, Springer-Verlag.

1985

Computation and Automata. Encyclopedia of Mathematics and Its Applications, Vol. 25. Cambridge University Press, Cambridge and New York, XIII+282 pp.

(with H. Jürgensen) Syntactic monoids in the construction of systolic tree automata. International Journal of Computer and Information Sciences 14, 35–49.

On a public-key cryptosystem based on parallel rewriting. Parcella-84, Proceedings of the International Conference on Parallel Processing, Berlin, 209–214.

Cryptography from Caesar to DES and RSA. EATCS Bulletin 26, 101–119.

The Ehrenfeucht conjecture: a proof for language theorists. EATCS Bulletin 27, 71–82.

Generalized number systems: decidability, ambiguity, codes. Proceedings of the 19th Nordic Congress of Mathematicians, Reykjavik, 213–214.

Tietosuojauksen kehittäminen. Matemaattisten aineiden aikakauskirja 49, 283–291.

On meta-normal forms for algebraic power series in noncommuting variables. Annales Academiae Scientiarum Fennicae, Ser. AI, Vol. 10, 501–510.

(ed. with G. Rozenberg) The Book of L. Springer-Verlag, Berlin and New York, xv+471 pp.

(with G. Rozenberg) When L was young. In: G. Rozenberg, A. Salomaa (eds.) The Book of L, Springer-Verlag, 383–392.

(ed. with W. Brauer and G. Rozenberg) 2 volumes of EATCS Monographs on Theoretical Computer Science, Springer-Verlag.

1986

(with W. Kuich) *Semirings, Automata, Languages.* EATCS Monographs on Theoretical Computer Science, Vol. 5, Springer-Verlag, Berlin and New York, vi+374 pp.

(ed. with J. Demetrovics and G. Katona) Algebra, Combinatorics and Logic in Computer Science, I-II. North-Holland, Amsterdam and New York, 887 pp.

Systolic tree and trellis automata. In: J. Demetrovics, G. Katona, A. Salomaa (eds.) Algebra, Combinatorics and Logic in Computer Science, North-Holland, 695–710.

Zhemtsuzhiny teorii formalnykh jazykov. Izd. "Mir", Moscow, 159 pp. (Translation of *"Jewels of Formal Language Theory"*.)

(with E. Kinber and Sheng Yu) On the equivalence of grammars inferred from derivations. EATCS Bulletin 29, 39–46.

(with K. Culik and J. Gruska) Systolic trellis automata: stability, decidability and complexity. Information and Control 71, 218–230.

(with H. Maurer, E. Welzl and D. Wood) Denseness, maximality and decidability of grammatical families. Annales Academiae Scientiarum Fennicae, Ser. Al, Vol. 11, 167–178.

(with Sheng Yu) On a public-key cryptosystem based on iterated morphisms and substitutions. Theoretical Computer Science 48, 283–296.

(ed. with W. Brauer and G. Rozenberg) 3 volumes of EATCS Monographs on Theoretical Computer Science, Springer-Verlag.

1987

Markov algorithms as language-defining devices. In: "The Very Knowledge of Coding", Univ. of Turku, 120–127.

(with S. Horvath, E. Kinber and Sheng Yu) Decision problems resulting from grammatical inference. Annales Academiae Scientiarum Fennicae, Vol. 12, 287–298.

Two-way Thue. EATCS Bulletin 32, 82–86.

Playfair. EATCS Bulletin 33, 42–53.

(ed. with W. Brauer and G. Rozenberg) 2 volumes of EATCS Monographs on Theoretical Computer Science, Springer-Verlag.

1988

On a public-key cryptosystem based on language theory. Computers and Security, Vol. 7, 83–87.

L codes: variations on a theme of MSW. In IIG Report 260, Ten years of IIG, 218.

Cryptography and natural languages. EATCS Bulletin 35, 92–96.

COSTOC: Tietokoneavusteisen opetuksen projekti. Korkeakoulujen ATK-Uutiset 2/88, 8–10.

(ed. with T. Lepistö) Automata, Languages and Programming, Proc. of ICALP-88. Springer Lecture Notes in Computer Science, Vol. 317, 741 pp.

Computation and Automata. Japanese translation. Information and Computing -28. x+332 pp.

Computation and Automata. HyperCOSTOC Computer Science, Vol. 5. Hofbauer Verlag AG. 84 pp. and 10 discs.

Cryptography and Data Security. HyperCOSTOC Computer Science, Vol. 32. Hofbauer Verlag AG. 41 pp. and 5 discs.

Cryptographic Transductions. EATCS Bulletin 36, 85–95.

(ed. with W. Brauer and G. Rozenberg) 6 volumes of EATCS Monographs on Theoretical Computer Science, Springer-Verlag.

1989

Knapsacks and superdogs. EATCS Bulletin 38, 107–123.

Tutorial: Cryptography and data security. Springer Lecture Notes in Computer Science, Vol. 381, 220–244.

Public-key cryptosystems and language theory. A Perspective in Theoretical Computer Science. Commemorative Volume for Gift Siromoney. World Scientific, Series in Computer Science, Vol. 16, 257–266.

(with G. Rozenberg) Complexity theory. In Encyclopaedia of Mathematics, Vol. 2, 280–283. Kluwer Academic Publishers.

(with G. Rozenberg) Cryptography. In Encyclopaedia of Mathematics, Vol. 2, 466-468. Kluwer Academic Publishers.

(with G. Rozenberg) Formal languages and automata. In Encyclopaedia of Mathematics, Vol. 4, 53–57. Kluwer Academic Publishers.

(ed. with W. Brauer and G. Rozenberg) 2 volumes of EATCS Monographs on Theoretical Computer Science, Springer-Verlag.

1990

Introduction à l'Informatique Théorique, Calculabilité et Complexité. Armand Colin, Paris, ix+372 pp.

Public-Key Cryptography. Springer-Verlag, Berlin, New York, London, Paris, Tokyo, x+245 pp.

Formal languages and power series. In Handbook of Theoretical Computer Science, Vol. II (J. van Leeuwen, ed.), Elsevier Science Publishers B.V., Vol. B, 103–132.

(ed.) Special issue of Theoretical Computer Science, Vol. 71, no. 1, 174 pp.

(with G. Rozenberg) L-systems. In Encyclopedia of Mathematics, Vol. 5, 325–327. Kluwer Academic Publishers.

Decidability in finite automata. EATCS Bulletin 41, 175–183.

Decision problems arising from knapsack transformations. Acta Cybernetica 9, 419–440.

Interaction. Japan Computer Science Association Reports 15, 4–8.

Formal power series: a powerful tool for theoretical informatics. Proceedings of the 300-Year Festival Congress of the Hamburg Mathematical Association, 1033–1048.

(with L. Santean) Secret selling of secrets with many buyers. EATCS Bulletin 42, 178–186.

(with G. Rozenberg) Mathematical theory of computation. Encyclopedia of Mathematics, Vol. 6, 146–148.

From number theory to cryptography: RSA. Arkhimedes 42, 526–535.

Mathematics and natural sciences. In: Finnish Council of University Rectors (ed.), University Research in Finland, 10–13.

(ed. with W. Brauer and G. Rozenberg) 4 volumes of EATCS Monographs on Theoretical Computer Science, Springer-Verlag.

1991

(with G. Rozenberg) Post correspondence problem. Encyclopedia of Mathematics, Vol. 7, 252–253.

(with H. Maurer and D. Wood) Bounded delay L codes. Theoretical Computer Science 84, 265–279.

A deterministic algorithm for modular knapsack problems. Theoretical Computer Science 88, 127–138.

(ed.) Special issue "Formal Language Theory" of Discrete Applied Mathematics, Vol. 32, no. 2, 142 pp.

(with H. Nurmi) A cryptographic approach to the secret ballot. Behavioral Science 36, 34–40.

Many aspects of formal languages. Information Sciences, Vol. 57–58 (Special issue "Information Sciences: Past, Present, Future"), 119–129.

(with H. Nurmi) Salaiset vaalit ja matemaattinen kryptografia. Politiikka 1, 11–18.

L codes and L systems with immigration. EATCS Bulletin 43, 124–130.

(with K. Salomaa and S. Yu) Primality types of instances of the Post correspondence problem. EATCS Bulletin 44, 226–241.

(with J. Honkala) L morphisms: bounded delay and regularity of ambiguity. Springer Lecture Notes in Computer Science 510, 566–574.

(with H. Nurmi and L. Santean) Secret ballot elections in computer networks. Computers and Security 10, 553–560.

Verifying and recasting secret ballots in computer networks. Springer Lecture Notes in Computer Science 555, 283–289.

(with M. Andrasiu, A. Atanasiu and G. Paun) A new cryptosystem based on formal language theory. Bull. Math. Soc. Sci. Math. Roumaine, to appear.

(with G. Paun) Thin and slender languages. Submitted for publication.

(ed. with W. Brauer and G. Rozenberg) 3 volumes of EATCS Monographs on Theoretical Computer Science, Springer-Verlag.

1992

(with G. Paun and S. Vicolov) On the generative capacity of parallel communicating grammar systems. International Journal of Computer Mathematics 45, 45–59.

(with J. Honkala) Characterization results about L codes. RAIRO 26, 287–301.

(with L. Kari, S. Marcus and G. Paun) In the prehistory of formal language theory: Gauss languages. EATCS Bulletin 46, 124–139.

(with G. Paun) Decision problems concerning the thinness of DOL languages. EATCS Bulletin 46, 171–181.

(with J. Dassow, A. Mateescu and G. Paun) Regularizing context-free languages by AFL operations: concatenation and Kleene closure. Acta Cybernetica, Szeged, vol. 10, no. 4, 243–253.

(with L. Kari, A. Mateescu and G. Paun) Deletion sets. Fundamenta Informaticae 19, 355–370.

(with L. Kari and G. Paun) Semi-commutativity sets for morphisms on free monoids. Bull. Math. Soc. Sci. Math. Roumaine, to appear.

(with H. Nurmi) Secret Ballot Elections and Public-Key Cryptosystems. European Journal of Political Economy 8, 295–303.

(with H. Nurmi) Tietokonevaalit ja Tengvallin credo. Politiikka XXXIV, 199–201.

(with H. Nurmi) Conducting Secret Ballot Elections in Computer Networks: Problems and Solutions. Presented at the IFAC workshop on Support Systems for Decision and Negotiation Processes, Warsaw June 24–26. Published in the preprints of the conference. Submitted for publication.

(with G. Paun) Semi-commutativity sets — a cryptographically grounded topic. Bull. Math. Soc. Sci. Math. Roumaine 35, 255–270.

(ed. with G. Rozenberg) *Lindenmayer Systems*. Springer-Verlag, 514 pp.

(ed. with W. Brauer and G. Rozenberg) 3 volumes of EATCS Monographs on Theoretical Computer Science, Springer-Verlag.

Public-Key Cryptography. Japanese translation published by Tokyo Denki Daigaku Shuppankyoku.

Nhap Mon Tin Hoc Ly Thuyet. Tinh Toan Vacac Otomat. Vietnamese translation of *Computation and Automata* published by Nha Xvat Ban Khoa Hoc Va Ky Thuat, Hanoi.

Recent trends in the theory of formal languages. Proceedings of the Conference "Salodays in Theoretical Computer Science", Bucharest, May 1992, 3 pp.

Different aspects of the Post correspondence problem. EATCS Bulletin 47, 154–165.

(with E. Neuhold, A. Björck, D. Parnas and D. Patterson) Informatikk: Research and Teaching in Norway. A critical evaluation. NAVF, Norway, 66 pp.

Nhung huong phat trien moi trong tin hoc ly thuyet. In the Vietnamese translation of *Computation* and *Automata*, 394–404.

(with T. Jiang, E. Kinber, K. Salomaa and S. Yu) Pattern languages with and without erasing. To appear in International Journal of Computer Mathematics.

1993

Simple reductions between D0L language and sequence equivalence problems. Discrete Applied Mathematics 41, 271–274.

(with A. Mateescu) PCP-prime words and primality types. RAIRO 27, 57–70.

(with M. Andrasiu, J. Dassow and G. Paun) Language-theoretic problems arising from Richelieu cryptosystems. Theoretical Computer Science 116, 339–357.

(with M. Andrasiu, A. Atanasiu and G. Paun) A new cryptosystem based on formal language theory. Bull. Math. Soc. Sci. Math. Roumaine 36, Nr. 1, 3–16.

(with G. Rozenberg) Undecidability. In Encyclopedia of Mathematics, Vol. 9, 310–311. Kluwer Academic Publishers.

Criptografie Cu Chei Publice. Romanian translation of *Public-Key Cryptography*, published by Editura Militara, 253 pp.

(ed. with G. Rozenberg) *Current Trends in Theoretical Computer Science.* World Scientific, Singapore, ix+628 pp.

(with L. Kari, S. Marcus and G. Paun) In the prehistory of formal language theory: Gauss languages. In: G. Rozenberg and A. Salomaa (eds.), Current Trends in Theoretical Computer Science, World Scientific, 551–562.

(with S. Marcus, A. Mateescu and G. Paun) On symmetry in strings, sequences and languages. Submitted for publication.

What Emil said about the Post Correspondence Problem. In: G. Rozenberg and A. Salomaa (eds.), Current Trends in Theoretical Computer Science, World Scientific, 563–571.

Decidability in finite automata. In: G. Rozenberg and A. Salomaa (eds.), Current Trends in Theoretical Computer Science, World Scientific, 572–578.

(with A. Mateescu) On simplest possible solutions for Post correspondence problems. Acta Informatica 30, 441–457.

(with A. Mateescu and V. Mitrana) Dynamical teams of cooperating grammar systems. To appear in Annals of University of Bucharest, Romania.

(with J. Dassow and G. Paun) On thinness and slenderness of L Languages. EATCS Bulletin 49, 152–158.

(with L. Kari) 50 EATCS Bulletins. EATCS Bulletin 50, 5–12.

(with G. Paun) Remarks concerning self-reading sequences. EATCS Bulletin 50, 229–233.

(with G. Paun) Closure properties of slender languages. Theoretical Computer Science 120, 293–301.

(with G. Paun) Thin and slender languages. Discrete Applied Mathematics, to appear.

(with H. Nurmi) Cryptographic protocols for Vickrey auctions. Ann. Univ. Turku, B 200, 9–22.

(with H. Nurmi) The nearly perfect auctioneer: cryptographic protocols for auctions and bidding. To appear in the Proceedings of "Decision Making: Towards the 21st Century", Madrid, June 2–5, 1993.

(with H. Nurmi) Cancellation and Reassignment of Votes in Secret Ballot Elections. European Journal of Political Economy 9, 427–435.

(with T. Jiang, K. Salomaa and S. Yu) Inclusion is undecidable for pattern languages. Springer Lecture Notes in Computer Science 700, 301–312.

Pattern languages: problems of decidability and generation. Springer Lecture Notes in Computer Science 710, 121–132.

(with A. Mateescu) Post correspondence problem: primitivity and interrelations with complexity classes. Springer Lecture Notes in Computer Science 711.

(with C. Calude) Algorithmically coding the universe. To appear in G. Rozenberg and A. Salomaa (eds.), Developments in Language Theory, World Scientific.

(with L. Kari, A. Mateescu and G. Paun) Multi-pattern languages. Theoretical Computer Science, to appear.

(with L. Kari, A. Mateescu and G. Paun) Teams in cooperating grammar systems. Journal of Experimental and Theoretical AI, to appear.

(with L. Kari, A. Mateescu and G. Paun) Grammars with oracles. Annals of University of Iassy, Romania, to appear.

(with L. Kari and G. Paun) Semi-commutativity sets of morphisms over finite monoids. To appear.

(with A. Mateescu) Nondeterminism in patterns. Springer Lecture Notes in Computer Science, to appear.

(with A. Mateescu) Pattern languages with a finite degree of ambiguity. RAIRO, to appear.

Slenderness and immigration: new aspects of L systems. To appear in the Proceedings of the 9th Conference on Automata and Formal Languages, Salgotarjan 1993.

(with A. Mateescu and G. Rozenberg) Geometric transformations on language families: the magic of symmetry. Submitted for publication.

(with L. Kari and G. Rozenberg) Generalized D0L trees. Submitted for publication.

(with J. Dassow and G. Paun) On the union of 0L languages. Information Processing Letters 47, 59–63.

(with J. Dassow and G. Paun) Grammars based on patterns. International Journal of Foundations of Computer Science 4, 1–14.

(with G. Paun and G. Rozenberg) Contextual grammars: erasing, determinism, one-side contexts. To appear in G. Rozenberg and A. Salomaa (eds.), Developments in Language Theory, World Scientific.

(with G. Paun and G. Rozenberg) Contextual grammars: parallelism and blocking of derivation. Submitted for publication.

(with G. Paun and G. Rozenberg) Contextual grammars: modularity and leftmost derivation. Submitted for publication.

(with T. Jiang, K. Salomaa and S. Yu) Decision problems concerning patterns. Submitted for publication.

(with L. Kari, A. Mateescu and G. Paun) On parallel deletions applied to a word. RAIRO, to appear.

(with A. Mateescu, K. Salomaa and S. Yu) P, NP and Post Correspondence Problem. Submitted for publication.

(ed. with G. Rozenberg) *Developments in Language Theory.* Manuscript 497 pp., to be published by World Scientific.

(with G. Rozenberg) *Cornerstones of Undecidability.* Manuscript 250 pp., to be published by Prentice Hall.

Author Index

Springer-Verlag
and the Environment

We at Springer-Verlag firmly believe that an international science publisher has a special obligation to the environment, and our corporate policies consistently reflect this conviction.

We also expect our business partners – paper mills, printers, packaging manufacturers, etc. – to commit themselves to using environmentally friendly materials and production processes.

The paper in this book is made from low- or no-chlorine pulp and is acid free, in conformance with international standards for paper permanency.

Lecture Notes in Computer Science

For information about Vols. 1–729
please contact your bookseller or Springer-Verlag